T0361388

ECONOMICS AND POLITICS
OF TRADE POLICY

World Scientific Studies in International Economics
(ISSN: 1793-3641)

The complete list of the published volumes in the series can be found at
http://www.worldscientific.com/series/wssie

33 World Scientific
Studies in
International
Economics

ECONOMICS AND POLITICS OF TRADE POLICY

Douglas R. Nelson
Tulane University, USA

 **World Scientific**

NEW JERSEY · LONDON · SINGAPORE · BEIJING · SHANGHAI · HONG KONG · TAIPEI · CHENNAI

Published by

World Scientific Publishing Co. Pte. Ltd.

5 Toh Tuck Link, Singapore 596224

USA office: 27 Warren Street, Suite 401-402, Hackensack, NJ 07601

UK office: 57 Shelton Street, Covent Garden, London WC2H 9HE

British Library Cataloguing-in-Publication Data
A catalogue record for this book is available from the British Library.

World Scientific Studies in International Economics — Vol. 33
ECONOMICS AND POLITICS OF TRADE POLICY

ISBN 978-981-4452-50-2

In-house Editors: Yvonne Tan/Lee Xin Ying

Typeset by Stallion Press
Email: enquiries@stallionpress.com

Printed in Singapore

Preface

Introduction

As recently as the late-1970s, when I was studying for my PhD in Political Science at the University of North Carolina, political economy was, at best, a peripheral area of study. Unlike today when many universities have entire departments given over to something called political economy and courses with "political economy" as core content are common, in the late-1970s if you encountered political economy at all, it was likely to be in a course on developing countries. It was my good luck, however, that in this period, positive political economy was beginning to emerge as a distinctive area of study. By way of context for the papers collected here, I will start this introduction with a brief overview of the state of political economy as I experienced it in the late 1970s. Following that, I will try to suggest a certain coherence among the papers here and their connection to the broader literature on the political economy of trade, of which they constitute a very small part.

Background

In political science in the 1960s and 1970s, "political economy" mostly meant "Marxism". As a graduate student, I read plenty of the Marxist literature, but focused particularly on Gramsci (because Craig Murphy was my office mate), Poulantzas (for the rigor and clarity) and Habermas (for the depth, and the obvious links to Weber).[1] In coursework, we were most likely to see systematic political economy in courses related to development (in my case, in a course on Latin America). These were the years of high dependency theory, which figured in a number of courses and in extensive

---

[1] Habermas also got me to Luhmann, whose own version of Weberian political economy developed in interaction with the German left, and Habermas in particular.

discussion with graduate students. This was already morphing into world systems theory (*a la* Wallerstein, 1974, 1976, 1989) and the Latin American literature on bureaucratic authoritarianism (O'Donnell, 1973; Kaufman, 1979).[2] The great virtue of the Marxist literature was that it was fundamentally positive, relentlessly materialist, and it treated the relationship between the economy and the political system as an obvious focus for study. The problems, at least for me, were a model of the economy that seemed underdeveloped (the classic problem that led to the development of neoclassical theory) and a political economy that ran, axiomatically, through class struggle. These problems would ultimately lead me to the general equilibrium theory of competitive markets, which offered both a compelling, though tractable, model of the economy, as well as a number of possible dimensions of conflict (e.g. inter-sectoral as well as class conflict).

Of course, many of the elements of a systematic, positive political economy were well-established in the political science literature. Most importantly, the pluralist tradition often saw organized interests as rooted in material interests (e.g. Schattschneider, 1935; Truman, 1951; McConnell, 1966; Lowi, 1969). This work was stimulating, and often provided institutionally rich case studies of particular policy domains that easily lent itself to formalization. In addition, Olson's (1965) classic *Logic of Collective Action* illustrated the power of economic theory applied to political science questions framed in group theoretic terms. The other major contribution of political science to the pre-history of modern political economy was the rapid growth in positive political theory *a la* Rochester and CalTech. But first, we need to look over the fence at what was going on in Economics departments.

As with Political Science, political economy was not a well-established part of the Economics curriculum in the late 1970s. At that point in time, political economy served two closely related purposes in mainstream economics: it served to account, without much systematic analysis, for deviations from welfare optima; and it was a way of adding additional costs to embarrassingly small welfare losses from policies that we find particularly problematic. The identification of something as a "political economy problem", especially in a seminar, meant that we, as economists, did not have to deal with it systematically, but that it might be fun to tell some

---

[2]One of my first publications, written for Traian Stoianovich's faculty seminar when I was at Rutgers, not included here, was a critical analysis of world systems theory (Nelson, 1983).

stories and possibly apply some partial equilibrium price theory of a loose, and not terribly compelling, sort as a framework for our discussion. At the University of Chicago and at Virginia Tech (eventually moving the George Mason University), this was treated much more seriously as a research topic. The Chicago school (Stigler, 1971; Peltzman, 1976) and the Public Choice school (Buchanan and Tullock, 1962; Niskanen, 1971) shared a view of the political system as a competitive market that could be reasonably analyzed in partial equilibrium terms, and a disinterest in decades of research by political scientists on the same and cognate questions. They also shared a fundamental normative purpose: the illustration of distortions created by democratic political process and the gains from blocking that process.

Thus, the two main strains of political economy theory when I was a student (Marxism and Public Choice) were fundamentally normative in nature. Marxism, by putting exploitation (extraction of surplus value) at the core of its model of the economy, not only rendered class struggle as the motor of history, but identified a clear normative valence in that struggle. Capitalism (like feudalism before it) is seen to be fundamentally unfair and, as a result, in the class struggle, the working class has moral right on its side. Similarly, both the Chicago school of political economy and the Public Choice school analyze government against a normative baseline in which government is seen as the object of "rent-seeking" (Tullock, 1967; Krueger, 1974) or "directly unproductive profit-seeking activity" (Bhagwati and Srinivasan, 1980; Bhagwati, 1982a). Political activity of a free people is seen as an additional source of costs, without any consideration of the positive benefits of free political activity in the context of a democratic polity. This yields an interesting inversion of the Marxist analysis: in the Marxist analysis, the economy generates unfairness and only the political system (revolution or, in later work by analysts like Gramsci and Habermas, democratic politics) can reverse the unfairness; in the Public Choice analysis, the market generates fair activities and politics generates inefficiency and unfairness. In either case, struggles at the core of democratic capitalism are seen to be problematic for the political economy and based on a fundamental unfairness that renders one side the defender of a morally right outcome and the other, a possibly misguided defender of moral wrong.[3] While it seemed to

---

[3]The very old question of the consistency of democracy and capitalism, in which scholars of both the right (Schumpeter, 1975) and the left (Polanyi, 1944) have argued for inconsistency, reflects the same concerns. For a fine survey and empirical extension of this question, see Rueschemeyer *et al.* (1992).

me that this sort of normative commitment produced a poor foundation for social scientific analysis, struggling with these questions of where fairness fits in a positive analysis is no doubt a source of my more recent interest in the way fairness norms affect individual behavior and aggregate outcomes in both the economy and the political system (see the papers in Section 3).

What drove the Public Choice and Chicago schools of political economy to the margins, where Marxists already dwelt, was the emergence of a body of analytical political science possessed of a high level of technical sophistication, with solid roots in the institutional and empirical results of contemporary political science. Building on decision-theoretic and, especially, game theoretic foundations, the Rochester-CalTech school developed their analytical framework free from any first-order normative commitments in the political struggles their analytical tools were developed to study.[4] This work had the additional virtue of being easily linked to mainstream neoclassical models of the economy, without being burdened with a view of the political system as just another market.

The Economics and Politics of Administered Protection

Although my training was in quantitative international relations, by the time I was ready to write a PhD thesis, I knew I was interested in political economy.[5] The political economy of international monetary policy was already developing rapidly in political science and economics, though the emphasis was on international political economy (e.g. policy coordination). As a result, there was little in the way of direction for someone interested in the domestic foundations of international policy. In addition, as someone untrained in economics, the links between obvious, macro-level groups and

---

[4] An excellent presentation of the main body of positive political theory can be found in Austen-Smith and Banks (1999, 2005).

[5] The University of North Carolina at this time was an early and committed convert to the behavioral revolution in political science. This was certainly the case in the study of international relations. I worked with Edward Azar, a brilliant innovator in the application of statistical methods to the study of conflict and peace. My MA thesis was an interrupted time series analysis of conflict between the US and the USSR. While well outside his area of expertise, Azar was amazingly supportive of my desire to pursue political economy. He bore some considerable cost because there was no one, in either Economics or Political Science, who was working in this area. The extraordinary Bill Keech was on the UNC faculty at that point, but he had only just returned from the sabbatical during which he retooled to become the major political economist he is today. Sadly, too late for me. As a result, Edward Azar chaired my PhD committee, making major contributions to its completion.

macroeconomic policy were just not clear to me.[6] As a result, I began to focus on the political economy of international trade policy — in particular, the political economy of protection. Trade policy is one of the few areas of policy that has been with the US since the Revolution, and as a major policy issue of such long standing, as well as journalistic treatments, it has been studied by historians, political scientists and economists. Much of this work was useful input to thinking about the political economy of trade policy, but three pieces were absolutely essential: Schattschneider's (1935) *Politics, Pressure and the Tariff*; Bauer *et al.*'s (1963) *American Business and Public Policy*; and Lowi's (1964) classic review of Bauer *et al.*[7] However, virtually all of this work focused on the politics of the tariff, which had ceased to be the main source of new protection following the Hawley–Smoot tariff. Instead, protection was constrained by commitments under the General Agreement on Tariffs and Trade (GATT) and, now, the World Trade Organization (WTO) to outcomes from administrative mechanisms (antidumping and countervailing duties, escape clause protection, and a number of minor sources of administered protection).

This is where I came in. None of the literature on the politics of protection had come to grips with the facts of administered protection. Thus, I began to read up on the law, institutions and politics of administered protection.[8] I also intended to base part of my thesis on interviews with people actively involved in the implementation of administered protection. Jim Ingram recommended that I talk with J. Michael Finger (a 1967 graduate of the University of North Carolina whose own PhD thesis Ingram had chaired), who was then the director of the US Treasury Department's Office of Trade Research and one of the very few experts on administered

---

[6] Certainly, there was already work on the political economy of domestic fiscal and monetary policy, but the models of both the economy and the political system were uncongenial to me. This should be seen as my failing, not a criticism of those literatures.

[7] It is not unreasonable to see virtually all research on the domestic politics of trade policy as linear combinations of Schattschneider and Bauer/Pool/Dexter, with Lowi providing a skeleton key to their relationship. As I will argue in the next section, most work has tended toward the Schattschneider end of this dimension.

[8] I also began to study the parts of economics with most direct application to trade policy — general equilibrium theory and its application to international trade and trade policy. Jim Ingram and Dennis Appleyard, both at the University of North Carolina, were very generous with their time in helping me negotiate this literature. Similarly, Steve Magee, at the University of Texas, provided much help and guidance on both trade theory and its application to building a systematic theory of political economy of trade policy.

protection that was not a lawyer. Mike ended up being the shadow chair of my thesis committee, taught me a good share of the trade theory I know, and even ended up hiring me to work at the Treasury and then (twice) at the World Bank. My thesis research fit well with Mike's own interests to such a degree that he and I, along with Keith Hall (who had just finished his undergraduate degree at Virginia), jointly wrote the paper that is the first chapter of this volume (Finger et al., 1982).

Like much of the political economy literature at that point in time, this paper was based on an informal, and not particularly carefully considered, mix of partial and general equilibrium reasoning about the underlying economy that generated demands for political action, but paid considerable attention to the legal, institutional and political details relating to the implementation of administered protection. We argued that these institutions needed to be understood as a reflection of the need to respond to political pressure for protection in the context of a GATT commitment not to legislate new protection. That is, the administered mechanism is a political safety valve. We argued that this mechanism had two "tracks": a technical track that handled the majority of cases (antidumping and countervailing duties); and a high track that handled cases too big, or politically visible, to be constrained to the technical track. On the technical track, cases are "determined" according to terms specified in the legislation; while the political track is less constrained, granting the President considerable discretion in responding to the results of the administered process. The econometric results were strongly consistent with our hypotheses relating to this structure.

In the fall of 1980, Keith Hall moved on to study for his PhD in Economics at Rochester (ultimately switching to Purdue, where he finished), while Finger and I went to the World Bank. I was trying to develop theoretical skills that would allow me to move beyond the informal theoretical framework that I had used in my PhD thesis and had the good fortune to be working at the World Bank at the same time Jagdish Bhagwati was visiting. Bhagwati was developing his interests in political economy; among other things, he had founded the journal *Economics & Politics*, and had recently organized a conference on the political economy of trade that would result in the important volume *Import Competition and Response* (Bhagwati, 1982b). Bhagwati was kind enough to share the papers from this conference with me, in particular the absolutely fundamental paper by Findlay and Wellisz (1982) and the accompanying comment by Leslie Young. It was clear that, since the collapse of trade policy as a major electoral issue sometime in the 1930s, trade policy had to be seen as primarily a lobbying issue, and Findlay and Wellisz provided a simple, tractable framework for the analysis of trade policy lobbying (and Young illustrated the gains to be had from applying duality theory to the Findlay–Wellisz model).[9]

Building on the Findlay–Wellisz framework, Keith Hall and I developed a model illustrating the difference between legislated and administered protection (Hall and Nelson, 1992). The basic idea is that lobbying for a sector-specific tariff, as was the norm under legislated protection, was fundamentally different than lobbying for the terms of a rule that would regulate access to protection under administered protection. Virtually all theoretical work to this day (and very much including the important work of Grossman and Helpman (1994) and the massive literature descending from it) treats protection as a sector-specific output of the political process which is essentially unconnected to the protection granted to other sectors. However, Finger, Hall and I demonstrated empirically, and as Hall and I argue in more explicit detail, administered protection proceeds under terms that are set in legislation of general applicability. Hall and I then argue that, where a legislated tariff line is like a private good for a sector (by comparison to other sectors), the legislation setting the terms under which administered protection is administered is like a public good. We then proceed to demonstrate that the equilibrium level of protection generated in the latter case is lower than for the case of legislated protection. Furthermore, we argue that this might help explain the fact that the average level of protection falls dramatically following the implementation of the Reciprocal Trade Agreements Act of 1934. We return to this in the next section.

Both of the preceding papers have the implication that the level of protection under an administered protection regime should be modest. Finger *et al.* (1982) follow Viner (1923) in assuming that administered protection provides political protection for a liberalizing regime. If it serves this purpose, it must generate lower protection than would be the result from the legislated protection system it replaced. Hall and Nelson (1992) provide a theoretical account of the way the switch from legislated to administered protection might support this goal. Contrary to this claim, in the two decades following this paper, the overwhelming majority of research on antidumping has sought to argue that the actual level of protection

---

[9]The Findlay–Wellisz analysis of trade policy appears to have helped Becker (1983, 1985) break decisively with the Chicago school tradition to produce a positive analysis of lobbying based on solid game theoretic foundations.

generated by antidumping is somehow much larger than it might initially appear — that there is a "global chilling effect" of antidumping (Vandenbussche and Zanardi, 2010). Peter Egger and I, in the paper reproduced as Chapter 3 of this volume (Egger and Nelson, 2011), examined this and a number of other hypotheses seeking to explain that there are actually large aggregate effects of antidumping. Building on Egger's work with structural gravity models, we are able to reject most of these accounts, in particular the global chilling effect. Especially given the quite modest protectionist response to the most serious recession since the Great Depression, our estimate of very small aggregate effects of antidumping on trade volumes (the major source of new protection in the core trading nations under the GATT/WTO regime), in the face of an essentially unchanged aggregate preference for protection, suggests that a substantial change in the political economy of protection occurred sometime after the passage of the Hawley–Smoot tariff.

The Broader Context of Trade Policy Making

The two workhorse models in research on the political economy of protection are the referendum model (Mayer, 1984) and the menu auction model of lobbying (Grossman and Helpman, 1994). These are tractable models that do a good job of accounting for the cross-section pattern of protection, but they do not tell us much about the broader political economy of protection. The papers in the second section of this volume are attempts to identify the context within which those models operate, and thus their limits.

The transition of the US from an isolationist, high-tariff country to an internationalist, low-tariff country provides a laboratory for thinking about the sources of large-scale change in political economic structures and institutions. As a matter of fact, the Tariff Act of 1930 (the Hawley–Smoot tariff) was the last tariff legislated by the US, and the Reciprocal Trade Agreements Act of 1934 (RTAA) created the basis for the contemporary system in which Congress grants the Executive the power to negotiate trade liberalization, as constrained by the terms of the legislation, and sets the terms under which administered protection will be granted. Prior to this period, US protection was high on average and highly variable. After this period, the US tariff dropped dramatically and has showed no general trend but down in the 80-plus years since. This timing has led some to suggest that Congress "learned" that protection led to depression and sought to avoid future problems by delegating to the less protectionist executive branch under terms that allowed them to complain about trade publicly, but actually to do nothing — the "cry and sigh syndrome" (Pastor, 1983). The Congressional learning account faces two problems: first, there is little evidence of a link between the Hawley–Smoot tariff and the depression (Eichengreen, 1989), so this would involve Congress "learning" something that was not, in fact, true; and the timing is poor for this account — protectionist Congresspeople did not change their voting records and partisan preferences on the tariff did not begin to change until the 1960s.

An alternative account runs through institutional change. As I have already noted, Chapter 2 (Hall and Nelson, 1992) argues that the institutional changes embedded in the RTAA produce a downward shift in the equilibrium tariff (also see Haggard, 1988; Schnietz, 2000). The problem with such institutional accounts is that they fail to explain the sustainability of the institutional changes. In 1953, with a Republican president and both houses with Republican majorities, and recognizing that Republicans were not strong supporters of the Trade Agreements Program, why did they not simply change the law? Nelson (1989), Chapter 4 in this volume, extends this account in a detailed analysis of the political and institutional context of this change, arguing that a key element is executive branch leadership and, in particular, the ability of the executive branch to attach trade policy to foreign policy. Thus, the combination of the Cold War and a notion that the Trade Agreements Program was seen as an essential element of Cold War strategy is surely part of the story, but the long-term stability of liberalization seems to require a more structural explanation.

One structural approach runs through factor mobility. In Hall and Nelson (1989), Chapter 5 in this volume, we develop the logics of short-run evaluation of policy effects (which generate sector-based politics) and long-run evaluation (which generate class-based politics) and link that to Lowi's (1964) typology of institutionalized policy types. An implication of this sort of analysis is that if, for some reason, the time horizon of political calculation changes, the form of politics would change. Hall and I merely sketch this as a theoretical possibility, but Michael Hiscox (2001) has developed this logic (completely independently of our work) in both theoretical and empirical detail. One might have doubts that the magnitudes of changes in factor mobility identified by Hiscox would be sufficient to drive rapid and fundamental change of the sort that occurred between the Hawley–Smoot tariff and the RTAA, but one cannot doubt that this is the single most complete and sophisticated attempt to provide an answer to the question of what structural change accounts for in the transition in US trade politics.

For sheer entertainment value, an account that runs through structural change in the electorate is hard to beat. From Mayer's (1984) foundational analysis of a referendum-based model of the political economy of trade policy, we know that a change in the makeup of the electorate can produce a shift in the identity of the median voter, and (via the Hotelling–Downs mechanism) a change in the equilibrium policy. Reading some of the political journalism of the period, I found a number of claims (by proponents of The Tariff System) that female franchise would be a deadly blow to The Tariff. It is notable that the claim was: first, that what was at stake was not any particular tariff line item, but The Tariff (a one-dimensional issue); and second, that women (who would be added to the pool of voters) would all be added to the free trade end of voter distribution. From Mayer, the implication was clear: this should lead to a structural reduction in the equilibrium tariff, even though the change was made for reasons unrelated to the issue of the tariff. Keith Hall and I had great fun developing the argument, but we needed help with the time series econometrics (as seminar participants and, ultimately, referees, told us). My colleague at Syracuse, Duke Kao, filled the bill perfectly, and the three of us wrote the final version of the paper which is Chapter 6 (Hall *et al.*, 1998). We not only explain the transition to the low tariff equilibrium, but we also explain the transition from the System of '96 to the New Deal electoral system. One would not want to take the claims of the paper too seriously, but this is unquestionably the most fun paper to give at seminars I have ever been associated with.

Informal discussions of trade policy are often, implicitly or explicitly, based on a straightforward spatial model of the sort presented in Mayer (1984). The claim is not that trade policy is determined in a referendum, it virtually never is, but that there is some kind of public opinion constraint on policies as they emerge from a complex, but unmodeled, political process. I think this is a useful application of the referendum model, but it is important to be clear about just what is being modeled. In particular, treating poll data as reflecting a relatively fixed representation of the state of public opinion and, in particular, shifts in opinion as reflecting public response to fundamentals (as any link to something like the Mayer model must presume), are problematic. In Chapter 7 (Hall and Nelson, 2004), Keith Hall and I looked at public opinion on NAFTA, finding large changes in the "public preference" for NAFTA, even in the face of no information release. That is, public statements moved opinion even though there were no changes in NAFTA fundamentals. We develop an illustrative model based on social learning models.[10] This is precisely what we would expect if a relatively poorly informed electorate is seeking to take cues at relatively low cost about issues of relatively low salience. Not only is this consistent with Downsian "rational ignorance" (Downs, 1957; Hinich and Munger, 1994), but it is also consistent with a more discursive theory of democracy in which the public discourse about policy is open-ended and unpredictable (e.g. Schattschneider, 1960). My most recent work with Carl Davidson and Steven Matusz (Davidson *et al.* 2006, 2012), Chapters 12 and 13 in the next section, seek to pursue this line in more detail. The point here is that public opinion on trade policy cannot really be treated as solidly anchored in material self-interest.[11]

One of the striking gaps between macroempirical research on the political economy of trade and theoretical models is the lack of attention to unemployment. It is clear in the time series studies on the correlates of protection that there is a strong counter-cyclical element in both the demand for protection (e.g. filings of administered protection cases) and protectionist output.[12] Standard competitive models, of the sort that constitute the core of endogenous policy models, are unsuited to raising this important issue. In fact, it is often asserted that trade does not affect unemployment. However, recent work on models with equilibrium (involuntary) unemployment find strong links (Davidson and Matusz, 2004, 2010). In my work with Noel Gaston, reproduced as Chapter 8, we develop a model of a small open economy with a unionized and a non-unionized sector characterized by equilibrium unemployment, and a government that provides an unemployment benefit determined in a menu auction lobbying model (Gaston and Nelson, 2004). We also present preliminary empirical results that are supportive of our claim that political economy pressures on trade policy are likely to be conditioned by the interaction of industrial/labor market structure and government policy that might not be picked up in standard political

---

[10]Morrissey and Nelson (2003, 2005), in papers not collected here, use similar models to study international social learning.

[11]This should probably also be borne in mind when evaluating the results in the now massive literature seeking to use survey data to identify such material interest — e.g. whether preferences are long-run ("Heckscher–Ohlin") or short-run ("Ricardo–Viner"). For an overview and substantial development of this literature see Scheve and Slaughter (2001).

[12]In Nelson (2006), I survey the macro literature with particular reference to administered protection.

economy empirics based on models that assume competitive markets (what we call "indirect" political economy effects to distinguish them from direct effects that are determined by direct tariff-to-price-to-factor price effects).

Building on Davidson and Matusz's (2010) fundamental work on trade with equilibrium unemployment, Davidson, Matusz and I (Davidson *et al.*, 2007), Chapter 9 here, consider an economy with equilibrium unemployment that must choose both an unemployment benefit and a trade policy via referendum. Among other results, we find that the sustainability of trade liberalization can depend on the order in which the referenda are voted.[13] The models in Chapters 8 and 9 are simple and stylized, but they illustrate the gains to be had from more systematic attention to unemployment in the political economy of trade.

The last paper in this section, Greenaway and Nelson (2010), compares the political economies of international trade and international migration in endogenous policy models to develop some insight on directions for future research in such models. We informally distinguish between accounting for the average level of a policy (trade or migration) and the dispersion of that policy, and whether the underlying model emphasizes welfare maximization (an ideal Weber/Samuelson policy maker) or a political economy account. We argue that the politics of trade and migration are very different and seek to account for those differences. Once again, the issue comes down to whether the issue involves public politics, which are highly uncertain, or the more well-disciplined politics of lobbying. In either case, we argue that broad notions like fairness play a role in determining outcomes. It is on those issues that the three papers in the next section focus.

Learning from Behavioral Economics: Fairness in Trade and Trade Policy

By this point, it is probably clear that I strongly believe that widely held notions about what is, for want of a better term, "fair" plays a significant role in politics generally, and in the politics of trade policy in particular. One of the many pleasures/benefits of my long association with the School of Economics at the University of Nottingham is time spent talking with various members of the behavioral economics group: Robin

---

[13]Spiros Bougheas and I (Bougheas and Nelson, 2012), in a paper not collected here, apply a similar model to evaluate the distributional effects of trade and migration policies.

Cubitt, Elke Renner, Martin Sefton, Chris Starmer and, especially, Simon Gaechter. They have proved an exceptionally useful source of information and a sounding board for my, at best, half-baked notions about fairness. It was also at Nottingham that I began both collaborations that have produced papers on this topic: with Udo Kreickemeier (now at the University of Tubingen) and with Carl Davidson and Steven Matusz (always at Michigan State, but with whom I developed the initial ideas in these papers during joint visits at Nottingham).

One straightforward way into both issues of fairness and unemployment is the fair wage version of the efficiency wage model (Akerlof and Yellen, 1988, 1990). This model has the virtues of being based on intuitively plausible and empirically well-supported assumptions about the link between perceived fairness and effort (Bewley, 1999). As a result, firms pay the wage necessary to extract optimal effort, but there is then an equilibrium relationship between unemployment and the wage paid to the factor for which the fairness constraint binds. Udo Kreickemeier joined the University of Nottingham in 2007 and it was my good luck that his office was directly across from the office I usually used. He was already well-versed in the application of fair wage models to issues of international trade and was working on an interesting paper developing an analysis of asymmetric national labor markets parallel to that of Davis (1998), but relying on differing degrees of the preference for fairness in the fair wage model, instead of a minimum wage, to generate the asymmetry between countries. Udo asked for comments on the paper and I happily gave them, since I learned a lot reading the paper. To my surprise, and a bit of embarrassment given the modest amount of my contribution, I ended up as a co-author (Kreickemeier and Nelson, 2006; Chapter 11 in this volume). Collecting the paper here gives me a chance to come clean about this one, plus it is great to have this paper in any collection of papers on trade policy and political economy.

The next two papers are genuinely collaborative. As I noted above, Carl Davidson, Steven Matusz and I started discussing the political economy of trade under unemployment while we were all visiting at the University of Nottingham. They were already well-known as pioneers in the application of equilibrium unemployment models to the study of international trade and were interested in political economy applications. I was interested in the way that, when unemployment was associated with international trade, people became significantly more protectionist (Hiscox, 2006). It seemed to me that notions of fairness were an essential part of the political glue that held the public politics of trade together, but that this issue was essentially unstudied. Our first effort in this direction focused on the fairness issue directly, without any unemployment (Davidson *et al.*, 2006; Chapter 12 here). We considered a referendum model of the Mayer (1984) sort, but assumed that people had Fehr–Schmidt preferences for equality in income distribution — a simple, tractable representation of fairness (Fehr and Schmidt, 1999).[14] In this setup, it is easy to show that equilibrium tariffs will be higher when people possess such preferences and the importable good uses unskilled labor intensively.

Our other paper on this topic seeks to integrate fairness and unemployment in a model of the general public politics constraint on trade policy (Davidson *et al.*, 2012; Chapter 13 here). We argue that the social welfare component of government preferences in Grossman and Helpman's (1994) protection for sale model can be interpreted as the public political check I mentioned in the previous section. In that context, and reflecting the empirics on the aggregate political economy of trade, it then makes sense to directly incorporate resistance to unemployment. Thus, we construct a model economy with search-generated unemployment and evaluate trade policy in terms of an unemployment-averse government. This framework allows us to present an analysis of the role of unemployment insurance in supporting trade liberalization. The results seem empirically plausible and suggest directions for future empirical work.

Trade Theory

The final set of three papers is different from the others in that they are primarily exercises in trade theory. However, they are all papers of which I am (possibly without foundation) proud. So there they are.

The first is from my days at Washington University in St. Louis. I was still in the process of making the transition from Political Science to Economics and, through the good offices of Bob Bates, had been offered a visiting job in the School of Business. One of my colleagues there was Tom Gresik, a first-rate micro theorist with interests in implementation theory. We started to talk about regulation of transfer pricing when firms possess private information. Once we had the paper ready for submission, we discovered that Prusa (1990) had scooped us. In the process of producing a generalization, we discovered that there was a technical problem in applying

---

[14]There is another Nottingham connection here: Simon Gaechter recommended that I look at Fehr–Schmidt preferences as a way of incorporating fairness in our analysis.

the revelation principle to this problem (because the transfer price has both direct and indirect payoff relevance for the firm) so, as a result, it can be the case that the optimal regulation does not involve truthful revelation (Gresik and Nelson, 1994; Chapter 14 in this volume). Thomas Gresik left Washington University for the University of Pennsylvania, where he was able to develop this line of work in much greater sophistication with Eric Bond (Bond and Gresik, 1996, 1997, 2011).

I left Washington University for Syracuse University. This was my first job in an Economics Department and it is where I finally really learned how trade theory works. Mary Lovely and I taught the PhD trade sequence every year, and every year I sat in all of Mary's lectures. I truly cannot imagine a better teacher. That process also allowed us to develop common notation, common tastes, and an easy approach to collaboration. One of the fruits of that collaboration came initially from a Nottingham issue. Nottingham, beginning with David Greenaway and Chris Milner, has long been a hotbed of research on intra-industry trade (IIT). Someone suggested over drinks in the evening at a Nottingham conference on intra-industry trade that, while it was well-known since Balassa (1966), and I had even made the same argument informally (Nelson, 1990), that IIT was less disruptive than inter-industry trade, no one had ever demonstrated that this obvious fact could be derived as a necessary property of some standard model of IIT. Since people were using this fact as the basis of research on trade and labor markets, it seemed like an easy opportunity to write a paper that would be cited constantly in the IIT literature. It also seemed like a perfect topic for Mary and me. In the event, it turned out that the intuition was, at least technically, wrong. Mary and I wrote a paper using Ethier's (1982) model of monopolistic competition and trade, and showed that the intuition was false. This paper (Lovely and Nelson, 2000), not collected here, did not make us popular. People argued that the Ethier model was too special to be a framework for this analysis. Thus, we went back to the drawing board and developed a very simple model that embedded most types of models of IIT and showed that there cannot be a general presumption that IIT is less disruptive than inter-industry trade (Lovely and Nelson, 2002; Chapter 15 here). This did not make us any more popular, but the paper usually gets cited as a marginal annoyance. Oh well...

The last paper collected here is a favorite for a variety of reasons: Joe Francois is an old friend and current co-author; the paper was my attempt to present a model graphically with the same clarity of graphical exposition as Peter Neary (one of the great expositors of theory — to say nothing of being one of the great theorists); and finally, the exposition is of one of my favorite papers in trade theory — Ethier's (1982) great national and international returns to scale paper. This is a difficult paper to grasp because, with international trade in intermediates, the production set is not a technological fact, but is determined by the international division of labor itself. Joe and I (Francois and Nelson, 2002) developed a graphical framework that gets this core difficulty across in a transparent way. It may not be up to Neary's level, but it seems to get the job done.

Douglas R. Nelson
October 2013

References

Akerlof, George A. and Janet L. Yellen. 1988. "Fairness and Unemployment." *American Economic Review*, 78(2), 44–49.

————. 1990. "The Fair Wage-Effort Hypothesis and Unemployment." *Quarterly Journal of Economics*, 105(2), 255–283.

Austen-Smith, David and Jeffrey S. Banks. 1999. *Positive Political Theory I: Collective Preference*. Ann Arbor: University of Michigan Press.

————. 2005. *Positive Political Theory II: Strategy and Structure*. Ann Arbor: University of Michigan Press.

Balassa, Bela. 1966. "Tariff Reductions and Trade in Manufacturers among the Industrial Countries." *The American Economic Review*, 56(3), 466–473.

Bauer, Raymond; Ithiel de Sola Pool and Lewis Anthony Dexter. 1963. *American Business and Public Policy: The Politics of Foreign Trade*. Chicago: Aldine.

Becker, Gary S. 1983. "A Theory of Competition among Pressure Groups for Political Influence." *Quarterly Journal of Economics*, 98(3), 371–400.

————. 1985. "Public Policies, Pressure Groups, and Dead Weight Costs." *Journal of Public Economics*, 28(3), 329–347.

Bewley, Truman F. 1999. *Why Wages Don't Fall During a Recession*. Cambridge, Mass.: Harvard University Press.

Bhagwati, Jagdish N. 1982a. "Directly Unproductive, Profit-Seeking (DUP) Activities." *Journal of Political Economy*, 90(5), 988–1002.

_____. (ed). 1982b. *Import Competition and Response*. Chicago: University of Chicago Press.

Bhagwati, Jagdish and T. N. Srinivasan. 1980. "Revenue Seeking: A Generalization of the Theory of Tariffs." *Journal of Political Economy*, 88(6), 1069–1087.

Bond, Eric W. and Thomas A. Gresik. 1996. "Regulation of Multinational Firms with Two Active Governments: A Common Agency Approach." *Journal of Public Economics*, 59(1), 33–53.

_____. 1997. "Competition between Asymmetrically Informed Principals." *Economic Theory*, 10(2), 227–240.

_____. 2011. "Efficient Delegation by an Informed Principal." *Journal of Economics and Management Strategy*, 20(3), 887–924.

Bougheas, Spiros and Douglas R. Nelson. 2012. "Skilled Worker Migration and Trade: Inequality and Welfare." *World Economy*, 35(2), 197–215.

Buchanan, James M. and Gordon Tullock. 1962. *The Calculus of Consent, Logical Foundations of Constitutional Democracy*. Ann Arbor: University of Michigan Press.

Davidson, Carl and Steven J. Matusz. 2004. *International Trade and Labor Markets: Theory, Evidence, and Policy Implications*. Kalamazoo, Mich.: W.E. Upjohn Institute for Employment Research.

_____. 2010. *International Trade with Equilibrium Unemployment*. Princeton, NJ: Princeton University Press.

Davidson, Carl; Steven J. Matusz and Douglas R. Nelson. 2006. "Fairness and the Political Economy of Trade." *World Economy*, 29(8), 989–1004.

_____. 2007. "Can Compensation Save Free Trade?" *Journal of International Economics*, 71(1), 167–186.

_____. 2012. "A Behavioral Model of Unemployment, Sociotropic Concerns, and the Political Economy of Trade Policy." *Economics and Politics*, 24(1), 72–94.

Davis, Donald R. 1998. "Does European Unemployment Prop Up American Wages? National Labor Markets and Global Free Trade." *American Economic Review*, 88(3), 478–494.

Downs, Anthony. 1957. *An Economic Theory of Democracy*. New York: Harper.

Egger, Peter and Douglas R. Nelson. 2011. "How Bad is Antidumping? Evidence from Panel Data." *Review of Economics and Statistics*, 93(4), 1374–1390.

Eichengreen, Barry. 1989. "The Political Economy of the Smoot-Hawley Tariff." *Research in Economic History*, 12, 1–43.

Ethier, Wilfred J. 1982. "National and International Returns to Scale in the Modern Theory of International Trade." *American Economic Review*, 72(3), 389–405.

Fehr, Ernst and Klaus Schmidt. 1999. "A Theory of Fairness, Competition, and Cooperation." *Quarterly Journal of Economics*, 114(3), 817–868.

Findlay, Ronald and Stanislaw Wellisz. 1982. "Endogenous Tariffs, the Political Economy of Trade Restrictions and Welfare," in J. Bhagwati (ed), *Import Competition and Response*. Chicago: University of Chicago Press/NBER, 223–234.

Finger, J. Michael; H. Keith Hall and Douglas R. Nelson. 1982. "The Political Economy of Administered Protection." *American Economic Review*, 72(3), 452–466.

Francois, Joseph F. and Douglas R. Nelson. 2002. "A Geometry of Specialisation." *Economic Journal*, 112(481), 649–678.

Gaston, Noel and Douglas R. Nelson. 2004. "Structural Change and the Labor-market Effects of Globalization." *Review of International Economics*, 12(5), 769–792.

Greenaway, David and Douglas R. Nelson. 2010. "The Politics of (Anti-) Globalization: What Do We Learn from Simple Models?," in N. Gaston and A. Khalid (eds), *Globalization and Economic Integration: Winners and Losers in the Asia-Pacific*. Cheltenham: Elgar, 69–92.

Gresik, Thomas A. and Douglas R. Nelson. 1994. "Incentive Compatible Regulation of a Foreign-owned Subsidiary." *Journal of International Economics*, 36(3–4), 309–331.

Grossman, Gene M. and Elhanan Helpman. 1994. "Protection for Sale." *American Economic Review*, 84(4), 833–850.

Haggard, Stephan. 1988. "The Institutional Foundations of Hegemony: Explaining the Reciprocal Trade Agreements Act of 1934." *International Organization*, 42(01), 91–119.

Hall, H. Keith and Douglas R. Nelson. 1989. "Institutional Structure and Time Horizon in a Simple Model of the Political Economy: The Lowi Effect." *The International Spectator*, 24(3/4), 153–173.

————. 1992. "Institutional Structure in the Political Economy of Protection: Legislated v. Administered Protection." *Economics and Politics*, 4(1), 61–77.

————. 2004. "The Peculiar Political Economy of NAFTA: Complexity, Uncertainty and Footloose Policy Preferences," in A. Panagariya and D. Mitra (eds), *The Political Economy of Trade, Aid and Foreign Investment Policies*. Amsterdam: Elsevier, pp. 91–109.

Hall, H. Keith; Chihwa Kao and Douglas R. Nelson. 1998. "Women and Tariffs: Testing the Gender Gap Hypothesis in a Downs-Mayer Political-Economy Model." *Economic Inquiry*, 36(2), 320–332.

Hinich, Melvin J. and Michael C. Munger. 1994. *Ideology and the Theory of Political Choice*. Ann Arbor: University of Michigan Press.

Hiscox, Michael J. 2001. *International Trade and Political Conflict: Commerce, Coalitions, and Mobility*. Princeton: Princeton University Press.

_____. 2006. "Through a Glass Darkly: Framing Effects and Individuals' Attitudes toward Trade." *International Organization*, 60(3), 755–780.

Kaufman, Robert R. 1979. "Industrial Change and Authoritarianism, a Concrète Review of the Bureaucratic-Authoritarian Model," in D. Collier (ed), *The New Authoritarianism in Latin America*. Princeton: Princeton University Press, 165–255.

Kreickemeier, Udo and Douglas R. Nelson. 2006. "Fair Wages, Unemployment and Technological Change in a Global Economy." *Journal of International Economics*, 70(2), 451–469.

Krueger, Anne O. 1974. "The Political Economy of Rent-Seeking Society." *American Economic Review*, 64(3), 291–303.

Lovely, Mary E. and Douglas R. Nelson. 2000. "Marginal Intraindustry Trade and Labor Adjustment." *Review of International Economics*, 8(3), 436–447.

_____. 2002. "Intra-Industry Trade as an Indicator of Labor Market Adjustment." *Weltwirtschaftliches Archiv-Review of World Economics*, 138(2), 179–206.

Lowi, Theodore J. 1964. "American Business, Public Policy, Case Studies and Political Theory." *World Politics*, 16(4), 676–715.

_____. 1969. *The End of Liberalism; Ideology, Policy, and the Crisis of Public Authority*. New York: Norton.

Mayer, Wolfgang. 1984. "Endogenous Tariff Formation." *American Economic Review*, 74(5), 970–985.

McConnell, Grant. 1966. *Private Power & American Democracy*. New York: Knopf.

Morrissey, Oliver and Douglas R. Nelson. 2003. "The WTO and the Transfer of Policy Knowledge: The Case of Trade and Competition Policy," in H. Bloch (ed), *Growth and Development in the Global Economy*. Cheltenham: Edward Elgar, 235–251.

_____. 2005. "The Role of the World Bank in the Transfer of Policy Knowledge on Trade Liberalisation," in D. Nelson (ed), *The Political Economy of Policy Reform: Essays in Honor of J. Michael Finger*. Amsterdam: Elsevier, 173–194.

Nelson, Douglas R. 1983. "Why World Systems Theory?: Accepting a New Paradigm." *International Interactions*, 9(4), 353–368.

_____. 1989. "Domestic Political Preconditions of US Trade Policy: Liberal Structure and Protectionist Dynamics." *Journal of Public Policy*, 9(1), 83–108.

_____. 1990. "The Welfare State and Export Optimism," in D. Pirages and C. Sylvester (eds), *The Transformations in the Global Political Economy*. London: St. Martin's Press, 127–152.

_____. 2006. "The Political Economy of Antidumping: A Survey." *European Journal of Political Economy*, 22(3), 554–590.

Niskanen, William A. 1971. *Bureaucracy and Representative Government*. Chicago: Aldine.

O'Donnell, Guillermo A. 1973. *Modernization and Bureaucratic-Authoritarianism; Studies in South American Politics*. Berkeley: Institute of International Studies.

Olson, Mancur. 1965. *The Logic of Collective Action*. Boston: Harvard University Press.

Pastor, Robert. 1983. "The Cry-and-Sigh Syndrome: Congress and Trade Policy," in A. Schick (ed), *Making Economic Policy in Congress*. Washington, DC: American Enterprise Institute for Public Policy Research, 158–195.

Peltzman, Sam. 1976. "Toward a More General Theory of Regulation." *Journal of Law & Economics*, 19(2), 211–240.

Polanyi, Karl. 1944. *The Great Transformation: The Political and Economic Origins of Our Time*. New York: Farrar & Rinehart.

Prusa, Thomas J. 1990. "An Incentive Compatible Approach to the Transfer Pricing Problem." *Journal of International Economics*, 28(1–2), 155–172.

Rueschemeyer, Dietrich; Evelyne Huber and John D. Stephens. 1992. *Capitalist Development and Democracy*. Chicago: University of Chicago Press.

Schattschneider, Edward Elmer. 1935. *Politics, Pressure and the Tariff*. Englewood Cliffs: Prentice Hall.

_____. 1960. *The Semisovereign People: A Realist's View of Democracy in America*. New York: Holt.

Scheve, Kenneth and Matthew J. Slaughter. 2001. *Globalization and the Perceptions of American Workers*. Washington, DC: Institute for International Economics.

Schnietz, Karen E. 2000. "The Institutional Foundation of U.S. Trade Policy: Revisiting Explanations for the 1934 Reciprocal Trade Agreements Act." *Journal of Policy History*, 12(4), 417–444.

Schumpeter, Joseph Alois. 1975. *Capitalism, Socialism, and Democracy*. New York: Harper & Row.

Stigler, George. 1971. "The Theory of Economic Regulation." *Bell Journal of Economics and Management*, 2(1), 3–21.

Truman, David Bicknell. 1951. *The Governmental Process; Political Interests and Public Opinion*. New York: Knopf.

Tullock, Gordon. 1967. "The Welfare Costs of Tariffs, Monopolies and Theft." *Western Economic Journal*, 5(3), 224–232.

Vandenbussche, Hylke and Maurizio Zanardi. 2010. "The Chilling Trade Effects of Antidumping Proliferation." *European Economic Review*, 54(6), 760–777.

Viner, Jacob. 1923. *Dumping: A Problem in International Trade*. Chicago: University of Chicago Press.

Wallerstein, Immanuel M. 1974. *The Modern World-System, I: Capitalist Agriculture and the Origins of the European World-Economy in the Sixteenth Century*. New York: Academic Press.

———. 1976. *The Modern World-System, II: Mercantilism and the Consolidation of the European World-Economy, 1600–1750*. New York: Academic Press.

———. 1989. *The Modern World-System, III: The Second Era of Great Expansion of the Capitalist World-Economy, 1730–1840s*. San Diego: Academic Press.

Acknowledgments

Like Blanche Dubois, in *A Streetcar Named Desire*, I have always relied on the kindness of strangers. Unfortunately, economists do not generally write books, and articles are not really the place to acknowledge those kindnesses. Thus, I take a couple of pages here to recall, fondly, the many institutional and personal kindnesses over the past nearly 40 years. The list is long, and space is short, so I can only hit some high points. I am well aware that my personal and professional debts extend well beyond those acknowledged here.

I was an undergraduate student at Miami University, in Oxford, Ohio. Miami has many virtues as an undergraduate institution, but for me, having David McClellan as a professor was literally life-changing. Professor McClellan was the sort of old-fashioned teacher that set very high standards and expected you to be able to meet them. In addition to instilling in me a desire to see problems in context, he also talked me out of applying to law school. My life is richer on both counts.

I have already noted that graduate school was at the University of North Carolina at Chapel Hill. The kindnesses from the faculty and my student colleagues are far too many to mention. I noted above that Edward Azar was an extraordinary scholar and a supportive thesis advisor. I had many friends in the PhD program, but one stands out. Craig Murphy to this day remains the friend I am most likely to call when I want to talk. His commitment to research and teaching is something I can only aspire to, but it is nice to have exemplars. We leave aside that he is only the second smartest person in his own house. Among the many others, Jim Ingram, Dennis Appleyard, Boone Turchi, Bill Keech, Claudio Cioffi-Revilla and, for somewhat different reasons, Carl Pletsch deserve special mention.

Similarly, I have already noted that the Treasury provided an opportunity to learn on the job, finish my dissertation, and work with Mike Finger and Keith Hall. I learned from both then, I continue to learn from both. What else is there to say.

The World Bank, through Mike's good offices, was twice a home. While there, I had an incredible collection of colleagues: David Tarr, Jaime DeMelo, Alan Winters, Julio Nogues, Andrzej Olechowski, Ellen Hanak, and Uma Lele. When the time came to leave, Bob Bates, who was visiting, suggested Washington University in St. Louis would be a good place, and he helped me secure a visiting job there.

The School of Business at Washington University was a splendid place to work. Although just a visitor, I was treated exceptionally well. On top of that, I had great colleagues. Tom Gresik, Jean Masson and Krish Ladha (and their three spouses), and Charlie Wasley were good friends as well as good colleagues. Gary Miller, the head of the political economy group, is an extraordinary scholar and was a true mentor. Cheryl Eavey and Phil Dybvig both joined the faculty a bit after I did and were good colleagues and friends. The culture of Washington University was unique in that the business school, Economics, Political Science, and Law all had good relations, shared seminars, etc. The group in Economics was particularly stimulating: Doug North, Norm Schofield, Art Denzau, John Nye and Hy Minsky were a fascinating group.

The move from Washington University to Syracuse was particularly notable because it gave me the opportunity to teach and do research in an Economics department. And what a great department it was. In addition to Duke Kao, there was Johnny Yinger, Jerry Kelly, Jan Ondrich, Mike Wasylenko, Dave Richardson and Jim Follain in Economics; Carol Nackenoff, Jim Greer, Mark Rupert, Fred Frohock and Kristi Andersen in Political Science. But mostly, there was Mary Lovely. If the weather had not been so bad, I would probably still be there.

But the weather was appalling (or so my wife tells me), and the offer from the Murphy Institute at Tulane University was too good to turn down. And, after a lifetime of travelling around, I have been here for 20 years. I have had, and have, some good friends and colleagues. The Murphy Institute has been my physical home and it has been great: Rick Teichgraeber, Jon Riley, Nick Baigent, Kevin Grier, Judy Schaefer, John Howard, Meg Keenan and Ruth Carter made and make it a great place to work. In Economics: Noel Gaston, Dave Malueg, Jon Pritchett, Yonsheng Xu, Stefano Barbieri, and now a whole new group of colleagues. I have had some exceptional students as well — Pia Law, Tim Wedding, Rodrigo Navia and Simone Silva. Outside of Murphy and Economics, I have been able to study with Graeme Forbes and gotten to know Molly Rothenberg. Like all places, Tulane has its challenges (most seem to come from the administration), but, on balance, it has been good.

Three other institutions deserve special mention. Starting in 1995, the School of Economics at the University of Nottingham has been a second home to me. The extraordinary David Greenaway (now Vice Chancellor of the University) invited me to visit in 1995 and still has not quite been able to get rid of me. From 2002–2009 I was a (part-time) Professor of Economics in the School. A quick glance at my CV shows the professional effect. In addition to providing me with a number of co-authors (Greenaway, Morrissey, Bougheas, Kreickemeier, Hijzen, and Jones were all members of the School), Davidson, Matusz, Egger and Egger were all close colleagues via their visits at the School. Perhaps even more important is the atmosphere of hard work and hard play in an exceptionally collegial environment. The list of friends runs essentially to the entire faculty, but in addition to those already mentioned, a few merit special note: Pete Wright, Michelle Haynes, Richard Upward, Chris Milner, Rod Falvey, Norman Gemmell, Simon Gaechter, Dan Seidmann, Dave Whynes, Richard Kneller, Marta Alloi, Zhihong Yu and, of course, Sue Berry. What a group. My life would be dramatically poorer without this group.

The next institution involves a much narrower acquaintanceship, but an extraordinary one. In August 2005, Hurricane Katrina hit New Orleans just as the school year was starting. Following the flooding, New Orleans was under mandatory evacuation, and it was not clear when we would be able to return. My wife's sister and her husband put us up at their home in Shreveport for months, making us feel more than welcome the entire time. Even so, it was not clear whether/when Tulane would reopen and I needed a place to work. Bob Flood, then of the IMF, who I had never met, thought the IMF should provide a temporary home for a displaced researcher from the area affected by Katrina and, for reasons unknown to me, decided it should be me. Because communications were disturbed, finding me was not easy. However, by contacting co-authors (Joe Francois and Mary Lovely), he tracked me down in Shreveport and offered me a job. In short order, I bought a couple suits, shoes, etc. (since all I brought from New Orleans were shorts, sneakers, tee shirts, my computer, and my guitars), and moved to DC. While there, I got to work with Shang-Jin Wei, Mary Amiti, Phillip McCalman and Stephen Tokarick. I owe Bob, as well as Anne Krueger and Raghuram Rajan, a real debt of thanks.

Finally, after my brief, unfortunate period as Chair of the Tulane Economics Department, I was able to take a sabbatical. Peter Egger arranged for me to spend the year visiting at ETH Zurich. Peter is an extraordinary mix of traits, talents and tastes. The year spent visiting in Zurich was not only exceptionally productive, but insanely fun. In addition to Peter, at his chair was an extraordinary group: Max von Ehrlich, Valeria Merlo, Georg Wamser, Doina Radulescu, Toby Seidel and Sergey Nigai. In addition to Peter's chair, Jan-Egbert Sturm, KOF and the Chair of Applied Macro were equally welcoming. Christoph Moser, Martin Gassebner, Michael Graff, and Andrea Lassmann were a great group.

And now, the best for last. My family has always been a source of strength, inspiration, and entertainment. My parents (Paul and Sue Nelson) raised us to be curious, skeptical and independent in thought. My siblings (Cindy, David and Eric) have always been the best of friends and a constant source of surprise and inspiration. Their spouses (Taylor, Laurie and Jamie) fit right in with the crowd. Letty has been my friend and partner for nearly 30 years. She has supported and tolerated occasional excessive focus, and still made it all fun. The most fun of all is the best girl in the world: Mariel Susana Vasquez Nelson.

Contents

Economics and Politics
of Administered Protection

The Political Economy of Administered Protection

By J. M. FINGER, H. KEITH HALL, AND DOUGLAS R. NELSON*

Trade restrictions are hardly ever voted directly by Congress. Though the threat of direct congressional action is frequently present, pressure for protection is usually applied through the major instruments for the administrative regulation of imports: the antidumping and countervailing duty procedures and the escape clause mechanism.

In this paper, we will examine these instruments for the administrative regulation of imports. The form of the paper is not novel —a theory of how these mechanisms work is developed, then operational implications of this theory are deduced and tested over the record of countervailing duty, antidumping, and escape clause cases decided from 1975 through 1979. This is the period over which the Trade Act of 1974 was in force. Because the nature of these mechanisms is relatively unfamiliar, a relatively large amount of institutional information is provided.[1]

I. Administrative Mechanisms

The distinction between "high" and "low" policy tracks is one which Richard Cooper has used in the international relations literature. The low, or technical, track is the "rules" track. Cases here are "determined," "decided," according to criteria established by law, administrative regulations and precedent. Higher-track decisions are less circumscribed by rules and regulations, and require considerable attention by government officials entrusted with discretionary authority and subject to political accountability. Political influence is applied directly in high-track cases, but comes to bear on low-track cases only indirectly, through the shaping of the laws and regulations which define their technocratic nature.

The highest, most open, decision mechanism in trade matters is, of course, Congress. Here decisions are made in the light of public awareness by decision makers directly responsible to the voters. At this level, decision criteria are very open—any industry seeking protection may present any reasons which it feels will be convincing.

Both the escape clause and the less-than-fair value mechanism are delegations of Congress' authority to regulate trade. One might assume that the same forces which would have come to bear on Congress will influence the delegated decision. We will, however, argue that the delegation of such decisions to a technical track will significantly affect their substance.

A. *The Escape Clause*

The more political of the administrative tracks created by Congress is the escape clause (Section 201 of the 1974 Trade Act). Under this clause, an industry may petition the International Trade Commission (ITC) to conduct an investigation of "injury" from imports. The ITC's investigation is limited to whether or not there has been or is likely to be injury to "the domestic industry producing an article like or directly competitive with the imported article." The ITC reports its findings to the president, and if injury to the domestic industry has been found, the report includes the ITC's recommendation as

*World Bank, University of Rochester, and Rutgers University, respectively. The original draft of this paper was completed while we were with the U.S. Treasury Department, Office of Trade Research. The positions taken and opinions expressed in this paper are our sole responsibility.

[1] Various sorts of information have gone into the development of this theory, much of it derived from firsthand observation of how things are done. The reaction of several readers to earlier drafts suggests that trained economists find "institutional information" (such as what the antidumping law actually says) repugnant, and that they are unwilling to admit such information as evidence in the testing of theories. Their position, it would seem, is that reading what the law *says* will not help one understand what it *means*. This meaning they seem to assume can only be grasped by interpreting regression results.

to the import restriction and/or adjustment assistance necessary to prevent or remedy the injury. The president, however, is not legally constrained by the ITC's recommendation. He may, if the ITC determines injury, decline to provide import relief or adjustment assistance, may decide to provide one when the other was recommended, or may negotiate orderly marketing agreements with exporting countries. Thus, the ITC's function is like that of a grand jury, the commissioners being charged with examining only one side of the issue which the president must decide. The ITC decides not the outcome of the case, but whether or not the case should be taken up by the president.

B. Less-than-Fair Value Cases

Countervailing duty cases are concerned with the sale of subsidized exports in the U.S. market, and antidumping cases with sales in the United States at a price below the foreign producer's long-run costs, or below his home-market price. Such cases are described as "less-than-fair value (LFV) cases," because the trade practices they are intended to control involve, in legal terms, the sale of products at less than their "fair value." The imposition of dumping duties requires both a determination of LFV pricing and a determination of resulting injury to domestic producers. Over the period covered by this study, a countervailing duty case included an injury test only if the product involved was duty free in the U.S. tariff schedule. During this period, LFV investigations were the responsibility of the Treasury Department and injury investigations were the responsibility of ITC.[2]

The LFV criteria are, by law, more technically precise than escape clause criteria. Dumping, for example, is defined by 300 lines of text in the antidumping act plus 1,000 Federal Register lines of administrative

[2] Since January 1, 1980, LFV investigations (in dumping and in countervailing duty cases) are done by the Commerce Department, and all countervailing duty cases include an injury test. Injury tests remain the responsibility of the ITC.

regulations. In contrast, the only criterion the Trade Act of 1974 imposed on the president's escape clause decisions was "the national economic interest of the United States," and the criteria by which the 1974 Trade Act charged the ITC with judging injury take up only 35 lines.

Further, the injury criteria are illustrative, while the dumping criteria are limiting. The Trade Act tells the ITC to take into account "all economic factors which it considers relevant, including (but not limited to)...[A list follows]." The antidumping act, in defining foreign value, specifies, for example, that "the amount for general expenses shall not be less than 10 percentum of the cost as defined in paragraph..., and the amount of profit shall not be less than 8 percentum of the sum of such general expenses and cost...."

That the technical criteria are followed is assured by the right of appeal. Any interested party can appeal a LFV determination into the federal courts. This right of court appeal does not apply to escape clause findings.

II. Nature of the Technical Track

A technical track is cheaper to operate than a political process. Discretion must be vested in relatively senior government officials, while a more tightly constrained process can be administered by a technically trained, as opposed to a broadly educated and politically astute, staff which could work out a political solution for their superior's signature.

A much more important characteristic of the technical track relates to the minimization of the political costs of making a decision. Protection involves large transfers of income—those from consumers to producers are typically eight to ten times the net costs of protection (Dale Larson). As Lester Thurow has pointed out, it is very difficult for democratic political systems to make such nearly zero-sum transfer decisions. Losses seem always to be more identifiable than gains; hence the optimal outcome is often to avoid a political decision.

454   THE AMERICAN ECONOMIC REVIEW   JUNE 1982

A. *Positive-Sum Decision*

When protection is the issue, the opposed interests are domestic producers, who want imports restricted, and domestic consumers or users, who want access to foreign sources of supply.[3] By specifying precisely how the interests of one group are to be taken into account, legal or technical criteria spare policy level officials from having to decide whose interests will be taken into account, and from having to explain why to those whose interests are left out. They provide solid reasons for the government's decision, and hence allow the government to point out to the losing side that no other decision was legally possible. This justification helps to diffuse the political costs of the decision without preventing the government from harvesting the gratitude of the winners.

In short, the technical track provides a way to decide between the courses of action which would be advocated by two directly opposed interest groups without facing up to the issue which divides them, that is, without weighing in comparable terms one side's interests against the other's. In terms of the interests *effectively* represented, the technical track turns a zero-sum situation into a positive-sum decision.

B. *Role of Misdirection and Obfuscation*

The key to the effectiveness of a technical track is that it disenfranchises one "side" with major interest in the decisions it makes. But the mechanism itself is established through democratic processes, hence, the disenfranchised "losers" from the decisions have the same right to shape its mechanisms as the "winners" do. That they do not is a reflection of their unawareness of what is going on. This unawareness in turn depends on two elements critical to an effective democratic decision mechanism—misdirection and obfuscation.

Misdirection has to do with the difference between the *LFV* mechanism's legal purpose and its economic function. In law, the mechanism is designed to impose import restrictions only in instances of "unfair" foreign pricing, for example, subsidized exports thereby priced below cost. (The *LFV* duties offset, in theory, the effects on import prices of unfair foreign practices.) But, as will be explained below, the economics of such mechanisms suggests that they will go "too far" and protect domestic producers from "fair" foreign competition as well.

As misdirection is the basis for establishing such mechanisms, obfuscation is what keeps them going. The *LFV* mechanism is an outlet for complaints by domestic producers, not domestic users or buyers, and hence at the initiation of each case, those who benefit from the possible import restriction will be better prepared than those who will lose. It is not likely that this discrepancy will disappear during the course of a case investigation. Lower-track procedures *are* technical, and thus incomprehensible without lengthy training. This means that such material is not likely to attract news media attention, and certainly not the attention which the more comprehensible political track events will receive. Thus technical procedures, whatever their purpose, tend to be obscure and the obfuscation they create allows the government to serve the advantaged interest group without being called to task by the disadvantaged.

C. *Nature of the Biases in the LFV Mechanism*

Our argument suggests that a low track will not function unless it is biased in favor of one or the other interest group in conflict. The direction of the bias in the *LFV* mechanism does not follow from the fact that it is technical, but simply from the fact that it is a channel for complaints about a surfeit of import competition, not a lack. Thus by design, it weighs domestic producers' interests more heavily than domestic users—it has the capacity to impose trade restrictions but not to remove them (other than those it imposes itself).

---

[3] This exposition assumes that the foreign exporter and/or government is not a major interest effectively involved in such decision mechanisms. This hypothesis will be tested below.

The characteristics of the *LFV* decision process come together in such a way as to suggest that the mechanism will be protectionist in more than the obvious sense just described. Control of the technocratic apparatus is ultimately political; hence the overall bias in the mechanism depends on how the political impacts of the disadvantaged interest's losses and of the advantaged interest's gains balance each other within it.

The existence itself of the mechanism demonstrates that one side has the advantage, and the obscure nature of its proceedings assures that that advantage can (to some degree) be exploited without generating opposition. Thus along whatever scale the *LFV* mechanism operates, it will be, as a central tendency, on the advantaged group's side of zero.[4]

The scale along which the *LFV* mechanism operates is the nature of the pricing practices which foreign sellers are allowed to employ in the U.S. market. Zero on this scale—the position accepted (as fair) by both conflicting interests, domestic producers and domestic consumers—is when foreign sellers are limited to the same pricing practices available to domestic sellers.[5] On the side of zero advantageous to domestic producers, foreigners will be more tightly restricted than U.S. sellers, that is, the *LFV* laws and mechanism will take pricing practices away from foreign sellers which the equivalent "domestic" law (for example, antitrust law) does not take away from domestic sellers. Thus our model predicts that the *LFV* mechanism imposes constraints on foreign sellers not imposed on domestic ones by equivalent domestic laws.

More than that, this approach suggests that protectionist pressure will bring about qualitative changes in the *LFV* mechanism and bring it to focus more on the question of comparative costs between domestic and foreign competitors for sales in the U.S. market than on the fairness of the foreigner's trade practices.

This argument is based on two propositions from social anthropology. The first of these is that the institutionalization of a social issue will attract, or cause to form, interest groups which stand to gain from that mechanism. The second is that institutional systems change over time, and that this change is significantly influenced by the interests of those groups which come to focus on it (Shmuel Eisenstadt, pp. 419–20; Walton Hamilton).

The legal objective of the *LFV* mechanism is to police the fairness of trade practices, and it pursues that objective by restricting imports (in design, from unfair exporters only). It is therefore an economic instrument with the power to restrict imports, and it will attract those with an interest in having imports restricted. This will include not only firms and industries beset by unfair competition, but more generally, those least favorably situated vis-à-vis their foreign competitors' costs. They will, the logic of social anthropology suggests, attempt to make their needs fit its scope, and its scope fit their needs. These tendencies, particularly the latter, suggest a convergence of the *economic* subject matter of *LFV* and escape clause (*EC*) cases—suggest that the *LFV* rules will tend toward protecting against the sort of injury from import competition which the escape clause goes at "officially."

III. Empirical Examination of *LFV* Determinations

A. *Empirical Questions*

In the most general sense, the purpose of our empirical examination of *LFV* and *EC* decisions is to demonstrate that the *LFV* system displays the characteristics of a technical track, and the *EC* mechanism those of a more political track. Several questions

---

[4] The logic of this paragraph applies to any delegation of authority to an administering agency. Hence OSHA is a good idea but we get too much of it. Likewise for Ralph Nader and factor-proportions model trade papers in this *Review*.

[5] The antitrust laws and enforcement mechanisms take up the general question of what trade practices are fair. Against this background, the *LFV* mechanisms deal only with the trade practices in the U.S. market of foreign sellers. The institutional basis for this separation may be that the mechanisms used to enforce the antitrust laws cannot be applied to foreign firms.

derived from the high-track, low-track model will be evaluated. The first and most obvious of these is that technical, not political, factors determine the outcome of cases on the lower track, and vice versa on the higher track.

The second point we want to make is that it is the relaxing of technical criteria rather than the direct specification of political criteria which allows political factors to influence a case outcome.

The difference between the *LFV* pricing and *LFV* injury determinations provide almost a controlled experiment for testing this hypothesis. Under the 1974 Trade Act, each dumping case and each countervailing duty case involving a duty-free product on which the Treasury Department's preliminary determination was affirmative then went to the ITC for an injury investigation. The decision environment of an injury investigation differed from that of a pricing determination in two important respects. First (as explained above), the technical criteria defining injury are much less precise than those defining *LFV* pricing. Second, the pricing, but not the injury determination, could be appealed in federal court—the pricing, but not the injury decision, is subject to a technical review which has the force of law behind it.

There is no formal political review of either determination. In form, the only difference is the relatively ambiguous technical definition of injury.

The third area we will examine is the nature of the bias in the *LFV* mechanism. We will take up two overlapping hypotheses. The first is that the technical rules which calibrate the mechanism not only prevent foreign sellers from using practices considered unfair (for all sellers) in the U.S. market, but spill over to protect U.S. producers against fair competition from foreigners. The second is that comparative costs have a major influence on *LFV pricing* decisions.

B. *Statistical Model*

The statistical objective of our data analysis is to determine the influence of political and economic variables on the likelihood of an affirmative determination in an *LFV* case. The dependent variable in this analysis was the case decision (affirmative or negative). The *LFV* pricing tests covered every case decided during 1975–79 for which we could develop values for the independent variables —183 of 208 cases, or 96 percent of the value of imports covered by the 208 cases.[6] Analysis of *LFV* injury determinations covered 57 cases of 68 decided—again, all the cases for which we could assemble the relevant data.

C. *Independent Variables*

Political Influences: International. Two variables in our model represent international political influences. The first of these measures the proportion of total U.S. exports (1976) which are imported by the country against which the *LFV* case was filed. The hypothesis which this variable tests is that nations with which we experience a high level of economic interdependence exercise greater influence on *LFV* outcomes than nations with which we are less interdependent.

The second international political variable is a dichotomous variable which identifies those cases brought against less-developed countries (*LDCs*). The hypothesis here is that the *LFV* decision process is prejudiced against the *LDCs*. The basis for this hypothesis is the argument by some proponents of "dependency" analysis that the institutional and legal structure in the advanced capitalist countries is rigged against *LDCs*.[7] A less conspiratorial way of viewing such an expectation is that the *LDCs* are simply not as well equipped to apply political pressure on their own behalf as other more developed countries.

Political Influences: Domestic. Our model will test two hypotheses that relate to domestic political influence:

HYPOTHESIS 1: *Industry size is positively related to success in the LFV mechanism.*

---

[6] The product coverage of each *case* is defined in terms of the TSUSA seven-digit import categories covered by the petition. The *industry* affected by a case is the four-digit SIC category into which the relevant TSUSA categories are mapped by the U.S. Bureau of the Census classifications.

[7] See, for example, Andre Frank.

HYPOTHESIS 2: *Industrial concentration is positively related to success in the LFV mechanism.*

Both of these hypotheses are based on the assumption that, at least on economic issues, industry structure translates directly into political power.

In our statistical model, we have used three alternative measures of industry size: total employment, the value of the physical capital stock, and value-added in the industry. We have also included "case size"—the value of 1978 imports of products covered by the case—as an indicator of the political influence of size.

The widely suggested relationship between industry concentration and political influence is rooted in the theory of collective goods. This theory suggests that decision-making costs are low in groups with one or a few dominant actors, allowing relatively effective political action.

A final hypothesis about political influence refers to the administrator's instinct for self-preservation. On January 1, 1980, responsibility for enforcement of the dumping and countervailing duty laws was shifted from the Treasury to the Commerce Department. According to government officials directly affected by this transfer, the movement for trade reorganization began in earnest in January 1979, as markup of the Trade Agreements Act of 1979 was completed. Behind this shift of responsibility was the presumption that the Commerce Department would find affirmatively more often than the Treasury Department. If the frequently expressed assumption that defense and expansion of "turf" are important arguments in the objective function of bureaucrats and of bureaucratic agencies, and if the *LFV* decision mechanism allowed for discretionary response to political pressure, then there should have been a detectable shift in 1979 of the *LFV* decision function toward the affirmative. We test this hypothesis by introducing a dummy variable which identifies all cases decided in 1979.

Comparative Costs. Comparative costs are virtually impossible to measure directly. We have used instead "factor proportions," which an extensive body of theoretical and

empirical work argue are the determinants of comparative costs, as an indirect measure. The variables employed are the industry physical capital-labor ratio;[8] industry average wage per worker, as a proxy for human capital intensity; and the extent of economies of scale in the industry.[9] If our hypothesis about the bias in the mechanism is valid, then *LFV* decisions will be influenced toward the affirmative by the existence of a cost disadvantage for the American industry.

In addition to supporting our hypothesis about the protectionist bias of the mechanism, a significant influence for factor proportions on *LFV* decisions would be consistent with our general hypothesis that the *LFV* mechanism is a technical, not a political, track.

This interpretation is supported by logic and by fact. As to logic, the advantaged interest has two ways to get what it wants: 1) to have the rules changed (further) in its favor; 2) to have the rules relaxed, so as to allow a more open, more expensive political track procedure. The former is the more direct, less risky, and less expensive alternative. As to fact, we will cite below examples of specific rules which bring comparative costs into the *LFV* pricing determination.

Precision. Our remaining technical variable measures the number of different products covered by the case—in operational terms, the number of 7-digit TSUSA lines. The logic behind this variable is that less than fair value is a pricing concept, and thus more appropriately applied to individual products than to large aggregates. Because the rules specify precisely what *LFV* pricing is, our hypothesis is that determinations will tend toward the status quo (negative) when the technical criteria for a decision are less clearly met. Thus the technical track hy-

[8] The physical capital stock was estimated, for 1975, by the Branson-Monoyios method; as the gross book value of plant and equipment, plus the capitalized value of supply and materials inventories. Data for all industry variables are from the *U.S. Census of Manufactures*.

[9] Estimated by Hufbauer's method. His measure of economies of scale is the coefficient a in the regression equation $\log v = k + a$ times $\log n + e$, where v is the ratio between value-added per man in plants employing n persons and value-added per man for the entire four-digit industry, and k is a constant. We used 1972 data.

TABLE 1—LOGIT ANALYSIS OF INFLUENCES ON LESS-THAN-FAIR VALUE PRICING DETERMINATIONS, 1975–79

Hypothesis and Variable	Hypothe- sized Sign	Results—Estimated Coefficient (t-Statistic)					
		(1)	(2)	(3)	(4)	(5)	(6)
Political Track Hypothesis							
International Political Influences							
Proportion of U.S. Exports to Country	−	−9.1 (−0.03)	76.2 (0.25)				
Against a Developing Country	+	−28. (−.61)	−.30 (−0.66)				
Domestic Political Influences							
Administrative Reorganization Threat	+	.69 (1.27)	.81 (1.53)	.80 (1.52)	.80 (1.52)		
Industry Concentration	+	−1.8 (−2.28)	−2.3 (−3.07)	−2.4 (−3.14)	−2.4 (−3.16)	−2.3 (−3.08)	
Case size	+	−.13 (−0.71)					
Industry Size							
Employment	+	2.9 (1.05)	−.13 (−0.14)	−0.4 (−0.04)			
Capital Stock	+	−0.3 (0.52)					
Value-Added	+	−.11 (−0.80)					
Technical Track Hypothesis							
Comparative Costs							
Capital-Labor Ratio	+	1.8 (2.20)[a]	1.8 (2.36)[b]	1.7 (2.33)[b]	1.7 (2.37)[b]	1.8 (2.39)[b]	1.6 (2.28)[b]
Average Wage	−	−.19 (−1.90)[a]	−.29 (−3.56)[b]	−.28 (−3.53)[b]	−.28 (−3.77)[b]	−.28 (−3.77)[b]	−.31 (−4.47)[b]
Scale Economies	−	−4.6 (−2.67)[b]	−5.2 (−3.05)[b]	−5.1 (−3.11)[b]	−5.1 (−3.12)[b]	−4.8 (−3.00)[b]	−3.5 (−2.40)[b]
Technical Precision							
Number of Products	−	−.90 (−1.54)	−.88 (−2.11)[a]	−1.0 (−2.39)[b]	−1.0 (−2.99)[b]	−1.0 (−3.11)[b]	−0.8 (−2.74)[b]
Constant		2.8 (2.75)[b]	4.1 (4.57)[b]	3.9 (4.97)[b]	3.9 (5.11)[b]	4.0 (5.20)[b]	3.2 (4.75)[b]
Proportion of Outcomes Successfully Predicted		69	71	71	71	71	68
Chi-Squared		168[b]	172[b]	171[b]	171[b]	172[b]	178[b]
Number of Observations		183	183	183	183	183	183

[a] Indicates *rejection* of the null hypothesis that the sign is not the expected one, at the 95 percent level of confidence (one-tail test).

[b] Same as fn. a, but at the 99 percent level of confidence (one-tail test).

pothesis suggests a negative relation between the number of products covered by a case and the likelihood of an affirmative determination.

D. Evaluation of Results

LFV Pricing. The technical nature of the *LFV* pricing determinations is most di-rectly illustrated by the language of the law and the related administrative regulations— the sort of information presented in Section I above. Our statistical results, presented in Table 1, are also consistent with this hypothesis. In our examination of the influences on *LFV* pricing determinations, we found each technical factor to be statistically influential. And as we hypothesized, the significant test on each political variable is inconsistent with the political track hypothesis. Most soundly rejected is the hypothesis of international political influence. The t-statistics on these two variables are much below unity (in absolute value) and the coefficient on the *LDC* variable has the wrong sign. Further, when these variables are removed from the equation (from col. 2 to col. 3), the coefficients and the t-statistics on the significant variables are virtually unaffected.

The domestic political influence variables fare only slightly better. Of the four size variables, only employment has the expected sign, and even it is a long way from statistically significant. The closest thing to a valid domestic political influence hypothesis seems to be the "turf defending" hypothesis about the administering agency. The coefficient on the administrative reorganization threat variable has the hypothesized sign, and though insignificant at the 95 percent confidence level, has a larger t-statistic than the other domestic political influence variables.

On the technical track side, there is not much to add to the message in the table. Each technical track variable has the expected sign and is significant, at the 99 percent level of confidence.

LFV Injury. When we deal with injury, where the technical rules are less precise, we expect political factors to be more influential. As tests of the impacts of the various factors, we expect the same signs on the coefficients as in the analysis of the *LFV* decision, with one exception. An affirmative *LFV injury* determination will become *more* likely as the number of products covered by the case increases. While price is a concept most readily made operational on an individual product basis, injury is more appropriately (for example, in the Escape Clause of the Trade Act) expressed in terms of capacity utilization, employment, or profits—concepts more readily made operational at the firm or industry level.

The results (Table 2) are consistent with our expectations. The political variables are much more significant here than they were in Table 1, and the technical variables much less. The hypothesized influence of the threat

of administrative reorganization is supported by our data, as is the hypothesized influence of the size of the petitioning industry's labor force.

International political influences again are not significant—it is domestic politics which counts.

John Odell obtained similar results in a study of twenty-five bilateral trade disputes between the United States and Latin American countries. He found that when the foreign country worked with common economic interests within the United States, the proportion of outcomes favorable to the foreign country was higher. But mobilizing the State Department or the National Security Council staff to make "foreign policy" arguments was not effective. Thus he found that foreign interests, to get what they want must work through allied domestic interests.

Protectionist Bias and Comparative Costs. In form, a *LFV* pricing investigation consists of observing the prices a foreign firm charges on home market sales and on sales in the United States, and then comparing the two. The details of the law and of the administrative regulations specify how the observations are to be made, and how one or the other is to be adjusted for different terms of sale (for example, lot size, payment terms, etc.), so as to make them comparable. William Dickey explains several ways in which these rules are more restrictive of foreign firms' than is comparable "domestic" law of domestic firms' sales practices in the U.S. market. For example, sales below full cost during periods of slack demand (i.e., sales which cover only variable costs) are normally not considered an unfair trade practice under the antitrust laws. But the antidumping law specifies that in determining the home market price charged by a foreign firm, observations of home market sales *below cost* must be disregarded.[10]

There are other, more direct illustrations that the *LFV* process now compares foreign and domestic costs. The administrative regulations for antidumping cases state that "Pe-

---

[10]See Dickey, p. 245. He provides several other, more complicated, examples.

TABLE 2—LOGIT ANALYSIS OF INFLUENCES ON ITC INJURY DETERMINATIONS IN LESS-THAN-FAIR VALUE CASES

Hypothesis and Variable	Expected Sign	Results—Estimated Coefficient (t-statistic)						
		(1)	(2)	(3)	(4)	(5)	(6)	(7)
Political Track Hypothesis								
International Political Influences								
Proportion of U.S. Exports to Country	−	−1276	−1205	−967	−922	−604		
		(−1.64)	(−1.57)	(−1.41)	(−1.44)	(−0.96)		
Against a Developing Country	+	−.5						
		(−0.44)						
Domestic Political Influences								
Administrative Reorganization Threat	+	2.5	2.6		2.8	2.7	3.0	2.9
		(1.90)	(2.07)[a]		(2.30)[a]	(2.20)[a]	(2.49)[b]	(2.43)[b]
Industry Concentration	+	−5.9	−6.1	−5.6	−3.9	−5.5	−5.6	−5.6
		(−2.22)	(−2.44)	(−2.39)	(−2.05)	(−2.34)	(−2.35)	(−2.34)
Case Size	+	2.3	2.5	2.2	1.7		1.0	
		(1.25)	(1.37)	(1.29)	(1.17)		(0.87)	
Industry Size								
Employment	+	36.1	36.0	27.5	22.3	27.9	27.9	28.4
		(1.85)[a]	(1.98)[a]	(2.22)[a]	(2.00)[a]	(2.22)[a]	(2.07)[a]	(2.14)[a]
Capital Stock	+	−.57	−.60	−.47	−.37	−.42	−.45	−.43
		(−1.87)	(−2.10)	(−2.45)	(−2.19)	(−2.27)	(−2.24)	(−2.19)
Value-Added	+	−0.7						
		(−0.12)						
Technical Track Hypothesis								
Comparative Costs								
Capital-Labor Ratio	+	1.5	1.5					
		(0.73)	(0.78)					
Average Wage	−	.35	.34	.39	.24	.38	.37	.37
		(1.25)	(1.48)	(1.83)	(1.39)	(1.75)	(1.67)	(1.68)
Scale Economies	−	−2.2	−2.2					
		(−0.64)	(0.73)					
Technical Precision								
Number of Products	+	−55.6	−54.3	−49.8		−46.7	−50.0	−48.3
		(−1.86)	(−1.82)	(−1.84)		(−1.73)	(−1.80)	(−1.76)
Constant		−.75	−.71	−1.2	−1.2	−1.2	−1.4	−1.4
		(−0.28)	(−0.34)	(−0.61)	(−0.67)	(−0.63)	(−0.70)	(−0.72)
Proportion of Outcomes								
Successfully Predicted		84	81	81	79	79	83	83
Chi-Squared		127	126	130	84	129	149	145
Number of Observations		57	57	57	57	57	57	57

[a, b] See Table 1.

titioners unable to furnish information on foreign sales or costs may present information concerning US domestic producers' costs adjusted for differences in the foreign country in question...."[11]

Our own analysis provides corroborating evidence. Each of the determinants of com-

[11]*Federal Register*, No. 26, p. 8199, col. 1. This evolution continues. Matthew Marks (p. 432) points out that the shorter time limits put into effect by the Trade Agreements Act of 1979 will make the administering agency more dependent on such cost information supplied by the petitioner.

parative advantage has the hypothesized sign and is significant at the 99 percent level of confidence.[12]

[12]We assume that scale economies and human capital intensity are positively related and physical capital intensity negatively related to U.S. comparative advantage. Virtually all relevant empirical work supports the assumed signs on the first two variables. As to our "Leontief paradox" assumption on the third variable, Robert Stern (pp. 86–90), reviewing recent cross-section studies of the trade position of U.S. industries, indicates that in each of them only when "resource intensive" industries are excluded does the relation between physical capital intensity and U.S. comparative advantage

E. Anomalies

The coefficients on several variables do not have the signs we expected. For example, we interpreted the concentration ratio as a reflection of political influence, and expected it to have a positive coefficient in Tables 1 and 2. It is, however, negative in both cases. This result might be consistent with a technical interpretation of the variable. According to the technical track hypothesis, the outcome of a case, once it is filed, depends on technical factors not affected by the petitioner's lobbying. Protection, from a successful petition, will add to the profitability of each domestic sale by the industry—not just to those sales by the petitioning firm or firms. But in a concentrated industry, a larger share of the benefits from a successful petition will be captured by the petitioner and a smaller share will spill over to firms which did not help finance it. Hence, a firm's filing a petition will make economic sense at a lower likelihood of success if the industry is concentrated.

As this paper examines influences on the *outcomes* of *LFV* cases (once they are filed), the negative coefficient on concentration can be consistent with the positive (but insignificant) cross-section relation Finger (forthcoming) found between concentration and the industry incidence of *LFV* complaints, and Robert Baldwin (1980) found between concentration and the depth of the tariff cut made by the United States at the Tokyo round. The Finger and the Baldwin results may indicate that the concentration ratio is not a reliable indicator of how well an industry is organized to take advantage of the avenues the government provides. And if the firms in concentrated industries tend to be multinational in scope, this weak result may simply indicate that restrictions on imports are not what they want from the government.

Several readers have suggested that the statistical significance of the wage variable might also be interpreted as evidence of political influence on *LFV* pricing decisions. One such interpretation is simply that the decision makers have sympathy for poor people, and will use the discretion the technical rules allow to protect them. A more cynical interpretation is that the politically sensitive decision makers "buy them off" by providing trade protection.

Serious questions can be raised about the analytical soundness of the latter proposition and about the validity of both.

If we accept the buy-them-off interpretation, then we are assuming that it is the votes of the poor, not their well-being, which is the politician's concern. If so, the critical variable is how *many* there are, not how *poor* they are. If so, the *number* of workers, not their wage rate, is the better representation.

Furthermore, higher-wage workers will more likely be able to afford political action and are more likely to be organized in such a way as to be politically effective. This would make the political association between affirmative decisions and the wage rate positive, not negative.

As to the evidence, if one looks at the entire pattern of statistical results, and not just at one *t*-statistic, a political interpretation of the average wage variable becomes untenable. All *three* comparative cost proxies are significant, and it is difficult to explain the other two in political terms. Economies of scale might lead to size and/or concentration, which would produce political power, but scale economies itself is not a political influence. Similarly, the number of workers in an industry or the industry's wealth (capital stock) might measure political power, but not the ratio of one to the other.

Even more to the point, the political interpretation of the average wage variable cannot assume that the law or the administrative regulations specify that the income or need of the affected workers be taken into account. They simply do not. Political influence slips in (if it slips in) because the technical specifications are ambiguous and allow it. If so, the more obvious and direct political influences represented by our list of political variables should be significant. They are not.

---

become positive. Our analysis included the resource intensive industries, and in this analysis, capital intensity is used only as a *forecaster* of comparative advantage. Correlation between physical capital and natural resource intensity, which muddles the analysis of *cause* of comparative advantage, is of no consequence to our analysis.

TABLE 3—CHARACTERISTICS OF HIGH AND LOW ADMINISTRATIVE DECISION TRACKS

Track	Functional Criterion	Scope of Decision	Decision Criteria	Decision Type
Low	Public Unawareness (political insignificance)	Parochial— Petitioner's Interests	Precise and Limiting	Positive Sum (easy)
High	Public Awareness (political significance)	National Interest	Open	Zero Sum (hard)

Finally, the technical criteria for injury *are* less precise than those of *LFV* pricing. The hypothesized influence of sympathy for the poor should therefore have a stronger influence on the injury determination. This is not the case. Results in Table 2 show that the domestic political factors *are* significant influences in *LFV* injury determinations, but the average wage variable's coefficient does not even have the sign which a political influences interpretation suggests.

IV. The Escape Clause (*EC*) Decision

A. *Determinants of where Cases will be Resolved*

From the petitioner's point of view, the distinction between a *LFV* case and an *EC* case is not a technical one. The technical criteria for demonstrating injury are not precise, hence a petitioner who feels that he has sufficient *political* influence to win has considerable latitude in putting together his supporting case. The technical criteria on *LFV* pricing are much more precise, but as our model suggests and our data demonstrate, they overlap considerably with comparative disadvantage, or the likelihood of injury from import competition. The other part of an *LFV* case is the ITC injury test, hence the *technical* criteria for good *LFV* cases and for good escape clause cases are much the same and do not serve to restrict a complaint to one track or the other.

The functional characteristic which separates the low from the high track is the political significance of the cases it handles. This characteristic will be closely related to the degree of public awareness of the cases being processed. If the public is unaware of a petition to the government for protection, then (as outlined in Table 3) the scope of the decision on the case can be limited to the interests of the petitioner, and a decision can be reached with dispatch. The technical criteria of the lower track will serve both to control the decision process and to keep it from becoming a public issue. They can therefore be designed to evaluate only the petitioner's interests. The decision then is easy. Those who will lose are not aware that the decision is being made.

A high degree of public awareness changes the game. It is impossible, in a democratic country, to define out of a public decision parties who are aware that their interests are at stake. Thus such a decision cannot be bounded by technical constraints, and it cannot be limited to considerations only of the petitioner's interests. Among the participants in such a decision, there will be losers as well as winners and, as Lester Thurow suggests, such decisions will be hard to achieve.

Within limits, the high track can create public awareness and the low track obscure it, but public awareness is more an exogenous factor than an endogeneous one. This factor has no obvious quantitive measure, but is likely closely related to case size. Case size thus should serve to distinguish between cases which the low track can and cannot process effectively. Table 4 shows that the average case filed in the *EC* mechanism was three times as large as the average *LFV* case. If we exclude antidumping petitions for steel and autos (disputes which we shall argue below did not "belong" in this mechanism

TABLE 4— *LFV* AND *EC* MECHANISMS: NUMBER OF CASES, 1975–79 AND IMPORT COVERAGE

	LFV Cases		EC Cases	
	All Cases	Excluding Steel and Autos	ITC Decision	Presidential Decision
Number of cases				
Filed	245	214	43	–
Decided	208	177	40	25
Affirmative	73	73	25	8
(Percent of Decided)	35	41	62	32
Orderly Marketing Arrangements	–	–	–	3
(Percent of Affirmative)	–	–	–	38
Import Coverage of Cases ($ million)[a]				
Filed	$25,948	$5,991	$14,224	–
Decided	$25,085	$5,079	$13,016	$8,968
Affirmative	$2,860	$2,860	$8,968	$4,992
(Percent of Decided)	11	56	69	56
Orderly Marketing Arrangements	–	–	–	$3,888
(Percent of Affirmative)	–	–	–	78
Average Case Size ($ million)[a]				
Filed	$106	$28	$331	–
Decided	$121	$29	$325	$359
Affirmative	$39	$39	$359	$624
Orderly Marketing Arrangements	–	–	–	$1,296

[a]In terms of 1978 import values.

and were not resolved there), *EC* cases were more than eleven times as large as *LFV* cases.

B. *The Presidential Decision*

Protection cases decided in the spotlight of national attention are close to zero-sum decisions. The political net gain (or minimal net loss) is not on either side of such decisions, but in avoiding them. This has two implications for the presidential decision. First, it will push the president toward saying no. Negative decisions will discourage further petitions and hence reduce the number of times the president will have to say anything. A minimal political gain from saying yes on one case may be undone by the loss from having to decide the four others this yes encourages. Second, it will push a presidential affirmative decision as far toward a non-decision as his legally defined options allow. The president cannot avoid public scrutiny or political accountability by ordering the negotiation of an orderly marketing arrangement (*OMA*), but he can cloud the public's view and diffuse accountability somewhat.

The details of an *OMA* can be made quite complex, or put off to be worked out in the future, when they will be announced at a high, but lower than presidential level (for example, the Special Trade Representative). The other affirmative options give consumer interests a more precise dimension on which to focus—several percentage points added to price by a tariff, or taken away from supply by a quota, or the budgetary cost of adjustment assistance. As Table 4 shows, the three *EC* cases in which the president recommended an orderly marketing arrangement covered 78 percent of the imports on which affirmative decisions were returned.[13] In effect, ordering the negotiation of an *OMA* is a step toward disenfranchising domestic consumers, and hence a movement toward a

---

[13]Virtually every line in the U.S. tariff has been "conceded" under the GATT. Import relief would therefore involve nullification or impairment of a GATT concession for which the countries to whom the concession had been made could demand compensation. Negotiation of an *OMA* with these trading partners would incorporate the question of compensation and thus avoid its becoming a separate issue.

464 THE AMERICAN ECONOMIC REVIEW JUNE 1982

positive-sum decision environment. If domestic and foreign producers are the only influences at play, a minimal amount of political craft should be needed to induce the competing producers to do what the antitrust laws attempt to prevent them from doing voluntarily.

On the high track, the clearest pressures are away from a decision, not toward either a yes or a no. Accepting this, and looking deeper for some political or economic basis of forecasting the president's decision when he must make one, we note that both the degree of injury to the domestic producer of import replacements and the "gains from trade" to domestic consumers will concentrate on those sectors in which the United States has comparative disadvantage. Hence, *net* losses to the national economic interest should not vary much between industries (see Larson, Table 1), and in cases which are big enough to overcome the relative dispersion of consumers and/or public enough so that consumers as well as producers will be aware of their stake in them, there is no basis for predicting that comparative costs will consistently push the decision in one direction or the other. As protection, except in unlikely "optimum tariff" situations, is a negative sum proposition, the "national economic interest" will always push toward a negative decision. But as this net loss to the economy comes to only 10 percent of the gross gain for protected producers (see Larson, Table 1), the net national interest is not likely to be a powerful influence.

The president's decision is made, therefore, at the razor's edge. The economic gains to those who want protection are only marginally smaller than its costs to those who oppose it, and this margin will not vary much from case to case. Because of the level at which the decision is made, consumers (potential losers from protection) will not be in the dark, but if there is a marginal difference in the degree of public awareness of a case and of its implications, it should favor the producer's side. Thus, the economics and the politics of the decision will each favor one side or the other only marginally, with economics tipped toward one side and politics toward the other.

The ITC's findings will not be definitive. Their role in the decision process will be more political than technical or economic, and more facilitating than decisive. Their major functions are to make sure a politically significant petitioner gets his day before the president; to occupy time during which resolution of the case may be achieved by less focused means than a presidential decision; to provide a focal point so that the president may observe how the sides are drawn before the mechanism focuses on him.

We thus find it difficult to say what will define operationally the "clout" needed to win an affirmative decision from the president. Baldwin, as we predict, did not find the ITC decision a significant factor. Our own *Logit* analysis was plagued by convergence problems, due in part, we suspect, to the smallness of the number of presidential decisions—this smallness being consistent with our predictions. The obvious, though gross, measure of political clout behaved in the obvious way. On eight "Big Cases" (over $400 million of imports), the president said yes five times (three *OMAs*). On seventeen "Small Cases," he said yes only three times (no *OMAs*).

Our and Baldwin's generally poor results with statistical decision rules illustrate perhaps the nature of the presidency. Those things which can be reduced to rules will be decided at a lower level.

V. Conclusions

We have presented and tested an interpretation of how the administrative import restraint mechanisms function. This interpretation differs in some respects from more or less "official" interpretations, but this difference is not an indictment of the mechanisms. Their function is to resolve or diffuse complaints about import competition, and all in all they seem to serve this function efficiently.

A major difference between our view and others' has to do with what the *LFV* and *EC* mechanisms actually do. In law, the escape clause deals with injury to U.S. producers from import competition and the *LFV* mechanism with the fairness of business practices

TABLE 5—PERCENTAGE OF IMPORTS OF MANUFACTURED GOODS
COVERED BY *LFV* AND *EC* CASES, 1975–79

	Antidumping and Countervailing Duty Cases		Escape Clause Cases	
Year[a]	Filed	Affirmative	Filed	Affirmative
1975	15.4	0.3	4.1	0.0
1976	0.8	0.9	2.3	0.5
1977	4.1	0.6	2.6	2.8
1978	0.6	0.4	1.0	0.4
1979	0.4	0.1	0.5	0.0
1975–79	21.3	2.2	10.4	3.8

[a] The trade coverage of each case was measured by 1978 imports of the products covered by the case, for example, *LFV* cases filed in 1975 covered products which in 1978 accounted for 15.4 percent of manufactured imports. The 1975–79 figures measure the percentage of 1978 manufactured imports covered by cases filed (or affirmatively decided) in the five-year period.

used in the U.S. market by foreigners. But in economics we find that they both deal with the same thing—injury from imports and the associated gains from trade. The functional difference between the cases which belong on one track or the other is the size and perhaps the degree of public awareness of the interests at stake, not the nature of those interests. Antidumping and countervailing duties are, functionally, the poor (or small) man's escape clause.[14]

The administrative mechanism is in part self-policing, but its effective function depends in part on the good citizenship of its users. It is not likely that a politically obscure case will be filed on the high track. It is less costly to provide data for technocrats to fit into their formulae than to establish the political basis for a presidential decision. Besides, the lower-track decision weighs the petitioner's interests more heavily than does the higher. In short, if you are politically obscure, the lower track will work *for* you. But if you are politically prominent, the lower track will not work. Highly visible petitions will attract political opposition which the technical rules of the track will not be able to depose, or even effectively express. Because they have no technical outlet, buyers must press their interests at the political level,

hence such cases will escalate into political issues.

The antidumping mechanism did not resolve the steel and auto cases. Though these antidumping cases were terminated, the conflicts they represented went on—autos became an escape clause case and finally an *OMA* with Japan, and the steel issue has led to high level administrative protection through the Trigger Price Mechanism. This is not to argue that the petitioner will not gain from such a filing. He will, through the news generated by such a petition and the opportunities it will create to complain about the ineffectiveness of the government and the bureaucracy, publicize his complaints about the "unfairness" of foreign competition. In so doing, he will be building the broad base of public support needed to win a favorable political decision at the national level.[15]

But using the mechanism to publicize a particular case will create public awareness of the mechanism, and hence reduce its capacity to process efficiently those cases for which it would have been appropriate. The recent trade reorganization act not only transferred administration of *LFV* cases from Treasury to Commerce, but made its procedures considerably more Byzantine—so

---

[14] And seems, in a way, to define having comparative advantage as an unfair trade practice.

[15] The uncertainty of the case outcome might slow foreign development of a market in the United States. For details and empirical tests, see Finger.

much so that its drafters describe it as a "Lawyer's Relief Act." The motive behind this might have been protectionist, but it may also have been to restore the degree of obscurity (and therefore effectiveness)[16] which use of the mechanism by the steel and auto industries took away.

Table 5 is presented to assure the reader that a cynical or despondent interpretation of the institutions we have described is not warranted. We have argued that in their central tendency these mechanisms are biased toward protectionism. But this bias is not large. In the five years, 1975–79, only 2.2 percent of U.S. manufactured imports have been granted relief under the *LFV* statutes, and only 3.8 percent under the escape clause.[17] The costs of gathering and disseminating information needed to reduce this bias would probably exceed the benefits. The dark side of the force is more protectionist than the light, that is, it is the openness of the system which keeps the bias as small as it is.

[16] Which suggests that the social value of lawyers lies in the confusion they create, not in that they dissolve.

[17] Of the imports subject to relief under the escape clause, 68 percent are covered by the *OMA*s for footwear and television receivers. Larson argues that these *OMA*s have had no effect on the trends of U.S. imports of footwear and television sets.

REFERENCES

Baldwin, Robert E., "U.S. Political Pressures Against Adjustment to Greater Imports," paper presented at the Eleventh Pacific Trade and Development Conference, Korean Development Institute, Seoul, September 1–5, 1980.

Branson, William H. and Monoyios, Nikolaos "Factor Inputs in U.S. Trade," *Journal of International Economics*, 7, May 1977, 111–31.

Cooper, Richard N., "Trade Policy is Foreign Policy," *Foreign Policy*, No. 9, Winter 1972–73, 18–36.

Dickey, William L., "The Pricing of Imports into the United States," *Journal of World Trade Law*, May–June 1979, *13*, 238–56.

Eisenstadt, Shmuel N., "Social Institutions" in *International Encyclopedia of the Social Sciences*, New York: Macmillan and the Free Press, 1968, *14*, 409–29.

Finger, J. M., "The Industry-Country Incidence of 'Less Than Fair Value' Cases in the United States Import Trade," in Malcolm Gillis and Werner Baer, eds., *Export Diversification and the New Protectionism*, National Bureau of Economic Research, forthcoming.

Frank, Andre G., *Capitalism and Underdevelopment in Latin America*, New York: Monthly Review Press, 1967.

Hamilton, Walton H., "Institution" in *Encyclopedia of the Social Sciences*, Vol. 8, New York: Macmillan, 1937, 84–89.

Hufbauer, Gary C., "The Impact of National Characteristics and Technology on the Commodity Composition of Trade in Manufactured Goods," in Raymond Vernon, ed., *The Technology Factor in International Trade*, National Bureau of Economic Research, New York: Columbia University Press, 1970.

Larson, Dale W., "The Cost of Import Protection in the United States," U.S. Treasury Department, processed, 1979.

Marks, Matthew J., "Recent Changes in American Law on Regulatory Trade Measures," *The World Economy*, July 1980, *2*, 427–40.

Odell, John S., "Latin American Trade Negotiations with the United States," *International Organization*, Spring 1980, *34*, 207–28.

Stern, Robert M., "Changes in U.S. Comparative Advantage: Issues for Research and Policy" in National Science Foundation, *International Economic Policy Research*, papers and proceedings of a colloquium held in Washington, D.C., October 3 and 4, 1980.

Thurow, Lester C., *The Zero Sum Society*, New York: Basic Books, 1980.

Federal Register, No. 26, Vol. 45.

U.S. Bureau of the Census, *Census of Manufactures*, Washington, various years.

ECONOMICS AND POLITICS   0954-1985
Volume 4   March 1992   No. 1

INSTITUTIONAL STRUCTURE IN THE POLITICAL ECONOMY OF PROTECTION: LEGISLATED V. ADMINISTERED PROTECTION

H. KEITH HALL AND DOUGLAS NELSON

In endogenous tariff theory the outcome of the political process (the tariff) is a strictly private good from the perspective of the specific-factors in an industry. That is, the benefits from participation in the political process are fully captured by the participant group. We argue that this is an institutional assumption by showing that an alternative, administered protection, involves the enforcement of a rule that, once written, is applied to all industry groups, where applicable. Attempts to increase protection therefore result in benefits to all import competing industry groups. In a short-run neo-classical model of trade with no intermediate goods, you therefore get a political free rider problem that you do not get with legislated tariffs. Further, it is argued that the distinction between these forms of protection is of both empirical and philosophical relevance.

The fundamental importance of institutions to the study of political economy is undeniable. To most economists, however, the paramount institutional issues relate to the organization of exchange and production. On these topics we find two hundred years of cumulative theoretical and empirical research, defining the core of modern research on welfare theory and microeconomic theory. More recently, we have seen the development of a new area of research by economists applying the standard techniques of economic analysis to human behavior outside the economy, including the creation and evolution of social institutions.[1] Virtually all of this research examines institutional form as a function of rational choice. With the exception of some very recent research on constitutional theory (most of it by James Buchanan and his school), there is very little systematic research by economists on the inverse relationship: the effect of institutional form on individual choice in socio-political environments.

Consider the case of endogenous tariff theory.[2] It is clear enough that a tariff increase has redistributive consequences. In the short-run, factors that are mobile and specific (immobile) to the protected industry gain at the expense of factors specific to other industries (Jones, 1971, 1975; Mayer, 1974; Mussa, 1974; Neary, 1978). In the long-run, the returns to factors used relatively intensively in the protected industry are unambiguously raised (the Stolper-Samuelson theorem).

---

[1] See Hirshleifer (1985) for a brief survey of this "economics imperialism." With regard to the microeconomic/choice-theoretic analysis of social institutions, in addition to the classic work of Hicks (1969), North (1981), and the property rights theorists on the evolution of economic institutions, there has been substantial recent growth of more general work on the evolution of normative systems (e.g. Field, 1984; Leibenstein, 1984; Axelrod, 1986; Sah, 1987).

[2] See Nelson (1988) for a survey of endogenous tariff theory.

62   HALL AND NELSON

If we suppose that a tariff is the sole institutional mechanism for seeking such redistribution, we would expect to find economically rational agents engaging in both directly productive (i.e. economic) and directly-unproductive (i.e. political/tariff-seeking) activity until their relative marginal returns are equalized.[3] Endogenous tariff theory proceeds by permitting tariff-seeking as an economic activity and solving for the overall equilibrium.

To date, most research on endogenous tariff theory has emphasized either the demonstration that stable equilibria exist and/or the effect of various "demand side" considerations on the effective preferences of economic actors in the arbitrage between economic and "non-economic" investment. The only genuinely institutional consideration that has received sustained analysis in this literature relates to the object of choice of redistribution mechanism (i.e. tariff v. QR v. VER).[4] Most of these analyses have been concerned primarily with explaining the relative preference for one or another of these options and therefore explaining their relative prevalence in the overall structure of protection from foreign competition (or marginal changes in the structure). Institutional form is therefore modeled as a function of rational choice. Though focusing on different institutions, we take an alternative approach by reversing this view and examine the effect on both the level of non-economic activity and the demand for protection of limiting economic actors to each of two specific institutional forms. We therefore examine the effect of alternate institutional forms on rational choice.

Virtually all of the work on endogenous tariff theory shares a fundamental institutional assumption: that, in a short-run model with no intermediate goods, the outcome from the political process (the tariff) is a strictly private good from the perspective of the specific-factors in an industry. That is, the benefits from participation in the political process may be fully captured by the participant.[5] In the next section of this paper we argue that this is, in fact, an institutional assumption by showing that alternative institutional forms are possible. Specifically, we will argue that *legislated protection* tends to treat protection as a strictly private good (from the perspective of the politically active specific factors), while *administered protection* treats protection as a public good in that

---

[3] Mayer and Riezman (1987a,b) have begun to examine the case of choice among redistributive instruments. As long as government mediated (i.e. policy-based) redistribution is the only mechanism for non-market redistribution, we would expect political activity on the part of some rational economic actors. As J. M. Finger and T. N. Srinivasan have pointed out, this will not be the case if direct (i.e. unmediated) transfers are possible because such transfers do not entail the dead-weight losses of government-mediated transfers, and will thus dominate mediated transfers.

[4] The only significant exception to this claim is Mayer's (1984) analysis of the comparative static effects of factor-based limitations on the right to vote (in a model in which the tariff is determined by direct referendum). While our underlying model of the poltical process differs from Mayer's, his paper is the closest to ours in inspiration.

[5] There are equivalent sets of politically relevant assumptions about the characteristics of returns to protection in short-run models with intermediate goods. See, for example, Lloyd's 1987 extension of Jones and Scheinkman (1977) and Cassing's (1981) model of natural friends and enemies. The equivalent assumption in the long-run two factor model, that the returns to protection are strictly private from the perspective of a given factor owner, lacks the political significance to this paper's analysis of the short-run case.

returns from increased protection necessarily cut across industries.[6] Further, it is argued that the distinction between these forms of protection is of both empirical and philosophical relevance. The second section presents the basic model of endogenous tariffs and the third section presents the main result of the paper: that administered protection induces both a lower level of unproductive activity (lobbying) and a lower equilibrium level of protection than legislated protection.

I. LEGISLATED AND ADMINISTERED PROTECTION IN PRACTICE AND THEORY

A. *Distributive v. Regulatory Issues*

Before distinguishing between legislated and administered protection, it will be useful to make a distinction originally due to Lowi (1964, 1969), that is now a standard in political science, between distributive and regulatory definitions of political issues.[7] For our purposes the major attribute of distributive politics is that its direct outcome is comparable to a collection of private goods, unrelated in administration by any logic external to the legislative choice process. By contrast, the direct outcome of regulatory politics is a general rule for administering demands for government output. If we assume, for simplicity, that government is nothing more than a passive register of citizen demand and that this demand is organized into a number of non-overlapping groups, then we may characterize a *distributive* outcome on a given issue by a set:

$$g^1(d_1^1, d_2^1, \ldots, d_n^1), g^2(d_1^2, d_2^2, \ldots, d_n^2), \ldots, g^n(d_1^n, d_2^n, \ldots, d_n^n)$$

where g^i represents the government output directly affecting only group i and d_i^j represents group i's demand for the output affecting group j. Even if a group does not explicitly oppose government output for other groups, in the absence of inter-group agreements and with limited government resources, we would expect that increased output for one group, g^i, reduces the government's ability to increase output for another, g^j. A *regulatory* outcome may be characterized as the formulation of a general rule $R(d_1, d_2, \ldots, d_n)$ which allows group demand to affect government output indirectly as follows:[8]

---

[6] Rodrik (1986) presents a result that bears a close family resemblance to our major result. In a discussion related to the normative theory of trade policy, Rodrik also notes the importance of the public-good nature of a political outcome. In comparing the welfare effects of tariffs and subsidies, he shows that if tariffs are more "public" than subsidies, the usual welfare ranking of the two may be reversed. The results in this paper are rooted in assumptions based on observed underlying properties of political outcomes (see section I) and are therefore related to the political economy of trade policy.

[7] See Hall and Nelson (1989) for a more detailed examination of these concepts in the context of an endogenous economic policy model.

[8] A number of readers to have been troubled by the fact that $g^i(R(\mathbf{d}))$ could be written as, say, $g^{i*}(\mathbf{d})$. The source of the concern appears to be the erroneous assumption that $g^i(\mathbf{d}) = g^{i*}(\mathbf{d})$ for all $\mathbf{d}$. The key to resolving this confusion is the recognition that $g^i(\mathbf{d})$ and $g^{i*}(\mathbf{d})$ are different functions. By way of analogy, consider the case of constant versus increasing returns to scale production functions. Both are mappings from input-space to outputs. Thus, both can be written as $x^i(\mathbf{y})$, where x^i is

$g^1(R)$, $g^2(R)$, ... , $g^n(R)$.

The important difference between these two types of political issues is that in the former, a group may demand and receive higher government output affecting their group alone (as with consumer demand for an excludable private good). That is, it would be possible for a group i to support higher government output to themselves, ($\partial g^i/\partial d_i^i$ is positive) while opposing higher government output to another group ($\partial g^j/\partial d_i^j$ is negative). In the latter situation, increasing government output affecting one group must necessarily involve strengthening the rule and thereby increasing government output affecting all other groups as well (as in consumer demand for a non-excludable public good). That is, if a group i supports higher government output they must have a positive $\partial R/\partial d_i$ which necessarily increases g^j, for any other group j (since $\partial g^j/\partial R$ is defined to be positive).

An additional attribute of a distributive political issue is the property that Lowi referred to as "reciprocal non-interference". This property amounts to an agreement between groups not to interfere with the government output affecting another group. With this additional property (and therefore less generally), a distributive outcome on an issue may be represented as

$g^1(d_1)$, $g^2(d_2)$, ... , $g^n(d_n)$

where g^i represents the government output affecting only group i and d_i represents group i's demand for that output. That is, there is no expressed demand by a group i for or against the government output affecting another group j ($d_i^j = 0$, for $i \neq j$).[9]

B. Legislated v. Administered Protection in the U.S.

In the United States, legislated protection has historically involved a distributive definition of the protection issue, while administered protection has involved a regulatory definition.[10] In fact, the relationship between legislated protection

the output of good i and y is a vector of inputs. The properties of the two functions are different, which is why we usually use some fairly obvious means of differentiating the two. In the case of the distinction between distributive and regulatory issues we use the intermediate function $R(\mathbf{d})$ to represent the difference. For the specific case of legislated versus administered protection, this has the additional virtue of formally representing the institutional distinction between setting a rule (the legislature's job) and implementing the rule (the bureaucracy's job).

[9] Clearly, there are other cooperative agreements possible between groups on distributive political issues (at least as we've defined them) than reciprocal non-interference. Typically, distributive issues are viewed as providing government output for one of a very large number of groups, so that an individual group fails to recognized any interdependence with another group. This is much like the assumptions about a single firm within a perfectly competitive market.

[10] Administered protection results from the application of a bureaucratic mechanism to provide protection from foreign competition in the home market. The major instruments of administered protection in the U.S. are the anti-dumping, countervailing duty, and escape clause mechanisms.

THE POLITICAL ECONOMY OF PROTECTION 65

and distributive politics is nearly tautological. The key attribute of tariff legislation is that its basic unit is the industry (fairly narrowly and politically defined). As long as protection is available only in the form of tariff legislation, and given that both Houses of Congress lack any inherent mechanism for imposing an external logic on decision (e.g. efficiency), protection is necessarily defined in distributive terms.

The Reciprocal Trade Agreements Act (RTAA) of 1934 and subsequent acquiescence to active participation in the General Agreement on Tariffs and Trade (GATT) fundamentally changed the definition of protection as a political issue in the U.S. Congress, and thus in the polity as a whole (given Congressional control of trade/tariff issues under Article I, Section 8 of the U.S. Constitution). By delegating to the Executive the responsibility to negotiate reciprocal reductions in the barriers to international trade, Congress implicitly agreed not to legislate tariffs.[11] In exchange for this delegation, however, Congress did insist that the Executive undertake to insure American business against "serious injury" from international competition. That is, in addition to delegating the responsibility for liberalization, Congress also delegated the responsibility for protection. It is the latter delegation that concerns us in this paper.[12]

Giving statutory content to the "no serious injury" norm is what transformed protection from a distributive issue into a regulatory issue. That is, Congress had to define the terms under which the Executive would grant protection. This required the identification of a logic (external to the political process in Congress) that was *generally applicable* to the issue of protection and sustainable in the Congressional political process. In simple terms, Congress has to establish a rule determining the conditions under which protection would be provided and the level of protection given those conditions. However, given that the key attribute of a general rule is that it cannot be divided into a large number of effectively private concessions, the necessary condition for distributive politics cannot be met.

While the RTAA/GATT system implied the end of legislated protection, the emergence of this administered protection did not necessarily imply the end of trade as a distributive issue. If, for example, the delegation had involved substantial Executive discretion, tariff-seeking/tariff-avoiding forces could still hope to pursue their private interests via Congressional pressure. For the purposes of this paper we will consider a delegation without discretion. That is, once the rule is set, protection-seekers have no influence at the bureaucratic level and therefore receive a determinant level of protection, with certainty, and at no cost. Thus, the only tariff-seeking/tariff-avoiding costs will be those directed to the determination of the rule. In this case, the shift to administered protection implies a shift to regulatory politics in Congress.

---

[11] It should be made clear, however, that until very recently Congress did not explicitly make any such commitment. In fact, Congress was very clear in the extensions of negotiating authority to explicitly state that such extensions were not to be taken as ratification of the GATT itself.

[12] See Nelson (1989a) for a discussion of the implications of constituting protection and liberalization as distinct political issues.

66   HALL AND NELSON

In fact, the bureaucratic structure of trade management in the U.S. involves a low-track characterized by rules very closely approximating the condition of "delegation without discretion", and a high track involving Executive discretion and legislative intervention.[13] We justify an emphasis on purely distributive and purely regulatory politics in two ways. First, the formal results clearly indicate the importance of institutional assumptions in a simple, intuitively reasonable framework. Second, as we suggest above, the assumption of delegation without discretion is closely paralleled in fact by a significant part of the U.S. trade protection system (i.e., the low-track of anti-dumping and countervailing duties).

We now turn to the development of a simple model of the tariff-seeking process under either legislated or administered protection. In the context of a conventional short run general equilibrium model (the specific factors model) we permit the possibility of lobbying for (or against) either an industry-specific tariff (section II) or the rule regulating administered protection (section III).

II. OPTIMAL LOBBYING BY INDUSTRY—LEGISLATED PROTECTION

In order to compare the effects of institutional structure on both the politics and the resulting level of protection from foreign competition, we will use as our base model a simple version of the standard neo-classical model of trade (the specific factors model). In our analysis, then, we start from a very simple view of the interaction of economics and politics: that the politics and resulting political outcomes (in this case, the level of protection from foreign competition) will be entirely determined by the economic effects of these outcomes. Although firms within an industry will be perfectly competitive (the standard neo-classical assumption), we will further simplify things by assuming that with respect to trade policy, lobby groups will form at the industry level and behave as a single economic/political agent.

On a theoretical level, we justify this industry-level collusion by noting the well-known welfare effects of protection at the factor ownership level in the specific factors model of trade. The returns to ownership of units of a specific factor in a tariff-protected industry increase with the level of protection while the returns to ownership of other specific factors decline. Further, the magnification effect of industry level price changes insures that an individual owning only units of the protected specific factor will have an increase in real income (and therefore welfare) and an individual owning only units of other specific factors will have a decrease in real income (and therefore welfare). For this reason, allowing individual ownership of units of one specific factor alone, we expect that lobby groups may be easily formed within an industry around specific factor types. Further, members of such a lobby group have a common benefit from higher

---

[13] Nelson (1989a,b,c) examines the statutory and political details of this two-track system while Finger, Hall and Nelson (1982) provide some empirical evidence for the two-track hypothesis.

prices regardless of individual demand preferences (as long as they are "well-behaved" in the microeconomic sense). Also, since the real returns from ownership of the mobile factor are ambiguous,[14] we focus only upon lobby groups formed by specific factor ownership and politically ignore the mobile factor.[15]

In addition to having full industry level collusion to form the lobbying groups we allow no inter-industry collusion. This does two things for us. First, it simplifies the analysis by eliminating coalitional questions that would distract from the main thrust of the paper. Second, it may be a reasonable characterization of the inter-industry politics surrounding trade policy in the U.S. Certainly in the U.S. prior to the RTAA of 1934, Lowi's reciprocal non-interference seems to have been the norm for legislated protection.

In this section, our model is formulated under a legislative institutional structure (providing Legislated Protection). In the first two parts, the basic model is formally described. In part C we note that exogenous changes in industry price (tariff) levels have no predictable effect on the equilibrium levels of lobbying[16] and therefore tariff levels, while changes in government marginal responsiveness to lobbying are directly related to equilibrium lobbying levels.

A. The Net Return to Lobbying

We consider a small open economy in which fixed amounts of labor and capital are used to produce two import competing goods, M_1 and M_2, and an exported good, X. Labor, L, is perfectly mobile between industries and capital is assumed to be industry specific (K_1, K_2, K_x), all markets are competitive, and production functions are twice differentiable, strictly quasi-concave, and have positive first derivatives.[17] The total return from ownership of a specific factor is $r_i K_i$, $i = 1,2,x$, where r_i is the per unit cost of the specific capital in industry i in units of the exported good. Since the welfare effects of price changes are ambiguous for the owners of mobile labor, owners of specific capital will employ labor (perfectly substitutable with labor employed in production of any of the goods)

---

[14] Specifically, individual owners of the mobile factor who spend a relatively large portion of their income on consumption of the protected good will be worse off while those who spend a relatively small portion will be better off. This is the well-known "neoclassical ambiguity" of Ruffin and Jones (1977).

[15] This assumption eliminates the concern with individuals owning more than a single factor of production. We therefore avoid a number of issues related to the demand preferences of individual group members that don't have a substantive effect on our final result. See Mayer (1984).

[16] Using Bhagwati's (1982) terminology, this is the level of directly unproductive profit (DUP) seeking behavior in the economy.

[17] We assume the existence of two import competing industries to allow either or both to politically oppose protection for the other under a discretionary tariff (LP). This allows us to compare this result with one where protection comes only from the application of a rule (AP) and changes in protection levels in these two industries are tied together. As with the welfare results of the standard specific factors model, our results generalize straightforwardly to any number of industries ($n + 1$ factors, n goods).

68   HALL AND NELSON

to lobby for or against protection from foreign competition, $\mathcal{L}_i$. Specific factor returns, in export units, net of lobbying, are

$$N_i = r_i K_i - w \mathcal{L}_i$$

where w is the cost of labor, also in export units.[18] Further, the total (fixed) labor supply in the economy is

$$\bar{L} = L_d + \mathcal{L}_1 + \mathcal{L}_2 + \mathcal{L}_x$$

where $L_d = L_1 + L_2 + L_x$ is the labor used directly in production.

Taking the existence of political mechanisms as given, the supply side of the market for protection from foreign competition for either of the import competing industries may be described by a simple supply function, using as inputs the lobbying resources employed by the relevant special interest groups. If we make the assumption that owners of capital must own only capital and employ it in only one industry and if the political mechanism supplying protection from foreign competition is a form of *legislated protection*, LP, the service provided is a set of industry level tariffs:

$$t_i = t_i(\mathcal{L}_1, \mathcal{L}_2, \mathcal{L}_x), \ i = 1, 2.$$

If dU/dp_i is positive (negative), then $dt_i/d\mathcal{L}$ will be assumed to be greater (less) than zero. The domestic relative price of the import competing goods in export units will simply be:

$$p_i = (1 + t_i)\pi_i$$

where π_i is the world price of good i.[19]

The return to specific factor owners in industry i, $i = 1, 2, x$, net of lobbying both for or against protection in each of the import competing industries, for a given

---

[18] The net return to lobbying would be $N_i - r_i^0 K_i$ where r_i^0 is the return to the specific factor without lobbying. Since K_i is fixed, any changes in the net return to lobbying will occur through N_i alone. We will therefore be able to use N_i in place of the net return to lobbying, for convenience. Also, to avoid complications of revenue seeking, we will assume that tariff revenue is not distributed to industry groups. While this may make the story seem incomplete, all we really need here is the reasonable assumption that an industry group doesn't view marginal changes in a tariff level as significantly changing their share of the total tariff revenue collected by the government.

[19] In denoting the total lobbying by specific factors in industry i by $\mathcal{L}_i$, we have not distinguished between the portion of these resources devoted to lobbying for or against the tariff level in industry 1 from the portion devoted to lobbying for or against protection in industry 2. We simply assume that lobbying efforts are spread out efficiently between the two tariffs as to maximize the net benefits to the group. Each price level is therefore a function of total lobbying by an industry group in the same way that total cost is a function of output in the economic theory of the firm. In the latter, the firm is implicitly assumed to hire inputs so as to minimize cost for every given level of output.

THE POLITICAL ECONOMY OF PROTECTION 69

level of lobbying by all other specific factor owners, is therefore affected by changes in their level of lobbying as follows:

$$\frac{\partial N_i}{\partial \mathcal{L}_i} = \sum_{j=1}^{2} \left(K_i \frac{\partial r_i}{\partial p_j} - \mathcal{L}_i \frac{\partial w}{\partial p_j} \right) \frac{\partial p_j}{\partial \mathcal{L}_i} - w - \left(K_i \frac{\partial r_i}{\partial L_d} - \mathcal{L}_i \frac{\partial w}{\partial L_d} \right). \tag{1}$$

First, there are the own and cross price effects, each being the increase in industry specific factor returns from politically influencing an industry price: (i) the direct effect on specific factor returns, $K_i \dfrac{\partial r_i}{\partial p_j} \dfrac{\partial p_j}{\partial \mathcal{L}_i}$, minus (ii) the increased lobbying costs from higher wages, $\mathcal{L}_i \dfrac{\partial w}{\partial p_j} \dfrac{\partial p_j}{\partial \mathcal{L}_i}$. Then there is the cost of hiring an additional unit of lobbying labor: (iii) the current wage, w, plus the indirect cost of the resulting reduction in "productive" labor through (iv) the decrease in specific factor returns, $K_i \dfrac{\partial r_i}{\partial L_d}$, and (v) higher lobbying wages, $\mathcal{L}_i \dfrac{\partial w}{\partial L_d}$.

The net effects of lobbying on the returns to specific factors may also be seen using the familiar two sector diagram in Figure 1. Focusing on the own price effect of lobbying for protection alone (that is, ignoring the portion of lobbying devoted to influencing tariffs in other industries—as if under a reciprocal non-interference agreement with the other import competing industry), each additional unit of

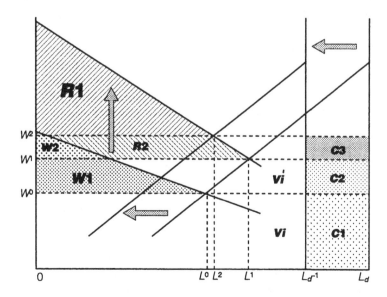

Figure 1.

70   HALL AND NELSON

lobbying resources shifts an industry value of marginal product curve upward, V_i to V_i', while simultaneously reducing the total productive labor available in the economy. The former drives up wages from w^0 to w^1 and increases industry employment from L^0 to L^1. The latter increases wages further to w^2 and reduces industry employment from L^1 to L^2. The net return to specific factors in the industry is the difference between the gain of area $(R1)$ and the loss of area $(W1 + W2 + C1 + C2 + C3)$.[20]

B. The Industry Problem

If we define the industry problem as hiring lobbying labor to simply maximize the return to specific factors net of lobbying costs then the equilibrium levels of lobbying will be sensitive to the units used (i.e. whether we measure net return in dollar terms, units of good X, or in units of one of the import competing goods). Although our main results that follow are not sensitive to the units, we will formulate the industry problem using an indirect utility function representing the trade-off between changes in the relative price levels and the return to specific factors net of lobbying as follows:

$$\max_{\mathfrak{L}_i}\ U^i(p_1, p_2, N_i).$$

Letting each utility function be twice continuously differentiable and strictly concave in lobbying, the necessary and sufficient condition for industry i will be[21]

$$U_i^i = \sum_{j=1}^{2} \frac{\partial U^i}{\partial p_j}\frac{\partial p_j}{\partial \mathfrak{L}_i} + \frac{\partial U^i}{\partial N_i}\frac{\partial N_i}{\partial \mathfrak{L}_i} = 0.$$

Since an industry is also maximizing utility through consumption of the three goods, we may use Roy's identity (Varian, 1984), substitute equation (1) into the above, and rearrange to get

$$\sum_{j=1}^{2}\left(K_i\frac{\partial r_i}{\partial p_j} - \mathfrak{L}_i\frac{\partial w}{\partial p_j} - D_j^i\right)\frac{\partial p_j}{\partial \mathfrak{L}_i} = w + \left(K_i\frac{\partial r_i}{\partial L_d} - \mathfrak{L}_i\frac{\partial w}{\partial L_d}\right)$$

where each D_j^i denotes the Marshallian demand function for import competing good M_j by specific factors in industry i. Defining θ_L^i, θ_1^i, θ_2^i, and θ_x^i as the

---

[20] The net return to specific factors is the gain from shifting the industry value of marginal product curve from V_i to V_i': (i) the direct effect on specific factor returns, area $(R1 + R2 - W1)$, minus (ii) the increased lobbying costs from higher wages, area $C2$; minus (iii) the cost of hiring an additional unit of lobbying labor, area $C1$, minus the indirect cost of the reduction in "productive" labor: (iv) the reduction in specific factor returns, area $(W2 + R2)$, and (v) higher lobbying wages, area $C3$. These areas labeled on the graph match with the terms in equation (1), also denoted (i) through (v).

[21] Subscripts on U^i will denote partial derivatives with respect to lobbying.

proportions of specific factor i's income spent on lobbying efforts and consumption, respectively, we can convert the above into elasticity form for the import competing industries ($i, j = 1,2, i \neq j$) to get:

$$(\epsilon_{ii} - \theta^i_L \epsilon_{wi} - \theta^i_i)\varrho_{ii} + (\epsilon_{ij} - \theta^i_L \epsilon_{wj} - \theta^i_j)\varrho_{ij} = \theta^i_L + \frac{\mathcal{L}_i}{L_d}(\eta_i - \theta^i_L \eta_w) \tag{2}$$

where ϵ_{ij} and ϵ_{wj} are the price j elasticities of r_i and w, respectively, η_i and η_w are the elasticities relating a change in directly productive labor to r_i and w, respectively, and ϱ_{ij} is the elasticity of the price level in industry i from a change in the lobbying levels by industry j.[22]

The right hand side of equation (2) represents the marginal costs of lobbying and is unambiguously positive.[23] The two terms on the left hand side represent the marginal benefits of influencing protection levels through own-price changes and cross-price changes, respectively. The cross price effect of lobbying, $(\epsilon_{ij} - \theta^i_L \epsilon_{wj} - \theta^i_j)$, is unambiguously negative and, given that the marginal cost of lobbying is positive, it would therefore never benefit an industry group, in the absence of inter-industry collusion, to lobbying for protection in another industry (they would choose $\varrho_{ij} \leqslant 0$, $i \neq j$).[24] We may sign the own price effect by first substituting for θ^i_i in the first term above and rearranging to get: $((\epsilon_{ii} - 1) - \theta^i_L(1 - \epsilon_{wi}) + \theta^i_i + \theta^i_j)$. The magnification effect of price level change insures that the own price elasticity of a specific factor return will always be greater than one ($\epsilon_{ii} > 1$) and the price elasticity of the return to labor will always be between zero and one ($0 < \eta_i < 1$). The own price effects of lobbying is therefore unambiguously positive and it would never benefit a specific factor, in the absence of inter-industry collusion, to lobbying against their own tariff level (they would choose $\varrho_{ii} \geqslant 0$).

The necessary condition for the export industry problem may also be converted to elasticity form as follows:

$$(\epsilon_{x1} - \theta^x_L \epsilon_{wi} - \theta^x_1)\varrho_{x1} + (\epsilon_{x2} - \theta^x_L \epsilon_{w2} - \theta^x_2)\varrho_{x2} = \theta^x_L + \frac{\mathcal{L}_x}{L_d}(\eta_x - \theta^x_L \eta_w). \tag{3}$$

Note again that each of the cross lobbying price effects, $(\epsilon_{xi} - \theta^x_L \epsilon_{wi} - \theta^x_i)$ for $i = 1,2$, is negative, and it would never benefit the export industry, in the absence

---

[22] Note that the lobbying elasticity of the supply of productive labor, $\dfrac{\partial L_d}{\partial \mathcal{L}_i} \dfrac{\partial \mathcal{L}_i}{L_d}$, equals the $-\dfrac{\mathcal{L}_i}{L_d}$ term above.

[23] From the standard results of the specific factors model of trade, we know that changes in the supply of productive labor is directly related to specific factor returns and inversely related to wages ($\eta_i > 0$ and $\eta_w < 0$).

[24] Again, from the standard results of the specific factors model of trade, we know that changes in the price level in an industry are directly related to wages and inversely related to specific factor returns in other industries ($\epsilon_w > 0$ and $\epsilon_{ij} < 0$, for $i \neq j$).

72   HALL AND NELSON

of inter-industry collusion, to lobby for a tariff in an import competing industry (they would choose $\varrho_{xi} \leqslant 0$, for $i = 1,2$).

The optimal choice of a lobbying level by a factor group will be a function of the lobbying levels of the two other groups. With Cournot conjectures by all industry groups, there are two reaction curves for each industry problem. If the sufficient condition for a unique solution to the industry problem is met (utility is strictly concave in lobbying), then signing the slope of a reaction function becomes the problem of identifying the effect of a change in the lobbying level of industry k ($k \neq i$) on the marginal utility of lobbying by an industry group:

$$U^i_{ik} = \partial \left(\frac{\partial U_i}{\partial p_j} \frac{\partial p_j}{\partial \mathcal{L}_i} + \frac{\partial U_i}{\partial N_i} \frac{\partial N_i}{\partial \mathcal{L}_i} \right) \Big/ \partial \mathcal{L}_k.$$

This is, however, a long succession of terms involving second derivatives whose signs are not derivable without further assumptions on the model.[25] Whether the reaction functions are positively or negatively sloped, we will simply assume that there is a unique, stable Cournot solution between the three groups.

C. The Supply Side of Protection

In this short section we want to note the comparative static effects of two types of supply side changes in our model as thus far developed. First, if an *industry price level* changes (reflecting an exogenous change in the tariff rate due to changes in government preferences or in foreign competitiveness), there is no clear effect on the marginal utility of lobbying by any industry.[26] Second, a change in the *marginal responsiveness of a tariff to lobbying* by a particular industry group (which may reflect a change in the political institution providing tariff protection) will be directly related to the marginal utility of lobbying

$$dU^i_i = (\epsilon_{ij} - \theta^i_L \epsilon_{wj} - \theta^i_j) d\varrho_{ij} > 0$$

for $i = 1,2,x$ and $j = 1,2$.[27] Given concave utility in lobbying and a stable Cournot solution, an increase in marginal responsiveness toward any single industry group

---

[25] In particular, when a price level is changed, although there is a predicable direct effect on the marginal utility of lobbying by an industry group as consumers (since utility in the neo-classical model of the consumer is typically quasi-convex in prices alone), there is an indirect effect on them as owners of immobile factors. Further, an import competing industry will lobby to raise one price level but lower another, tending to cancel out the above direct effects on the marginal utility of lobbying to all industry groups.

[26] The complication here is much the same as with determining the sign of the slope a reaction function as discussed above. While the direct effect of a price increase on marginal utility is clear (with utility quasi-convex in prices), there is an indirect effect on income through changes in factor returns.

[27] Note that when $i \neq j$, ϱ_{ij} will be less than zero and an increase in the marginal responsiveness of the tariff to lobbying means that $d\varrho_{ij} < 0$. Also, note that the results are the same when the marginal responsiveness of more than one tariff increases:

$$dU^i_i = (\epsilon_{i1} - \theta^i_L \epsilon_{w1} - \theta^i_1) d\varrho_{i1} + (\epsilon_{i2} - \theta^i_L \epsilon_{w2} - \theta^i_2) d\varrho_{i2} > 0.$$

will increase their equilibrium lobbying level while the direction of change in lobbying levels by other industry groups will depend upon the slopes of the appropriate reaction functions.

III. LEGISLATED VERSUS ADMINISTERED PROTECTION

In our model so far, protection from foreign competition has been applied at the industry level only and an import competing industry has been able to completely appropriate the benefits of their political activity. In this section we introduce the possibility that an alternate political institutional structure is possible where protection must necessarily be raised to both import competing industries simultaneously. An import competing industry now must not only end lobbying opposition to protection for the other import competing industry[28] (or oppose protection in their own industry), but their own-industry lobbying efforts raise the protection level in the other industry. Since they compete for the employment of mobile labor, they are harmed by increases in other industry price levels (or, if they oppose protection, they are harmed by a lowering of their own industry price level) and the marginal benefit of political activity for import competing industry groups declines (*much the same as if government simply became politically less responsive to their efforts to gain protection*). This is essentially a free-rider effect of lobbying for both import competing industries that does not exist for the export industry. While depending exactly upon lobby group reaction functions in the Cournot equilibrium, this strongly suggests a bias towards a lower overall equilibrium level of protection in the economy. In terms of its effect, this institutional change offers government an alternative way of expressing an increased commitment to trade liberalization similar to lowering their political responsiveness to all import competing industries.

To begin, suppose that marginal changes in protection levels are entirely legislated (as above) and there is a political equilibrium. Then, in an institutional change, marginal changes in protection are provided entirely through a *rule* that, once written, applies to all imported goods. To isolate the effects of the change in institutional structure (from an LP mechanism to an AP mechanism), the marginal responsiveness to lobbying (as described in the previous section) is held constant. Let $R_j(\mathcal{L}_1, \mathcal{L}_2, \mathcal{L}_x)$ denote the percentage increase in the price level in industry $j(=1,2)$ resulting from a one percent increase in the level of the rule (this is assumed positive), and ϱ_{iR} denote the percentage increase in the rule resulting from a one percent increase in political activity by industry group $i(=1,2,x)$. Holding marginal responsiveness to lobbying by every industry group constant ensures that the absolute value of ϱ_{ij} will equal $\varrho_{iR}R_j$ (responsiveness under AP). The difference, however, is that the assumption of a rule (where $R_j > 0$ for

---

[28] There may not have even been any anti-protection lobbying against another import competing industry if tariffs had been a fully distributive political issue and Lowi's reciprocal non-interference property was the norm.

74   HALL AND NELSON

all i) forces the a group to be generally pro-protection or anti-protection since

$$\text{sgn}(\varrho_{ir}R_i) = \text{sgn}(\varrho_{ir}R_j).$$

The industry must now make a decision. If they choose to continue to seek protection in their own industry, they will also raise the protection level in the other import competing industry ($\varrho_{iR}R_j > 0$ while previously $\varrho_{ij} < 0$, for $i \neq j$). If they choose to continue to oppose protection in the other import competing industry, they will lower the protection level of their own industry ($\varrho_{iR}R_i < 0$ while previously $\varrho_{ii} > 0$). Either way, we clearly find that at existing levels of political activity (replacing ϱ_{ij} on the left with $\varrho_{iR}R_j$ on the right) we have, for $i, j = 1,2$

$$(\epsilon_{ii} - \theta_L^i \epsilon_{wi} - \theta_i^i)\,(\varrho_{iR}R_i - \varrho_{ii}) + (\epsilon_{ij} - \theta_L^i \epsilon_{wj} - \theta_j^i)\,(\varrho_{iR}R_j - \varrho_{ij}) < 0. \qquad (4)$$

That is, the marginal benefit of political activity for each import competing industry group, at existing lobbying levels by all industry groups, will decline.

For the export industry, holding government responsiveness constant ensures that their marginal benefit from political activity is unchanged. That is, since they lobbied against all protection prior to the institutional change, they may continue to do so with equal effectiveness through the rule. With the political activity of the interest groups supporting protection reduced and the political activity of the export industry unchanged, there is not only a lower overall level of political activity but also a bias toward lower equilibrium protection levels. This lowered marginal benefit of political activity is a "political free-rider effect" which, by the same argument as with the free-rider effect on the market provision of a public good, may lead to a lower equilibrium level of political output (in this case, protection from foreign competition).

IV. CONCLUSION

The endogenous economic policy approach to the study of political-economic interaction constitutes a major theoretical advance. To date, most research in this tradition has emphasized the link between endogenously determined political preferences and policy outcomes. As Nelson (1988) argues, this has resulted in a lack of attention to the "supply side" of the political market. This paper takes a first step toward the explicit analysis of supply side assumptions. Our contribution in this regard is two-fold: we offer a simple formal method for characterizing state preference (i.e. noting the differing effects of changes in tariff levels and the marginal responsiveness of tariffs to political pressure); and we demonstrate the significance of supply side considerations. Specifically, we demonstrate that direct legislation of industry-specific tariffs (i.e. distributive politics) entails higher marginal benefits from protection seeking than delegation (without administrative discretion) under a generally applicable rule (i.e. regulatory

THE POLITICAL ECONOMY OF PROTECTION   75

politics). The intuition behind this result is quite straight-forward: the benefits of a distributive process are appropriable by the individual policy-seeking groups, while the benefits of a regulatory process are not. As a result, by comparison to the distributive process, the regulatory process may "underproduce" protection. In economic terms, the welfare implications are clear. Endogenous distortions may be lower under a regulatory system (recall that our definition of regulation entails delegation without administrative discretion)—both because the levels of intervention and policy-seeking may be lower. What is not at all clear, however, is that a strictly economic definition of welfare is appropriate in this context. After all, *the economic improvement is achieved by making the political system less responsive.* Making this sort of judgment would seem to require some broader notion of social welfare than economic optimality. Such speculations are well beyond the bounds of this paper.

To end on a less speculative note, we should recognize the implications of this research for system design. Suppose that politicians seek to service constituents at minimal economic cost to the economy as a whole.[29] The research reported here suggests that they should explicitly consider institutional form. This is obviously of far more than abstract interest. Many countries are currently engaged in attempts to restructure their trade management systems (generally as part of their ongoing participation in the GATT). Given the extreme simplicity of the model used here, it would be unwise to draw much more than very general lessons from our results. Nonetheless, the suggestiveness of these results would seem to indicate that additional research of this sort could be of considerable value.

H. KEITH HALL   DOUGLAS NELSON
US International Trade Commission *   *Economics Department*
500 E. Street, SW   *Syracuse University*
Washington, DC 20436   *Syracuse*
                                                         NY 13244

REFERENCES

Axelrod, Robert, (1986). "An Evolutionary Approach to Norms", *American Political Science Review*, vol. 80, no. 4, pp 1095–1111.
Bhagwati, Jagdish, (1982). "Directly Unproductive, Profit-seeking (DUP) activities", *Journal of Political Economy*, vol. 90, no. 5, pp 988–1002.
Cassing, James, (1981). "On the Relationship Between Commodity Price Changes and Factor Owner's Real Positions". *Journal of Political Economy*, vol. 89, no. 3, pp 593–595.
Feenstra, Robert and Jagdish Bhagwati, (1982). "Tariff-Seeking and the Efficient Tariff", in J. Bhagwati, ed., pp 245–258.

[29] This is effectively the assumption applied by Feenstra and Bhagwati (1982) in their analysis of the efficient tariff.

* This paper is meant to represent the opinions of the author(s) and is not meant to represent in any way the views of the International Trade Commission or its members.

76   HALL AND NELSON

Field, Alexander, (1984). "Microeconomics, Norms, and Rationality", *Economic Development and Cultural Change*, pp 683–711.

Finger, J. M., H. Keith Hall and Douglas R. Nelson, (1982). "The Political Economy of Administered Protection", *American Economic Review*, vol. 72, no. 3, pp 452–466.

Hall, H. Keith and Douglas Nelson, (1989). "Institutional Structure and Time Horizon in a Simple Model of the Political Economy: The Lowi Effect", *International Spectator*, vol. XXIV, no. 3/4, pp 153–173.

Hicks, John, (1969). *A Theory of Economic History*, Oxford Clarendon Press.

Hirshleifer, Jack, (1985). "The Expanding Domain of Economics", *American Economic Review*, vol. 75, no. 6, pp 53–68.

Jones, Ronald, (1971). "A Three Factor Model in Theory, Trade, and History", in Bhagwati, *et al.* (1971), *Trade, Balance of Payments, and Growth*, Amsterdam: North-Holland, pp 3–21.

Jones, Ronald, (1975). "Income Distribution and Effective Protection in a Multicommodity Trade Model", *Journal of Economic Theory*, vol. 11, no. 1, pp 1–15.

Jones, Ronald and Jose Scheinkman, (1977). "The Relevance of the Two-Sector Production Model in Trade Theory", *Journal of Political Economy*, vol. 85, no. 5, pp 909–1035.

Leibenstein, Harvey, (1984). "On the Economics of Conventions and Institutions: An Exploratory Essay", *Zeitschrift fur die Gesamte Staatswissenschaft*, vol. 14, no. 1, pp 74–86.

Lloyd, Peter, (1987). "Protection Policy and the Assignment Rule". In H. Kierzkowski, ed., *Protection and Competition in International Trade*, Oxford: Blackwell, pp 4–21.

Lowi, Theodore, (1964). "American Business, Public Policy, Case Studies and Political Theory", *World Politics*, vol. 16, no. 4, pp 347–382.

Lowi, Theodore, (1969, revised 1979). *The End of Liberalism*, New York: Norton.

Mayer, Wolfgang, (1974). "Short-run and Long-run Equilibrium in the Small Open Economy", *Journal of Political Economy*, vol. 82, no. 4, pp 955–967.

Mayer, Wolfgang, (1984). "Endogenous Tariff Formation", *American Economic Review*, vol. 74, no. 5, pp 970–985.

Mayer, Wolfgang and Raymond Riezman, (1987a). "Endogenous Choice of Trade Policy Instruments", *Journal of International Economics*, vol. 23, no. 3, pp 377–81.

Mayer, Wolfgang and Raymond Riezman, (1989). "Tariff Formation in a Multi-dimensional Voting Model", *Economics and Politics*, vol. 1, no. 1, pp 61–79.

Mussa, Michael, (1974). "Tariffs and the Distribution of Income: The Importance of Specificity, Substitutability and Intensity in the Short and Long Run", *Journal of Political Economy*, vol. 82, no. 5, pp 1191–1203.

Neary, J. Peter, (1978). "Short-run Capital Specificity and the Pure Theory of International Trade", *Economic Journal*, vol. 88, 488–510.

Nelson, Douglas, (1988). "Endogenous Tariff Theory: A Critical Review", *American Journal of Political Science*, vol. 32, no. 3, pp 796–837.

Nelson, Douglas, (1989a). "Domestic Political Preconditions of US Trade Policy: Liberal Structure and Protectionist Dynamics", *Journal of Public Policy*, vol. 9, no. 1, pp. 83–108.

Nelson, Douglas, (1989b). "On the High Track to Protection: Automobiles, 1979–1981", in S. Haggard and C. I. Moon eds., *Pacific Dynamics*, Denver: Westview Press, pp 97–128.

Nelson, Douglas (1989c). "The Political Economy of Trade Policy", *Economics and Politics*, vol. 1, no. 3, pp 301–314.

North, Douglas, (1981). *Structure and Change in Economic History*, New York: Norton.

Rodrik, Dani, (1986). "Tariffs, Subsidies and Welfare with Endogenous Policy", *Journal of International Economics*, vol. 21, pp 285–299.

Ruffin, Roy and Ronald Jones, (1977). "Protection and Real Wages: The Neoclassical Ambiguity", *Journal of Economic Theory*, vol. 14, pp 337–348.

THE POLITICAL ECONOMY OF PROTECTION 77

Sah, Raj Kumar, (1987). "Persistence and Pervasiveness of Corruption: New Perspectives", ms.: The World Bank.

Stolper, Wolfgang and Paul Samuelson, (1941). "Protection and Real Wages", *Review of Economics and Statistics*, vol. 9, no. 1, pp 58–73.

Varian, Hal R., (1984). *Microeconomic Analysis*, New York: Norton.

HOW BAD IS ANTIDUMPING? EVIDENCE FROM PANEL DATA

Peter Egger and Douglas Nelson*

Abstract—Current research on antidumping suggests a number of channels through which antidumping affects the volume of world trade. This paper uses a structural approach to the gravity model framework to evaluate these hypotheses using data on trade volume over the period 1948 to 2001. We conclude that the volume and welfare effects have been negative but quite modest.

I. Introduction

A S with the wave of interest in the "new protection" in the 1970s, we are now observing a new wave of concern with a rapid increase in the use of "nontraditional" protectionist instruments (Prusa, 2001; Zanardi, 2006). Once again, the main culprit is contingent protection (primarily antidumping and countervailing duties, though voluntary export restraints—mainly coming from the safeguards process—also figured prominently in the 1970s).[1] The main difference is that in the 1970s, the main users were industrial countries (mainly the United States, European Union, Canada, and Australia), the millennial new users, and the main source of growth in use, are developing countries and countries in transition (Argentina, Brazil, India, Mexico, South Korea, Taiwan, Turkey).[2] In this paper, we are primarily concerned with the impact of the spread of antidumping on trade.

Before turning to a discussion of the main issues, we can fix the essential facts drawing on an excellent paper by Zanardi (2006). Zanardi shows a strong upward trend in investigations and a more moderate rate of growth in the number of antidumping orders in place. Furthermore, although there may be some downward trend in the use of contingent protection by traditional users, the trend in new users is strongly upward. This suggests the potential for very wide adoption

and use of these mechanisms.[3] While the spread of contingent protection mechanisms, and their use, is an undeniable fact, the scale of their use and their effect on aggregate trade and welfare are considerably less certain. The public rhetoric, as well as that in much of the academic research on antidumping, could easily give the impression that these effects are sizable. In this paper, we develop a framework within which we can evaluate most of the common hypotheses relating to the aggregate effects of antidumping.

Our analysis is based on the gravity model framework, which has become a standard tool in establishing an empirical baseline for the analysis of equilibrium trade patterns and deviations therefrom (Feenstra, 2004). Such a baseline needs, in principle, to reflect the underlying general equilibrium of the world trading system. Early attempts to identify deviations generated by the presence of various forms of protection sought to use the structure provided by the Heckscher-Ohlin model but did not appear to produce convincing results (Leamer, 1987, 1990). With the development of theoretical foundations for the gravity model, along with its statistical success in accounting for trade patterns, the gravity model has increasingly become the econometric framework of choice when seeking to analyze deviations from expected trade between two countries.[4] More recently, the gravity model has also been used to evaluate the effect of fundamental institutions such as the WTO and various forms of preferential trade and currency arrangement.[5]

In the next section, we develop the motivation for our analysis of the link between antidumping and trade volume, followed by a presentation of our theoretical and econometric framework. Then we present our empirical results and robustness in the following sections. More specifically, the theoretical and empirical literature on which we draw suggests a number of causal channels by which antidumping can

Received for publication June 18, 2009. Revision accepted for publication May 4, 2010.

* Egger: Ifo Institute for Economic Research, Ludwig-Maximilian University of Munich, CESifo, and Leverhulme Centre for Research on Globalisation and Economic Policy, School of Economics, University of Nottingham; Nelson: Murphy Institute, Tulane University, and Leverhulme Centre for Research on Globalisation and Economic Policy, School of Economics, University of Nottingham.

We are grateful to the Leverhulme Centre for Research on Globalisation and Economic Policy at the University of Nottingham for providing support during the writing of this paper. We thank the editor and two referees for very helpful comments. The primary data set was made available by Chad Bown. In addition, we have had help on data from Peter Lloyd, Patrick Messerlin, and Maurizio Zanardi. We thank Tobias Seidel for excellent assistance with data collection. Peter Egger acknowledges funding from the Austrian Science Fund through grant P17713-G05.

[1] These forms of protection are "contingent" because they are dependent on a quasi-judicial/bureaucratic finding prior to application of the protection. By contrast, traditional protection is "statutory"; it is applied in every case, without any such finding. This is a more useful distinction than the common tariff-versus-nontariff barrier distinction since contingent protection is usually included in the latter even though it is implemented by tariffs.

[2] The industrial countries continue to be quantitatively the biggest users, but growth in use is coming from developing countries.

[3] This appears to be even more the case in the face of the current economic crisis. On the one hand, as Bown (2009) showed and as one would expect from previous research showing a strong response of protection in general, and antidumping in particular, to economic downturn, both developed and developing countries have increased their use of contingent protection. However, it is even more striking how muted this protectionist response has been.

[4] The key papers providing theoretical foundations for the gravity model are Anderson (1979), Bergstrand (1985, 1989), and Deardorff (1998). The industry standard, on which we also rely, is Anderson and Van Wincoop (2003). Wall (1999) provides a useful discussion of the gravity model as a framework for evaluating the effect of protection on trade.

[5] For instance, Rose (2004a, 2004b) finds that membership in the WTO has no systematic effect on trade pattern, while Subramanian and Wei (2007) find that WTO membership exerts a powerful and positive impact on trade for a subset of countries that adopt liberalizing policies as part of accession to the WTO. Baldwin (1994), Frankel (1997), and Baier and Bergstrand (2007) use the gravity model to examine the trade effects of regional trading blocs, while the results in Frankel and Rose (2002), Rose (2000), and Rose and Van Wincoop (2001) point to the relevance of (various forms of) currency arrangements on trade volume.

The Review of Economics and Statistics, November 2011, 93(4): 1374–1390
© 2011 by the President and Fellows of Harvard College and the Massachusetts Institute of Technology

affect trade patterns. Many papers just list these in an essentially ad hoc way to suggest that antidumping should reduce trade (Vandenbussche & Zanardi, 2006). By contrast, we are able to link each of these to specific predictions that can be evaluated in the context of our gravity model. With minor variation across the various hypotheses, our results show uniformly low but negative effects of antidumping on aggregate trade patterns. Because we have adopted a structural framework, we are able to report comparative static estimates of the effect of antidumping on trade volumes (section VD) and present estimates of the welfare effects of antidumping (section VI). In addition to the sensitivity analysis we provide with respect to econometric specification, in section VII, we also apply our analysis to three sectors that are known to face heavy use of antidumping: iron and steel, other metals, and chemicals. Finally, in section VIII, we divide our sample into developing and developed countries to look for evidence of country heterogeneity. For neither sectors nor countries do we find evidence of heterogeneity in the coefficient estimates. Note that this does not say that there is not heterogeneity across sectors or countries in use of antidumping. There is: given the nature of our model, homogeneous parameters are associated with heterogeneous comparative static effect, and, of course, heterogeneity in use. We see this in section VII, where we use our structural framework to calculate the effect of the level of antidumping applied by a developing country that is a heavy user of antidumping (India). There we find that the welfare cost is three times higher than for the United States, though still quite modest.

II.   The Link between Antidumping and Trade Volume

The literature on the economics and political economy of antidumping (AD) is large, but we can identify four classes of channel through which AD affects trade volumes:[6] direct protection effects, effects due to the contingent nature of protection, effects due to the non-MFN nature of protection, and effects due to the firm-specific nature of protection. We consider each in turn.

Direct effects of protection recognize that AD tariffs are protection, and protection reduces trade volumes and welfare.[7] As with all other forms of protection, a variety of strong cases can be made against protection as a policy instrument

for most uses. In particular, protection distorts incentives, leading to suboptimal use of scarce national resources. Especially in the context of very low statutory rates of protection, the often very high rates of contingent protection can imply substantial distortion. These effects should cause reduced trade between the country imposing the duty and the exporter to that country's market. However, the measured aggregate effects are rather low. Rough-and-ready analyses for the case of the United States suggest that the welfare cost of AD may be as low as $2 billion to $4 billion for the United States in 1993 (Gallaway, Blonigen, & Flynn, 1999).[8] This is hardly surprising since the amount of trade directly affected by contingent protection is quite small—less than 5% of trade flows.[9]

A related direct effect has to do with retaliation. Following research on retaliation in general models of protection, recent research has suggested that the trade volume effects (and welfare effects) of protection could be worse if the trading partner retaliates (Prusa & Skeath, 2002). On the other hand, as Blonigen and Bown (2003) argue, protection may be less likely in a dyad where both parties possess an AD mechanism. In the latter case, then, the spread of AD would be trade increasing.

Beyond the standard problems with protection, there are three additional classes of issues more or less unique to AD: one directly related to its contingent nature, a second related to its non–most favored-nation (MFN) nature; and a third related to its firm-specific nature. Because contingent protection is contingent on an administrative decision, it is in its nature uncertain. A foreign firm currently facing statutory protection would presumably prefer a positive probability of the fixed level of protection to that fixed level of protection with certainty (because the expected level of protection would be lower), but given the support of tariffs that the AD authorities draw from, they may well be averse to a more general AD duty lottery (that is, a lottery where both the outcome and the final rate are uncertain). Furthermore, firms that are not exposed to a statutory tariff will be unambiguously negatively affected by exposure to AD risk. There is considerable anecdotal evidence that foreign firms do in fact price in such a way as to avoid AD risk (though, for obvious reasons, there is essentially no systematic evidence on the extent of this practice). Nonetheless, it is perfectly plausible that protection against one line of goods from a given exporter, *i*, could have effects on exports of other goods from *i*, the same line of goods from other countries, and even producers of other goods from other countries. The breadth of this effect

---

[6] For surveys of the work on antidumping, see Blonigen and Prusa (2003), Falvey and Nelson (2006), and Nelson (2006).

[7] In our usage, *direct effects* refer to any effects induced by the standard, and *aggregate effects* of antidumping as protection. A referee reminds us that antidumping, in common with any other form of protection, might work through a variety of other mechanisms. First, downstream effects might induce increased imports of the good due to either declining competitiveness of the domestic industry or increased competitiveness (especially moving up the value chain) of the foreign industry. Alternatively, antidumping jumping by foreign multinationals might reduce imports by providing domestic supply and by joining a protectionist coalition to further reduce imports. Overall, we are predisposed to see these effects as rather small. That, however, is an empirical question. These remain direct effects, and we will try to evaluate them.

[8] According to the 2006 *Economic Report of the President*, in 1993 the U.S. GDP was $6.7 trillion.

[9] There are other sources of cost, most prominently rent-seeking and dynamic effects, but these are unlikely to affect the trade volumes that are the empirical focus of this paper. For example, for the United States, the costs of filing cases are moderate, and, at least over the sample period of this paper, revenues from antidumping went into general revenue and were not seekable as such. This changed with the adoption of the Byrd amendment in 2000, which was repealed in 2006.

leads Vandenbussche and Zanardi (2006) to refer to this as the "global chilling effect" of AD.

A third source of concern is that AD protection, because it responds to exports from specific countries, violates the fundamental GATT/WTO commitment to nondiscrimination by the MFN clause in article 1 of the GATT agreement. As an empirical matter, the problem of non-MFN protection is that the overall effects are ambiguous. Even if we presume that the net effect of an AD duty on total imports from the home country of firms named in the AD complaint is negative (as seems plausible, but which we can test for), the effect on exports from nonnamed firms, and especially firms from nonnamed countries, is not at all clear. On the one hand, Prusa (2001) finds that in addition to suppressing imports from named countries, AD protection seems to increase imports from nonnamed countries (this would be the equivalent of "trade diversion"). In addition, Bown and Crowley (2006, 2007) also find trade deflection (restricted exporters increase their exports to unrestricted third markets). On the other hand, where Bown and Crowley focus on the effects of AD duties on the export behavior of firms from a single country (Japan), Prusa (2001) and Vandenbussche and Zanardi (2006) argue that, for essentially the reasons outlined above, the active use of AD is expected to generally reduce imports.

Finally, as we have noted already, AD is firm-specific protection. Filing an AD complaint has positive costs, so we must presume that the expected gain from such a filing is positive. These gains may flow directly from filing or from the expected grant of protection. An enormous literature has sought to explicate and empirically identify these gains.[10] For home firms, the benefits of filing come in the form of harassment or, in a strategic context, signaling or raising rivals' costs.[11] Similarly, the benefits of a positive expectation of an AD duty flow from standard distributional effects of protection, rent-shifting, or supporting collusion like Krishna's (1989) trade restrictions as facilitating devices. Given the number of potential strategic variables and market structures, it is probably not surprising that virtually any outcome is possible here. Although there is some, usually rather indirect, evidence that such collusion may be present, identifying

magnitudes (or even direction of effect) has proved virtually impossible.[12]

In the next section we develop our empirical framework. Following that, we suggest how each of the above effects can be identified within that framework.

III. An Empirical Gravity Model for Panel Data

We consider an N country world where each country has a representative consumer whose preferences are given by a constant-elasticity-of-substitution (CES) utility function reflecting a love of variety (see Dixit & Stiglitz, 1977; Krugman, 1979).[13] That is, the utility of a representative consumer in country j is given by

$$u_j = \left[\sum_{i=1}^{N} (\beta_i c_{ij})^{\frac{\sigma-1}{\sigma}} \right]^{\frac{\sigma}{\sigma-1}}, \quad i,j = 1,\ldots,N, \quad (1)$$

where σ is the elasticity of substitution, c_{ij} is the consumption by consumers in j of a single product originating in i, and β_i is a distribution parameter that is inversely related to country i's fraction of world endowments. The budget constraint of consumers in j may be written as

$$Y_j = \sum_{i=1}^{N} p_i t_{ij} c_{ij}, \quad (2)$$

where Y_j is country j's income (GDP), p_i is the mill price of differentiated products in i, and $t_{ij} \geq 1$ is a trade cost index

---

[10] Much contemporary research, both theoretical and empirical, has focused on the strategic elements of administered protection, concluding that the costs of administered protection are probably far in excess of those implied by simply looking at amounts of trade covered by dumping orders and levels of protection in those lines. Surveys of this work can be found in Blonigen and Prusa (2003) and Nelson (2006).

[11] There is some evidence of a harassment motivation, though the most sophisticated attempt to identify such a motivation found only a very small number of cases of this sort (Staiger & Wolak, 1994, 1996). One channel through which the presence of a contingent protection mechanism affects outcomes, even if we do not observe cases filed, is that firms may alter their strategic behavior to take into account the possibility of filing a case. Because such behavior distorts the allocation of resources, it has been called indirect rent seeking (Leidy, 1994). For example, foreign firms may compete less aggressively so as to avoid an antidumping complaint. In addition to changing the terms of noncooperative interaction between home and foreign firms, it is also quite possible that the presence of contingent protection may support collusion among home and foreign firms where, once again, we need not observe contingent protection in equilibrium.

[12] While this work is clever and suggests a warning that standard measures of the cost of protection may be substantial underestimates of those costs, it is important to recognize that there is virtually no compelling empirical work here. In fact, there is a somewhat awkward tension between this conclusion and the work, from an antitrust perspective, which suggests that most cases could not pass a first-stage Joskow-Klevorik predation test (Shin, 1998). That is, most cases do not seem to involve the kind of market structure that would permit antitrust action. It is possible that the cases not filed (those in which the presence of the threat of an antidumping case supports collusion) really do yield high costs, but this seems improbable. It is ironic that in a literature that stresses the disconnect between norms in antitrust and norms in contingent protection, the implicit presumption among antidumping scholars is that markets are imperfectly competitive—mainly because this raises the costs of antidumping) rather than the Chicago presumption (that the market is presumed competitive).

While it may be true that most sectors involved in antidumping are broadly competitive and thus unlikely to support collusive activity, some sectors might well have such market structures. If these sectors account for a large number of cases, collusion and predation might play a significant role in the aggregate effects of antidumping. There is certainly some evidence that this is the case in the chemical industry (Bernhofen, 1995, 1996, 1998). Iron and steel, the other leading user of antidumping worldwide, is a harder case. For steel, the evidence is that it is precisely the increasing competitiveness of the industry that led to its problems and its use of antidumping (Nelson, 1996). Ultimately this is an empirical question. In fact, we are testing for whether these sectors respond differently to antidumping than other sectors do (see table 5), and there must if this hypothesis is correct. The short answer is that there is no evidence that these sectors respond distinctively to antidumping.

[13] In contrast to Dixit and Stiglitz (1977) and Krugman (1979), we model countries here as endowment economies, as in Anderson and Van Wincoop (2003). Hence, we do not introduce separate variables for the number of firms in each economy, but we use the distribution parameter β_i to indicate a country's mass in world supply.

such that $t_{ij} - 1$ is the fraction of consumer prices that accrues to (tariff and nontariff) trade costs. Maximizing equation (1) subject to equation (2) determines the aggregate demand of consumers in j for goods from i at market prices as

$$X_{ij} = Y_j \left(\frac{p_i t_{ij}}{P_j} \right)^{1-\sigma}, \tag{3}$$

where the aggregate price of the consumption bundle of consumers in j under CES preferences (P_j) is determined as

$$P_j = \left[\sum_{i=1}^{N} (\beta_i p_i t_{ij})^{1-\sigma} \right]^{\frac{1}{1-\sigma}}. \tag{4}$$

In an important contribution, Anderson and van Wincoop (2003) illustrate how the condition of goods market clearing reflected in $Y_i = \sum_{i=1}^{N} p_i t_{ij} c_{ij} = \sum_{i=1}^{N} X_{ij}$, together with that of symmetric trade frictions $t_{ij} = t_{ji}$, may be used to reformulate equation (3) as

$$X_{ij} = \frac{Y_i Y_j}{Y_W} \left(\frac{t_{ij}}{P_i P_j} \right)^{1-\sigma}, \tag{5}$$

where $Y_W \equiv \sum_{i=1}^{N} Y_i = \sum_{j=1}^{N} Y_j$ is world income.
Similarly, defining $\theta_i \equiv Y_i/Y_W$ and $\theta_j \equiv Y_j/Y_W$, expressions for price indices P_i, P_j that obey goods market clearing can be found as

$$P_i = \left[\sum_{j=1}^{N} \theta_j \left(\frac{t_{ij}}{P_j} \right)^{1-\sigma} \right]^{\frac{1}{1-\sigma}},$$

$$P_j = \left[\sum_{i=1}^{N} \theta_i \left(\frac{t_{ij}}{P_i} \right)^{1-\sigma} \right]^{\frac{1}{1-\sigma}}. \tag{6}$$

Since the price index functions in equation (6) are nonlinear in both trade frictions and the parameters, Anderson and van Wincoop (2003) derive a nonlinear estimation procedure that obtains estimates of the impact of trade frictions on trade volumes. Recently, Baier and Bergstrand (2009) suggested using a log-linear first-order Taylor series approximation of the Anderson and van Wincoop (2003) model. An advantage of the latter approach is its computational simplicity and its performance, which has been shown to obtain parameter estimates that are very close to the ones relying on the nonlinear

procedure. Baier and Bergstrand rewrite the price index terms in equation (6) as

$$e^{(1-\sigma) \ln P_i} = \sum_{j=1}^{N} e^{\theta_j + (1-\sigma) \ln t_{ij} + (1-\sigma) \ln P_j},$$

$$e^{(1-\sigma) \ln P_j} = \sum_{i=1}^{N} e^{\theta_i + (1-\sigma) \ln t_{ij} - (1-\sigma) \ln P_i}, \tag{7}$$

and then apply a first-order log-linear Taylor series expansion centered at the symmetric, nonzero trade cost equilibrium with cross-section data, $t_{ij} = t \neq 1$ and $P_i = P = t^{\frac{1}{2}} \neq 1$.[15] This yields the following approximate log-inverse price index expressions corresponding to equation (7) for a symmetric world with trade frictions:

$$-\ln P_i^{1-\sigma} = (\sigma - 1) \left[\frac{1}{N} \sum_{j=1}^{N} \ln t_{ij} - \frac{1}{2} \frac{1}{N^2} \sum_{i=1}^{N} \sum_{j=1}^{N} \ln t_{ij} \right],$$

$$-\ln P_j^{1-\sigma} = (\sigma - 1) \left[\frac{1}{N} \sum_{j=1}^{N} \ln t_{ij} - \frac{1}{2} \frac{1}{N^2} \sum_{i=1}^{N} \sum_{j=1}^{N} \ln t_{ji} \right]. \tag{8}$$

The first-order Taylor series approximation to the gravity model, evaluated at symmetric but nonzero trade frictions, for bilateral panel data in logs then reads

$$\ln X_{ijt} = \ln Y_{it} + \ln Y_{jt} - \ln Y_{W,t} - (\sigma - 1) \ln t_{ijt}$$

$$+ (\sigma - 1) \left[\frac{1}{N} \sum_{j=1}^{N} \ln t_{ijt} - \frac{1}{2} \frac{1}{N^2} \sum_{i=1}^{N} \sum_{j=1}^{N} \ln t_{ijt} \right]$$

$$+ (\sigma - 1) \left[\frac{1}{N} \sum_{i=1}^{N} \ln t_{jit} - \frac{1}{2} \frac{1}{N^2} \sum_{i=1}^{N} \sum_{j=1}^{N} \ln t_{jit} \right]. \tag{9}$$

Note that we have outlined only the deterministic part of the model in this analysis. We follow the majority of previous work on the estimation of bilateral trade flow models by assuming that the stochastic part is linearly separable in a specification in logs as in equation (9).[16] With panel data, the stochastic part of the model (we refer to it as u_{ijt}) distinguishes two components: one that is constant across periods (the between-country pairs dimension of the data) and the remaining part (the within-country-pairs dimension of the data, which Glick and Rose, 2002, refer to as the

---

[14] Their focus is on the border effect for trade across U.S. states and Canadian provinces relative to intranational trade among these regions. However, the argument naturally extends to estimating the impact of trade frictions on trade volumes in such a model in general.

[15] They provide an alternative linearization at the zero-trade-cost equilibrium $t_{ij} = t = 1$ and $P_i = P = 1$. However, the latter seems less plausible from an empirical point of view.

[16] See Santos Silva and Tenreyro (2006) for an exception.

time series dimension). In formal accounts, the overall stochastic component for country pair ij and year t may be written as

$$u_{ijt} = \mu_{ij} + v_{ijt}. \tag{10}$$

Clearly, μ_{ij} is the time-invariant part of the error term, while v_{ijt} is an idiosyncratic disturbance term. There are two main options for modeling μ_{ij}. First, assume a specific functional form μ_{ij} could be modeled as random. However, for this to obtain consistent model parameter estimates, all observables included in the model have to be independent not only of v_{ijt} but also of μ_{ij}. Otherwise the parameter estimates are biased and inconsistent. Second, one can estimate the parameter μ_{ij} for each country pair ij. Obviously this is less efficient than assuming μ_{ij} as random. Implicitly, it means that we have to estimate not only a single constant for the model but one for each country pair. Since the number of country pairs is much larger than the available time periods in typical gravity models, the parameters μ_{ij} will be highly inaccurate. However, usually we are interested not in the estimates of μ_{ij} but in the parameters of the covariates in the model. While their parameters will also be less accurate than in a model where μ_{ij} is random, the fixed country pair effects estimator is immune to the problem of possible correlation between the covariates and the μ_{ij}. Therefore, the model with a fixed μ_{ij} is a benchmark case, and the one with a random μ_{ij} needs to obtain parameter estimates for the covariates that are very similar to the fixed μ_{ij} estimator. Hence, the reliability of the random country pair effects model is testable (see Hausman, 1978), and with bilateral trade volume data, it is typically rejected against its fixed country pair effects counterpart (see Glick & Rose, 2002; Cheng & Wall, 2005). While this might be seen as a problem of panel data, in fact it raises serious concerns only about parameters in cross-section models. The random country pair effects estimator can be shown to be a weighted average of the fixed country pair effects model and a time-averaged cross-section model (see Baltagi, 2005). Under the outlined assumptions, rejection of the random effects model due to correlation between the covariates and the μ_{ij} implies that the cross-section estimates are biased and inconsistent. Since previous evidence on gravity models points in that direction, we focus on panel econometric fixed-effects estimates throughout.

While ours is not the first attempt to apply such techniques in the context of gravity models, their introduction in the literature on the quantification of trade volume response to trade policy is novel to the best of our knowledge.[17]

IV. Data Description

While the model of Anderson and van Wincoop (2003), and Baier and Bergstrand's (2009) approximation thereof, can be used for a gravity model–based quantification of the trade friction impact on trade volumes in general, previous work focused on the estimation of border effects.[18] By way of contrast, our goal is to analyze the bilateral and multilateral responses of trade volumes to trade impediments in general and AD investigations in particular.

A. Trade Volumes and GDP

We use bilateral export volumes (X_{ijt}) and exporter as well as importer GDPs (Y_{it}, Y_{jt}) as published by the IMF. The corresponding figures are expressed in nominal U.S. dollars. Exports span the period from 1948 to 2001 and GDPs from 1960 to 2001 at the annual level. Bilateral export data are based on the Direction of Trade statistics, and GDP is available from the International Financial Statistics. In most of the models we estimate, using GDPs is not necessary, since they may be controlled for by fixed country time effects. Then the sample period covers the period from 1948 to 2001. In specifications that employ GDPs, the sample period runs from 1960 to 2001.

B. Geographical and Cultural Trade Frictions

Geographical trade frictions are well known for their robust negative impact on bilateral trade flows. In particular, geographical distance and (the absence of) common borders should be mentioned here (Bergstrand, 1985, 1989; Anderson & Van Wincoop, 2004). We compute bilateral great circle distances ($DIST_{ij}$) between two countries' capitals based on the longitude and latitude as published in the *CIA World Factbook*. The same source provides information on a country's common borders with other economies. Since our focus is on trade frictions, we depart from previous research by designing a dummy variable that takes the value 1 in the absence of a common border and 0 otherwise ($NBORD_{ij}$). Furthermore, we follow the same principle by defining a cultural (language) distance variable that is 1 in the absence of a common official language and 0 otherwise ($NLANG_{ij}$).

C. Political Trade Frictions: Regional Trade Agreements and Antidumping Investigations

We use several different binary political trade friction indicators. Most important for the purposes of this paper, we employ variables giving the number of AD investigations of

---

[17] Baier and Bergstrand (2007) provide an analysis of the trade friction effects with panel data. While they include fixed effects to avoid biased estimates of the parameters, a compulsory quantification of the effect of trade frictions cannot be retrieved in their case (see Feenstra, 2004).

[18] More precisely, that research sought to provide an explanation of the strong, negative effect of national borders on trade volumes among Canadian provinces and U.S. states as compared to that of state and province borders on interregional trade within these two countries.

an importer against its exporting trading partner.[19] We use this information on AD activity to construct two variables (and lags thereof) for use in our empirical models. The first is a count variable reflecting the number of AD investigations importing country j has initiated against exporting country i in year t (AD_{ijt}). We expect the parameter of AD_{ijt} to be negative if concurrent AD investigations impede exports of a country whose firms have been filed on. In addition, we allow for a separate impact of an accumulation of investigations at the country pair level. Specifically, we use the cumulative number of AD investigations for a country pair, indicating how many AD investigations economy j has launched against country i until year t (CAD_{ijt}). This would reflect a particularly long memory in trade response to earlier investigations.

Following other work, we use information on (the absence of) common regional trade agreement membership for each country pair and year—one for customs unions (NCU_{ijt}) and the other one for free trade areas ($NFTA_{ijt}$) as notified to the WTO.[20]

D. Definition of the Trade Friction Variable t_{ijt}

While we used a single symbol t_{ijt} for trade costs in section III, the preceding subsections suggest that t_{ijt} is an aggregate

of AD_{ijt}, CAD_{ijt}, NCU_{ijt}, $NFTA_{ijt}$, $DIST_{ij}$, $NBORD_{ij}$, and $NLANG_{ij}$.[21] In the aggregation, we follow the literature by assuming a log-linear functional form,

$$
\ln t_{ijt} = \alpha_1 AD_{ijt} + \alpha_2 CAD_{ijt} \\
+ \alpha_3 NCU_{ijt} + \alpha_4 NFTA_{ijt} \\
+ \alpha_5 \ln DIST_{ij} + \alpha_6 NBORD_{ij} + \alpha_7 NLANG_{ij}.
$$
(11)

Following Anderson and van Wincoop (2003), we use $\ln x_{ijt} \equiv \ln X_{ijt} - \ln Y_{it} - \ln Y_{jt}$ instead of X_{ijt} as the left-hand-side variable in the sequel.

To implement the Baier-Bergstrand approximation, for each variable in $\ln t_{ijt}$ we collect terms in equation (9) into a variable indicated by a tilde. For instance, the term corresponding to $\ln DIST_{ij}$ is the first-order Taylor series approximation evaluated at an equilibrium with symmetric but nonzero trade frictions as in equation (9), which reads $\ln \widetilde{DIST}_{ij} \equiv \ln DIST_{ij} - \frac{1}{N}\sum_{j=1}^{N} \ln DIST_{ij} + \frac{1}{2}\frac{1}{N^2}\sum_{i=1}^{N}\sum_{j=1}^{N} \ln DIST_{ij}$, and similarly for all other trade barrier variables. Note that the latter approximation reveals an analogy to the two-way panel data within estimator (here, with fixed exporter-by-time and importer-by-time effects). Variable $\ln \widetilde{DIST}_{ij}$ is defined as the exporter-by-year and importer-by-year demeaned $DIST_{ij}$, and similarly for the other trade barrier variables. The only difference by comparison to the two-way within model is that the left-hand-side variable is not demeaned in the Baier and Bergstrand (2009) approach.

Inserting equation (11) in equation (9) and using the above definitions yields

$$
\ln x_{ijt} = -\ln Y_{W,t} - (\sigma - 1) \ln \alpha_1 \ln \widetilde{AD}_{ijt} \\
- (\sigma - 1)\alpha_2 \widetilde{CAD}_{ijt} - (\sigma - 1)\alpha_3 \widetilde{NCU}_{ijt} \\
- (\sigma - 1)\alpha_4 \widetilde{NFTA}_{ijt} - (\sigma - 1)\alpha_5 \ln \widetilde{DIST}_{ij} \\
- (\sigma - 1)\alpha_6 \widetilde{NBORD}_{ij} - (\sigma - 1)\alpha_7 \widetilde{NLANG}_{ij} + u_{ijt}.
$$
(12)

The specification in equation (12) could be estimated by adding $\ln Y_{W,t}$ to both sides of the model or, in a less restrictive approach, replacing $-\ln Y_{W,t}$ by fixed time effects.[22] If the number of country pairs in the data is as large as in our application, one can apply a country pair within estimator to eliminate the possible correlation of the covariates with μ_{ij}. The parameter estimates α_k for $k = 1, \ldots, 4$ are then the fixed effects benchmark coefficients.

---

[19] Data on antidumping investigations are collected from various sources. First, we take advantage of Chad Bown's series of antidumping cases from the year 1980 onward. The data are available as tables at http://people.brandeis.edu/~cbown/global_ad/. In fact, much more information is available there than we make use of, and these data may be a rich source for future research.

In addition to Bown's data, we have compiled data on bilateral antidumping investigations before 1980. In particular, data on the European Union's (then, the European Community's) investigations are collected in the appendix to Beseler and Williams (1986). The data on Australia, South Africa, United Kingdom, and the United States stem from the General Agreement on Trade and Tariffs (GATT), in particular the supplement to its *Basic Instruments and Selected Documents* and national sources, for example: Australian Customs Service, Canada Customs and Revenue Agency, the DTI (for South Africa), and other countries' agencies. Bruce Blonigen provides Web links on his homepage to a set of countries' administrative offices (pages.uoregon.edu/bruceb).

Unlike statutory tariffs, contingent protection is characterized by a multitude of details in implementation that vary across sectors, countries, and time. It would be nice to have access to data that control for this variability. However, like all other analyses dealing with cross-sectoral, cross-national, and cross-temporal contingent protection, we are constrained to work with count data. As with all other papers that share this problem, we hope (with more-or-less justification) that any biases imported in this fashion are small. Note that Zanardi (2006) provides information at the unilateral level by summarizing the investigations at the investigator country level as available from the GATT's supplement to its *Basic Instruments and Selected Documents* publication. While Zanardi's article is a rich source as well, it is not useful for our purpose due to the absence of country pair information for investigations.

[20] In the sensitivity analysis in table 2, we allow for a further impact of other preferential trade agreements notified to the WTO, WTO nonmembership of either one or two countries of a pair, and the absence of currency arrangements such as currency union, currency peg, or currency band membership as documented by the IMF. Also, we consider the role of once- and twice-lagged antidumping ($AD_{ij,t-1}$, $AD_{ij,t-2}$, $CAD_{ij,t-1}$, $CAD_{ij,t-2}$), and, finally, we use an exporter's antidumping investigations against the importer (AD_{jit}, CAD_{jit}) as additional control variables there to capture dynamic effects of antidumping and the sluggish response of trade flows to antidumping.

[21] Analogously, the other trade friction indicators mentioned above will be included in the sensitivity analysis of section VB.
[22] Then the coefficient of $-\ln Y_{W,t}$ no longer has to be unity.

1380   THE REVIEW OF ECONOMICS AND STATISTICS

V. Panel Data Estimates of the Impact of Antidumping Investigations on Trade Volumes

A. Baseline Results

In the empirical analysis, we proceed in two steps. First, we estimate the counterpart to equation (12) that uses non-demeaned trade friction variables on the right-hand side. While this model accounts for the possible influence of time-invariant variables, it ignores the impact of multilateral resistance on trade volume.[23] Second, we summarize the findings of the transformed model as in equation (12). A comparison of the corresponding model outcome with that based on the properly demeaned model sheds light on the importance of multilateral versus bilateral effects of trade frictions on trade volume in general and of AD in particular. The null hypothesis of a zero impact of multilateral resistance is even testable.

We run each of these two models by pooled ordinary least squares (OLS) and the fixed country-pair effects estimator. Pooled OLS assumes that the included explanatory variables are uncorrelated with the time-invariant unobservables that are collected in the between-error term (μ_{ij}) while the fixed-effects model does not. Since the geographical and cultural variables in the model ($\ln DIST_{ij}, NBORD_{ij}, NLANG_{ij}$) are time invariant, they will be wiped out by the fixed country pair effects estimator so that their coefficients are reported only with pooled OLS.

Table 1 provides a summary of results for the four models. The results suggest the following conclusions. First, the test statistics reject the pooled OLS models A and C against their fixed country pair effects counterparts B and D. Second, models A and B ignore the role of multilateral resistance and are rejected against their cum-multilateral-resistance-term counterparts, models C and D. Since model D is clearly preferable on econometric grounds over models A to C, we focus on the discussion of the corresponding parameters in the sequel.

The point estimates for the parameter of AD_{ijt} indicate that a single AD investigation exerts a significantly negative, direct, contemporaneous impact on bilateral exports of about $e^{-0.073} \simeq -7.03\%$.[24] According to the much smaller (in absolute value) and insignificant parameter of CAD_{ijt}, there is no indication of a long memory in trade responsiveness to AD in that model. Hence, investigations of an importer against an exporter in the past do not impede concurrent trade volume.

[23] With panel data, the multilateral resistance terms can principally be captured by fixed exporter-by-time and importer-by-time effects. See Baltagi, Egger, and Pfaffermayr (2003) for such a model. However, with a large data set such as ours, this involves a huge matrix of dummy variables that is infeasible to handle by standard computer hardware.

[24] This magnitude may strike the reader as quite large. However, note that this reflects only the direct impact of AD_{ijt} on trade flows within an overall highly nonlinear framework. A valid quantification of the effect of antidumping investigations is quite tricky, here, since we have to compute the associated change of AD_{ijt} through an increase in AD_{ijt} for all country pairs. We pursue this explicitly in section VD, where we will see that this ends up being a very small effect.

TABLE 1.—POOLED OLS AND FIXED COUNTRY PAIR EFFECTS ESTIMATES OF ANTIDUMPING INITIATION AND OTHER TRADE FRICTION EFFECTS ON BILATERAL EXPORTS, 1948–2001

| | Ignoring Multilateral Resistance (Untransformed Trade Frictions) | | | | Accounting for Multilateral Resistance (transformed Trade Frictions) | | | |
| | Model A: Pooled OLS | | Model B: Fixed Country Pair Effects | | Model C: Pooled OLS | | Model D: Fixed Country Pair Effects | |
Trade Friction Determinants of Normalized Bilateral Exports	Coefficient	S.E.	Coefficient	S.E.	Coefficient	S.E.	Coefficient	S.E.
Antidumping variables								
AD_{ijt}	-0.076	0.002	-0.068	0.005	-0.112	0.001	-0.073	0.004
CAD_{ijt}	0.037***	0.003	-0.007	0.091	0.039***	0.003	-0.014	0.097
Other trade frictions								
NCU_{ijt}	0.158	0.059	-0.107*	0.059	0.097	0.066	-0.227**	0.070
$NFTA_{ijt}$	-0.054	0.007	0.028**	0.003	-0.010	0.008	0.029**	0.003
$\ln DIST_{ij}$	-0.389	0.079	—		-0.352	0.084	—	
$NBORD_{ij}$	0.564	0.042	—		0.495	0.043	—	
$NLANG_{ij}$	0.043	0.013	—		-0.011	0.016	—	
Observations	294,356		294,356		294,356		294,356	
Country pairs	21,450		21,450		21,450		21,450	
Joint significance of all regressors (p-value of F-statistic)	0.000		0.000		0.000		0.000	
Joint significance of multilateral resistance (p-value of F-statistic)	—		—		0.000		0.000	
Hausman test (p-value of χ^2 statistic)	—		0.084		—		0.924	
Fixed country-pair effects (p-value of F-statistic)	0.000		0.000		0.000		0.000	
Fixed time effects (p-value of F-statistic)	0.000		0.000		0.000		0.000	

***, **, * significance at 1%, 5%, 10%, respectively. AD_{ijt}: number of bilateral antidumping investigations of country j against i in year t. CAD_{ijt}: cumulative number of AD_{ijt} until year t. $NCU_{ijt}/NFTA_{ijt}$: absence of pair ij's membership in customs union/free trade area in year t. $NBORD_{ij}/NLANG_{ij}$: absence of a common border/language between i and j. $\ln DIST_{ij}$: great circle distance between i and j.

TABLE 2.—SENSITIVITY ANALYSIS OF THE ANTIDUMPING EFFECT ON NORMALIZED EXPORTS
ACCOUNTING FOR MULTILATERAL RESISTANCE: TRANSFORMED TRADE FRICTIONS AS IN MODEL D OF TABLE 1

	Parameter of AD		Parameter of CAD	
Type of Model	Coefficient	S.E.[i]	Coefficient	S.E.[i]
Reference: Model D in table 1	−0.073	0.029**	0.004	0.003
Sensitivity analyses				
(i) Including further time-variant trade frictions[a]	−0.075	0.029***	0.005	0.003*
(ii) As in i plus lagged antidumping measures[b]	−0.133	0.051***	0.011	0.005**
(iii) As in ii plus twice lagged antidumping measures[c]	−0.131	0.059**	0.015	0.009**
(iv) As in iii plus AD and CAD of exporter[d]	−0.134	0.063**	0.013	0.007**
(v) As in iv but accounting for systematically missing trade flows[e]	−0.135	0.048***	0.013	0.008*
(vi) As in iv but using levels (incl. zeros) rather than the log of exports in a poisson QML model[f]	−0.212	0.041***	0.010	0.006
(vii) As in iv but using impositions of AD measures instead of investigations[g]	−0.107	0.052**	0.002	0.002
(viii) As in iv but using GDP-weighted rather than unweighted averages for third-country effects[h]	−0.046	0.027*	0.017	0.007**

All models include fixed country pair effects and fixed time effects. ***, **, and *: Significance levels of 1%, 5%, 10%, respectively.
[a] Beyond model D in table 1, the specification includes the following covariates: absence of WTO membership for one of the two countries; absence of WTO membership for both countries; absence of currency union membership; absence of currency peg membership; absence of currency band membership; absence of preferential (other than customs union or free trade area) membership.
[b] Beyond specification i, we include $AD_{ij,t-1}$ and $CAD_{ij,t-1}$ (jointly significant at 5%). The above coefficients are the accumulated effects.
[c] Beyond specification ii, we include $AD_{ij,t-2}$ and $CAD_{ij,t-2}$ (jointly significant at 5%). The above coefficients are the accumulated effects.
[d] Beyond specification iii, we include the exporter's AD_{jit} and CAD_{jit} (jointly significant at 1%).
[e] We apply Woolridge's (1995) sample selection estimator for panel data. We estimate annual selection models using the following determinants of the indicator for nonmissing/nonzero exports: all variables as in specification iv in this table; the means of these variables; time-invariant geographical determinants such as common language, adjacency, log distance, log area of exporter plus importer, location on a common continent, and their demeaned counterparts to account for multilateral resistance as in equation (12). There is an inverse Mill's ratio for each year. The inverse Mill's ratios are jointly significant at 1%.
[f] This model follows the suggestion of Santos Silva and Tenreyro (2006) by using a quasi-maximum likelihood Poisson model with robust standard errors, but with country pair fixed effects. Since this specification includes 0 trade flows, we cover 882,431 observations in this case. While the point estimate in this model turns out to be larger than that in iv, the two confidence intervals overlap enough so that the parameters for AD and CAD are not significantly different between iv and vi.
[g] The data are provided by Chad Bown and available only from 1980 onward. The total number of observations is 85,052, and there are 9,744 country pairs. Other than using impositions rather than investigations, the estimated specification is the same as that in iv in this table.
[h] See Baier and Bergstrand (2009) for this alternative approximation of the model by Anderson and Van Wincoop (2003). The exporter's antidumping investigations are jointly significant in this model.
[i] The figures for specifications i–vii are bootstrapped standard errors.

B. Sensitivity Analysis

Before turning to the quantification of the impact of AD investigations on trade volume, we provide a sensitivity analysis of the baseline estimates in table 1. Overall, we provide nine alternative sets of results for the parameters of interest (those of AD_{ijt} and CAD_{ijt}). Our findings are summarized in table 2A.

Experiment i—including further trade friction variables. In a first step, we augment our specification of model D by six additional covariates related to trade frictions: absence of preferential (other than customs union of free trade area) membership; absence of WTO membership for one of the two countries; absence of WTO membership for both countries; absence of currency union membership; and absence of currency peg membership; absence of currency band membership. Most of these variables have been shown to affect trade volumes. As we noted in section I, all of these variables have been shown, at least in some analyses, to significantly affect trade patterns. Indeed, we find that these variables exert a jointly significant (at 1%) impact on bilateral export volume. However, their omission does not influence the point estimates of the parameters of interest, $\beta_{AD_{ijt}}$ and $\beta_{CAD_{ijt}}$.

Experiments ii and iii—dynamic effects of antidumping. By including CAD_{ijt} along with AD_{ijt}, model D accounts for a dynamic effect of AD on trade volume but in a very crude way. In experiment ii, we include once-lagged levels of our AD variables ($AD_{ij,t-1}, CAD_{ij,t-1}$) to the specification in experiment i, and in experiment iii, we additionally include the twice-lagged levels thereof ($AD_{ij,t-2}, CAD_{ij,t-2}$). Hence, these specifications capture the time-variant influence of

contemporaneous versus lagged AD investigations as in autoregressive distributed lag models.[25] Since we are interested in the long-run effects of AD, we report its cumulated impact with these two experiments: $\beta_{AD_{ijt}} + \beta_{AD_{ij,t-1}}(+\beta_{AD_{ij,t-2}})$ and $\beta_{CAD_{ijt}} + \beta_{CAD_{ij,t-1}}(+\beta_{CAD_{ij,t-2}})$, respectively. We find that the fixed effects estimator of model D substantially underestimates the impact of both current and cumulative investigations; however, we also find that the inclusion of a second lag provides essentially no additional impact on trade volume.[26]

Experiment iv—the exporter's investigations and their impact on bilateral export volume. In the next experiment, we include the exporter's AD investigation variables AD_{jit} and CAD_{jit}, respectively, in addition to the covariates in experiment iii. We do so to make sure that we do not ascribe an effect to the importer's investigations that in fact is due to exporter activity. Again, these two variables contribute significantly to the explanation of bilateral, normalized export volume. However, the parameters of interest are not statistically different from those in experiment iii, as can be seen from the point estimates and the *t*-statistics reported in table 2.

Experiment v—systematically missing trade values. Research provides an explanation of zero trade among trading partners with particular characteristics (Evenett & Venables, 2002; Felbermayr & Kohler, 2006; Helpman, Melitz, &

[25] We have a wide variety of ways that we might motivate such dynamic effects, and empirical papers on antidumping have certainly used them. One example is Blonigen and Haynes (2002).
[26] This holds true, although not only the once-lagged but also the twice-lagged antidumping investigation variables contribute significantly to the model. We have run specifications with even more than two lags, but the results remain stable.

Rubinstein, 2008). With a log-linear model like ours, the dependent variable may be missing for three reasons: bilateral trade is truly, 0, bilateral trade values are not reported[27] or GDP values are not available. As a result, selection into the sample might lead to a biased impact of the AD investigation parameters of interest. We check for the sensitivity of the findings by correcting the specification as in experiment iv for sample selection bias.[28] We follow Wooldridge (1995) by applying a sample selection model that is suitable for panel data with fixed effects.[29] This model rests on inverse Mill's ratios as selection correction variables that are based on annual probit models. These probit models employ the multilateral resistance transformed and untransformed variables as in experiment iv and time-invariant geographical and cultural determinants (see note f in table 2 for details). In all years, these variables possess high joint relevance (they are significant at 1% throughout). A test of sample selection following Wooldridge (1995) indicates that there is significant (at 1%) selection into the sample conditional on this specification. However, there is little impact on the point estimates of the parameters of interest.

Experiment vi—accounting for 0 trade flows in a Poisson quasi-maximum-likelihood model. Santos Silva and Tenreyro (2006) have suggested accounting for 0 bilateral trade flows in a Poisson model. There, only the right-hand side of the specification is logarithmically transformed, not the dependent variable. Hence, 0 trade flows are not dropped via log-transforming the model. In our data set, there are 588,095 0 bilateral export values across all years. Hence, the number of observations in the Poisson model is 882,451, while it was only 294,356 in the log-export-based specifications. For the sake of consistent estimates, we follow the Mundlak-Chamberlain device and include country pair means of all explanatory variables in the model, along with the original variables.[30] This leads to parameter estimates for the original variables that are to be interpreted as within–country pair estimates as in the previous models. Additionally, the estimates are based on heteroskedasticity-robust standard errors as suggested by Santos Silva and Tenreyro (2006). The estimated impact of AD and CAD is similar to the baseline results. While the point estimate for the impact of AD on bilateral exports is higher than before, the parameter is not significantly different from the original estimates.

Experiment vii—using the number of impositions of preliminary antidumping measures instead of the investigations. We might reasonably expect that the primary effect of AD on trade comes only with the actual imposition of AD duties. Unfortunately, neither Bown's data (which begin in 1980) nor the data we have been able to collect permit us to treat this question over the entire GATT/WTO time period. Thus, as an additional experiment, we consider the subperiod from 1980. Interestingly, the results point to a somewhat smaller point estimate of the long-run impact of impositions than for investigations for the longer time span. However, the parameter estimates are not significantly different between experiments iv and vi.[31]

Experiments viii—using GDP-weighted rather than simple averages in the Baier and Bergstrand (2009) approach to account for multilateral resistance. Baier and Bergstrand suggest an alternative specification of multilateral resistance, where the original trade friction variables are not transformed by subtracting simple exporter and importer means but rather GDP-weighted ones. The latter transformation is associated with a Taylor series approximation around the 0 trade friction equilibrium. This specification leads to a lower point estimate of the AD impact. However, this effect is estimated at less precision than the original ones so that it is not significantly different from the baseline estimates.

Based on the analysis in this section, we will generally use the specification in experiment iv as our main framework. In addition, we will compare the results from this specification against ones that are based on applied measures as in experiment vii.

C. Discussion of Hypotheses on Trade Volume Effects of Antidumping

In section II, we presented four broad classes of channel that the literature on AD has identified as affecting trade volumes: direct protection effects, effects due to the contingent nature of protection, effects due to the non-MFN nature of protection, and effects due to the firm-specific nature of protection. In section III, we developed the model that resulted in our empirical specification in equation (12). In this section, we express the predicted effects as hypotheses of this model and present some estimates of these effects. Section VD will present our analysis of the quantitative magnitude of the major effects.

The most obvious implementation of our key question is to ask whether the use of AD by country j on the imports from country i (implemented as exports from i to j) reduces the volume of those imports. In terms of the specification in equation (12), this implies that $\alpha_1 < 0$. As the estimates

---

[27] Zero trade and missing trade values are typically not satisfactorily distinguishable in trade matrices.

[28] We do not use the model as of experiment v since the use of GDP in the selection model leads to an unnecessary loss of observations.

[29] Cross-section procedures as in Helpman et al. (2008) or Felbermayr and Kohler (2006) are not applicable in this case, as Wooldridge (1995) pointed out.

[30] Mundlak (1978), Chamberlain (1984), and Wooldridge (2002) suggest parameterizing the fixed effects in panel data models as an additive function of all time-averaged variables in the model. Unlike the dummy variables estimator, this procedure is applicable to both linear and nonlinear models, and it produces consistent parameter estimates even if some of the time-variant variables in the model are correlated with time-invariant unobserved effects.

[31] One explanation for this may be the high correlation between nontransformed and transformed antidumping investigations and the impositions of antidumping measures. The correlation coefficients amount to 0.64 and 0.62 (impositions), respectively.

reported in table 2 suggest, we find a statistically significant negative effect of AD in the year of initiation. In our sensitivity analysis, we also considered one- and two-period lags of AD, both of them significant. More important, it is clear that inclusion of one lag is necessary to capture the effects of AD on trade in a given period, but that the second lag contributes little to the analysis. Because the data on applied measures are not available for many countries over the entire time period of interest, we have defined our AD (and CAD) variables in terms of initiations. Given data availability and a reasonably high correlation between initiations and application of duties, this seems a sensible strategy. However, experiment iv directly examines the number of cases in which duties were applied as a robustness check. Consistent with our expectations, α_1 is negative and statistically significant with a magnitude roughly similar (in fact, slightly smaller) to the value of the parameter estimated in our baseline specification estimated on initiations.[32]

It is interesting to note that the coefficient on our CAD variable, α_2, is greater than 0. This variable is intended to pick up the long-run effects of AD in the relevant dyad. We capture the contemporaneous, the once-lagged, and the twice-lagged impact in α_1, so countries that applied many AD measures in the past now have fewer of them.[33] For the overall impact of AD, note that a country's cumulative number of AD actions grows by definition, while contemporaneous ADs may increase or fall over time. Altogether, the cumulative impact (through α_2) reduces the contemporaneous one. The smaller the change relative to a dyad's average number of AD actions across the years in a given time span, the smaller is the reduction of the direct impact of AD (through α_1; for a given dyadic change in AD over time) by that of the cumulative one (through α_2). Hence, $\alpha_2 \times CAD$ reduces the impact of $\alpha_1 \times AD$, and this reduction depends on the level and change in both AD and CAD.[34] This effect might be picking up some of the retaliation effects, which we consider explicitly below.

A second set of hypotheses relates to the firm-specific effects of AD protection. We considered two broad arguments here: harassment and strategic effects. In the case of harassment, we would expect the effect to flow from initiation, so we can use our full data set. The hypothesis would be $\alpha_1 < 0$. In the case of strategic effects, it is not clear

whether we should be focusing on initiations or implementations, but in either case, the hypothesis is $\alpha_1 < 0$. As with the hypothesis of general direct effects, we find a statistically significant negative impact of both initiation and implementation. Since these three hypotheses make observationally equivalent predictions, our results do not allow us to choose among hypotheses.[35] We can, however, consider the magnitudes involved. We consider this in the next section.

A third set of hypotheses derives from the non-MFN nature of AD protection. The essential issue here is trade diversion. In thinking about trade diversion in the context of a gravity model, there are several important things to note. First, the direct impact of a country's AD investigations on dyadic exports, given everybody else's actions, is identical to the parameter in table 2 (of course, our left-hand-side variable is in logs, so the elasticity in percent would be about $100 \times (e^{\alpha_1 - \text{Var}(\alpha_1)} - 1)$.[36] Second, the impact on the average dyadic number of AD investigations for the average exporter in year t is quite small, as is that on the average dyadic number of AD investigations for the average importer. The impact on the overall average dyadic number of AD investigations for all pairs is even smaller. The negative of the change in exporter-by-time average number of AD investigations minus that of the importer-by-time average number of AD investigations plus that of the time average number of AD investigations is the third-country change, that is, $\Delta(-\overline{AD}_{jt} - \overline{AD}_{it} + \overline{AD}_t)$, where Δ is the first difference operator. Recall that, in contrast to the following table, we are talking about the marginal impact of a single AD investigation on bilateral trade here. Clearly the direct impact of AD on trade is captured by $\alpha_1 \Delta AD_{ijt} = \alpha_1$ from which it follows that the effect due to multilateral resistance is $\alpha_1 \Delta(-\overline{AD}_{jt} - \overline{AD}_{it} + \overline{AD}_t) < 1$. Since the parameter for both effects is the same, the diversion effect is smaller than the creation effect (of course, since $\alpha_1 < 0$, here, we face a negative creation effect). Beyond that, we may say that with a worldwide increase of use, the diversion effect will decline, since the means will be affected less than before by a unitary increase of a single country's AD investigations but the direct effect is always multiplied

---

[32] Using data from Bown's data set covering the period 1980–2001, we also considered specifications in which AD was implemented as each component: duties, suspension agreements, and price undertakings. For specifications involving the contemporaneous values, we considered one and two lags of these variables. With the exception of a specification in which two lags of price undertakings were considered, none of these achieved conventional levels of significance. The specification involving one and two lags of the price-undertaking variable was significantly negative, though the cumulative impact of the two lags was not significant. Full results are available on request.

[33] This is precisely the pattern found by Zanardi (2006), where both initiations and implementations by traditional users have declined over time while use by new users has increased dramatically.

[34] Since our framework explicitly incorporates multilateral resistance, the overall impact of AD activity (both contemporaneous and cumulative) also depends on what happens in the other dyads.

[35] As we noted in section II, for strategic effects to be macroeconomically significant (and thus show up in analysis of the sort we consider here) would require implausible market structure conditions at the global level. The empirical work that speaks directly to this issue would seem to be unsupportive of the existence of such market structures (Shin, 1998). Furthermore, the work we report in section VII, on the most significant sectors, where such market structures might exist and might affect aggregate outcome, does not find evidence of difference between these sectors and the aggregate.

Harassment is a somewhat different story. Empirical research, especially by Staiger and Wolak (1994, 1996), has found some some evidence of harrassment. While Staiger and Wolak find evidence of harassment effects and the presence of participants in the process who are primarily interested in those effects ("process filers"), they ultimately conclude that "for most industries, the prospect of a dumping finding is an important ingredient in the decision to file and thus that outcome filers are the predominant users of antidumping law" (1994, p. 53). Overall, we are predisposed to believe that the effects we have identified flow from direct effects.

[36] Note that the effect of a unitary change in AD on exports is not well approximated by $100 \times (e^{\alpha_1} - 1)$ in a semi-log model as indicated by Van Garderen and Shah (2002).

TABLE 3.—FURTHER RESULTS

A: Further Results Using Price Undertakings (Aggregate AD Investigation or Imposition Case Numbers)	Coefficient	S.E.
Case 1: Using the sum of antidumping investigations of country *j* against all countries in year *t* in addition to the dyad-by-year specific ones (in the spirit of Vandenbussche and Zanardi)[a]		
Variable: Sum of all contemporaneous investigations of country *j* in year *t*	0.090	0.100
Case 2: Using the sum of antidumping impositions of country *j* against all countries in year *t* in addition to the dyad-by-year specific ones (in the spirit of Vandenbussche and Zanardi)[a]		
Variable: Sum of all contemporaneous impositions of country *j* in year *t*	−0.046	0.143
Case 3: Using the sum of antidumping investigations and that of impositions of country *j* against all countries in year *t* in addition to the dyad-by-year specific ones (in the spirit of Vandenbussche and Zanardi)[a]		
Variable: Sum of all contemporaneous investigations of country *j* in year *t*	−0.160	0.143
Sum of all contemporaneous impositions of country *j* in year *t*	0.111	0.199
B. Further Results Inferring the Impact of Retaliation	**Coefficient**	**S.E.**
Case 4: Using the specification as in iii of table 2 plus a retaliation dummy that is unity if the exporter used AD investigations against the importer in year *t* or any other year before		
Variable		
Retaliation dummy$_{ijt}$	0.204	0.161
AD_{ijt}	−0.139	0.039**
CAD_{ijt}	0.014	0.004**
Case 5: Using the specification as in iii of table 2 plus a retaliation dummy that is unity if the exporter used AD investigations against the importer in year *t* or any other year before interacted with the number of AD investigations[a]		
Variable		
Retaliation dummy$_{ijt}$	0.040	0.060
AD_{ijt}	−0.139	0.041**
CAD_{ijt}	0.014	0.004**
Case 6: Using the specification as in iv of table 2 plus a retaliation dummy that is unity if the exporter used AD investigations against the importer in year *t* or any other year before		
Variable		
Retaliation dummy$_{ijt}$	0.026	0.165
AD_{ijt}	−0.135	0.040**
CAD_{ijt}	0.013	0.005**
Case 7: Using the specification as in iv of table 2 plus a retaliation dummy that is unity if the exporter used AD investigations against the importer in year *t* or any other year before interacted with the number of AD investigations[a]		
Variable		
Retaliation dummy$_{ijt}$	−0.011	0.061
AD_{ijt}	−0.132	0.044**
CAD_{ijt}	0.013	0.004**
Case 8: Using the specification as in iv of table 2 plus three dummies: AD—law adoption of exporter; AD—law adoption of importer and the interactive term of the two. The dummies are set at 1 in any year of AD-law adoption and thereafter		
Variable		
Exporter's AD law dummy	14.743	3.276***
Importer's AD law dummy	−7.422	3.284**
Interaction effect of exporter and importer AD-law dummy (both apply the law)	0.023	0.032
AD_{ijt}	−0.135	0.039**
CAD_{ijt}	0.013	0.004**

All models include fixed country pair effects and fixed time effects. ***, **, and *: Significance levels of 1%, 5%, and 10%, respectively.
[a]The exporter's AD investigations are included as well, and they enter significantly at 1%. Hence, the exporter's investigations matter, but not in a way that is interrelated with the importer's investigations as presumed in the retaliation literature.

by $\Delta AD_{ijt} = 1$. The latter has some interesting implications. For instance, if there is a clustered entry into the group of AD users, the diversion effect for a single country is smaller in the phase of clustered entry, while it is relatively larger in a phase without clustered entry and usage. On the other hand, the worldwide overall diversion effect is then large, since all countries together have a sizable impact on the change of the means.

A third set of hypotheses involves contingent protection effects, or what Vandenbussche and Zanardi (2006) call the "global chilling effect"—the effect on all trading partners of AD protection levied on any trading partner. In table 3A we report three specifications in the spirit of Vandenbussdre and Zanardi, using the sum of all AD initiations by country *j* against any country in year *t*, in addition to the dyad-by-year

specific terms (table 3A, case 1); using the sum of all AD implementations by country *j* against any country in year *t*, in addition to the dyad-by-year specific terms (table 3A, case 2); and introducing both of these variables at the same time (table 3A, case 3).[37] That is, we consider AD_{jt} and CAD_{jt} in addition to AD_{ijt} and CAD_{ijt}. In no case are these variables significant, and the sign pattern among specifications is also unstable. Thus, we find no evidence in favor of global chilling.

Retaliation is a more complex direct effect of AD. We saw in section II that retaliation has both a trade-reducing and a trade-increasing effect and that these effects might be conveyed by simply adopting an AD mechanism—by initiation

[37] We can use only the full sample for the first specification. For the other two, we can use only 1980–2001.

TABLE 4.—QUANTIFYING THE ANTIDUMPING INITIATION EFFECT ON EXPORT VOLUME
PERCENTAGE POINT CHANGES OF NORMALIZED EXPORTS FROM 1960 TO 2000

Effect on Exports of All Countries into:	Total Effect	Effect due to Multilateral Resistance
Average country pair in the sample	−0.119	−0.024
Average country pair with violating importer in the sample	−1.597	−0.575
Average country pair with nonviolating importer in the sample	0.035	0.035

The reported effects are trade-weighted averages.

or by implementation (or both). Thus, we consider a number of specifications. Specifically, we construct a dummy that takes the value of unity if the exporter (country i) initiated an AD action against the importer (country j) in period t or any other year before. We also consider this variable interacted with the number of AD actions. We then use these variables in both specifications iii and iv (table 3B, cases 4–7). It turns out not only that these new variables are not significant, but as the first four cases in table 3B show, the values of α_1 and α_2 are essentially unchanged. Finally, we consider a specification with three dummy variables: one each for whether the importer and exporter possess an AD mechanism (variable takes a value of unity if yes) and an interaction term if both possess an AD mechanism (table 3B, case 8). If retaliation were significant, we would expect the interaction term to be significant.[38] This is not the case. Thus, unless we want to consider CAD and $\alpha_2 \times CAD$ as evidence of retaliation, we find no evidence in favor of this hypothesis.

D. Quantification of the Antidumping Effect on Trade Volume between 1960 and 2000

Because we expect AD activity to affect long-run as well as current trade, we use the model as in experiment iv of table 2 to quantify the impact on exports among the covered economies. For this, we compare the contribution of AD alone to the predicted change in various aggregates of the normalized export volume between 1960 and 2000. Denote the predicted change in normalized exports by $\Delta \ln \hat{x}_{ij} \equiv \ln \hat{x}_{ij,2000} - \ln \hat{x}_{ij,1960}$ and the corresponding counterfactual change, where $\widehat{AD}_{ij,2000}$ and $\widehat{CAD}_{ij,2000}$ (and their lags) are replaced by $\widetilde{AD}_{ij,1960}$ and $\widetilde{CAD}_{ij,1960}$ (and their lags) in $\ln \hat{x}_{ij,2000}$. Denote the corresponding counterfactual change by $(\Delta \ln \hat{x}_{ij,c})$. The difference between the two, $\Delta \ln \hat{x}_{ij} - \Delta \ln \hat{x}_{ij,c}$ is an estimate of the impact of AD investigations on trade between 1960 and 2000. The overall impact on export volume is the net effect of recent (AD) and past (CAD) changes in the number of AD investigations.

We consider the effect of AD investigations on three different averages of world trade volume: the average country pair in the sample (trade weighted); the average (trade-weighted) country pair with an investigation importer (being defined as one where the cumulative number of investigations is greater than 0 in the year 2000, $CAD_{ij,2000} > 0$); and the

(trade-weighted) average impact on country-pairs where the importer has never been investigated ($CAD_{ij,2000} = 0$). Table 4 summarizes our findings.

The table suggests that the impact on exports is rather small. The reason for this is that, on average, $\widetilde{AD}_{ij,1960}$, $\widetilde{AD}_{ij,2000}$, $\widetilde{CAD}_{ij,1960}$, $\widetilde{CAD}_{ij,2000}$, and, most important, their changes are rather small (see table A1 in the Table Appendix). For the average country pair, the decline in bilateral exports between 1960 and 2000 that is attributable to AD investigations is slightly more than one-tenth of a percentage point. Of this, about 80% is due to the direct effect of bilateral AD rather than multilateral resistance. However, multilateral resistance tends to raise the impact and, on average, works in the same direction as the direct effect. Exports into AD-applying importers declined by about 1.6 percentage points over the same four decades. For these pairs, multilateral resistance accounted for more than a third of the effect. Exports into non-AD-applying importers increased marginally by about a third of a percentage point, which was entirely due to multilateral resistance.

VI. Welfare Effects of Antidumping

In addition to calculating the effect on trade volumes, we can also use our structural framework to estimate the welfare effects of antidumping as the equivalent variation in percentage associated with an annual change in AD and CAD for country i.[39] For this, we define the estimated contribution of the kth trade friction variable to country i's predicted bilateral log exports to country j in the year t as $\hat{\beta}_k \widetilde{\ln} t_{k,ij,t}$, according to equation (9). For instance, log bilateral trade due to contemporaneous antidumping would then be $\hat{\beta}_{AD} \widetilde{AD}_{ij,t}$. With unitary GDP coefficients, a prediction of GDP-normalized bilateral exports is then

$$\frac{\widehat{X_{ij,t} Y_{W,t}}}{Y_{i,t} Y_{j,t}} = e^{\sum_k \hat{\beta}_k \widetilde{\ln} t_{k,ij,t}}. \tag{13}$$

According to the model assumptions, $\sum_{j=1}^{N} \widehat{X}_{ij,t} = \widehat{Y}_{i,t}$. Using antidumping variables as of $t-1$ but other trade frictions as of the year t to construct counterfactual trade frictions in logs as of t, referred to as $\hat{\beta}_k \widetilde{\ln} t_{k,ij,c}$, we may estimate counterfactual bilateral exports ($\widehat{X}_{ij,c}$) and GDP ($\widehat{Y}_{i,c} = \sum_{j=1}^{N} \widehat{X}_{ij,c}$). Then the equivalent variation which in this model corresponds to

---

[38] The individual dummies take the same signs as the count variables tapping the same policies. Note that, again, the parameters of the AD and CAD variables are essentially unchanged.

[39] The welfare costs of AD are calculated as their impact on real GDP. It is not sufficient to aggregate predicted bilateral exports (including intranational exports), which corresponds to nominal GDP in the model adopted in the paper, but one has to divide the result by the price index.

the change in real GDP, for country i in percentage according to the observed change in AD and CAD between 2000 and t evaluated at other variable levels as of the year t is defined as

$$\widehat{EV}_{i,t} = 100 \left(\frac{\widehat{Y}_{i,t,c}}{\widehat{Y}_{i,t}} \frac{\widehat{P}_{i,t}}{\widehat{P}_{i,t,c}} - 1 \right), \tag{14}$$

where $\widehat{P}_{i,t} = (e^{\sum_{k=1}^{K} \{-\frac{1}{N} \sum_{j=1}^{N} \widehat{\beta}_k \ln t_{k,ij,t} + \frac{1}{2} \frac{1}{N^2} \sum_{i=1}^{N} \sum_{j=1}^{N} \widehat{\beta}_k \ln t_{k,ij,t}\}})^{\frac{1}{1-\sigma}}$ is the consumer price index defined as in equation (8) and evaluated at original trade frictions in the year t. $\widehat{P}_{i,t,c}$ is similarly defined for counterfactual trade frictions. Since the elasticity of the substitution parameter is not estimated directly, we follow Anderson and Van Wincoop (2003) by assuming a level of $\sigma = 5$. Under this assumption, we estimate an average annual welfare effect of antidumping that is about -0.01%. The average annual effect on AD-applying countries is about -0.05% percent and that on AD-nonapplying countries is about 0.002%, respectively. The maximum estimated annual welfare effect of AD amounts to less than 1.5%. The average annual reduction for the United States amounts to 0.06%.[40] The maximum estimated annual AD-induced reduction in welfare for the United States over the period 1960 to 2000 amounts to less than 0.23%. Hence, consistent with the small impact on trade flows, the estimated welfare effects of antidumping are small.

VII.   Effects Antidumping on Bilateral Trade of Specific Product Groups

The unambiguous result of our main analysis is that antidumping has small aggregate effects on trade and small aggregate welfare effects. That said, it is certainly the case that due to the high dumping margins and concentration on a small number of sectors, the microeconomic effects can be quite significant. More important for our purposes, as noted in notes 12 and 34, if these sectors (which might well be characterized by some form of oligopolistic interaction) are characterized by a distinctive response to antidumping, we might take that as evidence that such microeconomic interactions have significant macroeconomic effects. Thus, in this section, we pursue a sector-level analysis of sectors characterized by high levels of antidumping activity. It is widely known that antidumping by both developed and developing countries falls particularly heavily on the steel and chemical sectors (Bown, 2009).

For an analysis of the consequences of antidumping on specific product classes, we must use trade data from a different source. We employ data of bilateral exports, which are classified according to Revision 2 of the Standard International Trade Classification from the U.N. World Trade Database.

In particular, we use bilateral exports of products in three two-digit categories: Chemicals excluding Pharmaceuticals (category 52), Iron and Steel (category 67), and Other Metals (category 68). In order to assess the impact of antidumping on trade with these specific products, we had to merge the antidumping data by case, as collected by Bown, with the trade data. Fortunately, Bown's antidumping database contains the specific product measures applied so that such a match between data sources was possible. After merging the trade and antidumping data, we obtain a panel data set of 10,201 country pairs, which we observe annually over the years 1980 to 2004. In that data set, antidumping measures are quite concentrated on the products just mentioned: the three product groups together account for about 64% of all antidumping cases for the countries and years in the sample. Of the 64%, about 28 percentage points are contributed by Chemicals and by Iron and Steel each, and Other Metals make up for the rest of it. However, while Chemicals, Iron and Steel, and Other Metals are quite important when it comes to the use of dumping and antidumping, they account for less than 10% of total exports in the sample.[41]

How does antidumping affect trade in the three product categories? To shed light on this matter, let us estimate Poisson QMLE models as in experiment vi of table 2.[42] Table 5 summarizes the associated findings by focusing on the antidumping measures AD and CAD only, akin to table 3.[43]

Before turning to the discussion of the estimated effects themselves, a few remarks are in order. First, although we allow the dependent variable to be 0 in general, the number of observations and country-pairs differs across the three product categories. The reason lies in the fact that we may exclude country pairs from the sample if they never traded goods in a specific category in any of the years between 1980 and 2004 without any effect on the results. This is because we employ fixed-effects Poisson QMLE, which conditions on those country pairs that displayed some change in trade over the years. Therefore, the number of country pairs varies between 8,958 and 10,201 in the table, and the number of observations varies between 223,950 and 255,025, respectively. Second, while observations may be excluded from the regressions for statistical reasons, the calculation of multilateral resistance terms has to and does rely on the full sample of country pairs and years.[44] Third, similar to aggregate trade flows, fixed effects and multilateral resistance terms

---

[40] The only other estimate of the welfare effect of antidumping that we know of is that of Gallaway et al. (1999). As we note above, they estimate that antidumping in 1993 reduced U.S. welfare a maximum of 0.06% (a $2 billion to $4 billion welfare reduction in a year where U.S. GDP was estimated to be $6.7 trillion). This is remarkably close to our average annual estimate for the United States. In any event, both estimates are very small.

[41] This makes us even more confident about our identification of modest aggregate effects of antidumping: a large concentration of antidumping measures applied to what appears to be a tiny fraction of total trade would unlikely cause large aggregate effects.

[42] Notice that we do not use linear regressions here for good reason: at the product level, the problems of zero trade and heteroskedasticity become even more important than in the aggregate. Therefore, it seems even more advisable to resort to nonlinear QMLE estimation with the disaggregated data at hand than with aggregate bilateral trade flows.

[43] Since the models are estimated by Poisson QMLE, the test statistics reported on in the table are χ^2-statistics rather than F-statistics.

[44] Obviously zero bilateral trade implies that the corresponding weights for trade frictions in calculating the averages across exporters and importers have to be set to 0.

TABLE 5.—ANTIDUMPING EFFECTS ON TRADE OF CHEMICALS, IRON AND STEEL, AND OTHER METALS, 1980–2004

Effects of Antidumping	Chemicals (excluding Pharmaceuticals)		Iron and Steel		Other Metals	
	Coefficient	χ^2 statistic	Coefficient	χ^2 statistic	Coefficient	χ^2 statistic
Joint effect of AD_{ijt}, $AD_{ij,t-1}$, and $AD_{ij,t-2}$	−0.112	0.045**	−0.117	0.042***	−0.098	0.002***
Joint effect of CAD_{ijt}, $CAD_{ij,t-1}$, and $CAD_{ij,t-2}$	0.015	0.001***	0.024	0.010**	0.055	0.003***
Observations	252,600		255,025		223,950	
Country pairs	10,104		10,201		8,958	
Joint significance of all regressors (p-value of χ^2 statistic)	0.000		0.000		0.000	
Joint significance of multilateral resistance (p-value of χ^2 statistic)	0.000		0.000		0.000	
Fixed country pair effects (p-value of χ^2 statistic)	0.000		0.000		0.000	
Fixed time effects (p-value of χ^2 statistic)	0.000		0.000		0.000	

*** and **: Significance levels of 1% and 5%, respectively. All models include fixed country pair, fixed time effects, and multilateral resistance terms and are estimated by Poisson QMLE based on a specification as in model vi of table 2. Standard errors are robust to heteroskedasticity of arbitrary form. The number of observations differs across models only because country pairs that do not trade the type of products in any year (or whose exports are always the same) are excluded from the sample. Chemicals correspond to the two-digit category 52 of the SITC revision 2 classification, Iron and Steel, corresponds to the two-digit category 67, and Other Metals corresponds to the two-digit category 68. Bilateral exports for these categories are taken from the United Nations World Trade Database. The fraction of antidumping measures applied to Chemicals in our sample accounts for 28.4% of all measures (Chemicals' share in total trade is 3%), the one for Iron and Steel accounts for 28.5% of all measures (Iron and Steel's share in total trade is 3%), and the one for Other metals accounts for 7.2% of all measures applied in the average year and country-pair (Other metals' share in total trade is 2%). Only effects of antidumping are displayed.

are statistically significantly different from 0 and should not be ignored.

As to the impact of AD and CAD on bilateral exports in year t, notice that we allow for a distributed impact across three years as in experiment vi of table 2, where both AD and CAD of years t, $t − 1$, and $t − 2$ are allowed to matter for exports in t. What we report in table 5 is the joint (that is, accumulated long-run) effect of the corresponding measures in the three periods together, as in table 2. Similarly, the standard errors to the right of the long-run coefficients refer to the long-run impact.

The estimated long-run effects in table 5 suggest the following conclusions. First, the point estimates for AD are somewhat lower than the reference estimate for aggregate trade flows in the longer panel as in experiment vi of table 2 (the corresponding parameter was −0.212, there), but they are similar to the ones of the linear models as in experiment iv of table 2 (the corresponding parameter was −0.134). The estimated effect is largest for Iron and Steel (amounting to −0.117) and smallest for Other Metals (amounting to −0.098), but the variance across the point estimates is quite small. The parameter estimates of CAD are positive as they were in the previous tables, and they range from 0.015 (for Chemicals) to 0.055 (for Other Metals). Altogether we may conclude that the responsiveness (in terms of parameter estimates) of trade to antidumping is similar in the three considered product categories, which are heavy users of antidumping. We note that this result is not consistent with macroeconomically significant strategic effects in any of these sectors. It is, however, important to note that antidumping is more harmful for industries engaging in the trade of these products than on average, since the use of dumping and antidumping measures is more extensive there: about 64% of initiated antidumping cases affect about 8% of all trade flows, while the remaining 36% are spread across product categories, which together account for 92% of total world exports.

Hence, we may conclude that antidumping is harmful for trade, in particular, of specific product categories such as Chemicals, Iron and Steel, or Other Metals. Yet the main

damage of antidumping in the corresponding industries is brought about not by their greater responsiveness to the initiation of antidumping cases than in other industries but to the more frequent use of antidumping. However, on average these products account for a relatively small fraction of world trade so that potentially important effects on specific products turn out small when it comes to aggregate effects on trade flows, GDP, or welfare.

VIII. Effects of Antidumping on Bilateral Trade of Specific Subsamples of Countries or Product Groups

One problem with the results discussed so far may be that by pooling the data across a large number of quite heterogeneous countries, they conceal dramatically different coefficients on antidumping in specific subgroups of countries. While we are bound to focus on aggregate effects of antidumping and do not want to venture into too detailed an analysis of the heterogeneity of antidumping coefficients, an obvious question to ask is whether antidumping affects less developed countries differently from the developed ones in terms of the estimated coefficients. This seems reasonable to ask since the use of antidumping measures historically pertained mainly to developed countries against less developed ones. However, this pattern changed over the previous decade as countries such as Brazil, China, and India started using antidumping measures intensively.

To shed light on the issue of development status and trade responsiveness to antidumping, we may split the sample used in the previous tables according to some rule of thumb. Here, we apply the World Bank's classification of countries into high-income versus other economies. According to that classification, the sample used before consists of 54 high-income countries and 122 low-income economies (the classification of countries is available from the authors on request). Using this classification, we distinguish three types of country pairs: ones that involve high-income countries as both an exporter and an importer (1,570 country pairs and 22,390 observations), ones that involve a high-income exporter and

TABLE 6.—ANTIDUMPING EFFECTS IN LOW- VERSUS HIGH-INCOME COUNTRIES, 1948–2001

	Among High-Income Countries		Country Subsamples Between High- and Low-Income Countries		Among Low-Income Countries	
Effects of Antidumping	Coefficient	S.E.	Coefficient	S.E.	Coefficient	S.E.
Joint effect of AD_{ijt}, $AD_{ij,t-1}$, and $AD_{ij,t-2}$	−0.204	0.073***	−0.201	0.111*	−0.197	0.807
Joint effect of CAD_{ijt}, $CAD_{ij,t-1}$, and $CAD_{ij,t-2}$	0.007	0.022	0.041	0.015***	0.062	0.514
Observations	22,390		96,174		102,516	
Country pairs	1,570		7,062		7,812	
Joint significance of all regressors (p-value of χ^2 statistic)	0.000		0.000		0.000	
Joint significance of multilateral resistance (p-value of χ^2 statistic)	0.000		0.000		0.000	
Fixed country pair effects (p-value of χ^2 statistic)	0.000		0.000		0.000	
Fixed time effects (p-value of χ^2 statistic)	0.000		0.000		0.000	

*** and *: Significance levels of 1% and 10%, respectively. All models include fixed country pair, fixed time effects, and multilateral resistance terms and are estimated by Poisson QMLE based on a specification as in model vi of table 2. Standard errors are robust to heteroskedasticity of arbitrary form. Country samples were determined according to the World Bank's classification of high-income economies. Only antidumping provisions are displayed.

a low-income importer or vice versa (7,062 country pairs and 96,174 observations), and ones that involve low-income countries both as an exporter and as an importer (7,812 country pairs and 102,516 observations). Table 6 summarizes the parameter estimates on antidumping and cumulative antidumping using the same technique, specification, and multilateral resistance terms (which are calculated from the full sample of countries) as in experiment vi of table 2.

There are two remarkable findings in table 6. First, the point estimates of the effects of AD on bilateral exports across the three subsamples are very close to each other and close to the reference estimate in table 2, which was 0.212. However, the parameter estimate is not statistically different from 0 in the subsample of low-income countries only. The reason for the latter is that the corresponding parameter is estimated from a relatively small number of users and heteroskedasticity is quite pronounced within this subset of countries. Second, the point estimates of CAD are also relatively similar to both each other and the reference value, which was 0.010 (and not statistically significantly different from 0) in table 2. The estimate of CAD is not statistically different from 0 in the subsamples of high-income-only and low-income-only countries.

Overall, we may therefore conclude that what distinguishes the three considered subsamples from each other is not so much the degree of responsiveness of trade flows with regard to antidumping (in terms of parameter estimates) but the extent of antidumping initiations and the use of corresponding antidumping measures. Admittedly, there are stronger users of antidumping than the United States, and we would not want to give the impression that all countries would experience welfare effects of abandoning antidumping of the magnitude as the United States did. For comparison, let us compute the welfare costs of antidumping of India, a heavy user, with those of the United States. India used antidumping measures much more extensively than the United States did over the last decade covered by our sample (1992–2001). Accordingly, the total direct impact of abandoning antidumping is bigger. However, abandoning antidumping has not only direct expansionary effects on trade but also indirect dampening effects

through the multilateral resistance terms. Obviously the latter will not outweigh the former, but they cushion the detrimental effects of trade costs and reduce expansionary effects of trade liberalization and the reduction of protection. Altogether, this leads to predicted effects on India's welfare within the last decade of the sample of about 0.8% per annum. While this is about three times as large as the welfare effects on the United States, it is still small when keeping India's growth of trade and GDP over that period in mind.

IX. Conclusion

Overall our analysis suggests that the aggregate effects of AD in the context of the GATT/WTO system are modest. This should not be taken to imply that AD is not, or should not be, a matter of concern to the liberal international trading system. Given the magnitude of duties, the sectoral distortions can be sizable. In addition, the control of protection and the advance of liberalization are the centerpieces of that system, and AD protection is protection. At the same time, it does not seem useful to oversell the consequences of AD. Since it seems likely that contingent protection has played an important role in supporting trade liberalization, reflexive rejection seems particularly inappropriate.

This last point strikes us as important. As economists, our first line of response to AD is surely negative. We applaud the reductions in tariffs associated with various trade liberalizations but abhor the backsliding associated with administered protection. The moral language is used advisedly: most of us view liberalization as an act of moral courage and reversals as moral weakness. Close students of AD, however, have long been clear that the reality is considerably more complex. The effects on which this paper has focused are essentially microeffects. That is, they refer to the effects within country pairs (and, at least intuitively, are driven by firm- and sector-level effects). While such microeffects have been the focus of the great majority of both theoretical and empirical research on AD, systemwide (macro) effects have also been noted (Nelson, 2006). The global chilling effect is in principle a macroeffect, but we were unable to find any evidence of its presence. Strongly positive macroeffects have also been commented on. From the very earliest research on AD (Viner, 1923), it has been recognized that AD can be a central part of a political strategy to support liberalization. Finger and Nogues (2005) have provided strong case study evidence that at least in a number of Latin American countries engaged in liberalization episodes in the 1980s, AD was used in precisely this way. To the extent that the liberal trading system that began to emerge in the late 1930s and was institutionalized in the GATT/WTO system relied on U.S. leadership and that that leadership was conditional on the various reciprocal trade acts and their more modern descendants, it is clear that administered protection played a central role in underwriting the system as a whole. While such systemwide macroeffects are purely speculative, the generally small microeffects suggest at a minimum that we need much more information on the way contingent protection interacts with statutory protection and multilateral liberalization.

REFERENCES

Anderson, James E., "A Theoretical Foundation for the Gravity Equation," *American Economic Review* 69:1 (1979), 106–16.

Anderson, James E., and Eric Van Wincoop, "Gravity with Gravitas: A Solution to the Border Puzzle," *American Economic Review* 93:1 (2003), 170–192.

——— "Trade Costs," *Journal of Economic Literature* 42:3 (2004), 691–751.

Baier, Scott L., and Jeffrey H. Bergstrand, "Do Free Trade Agreements Actually Increase Members' International Trade?" *Journal of International Economics* 71:1 (2007), 72–95.

——— "Bonus Vetus OLS: A Simple Method for Approximating International Trade-Cost Effects Using the Gravity Equation," *Journal of International Economics* 77:1 (2009), 77–85.

Baldwin, Richard, *Towards an Integrated Europe* (London: Centre for Economic Policy Research, 1994).

Baltagi, Badi, *Econometric Analysis of Panel Data* (Hoboken, NJ: Wiley, 2005).

Baltagi, Badi, Peter Egger, and Michael Pfaffermayr, "A Generalized Design for Bilateral Trade Flow Models," *Economics Letters* 80:3 (2003), 391–397.

Bergstrand, Jeffrey H., "The Gravity Equation in International Trade: Some Microeconomic Foundations and Empirical Evidence," this REVIEW 67:3 (1985), 474–481.

——— "The Generalized Gravity Equation, Monopolistic Competition, and the Factor-Proportions Theory in International Trade," this REVIEW 71:1 (1989), 143–153.

Bernhofen, Daniel M., "Price Dumping in Intermediate Good Markets," *Journal of International Economics* 39:1–2 (1995), 159–173.

——— "Vertical Integration and International Predation," *Review of International Economics* 4:1 (1996), 90–98.

——— "Intra-Industry Trade and Strategic Interaction: Theory and Evidence," *Journal of International Economics* 45:1 (1998), 77–96.

Beseler, Johannes F., and A. N. Williams, *Antidumping and Antisubsidy Law: The European Communities* (London: Sweet and Maxwell, 1986).

Blonigen, Bruce A., and Chad Bown, "Antidumping and Retaliation Threats," *Journal of International Economics* 60:2 (2003), 249–273.

Blonigen, Bruce A., and Stephen E. Haynes, "Antidumping Investigations and the Pass-Through of Antidumping Duties and Exchange Rates," *American Economic Review* 92:4 (2002), 1044–1061.

Blonigen, Bruce A., and Thomas Prusa, "Antidumping" (pp. 251–284), in James Harrigan and E. Kwan Choi (Eds.), *Handbook of International Trade* (Oxford: Blackwell, 2003).

Bown, Chad, "The Global Resort to Antidumping, Safeguards, and Other Trade Remedies amidst the Economic Crisis" (pp. 91–118), in Simon Evenett, Bernard Hoekman, and Olivier Cattaneo (Eds.), *Effective*

Crisis Response and Openness: Implications for the Trading System (Washington, DC: World Bank, 2009).

Bown, Chad, and Meredith Crowley, "Policy Externalities: How US Antidumping Affects Japanese Exports to the EU," *European Journal of Political Economy* 22:3 (2006), 696–714.

——— "Trade Deflection and Trade Depression," *Journal of International Economics* 77:1 (2007), 176–201.

Chamberlain, Gary, "Panel Data" (pp. 1248–1318), in Zvi Griliches and Michael D. Intriligator (Eds.), *Handbook of Econometrics* (Amsterdam: North-Holland, 1984).

Cheng, I-Hui, and Howard Wall, "Controlling for Heterogeneity in Gravity Models of Trade," *Federal Reserve Bank of St. Louis Review* 87:1 (2005), 49–63.

Deardorff, Alan, "Determinants of Bilateral Trade: Does Gravity Work in a Neoclassical World?" (pp. 7–22), in Jeffrey Frankel (Ed.), *The Regionalization of the World Economy* (Chicago: University of Chicago Press/NBER, 1998).

Dixit, Avinash K., and Joseph E. Stiglitz, "Monopolistic Competition and Optimum Product Diversity," *American Economic Review* 67:3 (1977), 297–308.

Evenett, Simon, and Anthony Venables, "Export Growth by Developing Economies: Market Entry and Bilateral Trade," unpublished manuscript (2002).

Falvey, Rodney E., and Douglas R. Nelson, "100 Years of Antidumping," *European Journal of Political Economy* 22:3 (2006), 545–553.

Feenstra, Robert C., *Advanced International Trade: Theory and Evidence* (Princeton, NJ: Princeton University Press, 2004).

Felbermayr, Gabriel J., and Wilhelm Kohler, "Exploring the Intensive and Extensive Margins of World Trade," *Review of World Economics* 142:4 (2006), 642–674.

Finger, J. Michael, and Julio Nogues, *Safeguards and Antidumping in Latin American Trade Liberalization: Fighting Fire with Fire* (Houndmills, Basingstoke, Hampshire: Macmillan Palgrave, 2005).

Frankel, Jeffrey, *Regional Trading Blocs in the World Economic System* (Washington, DC: Institute for International Economics, 1997).

Frankel, Jeffrey, and Andrew Rose, "An Estimate of the Effect of Currency Unions on Trade and Growth," *Quarterly Journal of Economics* 117:2 (2002), 437–466.

Gallaway, Michael, Bruce A. Blonigen, and Joseph Flynn, "Welfare Cost of the US Antidumping and Countervailing Duty Law," *Journal of International Economics* 49:2 (1999), 211–244.

Glick, Reuven, and Andrew Rose, "Does a Currency Union Affect Trade? The Time Series Evidence," *European Economic Review* 46:6 (2002), 1225–1251.

Hausman, J. A., "Specification Tests in Econometrics," *Econometrica* 46:6 (1978), 1251–1271.

Helpman, Elhanan, Marc Melitz, and Yona Rubinstein, "Estimating Trade Flows: Trading Partners and Trading Volumes," *Quarterly Journal of Economics* 123:2 (2008), 441–487.

Krishna, Kala, "Trade Restrictions as Facilitating Devices," *Journal of International Economics* 36:3–4 (1989), 251–270.

Krugman, Paul R., "Increasing Returns, Monopolistic Competition, and International Trade," *Journal of International Economics* 9:4 (1979), 469–479.

Leamer, Edward E., "Cross Section Estimation of the Effects of Trade Barriers" (pp. 52–82), in Robert C. Feenstra (Ed.), *Empirical Methods for International Trade* (Cambridge, MA: MIT Press, 1987).

——— "The Structure and Effects of Tariff and Nontariff Barriers in 1983" (pp. 224–260), in Ronald W. Jones and Anne O. Krueger (Eds.), *The Political Economy of International Trade* (Oxford: Blackwell, 1990).

Leidy, Michael, "Trade Policy and Indirect Rent Seeking: A Synthesis of Recent Work," *Economics and Politics* 6:2 (1994), 97–118.

Mundlak, Yair, "Pooling of Time-Series and Cross-Section Data," *Econometrica* 46:1 (1978), 69–85.

Nelson, Douglas R., "The Political Economy of U.S. Automobile Protection" (pp. 133–191), in Anne O. Krueger (Ed.), *The Political Economy of American Trade Policy* (Chicago: University of Chicago Press/NBER, 1996).

——— "The Political Economy of Antidumping: A Survey," *European Journal of Political Economy* 22:3 (2006), 554–590.

Prusa, Thomas, "On the Spread and Impact of Antidumping," *Canadian Journal of Economics* 34:3 (2001), 591–611.

Prusa, Thomas, and Susan Skeath, "The Economic and Strategic Motives for Anti-Dumping Filings," *Weltwirtschaftliches Archiv* 138:3 (2002), 389–413.

Rose, Andrew K., "One Money, One Market: The Effect of Common Currencies on Trade," *Economic Policy* 15:30 (2000), 9–45.

——— "Do We Really Know That the WTO Increases Trade?" *American Economic Review* 94:1 (2004a), 98–114.

——— "Do WTO Members Have a More Liberal Trade Policy?" *Journal of International Economics* 63:2 (2004b), 209–235.

Rose, Andrew K., and Eric Van Wincoop, "National Money as a Barrier to Trade: The Real Case for a Currency Union," *American Economic Review* 91:2 (2001), 386–390.

Santos Silva, J.M.C., and Silvana Tenreyro, "The Log of Gravity," this REVIEW 88:4 (2006), 641–658.

Shin, Hyun Ja, "Possible Instances of Predatory Pricing in Recent U.S. Antidumping Cases" (pp. 81–97), in Robert Lawrence (Ed.), *Brookings Trade Forum* (Washington, DC: Brookings Institution, 1998).

Staiger, Robert, and Frank Wolak, "Measuring Industry-Specific Protection: Antidumping in the US," *Brookings Papers on Economic Activity Microeconomics* (1994), 51–118.

——— "Differences in Uses and Effects of Antidumping Law across Import Sources" (pp. 385–415), in Anne O. Krueger (Ed.), *The Political Economy of American Trade Policy* (Chicago: University of Chicago Press/NBER, 1996).

Subramanian, Arvind, and Shang-Jin Wei, "The WTO Promotes Trade, Strongly But Unevenly," *Journal of International Economics* 72:1 (2007), 151–175.

Van Garderen, Kees Jan, and Chandra Shah, "Exact Interpretation of Dummy Variables in Semilogarithmic Equations," *Econometrics Journal* 5 (2002), 149–159.

Vandenbussche, Hylke, and Maurizio Zanardi, "The Global Chilling Effects of Anti-Dumping Law Proliferation," CEPR discussion paper no. 5597 (2006).

Viner, Jacob, *Dumping: A Problem in International Trade* (Chicago: University of Chicago Press, 1923).

Wall, Howard, "Using the Gravity Model to Estimate the Costs of Protection," *Federal Reserve Bank of St. Louis, Review* (January–February 1999), 33–40.

Wooldridge, Jeffrey M., "Selection Corrections for Panel Data Models under Conditional Mean Independence Assumptions," *Journal of Econometrics* 68:1 (1995), 115–132.

——— *Econometric Analysis of Cross Section and Panel Data* (Cambridge, MA: MIT Press, 2002).

Zanardi, Maurizio, "Antidumping: A Problem in International Trade," *European Journal of Political Economy* 22:3 (2006), 591–617.

APPENDIX

Country Coverage

Afghanistan, Albania, Algeria, Angola, Argentina, Armenia, Aruba, Australia, Austria, Azerbaijan, the Bahamas, Bahrain, Bangladesh, Barbados, Belarus, Belgium, Belize, Benin, Bermuda, Bolivia, Bosnia and Herzegovina, Botswana, Brazil, Brunei, Bulgaria, Burkina Faso, Burundi, Cambodia, Cameroon, Canada, Cape Verde, Central African Republic, Chad, Chile, China, Colombia, Comoros, Republic of Congo, Costa Rica, Cote d'Ivoire, Croatia, Cuba, Cyprus, Czech Republic, Denmark, Djibouti, Dominican Republic, Ecuador, Egypt, El Salvador, Equatorial Guinea, Eritrea, Estonia, Ethiopia, Fiji, Finland, France, French Polynesia, Gabon, the Gambia, Georgia, Germany, Ghana, Greece, Guatemala, Guinea, Guinea-Bissau, Guyana, Haiti, Honduras, Hong Kong (China), Hungary, Iceland, India, Indonesia, Islamic Republic of Iran, Iraq, Ireland, Israel, Italy, Jamaica, Japan, Jordan, Kazakhstan, Kenya, Republic of Korea, Kuwait, Kyrgyz Republic, Lao People's Democratic Republic, Latvia, Lebanon, Lesotho, Liberia, Libya, Lithuania, Luxembourg, Macao (China), Former Yugoslav Republic of Macedonia, Madagascar, Malawi, Malaysia, Mali, Malta, Mauritania, Mauritius, Mexico, Federal States of Micronesia, Moldova, Mongolia, Morocco, Mozambique, Myanmar, Namibia, Nepal, Netherlands, Netherlands Antilles, New Caledonia, New Zealand, Nicaragua, Niger, Nigeria, Norway, Oman, Pakistan, Palau, Panama, Papua New Guinea, Paraguay, Peru, Philippines, Poland, Portugal, Puerto Rico, Qatar, Romania, Russian Federation, Rwanda, Samoa, São Tomé and Principe, Saudi Arabia, Senegal, Sierra Leone, Singapore, Slovak Republic, Slovenia, Somalia, South Africa, Spain, Sri Lanka, St. Lucia, Sudan, Suriname, Swaziland, Sweden, Switzerland, Syrian Arab Republic, Tajikistan, Tanzania, Thailand, Togo, Tonga, Trinidad and Tobago, Tunisia, Turkey, Turkmenistan, Uganda, Ukraine, United Arab Emirates, United Kingdom, United States, Uruguay, Uzbekistan, Vanuatu, RB Venezuela, Vietnam, Republic of Yemen, Zambia, Zimbabwe.

TABLE APPENDIX

TABLE A1.—DESCRIPTIVE STATISTICS

Variables	Untransformed		Demeaned as in Baier and Bergstrand (2007)	
	Mean	S.D.	Mean	S.D.
Antidumping investigations *(AD)*				
Contemporaneous *(AD$_{ijt}$)*	0.0067	0.1515	0.0002	0.1424
Once lagged *(AD$_{ij,t-1}$)*	0.0063	0.1480	0.0003	0.1392
Twice lagged *(AD$_{ij,t-2}$)*	0.0059	0.1418	0.0003	0.1336
Cumulative antidumping investigations				
Contemporaneous *(CAD$_{ijt}$)*	0.0577	2.1188	0.0076	2.0497
Once lagged *(CAD$_{ij,t-1}$)*	0.0522	2.0465	0.0073	1.9812
Twice lagged *(CAD$_{ij,t-2}$)*	0.0490	2.0416	0.0076	1.9798
Absence of regional trade agreements				
Customs unions *(CU$_{ijt}$)*	0.9956	0.0664	0.0007	0.0633
Free trade areas *(FTA$_{ijt}$)*	0.9918	0.0902	0.0003	0.0799
Other preferential trade agreements *(PTA$_{ijt}$)*	0.9836	0.1272	−0.0004	0.1081
WTO nonmembership of:				
One country in a pair	0.4315	0.4953	−0.0004	0.4377
Both countries in a pair	0.3460	0.4757	0.0001	0.2187
Absence of currency arrangements				
Currency unions	0.9910	0.0947	0.0001	0.0356
Currency pegs	0.9628	0.1892	−0.0011	0.1665
Currency bands	0.9926	0.0856	−0.0002	0.0791
Geographical and cultural variables				
Log bilateral distance (ln *DIST$_{ij}$*)	8.7524	0.7796	−0.0053	0.6690
Absence of a common border	0.9852	0.1206	0.0013	0.1193
Absence of a common language	0.8423	0.3645	−0.0025	0.3114

The dependent variable is the log of bilateral exports over exporter-times-importer GDP (mean = −46.2346; s.d. = 2.5988). In some of the regressions, we use the nondemeaned log exporter GDP (mean = 23.8455; s.d. = 2.3315) and log importer GDP (mean = 23.9068; s.d. = 2.2935) as additional control variables.

The Broader Context of Trade Policy Making

Jnl Publ. Pol., **9**, *1*, 83–108

Domestic Political Preconditions of US Trade Policy: Liberal Structure and Protectionist Dynamics

DOUGLAS NELSON *School of Business, Washington University*

ABSTRACT

This paper examines the set of norms, rules and institutions (the regime) which regulate the domestic politics of international trade policy in the US. It is particularly concerned to explain the simultaneous occurrence of successful participation in multilateral trade liberalization in the GATT and rising levels of protection via the administered protection mechanisms (e.g. anti-dumping and countervailing duty, and escape clause). The explanation of this phenomenon is the development of a new institutional definition of trade policy that permitted executive dominance of trade policy, in conjunction with a changed perception of the role of trade policy by the executive branch. Specifically, it is argued that post-war executives (at least until Reagan) came to associate trade policy with broader foreign policy goals.

By any measure, the US is a key member of the international trading system: it has played a fundamental role in the creation and maintenance of the multilateral trading order based on the General Agreement on Tariffs and Trade (GATT); and it could play an equally key role in destroying that system with a decision to revert to the protectionist policies of its early history. While it is often convenient and interesting to evaluate international economic policy from the perspective of interna-

Prepared for Conference on Political Economy: Theory and Policy Implications. The World Bank, 17–19 June 1987. This paper was prepared while I was a consultant with the International Economic Research Department of the World Bank. I would like to thank Mike Finger, Patrick Messerlin, and Stephan Haggard for useful comments on earlier drafts of this paper. At the conference, I.M. Destler, John Ruggie and Robert Baldwin made extensive and very useful comments. The contribution of Jagdish Bhagwati went well beyond that of a conference organizer. While I acknowledge, with thanks, all of these contributions, I alone am responsible for any errors of fact, analysis, or judgement.

The World Bank does not accept responsibility for the views expressed herein which are those of the author and should not be attributed to the World Bank or to its affiliated organizations. The findings, interpretations, and designations employed, the presentation of material, and any maps used in this document are solely for the convenience of the reader and do not imply the expression of any opinion whatsoever on the part of the World Bank or its affiliates concerning the legal status of any country, territory, city, area, or of its authorities, or concerning the delimitation of its boundaries, or national affiliation.

84   *Douglas Nelson*

tional political and/or economic structures,[1] any attempt to explain current policy or make projections about the future needs to start with an examination of the domestic political-economy. It will be one of this paper's basic arguments that, while trade policy may be used as an instrument of international policy, such uses are ultimately constrained by the fact that, to turn Cooper's (1972) well-known formulation on its head, trade policy is domestic policy.

The distinction between domestic and international policy is fundamental to the analysis of this paper, but it is not an easy distinction to make clearly. The primary source of confusion is the tendency to define categories of choice either in terms of consequences or immediate subjects of choice. In the first case, since most of the politically relevant benefits and costs of trade are domestic (e.g. those considered in standard economic analysis of gains from trade), one might view virtually all economic policy (including trade policy) as domestic. On the other hand, if the immediate subjects of the choice are goods crossing borders, then trade policy is demonstrably international in nature. The coexistence of these two common definitions leads some to suggest that the distinction is not useful.

In contrast to both of these approaches, I want to distinguish between domestic and international policy in terms of the immediate *subjects* of choice for the relevant decision-maker. Thus, I argue that, when making trade policy, members of Congress are primarily concerned with effectively organized constituent demand—for them, trade policy is generally domestic policy. For the president, on the other hand, this paper argues that trade policy (at least since the Depression) has often been, to some significant degree, about such foreign policy issues as alliance building/maintenance and anti-communism. One of this paper's major points is that the Reciprocal Trade Agreements program and, later, the GATT created a system of policy-making in which liberalization policy came to be dominated by the executive, while protection policy remained the preserve of Congress. This has had the effect of making trade liberalization policy a branch of foreign policy (though still heavily constrained by domestic considerations), while trade protection policy remains overwhelmingly domestic policy. It should be noted that under this definition, those who believe that Congress is primarily concerned with, say, the construction of a liberal international economic order would characterize trade policy in Congress as foreign policy.

A secondary consideration, that will not be pursued in this paper, is the relative weight of political and economic factors in trade policy choice. While it is perfectly reasonable to analyze policy choice in terms of economically optimal choice (e.g. the general welfare superiority of freer trade, optimal tariffs, or Bhagwati/Johnson optimal interventions), I do

The Domestic Political Preconditions of US Trade Policy   85

not believe that these considerations play a major role in policy choice. Economic considerations certainly affect the sustainability of a policy, and thus act as a fundamental long-run constraint on policy, but they are rarely the primary determinants of policy.

The basic structure of this paper is simple. In addition to presenting the argument that trade policy is ultimately domestic policy, the first section presents two preliminary steps in the argument that the underlying political dynamic of trade policy is protectionist: 1) that Congress is responsive to effective political pressure; and 2) that political asymmetries favor protection-seekers. The second section argues that the institutional definition of a given policy has a strong affect on the form of politics surrounding that policy. In particular, it is argued that the Reciprocal Trade Agreements Act of 1934 (RTAA) fundamentally changed the domestic politics of international trade, permitting (but not in itself causing) the sustained liberalization of trade witnessed over the last fifty years. Finally, it is argued that the active force driving that liberalization in the US was the executive branch; but that its commitment to multilateral liberalization was primarily related to goals which were neither domestic nor economic. The paper concludes with a discussion of the prospects for change in the set of domestic norms, rules and institutions (the domestic regime for the politics of trade) that underlie continued US support for international cooperation on the liberalization of international trade.

Congressional Responsiveness, Asymmetric Political Pressure, and Structural Protectionist Bias

When Richard Cooper (1972, 1987) says 'trade policy is foreign policy', he is saying three things: that trade policy can be an effective instrument of foreign policy (this certainly has been the State Department's argument, at least since Cordell Hull); that trade policy has been used, with varying effectiveness, as an instrument of foreign policy (most generally as an instrument of alliance creation and maintenance; but also as an instrument of coercion—e.g. sanctions); and that trade policy should not be domestic policy (i.e. that trade policy should not be determined by domestic political pressure). One thing he is not saying, however, is that trade policy *is* not domestic policy. While we can identify a large number of instances in which trade policy has been used as an instrument of foreign policy (Cooper, 1987), we should not lose sight of the fact that trade policy is now, and for the entire history of the US has been, dominated by domestic politics (first for raising revenue, then in an attempt to stimulate local industry, and then as one of Congress' major pork-barrels).

86   *Douglas Nelson*

Congressional control of the regulation of international commerce (explicitly granted in Article 1, section 8 of the US Constitution) alone would tend to induce a domestic and sectional orientation to trade policy, relative to executive control. This follows simply from the definition of their respective constituencies. It is a fairly standard argument in political science that the difference in electoral constituencies for the presidency and Congress yield systematic differences between the branches of government (Burns, 1963; Kemp, 1984). Of particular importance is the conclusion that presidents (and to some extent presidential aspirants) tend to be more internationalist than members of Congress. Given the importance of institutional structure to the argument of this paper, it is interesting to note that while the logic of this paragraph would lead one to expect that Senators (with a broader constituency than Representatives) would be generally more liberal, it turns out that Senate language in Trade Bills is often more specific and more protectionist than in House trade bills. The primary reason would seem to be the much more restrictive rules under which trade bills are handled on the floor of the House—rules that are not available in the Senate.[2] It should be clear that no such problems affect our analysis of the executive.

Another aspect of Congressional policy choice, perhaps more important than its general predisposition to emphasize domestic considerations, is issue-specific responsiveness to political pressure. Most modern research on Congress suggests that the analysis of Congressional behavior should generally proceed from the assumption that members of Congress act to maximize the prospect of reelection (Mayhew, 1974; Fiorina, 1977). This does not necessarily mean that members of Congress represent the median preference of their total constituency, but that they represent the preferences of their 'reelection constituency' (Fenno, 1978; Cox, McCubbins and Sullivan, 1984; McCubbins and Sullivan, 1984). That is, they will be particularly concerned with interests that have strong preferences over some set of policy choices, are well-organized for political action, and are seen as strong supporters of one's candidacy. With particular reference to economic policy, there is considerable evidence that Congressmen do, in fact, represent the economic interests of their constituents (Kingdon, 1973; Peltzman, 1984, 1985).

As with any relationship between principal (constituent) and agent (representative), however, there is always the possibility of shirking—in this case interpreted as voting against the preferences of a reelection constituency. While recent analyses have presented some systematic evidence of such shirking (Kau and Rubin, 1982; Kalt and Zupan, 1984), it is important to recognize that such shirking has a distinct pattern. As with principal-agent relations generally, the better is the information (in terms of cost and clarity) on what the agent does, and the better the

The Domestic Political Preconditions of US Trade Policy   87

link between the actions of the agent and the interests of the principals, the more likely is the agent to effectively represent the principal. Thus, the clearer is the outcome of a piece of legislation with regard to a given interest, the more directly will a member of Congress be expected to represent that interest—if that interest is in the Congressman's reelection constituency (Nelson and Silberberg, 1987). As will be seen below, this is a point of some significance to an understanding of the change in US trade policy brought about by the RTAA.

It is virtually common knowledge in research on the domestic politics of trade policy that benefits of protection (costs of liberalization) are distributed asymmetrically. That is, the benefits of a given act of protection are concentrated on a relatively small number of firms producing the same product, while the costs are spread across all consumers of the product. Furthermore, the costs of not receiving protection to the marginal firm (or marginal factor-owners throughout the industry) may be quite high relative to costs borne by the marginal consumers (i.e. unemployment versus foregoing consumption of the good). The expected result of these asymmetries (in size of group and intensity of interest), by standard Olson-type logic of collective action, is that protection-seekers are more likely to be organized, and/or more likely to be better organized, than protection-avoiders. There is, thus, a presumption that the politically effective preference in society will be for protection. The point here is not that a majority of people will not favor liberal trading relations as a general principle (though time series evidence suggests that a relatively stable majority—i.e. 60–70 percent—has favored trade restrictions on 'goods priced lower than American goods of the same kind', at least since the early 1970s; Phillips, 1985), but that the balance of effectively organized people will prefer protection *for themselves*.

The evidence supporting both hypotheses (i.e. Congressional responsiveness and protectionist preference) is strong, and effectively unquestioned for the period prior to the adoption of the RTAA of 1934 (Taussig, 1931; Ratner, 1972). Although the specific conception of the issues relevant to tariff-making and the modalities of interest representation changed considerably over the period from independence to 1934, the politics of the tariff revolved primarily around the individual firm- and industry-level returns to protection (except for a brief period during which revenue motives prevailed). In the immediately post-independence period (1789–1816) industrial and sectoral interests were subordinated to the revenue needs of the new nation, but these needs were increasingly supplanted by explicitly protectionist justifications (especially following the Civil War which saw the development of many new industries in the North and the military defeat of the traditionally low-tariff South). That is, the tariff was increasingly seen as an instrument of domestic economic

88   Douglas Nelson

policy and domestic distributive policy. The politics of tariff policy did not show quite the degree of direct industry orientation because industry interests were only weakly institutionalized at the national level. As a result, tariff politics in the 19th century were primarily sectoral and partisan (with Democrats tending to represent low tariff regions and Republicans high). Had a Congressman (for some reason) possessed a free-trade ideology, this distance might have provided some political protection (though the fact that the tariff was a—if not the—major party issue would tend to reduce the value of this protection).

Not only did innovations in transportation and communication reduce the cost of monitoring the behavior of elected representatives, but the 20th century saw a number of other political and economic changes affecting tariff politics. In addition to stimulating a new flock of 'infant industries', the attempt to organize the economic effort of the first world war involved the creation of a number of well-institutionalized, industry-based groups experienced in dealing with Congress and the bureaucracy which were added to those which had developed in response to the regulatory innovations of the progressive era (Herring, 1929; Kolko, 1963; Wiebe, 1962, 1967; Weinstein, 1968). As a result, by the end of the first world war, the politics of the tariff had taken on the characteristic attributes of distributive politics as described by Lowi:

> . . . in the short-run certain kinds of government decisions can be made without regard to limited resources. Policies of this kind are called 'distributive' . . . Distributive policies are characterized by the ease with which they can be disaggregated and dispensed unit by small unit, each unit more or less in isolation from other units and from any general rule . . . These are policies that are virtually not policies at all but are highly individualized decisions that only by accumulation can be called a policy. They are policies in which the indulged and the deprived, the loser and the recipient, need never come into direct confrontation. (pg. 690)

Schattschneider's (1935) classic description of the making of the Smoot-Hawley tariff should leave no doubt as to the dominance of protectionist interests and the responsiveness of members of Congress to their requests.

It is sometimes suggested that one effect of the Smoot-Hawley tariff, and its historical proximity to the Depression and the second world war, was to induce a change in Congressional attitudes toward the tariff—effectively making them less responsive to protectionist demands from their constituents (Pastor, 1980). We would, however, expect such a change to induce new patterns of Congressional behavior with regard to trade legislation, especially high degrees of cooperation across party lines. Unfortunately, as Watson's (1956) study of voting on bills and amendments related to the reciprocal trade agreements program demonstrates,

The Domestic Political Preconditions of US Trade Policy 89

partisan voting patterns remained consistent with the pre-1934 patterns until the early 1950s when party discipline on trade began to break down. Furthermore, as Watson notes, the new coalitions on trade legislation were explainable primarily in terms of changes in the distribution of industry among geographical constituencies.

The thesis of this section (that Congress is responsive to political pressure; and that effective political pressure on the trade issue continues to reflect the protectionist bias it has always had) raises a clear problem: if Congress continues to respond to protectionist pressure, what accounts for the unprecedented period of US participation in multilateral tariff-cutting? I offer an answer in two parts. The next section argues that the RTAA effectively redefined trade policy as a political issue, with substantive effects on the politics of trade. Specifically, the political and institutional foundations were created from which a policy of liberalization could be launched. But, although a liberalization policy could be launched from Congress, for precisely the reasons outlined in this section, it could not be sustained from Congress. Thus, the second part of my answer has to do with the motivation of the executive branch in sustaining the policy of liberalization.

The Reciprocal Trade Agreements Act of 1934; Institutional Foundation for a Revolution in US Trade Policy

As the introduction noted, the RTAA of 1934 created the institutional foundations on which a revolution in the politics of US international trade policy was built (also see: Haggard, 1988). The statutory content of the RTAA was simple: it gave the President the right to negotiate tariff reductions (within Congressionally set limits). The RTAA's effect on the domestic politics of trade, however, was far from simple, and almost certainly not generally understood at the time. We can divide these effects into those flowing from the redefinition of the trade issue; and those flowing from the separation of liberalization from protection as political issues. We will consider each briefly.

The main concern of this section is with what I will call Lowi-effects, after Lowi's (1964) well-known reconciliation of the apparently contradictory findings in Schattschneider's (1935) study of the politics of the Smoot-Hawley tariff, and Bauer, Pool and Dexter's (1963) study of the politics surrounding extensions of the RTAA during the 1950s. He argued that a policy issue takes concrete form in the specific language Congress uses in drafting legislation, and that language directly induces characteristic patterns of political interaction in Congress as well as in the polity at large. Thus, he suggests that Schattschneider, and Bauer, Pool and Dexter were studying politics under fundamentally different institutional

90   *Douglas Nelson*

definitions of the issue at hand. The changes in political behavior induced by such a redefinition are what I call Lowi-effects.[3]

Prior to the RTAA, tariff levels were generally perceived to be primarily a distributive issue: a policy whose benefits are concentrated in a particular sub-set of the population (generally some politically relevant geographic area); but whose costs are dispersed over the entire population. The effect of such a definition in Congress, as Lowi conjectured, and recent choice-theoretic research has confirmed, is to induce norms of universalism and reciprocity (Weingast, 1979; Fiorina, 1981a; Shepsle and Weingast, 1981). Universalism is a norm under which all requests are accommodated ('something for everyone'), yielding what Lowi called 'coalitions of uncommon interest'. In the case of the tariff, this simply implied that if a member of Congress requested protection, his request should be accommodated. Reciprocity supports the universalism norm through generalized log-rolling in the issue area, or what Schattschneider called 'reciprocal non-interference' and demonstrated extensively for the tariff case. A similar pattern of behavior was elicited from the polity at-large, with requests for protection coming primarily from firm and, to a lesser extent, industry-level participants (for whom the tariff was effectively a private good). Protection opponents were not a major part of the process, and firms expecting injury from protection generally found their only available recourse to be additional protection for themselves.

Under the RTAA (and its successors to date), the issue ceased to be the degree of accommodation of discrete, individual interests and became (simplifying only somewhat) the determination of two general rules: one regulating the degree of tariff-cutting authority available to the executive; and the other regulating the ease of access to an administered protection mechanism and the conditions necessary for accommodation within that mechanism. The latter general rule, initially institutionalized through the peril point and the escape clause, embodies what Wilkinson (1960) calls the 'no serious injury norm'. That is, the executive promises Congress that its use of trade policy as an instrument of foreign policy will not result in serious deterioration of welfare for any significant group of people or industry. Thus, the effective 'right to protection' discussed by Schattschneider is not lost under the RTA system, but is redefined as the 'no serious injury norm'.[4] Economic interests were no longer able to lobby for an outcome with effectively private effects (i.e. a tariff on a specific line-item in the tariff schedule). Instead they had to lobby over the general (i.e. applicable to all firms/industries on the same terms) rules under which the administered protection mechanisms operated. That is, trade became what Lowi calls a regulatory issue.

We can identify two major effects of the shift from a distributive to a regulatory definition of trade: change in the organization of group

The Domestic Political Preconditions of US Trade Policy 91

activity; and change in the levels of group activity. The first of these is a direct extension of Lowi's point that issue type determines the form of politics. By contrast to distributive issues (which induce cooperation under norms of universalism and reciprocity), regulatory issues induce conflictive patterns of behavior because of the broader definition of the issue. That is, groups form (in the polity and in the legislature) as a function of their common interests vis-a-vis the general rule: preferences toward greater-or-lesser liberalization; and greater-or-lesser administered protection. The hypothesized effect of organized pressure for liberalization and against protection *in general* is first, to reduce a Congressman's preferred level of protection from what it would have been under the distributive regime. When trade was a distributive issue, members of Congress received pressure almost exclusively from protection-seekers; but under the regulatory definition, while protection-seekers would be expected to dominate for the reasons outlined in the preceding section, the presence of active anti-protection groups would be expected to moderate their effect. This was a major theme of Bauer, Pool and Dexter's (1963) work on the 1950's, is mentioned by Lindeen for the 1960s. A number of scholars have noted the increasing role of anti-protectionist interests (e.g. agricultural exporters and firms with extensive international interests) in the trade policy-making process (Destler and Odell, 1987; Milner, 1988).

A second effect on the organization and effectiveness of group behavior is related to the principal-agent problem between constituents and representatives noted above. As we have already suggested, the domestic politics of trade under the distributive definition involved a very clear link between agent behavior (i.e. support of an increase on the relevant line item in the tariff schedule) and principal interests. Under the regulatory definition, not only is the firm- or industry-specific protectionist impact less clear, but the additional statutory content related to negotiating authority further confuses the overall, interest-specific impact of trade legislation. That is, in addition to establishing the terms of access to administered protection and the grant of negotiating authority, Congress also specifies: the duration of the grant; limitations on the authority to liberalize (e.g. how much tariffs can be cut, exceptions for specific industries); procedural safeguards (peril points and escape clauses); requirements to consult with affected industries as well as Congress; and even the bureaucratic organization of responsibility for trade negotiation (i.e. the creation of the USTR).

The result of all this is legislation with distributive effects so obscure that only those legislators with rigidly protectionist or free-trade preferences have been dissatisfied. It is for this reason that any evaluation of Congressional sentiment should not be based simply on support for

92   *Douglas Nelson*

extensions of negotiating authority (as the ideology-shift arguments generally do), but must consider the total content of the legislation extending that authority. For example, although extension legislation was passed with substantial majorities in both the 80th and 83rd (Republican majority) Congresses, those bills were seen as major victories for the protectionist forces precisely because of the heavy constraints on negotiating authority (Wilkinson, 1960). The increased ease of access and relaxed conditions for affirmative findings in escape clause, countervailing duty and anti-dumping duty cases in recent legislation similarly involves protectionist content, as does explicit Congressional pressure for the application of non-tariff barriers of various sorts. Thus, we should not be surprised when Bauer, Pool and Dexter argue that members of Congress had considerable discretion on the trade issue under the RTAA's regulatory definition of the trade issue. I will argue in the next section that members of Congress used this discretion to accommodate strong requests from the executive for negotiating authority, and not out of ideological support for freer trade.

At least as important as its effect on the organization of group interests, however, is the effect of the redefinition of the domestic regime for trade politics on incentives to group action. On the basis of an Olson-type logic of collective action argument, it is usually argued that the major bias toward protection in democratic political systems emerges from an asymmetry in the distribution of benefits from protection and liberalization. That is, the benefits of protection are concentrated on a relatively small, easily identifiable group; while the costs (benefits of liberalization) are considerably more diffused. As a result, the gainers from protection are more likely to organize for collective action, and/or more likely to be effectively organized, than opponents of protection (proponents of liberalization).[5]

What is not generally recognized is that this argument rests on the pre-RTAA definition of the domestic political regime: each act of protection is seen as a function of a discrete (firm- or industry-specific) choice, with easily identifiable (and effectively privatized) effects at the firm or industry level. Instead, under the RTAA, each act of protection is the outcome of a bureaucratic process administered by the executive branch under a general rule adopted by Congress. (In fact the system is somewhat more complicated than this by the 'two-track' nature of the process (Nelson, 1981; Finger, Hall and Nelson, 1982). That is, demands for protection from politically 'large' interests may gain protection through a less technical (high track) bureaucratic process, or even through direct recourse to Congress. This complication, however, does not fundamentally alter the argument of this paper, and since we have treated it in detail elsewhere, we will not pursue it any further here.) Thus,

The Domestic Political Preconditions of US Trade Policy   93

the expected beneficiaries of protection find themselves lobbying for something approaching a public good (in the public choice, not the normative, sense) and not a policy approaching a private good (as in the distributive case). The result of dramatically enlarging the coalition and eliminating the direct link between lobbying and outcome in Congress should be 'underproduction' of protection, by the standard collective action logic.[6]

As institutionalists like Pastor suggest, the Lowi-effects should unambiguously lower both group pressure for protection and the propensity of Congress to offer protection for any given level of pressure. Furthermore, they are absolutely correct to point to the dramatic drop in levels of protection and sustained participation in multilateral liberalization efforts as evidence of the operation of these Lowi-effects. What these analyses miss is the effect of making liberalization and protection effectively distinct issues. The same piece of legislation that involves a major grant of negotiating authority (or ratification of the results of the application of such authority) can also involve a major increase in the protectionist content of the administered protection mechanisms. The Trade Act of 1974, for example, involved both the substantial grant of authority to negotiate on tariff and non-tariff barriers necessary to US participation in the Tokyo Round of GATT negotiations, and a major loosening of the conditions regulating access to administered protection. A complete evaluation of the domestic trade policy regime cannot be had by studying either liberalization or protection under the regime but, because both are treated as effectively distinct issues, both must be explicitly taken into account.

On the basis of the analysis suggested above, we would hypothesize a discontinuous downward shift in the level of protection (reflecting the effect of the changed institutional setting and executive pressure), followed by a continuing rise in the level of protection (reflecting continuing asymmetrical interest group pressure and Congressional vulnerability to that pressure). However, by the collective action argument, we would expect that rise to be slower and more stable than under the pre-RTA system. Furthermore, as a result of the procedural division between the protection and liberalization processes, we expect no necessary relationship between marginal changes in protection and liberalization (in fact, as long as the executive controls liberalization policy and Congress controls protectionist policy, we might find marginal changes to be inversely related).

I can think of no one who seriously disputes the proposition that there has been a discontinuous drop in the overall level of US protection dating from the RTA program. The matter of steadily increasing protection at the margin is a matter which may command somewhat less support (a fact

94   *Douglas Nelson*

which in itself provides some indirect support for the third proposition). In assessing the claim that protection has been steadily increasing, it is necessary to recall that marginal changes (i.e. changes that do not result in an immediate transformation of the system) in the post-RTA Act domestic trade regime take the form of changes in the rules regulating the administered protection mechanisms, not direct acts of protection by Congress. On this point there is also virtually no dispute, it is clear that there has been a systematic process of easing access to the administered protection mechanisms and reducing the conditions necessary to affirmative findings (Wilkinson, 1960; Nelson, 1981; Destler, 1986—chapter 6); as well as evidence that such changes result in more filings (Feigenbaum and Willett, 1985). Furthermore, there is considerable evidence of increasing coverage of trade affected by various forms of administered protection (Nowzad, 1978; Ajaria et al., 1982; Nogues, Olechowski, and Winters, 1986; Hufbauer et al., 1986), and evidence that these measures have the predicted trade diversion effects (Finger and Olechowski, 1986), and welfare effects (Magee, 1972; Tarr and Morkre, 1984; Baldwin and Krueger, 1984). Finally, however, we must also note that (as suggested above) the growth in protection has been more stable and slower in the 50 year period after 1934 than in the 50 year period preceding 1934, a fact which is often offered as evidence of a fundamental change in political attitudes toward protection (Pastor, 1980, 1983; Goldstein, 1986). It has been my argument to this point that an institutional-structural explanation accounts for the observed changes in policy at least as well as the ideological-shift argument, and does a better job of accounting for timing. What it does not do, that the ideological-shift argument does do, is account for the continued commitment to the multilateral liberalization process which is the anchor of the regulatory definition of the domestic political regime for trade policy (i.e. without that commitment there is no reason why the domestic trade policy regime should not revert to a distributive politics definition). My argument, which is no less *ad hoc* than the ideological-shift argument, has to do with a changed perception of the foreign policy role of trade policy by the executive, and changed power of the executive over foreign policy vis-a-vis Congress. The next section develops this argument.

Before turning to that argument, a brief summary of this paper's position to this point is in order. It has been argued: first, that there has been no change in the fundamental asymmetry between the economic interests of protection-preferring citizens and liberalization-preferring citizens; and second, that members of Congress remain generally responsive to effectively organized constituent demands. The Lowi-effects produced a one-time shift in both the level of protection and the rate at which protectionist pressure is accommodated, but that rate remains positive.

The Domestic Political Preconditions of US Trade Policy 95

The underlying *dynamic* remains protectionist. As long as the RTAA and post-RTAA definitions of the trade issue remain in place, this protectionist dynamic is to a significant extent contained; but those definitions are tied to a commitment to multilateral trade liberalization which did not emerge from Congress in the first place, and cannot (on the argument presented thus far) be sustained independently by Congress.

The Rise of the National Security State and the Executive's Preference for Trade Liberalization

In terms of understanding the shift in US trade policy, then, it is the shift in executive branch behavior and not the conversion of Congress that must be the explained. However, as I have already suggested, this shift cannot be explained simply in terms of a changed perception of the economic returns to liberal trading relations on the part of the executive, Congress, or some significant set of economically defined interests. Instead, we need to see trade policy as an instrument of some other policy concern.

With Democrat majorities in Congress and the most popular president in the 20th century in the White House, the Roosevelt administration was able to sustain the RTA program against increasing Congressional dissatisfaction. It is notable that the three extensions of the RTA program between 1940 and 1945 (1940, 1943, 1945) were justified primarily in terms of the need to build and sustain wartime solidarity among allies. Such requests would be hard to deny any wartime president, especially when the short-run economic and political costs were likely to be minimal. Thus, as with so many other domestic and international policies with roots in the early New Deal, the real moment of truth for the RTA program came in the transition from war to peace, and Roosevelt to Truman.

Although it is clear in retrospect that the US had little choice but to adopt an active leadership role in international political, military, and economic relations, this was far from clear at the time. As William Diebold (1983) recently observed in reference to the immediate post-War period:

. . . for a long time Americans did not realize how strong they were. Plans for the postwar economy assumed that London would continue to be a primary financial center, the pound a key currency, and Britain a leading element in a multilateral trading system. Continental Europe was expected to return to a central position in the world economy—provided Germany could be kept from becoming a menace once again. Much of Asia and Africa was still ruled from European capitals. (pg. 84)

96   *Douglas Nelson*

Thus, while the roots of US international leadership go back to the 1930s, the conjunctural moment for that leadership was the three year period 1945–1947. During this period the administration struggled within itself to define the nature and form of the US relation to the post-war international order (Gaddis, 1972, 1982; Yergin, 1977). Against the strong claims that the US should revert to a more-or-less isolationist stance consistent with the previous 150 years of US history (a position particularly strong among the Republican party's senior Congressmen— Taft, Vandenburg, Milliken, Gearhart, Simpson, Reed), Wilsonian internationalists (like Cordell Hull and James Byrnes—Hull's successor as Secretary of State) and cold war realists (e.g. Harriman, Bohlen, Kennan) promoted a more active role for the US. With the unintended cooperation of Josef Stalin, the cold war realists succeeded in defining the strategic vision of the Truman administration over the Wilsonian internationalists as well as the isolationists. Emphasizing the Soviet threat to world peace, the realists argued persuasively for strong, centralized executive control over a broad national security/foreign policy mandate. This vision received Congressional approval and institutional form in the National Security Act of 1947 (creating the National Security Council, the CIA, and the legislative basis of the 'peace-time' military—the creation of the Department of Defense at the cabinet level).

George Kennan, one of the primary architects of the new strategic vision, particularly emphasized the importance of economic instruments to the containment of the communist threat (Gaddis, 1982; chapters 2 & 3). This reflected both the successful experience of using US economic and productive power (rather than military manpower) to fight the second world war, and Kennan's carefully constructed vision of the creation of world order through a multilateral balance of power. As a result, the instruments of international economic policy (including trade policy) were seen as fundamental instruments of national security policy. The first task to which these instruments were turned was the reconstruction of a Europe seen as poised on the brink of economic collapse, with local Moscow-oriented communist parties waiting in the wings. The Marshall plan transferred needed financial resources directly, and liberalization of the US trade regime (without effective European reciprocity) was expected to transfer resources indirectly. This point is fundamental. The major policy-makers in the Truman White House and State Department (Secretaries of State Marshall and Acheson in particular) not only did not perceive trade as economically advantageous but, to the extent that they considered its economic effects at all, tended to see it primarily in terms of costs (Wilkinson, 1960; Pollard, 1985). They defended the program primarily as a necessary instrument of contain-

The Domestic Political Preconditions of US Trade Policy 97

ment. That is, the costs of liberal trade were seen as one of the costs of international leadership.

The fragility of the RTA program and its reliance on sustained executive leadership can be seen in its near collapse in the early years of the Eisenhower administration. Concerned primarily with response to a global communist threat that seemed to have taken concrete military form in Korea, the Eisenhower administration (and especially Secretary of State Dulles) focussed primarily on the strategic/military aspects of containment. At the same time, the administration faced a Republican Congress with strong hostility to the RTA program in the key committees (House Ways and Means and Senate Finance). In the hearings on the 1953 extension of RTA negotiating authority, Dulles apparently seemed uninformed and uninterested in the program, even expressing support for 'a considerable measure of protection' against foreign competition (Wilkinson, 1960; pg. 75). With weak leadership from the executive and strong hostility in Congress the program floundered for two years until the President and the Secretary of State reassessed the role of the RTA program as an instrument of foreign and national security policy, and the 1954 elections returned a Democrat majority to Congress.

Thus, in the context of the cold war and the development of what Yergin (1977) calls the 'national security state', the institutional structure established under the RTA Act became the new basis for the domestic politics of international trade. In turning to an examination of that structure, we need to remain constantly alert to the fact of the instrumental relationship of trade policy to national security policy as a condition of its stability in the face of underlying domestic pressures to use trade policy for distributive purposes.

We are now in a position to answer the central question of this section: how was the US able to sustain the commitment to multilateral trade liberalization which not only was fundamental to the success of that process, but also was the political glue that held in place the institutional structure that constrained the effectiveness of protectionist pressure in Congress? We have seen that, for reasons that varied over time, key decision-makers in the executive branch (especially in the State Department) were determined to use international trade policy as an instrument of national security policy. We have also seen that (more as a function of good fortune than good planning), the changed institutional environment made it possible for the executive branch to establish political control over an issue (trade policy) which had previously been controlled by the legislative branch. In exchange for guarantees that no significant sectors of the population would suffer sustained injury, the executive branch was given the power to pursue a sustained policy of trade liberalization. That

98   *Douglas Nelson*

is, by focussing the domestic politics of protection on the administered
protection process (i.e. the institutionalization of the 'no serious injury'
norm), the executive branch was freed to pursue liberalization with a
relatively free hand. The final issue we treat in this paper is the future of
these arrangements.

Domestic Political-Economic Dynamics and the Prospects for Regime Stability

There were two key factors in our explanation of US commitment to
multilateral liberalism: an institutional structure that permits such a
commitment; and strong executive leadership that takes advantage of
that structure. Since the latter is difficult to predict, we will be more
concerned in this section with forces for change that operate primarily
through their effect on the prospects for the continued stability of the
institutionalized regime regulating the domestic politics of trade policy.
We will consider four in particular: microeconomic dislocations; macroeconomic dislocations; international/imported political-economic disturb-
ances; and changes in the international strategic environment.

Microeconomic, and Sectoral Dislocation:

We have already noted that the process of adjustment to economic change
in a market-oriented political-economy tends to result in concentrated
costs and diffuse benefits. Under reasonably democratic (or pluralistic)
political arrangements, this asymmetry can be expected to create a bias
toward accommodation of demands for some form of protection from the
costs of adjustment. While the source of this protection need not be the
state, in societies with broadly individualist and secular social orders the
state is the most likely provider of such protection;[7] and it is certainly the
case that in virtually all of the core members of the international trading
system the state is in fact the major provider of such protection.

Although there is no necessary reason why this generalized predisposition to state protection should take the specific form of trade protection, it
has been recognized for some time that welfare state commitments and
GATT commitments are, at least, inconsistent (Krauss, 1978; Tumlir,
1978, 1981; Nelson, forthcoming a). The fundamental source of this
inconsistency lies in the fact that a commitment to liberal trade relations,
like any commitment to market discipline, implies adjustment costs
which are almost certain to be asymmetrically distributed through the
society. Furthermore, by standard trade theoretic analysis, the larger are
the collective gains, the larger will be the concentrated costs.[8] Thus, to the
extent that liberalization follows comparative advantage, we might
expect the costs to be considerable.

The Domestic Political Preconditions of US Trade Policy 99

Since there is not much evidence to suggest that the liberalization process is particularly driven by considerations of comparative advantage,[9] however, the use of trade policy instruments in response to various forms of microeconomic distress (whether directly trade related or not, but generally not directly related to specific acts of trade liberalization) is probably a more significant consideration. In addition to the asymmetries in the distribution of costs and benefits that we have already considered, the use of trade policy instruments in response to microeconomic crisis has the dubious political virtue of implying a cause of injury external to the domestic economy and, more importantly in an era in which international 'competitiveness' (measured by a current account surplus) is as an indicator of national fitness (very much in the Darwinian sense), external to the domestic political system as well. While there is no direct evidence in support of this conjecture, recent research by Hufbauer and his colleagues (Hufbauer and Rosen, 1986; Hufbauer, et al., 1986) provides some interesting indirect evidence. One of their findings is that, contrary to general expectations, a number of industries receiving administered (what they call 'special') protection do, in fact, adjust under administered protection. While Hufbauer's explanation that firms take legal time limits seriously is surely part of the story, it seems plausible that domestic/nontrade sources of microeconomic distress continue to generate adjustment pressures. Although this could be taken to imply some kind of policy-illusion on the part of protection seekers (in that some alternative, more direct, form of policy intervention would provide more complete relief from costs related to adjustment), a more plausible explanation is that the costs of receiving trade related protection are sufficiently lower than those associated with other forms of protection that protection-seekers tend to pursue the former.[10] These factors underlie the general systemic bias toward trade protection that I have outlined above and elsewhere (Nelson, forthcoming b).

As I demonstrate above, the structure of the system (i.e. the institutional division between the liberalization and protection processes) has allowed the accommodation of protectionist pressures through administered protection without undermining the liberalization process. Nonetheless, it should be clear that there are limits to the sustainability of that structure. Beyond some point, the accommodation of protectionist pressures at the domestic level must surely compromise the operation of the liberalization process at the international level. Beyond that point, the whole domestic institutional structure on which US participation in the international political economy has rested would be called into question. While such a situation could well emerge as a result of the normal functioning of the system, there are greater threats to its continued integrity outside the system.

100 *Douglas Nelson*

Macroeconomic Dislocation.

Most of this paper's analysis has assumed that, while firm or sector-level incentives to seek protection are subject to change, the system-level incentives are not. As a number of recent analyses have pointed out, however, this is not the case. The most important consideration here is the effect of trends in the macro-economy (i.e. the business cycle) on the arbitrage between economically productive investment and protection-seeking. Recent contributions by McKeown (1984), and Cassing, McKeown and Ochs (1986) develop a theory of tariff cycles based directly on such a consideration, in the course of which they develop the firm-level logic in some detail. Furthermore, recent empirical research provides further evidence of this connection. Takacs (1981), Feigenbaum, Ortiz and Willett (1985), and Feigenbaum and Willett (1985) all confirm statistically significant relationships between macroeconomic conditions and protectionist pressures (measured by escape clause case filings), but not between macroeconomic conditions and case outcomes. Since the administered protection process is not set up to respond to changed macroeconomic conditions, this is precisely the finding our institutional analysis would predict. In our more detailed analyses of the administered protection mechanism (Nelson, 1981; Finger, Hall and Nelson, 1982) we argue that it is characterized by a two-track system in which the 'low-track' (anti-dumping and countervailing duties) is tightly constrained by the rules under which it operates; and the 'high-track' (escape clause), while less rule-constrained, will tend to use its relative freedom to respond to politically significant cases (and thus also will be unresponsive to general changes in macroeconomic variables). Thus, macroeconomic deterioration would be predicted to result in: increased action in the administered protection mechanism reflecting generally decreased returns to economic activity relative to political activity; but stable response from the mechanism reflecting its role as a processor of high-track cases.

More importantly, with regard to the question of system transformation, while these analyses provide evidence on the effect of changes in the rules on protection-seeking,[11] they do not explicitly treat the reverse question: the effect of changing returns to political activity (relative to economic activity) on the structure of the rules. The institutional analysis presented in this paper suggests that Congress is responsive to constituent pressure, but that its degree of responsiveness was greater under the pre-RTA Act domestic regime than under the post-RTA Act regime. Thus, in addition to generating more business for the administered protection mechanism, we would expect the improved returns to politics to induce greater pressures for change in the rules. A large enough macroeconomic

The Domestic Political Preconditions of US Trade Policy 101

deterioration could conceivably produce a dramatic shift toward legislated protection of the pre-RTA Act sort even under a fixed responsiveness to protectionist pressure.

It is unlikely, however, that Congressional responsiveness to protectionist pressure would remain constant in the context of a significant macroeconomic deterioration. Most research on modern members of Congress gives the strong impression of strong risk averseness, in the sense that they are generally unlikely to pursue fundamental changes in policies and institutional structures that: 1) have politically effective constituencies; and/or 2) seem to be doing what they were set up to do. Instead, they prefer to engage in direct constituency service and pork-barrelling, neither of which requires changing the rules of the system (Mayhew, 1974). The primary source of this conservatism is the fact that most members of Congress are career politicians, seeking to remain in their current jobs (Fiorina, 1977). Thus, during periods of strong economic performance we would expect most members of Congress to attempt only marginal alterations in the overall structure of economic policy. However, during periods of general economic deterioration we would expect an increased willingness to accept (and participate in) fundamental change.

Combined with increased constituent pressure, this increased willingness to accept fundamental change could result in strongly discontinuous change not only in levels of intervention, but in the entire structure within which decisions to intervene are made. Trade policy is an obvious case. In the 1930s Congress produced a discontinuous increase in the level of trade intervention (although there was no obvious relationship between decreased trade and the solution of current macroeconomic problems), followed by a discontinuous decrease combined with a change in institutional structure (again without an obvious relationship between increased trade and the solution of current macroeconomic problems). Faced with massive trade deficits and an equally massive foreign debt, both parties in Congress seem increasingly interested in experimenting with trade policy responses to problems that do not have an obvious causal relationship to the state of the current account. At the same time, the Reagan administration revealed little capacity for sustained trade policy leadership, has accommodated more protectionist pressure than any president since Hoover, and participated in less liberalization. Unfortunately, there is no sign that his successor plans a substantial deviation from the Reagan (non)approach.

102   *Douglas Nelson*

International Economic Dislocation.

The fact that this paper's analysis has focussed on US trade policy should not be taken to imply that other countries have significantly less severe problems in sustaining international cooperation on trade liberalization. The same underlying pressures exist in all the core countries of the international trading regime: they are all liberal democratic political systems with strong welfare state commitments; as a result, adjustment costs associated with relatively liberal trading relations are easily transmuted into political demands for protection (as are general micro and macroeconomic problems). Research on European trade and industrial policy suggests that European governments face the same types of pressures and are moving toward the same types of responses as the US government (Strange, 1979; Tsoukalis and da Silva Ferreira, 1980; Kahler, 1985).

The importance of this lies in our conclusion that continued coopera-tion on trade liberalization requires that states be able to contain domestic protectionist pressures, permitting them to act more-or-less auto-nomously (i.e. as if they were unitary-rational) in their international relations over trade. Not only does a break-down in cooperative behavior threaten the international political-institutional structure through which their cooperation is mediated, but it puts enormous strain on the domestic political arrangements of the other countries which are as fundamental to the liberalization process as the equivalent institutional arrangements in the US that have been the concern of this paper. The effect of a major deviation by, say, England, France, Germany or Japan, on a Congress whose analysis of trade is dominated by the logic of 'fair trade' and 'the level playing field' would probably be catastrophic.

Transformation of US-Soviet Strategic Relations.

Given this paper's emphasis on the linkage between national security/ foreign policy and trade policy, I will close with a brief consideration of the effect of changing US-Soviet relations on the domestic politics of international trade. I argued that executive control over trade policy was effectively institutionalized during the early years of the Cold War as a subsidiary (but important) part of the containment strategy. The development of the Detente strategy during the Nixon-Kissinger era (Gaddis, 1981; chapters 9 and 10) resulted in a reduction in US-Soviet tension, but resulted in a return to an increased emphasis on economic containment (as during the Marshall/Kennan years). As one might expect, trade liberalization policy figured prominently in the Nixon and Carter administrations.

The Domestic Political Preconditions of US Trade Policy   103

As with domestic policy, the Reagan administration's lack of direction on strategic policy has had a negative effect on trade policy leadership. Very much like the Eisenhower administration, the Reagan administration's strategic policy has tended to emphasize strategic/military conflict with the Soviet Union (the 'evil empire'). Thus, while US hostility toward the Soviet Union rose dramatically during the Reagan administration (fortunately met by more temperate leadership from a Soviet Union too concerned with internal economic and political crisis to notice the US executive's hysteria), the administration's lack of concern with alliance building and non-military containment has, again like the Eisenhower administration, caused it to ignore the domestic-political linkage between trade policy and foreign policy. Rather than tending the delicate relationship with Congress over trade, aid, and other elements of international economic policy, the main emphasis was on increasing military spending. This surrender of leadership on international economic issues by the US seems to have led to the interesting phenomenon of renewed (at least intellectual) leadership by Britain's Margaret Thatcher. While this may or may not be good news at the international level, the domestic political result has been increasing Congressional trade activism.

Conclusion

Notwithstanding the considerations of the previous section, from the Roosevelt administration through the Carter administration, the executive branch (having chosen to pursue an active leadership role in international politics) has attempted to pursue a policy of trade liberalization as an instrument of its broader foreign/national security policy. Congressional acceptance of this linkage (under the 'no serious injury' norm) has permitted sufficient degrees of freedom from domestic protectionist pressure that the executive branch has achieved an impressive degree of success in promoting multilateral liberalization. That is Congress has granted increasingly deep tariff-cutting powers, has permitted the extension of negotiation to non-tariff barriers, and has made these grants for increasingly long periods of time. But that is only part of the story, the Congress has also made access to administered protection increasingly easy, has shown itself increasingly willing to legislate new protection, and individual members of Congress have come to play an increasingly active role in 'over-seeing' the liberalization process as well as promoting the protectionist process. This paper has argued that, without substantial executive leadership on the trade issue, it is the protectionist dynamic that will dominate trade policy-making in the foreseeable future. The politics of trade policy during the Reagan administration shows only too clearly the validity of this assertion.

104   *Douglas Nelson*

NOTES

1. In fact, the great majority of research on international trade policy in both political science and economics emphasizes considerations of international structure. Regime theory, in political science, attempts to explain the emergence of patterns of international order primarily in terms of the distribution of (issue-specific and/or general) power at the international level. See Nelson (1987) for a survey of international structural theories of the political economy of trade. While there is a substantial body of research in economics on both the domestic effects of trade policy (i.e. analysis of the distributional and welfare effect) and the optimal policy for a given policy goal, normative economic arguments for trade policy generally relate to international structure. That is, if the international economic structure is free of imperfections, liberal trading relations are generally preferred; on the other hand, the presence of imperfections *at the international level* constitutes a basis for trade intervention. The optimal tariff, for example, emerges from the possession of monopoly power; while most of the current research on strategic trade policy also rests on considerations of relative market structure between trading partners.

2. I am grateful to I. M. Destler for this point.

3. For an illustration of the capacity of institutional structure to induce characteristic patterns of interest group behavior on a trade-related issue, see my study of the changing politics of protection, between 1979 and 1981, relating to the VER agreement on automobiles with Japan.

4. It is interesting to note the similarity of this to Corden's (1974; pp. 107–112) 'conservative social welfare function' and Ruggie's (1982) 'embedded liberalism'.

5. The same argument could be used as part of an attempt to demonstrate that Congress acts ideologically to support liberalization. Thus, it could be argued that a change in Congressional ideology accounts for the apparent finding that the response to protectionist pressure has been weaker, and support of liberalization stronger since the stabilization of the RTA program. Krasner (1976), Pastor (1980), and Goldstein (1986) all seem to suggest something like this argument. The majority of the first part of this section argues that it is hard to find any direct support for this position in the expressions or action of Congress. The point of this paragraph is that the change in the logic of collective action attendant on the change in the domestic politics of the trade issue supports the interest group explanation of Congressional action, not an ideology explanation.

6. Hall and Nelson (1983) present a simple formal demonstration of this result. One of the key assumptions of that analysis is that the administered protection process which handles most of the cases is rule-bound. Empirical support for this assumption is presented in Nelson (1981, forthcoming b) and Finger, Hall and Nelson (1982).

7. The argument that the transition to capitalism tends to destroy the social relations providing what we might now call 'protection' (in the broad sense of the above paragraph) or 'adjustment assistance' is fairly standard (Polanyi, 1944), as is the argument that the individualist basis of capitalism tends to limit the capacity of the system to generate alternative mechanisms (Schumpeter, 1954; Hirsch, 1976). These arguments do not suggest that we do not find contemporary examples of private and/or non-secular protection (i.e. charity), but that these constitute an incomplete and unreliable system; and that, especially in broadly democratic political systems, this creates pressures for some form of state intervention.

8. That is, large gains will usually imply large adjustments necessary to realize the gains. In partial equilibrium this is the adjustments necessary to achieve the transfer from domestic producers to domestic consumers. Although the total gain to consumers will be larger than the loss to producers, the magnitudes will covary. Similarly, in general equilibrium, we would expect the magnitude of gain to covary with the magnitude of the shift in production.

9. In fact, to the extent that the advanced industrial countries that constitute the core of the liberal international trade system are presumed to be intensively endowed with capital or human-capital, there is considerable evidence to the contrary. That is, it is a common finding that reductions in tariffs, as well as existing tariff structures, protect labor: Cheh (1974), Bale (1977), and Marvel and Ray (1983) relate directly to the relationship between labor adjustment costs and GATT negotiation by the US; Baldwin (1984) and Hughes (1986) provide general surveys of the relevant empirical literature on the political economy of trade in industrial countries. Such findings are at least consistent with the operation of a 'no serious injury' norm.

10. If this is part of the explanation it has interesting (though hard to analyze) implications for the optimal economic policy literature (Bhagwati and Ramaswami, 1963; Johnson, 1965; Bhagwati,

The Domestic Political Preconditions of US Trade Policy 105

1971). One of the fundamental results of this literature is the proposition that, if an intervention is necessary (for whatever reason), it is best (in the sense of least costly) to use an intervention which responds directly to the cause of the intervention. However, if protection-seekers (i.e. adjustment avoiders) can be induced to accept a 'leaky' intervention because it is less costly to acquire, it is possible that such interventions may have a lower long-run cost than the 'correct' short-run intervention.

11. Specifically, Feigenbaum and Willett (1985) show a positive and statistically significant response of protectionist pressure to a change in the rules (proxied by a dummy reflecting the 1974 Trade Act) which eased the conditions of access to the mechanism.

REFERENCES

Allen, William (1954). 'Issues in Congressional Tariff Debates, 1890–1930'. *Southern Economic Journal*, 20, 2, pp. 340–355.

Anjaria, Shailendra, Zubair Iqbal, Naheed Kirmani, and Lorenzo Perez (1982). *Developments in International Trade Policy*. Washington, DC: IMF (Occasional Paper, 16).

Baldwin, Robert E. and Anne O. Krueger (1984). *The Structure and Evolution of Recent U.S. Trade Policy*. Chicago: University of Chicago Press.

Baldwin, Robert E. (1984). 'Trade Policies in Developed Countries'. in R. Jones and P. Kenen, eds. *Handbook of International Economics* (V.1). Amsterdam: North-Holland, pp. 571–619.

Bale, Malcolm (1977). 'US Concessions in the Kennedy Round and Short-Run Labor Adjustment Costs: Further Evidence'. *Journal of International Economics*. 7, 2, pp. 145–148.

Bauer, Raymond A., Ithiel de Sola Pool and Lewis Anthony Dexter (1963). *American Business and Public Policy: The Politics of Foreign Trade*. Chicago: Aldine.

Bhagwati, Jagdish (1971). 'The Generalized Theory of Distortions and Welfare'. In Bhagwati, et al. *Trade, Balance of Payments and Growth*. Amsterdam: North Holland.

Bhagwati, Jagdish (1982). 'Directly Unproductive, Profit-Seeking Activities'. *Journal of Political Economy*. 90, 5, pp. 988–1002.

Bhagwati, Jagdish and V. K. Ramaswami (1963). 'Domestic Distortions, Tariffs and the Theory of Optimum Subsidy'. *Journal of Political Economy*. 71, 1, pp. 44–50.

Bhagwati, Jagdish and T. N. Srinivasan (1982). 'The Welfare Consequences of Directly Unproductive Profit-Seeking (DUP) Activities'. *Journal of International Economics*. 13, 1/2, pp. 33–44.

Burns, James MacGregor (1963). *The Deadlock of Democracy*. Englewood Cliffs: Prentice-Hall.

Cassing, James, Timothy McKeown and Jack Ochs (1986). 'The Political Economy of the Tariff Cycle'. *American Political Science Review*. 80, 3, pp. 843–862.

Cheh, John H. (1974). 'United States Concessions in the Kennedy Round and Short-Run Labor Adjustment Costs'. *Journal of International Economics*. 4, 4, pp. 323–340.

Cole, Wayne (1983). *Roosevelt and the Isolationists, 1932–1945*. Lincoln: University of Nebraska Press.

Cooper, Richard (1972). 'Trade Policy is Foreign Policy'. *Foreign Policy*. 9, pp. 18–36.

Cooper, Richard (1987). 'Trade Policy as Foreign Policy'. In R. Stern, ed. *US Trade Policies in a Changing World Economy*. Cambridge: MIT Press; pp. 291–322.

Corden, W. Max (1974). *Trade Policy and Economic Welfare*. Oxford: Oxford University Press.

Cox, Gary, Matthew McCubbins and Terry Sullivan (1984). 'Policy Choice as an Electoral Investment'. *Social Choice and Welfare*. 1, 2, pp. 231–242.

Destler, I. M. (1986). *American Trade Politics: System Under Stress*. Washington, DC: Institute for International Economics.

Destler, I. M. and John Odell (1987). 'Antiprotection: Changing Forces in United States Trade Politics'. *Policy Analyses in International Economics—No. 21*. Washington, DC: Institute for International Economics.

Diebold, William jr. (1952). 'The End of the ITO'. *Princeton Essays in International Finance*, No. 16.

Diebold, William (1983). 'The United States in the World Economy: A Fifty Year Perspective'. *Foreign Affairs*. 62, 1, pp. 81–104.

Feigenbaum, Susan, Henry Ortiz and Thomas Willett (1985). 'Protectionist Pressures and Aggregate Economic Conditions: Comment on Takacs'. *Economic Inquiry*. 23, 1, pp. 175–182.

Feigenbaum, Susan and Thomas Willett (1985). 'Domestic versus International Influences on Protectionist Pressures in the United States'. In S. Arndt et al. *Exchange Rates, Trade and the US Economy*. Cambridge: Ballinger; pp. 181–190.

106   *Douglas Nelson*

Fenno, Richard (1978). *Home Style: House Members in their District.* Boston: Little, Brown.
Finger, J. M., H. Keith Hall and Douglas R. Nelson (1982). 'The Political Economy of Administered Protection'. *American Economic Review.* 72, 3, pp. 452–466.
Finger, J. M. and Andrzej Olechowski (1986). 'Trade Barriers: Who Does What to Whom'. ms: World Bank (DRDIE).
Fiorina, Morris (1977). *Congress: Keystone of the Washington Establishment.* New Haven: Yale University Press.
Fiorina, Morris (1981a). 'Universalism, Reciprocity, and Distributive Policy-Making in Majority Rule Institutions'. *Research in Public Policy Analysis and Management.* 1, pp. 197–221.
Fiorina, Morris (1981b). *Retrospective Voting in American National Elections.* New Haven: Yale University Press.
Frankfurt, Harry (1971). 'Freedom of Will and the Concept of a Person'. *Journal of Philosophy.* 68, 1, pp. 5–20.
Gaddis, John (1972). *The United States and the Origins of the Cold War, 1941–1947.* New York: Columbia University Press.
Gaddis, John (1982). *Strategies of Containment: A Critical Appraisal of Post-War American National Security Policy.* New York: Oxford University Press.
Goldstein, Judith (1986). 'The Political Economy of Trade: Institutions of Protection'. *American Political Science Review.* 80, 1, pp. 161–184.
Haggard, Stephan (1988). 'The Institutional Foundations of Hegemony: Explaining the Trade Agreements Act of 1934'. *International Organization.* 42, 1, pp. 91–119.
Hall, H. Keith and Douglas Nelson (1983). 'Modeling the Market for Protection: Administered Versus Legislated Protection,' presented at American Political Science Association.
Herring, E. Pendleton (1929). *Group Representation Before Congress.* Baltimore: Johns Hopkins University Press.
Hirsch, Fred (1976). *Social Limits to Growth.* Cambridge: Harvard University Press.
Hufbauer, Gary, Diane Berliner and Kimberly Elliott (1986). *Trade Protection in the United States: 31 Case Studies.* Washington, DC: Institute for International Economics.
Hufbauer, Gary and Howard Rosen (1986). 'Trade Policy for Troubled Industries'. *Policy Analyses in International Economics—No. 15.* Washington, DC: Institute for International Economics.
Hughes, Helen (1986). 'The Political Economy of Protection in Eleven Industrial Countries'. In R. Snape, ed. *Issues in World Trade Policy: GATT at the Crossroads.* London: Macmillan, pp. 222–237.
Johnson, Harry G. (1965). 'Optimal Trade Intervention in the Presence of Domestic Distortions'. R. Baldwin et al., *Trade, Growth and the Balance of Payments.* Chicago: Rand-McNally, pp. 3–34.
Kahler, Miles (1985). 'European Protectionism in Theory and Practice. *World Politics.* 37, 3, pp. 475–502.
Kalt, Joseph and Mark Zupan (1984). 'Capture and Ideology in the Economic Theory of Politics'. *American Economic Review.* 74, 3, pp. 279–300.
Kau, James and Paul Rubin (1982). *Congressmen, Constituents and Contributors.* Boston: Nijhoff.
Kemp, Kathleen (1984). 'Industrial Structure, Party Competition and the Sources of Regulation'. In T. Ferguson and J. Rogers, eds. *The Political Economy: Readings in the Politics and Economics of American Public Policy.* Armonk, N.Y.: Sharpe, pp. 104–111.
Keohane, Robert (1984). *After Hegemony: Cooperation and Discord in the World Political Economy,.* Princeton: Princeton University Press.
Kiewiet, D. Roderick (1983). *Macroeconomics and Micropolitics: The Electoral Effects of Economic Issues.* Chicago: University of Chicago Press.
Kingdon, John (1973). *Congressmen's Voting Decisions.* New York: Harper and Row.
Kolko, Gabriel (1963). *The Triumph of Conservatism: A Reinterpretation of American History, 1900–1916.* New York: Free Press.
Krasner, Stephen (1976). 'State Power and the Structure of International Trade'. *World Politics.* 28, pp. 317–347.
Krasner, Stephen (1979). 'The Tokyo Round: Particularistic Interests and Prospects for Stability in the Global Trading System'. *International Studies Quarterly.* 23, 4, pp. 491–531.
Krauss, Melvyn (1978). *The New Protectionism: The Welfare State and International Trade.* New York: NYU Press.
Lenway, Stefanie (1984). *The Politics of US International Trade: Protection, Expansion and Escape.* Boston: Pitman.
Lindeen, James (1970). 'Interest Group Attitudes Toward Reciprocal Trade Legislation'. *Public Opinion Quarterly.* 34, 1, pp. 108–112.
Lowi, Theodore (1964). 'American Business, Public Policy, Case Studies and Political Theory'. *World Politics.* 16, 4, pp. 347–382.

The Domestic Political Preconditions of US Trade Policy   107

Magee, Stephen and Leslie Young (1987). 'Endogenous Protection in the United States, 1900–1984'. In R. Stern, ed. *US Trade Policies in a Changing World Economy*. Cambridge: MIT Press, pp. 145–195.

Magee, Stephen (1972). 'The Welfare Effects of Restrictions on US Trade'. *Brookings Papers in Economic Analysis*. 3, pp. 645–701.

Marvel, Howard P. and Edward J. Ray (1983). The 'Kennedy Round: Evidence on the Regulation of International Trade in the U.S'. *American Economic Review*. 73, 1, pp. 190–197.

Matthews, Donald (1960). *US Senators and Their World*. New York: Vintage Books.

Mayhew, David (1974). *Congress: The Electoral Connection*. New Haven: Yale University Press.

McCubbins, Matthew and Terry Sullivan (1984). 'Constituency Influences on Legislative Policy Choice'. *Quality and Quantity*. 18, 2, pp. 299–319.

McKeown, Timothy J. (1984). 'Firms and Tariff Change: Explaining the Demand for Protection'. *World Politics*. 36, 2, pp. 215–233.

Milner, Helen (1988). *Resisting Protectionism: Global Industries and the Politics of International Trade*. Princeton: Princeton University Press.

Nelson, Douglas (1981). 'The Political Economy of the New Protectionism'. *World Bank Staff Working Paper—No. 471*.

Nelson, Douglas (1986). 'Notes on the Application of Social Choice Theory to the Political-Economy of Development Policy. Part I: Aggregation of Political Preferences; Part II: State Production of Political Output'; ms: The World Bank (DRDDS: MADIA).

Nelson, Douglas (1987). 'Structural Theories of the International Political Economy of Trade: A Short Review'. ms.: The World Bank (DRDIE).

Nelson, Douglas (1988). 'Endogenous Tariff Theory: A Critical Survey'. *American Journal of Political Science*. 32, 3, pp. 796–837.

Nelson, Douglas (forthcoming a). 'The Welfare State and Export Optimism'. In D. Pirages and C. Sylvester, eds. *The Transformation of the Global Political Economy*. London: Macmillan.

Nelson, Douglas (forthcoming b). 'The Public Politics of Protection: Automobiles, 1979–1981'. In S. Haggard and C. Moon, eds. *Pacific Dynamics*.

Nelson, Douglas and Eugene Silberberg (1987). 'Ideology and Legislator Shirking'. *Economic Inquiry*. 25, 1, pp. 15–25.

Nogues, Julio, Andrzej Olechowski and Alan Winters (1986). 'The Extent of Nontariff Barriers to Industrial Countries' Imports'. *World Bank Economic Review*. 1, 1, pp. 181–199.

Nowzad, Bahram (1978). 'The Rise in Protectionism'. *IMF Pamphlet Series—No. 24*.

Pastor, Robert (1980). *Congress and the Politics of U.S. Foreign Economic Policy: 1929–1976*. Berkeley: University of California Press.

Pastor, Robert (1983). 'The Cry-and-Sigh Syndrome: Congress and Trade Policy'. In A. Schick, ed. *Making Economic Policy in Congress*. Washington, DC: AEI; pp. 158–195.

Peltzman, Sam (1984). 'Constituent Interest and Congressional Voting'. *Journal of Law and Economics*. 27, 1, pp. 181–210.

Peltzman, Sam (1985). 'An Economic Interpretation of Congressional Voting in the Twentieth Century'. *American Economic Review*. 75, 4, pp. 656–675.

Phillips, Kevin (1985). 'The Politics of Protectionism'. *Public Opinion*. April/May, pp. 41–46.

Polanyi, Karl (1944). *The Great Transformation*. Boston: Beacon Press.

Pollard, Robert (1985). *Economic Security and the Origins of the Cold War, 1945–1950*. New York: Columbia University Press.

Ratner, Sidney (1972). *The Tariff in American History*. New York: D. van Nostrand.

Rosen, Elliot (1966). 'Intranationalism vs. Internationalism: The Interregnum Struggle for the Sanctity of the New Deal'. *Political Science Quarterly*. 81, 2, pp. 274–297.

Ruggie, John (1982). 'International Regimes, Transactions, and Change: Embedded Liberalism in the Postwar Economic Order'. *International Organization*. 36, 2, pp. 379–415.

Schattschneider, E.E. (1935). *Politics, Pressures and the Tariff*. New York: Prentice Hall.

Schumpeter, Joseph (1954). *Capitalism, Socialism, and Democracy*. New York: Harper.

Shepsle, Kenneth and Weingast, Barry (1981). 'Political Preferences for the Pork Barrel: A Generalization'. *American Journal of Political Sciences*. 25, 1, pp. 96–111.

Strange, Susan (1979). 'The Management of Surplus Capacity'. *International Organization*. 33, 3, pp. 303–334.

Takacs, Wendy (1981). 'Pressures for Protectionism: An Empirical Analysis'. *Economic Inquiry*. 19, 4, pp. 687–693.

Tarr, David and Morris Morkre (1984). *Aggregate Costs to the U.S. of Tariffs and Quotas on Imports*. Washington, DC: Federal Trade Commission.

Taussig, Frank (1931). *The Tariff History of the United States* (8th ed.) New York: A.M. Kelley.

108   *Douglas Nelson*

Tsoukalis, Loukas and Antonio da Silva Ferreira (1980). 'Management of Industrial Capacity in the European Community'. *International Organization*. 34, 3, pp. 355–376.

Tufte, Edward (1978). *Political Control of the Economy*. Princeton: Princeton University Press.

Tumlir, Jan (1978). *National Interest and International Order*. London: Trade Policy Research Centre.

Tumlir, Jan (1981). 'Evolution of the Concept of International Economic Order, 1914–1980'. In F. Cairncross, ed. *Changing Perceptions of Economic Policy*. New York: Methuen, pp. 152–193.

Watson, Richard (1956). 'The Tariff Revolution: A Study of Shifting Party Attitudes'. *Journal of Politics*. 18, 4, pp. 678–701.

Weingast, Barry (1979). 'A Rational Choice Perspective on Congressional Norms'. *American Journal of Political Science*. 23, 2, pp. 245–262.

Weinstein, James (1968). *The Corporate Ideal in the Liberal State, 1900–1918*. Boston: Beacon Press.

Wiebe, Robert (1962). *Businessmen and Reform: A Study of the Progressive Movement*. Chicago: Quadrangle.

Wiebe, Robert (1967). *The Search for Order, 1877–1920*. New York: Hill and Wang.

Wilkinson, Joe R. (1960). *Politics and Trade Policy*. Washington: Public Affairs Press.

Yergin, Daniel (1977). *Shattered Peace: The Origins of the Cold War and the National Security State*. Boston: Houghton Mifflin.

The International Spectator
Volume XXIV, No 3/4 July-December 1989

Institutional Structure and Time Horizon in a Simple Model of the Political Economy: The Lowi Effect

H. Keith Hall and Douglas R. Nelson

Institutional structure affects political process and, via that mechanism, political outcomes. All but the most religious structuralists and individualists have come to a new recognition of the fundamental role played by institutions in social processes.[1] There have been two major responses to this recognition. From the structuralist side has come a renewed commitment to the structurally focused case study.[2] This work emphasizes the importance of institutionally situated elites in responding to changes in domestic and international social structures. Given the case study orientation, it is not surprising that the interaction of very specific institutionally located elites becomes a major concern of these studies. From the individualist side has come the attempt to identify the effect of institutional structure on collective behaviour, as well as the attempt to identify 'institution-free' properties of collective behaviour.[3] This literature tends to operate under very general definitions of both individual preference and institutional structure.

This paper proposes an approach which is, in some loose sense, intermediate between these two approaches: endogenous economic policy modeling. Endogenous policy models attempt an explicit representation of the processes that generate payoffs to political activity in a general political-economic equilibrium.[4] The simplest form of this approach assumes that citizen preferences over economic policy are strictly determined by their relationship to the economy. While most research of this type has assumed a very simple institutional structure (direct referendum/lobbying), alternative institutional assumptions are now receiving some attention. This paper develops a formal link between the institutionalist and individualist theory by illustrating the effect of institutional structure on the incentives to po-

litical action. Since the results yield a typology similar to that observed in Lowi's now classic work (1964, 1972) linking institutionalized policy types to political action, this will be referred to as the *Lowi effect*.

The first section of the paper presents a brief discussion of the literature growing out of Lowi's work to establish the categories and the intuition behind the more formal analysis. This is followed by an overview of the endogenous policy approach to modelling political-economic interaction. The bulk of the paper is a step-by-step geometric development of the simplest endogenous policy model (a 2×2 economy with a passive register state). The paper concludes with a discussion of the derived Lowi-effect and some suggestions for future research.

---

[1] This does not imply that it is a new phenomenon. Social analysts have recognized the importance of institutional structure for as long as records of social analysis exist. The current wave of 'neo-institutionalism' in economics and political science, however, is a response to a rather long period from the late 1960s during which rather strong forms of structuralism prevailed in political science and sociology, at the same time that 'economics imperialism' brought strong forms of institution-free, individualist models from economics into political science and sociology. For a useful discussion of the 'new institutionalism', see March and Olsen (1984).

[2] Two recent collective efforts are exemplary: the work of Theda Skocpol and her colleagues on the development of the welfare state in the US, especially during the New Deal (Skocpol 1980; Skocpol and Finegold 1982; Skocpol and Ikenberry 1983; Orloff and Skocpol 1984; Amenta and Skocpol 1988) and the work of Ikenberry *et al.* reported in 'The State in American Foreign Economic Policy' (*International Organization* 1988).

[3] The seminal work on institutional structure is that of Shepsle (1979). A convenient survey of this growing literature can be found in Shepsle (1986). With regard to the institution-free aspects of social choice, see the important paper by McKelvey (1986).

[4] By *general* political-economic equilibrium, it is meant that (subject to behavioural and institutional assumptions) the level of political intervention and the state of the economy are endogenously determined. Comparative static analysis involves evaluating the effect of changes in the political and economic parameters of the model on the level of intervention and the state variables of the economy.

H. Keith Hall is Professor of Economics at the University of Arkansas. *Douglas Nelson* is Professor of Economics at Syracuse University, Syracuse, New York.

A Simple Model of the Political Economy: The Lowi Effect

The Lowi Literature

Lowi's typology seems to have emerged from an attempt to reconcile the apparently contradictory conclusions of the voluminous case study literature on politics at the local and national levels.[5] Lowi argues that much of the debate between various schools of thought on politics in liberal democratic systems (pluralists vs. elitists vs. state autonomists) arises from the erroneous notion that there is a single, best model of the political process. Instead, Lowi argues that there is a small number of 'arenas of power', each of which is characterized by its own distinctive politics. That is, the attributes of a policy tend to induce characteristic patterns of politics, or to use Lowi's own simple formula: 'policies determine politics' (Lowi 1972, p. 299).

In the 1964 review of Bauer, Pool and Dexter, the arenas of power analysis takes the form of an empirical observation: the recognition that there are several distinctive patterns of political interaction coexisting in the American political system and that these patterns relate to the major schools of interpretation of that system. Specifically, Lowi argues that there are three arenas of power, each yielding characteristic politics and research traditions: distributive (elitist), regulatory (pluralist) and redistributive (state autonomist).

Distributive policies 'are characterized by the ease with which they can be disaggregated unit by small unit, each unit more or less in isolation from the other unit and from any general rule. These are policies that are virtually not policies at all but are highly individualized decisions that only by accumulation can be called a policy. They are policies in which the indulged and the deprived, the loser and the recipient, need never come into direct confrontation'.

Regulatory policies 'are distinguishable from distributive in that in the short run the regulatory decision involves a direct choice as to who will be indulged and who deprived... So, while implementation is firm-by-firm and case-by-case, policies cannot be disaggregated to the level of the individual or the single firm (as in distribution), because individual decisions must be made by application of a general rule and therefore become interrelated within the broader standards of law'.

Redistributive policies 'are like regulatory policies in the sense that relations among broad categories of private individuals are involved and, hence, individual decisions must be interrelated... [But the] categories of impact are much broader, approaching social classes'.

In common with all empirical typologies, the arenas of power typology is a pre-theoretic construction. Abstracting from nihilistic assertions that reality is simply too complex to support any useful generalizations (e.g. Greenberg *et al.* 1977), research based on empirical typologies takes two general forms: attempts to apply the typology in additional empirical work[6] and attempts to develop the theoretical foundations in more detail. With regard to theoretical development, two major bodies of research can be identified; attempts to provide firmer theoretical foundations for the typology[7] and attempts to derive the properties of political activity within a given category.[8] The former issue will be dealt with in this paper.

The choice theoretic foundations of the Lowi effect are quite straightforward. Individuals are as-

---

[5] The first significant presentation of Lowi's approach is in a review of Bauer, Pool and Dexter's (1963) massive study of the politics leading up to passage of the 1962 Trade Expansion Act. In that book, Bauer *et al.* seem to argue against both pluralist and elitist schools of research by demonstrating the independence of congressmen. In particular, they reject the findings of Schattschneider's (1935) earlier study of the politics of the tariff. In his review, Lowi suggests that there is no fundamental conflict between these two classic studies, because trade policy was in the process of shifting arenas (from the distributive to the regulatory). In that review Lowi refers to a larger project that examines a wider range of policies. For the original presentation, see Lowi (1964). Later presentations that attempt to extend the analysis both theoretically and empirically can be found in Lowi (1970, 1972, 1985).

[6] Although this paper is concerned with theoretical development of the Lowi effect, it should be noted that the arenas of power typology has given rise to an extensive empirical literature. With regard to American domestic politics, the arenas typology has been used to organize research on: the presidency (Spitzer 1979); the executive bureaucracy (Lowi 1985); and most extensively, the Congress (Vogler 1890; Ripley and Franklin 1984). In addition to these applications, the arenas typology has also been used to organize research on foreign policy (Lowi 1967; Brewer 1973; Zimmerman 1973; Walker and McGowan 1982) and comparative politics (Smith 1969; Peters *et al.* 1977).

The wide acceptance and use of the arenas typology in empirical research has two important implications for attempts to extend the theoretical foundations of the typology. First, even though there are considerable difficulties in applying the typology, scholars and practitioners seem to think that it taps an important aspect of political life. Second, the broad application (across time, institutions and countries) suggests that some general process is at work. It is this general element that theoretical treatments like the one reported here to begin to capture.

[7] In addition to research on the theoretical foundations of the Lowi effect, there is also a closely related body of research that uses the arenas of power categories but returns to the more traditional question of the effect of political organization on policy type. We refer to the linkages between interest structure and political patterns detailed in this research as the *Salisbury effect* in recognition of the original contributions by Robert Salisbury, modelled below, from which much of this work arises (Salisbury 1968, 1970). Additional work on the Salisbury effect can be found in Hayes (1978, 1981) and Kofford (1987).

Research on the Lowi effect assumes that choice among arenas is somehow independent of (and certainly prior to) the organization of social interests; research on the Salisbury effect assumes that organization is logically prior to issue identification. These two are clearly intimately related, but they imply very different modelling programs. The first seeks to find optimal organization subject to given policy attributes; the latter seeks to find optimal policy attributes subject to given political organization.

[8] This research is effectively a search for more complete microfoundations for the Lowi effect. This research has tended to focus on distributive issues (Weingast 1979; Fiorina 1981; Shepsle and Weingast 1981; Niou and Ordeshook 1985); and regulatory issues (Fiorina 1982, 1986; McCubbins 1985; McCubbins and Schwartz 1984; Moe 1985, 1987).

H. Keith Hall, Douglas R. Nelson

sumed to be rational in terms of both economic and political calculation. That is, individuals are assumed to prefer policies that yield a net balance of benefits (economic rationality) and to engage in political action only when the returns to that action are positive (political rationality). Policies are given institutional form in a piece of legislation that specifies a distribution of costs and benefits, as well as the terms of access to the costs and benefits. Once a policy is institutionalized, Lowi conjectures that the institutional form tends to induce a characteristic pattern of politics. The causality runs strictly from policy (institutional form) to politics (patterns of activity).[9]

Lowi's (1972) own attempt to provide theoretical motivation for his empirical typology remains the most significant contribution of this sort. Generalizing his earlier discussion of the attributes of the arenas, Lowi argues that an issue can be characterized in terms of the applicability and likelihood of coercion expected from adoption of the policy in question. In his later work, Lowi drops the emphasis on coercion in favor of the more general 'impact' (e.g. Lowi 1985). Instead of applicability of coercion, this paper follows Lowi in emphasizing *form of intended impact*, which refers to whether the policy is expected to operate on individual conduct or on the environment of conduct. That is, whether decisions on individual cases reflect the operation of discretion or rules on the part of the decision-making entity.[10] In a sense, discretion permits the relevant

decision makers to treat each individual independently of any other, while rules create groups by aggregating individuals on the basis of some shared attribute or behaviour.[11]

While the rules vs. discretion dimension seems to be a fairly constant part of the literature on the Lowi effect, the other dimension has proven to be somewhat problematic. As with the previous dimension, Lowi's approach has been to focus directly on the statutory content of the legislation/regulation that gives a policy its official form. Thus, generalizing his earlier emphasis on applicability of coercion, Lowi's (1985) later work has emphasized the degree to which a policy works through incentives or constraints. That is, he asks whether the policy is implemented primarily by allocating benefits ('powers or privileges') or imposing costs ('obligations or positions').

A closely related approach stresses the distinction between policies with symmetrical and asymmetrical effects (Zimmerman 1973). Whereas Lowi emphasizes a policy's statutory content in identifying arenas, Zimmerman emphasizes the consequences of a policy by focusing on the relative distribution of costs and benefits across citizens. Thus, a policy with symmetrical effects treats all citizens equally, while a policy with asymmetrical effects distributes costs and/or benefits unequally. As with Lowi's analysis, the actual causal mechanism linking policy-type to behaviour is never analyzed in detail. The discussions in the relevant texts suggest two such mechanisms: information costs and collective action costs.[12] With regard to the former, it is implicitly assumed that symmetrically distributed costs may be so small that it would not be rational to notice them (i.e. the costs of learning about them are higher that the costs imposed by the policy). Even if individual costs rise above the level at which they are noticed when symmetrically distributed, there may be collective action problems in organizing for effective political action.

The difficulty with this construction is that is fails to recognize that asymmetries may be of various types, each with distinctive behavioural implications.

---

[9] It might be useful to note the relationship of this logic to that of the Salisbury effect. If it is assumed that there exists an *a priori* issue-cleavage pattern, and if politicians are simply passive registers of citizen demand (i.e. there is no political entrepreneurship), then there is no real difference between the Lowi and Salisbury effects. The first assumption asserts that one attribute of a political issue (prior to its institutional definition) is a fixed distribution of preferences over that issue. The second assumption asserts that politicians are unable to deviate from the outcomes established by that distribution of preferences. Under these assumptions, identification of an issue implies knowledge of the underlying pattern of political conflict and, thus, of the political arena. Another way of saying this is that issue is not *per se* important to the identification of arena, what is important is pattern of conflict. This logic is probably most useful in comparative political studies where it might be assumed that there is some pattern of conflict characteristic to a given country, which defines a central tendency in the politics of that country (Smith 1969; Peters *et al.* 1977; Nelson 1983; Rogowski 1988).

The Lowi effect, by its strict emphasis on the causal link from policy to politics, permits an independent analysis of the politics of issue institutionalization and transformation. This makes it possible to incorporate notions of the relatively autonomous state into a model with explicit micro-foundations.

[10] The rules-discretion dimension will, at first, seem quite different from Lowi's 'form of intended impact' dimension. This problem, however, can be easily clarified. Virtually all of the literature on the Lowi effect seeks to explain the effect by reference to the behaviour of rational individuals. Thus, all policies ultimately work through individual conduct. Similarly, all policies (no matter how individually oriented) involve some reference to more-or-less general principles (i.e. attempts to define an environment of conduct). The real issue is whether the legislation/regulation that embodies the policy is seen to permit an individual relationship to the political/regulatory process that generates costs and benefits, or whether that legislation/regulation permits only

a collective relationship. The former case requires discretion on the part of the relevant decision maker, the latter requires the absence of discretion.

[11] Note that in this analysis the term 'individual' is used to refer to the smallest effective unit of analysis. For example, if households and firms are the basic units of analysis, the rule must treat classes that include many households (e.g. a community) or firms (e.g. an industry). However, in the general equilibrium model developed later in the paper, although firms and households are the atomic elements of the analysis, the assumption that consumers possess identical tastes and that all firms in an industry possess a common production function implies that the industry is the smallest effective unit of analysis.

With regard to its impact on the incentives to individual action, the authors have recently shown that this distinction is formally quite similar to that between a private good and a public good (Hall and Nelson 1987).

[12] These are both subcases of the more general phenomenon of *transaction costs* (Arrow 1974; Williamson 1975, 1985).   **155**

A Simple Model of the Political Economy: The Lowi Effect

Once it is recognized that virtually all policies imply both benefits and costs, the importance of the distribution of benefits and costs becomes equally apparent. Drawing on the work of Wilson (1974), one might ask whether the benefits of a policy are distributed among citizens in a concentrated or a diffused manner, and made similar considerations about the costs. [13] Introducing these considerations along with the rules-discretion distinction yields what might be called a Lowi-Wilson typology.

Benefits Are:	Political Mechanism Operates Under			
	Rules		Discretion	
	Costs are:		Costs are:	
	Diffused	Concentr.	Diffused	Concentr.
Diffused	I	II	V	VI
Concentrated	III	IV	VII	VIII

Figure 1: Lowi-Wilson Typology of Policy Induced Arenas.

Assuming that individuals are rational in the sense that they support policies yielding a net balance of benefits and oppose policies yielding a net balance of costs, and that concentrated benefits or costs are more likely to stimulate political action than diffused benefits or costs, this typology allows for identification of several of the characteristic arenas of power. In arenas 1-4, the policy is administered under a general rule which treats individuals as members of a class on the basis of some relevant attribute.

1. *Public good*: The government provides many goods and services that are widely available (i.e. the benefits are diffused). Whether or not such goods are, in fact, non-excludable is not relevant. The terms of the policy define access to a broad class (e.g. all citizens). The funding of such goods and services (i.e. the costs) are provided out of general revenues and, thus, are also diffused. Research on the theory of collective action suggests that such policies are unlikely to stimulate strong political action on either side (i.e. for or against). [14] As a result, such issues are expected to be dominated either by the executive or by political entrepreneurs. In either case, the politics are expected to be very public.

2. *Regulatory* (Type I): Like the public good case, a good or service is being provided whose benefits are widely diffused. Unlike that case, however, the costs are clearly seen to fall on some identifiable class. In this case the rule identifies the class of individuals or behaviours that bears the cost. This is the general case of regulation in the public interest. Thus, legislation regulating the introduction of pollutants into the environment is seen to produce the diffused benefit of cleaner air, with concentrated costs to polluters and potential polluters. Like the public good case, the executive and/or entrepreneurs would be expected to play a major role in promoting such policy, while opposition is expected to be self-organizing.

3. *Regulatory* (Type II): Type II regulation is just the reverse of Type I regulation — the benefits of the policy are concentrated, but the costs are diffused. As in the Chicago School accounts of regulation, beneficiaries are easily organized to capture the regulatory policy to the detriment of those who bear the (diffused) costs of the policy. In this case, organized interests are expected to dominate the political process. [15] Subgovernments (or 'iron triangles') made up of committee elites, bureaucratic elites, and beneficiary elites are expected to manage Type II regulatory politics in a low visibility fashion.

4. *Redistributive*: In this case, the costs and benefits are concentrated such that the rule under which the policy takes place is clearly seen to redistribute value (e.g. wealth) from one class of people to another. Both gainers and losers would be expected to be effectively organized for political action in this case, and, as a result, substantial political conflict would be expected. Instead of the low politics of a subgovernment, one would expect to find high politics (i.e. President-floor-peak association).

Where the previous policy arenas are defined by the presence of some form of general rule under

---

[13] Alternatively attention could be focussed on relative degrees of information about the policy between gainers and losers, or relative degrees of access to the political system. While both of these are distinct from each other and from the relative concentration of benefits and costs, they are all closely enough related that the additional analytical leverage from their explicit inclusion in the analysis would not be sufficient to justify the substantial increase in complexity.

[14] The public good case illustrates well the importance of both perception and entrepreneurship in the Lowi literature. With regard to perception, it is important to note that the theory does not imply that a public good cannot have concentrated costs or benefits, but that the policy is accepted as being about something

other than those costs and benefits. Consider 'national security'. National security is clearly a public good in the sense that all members of the class 'citizen' consume it. There are, however, concentrated benefits (e.g. defense contractors) and concentrated costs (citizen soldiers).

As a result of its attributes, there may be no natural constituency for a policy of the public good type. This suggests the importance of political entrepreneurs with regard to these issues. Such entrepreneurs may be 'sincere' in the sense that they genuinely believe in the importance of the issue, or they may be 'strategic' in the sense that they are attempting to defuse conflict by hiding the interest of some constituent under the public interest label. Which of these is the case is of fundamental importance for predicting policy arenas (i.e. the Salisbury effect), but it is immaterial to the effect of policy on politics (i.e. the Lowi effect). [15] It is interesting to note that the regulatory life cycle hypothesis (Bernstein 1955) simply implies a temporal shift from Type I to Type II regulation. This, in turn, implies a substantial shift in the organization of politics: from public, entrepreneurial politics on the floor of the legislature; to private, subgovernmental politics.

H. Keith Hall, Douglas R. Nelson

which policy is administered, in arenas 5-8 the policy is perceived to operate through the allocation of costs and/or benefits on an individual basis.

5. *Routine constituent/administrative service*: In this case the government's relationship to civil society is defined in such a way that the relationship is highly individualized (reflecting a high degree of discretion). However, while the benefits of this relationship are seen as specific to individuals, they are open to the citizenry as a whole (diffused benefits). Furthermore, the costs of each act of accommodation are seen to be spread across the whole system (diffused costs). Research on Congress suggests that a substantial amount of a Congress-person's time is spent performing a wide range of small services for constituents (Fiorina 1977). These benefits are diffused in the sense that they are available to virtually everyone at low individual costs, while the costs are diffused both because the direct costs of any individual act of constituent service are low and are covered by general revenues.[16] We would expect the politics of such issues to be very non-conflictual, rarely involving floor action or high level executive officials.

6. *Adjudicative regulations*: In this case, concentrated costs are imposed on individuals in such a way that substantial discretion permits the relevant decision makers to distinguish between individuals in the allocation of such costs, but the benefits are diffused across the entire community.

7. *Distributive*: In this case, concentrated benefits are distributed to individuals, while the costs are diffused across the entire (tax paying) community. The politics in this case are characterized by log-rolling. The executive and the floor of the legislature are expected to be dominated by the operation of committees and organized pressure by the beneficiaries of the policy. Unlike Type II regulatory issues, however, the beneficiaries do not form an institutionally organized group; they are a 'coalition of uncommon interest'.

8. *Adjudicative redistribution*: In this case, the relevant authority identifies both the individual to be accommodated and the individual to bear the cost. The political effect of this sort of policy is to drive a wedge into an existing group — between those expecting to be accommodated and those expecting to be disadvantaged.[17]

---

[16] Note that the 'good' in question here is the intervention. The testimony of one's Representative in an International Trade Commission hearing is a good independent of the legal structure that yields outcomes with an economic value. That is, intervention in such a proceeding is independent of how one's Representative voted on the legislation regulating, say, Countervailing Duty proceedings.

[17] One clear example would be an industrial policy premised on the notion of 'picking winners'. In this case, some state agency is expected to identify some subset of an industry for discriminatory treatment, while the remainder of the industry expects to be forced out of business either by state fiat or by competition.

Since a primary goal of this paper is to present the endogenous policy approach in its simplest possible form, only the cases involving concentrated benefits will be analyzed. In these cases it is not unreasonable (at least as a first approximation) to abstract from activist political entrepreneurs (within the state and/or the polity). As with much work in the pluralist tradition, this simplification makes it possible to treat 'the state' as a passive register of effective demand by citizens and to focus on the equilibrium levels of political activity in the polity.[18]

The Endogenous Policy Approach to Political Economic Analysis

Given some reasonably coherent social entity (e.g. a nation-state), political economic analysis seeks to understand the interaction between its civil society, state and economy. Such an understanding can, conceivably, be advanced in a variety of ways, among them: philosophical reflection, case studies of particular policy choices and comparative analysis across countries and/or policy choices. Formal modelling is one form of philosophical reflection and the endogeneous policy approach to political economic analysis is one formal modelling strategy.

The strategy of endogenous policy modelling is deceptively simple. The actions of the state are taken to be a function of effective citizen demands.[19] These demands are, in turn, functions of citizen preferences and the opportunity cost of political activity; preferences are taken to be determined by the economic attributes of the citizen (tastes, factor ownership and industrial affiliation). The system is closed via the effect of policy on citizen interests as determined by their position in the economy (i.e. their attributes). On first reading, this structure may appear to be too simple to yield valuable insights. A moment of reflection, however, should lead one to the realization that it is precisely this sort of logic which is lurking just below the surface of the great majority of treatments of political-economic interaction. One of the great virtues of formal modelling is that it forces users to face up to the assumption structure necessary for their conclusions.[20]

---

[18] See Nelson (1988) for a discussion of alternative assumptions about the state in the context of endogenous economic policy models.

[19] Two points of clarification may prove useful here. First, although this paper operates with a minimal (passive register) state, a wide variety of assumptions about the function that transforms effective citizen demand into state action are possible. Second, it should be noted that the relevant political force here is *effective* political demand, not the more general notion of political preference. Since political action is costly and individual resources are finite, individuals are constrained in the combinations of economic and political activity available to them.

[20] Formal analysis often has the salutary effect of demonstrating the 'non-simplicity' of widely held notions. Perhaps the most striking of these relates to the general impossibility of social choice functions in minimally complex choice environments (Arrow 1951; McKelvey 1976; Schofield 1985). The point of these findings is (perhaps) not that there is no necessary link between collective preferences and social outcomes, but that the link is not as straightforward (i.e. simple) as many thought/hoped it was.

A Simple Model of the Political Economy: The Lowi Effect

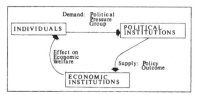

Figure 2

Since the goal of this paper is illustrative as well as analytical, an extremely simple set of behavioural, technological, and institutional assumptions is adopted. This strategy not only permits a direct focus on political economic interdependence in a clear and intuitively appealing way, but the fact that this simple structure is rich enough to generate the Lowi effect suggests the value of endogenous policy modelling as an instrument of political economic discourse.

The basic units of analysis in this work are citizens and firms. As has already been suggested, the former are defined in terms of three basic attributes: tastes (i.e. preferences over available consumption goods); factor ownership (the services of these factors are employed by firms as inputs into the production of consumption goods); and industry (i.e. which industry employs the services of a factor of production). The sole source of individual income is the sale of the services of factors of production (called the 'return' to a factor). Along with the price of each consumer good, factor income defines a set of affordable consumption bundles from which an individual consumer may choose. One of the primarily behavioural assumptions presented here is that individuals are economically rational utility maximizers.[21] Primarily for geometric tractability, most of the exposition in this paper proceeds under the assumption that there are just two goods (X and Y) and two factors of production (capital and labour). For reasons discussed later in the description of the basic model of the economy, each individual is classified as either an owner of capital (K) or labour (L), but not both, and an individual's capital can be employed in only one industry at a time. Finally, it will be assumed that labour is instantaneously mobile between sectors, but that once capital has been located in one of the industries, it cannot be instantaneously relocated to the other industry.[22]

Firms are very simple entities in this model. Like consumers, firms are assumed to be economically

rational, where rationality is defined as profit maximization. Each firm is characterized by a production function which specifies how the services of capital and labour can be combined to produce outputs of X or Y. Specifically, it will be assumed that production in each industry is characterized by constant returns to scale and positive but diminishing returns to both factors of production.[23] Unessential complications relating to specialization will be avoided by assuming that some of each good is always produced. Finally, it will be assumed that firms in each industry produce with the same production function, but that Y production relative to X production at all relative product prices.[24]

The following are major institutional assumptions. In the economy, it is assumed that there is a complete system of property rights and a complete system of markets for goods and factors of production, and that perfect competition obtains in all markets. With regard to the state, it is assumed that state choices are a function of the balance of effective political demand. That is, the state is a passive register of effective demand. This will be seen to be a lobbying model, not an electoral model. The analysis is further simplified by assuming that the state possesses only a single policy instrument: the capacity to change relative product prices by some combination of taxes and/or subsidies.[25]

Having defined terms and outlined assumptions, the model itself can now be developed. First a model of the economy is developed in some detail, with particular reference to the effects of state intervention on factor returns in the short run and in the long run. This emphasis follows from the fact that, given the assumptions about individuals, the welfare effects of government intervention operate through their effects on factor returns. Furthermore, the time horizon relative to the given issue will affect the organization of interests via the opportunities for adjustment to the policy change in the short and long run. From there the cost of influencing state action is introduced into the analysis. The opportunity to engage in political activity (yielding some direct economic benefit) at a positive cost im-

---

[21] In fact, a very strong form of rationality is used: individuals are assumed to be strictly self-regarding. That is, utility is derived solely from personal consumption. Alternative assumptions are possible, but for the purposes of this paper they add considerable complexity without additional benefit.
[22] This will be the basis of the distinction between the long run and the short run. That is, the long run is defined as the period in which all factors are mobile between sectors.

[23] More formally, it is assumed that production functions are linear homogeneous, twice differentiable and strictly quasi-concave, with positive first derivatives.
[24] This assumption means that the K/L ratio in Y production is always greater than the K/L ratio in X production.
[25] The standard practice is adopted here of assuming that the tax-cum-subsidy policy is constructed in such a way that it has no effect on relative product prices.
Given the technological and institutional assumptions made, the limitation of intervention to price instruments is not as limiting as it seems. It turns out that under constant returns and perfect competition there is a direct equivalence between price and quantity instruments. If the analysis permitted a more active role for the state, or some other political entrepreneurs, the limitation to a single instrument (of any kind) would be a considerably more significant simplification.

H. KEITH HALL, DOUGLAS R. NELSON

plies that economically rational individuals will allocate their resources between economic and political activity (i.e. between the production of goods and lobbying to influence government policy).[26]

One of the fundamental results illustrated in this paper is that once lobbying costs are introduced into the model, the institutional form through which state output is delivered has an effect on the organization of lobbying activity and, thus, on its level. The intuition behind this result is quite straightforward. Suppose a distinction is made, as in the discussion of the Lowi effect presented above, between delegation under a general rule and delegation with discretion (or, more appropriately, direct accommodation). In the former case, the output (loosely speaking) is like a public good in that it applies in the same form to all members of a given class, while in the latter case the output is (again, loosely speaking) like a private good. As a result, not only will there be some tendency to underproduce the public good on standard collective action logic, but the opposition will form in a more coherent fashion than in the privatized output case.

The Basic Model of the Economy

In this section the model of the economy is presented in somewhat more detail. As suggested above, it is a two sector, two factor general equilibrium model.[27] A particular goal of this section is to discuss the use of a graphic technique for depicting both a short-run and a long-run equilibrium in our simple economy. This technique will be used in the following section to discuss the real income effects of a price change in the economy brought about by a political process (the price change is, therefore, assumed to be the 'outcome' of the political process). The discussion will concentrate on the simple two sector version of this model, since the results may be presented graphically and the important effects of political outputs (price changes) on the distribution of income in the economy are preserved when generalized to any number of goods.

Given the assumptions, profit maximization will lead to the result that an industry will hire additional units of each factor of production up to the point

that the revenue generated by the additional output equals the cost of the factors. That is, each factor will be employed until its value of marginal product (price of the output times the marginal productivity of the factor) equals its cost (factor return). It will be recalled that in the short run, labour (L) is assumed to be fully mobile between industries while capital (K) is assumed to be fully immobile and, therefore, 'specific' to an industry. In the long run, capital is also fully mobile. Since labour is mobile in the short run, it will shift between industries until its return, w, is the same in each industry. Since capital is immobile in the short run, its returns in the two industries, r_x and r_y, may differ in the short run. These short-run equilibrium conditions are summarized below:

$$V_x = w \qquad (1.1)$$
$$V_y = w \qquad (1.2)$$
$$R_x = r_x \qquad (1.3)$$
$$R_y = r_y \qquad (1.4)$$

where V_x, V_y, R_x and R_y are the value of marginal products for labour and capital (respectively) in each industry. Over a long-run time period capital will be mobile and, therefore, will also shift between industries until factor returns are equalized as follows:

$$r_x = r_y. \qquad (1.5)$$

Labour market equilibrium

Graphically, we may represent short-run equilibrium in the labour market (where labour shifts between industries until returns are equalized as in equations 1.1 and 1.2 above) as follows in Figure 3.

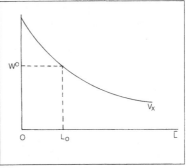

Figure 3

The value of marginal product of labour in industry X at each level of employment is represented by the height of the V_x curve. For any given cost of labour services, w, a profit maximizing industry **159**

[26] Bhagwati (1982) refers to 'directly productive' and 'directly unproductive' profit-seeking activities in making this distinction.
[27] This set up is standard in international trade theory and in much of public finance. The long-run version of the model is generally referred to as the Heckscher-Ohlin-Samuelson (H-O-S) model by trade theorists, and the short-run version as the specific-factors or Ricardo-Viner (R-V) model. These two models are fully described in the international trade theory literature. For a basic presentation of these models (both mathematically and graphically) and their implications for international trade theory, see appendix A of Ethier (1988). For a more detailed survey of these models in international trade, see Jones and Neary (1984). For applications to public finance, see McClure (1971a, b, 1975).

A Simple Model of the Political Economy: The Lowi Effect

will employ labour until the height of the V_x curve equals the given return. For example, if the cost of labour is w^0, then employment by industry X would be L^0. Letting $\overline{L}$ be the total amount of labour in the economy, full employment requires that the labour not used in industry X be employed in industry Y. The distance ($\overline{L} - L^0$) would, therefore, equal the employment of labour in industry Y. In Figure 4, we have added the value of margi-

total revenue of an industry equals the total payments to the two factors of production,[29] $wL + rK$, and the area of the rectangle below the equilibrium wage equals the total payments to labour, wL, then the area below the value of marginal product curve and above the wage represents the total payments to specific factors, rK. These areas are shown in Figure 5 below for both industry X and industry Y.

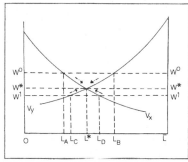

Figure 4

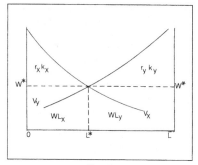

Figure 5

nal product curve for labour in industry Y using $\overline{L}$ as the origin and movement left as increases in employment of labour in industry Y.

If the cost of labour is w^0, then the distance L_A would equal the profit maximizing level of employment by industry X while ($\overline{L} - L_B$) would equal the profit maximizing level of employment of L in industry Y. The distance ($L_B - L_A$) would, therefore, represent unemployment of labour at w^0 and since it is greater than zero it would result in downward pressure on the wage. Similarly, given a wage of w^1, a labour shortage equal to ($L_D - L_C$) would result, creating upward pressure on the wage. The value of w at the intersection of V_x and V_y, w^*, therefore represents the only return to labour that will result in full employment of labour under conditions of profit maximization. In this equilibrium industry X would employ L^* units of labour and industry Y would employ ($\overline{L} - L^*$) units of labour.[28]

If industry output is assumed to be zero units of labour hired, then the area under a value of marginal product curve equals the total revenue in that industry. Further, since the assumption of perfect competition in the output market ensures that the

Short-run factor returns

A graphic representation of the short-run equilibrium returns to the immobile factor in each industry (as opposed to the total payments to each)[30] will be made, based on the fact that the assumption of perfect competition in all markets implies that the price of the output in an industry will always equal its per unit cost of production. Concentrating for the moment on industry X, this may be represented algebraically as follows:

$$P_x = \left\{ \frac{L_x}{X} \right\} w + \left\{ \frac{K_x}{X} \right\} r_x. \qquad (2)$$

Because of the further assumption of constant returns to scale (linear homogeneous) production functions in all industries, the factor to output ratios (representing the units of labour needed per unit of output) are independent of the level of output in each industry (by the definition of constant returns to scale production) and will, therefore, be functions of w and r_x alone. For any given output price (and, therefore, any given per unit cost of production) there will, therefore, be a functional relationship be-

---

[28] Note that the assumption of quasi-concave production functions leads to the result that both values of marginal product curves are downward sloping which ensures a unique equilibrium allocation of labour between the two industries.

[29] Note that although there is zero economic profit with perfect competition in output markets, rK may still represent entrepreneurial profit (accounting not economic profit).

[30] See equations 1.3 and 1.4 above.

H. KEITH HALL, DOUGLAS R. NELSON

tween w and r_x consistent with zero profit. Further, this relationship will be dependent only upon the technology of the industry and will be unaffected by the mobility of the factors between industries.[31] For a given price of output in industry X, feasible combinations of w and r_x may be mapped out consistent with zero profit (and, therefore, reflecting the efficient use of factor inputs for a given cost of production). The resulting curve, which will be labelled C_x, is generally referred to as an isocost curve for industry X. Similarly, the isocost curve for industry Y, C_y, may be derived. Both curves, for a given pair of output prices, may be seen in Figure 6.

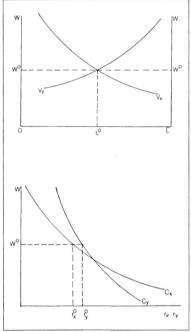

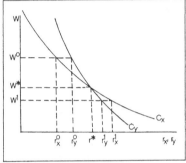

Figure 6

Note that rearrangement of equation (2) above will show that the absolute value of the slope of either curve at a given point will equal the equilibrium capital to labour ratio in that industry.[32] Once the return to labour, w, is determined in the labour market (as in the value of marginal product diagram in Figure 4), the isocost curves of Figure 6 will show the short-run equilibrium returns to capital in each industry, r_x and r_y, completing the description of the short-run economy. The labour market and isocost curve diagrams are shown together in Figure 7 where w^0, r_x^0, and r_y^0 represent short-run equilibrium returns to labour and the two specific factors for a given pair of output prices and value of marginal product curves.

Long-run factor returns

In the long-run time period, capital is mobile be-

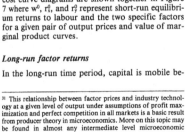

Figure 7

tween industries and will be attracted to the industry with the higher return (industry X if $r_x > r_y$, or industry Y if $r_y > r_x$). As capital flows into (out of) an industry, its marginal productivity will decline (increase), driving down (up) the returns in that industry. This will continue until the returns to capital in each industry are equalized, eliminating the incentive for the movement.[33] Further, as capital flows into (out of) an industry, the marginal productivity of labour in that industry and, therefore, its value of marginal product will increase (decline). This will then cause a shift in the employment of labour until the returns to the labour are equalized between industries.[34] This results in a unique combination of returns to labour and capital in both in-

---

[31] This relationship between factor prices and industry technology at a given level of output under assumptions of profit maximization and perfect competition in all markets is a basic result from producer theory in microeconomics. More on this topic may be found in almost any intermediate level microeconomic textbook.
[32] Thus the assumption that Y is capital intensive relative to X is shown by the fact that C_y is steeper than C_x in Figure 6.

[33] See equation 1.5 above for a statement of this equilibrium condition. Neary (1978) presents an admirably clear discussion of the adjustments referred to in this paragraph.
[34] Note again that the assumption of quasi-concave production function in all industries is important in that it guarantees that the isocost curves cross only once. Therefore, there will be a unique pair of factor returns, w^* and r^*, that denote equal returns to factors in both industries.

A Simple Model of the Political Economy: The Lowi Effect

dustries that represents a long-run equilibrium in the economy. To illustrate this adjustment process, suppose that the economy begins in a short-run equilibrium situation at the intersection of V_x^0 and V_y^0 as in Figure 8.

services of factors of production. Thus, we identify actors in terms of their preferences over consumption of X and Y, and their ownership of either K or L.[36] Since individuals are seen to purchase goods and services at given price levels, P_x and P_y,

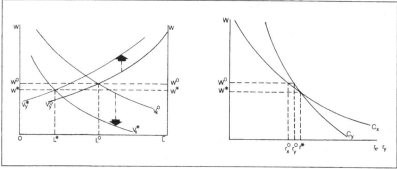

Figure 8

The short-run equilibrium returns to factors and allocation of labour between industries may all be seen in the diagram and are denoted with the null superscript. Since the return to capital in industry Y is greater than in industry X, capital will, over the long-run time period, shift from industry X to industry Y. As it does, the value of marginal product of labour curve in industry X shifts down as labour becomes less productive with less capital and the value of marginal product of labour curve in industry Y shifts up as labour in industry Y becomes more productive with more capital. The intersection of V_x and V_y in the long run will be determined by the technology of the two industries and will, therefore, eventually intersect at the same w* as the isocost curves do in the right hand diagram, with a long-run equilibrium return to capital of r*.[35]

Characterizing the political economic rationality of individuals

Since individuals are assumed to have preferences over government policy outcomes based only on the way the relevant policy affects their economic welfare, the possible economic welfare effects of different policy outcomes must be better described. In this simple model, individuals engage in only two types of behaviour: they consume goods and they sell the

and do so with a given amount of income, I, (derived from ownership of factors of production) each may, therefore, be seen to have preferences over different possible price and income levels that are representable by some real valued function $U(P_x,P_y,I)$. This 'indirect' welfare (or utility) function will reflect an inverse relationship between the price level in either industry and the welfare of the individual and a direct relationship between an individual's income level and welfare.[37]

Further, it is clear that if the income of an individual is increased by a greater percentage than the price level in either industry, then real income and, therefore, the welfare of an individual, as measured by this 'indirect' welfare function, is increased.[38] Using a 'hat' (ˆ) to denote a proportional change, this implies that an individual will support any government policy that proportionally increases income by a greater amount than the price level in either industry: $\hat{I} > \hat{P}_x$ and $\hat{I} > \hat{P}_y$. If a government

---

[35] Note the importance of the fact that the isocost curves for each industry are dependent solely upon the technology of the industry and are, therefore, unaffected by the shifting factors of production.

[36] Since capital will be assumed immobile in the short run it turns out to be important to note which industry employs a unit of capital.
[37] This is called the 'indirect' utility function in microeconomic theory since individual preferences are not assumed to be based directly upon prices and income, but upon the consumption of goods and services alone. For a given set of preferences over goods and services, the utility (or welfare) of an individual will, therefore, depend *indirectly* upon his/her income and the price levels of all goods in the economy.
[38] This follows from the fact that if real income is increased, then the buying power of the individual has increased in that the old purchases are still affordable while previously unaffordable bundles of goods are now attainable.

H. KEITH HALL, DOUGLAS R. NELSON

policy increases income by a greater percentage than the price level in one industry but not the other, then the preferences of the individual with regard to that policy are ambiguous. Specifically, support for such a policy will depend upon the consumption patterns of the individual. For example, if little good Y is consumed by the individual, then the fact that $\hat{P}_y > \hat{I}$ imposes little loss of welfare compared to the increased utility of the fact that $I > \hat{P}_x$.[39]

In order to simplify the determination of the income level of an individual (which is solely from ownership of factors of production and, therefore, dependent upon returns to factors owned), it is assumed that individual income flows from the returns to ownership of only one unit of either K or L.[40] Furthermore, with regard to ownership of capital, an individual will be involved with only one industry at a time. In the short run, therefore, a distinction may be made between an owner of capital in industry X, an owner of capital in industry Y and an owner of labour services. The indirect utility function of an individual will, therefore, have one of the following three forms: $U(P_x,P_y,r_xK)$, $U(P_x,P_y,r_yK)$, or $U(P_x,P_y,wL)$.[41] Further, income will change for each of these individuals through their factor returns: $\hat{I} = \hat{r}_x$, $\hat{I} = \hat{r}_y$, or $\hat{I} = \hat{w}$, respectively.

To sum up the neo-classical microeconomic view of an (economic and political) individual decision maker, if a government policy increases the returns to a factor by a proportionally greater amount than the price levels in both industries (or decreases returns proportionally less), then owners of that factor will unambiguously be better off. Conversely, if the returns to a factor increase proportionally less than both price levels (or decrease by a proportionally greater amount than both price levels), then owners of that factor will unambiguously be worse off. Also, if a factor return increases proportionally more than one price level but less than the other, then owners of that factor may or may not be better off since they may be consumers of the latter good.

Short-run Versus Long-run Effects of Price Changes

In order to examine the economic effects of politi-

cal outcomes on individuals, it will be assumed that policy outcomes affect only prices in an economy and do not affect the welfare of individuals directly. Of interest in the present work, therefore, is the effect of an exogenous change in the price level in an industry on the distribution of real income in the economy. It will be shown here that there are two distinct effects on real income in this model and, therefore, two distinct effects on individual welfare from a price change: a short-run and a long-run effect. Specifically, a price change will influence factor returns (and, therefore, individual welfare) at the industry level in the short run, but will cut across industries to the factor ownership level in a long-run time period.

Given the characterization of the foundations of political economic rationality in the previous section, the distinction between short-run and long-run results has an interesting implication for the formation of interest groups. Assuming that there are many more industries than factors of production,[42] when the time horizon over which political calculation is made is short, the gains from participation in the political process will fall to owners of an immobile factor in one industry at the expense of owners of immobile factors in other industries. Thus, as Lowi describes in distributive arenas, political action on behalf of a large number of relatively small, industry-specific interest groups would be expected. However, when the time horizon over which political calculation occurs is long, even when a political outcome increases the price level in a single industry, the benefits from participation will fall to a single factor, cutting across all industry prices. That is, in the case of two factors, either owners of labour will benefit at the expense of owners of capital, or owners of capital will benefit at the expense of owners of labour. Thus, as with Lowi's redistributive arenas, factor-based interest groups that cut across industries will form.

Short-run effects

Suppose the state acts to increase the price of industry X's output.[43] Since the value of marginal product of a good equals the output price times marginal productivity (unaffected by price change) the V_x curve will shift upward proportionally to the height of the curve (the V_y curve will, of course, re-

---

[39] This problem is encountered with the effects of relative price changes on the returns to labour in the model of the economy used (the specific factors model). For a discussion and partial solution to this problem, termed the 'neo-classical ambiguity', see Ruffin and Jones (1977).

[40] Though this assumption is mainly for convenience, its importance lies in that it eliminates the complication of individuals who may, due to a political outcome, simultaneously gain income from the ownership of units of one factor while losing income from the ownership of units of another. For this same reason, the capital of an individual will be assumed to be employed in one industry only. For a presentation of a model where similarly defined individuals are permitted to own both types of factors of production, see Mayer (1984).

[41] Note that K and L here refer to only one unit of capital and labour, respectively, and not industry totals.

[42] As this condition suggests, these results take on greater importance in a more 'realistic' model, i.e. one characterized by higher dimensionality than 2×2. While it is not a universally held opinion, the authors tend to believe that in the long run industries outnumber factors of production (probably by several orders of magnitude). That is, it is not too radical a simplification to suppose that basic factors can be limited to land, labour, capital and possibly human capital, while the number of industries can only be considered enormous.

[43] Note that any of the following analysis could be expressed in units of one of the two goods. In this case, an increase in the *relative* price of one good would represent either an increase in the dollar price of the good, or a decrease in the dollar price of the other good, or any combination of the two as long as the ratio of the prices increases.

A Simple Model of the Political Economy: The Lowi Effect

main unchanged). Since the isocost curve represents zero profit in the face of constant returns to scale, the C_x curve will shift outward proportionally to its distance along a ray from the origin (C_y is also unchanged). An example of these shifts is shown in Figure 9.

tion that r_y declines, as seen on the righthand side of Figure 9, the following is seen to hold:

$$\hat{P}_x > \hat{w} > \hat{P}_y (= 0) > \hat{r}_y.$$

Finally, again from the right side of Figure 9, it can

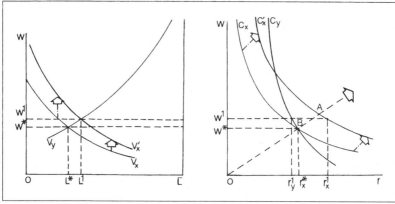

Figure 9

If V_x increases to V_x' and C_x increases to C_x', the equilibrium wage will increase from w^* to w^1, as seen in the labour market diagram on the left, and the returns to the two immobile factors may be read to be r_x^1 and r_y^1 in the isocost curves diagram on the right. Note that returns to all labour and to capital in industry X alone will increase while the returns to capital in industry Y will decline.

So far the analysis has been carried out in dollar terms, but as mentioned in the previous section, in order to discuss the welfare implications of a price change on the individual factor owner, it is necessary to examine the changes in proportional (percentage) terms. Beginning with the lefthand side of Figure 9, it can be seen that the proportional increase in the price level in industry X shifts the V_x curve up *proportionally* to its height. Therefore, at current employment, L^*, $\hat{P}_x$ will equal the distance between V_x and V_x' divided by the height of V_x. The wage will increase from w^* to w_1, so that $\hat{w}$ will equal the difference between w^1 and w^* divided by w^*. It can be seen that since w^* equals the height of V_x at L^*, the wage has risen proportionally less than the price of X.[44] Adding the trivial observa-

be seen that r_x increases by more than P_x. Since C_x shifts outward proportionally to the price change in industry X along a ray from the origin, the proportional change in P_x will equal the ratio of the distance AB/OB. Thus, a perpendicular dropped from A to the r axis would show a new return to capital in industry X, whose proportional increase is identical to that of the price level in industry X. It can, however, be seen that the new return (r_x^1) is greater than this. Thus, the complete result is:[45]

$$\hat{r}_x > \hat{P}_x > \hat{w} > \hat{P}_y > \hat{r}_y.$$

That is, when the government causes an increase in the relative price of one of the goods (X), the factor specific to that industry benefits unambiguously (i.e. experiences an unambiguous increase in welfare); the factor specific to the other sector (Y) loses unambiguously; and the effect on the mobile fac-

---

[44] The economic intuition behind this relationship is quite straightforward. If both L and K are fixed in the short run, an increase in the price of X raises the returns to both factors in the same proportion (by linear homogeneity of the production function and perfect competition). L, however, is mobile in the short run, so the incipient increase in wages in X causes labour

to move from Y to X until the labour market is back in equilibrium — at a wage whose proportional change is intermediate between the changes in P_x and P_y.

[45] The economic intuition behind this result is also quite straightforward. With zero profit, the benefits of an industry price increase must be distributed in the form of increased returns to the two factors of production. Since the proportional increase in the return to labour is below that of the industry price level, the returns to capital must be greater. Furthermore, since the return to labour in both industries goes up and there is no change in the price level in industry Y, the return to capital in that industry must decline.

H. Keith Hall, Douglas R. Nelson

tor's welfare is dependent on the mix of the two goods in consumption. Extensions of this result to policies that lower the relative price of Y or raise the relative price of X are trivial and can be left as exercises for the interested reader. The primary point is that this result yields clear predictions about the preferences of individuals over policies that affect the relative prices of products.

When policies are such as to induce short time horizons in political calculation, the gains from participation in the political process will fall to owners of an immobile factor in one industry at the expense of owners of immobile factors in other industries.[46] It would, therefore, be expected, as Lowi describes in distributive arenas, that relatively small interest groups will form on those political issues that affect a single industry and will be formed by owners of the specific capital employed in that industry. As for the mobile factor, those owners of the mobile factor with particular taste biases toward (or away from) goods or services from an affected industry, would tend to support government actions that increase (or decrease) the price level in that industry.

Long-run effects

The long-run effect of a price change may also be seen using these two diagrams. Suppose again that policy induces an increase in the relative price of Y, as in Figure 10-1.

While the returns to capital in industry Y increase and the returns to capital in industry X decrease in the short run, over time (in the long run) capital will shift between industries. As capital moves from industry X to industry Y, labour will also move from industry X to industry Y (as it becomes more productive with the increased capital) and returns to labour and capital will eventually adjust until factor returns in all industries are equalized. This will be at the new intersection, w** and r**, of the isocost curves, C_x and C_y'. Note in the example depicted in Figure 10-1, that although returns to capital in industry X initially decline to r_x^1, they will increase to r** in the long run. Also, note that wages will unambiguously decline in the long run to w**. In the notation used in the analysis of short-run effects:

$$\hat{r} > \hat{P}_y > \hat{P}_x > \hat{w}.$$

This result depends fundamentally on our assumption that Y production is always capital intensive relative to X production, as reflected in the steeper slope of the Y isocost curve. Thus, if the government chose instead to increase the relative cost of X (the labour-intensive good), as in Figure 10-2, the long run effect would be an increase in wages and a decrease in the return to capital. That is, the long-run effects of a relative price increase on the returns to factors as described above would

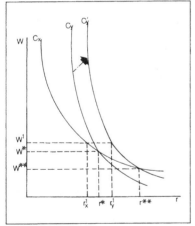

Figure 10-1

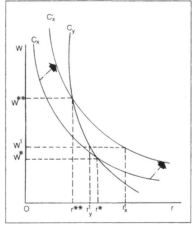

Figure 10-2

---

[46] It is arguable that the time horizon of political calculation should be treated as a parameter that varies across political communities. If community time horizon were a function of, for example, the average duration of government, we could use this

result in cross-national analysis of the Salisbury effect. The hypothesis would be that political conflict in countries with historically stable states (e.g. stable hereditary monarchs) would more likely be characterized by factor (i.e. class) based conflict, while

A Simple Model of the Political Economy: The Lowi Effect

be reversed. The new long-run equilibrium returns would be w** and r** and would reflect the result that although returns to capital in industry X initially increased to r_x^1, they will decrease to r** in the long-run. Further, returns to labour will unambiguously rise in the long run to w** in terms of either good. This is one of the most fundamental results of general equilibrium theory and is generally called the Stolper-Samuelson theorem. It may be expressed as follows:

An increase in the price of one good relative to the other will result in an increase in the price of the factor used intensively in the production of that good relative to the prices of both goods and a decrease in the return to the other factor relative to both goods (regardless of the industry in which the factors are employed).[47]

This result has an interesting implication with regard to the incentives for political action. Although the gains from participation in the political process will fall to owners of an immobile factor in one industry at the expense of owners of immobile factors in other industries in the short-run, when individuals are concerned about the long-run effects of a political decision, their natural political allies are other individuals with the same factor-endowment (regardless of the industry in which that factor is employed). Specifically, labour would benefit (be harmed) in the long run from an increase (decrease) in the price of a labour-intensive good and would be harmed (benefit) in the long-run by an increase (decrease) in the price of a capital-intensive good. It would, therefore, be expected, as in Lowi's redistributive arenas, that when considering long-run effects, large interest groups will form around ownership of factors of production regardless of their employment in the economy.

Toward a Model of General Political Economic Equilibrium: Endogenizing Political Choice

It is clear from the above discussion that in this simple short-run model, an increase in an industry's price level benefits owners of industry specific factors of production at the expense of owners of factors specific to other industries. If a political institution existed whose outcomes affected the price level in an industry, then one would expect to find economically rational individuals (utility maximizing through the consumption of goods and services only) engaging in two kinds of activities: directly produc-

tive (i.e. earning income through the rental of factors of production to firms) and political (i.e. lobbying government to influence prices, which then affect the returns to ownership of factors of production). Given that such political activity is costly, an implication of this is that economically rational individuals will recognize this trade-off between the gains from a higher (or lower) industry price level and the cost of attempting to influence government output and devote resources to political activities until the marginal benefit equals the marginal cost of doing so. Further, to the extent that the institutional form through which state output is provided affects the cost of political activity relative to its value, institutional form would be expected to have an effect on the incentives to engage in political action. In this section, the simple model will be expanded to include the trade-off between the gains from changes in the price level in an industry(s) and the cost of influencing the government output that causes this price change. Then, this expanded model will be used to discuss the effect of two alternate institutional forms of supply of government output.[48]

Costly lobbying

It will be assumed that individuals who participate in the political process are rational economic actors who influence the political process through lobbying (as opposed to voting). A measure of the resources used by a group in affecting government policy output will be denoted by LL. This variable will be referred to as 'lobbying labour' since it will be further assumed that this input is perfectly substitutable for the labour in the production of goods and services. The cost, then, of influencing government output is simply the return to the mobile factor, labour, times the amount of the mobile factor used in lobbying government, wLL. Since the benefits from a higher price level in a given industry fall unambiguously to the owners of specific factors in that industry, it will be assumed that they hire the labour resources to influence government output. Full employment in the economy, therefore, implies that:

$$\bar{L} = L_D + LL_x + LL_y$$

where LL_x and LL_y are the labour used in lobbying by specific factors in industry X and Y, respectively, and L_D is defined as 'productively' employed labour ($L_D = L_x + L_y$). Since government output will be seen to affect individuals only through

---

that in countries with unstable states (or states with institutionalized instability) would more likely be characterized by small-group based conflict.
[47] In the more general case of many industries and factors, this generalizes to the result that an increase in the price level in an industry results in a proportionally greater increase in the return to at least one factor (maybe more) of production while reducing the return to at least one other (also, maybe more).

[48] Note that gain to specific factors in an industry from an increased price level is at the expense of specific factors in all other industries. Specific factors in industries whose price levels are not increased by a government output will, therefore, oppose increases in this government output. Further, if an industry's price level increases only slightly by an increase in the rule, while a number of other industries' price levels increase, specific factor owners in the industry may prefer a decrease in the rule.

H. KEITH HALL, DOUGLAS R. NELSON

its economic effects, the price level in an industry will either go up or down as a result of political decision. Taking the existence of political mechanisms as given and letting p be the relative price of good X in terms of good Y (that is, $p = P_x/P_y$), the passive register state can be represented as a political output function, using as inputs the lobbying resources employed by the relevant special interest groups:

$$p = p(LL_x, LL_y).$$

To examine the effect of lobbying for government output graphically, the effect of using lobbying resources to influence the relative price level in the two industries will be considered. For simplicity, the analysis will concentrate on the benefits of lobbying to specific factors in industry X, hold the returns to the mobile factor constant, and keep factor returns in units of good Y. In Figure 11 below, it may be seen that when the relative price level goes up, the value of marginal product curve in industry X shifts up proportionally to its height.

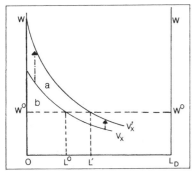

Figure 11

As discussed above in Figure 5, since there is perfect competition in all markets, the area below the V_x curve out to current employment of labour in the industry represents total industry revenue, which is divided between the total return to owners of specific factors (the area below V_x but above the current return to labour) and mobile factors (the rectangle below the current return to labour). Therefore, ignoring the labour market effects (i.e. holding w constant), when the relative price level increases, returns to owners of specific factors in industry X increase as shown by area (a).

Suppose, however, that wages are no longer assumed fixed and the effects of the relative price level increase on the market for the mobile factor are taken into account. When the value of marginal product curve for industry X shifts up, the return to the mobile factor will increase as it is bid away

from industry Y. Adding the value of marginal product curve for industry Y in Figure 12, it can be seen that this increase in w, from w^0 to w^1, reduces the demand by industry X for additional units of the mobile factor (employment increase to L^1 instead of L').

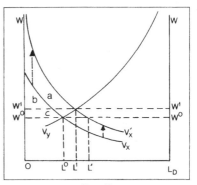

Figure 12

The total return to owners of specific factors in industry X before the price change was area (b + c) (above wage w^0 and below V_x, out to employment level L^0) and after the price change will be area (a + b) (above the new equilibrium wage, w^1, and below the new value of marginal product curve, V'_x, out to employment level L^1). The increase in returns to specific factors in industry X from the relative price increase is, therefore, equal to area (a + b) minus area (b + c) — or, simply, area (a − c). Note that, as previously discussed, the returns to specific factors in industry X must increase with this

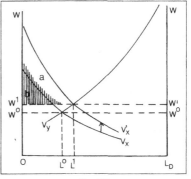

Figure 13   **167**

A Simple Model of the Political Economy: The Lowi Effect

price increase. Area $(a-c)$ must, therefore, be greater than zero. This is easily demonstrated graphically by noting that the height of area $(a+b)$ is greater at every given level of employment of labour than area $(b+c)$ (since the value of marginal product curve shifts upward proportionally to its height) while at the same time being wider (since L^1 must be larger than L^0 with a downward sloping V_y curve). This is shown in Figure 13 by moving shaded area $(b+c)$ on top of the larger area $(a+b)$.

When costly labour must be hired by specific factors in industry X to lobby for a relative price level increase, the supply of productive labour in the economy is reduced, as seen in Figure 14, shifting the origin for industry X inward, as well as the value of marginal product curve rightward (since its distance from the origin will not change).

Note that this decrease in the amount of productive labour in the economy increases the return to the mobile factor in the economy. This reduces the employment of labour by industry X, reducing the marginal productivity of the specific factor and thereby reducing the return to the specific factors in the industry. This may be seen to be the shaded area in Figure 14.

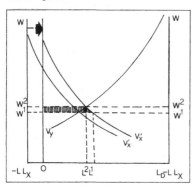

Figure 14

The industry problem

The model of the political economy is now complete. The basic framework may be see in Figure 15.

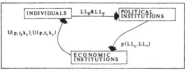

Figure 15

Since the total return to specific factors in industry X is $r_x K_x$ and owners of specific factors in each industry employ the lobbying resources to influence the industry price level, the net return to this political activity, noted by N_x, is

$$N_x = r_x K_x - w L L_x.$$

The problem, solved by the owners of specific factors in industry X, is to choose an amount of resources, LL_x, to employ that maximizes N_x for a given level of lobbying by factor owners in industry Y, LL_y. When lobbying labour is hired, several effects may be seen graphically. The combination of a simultaneous increase in the relative price level V_x to V'_x, and a decrease in productive labour due to the use of lobbying resources (the rightward shift in the left vertical axis) is show in Figure 16.

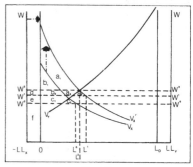

Figure 16

Note that this is simply adding the movements in Figure 12 and 14, and their resulting effects together into one diagram. The increase in the mobile factor returns from w^0 to w^1 and change in the allocation of the mobile factor from L^0 to L^1 are the same as in Figure 12 and due to the higher relative price level in industry X. Also, the increase in the return to the mobile factor from w^1 to w^2 and change in use of the mobile factor from L^1 to L^2 are the same as in Figure 14. Due to the reduction of productive labour in the economy, industry X hires more lobbying labour. The returns to specific factors in industry X will increase by an amount equal to

1) the increase due to the higher relative price level — equal to area $(a_1 + a_2 + a_3 - c_1 - c_2)$[49]

2) the decrease due to the increase in mobile factor returns from the reduction in productive labour — equal to area $(b_2 + a_2 + a_3)$[50].

---

[49] Note that areas $(a_1 + a_2 + a_3)$ and $(c_1 + c_2)$ in Figure 15 are the same as areas (a) and (c) in Figure 12, respectively.
[50] Note that area $(b_2 + a_2 + a_3)$ in Figure 15 equals the shaded area in Figure 14.

H. KEITH HALL, DOUGLAS R. NELSON

The cost to the specific factors of influencing the price level will be
3) the cost of hiring lobbying labour at the current wage level — equal to area (f)
4) the increased cost of hiring the lobbying labour due to the relative price increase — equal to area (e)
5) the increased cost of hiring lobbying labour due to the reduction of productive labour — equal to area (d).

In total, the increase in the net return to specific factors in industry X from lobbying for a higher relative industry price level equals area $(a_1 - c_1 - c_2 - b_2 - e - f - d)$. This may also be shown mathematically. The change in N_x from the use of additional units of lobbying resources, for a given level of lobbying by specific factors in industry Y, will be

$$\frac{\delta N_x}{\delta LL_x} = K_x \frac{\delta r_x}{\delta p} \frac{\delta p}{\delta LL_x} - K_x \frac{\delta r_x}{\delta L_D} - w -$$

$$- LL_x \frac{\delta w}{\delta p} \frac{\delta p}{\delta LL_x} - LL_x \frac{\delta w}{\delta L_D}.$$

The first term, $K_x \frac{\delta r_x}{\delta p} \frac{\delta p}{\delta LL_x}$, represents the direct effect on the revenue to specific factor from a relative price increase due to increased lobbying by industry X. An increase in LL_x would increase area $(a_1 + a_2 + a_3 - c_1 - c_2)$ from Figure 16 through this term.[51]

The second term, $K_x \frac{\delta r_x}{\delta L_D}$, shows the reduction in the total returns to specific factors from the increase in returns to mobile factors when productive labour is reduced by an increase in lobbying by industry X. An increase in LL_x increases the area $(b_2 + a_2 + a_3)$ in Figure 16 through this term. The cost of hiring lobbying labour services is the sum of the next three terms, w, $LL_x \frac{\delta w}{\delta p} \frac{\delta p}{\delta LL_x}$, and $LL_x \frac{\delta w}{\delta L_D}$. An increase in LL_x increases the area $(d + e + f)$ from Figure 16.[52]

---

[51] Note that this term is always positive since area $(a - c)$ must always increase with an increase in the relative price level.
[52] If the industry problem is defined as hiring lobbying labour simply to maximize the net return to lobbying, then the necessary and sufficient conditions will be sensitive to the units used (i.e. whether net return is measured in units of good X, good Y, or in dollar terms). Although the main results that point out the trade-off in benefits and costs of employing lobbying resources are not sensitive to the units, the industry problem could simply be formulated using a utility function representing the trade-off between changes in the relative price level and the net return to lobbying as follows:

$$\max_{LL_x} U_x(p, N_x).$$

The necessary condition for industry X would be

Rules versus discretion in determination of intervention levels

As argued in the discussion of the Lowi effect at the beginning of this paper, one of the attributes of a policy that is taken to affect the organization of political activity directed toward that policy is whether access to the policy output (in this case a change in relative prices) is a direct result of the lobbying process or an indirect result. In the first case, discretionary accommodation, the state makes case-by-case determinations on the basis of lobbying effort. This is in contrast to rule-based decision making in which the lobbying effort determines a general rule under which all efforts to change relative prices are determined.[53] An excellent example of this distinction is found in the original development of the Lowi effect (Lowi 1964). In mediating between the findings of Schattschneider (1935) and those of Bauer, Pool and Dexter (1963), Lowi argued that the Reciprocal Trade Agreements Act of 1934 and the emergence of multilateral tariff bargaining in the GATT changed the institutional definition of tariff politics from a distributive issue toward a regulatory issue. The authors have argued elsewhere that the core of this change was a shift from direct accommodation of tariff-seeking by Congress to rules-based accommodation by the executive under a delegation from Congress.[54]

In light of the foregoing, the last two results may now be presented: discretionary accommodation will tend to result in more political activity than rule-based accommodation and discretionary accommodation will more often result in increases in price levels than will rule-based accommodation. Once the cost of political activity is explicitly recognized, the logic behind the first result is quite straightforward:

$$\frac{\delta U_x}{\delta LL_x} = \frac{\delta U_x}{\delta p} \frac{\delta p}{\delta LL_x} + \frac{\delta U_x}{\delta N_x} \frac{\delta N_x}{\delta LL_x} = 0.$$

Since an industry is also maximizing utility through consumption of the two goods, Roy's identity may be used (Varian 1978), and rearranged to give

$$\left(K_x \frac{\delta r_x}{\delta p} - LL_x \frac{\delta w}{\delta p} - D_x \right) \frac{\delta p}{\delta LL_x} =$$

$$w + \left(K_x \frac{\delta r_x}{\delta L_A} - LL_x \frac{\delta w}{\delta L_A} \right)$$

where D_x is industry X's Marshallian demand function for good X (as a function of relative prices, p, and income, N_x). Note that since N_x is a function of p and L_A alone, D_x is also.
[53] To make the difference as stark as possible, it is assumed that the general rule operates costlessly and with certainty. As a result, the only political costs are those associated with setting the rule. Thus complete discretion is compared with a completely specified rule.
[54] The historical argument is made most clearly in Nelson (1987). In Finger, Hall and Nelson (1982) econometric evidence is presented supporting the hypothesis that the delegation from Congress (at least up to 1980) is precise enough for anti-dumping and countervailing duty cases to be decided 'on their merits'. A formal development of this argument for the case of tariff policy can be found in Hall and Nelson (1988).

169

A Simple Model of the Political Economy: The Lowi Effect

the benefits of discretionary accommodation are appropriable by the individual policy-seeking groups (industries, in our model) while the benefits of rule-based accommodation are not. As a result, by comparison to discretionary accommodation, rule-based accommodation results in lower levels of lobbying activity for the directly affected industry. The second result is also fairly straightforward: while there is a lower overall level of political activity under rule-based accommodation, there is also a bias in favor of individuals who are not owners of specific factors employed in industries whose price levels are directly affected by the government output.

As has been assumed up to this point, government output that influences price levels is completely determined by the lobbying resources used at the industry level. Momentarily dropping the assumption of just two industries, if a set of government outputs, g_1, g_2, ..., g_m, is considered, affecting a number n of industries, it can be seen that their values are simple functions of the lobbying resources expended by the industries:

$$g_j (LL_1, LL_2, ..., LL_n) \text{ for } j = 1, 2, ..., m.$$

Each of these government outputs, if assumed to influence only one industry price level (for simplicity), will affect only one set of industry-specific factors (in the short run). The price level in an industry X, for example, that is affected by a particular government output will, therefore, be determined by the lobbying resources used to influence that government output:

$$P_x (LL_1, LL_2, ..., LL_n).$$

For this reason, any lobbying resources used by this industry or small group of industries impart benefits that are fully or almost fully capturable. As a result, output under discretion may loosely be referred to as a 'private good'. Further, gain of that industry or small groups of industries is at the expense, to varying degrees, of all other industries indirectly through factors markets.

Suppose now that there is a different form of government output. It no longer results directly from industry level lobbying but from the application of a general rule which is itself simply determined by lobbying. The rule, therefore, may be represented as was each separate government output previously, as a simple function of the industry specific factors employment of lobbying resources

$$R (LL_1, LL_2, ..., LL_n).$$

This rule is applied to government output (which allows lobbying to indirectly influence government outputs) and, even if it is again assumed that each of these government outputs influences only one industry price level (for simplicity), it affects price levels in several industries at once:

$$P_x(R), P_y(R), ..., P_z(R).$$

Since the benefits of lobbying for rule-based accommodation will not be fully appropriable by a single group of industry-specific factors, the output in this case may loosely be referred to as a 'public good'. Instead, resources used by the specific factors in an industry must benefit several industries simultaneously. The effect that this public type of government output will have on the incentive for lobbying resources may be seen graphically using the same basic diagram as in Figure 16. Taking an arbitrary industry X, whose price level will be increased by the government output, if its resource use is compared to that of another industry not affected by the government output, then there will be a difference in their industry problem solution as in Figure 16. If its resource use is compared to that of another industry whose price level was also increased by the government output, then any resources used by this industry to increase its price level also must increase the price level in the other industry. This is shown in Figure 17.[55]

Note that the same rewards to lobbying pertain as in Figure 16, but now as LL_x increases P_x as before, P_y must now also increase. The result is that the value of marginal product curve in industry Y will now also shift upward proportionally to its height. The loss to specific factors in industry X from this addition shift is seen by the shaded area in Figure 17. Now, instead of simply gaining specific

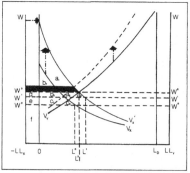

Figure 17

---

[55] Note that the returns to factors and value of marginal product curves have been switched into units of another good besides the output of industry Y (or, they could have been kept in units of dollars). This is for convenience only in that this permits an upward shift in the V_y curve, reflecting an increase in the price level in industry Y. Had things been kept in units of good Y as before, the V_x curve would simply (though not so clearly in the diagram) have been shifted downward. This would have further complicated things in that the returns would all have changed, since they were in units of good Y.

H. Keith Hall, Douglas R. Nelson

factor returns equal to area (a_1) minus area $(c_1 + c_2 + b_2 + e + f + d)$, there will be the additional loss of the shaded portion of the diagram. The result will be less of an incentive for lobbying by industry X, since the net gains from doing so will be reduced. In fact, the industry may even now prefer that its own price level be *decreased* by the government output. The potential benefits to specific factors from lowering its own price level would simply be the reverse of those from raising it: area $(c_1 + c_2 + b_2 + e + f + d)$ minus area (a_1) plus the shaded portion of Figure 17.

There will also be a bias in this public good government output. That is, this reduced incentive to lobby affects only industries whose price levels are affected. Those industries that are lobbying against the government output will have the same incentive as before.

Conclusions

The relationship between the results presented above and what has been called the Lowi effect should be clear. In the context of the model developed here, a policy will have two attributes: the time horizon (short or long) and the terms of access to output (discretionary or rule-based). Once these attributes have been specified, the organization of political action is determined along the lines shown in Figure 18.

	Short Horizon	Long Horizon
Rules	Regulatory	Redistributive
Discretion	Distributive	

Figure 18: The Lowi Effect.

A policy that induces a short time horizon in political calculation and discretion in accommodation of demands results in industry-based lobbying. In this model, industries are the smallest possible unit of collective identification, so this defines the kind

of limit conceived by Lowi in his definition of a distributive policy. Maintaining the short time horizon but shifting to a rule-based system for accommodating demands induces the creation of larger groups along the lines defined by the rule, which is the classic pattern of regulatory policy as analyzed by Lowi. Finally, if the rules orientation is retained but the definition of the policy induces long-run calculation, factor-based groups will form. If the presumption that there are far fewer 'basic factors' than industries is correct, this yields Lowi's redistributive case with its broad-based (approaching class struggle) groupings.[56]

The purpose of this paper has been to illustrate the use of a class of formal models in political economic analysis. The development was intentionally simple (both in terms of technique and assumption structure). Many interesting extensions present themselves immediately. With regard to the economy, it is possible to introduce various alternative assumptions about technology of production and market structure. With regard to behavioural assumptions, it is possible to include non strictly self-interested behaviour. Perhaps most importantly, it is possible to introduce more active political entrepreneurship and coalition behaviour. For example, if the state is able to play an active role, policy type can become a strategic variable.[57] The fact that such complications will undermine (to a greater or lesser degree) the conclusions of the simple model presented in this paper, however, should not be taken to detract from the value of simple models in the development of intuition and as a step on the way to a more well-grounded theory of political economy.

---

[56] The fourth (empty) cell is what is called adjudicative redistribution and is fully consistent with the above discussion. It involves factor-based interest identification, but the discretion allowed can have the effect of disorganizing the interest groups. This is not pursued here because it requires an additional structure that would undermine the simple presentation that was one of the goals of this paper.

[57] See Nelson (1983) for a discussion of such strategies in the case of industrial policy.

References

Amenta, E., Skocpol, T. (1988), 'Redefining the New Deal: World War II and the Development of Social Provision in the United States', in M. Weir, A.S. Orloff and T. Skocpol (eds.), *The Politics of Social Policy in the United States*, Princeton University Press, Princeton, pp. 81-122

Arrow, K. (1951), *Social Choice and Individual Values*, Yale University Press, New Haven.

Arrow, K. (1974), *The Limits of Organization*, Norton, New York

Bauer, R.A., Pool, I., Dexter, L.A. (1963), *American Business and Public Policy: The Politics of Foreign Trade*, Aldine, Chicago

Bernstein, M. (1955), *Regulating Business by Independent Commission*, Princeton University Press, Princeton

Bhagwati, J. (1982), 'Shifting Comparative Advantage, Protectionist Demands and Policy Response', in J. Bhagwati (ed.), *Import Competition and Response*, University of Chicago Press/NBER, Chicago, pp. 153-84

Brewer, T. (1973), 'Issue Context and Variations in Foreign Policy: Effects on American Elite Behaviour', *Journal of Conflict Resolution, 1*, pp. 89-114

Ethier, W. (1988), *Modern International Economics*, Norton, New York

Findlay, R., Wellisz, S. (1982), 'Endogenous   **171**

A Simple Model of the Political Economy: The Lowi Effect

Tariffs, the Political Economy of Trade Restrictions, and Welfare', in J. Bhagwati (ed.), *Import Competition and Response*, University of Chicago Press/NBER, Chicago, pp. 223-34

Finger, J.M., Hall, H.K., Nelson, D.R. (1982), 'The Political Economy of Administered Protection', *American Economic Review, 3*, pp. 452-66

Fiorina, M. (1977), *Congress: Keystone of the Washington Establishment*, Yale University Press, New Haven

Fiorina, M. (1981), 'Universalism, Reciprocity, and Distributive Policy Making in Majority Rule Institutions', *Research in Public Policy Analysis and Management*, pp. 197-221

Fiorina, M. (1982), 'Legislative Choice of Regulatory Forms: Legal Process or Administrative Process', *Public Choice, 1*, pp. 33-66

Fiorina, M. (1986), 'Legislator Uncertainty, Legislative Control, and the Delegation of Legislative Power', *Journal of Law, Economics and Organization, 1*, pp. 33-51

Hall, H.K., Nelson, D. (1987), 'Modelling the Market for Protection: Administered versus Legislated Approaches', manuscript, The World Bank/University of Arkansas

Hayes, M. (1978), 'The Semi-Sovereign Pressure Groups: A Critique of Current Theory and an Alternative Typology', *Journal of Politics, 1*, pp. 134-61

Hayes, M. (1981), *Lobbyists and Legislators: A Theory of Political Markets*, Rutgers University Press, New Brunswick

Jones, R., Neary, P. (1984), 'The Positive Theory of International Trade', in R. Jones and P. Kenen (eds.), *Handbook of International Economics (Vol. 1)*, North Holland, Amsterdam, pp. 1-62.

Kofford, K. (1987), 'Different Preferences, Different Politics: A Demand-And-Structure Explanation', manuscript, *Social Science Working Paper* No. 640, Caltech

Lowi, T. (1964), 'American Business, Public Policy, Case Studies and Political Theory', *World Politics, 4*, pp. 347-82

Lowi, T. (1967), 'Making Democracy Safe for the World: National Politics and Foreign Policy', J. Rosenau (ed.), *Domestic Sources of Foreign Policy*, Free Press, New York, pp. 295-331

Lowi, T. (1970), 'Decision-Making vs. Policy-Making: Toward an Antidote for Technocracy', *Public Administration Review, 3*, pp. 314-25

Lowi, T. (1972), 'Four Systems of Policy, Politics, and Choice', *Public Administration Review*, pp. 298-310

Lowi, T. (1985), 'The State in Politics: The Relation Between Policy and Administration', in Noll (ed.), *Regulatory Policy in the Social Sciences*, pp. 67-110

Magee, S., Brock, W., Young, L. (1988), *Black Hole Tariffs: Endogenous Policy Theory: Political Economy in General Equilibrium*, manuscript, University of Texas

March, J., Olsen, J. (1984), 'The New Institutionalism: Organizational Facts in Political Life', *American Political Science Review, 3*, pp. 734-49

Mayer, W. (1984), 'Endogenous Tariff Formation', *American Economic Review, 5*, pp. 970-85

McClure, C. (1971a), 'The Theory of Tax Incidence with Imperfect Factor Mobility', *Finanzarchiv, 1*, pp. 27-48

McClure, C. (1971b), 'The Theory of Expenditure Incidence', *Finanzarchiv, 4*, pp. 432-53.

McClure, C. (1975), 'General Equilibrium Incidence Analysis: The Harberger Model After Ten Years', *Journal of Public Economics, 2*, pp. 125-61

McCubbins, M. (1985), 'The Legislative Design of Regulatory Structure', *American Journal of Political Science, 2*, pp. 721-48

McCubbins, M. Schwartz, T. (1984), 'Congressional Oversight Overlooked: Police Patrols versus Fire Alarms', *American Journal of Political Science, 1*, pp. 165-79

McKelvey, R. (1976), 'Intransitivities in Multidimensional Voting Models and Some Implications for Agenda Control', *Journal of Economic Theory, 3*, pp. 472-82

McKelvey, R. (1986), 'Covering, Dominance, and Institution-Free Properties of Social Choice', *American Journal of Political Science, 2*, pp. 283-314

Moe, T. (1985), 'Control and Feedback in Economic Regulation: The Case of the NLRB', *American Political Science Review, 4*, pp. 1094-116

Moe, T. (1987), 'An Assessment of the Positive Theory of Congressional Dominance', *Legislative Studies Quarterly, 4*, pp. 475-520

Neary, J.P. (1978), 'Short-Run Capital Specificity and the Pure Theory of International Trade', *Economic Journal, 351*, pp. 488-510

Nelson, D. (1983), 'On Political Response to Economic Crisis in Advanced Industrial Countries: A Conflict Theory Approach', presented at the 1983 Annual Meeting of the American Political Science Association, Chicago

Nelson, D. (1987), 'The Domestic Political Preconditions of US Trade Policy: Liberal Structure and Protectionist Dynamics', presented at World Bank Conference on Political Economy: Theory and Evidence

Nelson, D. (1988), 'Endogenous Tariff Theory: A Critical Survey', *American Journal of Political Science, 3*, pp. 796-837

Niou, E., Ordeshook, P. (1985), 'Universalism in Congress', *American Journal of Political Science, 2*, pp. 246-58

Orloff, A.S., Skocpol, T. (1984), 'Why Not Equal Protection? Explaining the Politics of Public Social Spending in Britain, 1900-1911, and the United States, 1880s-1920', *American Sociological Review, 6*, pp. 726-50

Peters, B.G., Doughtie, J., McCulloch, M.K. (1977), 'Types of Democratic Systems and Types

H. KEITH HALL, DOUGLAS R. NELSON

of Public Policy: An Empirical Examination', *Comparative Politics, 3*, pp. 327-55

Ripley, R., Franklin, G. (1984), *Congress, The Bureaucracy and Public Policy* (3rd Ed.), Dorsey Press, Homewood

Rogowski, R. (1987), 'Political Cleavages and Changing Exposure to Trade', *American Political Science Review, 4*, pp. 1121-37

Ruffin, R., Jones, R. (1977), 'Protection and Real Wages: The Neoclassical Ambiguity', *Journal of Economic Theory, 2*, pp. 337-48

Salisbury, R. (1968), 'The Analysis of Public Policy: A Search for Theories and Roles', in A. Ranney (ed.), *Political Science and Public Policy*, Markham, Chicago, pp. 151-75

Salisbury, R. Heinz, J. (1970), 'A Theory of Policy Analysis and Some Preliminary Applications', in I. Sharkansky (ed.), *Policy Analysis in Political Science*, Markham, Chicago, pp. 39-60

Schattschneider, E.E. (1935), *Politics, Pressures and the Tariff*, Prentice Hall, New York

Schofield, N. (1985), *Social Choice and Democracy*, Springer-Verlag, Berlin

Shepsle, K. (1979), 'Institutional Arrangements and Equilibrium in Multidimensional Voting Models', *American Journal of Political Science, 1*, pp. 27-59

Shepsle, K. (1986), 'Institutional Equilibrium and Equilibrium Institutions', in H.F. Weisberg (ed.), *Political Science: The Science of Politics*, Agathon Press, New York, pp. 51-81

Shepsle, K., Weingast, B. (1981), 'Political Preferences for the Pork Barrel: A Generalization', *American Journal of Political Science, 1*, pp. 96-111

Skocpol, T. (1980), 'Political Response to Capitalist Crisis: Neo-Marxist Theories of the State and the New Deal', *Politics and Society, 2*, pp. 155-201

Skocpol, T., Finegold, K. (1982), 'State Capacity and Economic Intervention in the Early New Deal', *Political Science Quarterly, 2*, pp. 255-78

Skocpol, T., Ikenberry, J. (1983), 'The Political Formation of the American Welfare State in Historical and Comparative Perspective', *Comparative Social Research, Vol. 6*, pp. 87-148

Smith, T. (1969), 'Toward a Comparative Theory of the Policy Process', *Comparative Politics, 4*, pp. 498-515

Spitzer, R. (1979), 'The Presidency and Public Policy: A Preliminary Inquiry', *Presidential Studies Quarterly*, pp. 441-57

Varian, H. (1978), *Microeconomic Analysis*, Norton, New York

Vogler, D. (1980), *The Politics of Congress* (3rd ed.), Allyn and Bacon, Boston

Walker, S., McGowan, P. (1982), 'US Foreign Economic Policy Formulation: Neo-Marxist and Neopluralist Perspectives', in W. Avery and D. Rapkin (eds.), *America in a Changing World Political Economy*, Longman, New York, pp. 207-24

Weingast, B. (1979), 'A Rational Choice Perspective on Congressional Norms', *American Journal of Political Science, 2*, pp. 245-62

Williamson, O.E. (1975), *Markets and Hierarchies: Analysis and Antitrust Implications*, Free Press, New York

Williamson, O. (1985), *The Economic Institutions of Capitalism: Firms, Markets, Relational Contracting*, Free Press, New York

Wilson, J.Q. (1974), 'The Politics of Regulation', in J. McKie (ed.), *Social Responsibilities and the Business Predicament*, Brookings, Washington DC, pp. 135-68

Zimmerman, W. (1973), 'Issue Area and Foreign Policy Process: A Research Note in Search of a General Theory', *American Political Science Review, 4*, pp. 1204-12

WOMEN AND TARIFFS: TESTING THE GENDER GAP HYPOTHESIS IN A DOWNS-MAYER POLITICAL-ECONOMY MODEL

H. KEITH HALL, CHIHWA KAO, and DOUGLAS NELSON*

This paper tests a variant of the standard endogenous tariff model under direct democracy (the Downs-Mayer model) with a gender gap. Specifically, we argue that, if there is a division of economic activity between men and women, and political preferences are affected by one's relationship to the economy, there will be a gender gap in political activity. We test this hypothesis with respect to the effect of political enfranchisement of women on the level of the U.S. tariff. The empirical results strongly support the hypothesis. (JEL F4, D7, N4)

"I am convinced that at least two out of every three women have a grudge against the tariff, and a grudge which is all too frequently increased to an indignation by the subtle suggestion, on the part of importers and retailers, that the tariff adds to the prices of the things they buy. It is the women of the household who spend the husband's earnings—she has to make them go around, and anything which she is told adds to the prices of the things she buys naturally finds little excuse in her mind. Her attitude, regardless of logic, is a natural one. She doesn't stop to consider the part the tariff may have played in making her husband's earnings what they are, or in fact in making them possible at all, nor does she stop to consider the relatively minor part the tariff plays in the retail prices of the things she buys. She has never seen the tariff law, and so she cannot know that with such commodities as coal, coffee, tea, cocoa, furs and shoes on the free list, some explanation other than the tariff must account for the increased price of these things."

(Barbour, 1928)[1]

The notion that women and men hold systematically differing political preferences, that there is a "gender gap," is an old one in American politics. Even before the national enfranchisement of women in 1920, analysts and commentators attempted to identify issues on which such a gender gap would affect policy outcomes. One such issue was the tariff, with which we are concerned in this paper. The above passage from the January 1928 issue of the *Tariff Review* serves as an excellent text for our sermon. The logic of the argument is interesting: American women prefer a low tariff because a high tariff raises the prices of the things they purchase. Our paper represents this hypothesis as an extension of the Downs [1957]–Mayer [1984] political-economy model and then presents a simple empirical test of the hypothesis.

* The authors would like to thank: Elias Dinopoulos, Kevin Grier, Doug Holtz-Eakin, Bill Kaempfer, Carsten Kowalczyk, Steve Marks, Jay Wilson, several referees for *Economic Inquiry* and seminar participants at the Claremont Graduate School, University of Alabama, University of Nottingham, and the Fall 1991 Midwest International Economics Meetings. None of these should be implicated in any errors in fact, logic or good taste. This paper is solely meant to represent the opinions of the authors, and is not meant to represent in any way the views of the International Trade Commission or its members.

Hall: Economist, U.S. International Trade Commission Washington, D.C., Phone 1-202-205-3245
Fax 1-202-205-2340, E-mail hhall@usitc.gov

Kao: Associate Professor, Department of Economics Syracuse University, New York, Phone 1-315-443-3233
Fax 1-315-443-1081, E-mail ckao@maxwell.syr.edu

Nelson: Associate Professor, Murphy Institute of Political Economy, Tulane University, New Orleans, La.
Phone 1-504-865-5317, Fax 1-504-862-8755
E-mail dnelson@mailhost.tcs.tulane.edu

1. W. Warren Barbour, in addition to being the President of the Linen Thread Company, was the President of the American Tariff League when the lecture from which this article was derived was given.

320

Economic Inquiry
(ISSN 0095-2583)
Vol. XXXVI, April 1998, 320–332

We present our analysis in four major parts. First, we set the stage with a brief discussion of the political-economy of the tariff during the period relevant to our analysis [1890–1934]. This discussion provides motivation for the details of the more formal analysis in the following section. Next we develop the logic of the classic tariff system in the context of the Downs-Mayer model. The third section presents the testable proposition that the enfranchisement of women results in a lower equilibrium tariff as an implication of this model. In the final section we present our methodology and results.

I. THE POLITICAL-ECONOMY OF THE CLASSIC TARIFF SYSTEM

It is not unreasonable to think of the period from the end of the Civil War until 1934 as the era of classic tariff politics in the United States. During this period the tariff was a significant, partisan, electoral issue. Republicans were the party of the protective tariff, Democrats were opposed to the "tariff system." While there was regional variation with respect to details at the level of specific products, this characterization is quite accurate over the entire period with respect to overall commitment to the tariff system. Whether one studies political platforms or campaign speeches, this split between Republicans and Democrats remains clear.[2] Furthermore, there seems to be a fairly direct relationship between sectional economic interests and strength of partisan support: the industrial northeast was the historical center of Republicanism, while the rural south and mid-west was the center of Democrat support.

Another important aspect of the electoral politics during the era of classic tariff politics (from the perspective of this paper) was the essential one-dimensionality of "the tariff" as an issue.[3] That is, partisan conflict revolved

primarily around support for, and opposition to, the tariff *system*—not the details of the tariff structure. It is important to recall that, during this period, the tariff was one of the few instruments of industrial policy available to the national government and, at least since the end of the Civil War, the tariff as an electoral issue was explicitly presented by both Democrats and Republicans as a system of support for American industry.[4] The details of the tariff schedule were determined by Congress, with the House Committee on Ways and Means taking the lead, in response to the lobbying pressure of organized economic interests, but the electoral competition between the Republicans and Democrats determined the context within which the lobbying took place. Thus, elections can be thought of as setting the average level of protection while lobbying determined the dispersion around that level. The one-dimensionality of the tariff as a political issue and the centrality of that issue to the political contest between Democrats and Republicans in the era of classic tariff politics is an essential element of the link between the theoretical development of this paper and the empirical work.

Given the centrality of the characterization of classic tariff politics to the research reported here, it is useful to briefly discuss the role of the tariff in the election of 1896. Political scientists and historians are in broad agreement that the McKinley-Bryan election

2. Thus, it should not be surprising that, over this entire period, final votes on tariff legislation consistently showed high levels of party-line voting. In fact, the tariff was usually one of the two or three most divisive issues.

3. In fact, this assertion does not meet with universal approval among historians of this period. While many assume that the close link between centers of partisan strength and aggregate economic interest signifies that the politics of the protective system reflected classic inter-regional re-

distributive politics (e.g. Taussig [1931]; Rogowski [1989]), a substantial school of research based on careful study of local political conditions suggests that this is too simple. Specifically, a number of prominent ethnocultural historians, have emphasized that "the tariff" had different meanings in different locations precisely because it was more important as a symbol than as a commitment to any particular policy. See especially: Jensen [1971]; Kleppner [1970]; and McSeveney [1972]. McCormick [1974] presents a convenient survey of this research. Thus, if "the tariff" was a sort of ideological portmanteau, our assumption that it is essentially one-dimensional is clearly problematic.

4. It is also important to recall that, unlike the modern trade policy system, it was the tariff (as legislated by Congress) that was the dominant instrument of industrial protection. For a detailed development of the argument that the classic tariff system was essentially one-dimensional while modern system is irreducibly multi-dimensional, see Nelson [1989].

was of particular political significance.[5] This was certainly true with respect to the tariff system, which faced its most sustained and explicit challenge in the 1896 election. Populists and Democrats under the general leadership of William Jennings Bryan offered a progressive income tax as a direct attack on the tariff system. Specifically, the income tax was to replace the tariff, which was seen not only as a symbol of the power of eastern industrial interests, but as a fundamental defender of those interests. At the same time, the populists sought to go beyond simply removing the tariff by proposing a progressive income tax that would fall most heavily on the holders of "money power."[6] Republicans, and conservatives generally (including important elements of the Democrat party), opposed the income tax. As Baack and Ray [1985a,b] point out, during the Civil War (the only U.S. experience with an income tax prior to the 20th century) the income tax fell particularly heavily on New York, Massachusetts and Pennsylvania— the centers of Republican power. The tariff, on the other hand, provided substantial benefits for those same states. Perhaps of equal importance, the tariff had for some time been an important symbol of government commitment to U.S. industry, while Bryan made the income tax a symbol of sectional and class struggle.

The rout of Bryan and the populists defended the classic tariff system from its most serious challenge and resulted in stable tariff politics until the emergence of the New Deal political system. A fundamental rethinking of the tariff system had to wait until the Reciprocal Trade Agreements Act of 1934. The reestablishment of control of the Democrat party by establishment Democrats permitted a

return to classic tariff politics. Furthermore, this ultimately permitted the institutionalization of the income tax as a revenue raising device subordinate to the tariff.[7] Thus, even when the Democrats gained control of the White House and the Congress: there was no attempt to replace the tariff *system* (although there was some tariff reduction); the income tax was not used for redistributive purposes; and, as Baack and Ray [1985] point out, the structure of increased federal expenditures involved substantial benefits for the centers of Republicanism.

The purpose of this section has been to argue that the tariff constituted a significant issue, possibly the most significant continuing issue, in American electoral politics during the last part of the 19th century and the first part of the 20th century. Furthermore, we have argued that the electoral politics of the tariff can reasonably be characterized as one-dimensional. Finally, we have argued that both the politics of the tariff and the relationship of the tariff to the electoral/political system as a whole was relatively constant over this period. These aspects of the political-economy of the tariff undergird the theoretical and empirical analysis which is developed in the remainder of the paper. In the next section, we sketch a simple formal model of the political-economy of the classic tariff system in which the gender gap hypothesis plays a significant role.

II. THE POLITICS OF THE CLASSIC TARIFF SYSTEM IN THE DOWNS-MAYER MODEL

The spatial analysis of partisan competition that constitutes one essential element of Downs' [1957] economic theory of democracy

---

5. In the language of modern research on political history, the 1896 election was one of a small number of "critical elections." In fact, the electoral system defined by that election is generally referred to as the "system of 1896." On the general concept of critical elections and the periodization of American politics in those terms, see Burnham [1970], Sundquist [1973], and Clubb, Flanigan and Zingale [1980]. For more critical perspectives on critical elections, see: McCormick [1982] and Lichtman [1982]. With particular reference to the election of 1896 and the "system of 1896," see: Burnham [1981; 1986] and McCormick [1986].

6. Stewart [1980] and Hansen [1980] for excellent presentations of the politics of the income tax and its relationship to critical election theory. Also of interest is Hansen [1990].

7. This is an important point to which we shall return. While it is true, as a number of scholars have noted (e.g. Riezman and Slemrod [1987]), that there is a general relationship between the development of an income tax and the elimination of the tariff as a revenue raising device, the above discussion should make clear that this connection is far from direct in any particular case. In the U.S. case, it was precisely the agreement that the income tax would not constitute a threat to the tariff *system* that made adopting one politically feasible in the context of the "System of 1896." It was only with the collapse of the "System of 1896" and the emergence of the "New Deal System" that the classic tariff system could be dismantled and replaced with something else. Thus, while the existence of an alternative source of government revenue is a necessary condition to elimination of a protective system, it is not sufficient.

rests on two fundamental results: Black's [1948] theorem that if agents preferences over a one-dimensional political issue are single-peaked, then the most preferred point of the median voter cannot be beaten in a majority rule contest; and Hotelling's [1929] theorem that the most preferred point of the median voter is the Nash equilibrium of two-party competition over that dimension.[8] An important paper by Mayer [1984] applies the spatial model to the case of trade policy determination by deriving voter preferences over the tariff from a standard (Heckscher-Ohlin-Samuelson) trade theoretic model. In the Mayer model, every household is characterized by an endowment of productive factors and tastes (i.e., preferences over the consumption of goods and services). These endowments then determine household preferences over policy choices as these policies affect equilibrium factor and commodity prices. A full political-economic equilibrium is then determined through a majority-rule referendum on the tariff. Specifically, assuming that indirect utility functions are concave in the tariff, Mayer uses Black's theorem to analyze the effect of restricted franchise on the equilibrium tariff determined by a simple referendum.

Downs, however, is less interested in single-issue referenda than in the functioning of representative democracy in a complex and informationally rich political environment. The key contribution of Downs here is the notion of *rational ignorance*. The basic idea is that, since each agent has only a minuscule effect on the final outcome of the electoral contest, it is in no agent's interest to invest large resources in collecting or processing political information. This process of economizing on political information costs involves: conditioning voting behavior on low cost information; and using a simple evaluative scheme for processing that information. Both of these elements will be important to our analysis, but at this point we focus on the role of simple evaluative schemes. There are three key elements of such a scheme: it must be in common use throughout the electorate; must

differentiate the parties; and it must be stable across time. The first point is obvious, if the evaluative scheme is not public and commonly understood, it cannot serve as a basis for partisan competition. The second is also straightforward, if parties engage in Hotelling-like clustering on the dimension it will not serve to reduce decision-making costs. The third element, intertemporal stability, is a bit less obvious, but very important: without such stability information costs would not really be reduced since voters would have to identify a new evaluative dimension in every election.

Downs discusses these issues in the context of a general left-right evaluative dimension.[9] Modern voters will normally conceive of this in terms of big government versus small government, or level of commitment to macroeconomic policy activism. That particular form of evaluative dimension is of fairly recent vintage. In fact, it is a property of what political scientists usually refer to as "the New Deal system." The main point of the first section of this paper, however, was to argue that from the end of the Civil War until some time in the early part of this century, The Tariff served as precisely such a Downsian issue. The purpose of the next section is to argue that female franchise marks the end of the tariff as such an issue.

III.   THE GENDER GAP, FEMALE FRANCHISE
AND THE EQUILIBRIUM TARIFF

We can capture the gender gap on the tariff issue with a simple extension of the Downs-Mayer model. We assume that every household consists of two individuals (with identical tastes) that specialize in their economic activities: one undertakes all factor-market transactions while the other undertakes all product market transactions. If, following Downs, we assume that individual agents economize on information costs in making their political choices by weighing more heavily the information they observe directly, then individuals within a single household have

---

8. See Enelow and Hinich [1984] for an excellent textbook treatment of the spatial model.

9. See Hinich and Munger [1994] for a current development of Downs theory of the role of ideology in electoral competition.

different political preferences.[10] For simplicity we use the assumptions that factor-market specialists (men) are only concerned with the effect of policy on returns to their household's factor endowment, while product market specialists (women) are only concerned with the effect of policy on the prices of consumption goods. In the language developed below, each household is seen as having a wealth effect voter and a consumption effect voter. We have therefore modeled exactly the "political gender gap" that concerned political activists at the time.

How reasonable are the special assumptions of our model for the classic tariff era in the United States? With respect to the specialization of household economic decisions, we are convinced that this assumption is completely unproblematic. Data on women's labor force participation in the period with which we are concerned [1890–1934] show a very clear pattern of exclusion of women from the formal workforce [Goldin, 1990].[11] With respect to the additional assumption that this

specialization results in a political gender gap, we offer two lines of defense. First, contemporary political discussions, like the one cited at the beginning of this paper, suggest that political activists during this time period believed that such a gender gap existed. Assuming that policy is driven by the desire for reelection, a general belief in such a gender gap may be enough to cause a shift in trade policy whether such a gender gap actually existed or not. Second, given the specialization of decision-making within the household and the observation that information is generally costly to obtain, is seems perfectly rational that a household member would weigh more heavily that part of economic reality with which they are most directly concerned (i.e., the effects of policy on either factor or consumer prices). For simplicity we adopt the strong assumption that each is exclusively concerned with that part of economic reality with which they are most directly concerned.

The logic of the model should now be clear.[12] Prior to female franchise, the distribution of factor-ownership among households was such that the tariff could function as the Downsian issue dimension along which parties could differentiate themselves. Female franchise introduces a substantial population of people into the electorate that have preferences skewed toward lower tariffs. This has two empirical implications: the median voter now has a lower optimal tariff, and thus the equilibrium tariff must be lower; and the system of partisan competition based on the tariff must collapse. Before we turn to the econometric analysis of the first empirical implication in the next section, we can briefly consider the second.

---

10. We see this as directly related to Downs' [1957] notion of rationally ignorant voters. That is, politically relevant information is costly to obtain. As a result, voters will economize on information gathering. Furthermore, some information is relatively cheap, while other information is more costly. In our model we are assuming that factor-price information is observed freely by men and not at all by women, while commodity price information is observed freely by women and not at all by men. Neither is particularly concerned with the overall state of the economy as a whole. Each conditions both economic and political behavior on the information that is freely observed. While information may be exchanged between household members, each considers the information directly observed to be the most accurate information and essentially ignores other information. Some readers of this paper have found this assumption *ad hoc*. We would argue that it is no more *ad hoc* than the assumption of perfectly reliable information transfer.

Others have argued that the existence of a gender gap may flow from sources other than differential information. Most of the alternative accounts that have been suggested vary from the unlikely (e.g. perhaps female employment was concentrated in export-oriented sectors) to the genuinely silly (e.g. perhaps women were free traders because liberalization would cause relative price shifts that would change the balance of household bargaining power in their favor). However, our purpose in this paper is not to explain the gender gap, but to incorporate it in the corpus of endogenous tariff theory in a relatively straightforward way. We would argue that our differential information story does this effectively. The fact that this is consistent with contemporary accounts is simply an additional bonus.

11. According to Goldin [1990, Table 2.1] female labor force participation in 1890 was 18.9%, 20.6% in 1900 and 23.7% in 1920. This pattern is even clearer if we focus on women who were likely to be voters—i.e. middle class, white women. We do not have data by economic status, but the percentages for white, married women were 2.5%, 3.2%, and 6.5%. This can be compared to the labor force participation of males in these census years of 84.3%, 85.7%, and 54.3% (*Historical Statistics of the United States*, series D30).

12. In fact, while the general logic is straightforward, formally proving that the claims follow from the assumptions is far from easy. Hall and Nelson [1995] provides a detailed development and formal analysis of the gender gap model.

In his discussion of "The Origin of New Parties" (pp. 127–32), Downs argues that new parties emerge when the distribution of voters shifts in such a way as to make the initial equilibrium unstable. Downs' example is the effect of the extension of franchise to working class voters in the late-nineteenth century with the demise of the Liberal party, the birth of the Labor party and the realignment of British electoral politics. While Downs' analysis implies that events like franchise extension have no effect on the underlying dimension defining political competition, it should be clear that this is not necessarily implied by the analysis. In fact, research on party systems proceeding from the foundational work of V. O. Key [1955] and Walter Dean Burnham [1970] makes it clear that political realignments are essentially about the content of political contests (see footnote 5). Thus, although the institutional parties may (or may not) exist after a realignment, the membership and the terms on which the parties compete will be fundamentally changed—they will in effect be new parties. In the case which concerns us, the adoption of female franchise undermined the system of partisan competition based on the tariff in a particularly strong way: it created an expected majority of voters opposed to the platform of the previously dominant party.[13] That is, the "system of 1896" was dominated by the high tariff Republicans and the new voters would be expected to enter the electorate on the low tariff side of the low tariff party, thus undermining the commitment of the Republicans to the system. The result was not the elimination of either party, but the disappearance of the tariff as an electoral issue and the concomitant collapse of the "system of 1896."[14] It is in fact

the case that the tariff played no role in partisan competition in the system that replaced the "system of 1896," generally referred to as the "New Deal system."[15]

Interestingly, while political scientists have been very clear on the political alignments that define the New Deal system, and their differences from the "system of 1896," there has always been a certain uneasiness in the dating of the system. The problem is that the alignments that define the system seem to have emerged from the politics of the depression, but the voting behavior that signals the realignment seems to precede the depression, or more precisely to phase in over a period of several years. Specifically, as Lichtman [1982] argues, it is difficult to find the kind of decisive changes in voting behavior over the period 1916–1940 that one would normally associate with a realignment. But this is exactly the kind of behavior predicted by the analysis developed in this paper: with the collapse of the tariff, both parties would seek to find a new issue around which to organize partisan competition; the search process would generate some period characterized by uncertainty; with a catastrophic event like the depression, however, a new system could form around alternative visions of the relationship between government and the economy. Thus, the macrohistorical evidence is consistent with our analysis. We now turn to an econometric evaluation of the microhistorical evidence.

IV. A SIMPLE TEST OF THE GENDER GAP HYPOTHESIS

The Downs-Mayer model is based on the notion of an equilibrium relationship between citizen preferences (derived from their factor-ownership positions and their consumption preferences) and policy outcomes. Previous

---

13. It is interesting to note that Downs explicitly rules out female franchise in this context: "A change in the number of voters *per se* is irrelevant; it is the distribution which counts. Hence, women's suffrage does not create any new parties, although it raises the total vote enormously." The main point of this paper is that, while Downs got the mechanism exactly right, female franchise did shift the distribution on the one issue that mattered to the stability of the system.

14. Note that the disappearance of the tariff as a political issue is not in any way the same thing as the disappearance of the tariff. In fact, once the tariff ceased to be an instrument of public partisan competition it was freed to become first an example of pure pork barrel politics and, with the recognition that the costs exceeded the benefits of

treating trade policy as distributive politics, the Reciprocal Trade Agreements Act of 1934 redefined those politics in an essential way. See Nelson [1989] for a detailed development of this argument.

15. Note the implication for the equilibrium tariff. With the tariff no longer a Downsian valence issue both parties will converge on the optimal tariff of the median voter in Hotelling-Black fashion. Since under Republican domination the political equilibrium involved a tariff that was higher than the optimal tariff of the median voter even without female franchise, this implies that the equilibrium tariff would be even lower with female franchise.

time series research on the political economy of the tariff suggests that the tariff is a function of business cycle effects (proxied by either level of GNP or unemployment), international competition (trade balance or import penetration), party (the equilibrium tariff is lower with Democrats).[16] Our extension of the Downs-Mayer logic to the extension of voting rights to women suggests a straight-forward empirical test of that logic. Thus, the research reported in this section differs in two fundamental ways from the previous research by Magee and Young [1987] and Bohara and Kaempfer [1991a,b]. First, we focus only on the period of classic tariff politics. As we argue in section I, this period is characterized by a stable relationship between the tariff and the political system. Following the New Deal realignment, of which the Reciprocal Trade Agreements Act of 1934 was a fundamental part, virtually every aspect of the politics of trade policy underwent fundamental change. Second, and of more direct relevance to the major argument of this paper, we explicitly test for the impact of female franchise on the political economic equilibrium. This section presents the results of our analysis using annual data for the period 1866–1934 and 1896–1934.[17]

16. The majority of empirical research on the political economy of the tariff emphasizes sectoral dispersion of the tariff. Baldwin [1984], Anderson and Baldwin [1987], and McCarthur and Marks [1989] are convenient surveys of the research on tariff dispersion. Of particular note for the research presented here are the papers explaining tariff dispersion in the era of classic tariff politics: Pincus [1975]; Baack and Ray [1983], Eichengreen [1989] and Conybeare [1991].

17. The dependent variable in the analysis is the average tariff (in logarithms: tariff revenue/total dutiable imports). Our measures of domestic macroeconomic conditions are the unemployment rate, the real wage, and GNP, and our measure of international competitive conditions is the trade balance (= export value − import value). The source for these data is the *Historical Statistics of the United States*: total imports (Series U194); total exports (series U191); total dutiable imports (series U209); total duties (series U210). The income tax revenue and total government revenue series are from the same source. Unemployment rate, nominal and real GNP, and inflation are from the series in the appendix to Gordon's *Macroeconomics*, and the real wage series is reported in Williamson [1995]. All variables are in logs except trade balance (which takes negative values) and income tax/total government revenue (which takes zero values in many years).

To examine the effect of female franchise, we used a dummy variable which takes a value of 0 for the period 1890–1919 and 1 from 1920–1934. As we suggest in the text, the parties had very clearly defined preferences on trade policy. We attempt to control for partisan effects with

Table I contains several interesting results consistent with our hypothesis.[18] As previous research has already shown, we find that the domestic business cycle, the trade balance, and Democrat presidents all have the predicted effects. With respect to the gender gap hypothesis, assuming that the dummy variable accurately reflects the effect of female franchise, we find a strong effect, and we find this effect using a variety of domestic business cycle indicators, and we find this effect both from 1866–1934 and 1896–1934. Also of considerable interest is the lack of a significant effect for the income tax (as measured by the share of income tax revenue in total government revenue). This latter result seems to be consistent with our argument that the existence of the income tax (or some alternative source of revenue) was a necessary but not sufficient condition to the collapse of the classic tariff system. It has been the main argument of this paper that the politically necessary condition was the collapse of the distribution of voter preferences that allowed the tariff to function as a key issue in partisan competition.

Before considering the significance of female franchise result in more detail, we first discuss several possible objections to the result. A first objection is methodological and relates to our use of a dummy variable to capture the effect of female franchise. The fundamental difficulty here relates to the possibility that the dummy variable is actually picking up some other politically significant phenomenon. Although our search for obviously compounding events has not turned up anything, it remains the case that a dummy variable is far from ideal.[19]

a dummy variable for party of the president (Democrat = 1; Republican = 0).

18. At the suggestion of a reviewer, we ran all six versions of the model in first differences as a simple specification test. In all cases, both the signs and the significance levels of the parameters are unchanged. These results are reported in the Appendix.

19. It is, however, the case that we have explicitly considered the effect of the most commonly mentioned alternative (the income tax) as well as trade balance, business cycle, and partisan competition. Since we have discussed this in detail elsewhere we simply note that the other events that have been suggested bear no essential relationship to the politics of the tariff, whereas the burden of the argument in this paper is that there is a good theoretical reason for believing that female franchise does bear such a relationship.

TABLE I

Tariff Regression with Correction for First-Order Auto Correlation

Dependent variable is: log average tariff: = log[(tariff revenue)/(dutiable imports)]

	Sample: 1866-1934*				Sample: 1896-1934	
Constant	4.567734 (1.873522)	5.843697 (2.812331)	5.471275 (0.004259)	6.193553 (0.542278)	6.04956 (3.37549)	9.187024 (1.216581)
Log Unemployment	0.082331 (3.386318)			0.068164 (2.531519)		
Log Real Wage	-0.681683 (-2.819363)					-0.555830 (-3.661883)
Log GNP			-0.406195 (-3.581158)		-0.383527 (-1.05812)	
Trade Balance	-1.38 E-07 (-5.757670)	-0.002044 (-4.789279)	-1.01 E-07 (-4.271370)	-1.36 E-07 (5.129258)	-1.30 E-07 (-3.85886)	-9.66 E-08 (-3.907073)
Income Tax/Gov. Rev.	-0.000833 (-0.443393)	-0.002044 (-1.125129)	0.000472 (0.256167)	-0.002218 (-1.076921)	-0.002703 (-1.26845)	-0.000533 (-0.277640)
Women (= 1 if ≥ 1920)	-0.618024 (-6.379683)	-0.505995 (-5.602589)	-0.375911 (-4.171849)	-0.606676 (-5.763565)	-0.454826 (-4.39304)	-0.398334 (-4.345118)
President (= 1 if Dem)	-0.59666 (-1.950104)	-0.058670 (-1.924111)	-0.066954 (-2.260095)	-0.128234 (-2.883867)	-0.137080 (-2.82323)	-0.129501 (-3.189056)
AR(1)	0.987012 (25.26011)	1.017366 (40.45140)	1.000009 (48.30749)	0.991312 (21.11983)	0.982319 (45.3261)	0.988495 (37.00511)
R-Squared	0.880247	0.873116	0.880989	0.918645	0.764261	0.932527
Adjusted R-Squared	0.897859	0.860837	0.869472	0.903391	0.728543	0.919876
S.E. of Regression	0.708161	0.078861	0.076375	0.082064	0.89538	0.074735
Durbin-Watson	1.730452	1.867852	1.651519	1.998700	1.39569	1.975787
F-statistic	71.05523	71.10577	76.49328	60.22272	19.3674	73.71084
Prob(F-statistic)	0.000000	0.000000	0.000000	0.000000	0.000000	0.000000

t-statistics in parentheses

*Detailed descriptions of variables are in footnote 17. Log unemployment is 1870–1934.

A second objection to our interpretation of the results flows from the fact that women did not vote in significant numbers even after they were enfranchised. First, it follows from the work of Fenno [1978] and Cain, Ferejohn and Fiorina [1989] that people need not vote to be considered in the political calculus of reelection maximizing politicians, they only need to be able to vote. Furthermore, some women did vote. Both of these facts are sufficient to change the location of the median voter if women's preferences are as characterized in section II.

A third objection is that women already had the franchise before 1920 in several states. The first line of response to this is that, as with the previous point, all that is necessary with respect to the model developed in section II is that a large group of women entered the electorate in 1920. The fact that some states had already experienced this phenomenon would weaken the effect and make it harder to establish the result. More importantly, virtually all the early franchise states were Western states and, thus, generally supporters of trade liberalization in any event. Thus the identity of the median legislator would not be affected by these early franchise states. The gender gap should be strongest in the Northeast.[20]

Finally, there were women in the labor force, and working women (by the logic of this paper) should have the same preferences as men with respect to the tariff. We have already noted that female labor force participation was considerably lower than male labor force participation and that this was even more striking for what we can think of as "voting women"—i.e. middle class women. These facts suggest that the median preferences of women with respect to the tariff are for lower tariffs. Furthermore, contemporary accounts suggest that politicians believed women to have a preference for lower tariffs.

Thus, we believe that the results reported here provide strong, preliminary evidence for the effect of female franchise on the level of the average tariff. That is, there was a gender gap on the tariff. If this result stands up to further scrutiny, it is important for several reasons. First, it has been an open question in political science for some time whether or not female franchise had any politically significant impact at the time it occurred. It has been argued that, as new voters, women were not well socialized and, therefore, did not vote or voted in ways that reduced their impact as a group with common interests. Most of this research proceeds by studies of their voting behavior (e.g. Kleppner [1982] on turnout) and/or the activities of women's political organizations [Andersen, 1990]. The research reported here, by focussing directly on an issue over which men and women were presumed to disagree, provides some direct evidence of an immediate political impact of female franchise. Furthermore, not only is the effect of female franchise positive but, from the macrohistorical perspective, it is of substantial historical interest. Specifically, we argued at the end of section III that female franchise caused the collapse of the system of 1896 and created the conditions in which the New Deal system could be born.

A similar logic provides a more compelling account for Congress' adoption and continued support for the Reciprocal Trade Agreements Act of 1934. This act institutionalized an alternative approach to Congressional management of U.S. trade policy. The standard account of support for the RTAA asserts that Congress collectively learned a lesson from the Smoot-Hawley tariff. Unfortunately, there are two serious problems with this account. First, there is virtually no contemporary evidence of such a change. That is, there are no significant instances of individual members of Congress making this connection. Second, the changes in voting behavior that would be assumed to go along with such learning do not occur until well into the 1950s [Nelson, 1989]. There is a good reason why we should not observe changed political behavior: there is no systematic evidence of a strong economic connection between the Smoot-Hawley tariff and the severity of the depression [Eichengreen, 1989]. This has led to an alternative account, based in part on Schattschneider's [1935] classic account of the making of the Smoot-Hawley tariff: Congress delegated the making of the trade policy to the President because the writing of tariffs

---

20. There may even be a certain degree of endogeneity here. That is, given the centrality of the tariff to political contestation, women were more easily enfranchised where they least threatened the political equilibrium.

had become too time consuming and too politically difficult. The problem with these accounts is timing. The logic is straightforward and compelling, but why after Smoot-Hawley? The argument of this paper suggests a simple answer: with the collapse of the tariff as an organizing structure in partisan competition, there was no longer any reason to continue.

V. BY WAY OF A CONCLUSION: IMPLICATIONS FOR FUTURE RESEARCH

One interesting implication of this result for future research is that, once the labor market status of women becomes more like that of men, we would expect their political preferences with regard to trade policy to become more similar.[21] Using labor market participation data, we should, in principle, be able to study this effect directly. We say "in principle" not because there are fundamental problems with measuring women's labor force participation, but because measuring the average level of protection during the GATT era is difficult. Not only is there no longer direct legislation of protection, but there has been steady substitution of non-tariff for tariff barriers over the entire period; and trade economists have still not found satisfactory ways of measuring the economic effects of such barriers. Nonetheless, we find it at least suggestive that trade policy activism has made a substantial recovery as a public political issue in the 1990s—a period of substantially increased female labor force participation.

The second contribution of this paper relates to the direct link between endogenous tariff theory and empirical tariff politics. Much of the casual empiricism which is attached to the theoretical work on endogenous tariff theory implies a fairly direct relationship between those models and the political-economy of current trade policy. This is

clearly inappropriate. As we have just commented, and as is well known in policy discussions: modern trade policy is not about tariffs; and modern trade politics has not been about elections. Most endogenous tariff theory is of direct application only to the period of classic tariff politics. Pincus [1975], Baack and Ray [1983], Eichengreen [1989], and Conybeare [1991] demonstrate the usefulness of lobbying models for the explanation of tariff dispersion, while the research reported here illustrates the value of voting models for the explanation of the average tariff.

This suggests two important directions for future research. First, we need to move toward models that integrate the electoral process (to set the average propensity to protect) with lobbying models (to determine dispersion). Preliminary steps are taken in this direction by Hall and Nelson [1992] via their introduction into a standard lobbying model of an explicit parameter for tariff resistance. Perhaps more importantly, we need to develop better models of the political-economy of protection in the GATT era. This is difficult primarily because trade policy has become inherently multidimensional. Instead of "the tariff" as an electoral issue there is market access, unfair competition, and trade liberalization to name only a few. This makes the formal characterization of trade policy as either an electoral or a lobbying issue difficult.

Third, and finally, the research reported here is significant because it links political exclusion to an economically relevant social category: gender. Mayer's [1984] important work showed the potentially significant impact of political exclusion on equilibria of endogenous policy models. However, Mayer's analysis is difficult to test because the relevant patterns of political exclusion (i.e. factor-based exclusion) have not generally been observed in modern American politics. By focussing on gender-based exclusion we have moved toward a more testable version of the Downs-Mayer model.

---

21. Recent research by Claudia Goldin [1991] suggests that World War II was not the major turning point in women's labor market status that it has sometimes been taken to be. However, this argument relates as much to the social context of increased employment as to the economic. With respect to the issue raised in this paragraph, while the actual social turning point with respect to women's labor force participation may have been later than the 1940s, it seems uncontroversial to suggest that it did come at some point in the post-War era.

APPENDIX
Tariff Regression in First Differences

Dependent variable is: d [log average tariff]: = d [log[(tariff revenue)/(dutiable imports)]]

	Sample: 1866–1934*			Sample: 1896–1934		
Constant	0.009552 (0.979583)	0.20797 (1.974730)	0.019926 (2.101442)	0.019020 (1.435564)	0.033281 (2.226918)	0.032407 (2.431645)
Log Unemployment	0.081981 (3.425589)			0.067682 (2.579471)		
Log Real Wage		−0.646623 (−2.646585)			−0.835209 (−2.214109)	
Log GNP			−0.410371 (−3.868734)			−0.453718 (−3.201624)
Trade Balance	−1.39 E-07 (−5.981067)	−1.17 E-07 (−4.852624)	−1.06 E-07 (−4.569455)	−1.35 E-07 (−5.432777)	−1.09 E-07 (−3.062661)	−9.79 E-08 (−3.811903)
Income Tax/Gov. Rev.	−0.000890 (−0.487831)	−0.001999 (−1.116589)	−2.30 E-05 (−0.012882)	−0.002223 (−1.137583)	−0.002923 (−1.494483)	−0.001032 (−0.525418)
Women (= 1 if ≥ 1920)	−0.624061 (−6.538465)	−0.496602 (−5.516869)	−0.417814 (−4.746529)	−0.607839 (−5.977995)	−0.497814 (−5.174526)	−0.410187 (−4.319155)
President (= 1 if Dem)	−0.060369 (−2.009776)	−0.057589 (−1.885484)	−0.066392 (−2.308896)	−0.129569 (−3.020194)	−0.121992 (−2.717732)	−0.138653 (−3.417684)
R-Squared	0.533236	0.491496	0.543429	0.681109	0.666373	0.707628
Adjusted R-Squared	0.493680	0.451139	0.507193	0.632792	0.615824	0.663329
S.E. of Regression	0.077561	0.078535	0.074417	0.080861	0.082709	0.077426
Durbin-Watson	1.740095	1.837231	1.697242	2.012333	1.998904	2.046971
F-statistic	13.48044	12.17857	14.99702	14.09670	13.18258	15.97396
Prob(F-statistic)	0.000000	0.000000	0.000000	0.000000	0.000000	0.000000

t-statistics in parentheses, all variables are differenced once.
*Detailed descriptions of variables are in footnote 17. Log unemployment is 1870–1934.

REFERENCES

Andersen, Kristi. "Women and Citizenship in the 1920's," in *Women, Politics and Change*, edited by Louise Tilly and Patricia Gurin. New York: Russell Sage Foundation, 1990, 177–98.

Anderson, Kym, and Robert Baldwin. "The Political Market for Protection in Industrial Countries," in *Protection, Cooperation, Integration and Development*, edited by A. M. El-Agraa. London: Macmillan, 1987, 20–36.

Baack, Ben, and Edward Ray. "The Political Economy of Tariff Policy: A Case Study of the United States." *Explorations in Economic History*, January 1983, 73–93.

_____. "Special Interests and the Adoption of the Income Tax in the U.S." *Journal of Economic History*, September 1985a, 607–25.

_____. "The Political Economy of the Origin and Development of the Federal Income Tax," in *Emergence of the Modern Political Economy*, edited by R. Higgs. Greenwich: JAI Press, 1985b, 121–38.

Baldwin, Robert. "Trade Policies in Developed Countries," in *Handbook of International Economics*, edited by R. Jones and P. Kenen. Amsterdam: North-Holland, 1984, 571–619.

Barbour, W. Warren. "The Protective Tariff—On the Defensive." *The Tariff Review*, January 1928, 3–6, and 29.

Black, Duncan. "On the Rationale of Group Decision-Making." *Journal of Political Economy*, February 1948, 23–34.

Bohara, Alok, and William Kaempfer. "A Test of Tariff Endogeneity in the United States." *American Economic Review*, September 1991a, 952–60.

_____. "Testing the Endogeneity of Tariff Policy in the U.S.: Further Evidence." *Economics Letters*, March 1991b, 311–15.

Burnham, Walter Dean. *Critical Elections and the Mainsprings of American Politics*. New York: Norton, 1970.

_____. "The System of 1896: An Analysis," in *The Evolution of American Electoral Systems*, edited by P. Kleppner, et al. Westport: Greenwood Press, 1981, 147–202.

_____. "Periodization Schemes and 'Party Systems': The System of 1896 as a Case in Point." *Social Science History*, Fall 1986, 263–314.

Cain, Bruce, John Ferejohn, and Morris Fiorina. *The Personal Vote*. Cambridge, Mass.: Harvard University Press, 1989.

Campbell, Bruce, and Richard Trilling. *Realignment in American Politics: Toward a Theory*. Austin, Tex.: University of Texas Press, 1980.

Clubb, Jerome, William Flanigan, and Nancy Zingale. *Partisan Realignment: Voters, Parties, and Government in American History*. Beverly Hills, Calif.: Sage, 1980.

Conybeare, John A. C. "Voting for Protection: An Electoral Model of Tariff Policy." *International Organization*, Winter 1991, 57–81.

Downs, Anthony. *An Economic Theory of Democracy*. New York: Harper-Collins, 1957.

Eichengreen, Barry. "The Political Economy of the Smoot-Hawley Tariff." *Research in Economic History*, 12, 1989, 1–43.

Enelow, James, and Melvin Hinich. *The Spatial Theory of Voting: An Introduction*. New York: Cambridge University Press, 1984.

Epstein, David, and Sharyn O'Halloran. "The Partisan Paradox and the U.S. Tariff, 1877–1934." *International Organization*, Spring 1996, 301–24.

Fenno, Richard. *Home Style*. Boston: Little-Brown, 1978.

Gardner, Grant, and Kent Kimbrough. "The Behavior of U.S. Tariff Rates." *American Economic Review*, March 1989, 211–18.

Goldin, Claudia. *Understanding the Gender Gap: An Economic History of American Women*. New York: Oxford University Press, 1990.

_____. "The Role of World War II in the Rise of Women's Employment." *American Economic Review*, September 1981, 741–56.

Hall, H. Keith, and Douglas Nelson. "Institutional Structure and the Political-Economy of Protection: Administered versus Legislated Protection." *Economics and Politics*, March 1992, 61–77.

_____. "Women and Tariffs, II: A Formal Analysis of the Gender Gap Extension of the Downs-Mayer Model." Massachusetts: Tulane University, 1992.

Hansen, John Mark. "Taxation and the Political Economy of the Tariff." *International Organization*, Autumn 1990, 526–49.

Hansen, Susan B. "Partisan Realignment and Tax Policy: 1789–1976." Campbell and Trilling, 1980, 288–323.

Hinich, Melvin, and Michael Munger. *Ideology and the Theory of Political Choice*. Ann Arbor: University of Michigan Press, 1994.

Hotelling, Harold. "Stability in Competition." *Economic Journal*, March 1929, 41–57.

Jensen, Richard. *The Winning of the Midwest: Social and Political Conflict, 1888–1896*. Chicago: University of Chicago Press, 1971.

Key, V. O. "A Theory of Critical Elections." *Journal of Politics*, February 1955, 3–18.

Kleppner, Paul. *The Cross of Culture: A Social Analysis of Midwestern Politics, 1850–1900*. New York: Free Press, 1970.

_____. "Were Women to Blame? Female Suffrage and Voter Turnout." *Journal of Interdisciplinary History*, Spring 1982, 621–43.

Lichtman, Allan. "The End of Realignment Theory? Toward a New Research Program for American Political History." *Historical Methods*, 15(4), 1982, 170–88.

Magee, Stephen P., and Leslie Young. "Endogenous Protection in the United States, 1900–1984," in *U.S. Trade Policies in a Changing World Economy*, edited by R. Stern. Cambridge, Mass.: MIT, 1987, 145–95.

Mayer, Wolfgang. "Endogenous Tariff Formation." *American Economic Review*, December 1984, 970–85.

McCarthur J., and S. Marks. "Empirical Analyses of the Determinants of Protection: A Survey and Some New Results," in *International Trade Policies: Gains from Exchange Between Economics and Political Science*, edited by J. Odell and T. Willett. Ann Arbor: University of Michigan Press, 1989, 105–39.

McCormick, Richard L. "Ethno-Cultural Interpretations of Nineteenth-Century American Voting Behavior." *Political Science Quarterly*, June 1974, 351–77.

_____. "The Realignment Synthesis in American History." *Journal of Interdisciplinary History*, Summer 1982, 85–105.

_____. "Walter Dean Burnham and the 'System of 1896'." *Social Science History*, Fall 1986, 245–62.

McSeveney, Samuel T. *The Politics of Depression: Political Behavior in the Northeast, 1893–1896*. New York: Oxford University Press, 1972.

Nelson, Douglas R. "The Domestic Political Preconditions of U.S. Trade Policy: Liberal Structure and Protectionist Dynamics." *Journal of Public Policy*, 9(1), 1989, 83–108.

Pincus, J. J. "Pressure Groups and the Pattern of Tariffs." *Journal of Political Economy*, August 1975, 757–78.

Riezman, Raymond, and Joel Slemrod. "Tariffs and Collection Costs." *Weltwirtschaftliches Archiv*, 123(3), 1987, 545–49.

Rogowski, Ronald. *Commerce and Coalitions: How Trade Affects Domestic Political Alignments*. Princeton: Princeton University Press, 1989.

Schattschneider, E. E. *Politics, Pressure and the Tariff*. New York: Prentice Hall, 1935.

Stewart, Charles. "The Federal Income Tax and the Realignment of the 1890s." Campbell and Trilling, 1980, 263–87.

Sundquist, James L. *Dynamics of the Party System*. Washington, D.C.: Brookings, 1973.

Taussig, F. W. *The Tariff History of the United States*. New York: G. P. Putnams, 1931.

Williamson, Jeffry. "The Evolution of Global Labor Markets Since 1850: Background Evidence and Hypotheses." *Explorations in Economic History*, April 1995, 1–54.

The Political Economy of Trade,
Aid and Foreign Investment Policies
D. Mitra and A. Panagariya (Editors)
© 2004 Elsevier B.V. All rights reserved

CHAPTER 5

The Peculiar Political Economy of NAFTA: Complexity, Uncertainty and Footloose Policy Preferences*

H. KEITH HALL[a] and DOUGLAS R. NELSON[b,c,*]

[a]*US Department of Commerce, 14th and Pennsylvania Avenue, Washington, DC 20230, USA*
[b]*Murphy Institute of Political Economy, 108 Tilton Hall, Tulane University,*
New Orleans, LA 70118, USA
[c]*Leverhulme Centre for Research on Globalisation and Economic Policy, School of*
Economics, University of Nottingham, University Park, Nottingham NG7 2RD, UK

Abstract

On a large number of dimensions, the domestic political economy of the North
American Free Trade Agreement (NAFTA) in the US was peculiar. In some
ways the most surprising aspect of the politics of NAFTA relates to the apparent
footlooseness of aggregate opinion. That is, since standard theories of political
economy assume that policy preferences are determined by material conditions,
those theories only predict changes when material (economic or political)
conditions change. In this chapter we provide evidence that aggregate
public opinion in NAFTA shifted dramatically in the absence of any change
in the underlying political and economic fundamentals. We will then sketch

---

* This chapter is solely meant to represent the opinions of the authors, and is not meant to represent in
any way the views of the US Government or the Department of Commerce.
*Corresponding author.
E-mail address: dnelson@tulane.edu

92   *H.K. Hall and D.R. Nelson*

the elements of a theory of footloose policy preferences that helps understand this sort of phenomenon and conclude with a discussion of the implications of the analysis for policy analysis and advice.

Keywords: Political economy, trade, NAFTA, learning

JEL classifications: D72, D83, F13

On a large number of dimensions, the domestic political economy of the North American Free Trade Agreement (NAFTA) in the US was peculiar. For example, at least from the perspective of standard endogenous policy models of trade policy, the coalitions that emerged would seem to be difficult to rationalize in an ex ante compelling way.[1] Similarly, the level of national political heat generated by a policy estimated to have only very modest effects is surprising. However, in some ways the most surprising aspect of the politics of NAFTA relates to the apparent footlooseness of aggregate opinion. That is, since standard theories of political economy assume that policy preferences are determined by material conditions, those theories only predict changes when material (economic or political) conditions change. In this chapter we will argue that aggregate public opinion in NAFTA shifted dramatically in the absence of any change in the underlying political and economic fundamentals. We will then sketch the elements of a theory of footloose policy preferences that helps understand this sort of phenomenon and conclude with a discussion of the implications of the analysis for policy analysis and advice.[2]

---

[1] We specifically have in mind the strong opposition of a number of unions in sectors where research suggested that NAFTA would permit rationalization of production involving increased production in the US. The most obvious case is the automotive sector where an end to domenstic content rules will permit rationalization of production that was estimated to increase US employment in that sector. Similarly with respect to environmental organizations where research was far from clear on the environmental effects of NAFTA (though here it is important to recall that environmental organizations were actually split on NAFTA). With respect to bizarre coalitions, we need only recall that the Democrat president and the Republican congressional leadership led one coalition, opposing a group led by Pat Buchanan, Ross Perot, Richard Gephardt, Jesse Jackson, and Ralph Nader. Note that this is not to say that such a rationalization cannot be produced. We have no doubt that several can. We are, after all, professionals. The question is whether such a rationalization can be produced that would have been compelling ex ante.

[2] The theory of footloose policy preferences is developed in detail in Nelson (1998).

The Peculiar Political Economy of NAFTA   93

5.1. THE FACT: FOOTLOOSE AGGREGATE PREFERENCES ON NAFTA

In this section we first provide evidence of a sizable shift in public opinion on NAFTA and then provide evidence that political and economic fundamentals were, at best, unchanged and, at least arguably, moved in such a way that would have generally been expected to increase support for NAFTA.[3] Figure 5.1 shows, from 1991 to 1995, the shares of responses to questions asking whether the respondent believes NAFTA "would be mostly good or mostly bad for the US" and, from 1996 to 2000, whether NAFTA has "had more of a positive impact or more of a negative impact on the US".[4] It is easy to see that from very high levels of positive evaluation and very low levels of negative evaluation in 1990 and 1991, the positives drop dramatically while the negatives rise more slowly, but still steadily, so that by the mid-1990s positive and negative evaluations are essentially balanced.[5] Figure 5.2 summarizes these two by taking the ratio of "good" to "bad" responses. We now want to argue that this shift in opinion occurs despite the fact that, although NAFTA had been officially "implemented" in January 1994, virtually nothing of economic substance had occurred, or was scheduled to occur for several years. Furthermore, we want to argue that nothing had changed in Mexican or US fundamentals that would lead to a policy reassessment of the sort revealed by these two polls.

First, NAFTA itself. In early 1990, as part of, and as a support to, extensive domestic economic reforms, Mexico's president (Carlos Salinas de Gortari) approached the Bush White House with a request to negotiate a bilateral free trade agreement with the United States.[6] Canadian concern with the implications of such an agreement for its recently negotiated trade agreement with the US led to

---

[3] Philip Levy (1998) discusses such a shift in terms of two polls asking: will NAFTA be "mostly good for the country" (1991); and has NAFTA had "more of a postive...or a negative impact" (1996). It turns out that these two polls are the most extreme polls on NAFTA in the Roper Center database.

[4] These data are drawn from the Roper Center for Public Opinion Research database (available from Lexis–Nexis), and include all questions in that database of the form described in the text. The number of polls in each year are 1990 (1); 1991 (2); 1992 (3); 1993 (3); 1994 (2); 1995 (0); 1996 (2); 1997 (8); 1998 (1); 1999 (3); and 2000 (1).

[5] Following a sizable jump, from 1 to 19%, between 1990 and 1992, undecided responses stay in a fairly narrow range around 20% (except for 1999 (32%)). Null responses—i.e., either "about the same" or "neither one nor the other"—also make up a small number of responses (usually less than 5%).

[6] It is useful to recall that Mexico acceded to GATT membership in 1986. This was part of a substantial trade liberalization begun by President de la Madrid in 1983. See Ten Kate (1992), Weiss (1992), Pastor and Wise (1994), and Tornell and Esquivel (1997) for useful discussions of the trade policy aspects of Mexican liberalization in the period leading up to NAFTA. For more on Mexican reforms generally, see Lustig (1998).

94   H.K. Hall and D.R. Nelson

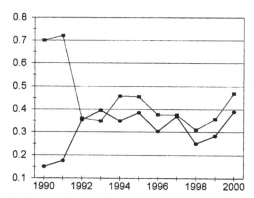

Figure 5.1:   Positive (■) and negative (●) evaluations of NAFTA.

the continental approach that eventually produced NAFTA. Virtually from the beginning, labor and environmental interests began organizing against NAFTA. The central issue in the early period was fast-track negotiating authority and, while there was substantial public opposition by labor and environmental groups, but consistent with the poll evidence cited above, fast track passed with substantial majorities on 23 (House) and 24 (Senate) May 1991.[7] NAFTA then became a major public issue in the Presidential campaign. However, only minor candidate Ross Perot opposed NAFTA (both George Bush and Bill Clinton came out publicly in support).[8] Perhaps surprisingly, NAFTA passed with nearly the same margins as had fast track, though in this case the outcome was considered highly uncertain until virtually the moment of the vote.[9] Under this legislation, NAFTA was scheduled to be implemented in January 1994.

One of the tricky things about implementation of complex legislation like NAFTA is the timetable. The NAFTA was completed in August 1992 and implementing legislation in the US became effective on January 1, 1994.

---

[7] 231–192 in the House and 59–36 in the Senate. These majorities are actually majorities against disapproval resolutions. These counts are from Destler (1995), which provides a fine treatment of the politics surrounding NAFTA, and all other aspects of US trade policy. Boadu and Thompson (1993) and Kahane (1996a,b) provide conventional econometric studies of the fast track vote.

[8] It should be noted, however, that candidate Clinton did express concern about both labor and environmental issues, stressing the importance of side agreements on both.

[9] House, 234–200 (17/11/93); and Senate, 61–38 (20/11/93). The NAFTA votes, especially in the the Senate, have been extensively studied, see Conybeare and Zinkula (1994), Steagall and Jennings (1996a,b), Kahane (1996a,b), Thorbecke (1997), Holian et al. (1997), Kamdar and Gonzalez (1998), Bailey and Brady (1998), and Baldwin and Magee (2000).

The Peculiar Political Economy of NAFTA   95

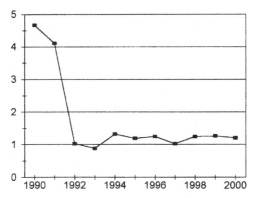

Figure 5.2:   Ratio of positive to negative evaluations.

It incorporated and expanded most of the provisions of the CFTA that was halfway into its 10-year phase-in period. While the agreement eliminated tariffs on many goods immediately (over half of US imports and nearly a third of exports with Mexico), it began the phasing-out of remaining tariffs over a 15-year period. Most of the anticipated effects of the agreement on the US economy, however, were through provisions covering a broad range of nontariff barriers, foreign direct investment, intellectual property rights, trade in services, and a number of other trade facilitating agreements (on customs administration, product standards, antitrust, and telecommunications). Many of these provisions were also to be phased-in over time. There were also two well-publicized side agreements on environmental and labor cooperation.

Prior to NAFTA implementation, the average US tariff rate on imports from Mexico was only around 3% and half by value already entered the US duty-free. By 1996, about three-fourths of US imports from Mexico were duty free with an average tariff of around 2.5% on the remainder (including sectors such as motor vehicles and motor vehicle parts, apparel and textiles, and fresh vegetables). The average tariff rate in Mexico on US goods started at around 10% prior to NAFTA and in 1996 was down to approximately 3% on NAFTA goods. Also, the share of US exports entering Mexico duty free increased from roughly one-third to two-thirds by 1996.

Most provisions on nontariff barriers were still being implemented in 1996. In particular, prohibitions, quantitative restrictions, and import licensing require-ments by Mexico were still being phased-out with the use of tariff-rate quotas. Additionally, implementation was not yet complete in a number of key industries. For example, Mexico is phasing-out trade and investment restrictions on

96   H.K. Hall and D.R. Nelson

automobiles over 10 years—including a slow reduction in local content requirements from 36% to only 34% in the first 5 years. Additionally, the US is phasing-out quotas on textiles and apparel made with foreign material over a 10-year period and both countries are phasing out nontariff barriers on agriculture (import licenses in Mexico and quota shares in the US) over 10 or 15 years using tariff-rate quotas. Implementation by Mexico is also not complete in the telecommunications, transportation services, and financial services industries. The provisions related to foreign direct investment, intellectual property rights, trade in services, customs administration, and product standards were fully in effect by 1996.[10]

Complicating an assessment of the impact of NAFTA on the US was the fact that the WTO Agreements entered into effect only 1 year later and addressed many of the same issues. In general, the WTO Agreements were broader than the NAFTA and went farther in sectors such as agriculture and telecommunication services, but fell short with respect to foreign direct investment and government procurement. Notable overlap includes areas such as sanitary measures, textile and clothing, antidumping, safeguards, intellectual property rights, and dispute settlement. The WTO Agreements also lowered US tariffs by nearly a third and began a 5-year phase-in period of tariff reductions on most products, with a 10-year phase-in period on sensitive sectors (such as textiles). Mexico did not reduce their MFN tariffs as a result of the WTO Agreements and, instead, merely bound their rates generally at 35%. In fact, in response to the peso crisis, Mexico raised MFN tariffs on 502 consumer goods in 1995 from an average of 20–35%. US exports to Mexico under the NAFTA were exempt from these tariff increases.

Thus, the major political event in the period 1991–1992 was the fast-track vote. The passage of the legislation, and thus the final legal form of NAFTA was not determined until the end of 1993, with "implementation" occurring in 1994.[11] It would be hard to argue that the sizable shift in opinion occurring between 1991 and 1993 was a function of the sort of shifts in political fundamentals that might be taken to account for changed policy preferences in standard political economy models. While the institutional environment had not changed significantly, it is entirely possible that a change in economic conditions induced the change in public trade policy preferences. We know from previous research on the correlates of trade policy that trade balance and general macroeconomic conditions are

---

[10] For a much more detailed discussion of the status of NAFTA implementation in 1996, see Chapter 2 of *The Impact of the North American Free Trade Agreement on the US Economy and Industries: A Three-Year Review*, US International Trade Commission, publication 3045.

[11] With reference to Levy's (1998) paper we simply note that (1) opinion shifts well before this date; and (2) actual implementation occurs much later (i.e., many of the most significant changes in US and Mexican law were scheduled to occur only with lags of up to 15 years).

The Peculiar Political Economy of NAFTA   97

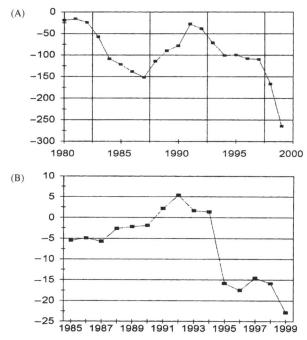

Figure 5.3:   (A) US balance on trade in goods and services. (B) US–Mexico merchandise trade balance.

associated with changes in trade policy demands. Figure 5.3A shows the balance on goods and services (1980–1999), where 1991 is the last year of a multi-year improvement in the trade balance and where 1992 and 1993 show positive performance by historical standards. By contrast, the large deteriorations in 1998 and 1999 do not appear to be particularly associated with changed evaluations. Similarly, Figure 5.3B shows the (possibly more relevant) merchandise trade balance with Mexico, where we see 1991 and 1992 are years of improving trade balances and, again, the large deterioration from 1994 to 1995 is not associated with changed evaluations. Aggregate economic indicators, shown in Figure 5.4, are equally unsupportive of an economic fundamentals story.[12] The period of

---

[12] It should also be recalled that this is the period of realignment of the US dollar from a period of very large overvaluation. It will be recalled that the dollar began accelerating in late 1980 or early 1981, reaching its peak in February 1985, and ultimately returning to something like an equilibrium level in late 1987 or early 1988. The essential fact would seem to be that 1991 is at the end of a period of exchange rate instability, while 1996 is in a relatively stable period.

98   *H.K. Hall and D.R. Nelson*

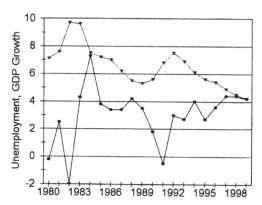

Figure 5.4:   Aggregate economic indicators: (▼) unemp; (●) drlGDP.

strongest support coincides with a period of low (even negative in 1991) growth and high unemployment, while the periods of weaker support are characterized by stronger growth performance and lower unemployment. The picture that emerges from these data is clear: standard theoretical and empirical models of trade policy preference/behavior would have predicted greater activism in 1990–1993 than in the latter half of the decade. Interestingly, this suggestion is supported by the data in Figure 5.5, which shows the number of Title VII (anti-dumping and countervailing duty) petitions initiated per year. Activity in the administered protection mechanisms, of which the Title VII mechanism is the most prominent, is well known to be a major indicator of protectionist activity. That figure shows a relatively smoothly rising trend in filings consistent with a period of deteriorating economic performance, and a drop in 1995 to a lower annual level of filings.[13] Thus, as we asserted at the outset of this section, it would be difficult to attribute to changed institutional or material conditions the shift in public attitudes with respect to NAFTA.

---

[13] The spikes in 1992 and 1997 are associated with massive steel industry filings that are determined institutionally (i.e., as a part of the steel industry's strategy relative to the mechanism) and are not in any obvious way associated with Mexico, Canada, or NAFTA.

Although, using annual data (1980–1999 and 1990–1999) there are too few data points for convincing analysis, simple regression of Title VII petitions on unemployment and trade balance suggests that both of these play a role in explaining filing behavior (with unemployment playing the larger role). Carrying out the same analysis using positive responses, negative responses, or their ratio yields no significant results at all.

The Peculiar Political Economy of NAFTA 99

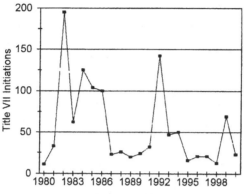

Figure 5.5: Title VII petitions initiated.

5.2. POLICY COMPLEXITY, SOCIAL LEARNING AND FOOTLOOSE PREFERENCES

As economists/political-economists, the conclusion of Section 5.1 leaves us in an awkward position. All positive political economy models operate by assuming that the policy preferences of individuals are derived in some relatively straightforward way from the effect of policy (and policy changes) on material well-being. But we have just displayed a case where policy preferences changed, and changed dramatically, with no relevant change in material or institutional conditions. In this section we argue that the complexity of NAFTA makes determining the effects of implementation difficult. It is under precisely such conditions that we might expect agents to condition their behavior on the actions of others, not for strategic reasons, but because those who have already taken actions might reasonably be expected to possess knowledge one does not possess. This attempt to learn from the behavior of others is called *social learning*.

From the point of view of the citizen, or policy-maker, trade policy is extremely complex. Trade policy rarely comes in the form of a single, discrete act of protection.[14] Instead, trade policy is embedded in legislative acts made up of complicated bundles of changes in the law regulating trade that even experts have a hard time evaluating. NAFTA is a very interesting example. NAFTA itself is

---

[14] Even in the days of the classic tariff system—say, 1870 to 1932—the political action revolved around tariff acts with hundreds of line items. In addition, as research on 19th century voting suggests, the social meaning of the tariff was highly variable across local electorates.

100   *H.K. Hall and D.R. Nelson*

a document of over 300 pages (not including the national tariff schedules and various other lists—with these the text runs over 2000 pages) covering trade in goods, technical barriers to trade, government procurement, investment, services, intellectual property, and the administrative and institutional conventions needed for implementation; the agreement on environmental cooperation is another 20 pages; as is the agreement on labor cooperation; all of these need to be implemented with specific national regulations in all three signatory countries. Some of these regulations will affect trade in goods, others will affect trade in factors of production; some will liberalize this trade, others will restrict it. In addition, while NAFTA officially became law in 1994, as we saw above, full implementation will not occur in sensitive sectors for periods of 10–25 years. In this environment even trade economists might be expected to have fairly diffuse priors with respect to NAFTA's aggregate and distributional effects.[15]

Clearly, in the case of NAFTA, some form of "learning" had occurred, since expressed evaluations had shifted fairly dramatically. What is completely unclear is what triggered this reassessment. There was virtually no NAFTA-specific information and the aggregate facts of the economy suggest the sort of environment in which trade is usually viewed relatively benignly. This would seem to be a virtually archetypal example of footloose preferences. Given the weakened domestic political institutions supporting trade liberalization in the US, and the concomitant likelihood of increased prominence for trade as a public political issue, such footlooseness of trade preferences could play a significant role in the future politics of trade.[16] As proponents of liberal trading relations, it behooves us to seek an understanding of such preferences.

While there may have been no change in the material or policy environment, the period from 1991 to 1996 (and especially 1991–1993) was characterized by an extraordinary amount of public discussion about NAFTA. It was the first instance of highly public trade politics since the heyday of the classic tariff system and, as such, it may tell us something about the politics of trade in years to come. NAFTA was in the news, it was dinner table and cocktail party conversation among non-economists, every politician had (and had to have) a public opinion (sometimes different from their private opinion). Perhaps most

---

[15] For the purposes of this chapter we abstract from the central importance to the US of locking in Mexican economic reforms. This is consistent with nearly all of the political-economy research on free trade areas in general, and NAFTA in particular. Though see the important series of papers by Ethier (1998a–c, 1999, 2002).

[16] The events surrounding the WTO meeting in Seattle (30 November 1999), illustrate this point even more clearly than does the politics of NAFTA. Nelson (1989) provides a discussion of the role and transformation of US trade policy institutions for the support of trade liberalism. Nelson (1995) discusses the collapse of those institutions in the early 1970s.

The Peculiar Political Economy of NAFTA   101

importantly, NAFTA was a major issue in the 1992 presidential election. Trade economists approached minor celebrity status, and the unanimity with which trade economists concluded that NAFTA was economically insignificant for the US was truly stunning. With similar unanimity we heaped well-earned scorn on dishonest claims about the "giant sucking sound".[17] But note that the timing is important. NAFTA really takes off as public issue only when candidate Ross Perot decided to focus on it, and this focus really comes after the change in public evaluations. While both Patrick Buchanan and Perot were critical in 1991 and 1992, it is only in 1993 (especially with the publication of Perot's book in September and the Gore–Perot debate in November) that there was wide discussion of the issue. Where economists appear to have been successful in convincing Congress that NAFTA's economic effects would be small, the public was clearly confused and worried (with "undecided" responses rising rapidly in 1991 and 1992).

Clearly, high uncertainty and learning play a major role in the NAFTA case. However, at least if we believe that the effects of NAFTA were likely to be small (and probably positive), as we claimed at the time, this is a peculiar kind of "learning". That is, instead of converging on the "true" facts of the matter, the public moved in the opposite direction. One useful way of approaching this phenomenon is to consider it as an example of herd behavior. Herding occurs whenever agents focus on a single behavior, with particular reference to cases in which there are multiple plausible candidate behaviors. The phenomenon of herd behavior is common enough that it has been used as the basis for a wide variety of economic analyses based on such things as demand interdependence (Leibenstein, 1950; Schelling, 1978; Becker, 1991) and network externalities (Dybvig and Spatt, 1983; David, 1985; Farrell and Saloner, 1985; Katz and Shapiro, 1985). An alternative explanation in terms of information cascades has recently been presented by Bikhchandani, Hirshleifer, and Welch (BHW, 1992), and further developed in a number of later papers.[18]

In an environment where individuals can learn about the environment from both private information and the behavior of others, an *information cascade* occurs when agents ignore their private information and follow the information implied by the behavior of others. Where the behavior of others is not perfectly informative with respect to their private information, an information cascade effectively traps socially useful information, thus permitting socially suboptimal

---

[17] It is probably useful, given the recent vogue among trade economists for attacking free trade areas, to recall that during the NAFTA debate support for NAFTA was seen as a litmus test of one's status as a serious economist.

[18] See Bikhchandani et al. (1998) and Nelson (1998) for surveys.

102   **H.K. Hall and D.R. Nelson**

outcomes. Thus, the essential elements of the information cascade model are coarse public signals and private signals of bounded accuracy. Without the first assumption, the law of large numbers suggests that, with a sufficiently large number of observations, the true state of the world is revealed (almost surely). In most information cascade models this assumption takes the form that agents observe the actions of other agents but not their signals, and that the actions are imperfectly informative with respect to signals. Without the second assumption, individuals might receive fully informative signals, allowing them to take actions that would break the cascade. In addition, BHW (1992) make a number of additional assumptions that permit a very simple expository model.

Consider the NAFTA case. Suppose that we start from an equilibrium and, thus, from a cascade involving all citizens. Specifically, suppose we start from a situation in which people have essentially no beliefs at all about NAFTA, and possibly have a weakly held belief that trade liberalization (whether NAFTA or multilateral) would have a negative effect on the economic interests of the US.[19] That is, we assume that citizens as a whole believe that trade liberalization is harmful, but this support of increased liberalization is highly conditional and subject to large shifts. Now recall that in the run up to the fast-track vote, virtually all respectable economists and the political leadership of both parties argued very publicly that, essentially, NAFTA was no big deal economically for the US, but that it was important politically (by being important economically for Mexico). The result, as we have already noted, was strong public support for NAFTA. However, the public had not *learned* that liberal trade was good, if by "learned" we mean "identified the true state of the world", but had simply shifted to another weakly held prior. With the campaigns in 1992 and the debate over NAFTA itself in 1993, the opposition forces began to receive considerable greater visibility and, even though there was no change in the material environment, people shifted their evaluations. Furthermore, once NAFTA was passed by Congress, economists in general (and trade economists in particular) not only lost interest in NAFTA, but began to argue that maybe NAFTA was not such a great idea after all. It is not really relevant that the free trade fundamentalist critique of NAFTA was that it distracted political attention from

---

[19] Both assumptions here strike us as plausible approximations for the purposes of this example. What poll data exist with respect to trade policy generally strongly suggests that a considerable majority believes further liberalization will be harmful to the US economy—though there is little evidence of support for general increases in protection (though support for sectoral increases is often strong)—see Scheve and Slaughter (2001). Furthermore, there is very little evidence that citizens make much of a distinction between preferential and multilateral liberalization. This makes sense. The difference in complexity, from the point of view of a citizen, between NAFTA and, say, a GATT agreement, is trivial.

The Peculiar Political Economy of NAFTA   103

broader trade liberalization. The public listens for the conclusion, not the argument—especially when the argument is, at best, arcane.[20] The result, in the face of continued aggressive public relations against NAFTA, as we have already noted, is that public opinion shifted back to opposition to NAFTA.

5.3. AN ILLUSTRATIVE MODEL

This section sets up a very simple political economy model of individual citizen preferences for or against the NAFTA under uncertainty over the impact of the agreement. Preferences over the trade agreement depend on two factors: an economic effect; and a political effect. The latter reflects the claim that NAFTA would help lock-in liberal political and economic reforms in Mexico. We will assume that this effect is certain, but has a relatively small weight in citizen welfare. The first reflects concerns with the economic effects of NAFTA on US labor. Poll data seem to suggest that negative evaluations of NAFTA were highly correlated with a perception of high labor adjustment costs in the US. If Mexico is economically small, we suppose that there are no significant adjustment costs; but if Mexico is large there will be significant adjustment costs. Furthermore, if Mexico is large, the adjustment costs are taken to outweigh the benefits of locking in Mexican reform. We will assume that these preferences are common and reflected in a common evaluation function $V(E, P) := v(E(S)) - P$, where E and P reflect the economic and political factors, S denotes the economic size of Mexico, and $v(\cdot)$ is the value of protecting displaced factors from adjustment costs, so a positive value of $V(\cdot)$ implies a preference for *rejecting* NAFTA.[21]

---

[20] Abstracting from details of trade creation and trade diversion, which are characterized by complexity considerations of the sort central to this chapter, it is notable that virtually all of the arguments against regionalism, whatever their validity, are arguments that only an economist would love. Unlike the simple models used to illustrate powerful, but difficult, notions of comparative advantage and gains from trade, which are based on assumptions that isolate the key causal relation generating gains from trade, the political economy arguments used to argue against free trade areas are based on assumptions that seem unrelated to the core processes involved. Their purpose seems more to be to stiffen the spine of the profession in its support of multilateralism than to persuade citizens or their representatives.

[21] That is we are assuming that citizens have a very simple form of *sociotropic preferences* (Kinder and Kiewiet, 1981; Mutz and Mondak, 1997), i.e., they evaluate policies in terms of the way policy affects community welfare. We simplify by assuming that the relevant community is the nation as a whole, and that the evaluation of community welfare is unaffected by individual preference. These latter two assumptions are generally false. We can prove the existence of cascades in more standard political economy models, but the additional analytical freight does not produce any additional insight relative to the central point of this chapter: footlooseness of policy preferences.

104   *H.K. Hall and D.R. Nelson*

We now assume that Mexico's size is uncertain. Each agent, therefore, faces a decision under uncertainty of whether or not to reject the trade agreement depending upon whether he/she expects it to be welfare improving. Specifically, we will assume that each citizen observes a conditionally iid signal $\sigma_i = \{L, S\}$ and that $\sigma_i > 0.5$ if the true value of Mexico's size is L and $1 - \sigma_i$ if the true value is S. In addition to the private signal, citizens take their action in a known order and each citizen observes the action (but not the signal) of all agents that precede them in this order. Thus, after the first citizen decides whether or not to reject NAFTA, all later deciders have two sources of information: one public, and one private. It is common knowledge that all agents are Bayesian rational. If we adopt BHW's normalization of $v(H) = 1$, $v(L) = 0$, $P = \frac{1}{2}$, and letting γ_i be the posterior probability that Mexico is large: $E[v_i] = \gamma_i \times 1 + (1 - \gamma_i) \times 0 = \gamma_i$; and $V_i > 0$ if $\gamma_i > \frac{1}{2}$. Finally, BHW adopt the tie-breaking convention that a citizen that is indifferent between rejecting and accepting NAFTA chooses to accept. This model is now identical to that of BHW's "specific model" (BHW, 1992, pp. 996–999).

The logic of cascades is straightforward in this model. Suppose that the first citizen observes $\sigma_1 = L$. She has no additional information, so $V_1 = 1 - \frac{1}{2} > 0$ and she rejects NAFTA. For citizen 2 there are two possibilities: $\sigma_2 = L$ and citizen 2 rejects; or $\sigma_2 = S$, so citizen 2 computes $E[v_2] = \frac{1}{2}$, $V_2 = 0$, and by the tie-breaking rule accepts. Citizen 3 is in one of three cases: both the previous citizens reject NAFTA, so citizen 3 rejects *independently of her private signal*; both previous citizens accepted, so citizen 3 accepts *independently of her private signal*; or 1 and 2 split, in which case 3 is in the same situation as 1—i.e., her private signal determines her action. Either of the first two cases is a cascade: all later citizens ignore their private signals and adopt the same action of those preceding them. In this simple framework it is easy to see that: cascades occur with probability 1; cascades occur more quickly the further is σ from 0.5; and good cascades occur more often the further is σ from 0.5. With reasonably high uncertainty, σ not terribly far from 0.5 (as we have argued may have been the case with NAFTA), but with a large number of citizens, everyone knows that they are in a cascade almost surely. This is the opening wedge for BHW's other key result that: (1) once an informational cascade has begun, individuals still value public information and (2) a small amount of public information can reverse a cascade. That is, even a strong informational cascade rejecting NAFTA can be suddenly reversed into an equally strong cascade supporting the agreement. The key result here is their result (3) "the release of a small amount of public information can shatter a long-lasting cascade, where a 'small amount' refers

The Peculiar Political Economy of NAFTA 105

to a signal less informative than the private signal of a single individual" (BHW, 1992, p. 1005).[22]

5.4. CONCLUSION: ON ECONOMISTS AS PARTICIPANTS IN THE POLITICS OF TRADE POLICY

It is important to be clear that, while the class of models considered here is positive, they are not predictive over the domain of final political-economic outcomes. These models do not avoid, in fact they rest on (or, more accurately, provide a formal representation of) the fact that, with appropriately chosen priors, we can reproduce virtually any final outcome.[23] Thus, any predictions of these models with respect to final outcomes are vacuous. Nonetheless, we hope that this chapter suggests that ignorance and learning in a social context are issues of first-rate importance, both as empirical phenomena and as potential determinants of trade policy outcomes. Furthermore, there are, we think, several implications of these models (and of ignorance/learning more generally) for us as policy analysts. We consider two: one with respect to evaluating the predictive content of our positive models; and the second with respect to the role of economists in the public discourse over trade policy.

There is no substitute for basing predictive political-economy models on political and economic fundamentals. We have good reason to expect such fundamentals to play a central role in determining trade policy, and we have equally good reason to predict the direction of the effects. However, if learning effects also play a, largely unpredictable, role, we also need to expect prediction errors that are occasionally large. That is, the right kind of ignorance can yield wildly different outcomes from those predicted by models. An excellent example, away from the trade policy focus of this chapter, is the poor performance of macro political-economy models in the 1992 Bush–Clinton election (Haynes and Stone, 1994). While the data seem to show recovery of the economy, and thus success for the

---

[22] BHW (1992) develop their analysis in a somewhat more general informational environment involving a sequence of possible signals and a more careful formalism. More importantly, it would be straightforward to extend their analysis to the case of preference heterogeneity, as generated, for example, in a standard endogenous tariff model, under full information about citizen types. In that case, while actions (e.g., accept, reject, abstain) will vary, so there need not be complete herding, there will still be good and bad cascades with strictly positive probability. More interesting possibilities emerge with type heterogeneity and uncertainty about types. Smith and Sørensen (2000) develop this case in detail. This is an important topic for future research, but beyond the needs of the simple point made in this chapter.

[23] It is the *re*production of outcomes that is most worrying in social scientific analysis. Thin predictions (unless strictly unfalsifiable) will not last, but compelling post-dictions ("stylized facts") can sustain empirically weak theoretical analyses for long periods.

106   *H.K. Hall and D.R. Nelson*

incumbent, there was widespread perception that the economy was still in an economic crisis ("It's the economy stupid"). The result, as they say, is history.

As noted in the introduction and suggested by the discussion of the NAFTA case, one of the most interesting implications of learning models with information cascades as a prediction is the suggestion of a major role for policy analysts. Some of the recent attempts to justify an active policy role for economists turn on difficult philosophical issues of freedom of choice that seem rather removed from the actual practice of participation by economists in the public policy discourse. The advice on how and whom to advise that emerges from this kind of argument seems of limited use.[24] The problem seems to emerge from taking our models seriously where we should not. We have just argued that these models serve a very useful positive purpose in understanding and predicting public policy. However, when we abstract from complexity and uncertainty in the interest of building parsimonious models, we have abstracted from the most obvious warrant for an active advisory role. When agents, whether citizens or policy-makers, are highly uncertain about the workings of the economy (i.e., most of the time), expert advice can have a substantial effect on final outcomes via precisely the channels identified in learning models.[25] It makes perfectly good sense for citizens and politicians to listen to, and even to seek out, the advice of economists because that advice is better informed than much of the policy advice that is given during a political process—though note that this need not be even vaguely perfect information. A public signal of strong agreement among economists, especially when supported by compelling evidence, during a political process can have the effect of a public information release in the models discussed above. Even if policy-makers, or citizens, believe that this information is less informative than any individual privately observed signal, such a public release can have the effect of reopening the public discussion and dramatically shifting the structure of governmental or public opinion.[26]

---

[24] This is the entering wedge for Dixit's (1997) comment on O'Flaherty and Bhagwati (1997).

[25] Just as trade and political economy models abstract from informational issues to focus on the causal forces of most immediate interest, learning models of the sort developed in this chapter abstract from a variety of complexities to highlight the effects of ignorance and learning in a social context. In particular, these models abstract from the important, and complementary, forces that make advisors participants (in a game theoretic sense) in the political process. Dixit (1997) provides a very nice sketch, with appropriate references, of models which highlight the role of advice giving in a strategic environment with asymmetric information.

[26] Although we are presumably better informed, as we noted above, economists are at least as prone to being trapped in cascades as any other rational agents engaged in learning about the world, possibly more so. Because economists have very similar understandings of the workings of the economy—due to strong socialization—we may behave more like the agents in the BHW models than any other group. Smith and Sørensen (2000) find much more complex aggregate behavior characterizing groups with heterogeneous preferences than in groups with homogeneous preferences.

The Peculiar Political Economy of NAFTA   107

It seems to us that a focus on this non-strategic, informational role of economic advice has useful implications. To the extent that the warrant for advice-giving is uncertainty, as much about the working of the economy as about simple facts, it seems particularly fruitless to give advice based on the presumption that those receiving it are well-trained economists.[27] We need to convince our auditors that a consensus on fundamental issues related to, say, trade policy, exists, and we need to do so in ways that are clear to relatively engaged, relatively intelligent non-economists. This clearly means that complicated arguments, requiring many closely argued steps, and knowledge of economic theory, are likely to be unsuccessful. However, as Matthew Slaughter (1999) argues, while outright lies may be successful in the short-run (e.g., "NAFTA will create thousands of jobs"), sooner-or-later they are likely to backfire. The most successful of our public representatives—e.g., Milton Friedman, Alan Blinder, Paul Krugman—seem to identify simple but compelling metaphors, which are mixed with a small number of striking facts, to argue for a single clear policy point. Finally, it should be noted that, if social learning does not produce knowledge of the intertemporally sturdy type, but rather of the type suggested by informational cascade models, we need to be prepared to stay engaged in the public discourse beyond the passage of any particular piece of legislation.

ACKNOWLEDGEMENTS

The authors would like to thank participants at the 1999 ASSA meetings, New York, NY and the 25th Anniversary Meeting of the International Economic Study Group, September 9–11, 2000, Isle of Thorns, Sussex. In particular, we are grateful to comments from Alan Winters and Devashish Mitra.

REFERENCES

Bailey, M. and Brady, D. (1998). Heterogeniety and representation: the senate and free trade. *American Journal of Political Science, 42*, 524–544.
Baldwin, R. and Magee, C. (2000). Is trade policy for sale? Congressional voting on recent trade bills. *Public Choice, 105*, 79–101.
Becker, G. (1991). A note on restaurant pricing and other examples of social influence on price. *Journal of Political Economy, 99*, 1109–1116.

---

[27] While admirable, the attempt to transform citizens and policy-makers into economists is almost certainly doomed to failure.

108   *H.K. Hall and D.R. Nelson*

Bikhchandani, S., Hirshleifer, D. and Welch, I. (1992). A theory of fads, fashion, custom, and cultural change as informational cascades. *Journal of Political Economy, 100*, 992–1026.

Bikhchandani, S., Hirshleifer, D. and Welch, I. (1998). Learning from the behavior of others: conformity, fads, and informational cascades. *Journal of Economic Perspectives, 12*, 151–170.

Boadu, F. and Thompson, M. (1993). The political economy of the U.S.–Mexico free trade agreement: analysis of the congressional fast track vote. *Journal of Agricultural and Applied Economics, 25*, 27–35.

Conybeare, J. and Zinkula, M. (1994). Who voted against the NAFTA. *World Economy, 19*, 1–12.

David, P. (1985). Clio and the economics of QWERTY. *American Economic Review. 75*, 332–337.

Destler, I. M. (1995). *American Trade Politics*, 3rd edn., Washington, DC: Institute for International Economics.

Dixit, A. (1997). Economists as advisers to politicians and society. *Economics and Politics, 9*, 225–230.

Dybvig, P. and Spatt, C. (1983). Adoption externalities as public goods. *Journal of Public Economics, 20*, 231–247.

Ethier, W. (1998). The international commercial system. *Essays in International Finance*, #210.

Ethier, W. (1998). The new regionalism. *Economic Journal, 108*, 1149–1161.

Ethier, W. (1998). Regionalism in a multilateral world. *Journal of Political Economy, 106*, 1214–1245.

Ethier, W. (1999). "Multilateral roads to regionalism," in *International Trade Policy and the Pacific Rim*, J. Piggot and A. Woodland (eds.), London: Macmillan, 131–152.

Ethier, W. (2002). Unilateralism in a multilateral world. *Economic Journal, 112*, 266–292.

Farell, J. and Saloner, C. (1985). Standardization, compatibility, and innovation. *Rand Journal of Economics, 16*, 70–83.

Haynes, S. and Stone, J. (1994). Why did economic models falsely predict a Bush landslide in 1992. *Contemporary Economic Policy, 12*, 123–130.

Holian, D., Krebs, T. and Walsh, M. (1997). Constituency opinion, Ross Perot, and roll-call behavior in the U.S. house: the case of the NAFTA. *Legislative Studies Quarterly, 22*, 369–392.

Kahane, L. (1996). Congressional voting patterns on NAFTA: an empirical analysis. *American Journal of Economics and Sociology, 55*, 395–409.

Kahane, L. (1996). Senate voting patterns on the 1991 extension of the fast track trade procedures: prelude to NAFTA. *Public Choice, 87*, 35–53.

Kamdar, N. and Gonzalez, J. (1998). An empirical analysis of the U.S. senate vote on NAFTA and GATT. *International Advances in Economic Research, 4*, 105–114.

Katz, M. and Shapiro, C. (1985). Network externalities, competition and compatibility. *American Economic Review, 75*, 424–440.

Kinder, D. and Kiewiet, D. (1981). Sociotropic politics: the American case. *British Journal of Politics, 11*, 129–161.

Leibenstein, H. (1950). Bandwagon, Snob and Veblen effects in the theory of consumer demand. *Quarterly Journal of Economics, 64,* 183–207.

Levy, P. (1998). "Learning from trade agreements," MS, Department of Economics, Yale University.

Lustig, N. (1998). *Mexico: The Remaking of an Economy,* 2nd edn., Washington, DC: Brookings.

Mayer, F. (1998). *The Science and Art of Policy Analysis,* New York: Columbia University Press.

Mutz, D. and Mondak, J. (1997). Dimensions of sociotropic behavior: group-based judgements of fairness and well-being. *American Journal of Political Science, 41,* 284–308.

Nelson, D. (1989). The domestic political preconditions of US trade policy: liberal structure and protectionist dynamics. *Journal of Public Policy, 9,* 83–108.

Nelson, D. (1995). "Political economy of protection for the US automobile industry," in *Political Economy of American Trade Policy,* A. Krueger (ed.), Chicago: University of Chicago Press, 133–191.

Nelson, D. (1998). "Footloose policy preferences and trade policy: the role of non-strategic social learning and information cascades," MS, Murphy Institute of Political Economy.

O'Flaherty, B. and Bhagwati, J. (1997). Will free trade with political science put normative economists out of work? *Economics and Politics, 9,* 207–219.

Pastor, M. and Wise, C. (1994). The origins and sustainability of Mexico's free trade policy. *International Organization, 48,* 459–489.

Schelling, T. (1978). *Micromotives and Macrobehavior,* New York: Norton.

Scheve, K. and Slaughter, M. (2001). *Globalization and the Perceptions of American Workers,* Washington, DC: Institute for International Economics.

Slaughter, M. (1999). Globalisation and wages: a tale of two perspectives. *World Economy, 22,* 609–629.

Smith, L. and Sørensen, P. (2000). Pathological outcomes of observational learning. *Econometrica, 68,* 371–398.

Steagall, J. and Jennings, K. (1996). Unions, PAC contributions, and the NAFTA vote. *Journal of Labor Research, 17,* 515–521.

Steagall, J. and Jennings, K. (1996). Unions and NAFTAs legislative passage: confrontation and cover. *Labor Studies Journal, 21,* 61–79.

Ten Kate, A. (1992). Trade liberalization and economic stabilization in Mexico: lessons of experience. *World Development, 20,* 659–672.

Thorbecke, W. (1997). Explaining house voting on the north American free trade agreement. *Public Choice, 92,* 231–242.

Tornell, A. and Esquivel, G. (1997). "The political economy of Mexico's entry into NAFTA," in *Regionalism versus Multilateral Trade Arrangements,* T. Ito and A. Krueger (eds.), Chicago: University of Chicago Press, 25–55.

Weiss, J. (1992). Trade liberalization in mexico in the 1980s: concepts, measures and short-run effects. *Weltwirtschaftliches Archives, 128,* 711–726.

Review of International Economics, 12(5), 769–792, 2004

Structural Change and the Labor-market Effects of Globalization

Noel Gaston and Douglas Nelson*

Abstract

The paper develops a simple political-economy model of unemployment benefit determination in a small open economy characterized by bargaining between firms and unions. The authors derive a number of comparative static results and present empirical results for a panel of OECD countries that are broadly consistent with the theory.

1. Introduction

Why is the average citizen so worried about globalization and the average economist so unworried? It is surely true, but unuseful, to say that the citizen and the economist simply do not understand the benefits and costs of globalization in the same way. There are good reasons why the economist feels comfortable arguing that, at least at an aggregate level, globalization is either no big deal or a substantial boon. It would be comforting to conclude that the citizen is simply wrong, with the obvious implication being that a little bit more effort at public education would help reduce globalphobia. There may be a significant element of truth here, but the consequences of introducing irrationality, ignorance, and learning into our models are substantial.[1] It seems to us to be useful to consider the possibility that the widespread concern with globalization emerges as a result of changes that are, to some extent, obscured when we apply standard trade-theoretic methods to understand globalization. In this paper we are interested in effects of globalization that operate on the labor market indirectly by transforming the structures that support one set of equilibria and induce change in those equilibria. We will develop our analysis in terms of the interdependence between economic and political structures in a given national economy. Because the economic and political structures are related, changes in the relationship of a national economy to the global economy can produce profound changes in the political–economic arrangements of a country. In addition to affecting equilibrium wages and employment, such changes could well be unsettling in themselves.

In section 2 we begin by briefly rehearsing the main framework within which most economists (at least trade economists) have considered the effects of globalization, and

* Gaston: School of Business, Bond University, Gold Coast, Queensland, Australia 4229. Nelson: Murphy Institute, Tulane University, New Orleans, LA 70118-5698; and School of Economics, University of Nottingham, Nottingham NG7 2RD, UK. In addition to comments from participants at the Leverhulme Centre for Research on Globalisation and Economic Policy conference on Adjusting to Globalisation, the authors are grateful for comments from participants at the Midwest International Economics Group, and seminars at the Development Bank of Japan, Tsukuba University, and the Kansai Institute for Social and Economic Research. In particular, the authors would like to thank Dyuti Banerjee, Simon Evennett, Jonathan Haskel, and Tim Lloyd for their comments; and Rob Franzese, Gilles Saint-Paul, Michael Wallerstein, and the OECD Social Policy Division for providing us with their data. Noel Gaston would like to acknowledge the collegial atmosphere provided by the Research Institute for Capital Formation at the Development Bank of Japan, while Doug Nelson benefited from comments and support during visits at Erasmus University and the University of Nottingham. The usual disclaimers apply.

found them to be essentially unproblematic. We refer to these as *direct effects* of globalization. In section 3 we review some of the research suggesting that globalization has effects on the returns to labor market participation that work through its effects on labor market and political institutions. We refer to these as *indirect effects* of globalization. We believe that this research supports a claim that indirect effects of globalization are sufficiently plausible to consider them in more detail.

Thus, in section 4, we develop a simple model of political economic equilibrium with firm–union bargaining and a welfare state. Using this model, we consider the impact of increased openness. Specifically, we show the effect of globalization on the bargain between the firm and the union (Proposition 1); as a baseline we derive the equilibrium unemployment benefit with a utilitarian policymaker in the closed economy (Proposition 2) and in the open economy (Corollary 1). Since the politics of labor figure prominently in existing work on indirect effects of globalization, we also formally characterize equilibrium with lobbying by labor (Proposition 3). In section 5, we present some empirical work based on a fixed-effects panel model for OECD countries. With respect to the effects of globalization, we find strong evidence of a positive relationship between openness and the unemployment benefit, but a negative relationship between openness interacted with the budget deficit and the unemployment benefit. This suggests that an increase in the government debt to GDP ratio lowers the response of the benefit replacement rate to openness. That is, there is some evidence that, as suggested by some of the work reviewed in section 3 and the model developed in section 4, globalization acts as a constraint on the political economy of labor market outcomes. Section 6 concludes.

2. The Direct Labor Market Effects of Globalization

The professional literature (to say nothing of the popular literature) on the direct labor market effects of globalization is enormous. The essential empirical issue is macroeconomic: accounting for the *economy-wide* rise of the skill-premium at a time when the share of skilled to unskilled workers is rising. Thinking systematically about the role of globalization in this context requires a model of the economy as a whole with sufficient structure that the link to the world economy can be treated explicitly, but simple enough that it generates guidance for both empirical work and policy. Standard low-dimensional trade-theoretic models provide just such a framework and, not surprisingly, they lie at the heart of a sizable majority of the theoretical work and an even larger share of the empirical work on trade (migration, foreign direct investment) and wages.[2]

As the story has now been told many times, in response to early work in the one-sector framework, trade economists successfully argued that the natural framework for thinking about the effect of trade on labor markets, at least from a maintained assumption of competitive markets, was the Stolper–Samuelson theorem and its various generalizations.[3] The theoretical account of trade shocks as running from commodity-price changes to factor-price changes provided a compelling equilibrium mechanism, and some useful rough empirical checks, but the real success came with the development and refinement of the mandated wage regression methodology (Baldwin and Cain, 2000). The solid theoretical foundations of the mandated wage regression approach led to the almost complete displacement of the factor-content study as a framework for empirical study. The interpretation of the empirical results, as well as the appropriate implementation of the framework, is not without controversy, but the aggregate professional prior would seem to have settled on the conclusion that trade has a small effect on the skill-premium (maybe 10–20%), but that other factors (especially technological change) are more important. The analysis of immigration would appear to be very different, but in fact contains strong similarities to the above story. The obvious problem with the trade-theoretic framework from the perspective of evaluating immigration shocks is that, as long as we assume the commodity and factor markets are competitive and, as seems quite the most plausible assumption, that the number of goods exceeds the number of factors, then we are stuck with what Leamer (1995) calls the *factor-price insensitivity theorem.* This result, which is the single-country analogue of the factor-price equalization theorem, asserts that, under the dimensionality and competitiveness assumptions already mentioned, as long as the economy produces the same types of goods before and after an immigration shock (the endowment remains inside the same cone of diversification), the change in endowment will leave relative factor-prices unchanged. Since the goal is to find globalization effects that might help account for the changing skill-premium, this feature of the trade-theoretic model would seem to be a problem. However, it turned out that most studies found only extremely small effects of immigration on the skill-premium.

To the extent that foreign direct investment (FDI) could be seen as capital arbitrage, factor-price insensitivity would apply there as well. The problem in this case is that economists had long become convinced that FDI was fundamentally not about capital arbitrage. This was the fundamental realization in Hymer's (1960) classic dissertation that is generally credited with beginning the modern theory of foreign direct investment. Starting with Caves (1971), a large body of research has incorporated the insights of the firm-theoretic approach by interpreting FDI as an arbitrage of firm-specific capital. Similarly, monopolistic competition models could be enlisted to analyze FDI by interpreting one input as managerial or headquarters services (Helpman, 1984). But this has always been only uneasily related to the firm-theoretic foundations of the modern theory of FDI. The problems become more obvious when outsourcing becomes part of the picture. We pick up that part of the story in the next section.

3. Indirect Labor Market Effects of Globalization: Some Preliminary Remarks

Implicit in all the comparative static analyses discussed in the previous section is the assumption that the underlying structure of the economy is unchanged by whatever is taken to be the relevant globalizing force—trade, immigration, FDI. However, one of the essential claims in much of the popular writing on globalization, and surely a major source of the general social concern about globalization, is its transformative nature. That is, globalization is taken to transform the economic and political structures in ways that might be obscured when we apply the standard toolkit of trade theory.

Consider the case of global outsourcing, one of the characteristic aspects of contemporary globalization (Feenstra, 1998). From a microeconomic or firm-theoretic point of view, outsourcing is just the reverse process of internalization, which has long been central to the theory of foreign direct investment. However, from the macroeconomic (e.g., trade-theoretic) perspective, internalization and externalization are radical innovations relative to the models used to understand trade and migration. That is, when we come to focus explicitly on outsourcing, it becomes clear that we are dealing with nonmarginal change in production structure that does not really permit simple extension of standard techniques. Where allocation of production among existing facilities is trade-theoretically straightforward, the decision to outsource creates new

772   *Noel Gaston and Douglas Nelson*

technologies and transforms the dimensionality of the underlying model.[4] This recognition is increasingly being made in the theoretical literature on outsourcing (Jones and Kierzkowski, 2001; Deardorff, 2001; Kohler, 2001), but empirical work on the link between outsourcing and wages continues to use a mandated wage approach that manifestly does not permit such nonmarginal change (e.g., Feenstra and Hanson, 1999).

In the case of outsourcing, because it directly transforms dimensionality in our standard models, we can see how structural change interferes with inference based on those tools in a straightforward way. The role played by broader social institutions in supporting economic and political–economic outcomes is less well understood, although elements of such an analysis are beginning to be developed in economics, drawing to a considerable degree on existing research in political science and sociology.[5] In this paper we are interested in the relationship between globalization, and welfare states. Loosely speaking, the idea is that part of the support for an equilibrium in which relatively unskilled workers receive high wages comes from the mutually supporting institutions of unions and welfare states. That is, as a result of labor market institutions, in this case a union, some workers receive a higher wage than other otherwise identical workers. There are insiders and outsiders. In addition, because there is unemployment in equilibrium, we will assume that there is some governmental transfer to the unemployed. It should be clear that globalization could change each of the components of this relationship, with implications for equilibrium relative wages. With respect to the first, there is now a sizable body of research examining the relationship between the institutional structure of the unionized sector of an economy (i.e., the extent and centralization of organization) and various measures of macroeconomic performance. Countries with encompassing labor market institutions (i.e., large unionized sectors with centralized bargaining) are characterized by: lower wage inequality (Rowthorn, 1992; Zweimüller and Barth, 1994; OECD, 1997); lower unemployment (OECD, 1997); and higher growth (Calmfors and Driffill, 1988; Rowthorn, 1992; Calmfors, 1993; Danthine and Hunt, 1994). The usual explanation involves the ability of centralized bargaining institutions to internalize negative wage externalities (Calmfors, 1993; Garrett, 1998). That is, where strong sectoral unions pursue wage gains relative to some perceived market wage, resulting in cost-push inflation, reduced employment, lower growth, and intersectoral inequality, the centralized union recognizes these negative externalities and takes them into account in its bargaining. Thus, as unionization has declined, there is some evidence that wage inequality has increased (Freeman, 1998).

Globalization is widely thought to have affected unions. On the one hand, globalization is generally taken to imply increased competition that, even without any change in relative bargaining power, will squeeze sectoral rents and lead to reduced wages in post-globalization bargains. In a closely related fashion, by raising the elasticity of demand for labor, imports can be seen to directly reduce the market power of unions. An alternative argument turns on the expectation that firms/capital are globally more mobile than labor. The existence of an exit option, even if not exercised, changes the relative bargaining power of the firm and the union. Thus, even without an observed increase in trade, unions should do worse in bargains after the cost of globalization of production (via importing, outsourcing, or FDI) fall. Finally, by affecting the return to union membership, the size of unions may decline, causing a further erosion of bargaining power.

Increased inequality, and real deterioration in the labor market outcomes of unskilled workers, is also directly related to changes in demand for welfare state provision. For example, it has been observed that despite increases in the dispersion of

STRUCTURAL CHANGE AND THE LABOR-MARKET EFFECTS   773

earned incomes that, in some countries at least, inequality in post-transfer and post-tax income inequality has *not* grown (e.g., Gottschalk and Smeeding, 1997; Aaberge et al., 2000). This suggests that political pressures have been brought to bear on the generosity of public transfers at a time when earned incomes have become more unequally distributed. From a political economic perspective, the growing inequality of income could be associated with strong compositional effects on the demand for public insurance. In particular, it seems to be the case that the growing size and economic significance of sectors of the economy that pay higher wages for certain types of workers could somewhat paradoxically result in political pressures that lead to higher levels of transfer payments to disadvantaged workers. It has been suggested that this could result from changes in the identity of the median voter (e.g., Alesina and Rodrik, 1994; Persson and Tabellini, 1994; Saint-Paul and Verdier, 1996) or as an optimal response to increased income risk in an increasingly open economy (e.g., Rodrik, 1998). In this paper we consider an alternative account in which self-interested behavior and institutional features of labor determine public insurance policy outcomes. Specifically, we examine how the demand for unemployment benefits may change during periods of trade liberalization, when collective bargaining is more or less centralized.

Where the effect of globalization on unions is taken to be generally negative, the effects on the welfare state are potentially more mixed. On the negative side, scholars such as Steinmo (1994) and Tanzi (1995) argue that increased mobility of capital not only erodes the tax base, reducing the state's ability to fund welfare state programs, but by shifting taxes onto labor, the capacity of the state to redistribute is reduced. In a similar fashion, Garrett (1998) has argued that, by forcing states to turn increasingly to borrowing to fund welfare state programs, the international capital market ends up imposing an increasing premium on large welfare states. In ways that are harder to quantify, but seem *prima facie* plausible, the decreasing cost of the exit option increases the relative power of business in policymaking (Huber and Stephens, 1998). Finally, it has been argued that globalization increases the general credibility of orthodox (i.e., market-oriented) policy advice, thus reducing the plausibility of arguments supporting welfare state expansion and enhancing the credibility of arguments in favor of welfare state retrenchment (Evans, 1997; Krugman, 1999). On the other hand, there are a number of reasons for believing that the sources of pressure for change are, at a minimum, not overwhelming. First, as has been widely noted for some time, the classic, large welfare states developed in the context of considerably more open economies than did the smaller, market conforming welfare states (Katzenstein, 1985; Huber and Stephens, 1998). As Rodrik (1998) has argued, this may be related to increased income risk. Interestingly, Bordo et al. (1999) carry this argument further, suggesting that the presence of sizable welfare states, and Keynesian macroeconomic policy, may have played an important role in providing sufficient indifference to globalization, that policies like support for the GATT/WTO system and the Bretton Woods institutions continued even in the face of recessions that might have had system closing consequences in earlier eras. In addition, current welfare states show considerable heterogeneity in response to the increases in globalization experienced over the last 15 to 20 years (Garrett, 1998; Swank, 2002). Here it has been widely argued that heterogeneity of domestic political, as well as labor market, institutions support heterogeneity of responses to globalization (Calmfors and Driffill, 1988; Garrett, 1998; Swank, 2002).

The next section develops a model in which, when collective bargaining is more centralized, or when unions are relatively more concerned with employment growth than with raising workers' wages, the workers seek to encourage policymakers to raise unemployment benefits. This happens because of the positive effect that higher reservation wages have on negotiated wages. In contrast, if wage and employment levels are negotiated in an extremely decentralized environment in which workers earn higher wages but are exposed to greater degrees of employment risk, then the workers whose employment is at greatest risk ally themselves with employers to lobby for reductions in transfer payments and benefits and the taxes which are necessary to finance them. That is, there is political pressure to decrease both unemployment benefits and taxes, but this tendency is largely reversed during times of greater openness to international competition.

In an era of rapid globalization, labor market deregulation and microeconomic reform, the associated decentralization of collective bargaining results in wages that are more closely aligned with productivity. However, these developments also expose the same workers to greater unemployment risk. Thus, they have an incentive to influence the direction of public insurance policies. There is considerable evidence that unions have played a prominent role in influencing policies that affect the welfare of their members. For example, there is the well-documented support by the trade union movement for higher minimum wages (e.g., Ehrenberg, 1994, pp. 44–45) and their active participation in the politics surrounding NAFTA (Mayer, 1998). In addition, Kau and Rubin (1981) found that US unions use their political contributions in a systematic and coordinated manner. Union campaign contributions are *always* significant in explaining not only voting on minimum wages, but also wage-price controls, benefits for strikers, OSHA (which regulates workplace safety) and CETA (i.e., manpower training programs) appropriations.

4. Indirect Labor Market Effects of Globalization: A Simple Model

Consider a small open economy populated by workers and shareholders. The economy has two sectors, a unionized sector and a non-unionized sector.[6] Our purpose in this section, and the next, is to determine the effects of trade liberalization (our measure of "globalization") on labor market outcomes via its direct effects on the wage bargain and indirect effects working through redistributive policies (e.g., the unemployment benefit).

Production in the Unionized Sector

The concave production technology for a representative firm in the unionized sector is represented by $x = f(n)$, where n is employment. Total profits are simply

$$\pi(n, w; p, t) = pf(n) - (1+t)wn, \tag{1}$$

where w is the wage and $t \in [0, 1)$ is a payroll tax levied on the total wage bill.[7]

The domestic relative output price of the good produced by the unionized sector is

$$p = (1 + \tau)p^*, \tag{2}$$

where p^* is the world price and τ is an *ad valorem* tariff. The tariff is assumed to be determined by multilateral trade negotiations in which the small country has negligible bargaining power, and therefore the tariff is taken as given by all domestic agents.

Workers and Shareholders

All individuals in the economy—shareholders, union, and non-union workers—are assumed to have the same preferences over consumption goods. The utility of each individual i is

$$U^i = c^{z^i} + u(c^{x^i}),$$ (3)

where c^{z^i} is consumption of the *numéraire* good produced by the non-unionized sector and c^{x^i} is consumption of the good produced by the unionized sector. $u(.)$ is increasing and concave. Individuals maximize utility subject to their expected income constraint.

The quasilinear form of equation (3) implies that the consumption of c^{x^i} depends only on p. Denoting the aggregate consumption of x by $C(p)$ and aggregate production of x by $X(p)$, the government's tariff revenue is

$$T(p) = \tau p^*(C(p) - X(p)),$$ (4)

where $C(p) - X(p)$ represents aggregate imports of good x.[8]

Union Leadership versus Union Workers

The unionized sector is assumed to have rents to bargain over. The firm and the union leadership, which represents workers, negotiate wages and employment levels. That is, the objectives pursued by a union's leadership and the welfare of individual workers are possibly quite distinct (Pemberton, 1988).

We assume that the union's objective function in bargaining can be represented by the Stone–Geary utility function; i.e.,

$$U(n, w) = (n - m)^\gamma (c^e - c^v)^\delta,$$ (5)

where m represents the number of incumbent union workers, c^e is the income for an employed worker, and c^v denotes the reservation alternative for an unemployed worker.[9]

In the following, we assume that the income for an employed worker is $c^e = w$. During the second stage of the game, we treat c^v as exogenous. For individual workers, c^v reflects the value of not working in the unionized sector. It is affected by the value of leisure time, home or nonmarket production, or the wage in the informal sector of the economy. For the purposes of this paper, we assume that the unemployment benefit or income transfer payable to those not employed in the unionized sector affects c^v.

The values of δ and γ in equation (5) indicate the relative importance of wages and employment in bargaining objectives. Pemberton (1988) interpreted a low value for δ as reflecting a relatively greater weight being placed on the desire for high membership on the part of union leadership *vis-à-vis* the desire for high wages on the part of the median union member.[10] Equation (5) results from interpreting the bargaining objective as deriving from a Nash game played between the union's leadership and the union's median member. The leadership wants a large union (high n), and consequently the lower wages that would achieve this growth or membership objective. The median union member, whose employment is assumed to be secure, is concerned only with maximizing wage rents.

One advantage of the Stone–Geary functional form is that it admits some interesting special cases (Farber, 1986, p. 1061). For example, if $\delta = \gamma$ and $m = 0$, then the union's objective is to maximize $U = n(c^e - c^v)$, the rents for employed union members. In this

776   Noel Gaston and Douglas Nelson

case, it is useful to think of all-encompassing labor market institutions where the bargaining over wages and employment is relatively centralized. When $\gamma = 1$ and $\delta = 0$, the objective is $U = n - m$, to maximize the size of the union. When $\delta = 1$ and $\gamma = 0$, the bargaining objective is $U = c^e - c^v$, the earnings for each of its members over and above their reservation alternative. That is, the union is completely "wage-oriented" in its negotiations with the firm (Carruth and Oswald, 1987). Consequently, the union places no importance on "internalizing" the adverse impact of higher wages on employment levels.

Wage and Employment in the Unionized Sector

We assume that bargaining over wages and employment is efficient and that the choice from the set of efficient contracts is the one that maximizes the symmetric Nash product; i.e.,[11]

$$S(n, w) = U(n, w)\pi(n, w). \tag{6}$$

We assume that the solution lies in the interior of the choice set and that S is strictly concave so that the solution is unique and may be characterized by the following first-order conditions (we suppress arguments where no ambiguity exists and use subscripts to denote partial derivatives):

$$S_w(.) = S(.)[\delta\Delta^{-1} - (1+t)n\pi^{-1}] = 0, \tag{7a}$$

$$S_n(.) = S(.)[\gamma(n - m)^{-1} + (pf_n - (1+t)w)\pi^{-1}] = 0, \tag{7b}$$

where $\Delta = c^e - c^v$ is the economic rent to employed workers. Substituting (7a) into (7b), we obtain the contract curve

$$(\gamma - \delta l)w = \gamma c^v - \frac{\delta l p f_n}{(1+t)}, \tag{8}$$

where $l = (n - m)/n$, $l \in (0, 1]$. From equation (8), and since $f(.)$ is concave, the contract curve has a positive (negative) slope when $\gamma > (<) \delta l$. Note that when $\gamma = 0$, labor is employed until its marginal revenue product equals its marginal cost; i.e., $pf_n = (1 + t)w$. When $\delta = 0$, $w = c^v$ and employment is maximized. In the following we refer to the former case as being equivalent to "decentralized bargaining" because wage and employment outcomes occur along the firm's demand-for-labor curve.[12] Likewise, the latter case is referred to as "centralized bargaining" because wages and employment are determined by the Nash bargaining condition and lie to the right of the firm's demand-for-labor curve.

The following proposition summarizes the comparative static results for wages and employment. For expositional purposes, we consider a production function with constant elasticity of employment, α. (Derivations are provided in the Appendix.)

PROPOSITION 1. $w(c^v, p^*, \tau, t, m, \gamma, \delta)$ and $n(c^v, p^*, \tau, t, m, \gamma, \delta)$. Suppose that $\alpha = nf_n f^{-1} > 0$. Then
   (i) $w_{c^v} > 0, w_{p^*} \geq 0, w_\tau \geq 0, w_t \leq 0, w_m < 0, w_\gamma < 0$, and $w_\delta > 0$;
   (ii) $n_{c^v} < 0, n_{p^*} \geq 0, n_\tau \geq 0, n_t < 0, n_m > 0, n_\gamma > 0$, and $n_\delta < 0$.

The sign patterns are quite standard. Higher prices, or import tariffs, for the unionized good increase employment and wages. (The possibility of a zero wage effect for the output price and the payroll tax are byproducts of adopting an isoelastic form for the demand-for-labor curve.) The wage and employment effects of more decentralized wage bargaining and higher values of δ (or lower values of γ) indicate the effect of an increased orientation to the pursuit of higher wages, as opposed to lowering the risk of unemployment. The effects of a higher m, given γ, are equivalent to the effects of a higher value of γ, given m. (Recall that m is the union leadership's threat point in a Nash bargaining game with the median union member. Hence, a higher m strengthens the union leadership's drive for employment growth.)

It is readily apparent that the owners of firms will always lose from any policy that involves increasing c^v. Doing so increases wages and lowers output and labor demand by firms. On the other hand, workers may adopt a variety of positions regarding the desirability of various labor market policies and public insurance programs depending on the size of tax increases needed to finance more generous benefits as well as the nature of their preferences. Specifically, whether workers are likely to support higher unemployment benefits depends on the extent to which payroll tax increases are shifted back onto workers (Ehrenberg, 1994, p. 8), the exposure of workers to unemployment, and the effect of higher reservation wages on negotiated wages. What is clear is that one of the main effects of higher unemployment benefits is to increase the wage pressure by insiders. Further, some authors (e.g., Saint-Paul, 1996) argue that, since incumbent workers are more numerous and better organized than the unemployed, labor institutions are determined by the interests of the employed. In turn, these decisive voters are likely to support policies and labor market institutions that increase the exclusion of outsiders.

5. Equilibrium Unemployment Benefits in a Small Open Economy

In this section, we study the political determination of unemployment benefits. In addition to understanding the effect of different labor institutions on the generosity of benefits, a primary objective is to investigate the relationship between trade liberalization and unemployment benefits.

The Lobby-group Model

The menu auction model of Bernheim and Whinston (1986) provides a useful framework for understanding the interaction between special interest groups and the government.[13] Interest groups are assumed to have organized exogenously and to consist of individuals with similar interests in policy outcomes. Our focus is upon the unemployment benefit, b. Denoting the set of lobby groups by L, political contributions are made by the various groups to an incumbent government in return for preferred labor market policies, $\Lambda^i(b)$, where $i \in L$. These functions relate the political contributions of lobby groups to feasible policy choices.

An incumbent government is assumed to choose b to maximize the weighted sum of aggregate political contributions and aggregate social welfare. The specific form of the government's objective function is

$$V^g(b) = \sum_{i \in L} \Lambda^i(b) + \sum_{j=k,u,n} a^j V^j(b), \tag{9}$$

where the $V^j, j = k, u, n$, are the gross indirect utility functions for each group of factor owners—capital, incumbent union workers, and non-union workers, respectively. The

778   *Noel Gaston and Douglas Nelson*

$a^j \geq 0$ are the "weights" that the government places on each group's social welfare, relative to revenues and political contributions. Equation (9) does not restrict the weights attached to the social welfare of each group in the economy to be equal. For example, $a^u > a^n$ would imply that the government places a higher weight on the welfare of union workers compared to the welfare of non-unionized workers (Rama and Tabellini, 1998; Fredriksson and Gaston, 1999). This particular feature of the model captures ideological or constituency-specific motives behind policymaking, reflecting a view that governments of different political persuasions treat the different groups differently.

Equilibrium unemployment benefits are the outcome of a two-stage game played between the government and the lobby groups.[14] Aggregating the government's welfare and the welfare of each group in society (net of political contributions), the policymaker's choice of b is given by

$$b^* = \operatorname{argmax} \sum_{i \in L} V^i(b) + \sum_{j=k,u,n} a^j V^j(b). \tag{10}$$

Budgetary Considerations

If we restrict our attention to balanced-budget methods of financing higher unemployment benefits, then the revenue available to fund unemployment benefits is given by the sum of payroll taxes and tariff revenues:

$$twn + T(p) = (1-n)b. \tag{11}$$

The effects of a trade liberalization are captured by reductions in τ. This holds true whether τ is an import tariff or subsidy, or an export tax or subsidy. Note that there are two avenues through which a reduction in trade barriers may have effects on unemployment benefits. First, in the case of an export subsidy or an import tariff, a lower τ reduces the internal relative price of the domestic good, thereby directly reducing employment in the protected sector. Second, in the case of an export tax or an import tariff, a lower τ reduces the revenue available to fund increases in benefits. Some authors have pointed to the possibility that the generosity of unemployment benefits, and hence the level of taxation needed to finance it, may well influence trade flows, at least in the short run (e.g., Ehrenberg, 1994). Equation (11) recognizes that, through the effect on government revenues, freer and more open trade will affect the budget used to fund unemployment benefits.

If tariff revenues are not used to fund unemployment benefits, then more generous unemployment benefits need to be matched with higher payroll tax revenues. Since higher benefits have adverse employment effects, this necessitates a higher payroll tax rate.[15] Hence, despite the possibility of beneficial wage effects for some workers, all workers and employers would unambiguously lose from the higher taxes needed to finance more generous benefits. Consequently, a balanced-budget constraint will serve to limit the size of equilibrium unemployment benefits (see below).

Impact of Higher Unemployment Benefits on Expected Income of Workers and Shareholders

Prior to wage and employment negotiations taking place, the income of all of the firm's shareholders is given by equation (1), evaluated at optimal values for w and n. In addition, using equations (2) and (11), and recalling that $C(p)$ is independent of expected income, yields

STRUCTURAL CHANGE AND THE LABOR-MARKET EFFECTS   779

$$I^k(b) = p^*f(n(b)) - w(b)n(b) - (1 - n(b))b. \qquad (12)$$

From the balanced-budget constraint, for a given level of b, it is clear that firms in the unionized sector with higher levels of unemployment are taxed more heavily. In this sense, the financing of unemployment benefits is fully "experience-rated." The total net income of the group of incumbent union workers, m, is

$$I^u(b) = mw(b). \qquad (13)$$

The expected income of $1 - m$ non-unionized workers is

$$I^n(b) = (n(b) - m)w(b) + (1 - n(b))(b + \kappa). \qquad (14)$$

The specification for workers assumes that they are risk-neutral and that they maximize expected utility. Note that only when $m = 0$ and $\delta = \gamma$ do the preferences of non-union workers coincide with those of the political leadership of the union. We assume that the income while unemployed for workers is given by $c^v = b + \kappa$, where b is the government-provided benefit or income transfer and κ represents the value of informal sector or nonmarket production (e.g., as in Benhabib et al., 1991).[16] Before proceeding it is useful to summarize the effects of changes in the generosity of higher unemployment benefits on the indirect utility of factor owners (see the Appendix for details):

$$V_b^k < 0, V_b^u > 0, \text{ and } V_b^n \gtreqless 0. \qquad (15)$$

Incumbent workers always prefer higher benefits, because their employment is secure and higher unemployment benefits increase the reservation wages of all workers (which, in turn, increase negotiated wages). Naturally, firms unambiguously prefer lower reservation wages. When $l = 1$, it is straightforward to show that

$$V_b^n = \begin{cases} \geq 0 & \text{if } \dfrac{\delta - \gamma - \alpha}{\alpha\delta} \leq v, \\[2mm] < 0 & \text{if } \dfrac{\delta - \gamma - \alpha}{\alpha\delta} \in (v, 1), \end{cases} \qquad (16)$$

where $v = 1 - n$ is the percentage of the workforce not employed in the unionized sector. A sufficient condition for a higher value of b to have a positive impact on worker welfare is $\gamma + \alpha > \delta$. In fact, this condition implies that the Nash bargaining condition (NBC) has a steeper slope than the union workers' indifference curve (evaluated at (w^*, n^*)).[17] Only when the rents from union bargaining become larger, which may result from very high levels of wage-oriented bargaining, do workers become concerned about the possible unemployment effects of higher levels of b.

Equation (16) also reveals that a sufficiently high probability of employment in the higher-wage and high-rent unionized sector lowers worker demand for public insurance. For example, if the unionized sector suffers falling output prices and higher unemployment, then the demand for higher unemployment benefits will increase. This result differs from a key finding of median voter models in which unemployment benefits are negatively related to unemployment. As Persson and Tabellini (2002, p. 31) note, this seems counterfactual when comparing Europe and the United States. Europe has both higher unemployment and higher unemployment benefits.

780   Noel Gaston and Douglas Nelson

Socially Optimal Unemployment Benefits

The presence of a non-lobby group population is important in the context of the Grossman–Helpman model because it admits the possibility that policies shaped by influence-seeking activities are likely to deviate from those chosen by a utilitarian social planner. From equation (10), it is clear that policies will always be socially optimal if the welfare of each group in society is equally weighted and if all groups are politically organized. The socially optimal unemployment benefit is defined as the benefit that maximizes aggregate social welfare (in the absence of any lobbying and political contributions). The utilitarian policymaker assumption is a useful benchmark for discussing the lobby-group model. In this case, b is chosen to maximize

$$\Omega(b) = \sum_{j=k,u,n} V^j(b), \tag{17}$$

subject to the government's balanced-budget constraint. Summing equations (12) to (14), and using equation (11), yields the following maximand:

$$\Omega(b) = p^* f(n(b)) + (1 - n(b))\kappa. \tag{18}$$

The optimal unemployment benefit is simply chosen to maximize the value of market and nonmarket production.[18]

Obviously, if workers are risk-neutral and if nonmarket production has no value (i.e., $\kappa = 0$), then employment in the unionized sector should be maximized and unemployment benefits should never exceed zero (Acemoglu and Shimer, 1999).[19] We summarize the key findings in Proposition 2.

PROPOSITION 2 (Utilitarian policymaker). *Suppose that $\kappa > 0$. Then:*
  (i) *Unemployment benefits are lower when the policymaker chooses balanced-budget or revenue-neutral policies.*
  (ii) *Unemployment benefits are positive only if collective bargaining is centralized.*

First, when a policymaker's balanced-budget constraint binds, unemployment benefits are lower than nonrevenue neutral benefits and transfers. Secondly, a more novel result is that $\gamma > \delta l$ is a necessary condition for the optimal unemployment benefit to be positive. Recall from equation (16) that this condition implies that the bargaining objective places relative greater weight on employment growth and job security. Hence, more centralized bargaining systems are likely to have higher unemployment benefits. Focusing on the effects of liberalizing trade, the key comparative static results are summarized next.

COROLLARY 1 (Open economy). $b^o(\kappa, p^*, \tau, m, \gamma, \delta)$, *where:*
  (i) $b_\kappa^o > 0$, $b_m^o > 0$, $b_\gamma^o > 0$, *and* $b_\delta^o < 0$.
  (ii) *If international competition lowers product prices and raises unemployment, then unemployment benefits are higher; i.e.,* $b_{p^*}^o \leq 0$.
  (iii) *The impact of trade liberalization depends on whether tariff revenues are used to fund unemployment benefits. Specifically:*
      (a) *If tariff revenues are not used to fund unemployment benefits, then:*
          1. *in the case of an import tariff or an export subsidy,* $b_\tau^o \leq 0$; *or*
          2. *in the case of an import subsidy or an export tax,* $b_\tau^o \geq 0$.
      (b) *If tariff revenues are used to partially, or to fully, fund unemployment benefits, then:*

STRUCTURAL CHANGE AND THE LABOR-MARKET EFFECTS   781

1. *in the case of an import tariff or an export subsidy, $b_\tau^o > 0$; or*
2. *in the case of an import subsidy or an export tax, $b_\tau^o < 0$.*

Part (i) indicates that unemployment benefits are higher when incumbent union workers, whose employment is secure, are more numerous. On the other hand, an aggressive pursuit of wage gains by union leaders, or wage contracts that expose workers to excessive amounts of unemployment risk, are balanced by lower unemployment benefits. The effect of higher values of κ on benefits reflects the increased value of time spent in nonmarket activities relative to time spent on production in the unionized sector.

Part (ii) indicates that, regardless of the method of financing, lower world prices raise unemployment benefits. That is, increased global competition is likely to lead to more generous unemployment benefits. The impact of trade liberalization, on the other hand, depends on whether tariff revenues are used to finance unemployment benefits and whether the unionized sector is protected or "antiprotected" (Vousden, 1990, p. 113).

Part (iii)(a) simply states that, for a small open economy liberalizing its unionized import-competing sector, optimal unemployment benefits will be higher. The lower tariff operates purely as an adverse domestic output price shock for the unionized sector. Of course, as unemployment benefits rise, income tax burdens are greater for workers and shareholders as well. Part (iii)(b) indicates that, when the unionized sector is protected and all tariff revenues are used to fund unemployment benefits, the effect of trade liberalization (assumed to lower tariffs and lower subsidies) is to reduce the value of unemployment benefits.[20] When the unionized sector is "antiprotected," benefits are increased. The effects of a trade liberalization are therefore twofold. First, lower import tariffs and export subsidies increase competition, which increases unemployment and raises benefits. Second, lower tariff or tax revenues affect the government's budgetary position. In the case of lower import tariffs there is pressure on b to rise due to greater import competition, but there is an offsetting pressure on b to fall due to fiscal concerns.[21]

The Effect of Lobbying Activities

Clearly, how a policymaker weights the welfare of the different groups of factor owners strongly influences the generosity of unemployment benefits. For example, if a higher weight is placed on the welfare of shareholders compared to the welfare of workers, whether organized or not (i.e., $a^k > a^u$ and $a^k > a^n$), then equation (15) implies that benefits are lower than they otherwise would be. That is, this suggests that countries with pro-business governments have lower unemployment benefits than those countries with labor-oriented governments, *ceteris paribus*.

Similarly, to understand the effect that lobbying by interest groups has on the determination of public insurance and other labor market policies, it is important to identify the groups in an economy that are politically organized and actively participate in the political process. If we assume that the political weights attached to each group of factor owners by the policymaker are equal, this is readily seen by rearranging the solution to equation (10) to obtain

$$(1 + a)\Omega_b = \sum_{i' \varepsilon L} V_b^{i'}. \tag{19}$$

Among others, Rama and Tabellini (1998) show that the policy distortion is proportional to the welfare effect of the policy on the unrepresented group in society.[22]

© Blackwell Publishing Ltd 2004

782   Noel Gaston and Douglas Nelson

Clearly, unemployment benefits are set at socially inefficient high (low) levels whenever the left-hand side of equation (19) is negative (positive). This result obtains
because of the nonparticipation by groups of factor owners in the political process who,
if represented, would press for lower (higher) benefits. Further, the degree of the distortion is decreasing in the relative weight placed on social welfare, a.[23]

The comparative static effects of unequal treatment of groups of factor owners in
the lobby group are transparent if we assume that only political contributions matter.
Compared to the maximization of social welfare alone, because the government values
contributions it weights more heavily the policy preferences of the organized groups
that contribute. It seems reasonable to assume that only organized labor and/or capital
owners make political contributions. In most OECD countries, non-unionized workers
are politically unorganized or sufficiently disenfranchised so as not to lobby (and contribute to) the government for preferred policy outcomes.

Naturally, which groups of factor owners are politically active differs from country
to country. In addition, it is not obvious that capital owners would be organized as a
lobby in every country.[24] For example, if the unionized firm is foreign-owned and
foreign shareholders do not participate politically or form a domestic lobby, then
unemployment benefits are set inefficiently high. That is, since the welfare of incumbent union workers is valued more highly, this places upward pressure on benefit
levels. To illustrate, the next proposition contains the results for the politically determined benefit, b^*, under the assumption that only organized labor makes political
contributions.

PROPOSITION 3 (Lobbying by organized labor). *Suppose that $\kappa > 0$, that $a^j = a$, and that
only organized labor lobbies. Then $b^* > b^o$. Further, b^* increases in (i) m, the number
of organized workers, and (ii) the elasticity of negotiated wages with respect to unemployment benefits. Further, b^* decreases in (i) a, the government's weight on general
welfare, and (ii) the elasticity of employment with respect to unemployment benefits.*

The results are straightforward. In terms of the comparative statics, note for the
model we consider in this paper that the demand for higher benefits by incumbent
union workers is driven by what Saint-Paul (1996) terms the "wage formation effect."
The stronger this wage effect, the higher are unemployment benefits. Likewise, an
elastic response of employment to higher benefits would counteract the wage formation effect.

6. Indirect Labor Market Effects of Globalization: Some Empirical Results

To test the main implications of the theory, our empirical analysis proceeds by
examining unemployment benefit entitlements both within and between countries
(see OECD, 1995 Jobs Study). In particular, we investigate whether openness of the
economy and labor market institutions might be responsible for the differences.
Amongst other things, in the empirical analysis our goal is to provide insights into
policy-related questions that remain largely unresolved. First, is greater openness to
trade correlated with the unemployment benefit generosity or stringency? Second, is
there a statistical association between the nature of union participation in the economy,
government indebtedness, partisan political effects, and unemployment benefits?

Using panel data for 17 OECD countries, we estimate the fixed-effects regression
model. The dependent variable in all cases is the OECD's gross benefit replacement
rate (BR): the proportion of expected income from work that is replaced by unem-

STRUCTURAL CHANGE AND THE LABOR-MARKET EFFECTS   783

Table 1. Descriptive Statistics and Summary of Hypotheses

Variable	Label	Hypothesis	Mean	Standard deviation
Benefit replacement rate (%)[a]	•	*BR*	24.018	14.309
Government gross debt as percentage of GDP (%)[b]	*Debt*	−	36.295	27.132
Union density (%)[c]	*Dentot*	+	44.415	19.111
Trade openness[d]	*Open*	+	58.338	28.003
Political orientation of government[e]	*Left*	+	2.354	1.533

Notes and data sources:
[a] Replacement rates (i.e., benefits before tax as a percentage of previous earnings before tax) as defined by legislated entitlements averaged across various circumstances in which an unemployed person may be. OECD (courtesy of OECD Social Policy Division).
[b] Consolidated central government gross debt as a fraction of GDP (Franzese, 1998).
[c] Total union membership (less self-employed) weighted by total dependent workforce, European countries from Ebbinghaus and Visser (2000). Data for Australia, Canada, Japan, and US from Golden et al. (1998).
[d] (Total exports of goods and services + total imports of goods and services)/GDP. OECD Main Economic Indicators, online access.
[e] *Left* = 1 if there is right-wing domination in both government and parliament; = 2 if right-wing or center parties make up between 33.3% and 66.6% of government; = 3 if center parties make up 50% or more of government; = 4 if left-wing or center parties make up between 33.3% and 66.6% of government; and = 5 if left-wing parties dominate the government. Woldendorp et al. (1998).

ployment and related welfare benefits.[25] Our model specification considers country fixed-effects and one-period lags of the independent variables, as well as a two-period lag of the dependent variable:[26]

$$BR_{i,t} = \gamma BR_{i,t-2} + \beta' X_{i,t-1} + \theta_i + \varepsilon_{i,t}, \qquad (20)$$

where $X_{i,t-1}$ is a vector including measures of openness, political orientation of the government (not lagged), union density, government debt, and a variable constructed by interacting the openness and debt variable; θ_i is the country-specific effect; and $\varepsilon_{i,t}$ is a random disturbance term. These are then stacked for estimation as a panel. Table 1 gives definitions, sources, and predicted signs of the variables in $X_{i,t-1}$.[27] In addition, we consider several variations on sample and specification.[28] The results are reported in Table 2.[29]

Before considering our preferred specification, consider the specification in column (2) of Table 2. This contains the main variables with which we are concerned. As we showed in the previous section, both left-wing governments and widespread coverage of workers by union bargaining are predicted to raise unemployment benefits, and both of these results are clearly present. Our results on these variables are consistent with those in the large empirical literature in comparative political economy focusing on the link between labor market institutions, political orientation, and welfare-state outputs.[30] As suggested by our model, and consistent with the widely remarked link between openness to international trade and size of welfare-state interventions, we find a significant, positive relationship between the trade openness variable and the size of the unemployment benefit. Finally, since the government faces a balanced budget constraint in our model, we introduce a measure of the magnitude of debt as an indicator of how closely the constraint binds. The sign of the coefficient is negative, as predicted,

784   *Noel Gaston and Douglas Nelson*

Table 2. *Determinants of Benefit Replacement Rates, 1963–95 (robust standard errors)*

	(1)	(2) No interaction	(3) Left lagged	(4) Contemporaneous	(5) With Italy
Left	0.260**	0.253**	0.162	0.257**	0.258**
	(0.106)	(0.115)	(0.121)	(0.103)	(0.105)
Union density	0.139***	0.133***	0.139***	0.158***	0.111**
	(0.046)	(0.052)	(0.046)	(0.041)	(0.047)
Openness	0.098***	0.044*	0.098***	0.102***	0.081**
	(0.034)	(0.027)	(0.036)	(0.035)	(0.035)
Government debt	0.043**	−0.015	0.043*	0.047**	0.025
	(0.022)	(0.018)	(0.023)	(0.023)	(0.019)
*Openness*Debt*10*	−0.007***		−0.007***	−0.007***	−0.006***
	(0.002)		(0.002)	(0.002)	(0.002)
Benefits(−2)	0.797***	0.812***	0.798***	0.782***	0.817***
	(0.072)	(0.072)	(0.072)	(0.066)	(0.079)
R^2	0.932	0.930	0.931	0.933	0.941
Observations	259	259	259	256	274

Notes: *Benefits* are lagged two years and *Left* is unlagged in all columns, except column (3) where *Left* is lagged one year. All other independent variables are lagged one year, except in column (4) where all variables are contemporaneous with the dependent variable. Column (5) adds Italy to the sample for the column (1) specification. ***,**,* denote significant at 1%, 5%, 10% level, respectively.

but it is not statistically significant. As in all specifications, the standard errors adjust for heteroskedasticity, and our tests reject the null of first- and second-order autocorrelation.

Now consider column (1) of Table 2, which contains the results for our preferred specification. The interpretations of our political orientation and union density variables are the same; but with the introduction of the interaction variable, which is highly significant though quantitatively small, the interpretation of trade openness and government debt become more delicate.[31] Specifically, the values of the coefficients on openness and government debt now vary with each other's levels. That is, they describe conditional relationships, not unconditional ones. In this case, the negative interaction term captures the notion that, at any given level of openness to trade, a standard deviation increase in the government debt to GDP ratio lowers the response of the benefit replacement rate to openness (i.e., the conditional slope) by about 1.1 percentage points (i.e., −0.0007 × 58.338 × 27.132). Having accounted for this relationship, we are concerned that the estimate of a positive relationship between the unemployment benefit and debt may reflect endogeneity problems that will need to be dealt with in future work on this topic. The remaining specifications of the model yield essentially the same results. Consequently, we find the empirical results reported in Table 2 to be quite consistent with the theoretical approach adopted in sections 4 and 5 of this paper.

7. Conclusions

We have argued that standard ways of looking at the link between globalization and labor markets, which consistently find small or zero effects, by focusing on what we have called direct effects, might obscure significant indirect effects. In addition to providing a review of research suggesting the significance of these indirect effects, we have constructed a model in which institutional features of the labor market help to explain observed trends in public insurance policies. That is, where related work has focused on the ways in which trade creates an outside option for domestic capital, we examined the link between trade and welfare-state provision. In our model, when wage bargaining is extremely decentralized, the lobbying influence of unions allied with the lobbying activities of employers encourages policymakers to ease tax burdens and cap increases in unemployment benefits. When the risk of unemployment is lower and collective bargaining is more centralized, workers prefer contracts with high unemployment risk and high wages, and this serves to increase the demand for publicly provided unemployment insurance. We then examined the impact of increased trade (in this case a reduction in the tariff) on the overall equilibrium. Trade has the effect of increasing sectoral unemployment, reducing the power of unions and increasing the demand for welfare-state provision. The particular channel of constraint is the budget deficit. The results of our empirical work are strongly consistent with the main predictions of the model.

We consider the results presented here to be sufficiently strong to support increased study of the indirect effects that are central to our story. We think several extensions are well worth considering. First, our model of lobbying is very simple—only organized labor lobbies and all groups are equally valued by government. Both of these assumptions should be examined. We clearly need to consider either politically active capital or a strong preference for capital in the government's objective function. As we note in section 3, a considerable body of research suggests that political valence (e.g., pro-labor/pro-capital) of the party in power is an important intervening variable in the relationship between globalization and sustainability of welfare states. In addition, it is not at all clear that trade is the empirically most significant force of globalization in determining these indirect effects. Given that the budget constraint plays an essential role here, it seems quite likely that international financial globalization should be considered in greater detail. We hope to pursue both of these in future work.

Appendix

Derivation of Comparative Statics in Proposition 1

Solving equations (7b) and (8) we have

$$w = \frac{(\gamma + \alpha l)c^v}{B} \quad \text{and} \quad \frac{f}{n} = \frac{(\gamma + l)(1 + t)c^v}{Bp},$$

where the elasticity of output is $\alpha = nf_n/f$, $l = (n - m)/n$ and $B = \gamma + \alpha l - (1 - \alpha)\delta l > 0$. It follows that

$$w_{c^v} = \frac{(\gamma + 1)\gamma + (\gamma + l)\alpha l}{y} > 0; \quad n_{c^v} = \frac{-(\gamma + l)Bn}{(1 - \alpha)yc^v} < 0; \quad w_p = \frac{(1 - l)\delta\gamma f}{yn} \geq 0;$$

$$n_p = \frac{(\gamma + 1)B(1 + t)n}{(1 - \alpha)yp} > 0; \quad w_\delta = \frac{w_{c^n}(1 - \alpha)lw}{(\gamma + \alpha l)} > 0; \quad n_d = \frac{-(\gamma + l)nl}{y} < 0;$$

$$w_\gamma = \frac{-(1 - \alpha)\delta l p f}{y(1 + t)n} < 0; \quad n_\gamma = \frac{(1 + \delta)nl}{y} > 0; \quad w_m = \frac{\gamma w_\gamma}{nl} < 0; \quad n_m = \frac{\gamma n_\gamma}{nl} > 0;$$

786   Noel Gaston and Douglas Nelson

where $y = (\gamma + l)B + (1 - l)(1 + \delta)\gamma > 0$. Furthermore, it follows that

$$w_{p^*} = \frac{(1+\tau)w_p}{(1+t)} \geq 0; \quad w_\tau = \frac{p^*w_p}{(1+t)} \geq 0; \quad w_t = \frac{-pw_p}{(1+t)^2} \leq 0; \quad n_{p^*} = \frac{(1+\tau)n_p}{(1+t)} \geq 0;$$

$$n_\tau = \frac{p^*n_p}{(1+t)} \geq 0; \quad n_t = \frac{-pn_p}{(1+t)^2} \leq 0.$$

Derivation of Equation (15)

Differentiating equations (12) to (14), using the results listed in the above subsection, and simplifying we have

$$V_b^k = \frac{-[(1-l)\gamma + (\gamma +l)\alpha l]n}{y} < 0, \quad V_b^u = mw_{c^u} > 0,$$

$$V_b^n = \frac{[(\gamma+1)\gamma + (\gamma+l)\alpha l - (\gamma+l)\delta]nl}{y} + (1-n).$$

Proof of Proposition 2

The solution to the maximization of equation (18) is

$$\Omega_b = (p^*f_n - \kappa)n_b = 0. \tag{A1}$$

When benefits are financed out of general revenues, the policymaker chooses b to maximize

$$\Omega(b) = p^*f(n(b)) + (1-n(b))(b+\kappa). \tag{A2}$$

The solution is given by

$$\Omega_b = (p^*f_n - \kappa) - b + \frac{(1-n)}{n_b} = 0. \tag{A3}$$

Comparison with equation (A1), and recalling that $n_b < 0$, yields part (i) of the proposition.

Next, use the first-order conditions (equations (7a) and (7b)) and the expression for the balanced-budget constraint (equation (11)) to obtain

$$b^o = \frac{(1-\alpha)\kappa n}{\alpha(\gamma+l)}\left[\frac{(\gamma+\alpha l)(\gamma-\delta l) - Bl\tau}{B+n(1-\alpha)\delta l}\right], \tag{A4}$$

where $B = \gamma + \alpha l - (1-\alpha)\delta l > 0$. Part (ii) of the proposition follows. □

Derivation of Comparative Statics in Corollary 1

From equation (A1), and using the results from above, the comparative statics in part (i) follow directly. Next, when tariff revenues are not used to finance b, then the policymaker's objective is $\Omega(b) = pf(n(b)) + (1 - n(b))\kappa$, rather than equation (18). Total differentiation of $(pf_n - \kappa)n_b = 0$ yields

STRUCTURAL CHANGE AND THE LABOR-MARKET EFFECTS   787

$$b_{p^*} = \frac{-(1-l)(1+\delta)\gamma c^v}{(\gamma+l)Bp^*} \le 0. \tag{A5}$$

Total differentiation of equation (A1) yields

$$b_{p^*} = \frac{-(1-l)(1+\delta)\gamma c^v}{(\gamma+l)Bp^*} \le 0 \quad \text{and} \quad b_\tau = \frac{-n_\tau}{n_b} > 0. \tag{A6}$$

In the case of an import tariff or an export subsidy, $n_\tau > 0$. In the case of an import subsidy or an export tax, $n_\tau < 0$. Parts (ii) and (iii) follow.

Proof of Proposition 3

The solution to maximization of equation (19) is

$$a(p^*f_n - \kappa)n_b = -mw_b. \tag{A7}$$

Defining $\varepsilon_w = bw_b/w > 0$ and $\varepsilon_n = bn_b/n < 0$, equation (A7) can be rewritten as

$$p^*f_n = \kappa - \frac{(1-l)w\varepsilon_w}{a\varepsilon_n}. \tag{A8}$$

Comparison with equation (A1), and noting that f_n increases in b, yields the proposition.   □

References

Aaberge, R., T. Wennemo, A. Bjorklund, M. Jantti, P. J. Pedersen, and N. Smith, "Unemployment Shocks and Income Distribution: How Did the Nordic Countries Fare During their Crises?" *Scandinavian Journal of Economics* 102 (2000):77–99.

Acemoglu, D. and R. Shimer, "Efficient Unemployment Insurance," *Journal of Political Economy* 107 (1999):893–928.

Alesina, A. and D. Rodrik, "Distributive Politics and Economic Growth," *Quarterly Journal of Economics* 109 (1994):465–90.

Baldwin, R. and G. Cain, "Shifts in Relative US Wages: the Role of Trade, Technology and Factor Endowments," *Review of Economics and Statistics* 82 (2000):580–95.

Benhabib, J., R. Rogerson, and R. Wright, "Homework in Macroeconomics: Household Production and Aggregate Fluctuations," *Journal of Political Economy* 99 (1991):1166–87.

Bernheim, B. D. and M. D. Whinston, "Menu Auctions, Resource Allocation, and Economic Influence," *Quarterly Journal of Economics* 101 (1986):1–31.

Blank, R. M. and R. B. Freeman, "Evaluating the Connection between Social Protection and Economic Flexibility," in R. M. Blank (ed.), *Social Protection versus Economic Flexibility*, Chicago: University of Chicago Press (1994):21–41.

Bordo, M., B. Eichengreen, and D. Irwin, "Is Globalization Today Really Different than Globalization a Hundred Years Ago?" *Brookings Trade Forum—1999*, Washington, DC: Brookings Institution (1999):1–72.

Calmfors, L., "Centralisation of Wage Bargaining and Macroeconomic Performance: a Survey," *OECD Economic Studies* 21 (1993):161–91.

Calmfors, L. and J. Driffill, "Bargaining Structure, Corporatism and Macroeconomic Performance," *Economic Policy* 6 (1988):14–61.

Carruth, A. A. and A. J. Oswald, "On Union Preferences and Labour Market Models: Insiders and Outsiders," *Economic Journal* 97 (1987):431–45.

Casamatta, G., H. Cremer, and P. Pestieau, "Political Sustainability and the Design of Social Insurance," *Journal of Public Economics* 75 (2000):341–64.

788   *Noel Gaston and Douglas Nelson*

Caves, R., "International Corporations: the Industrial Economics of Foreign Investment," *Economica* 38 (1971):1–27.

Clark, A. and A. J. Oswald, "Trade Union Utility Functions: a Survey of Union Leaders' Views," *Industrial Relations* 32 (1993):391–423.

Danthine, J. P. and J. Hunt, "Wage Bargaining Structure, Employment and Economic Integration," *Economic Journal* 104 (1994):528–41.

Deardorff, A., "Fragmentation across Cones," in S. W. Arndt and H. Kierzkowski (eds.), *Fragmentation: New Production Patterns in the World Economy*, Oxford: OUP (2001):35–51.

Doornik, J., D. Hendry, M. Arellano, and S. Bond, "PcGive, Panel Data Models," in J. Doornik and D. Hendry (eds.), *Econometric Modelling Using PcGive*, Vol. III, London: Timberlake Consultants Ltd (2001).

Ebbinghaus, B. and J. Visser (eds.), *Trade Unions in Western Europe since 1945*, London: Macmillan (2000).

Ehrenberg, R. G., *Labor Markets and Integrating National Economies*, Washington, DC: Brookings Institution (1994).

Evans, P., "The Eclipse of the State: Reflections on Stateness in an Era of Globalization," *World Politics* 50 (1997):62–87.

Farber, H. S., "The Analysis of Union Behavior," in O. Ashenfelter and R. Layard (eds.), *Handbook of Labor Economics*, Vol. 2, New York: Elsevier Science (1986):1039–89.

Feenstra, R., "Integration of Trade and Disintegration of Production in the Global Economy," *Journal of Economic Perspectives* 12 (1998):31–50.

Feenstra, R. and G. Hanson, "The Impact of Outsourcing and High Technology Capital on Wages: Estimates for the US, 1979–1990," *Quarterly Journal of Economics* 114 (1999):907–40.

Franzese, Jr, R. J., "The Political Economy of Public Debt: an Empirical Examination of the OECD Postwar Experience," paper for the Wallis Conference on Political Economy, Northwestern University (1998).

Friedrich, R., "In Defense of Multiplicative Terms in Multiple Regression Equations," *American Journal of Political Science* 26 (1982):797–833.

Fredriksson, P. G. and N. Gaston, "The 'Greening' of Trade Unions and the Demand for Eco-Taxes," *European Journal of Political Economy* 15 (1999):663–86.

———, "Environmental Governance in Federal Systems: the Effects of Capital Competition and Lobby Groups," *Economic Inquiry* 38 (2000):501–14.

Fredriksson, P. G. and J. Svensson, "Political Instability, Corruption and Policy Formation: the Case of Environmental Policy," *Journal of Public Economics* 87 (2003):1383–405.

Freeman, R. B., "War of the Models: Which Labour Market Institutions for the 21st Century?" *Labour Economics* 5 (1998):1–24.

Garrett, G., *Partisan Politics in the Global Economy*, Cambridge: Cambridge University Press (1998).

Gaston, N. and D. Nelson, "Unions and the Decentralisation of Collective Bargaining in a Globalising World," *Journal of Economic Integration* 17 (2002):377–96.

Gaston, N. and D. Nelson, "The Employment and Wage Effects of Immigration: Trade and Labour Economics Perspectives," in D. Greenaway, R. Upward, and K. Wakelin (eds.), *Trade, Investment, Migration and Labour Market Adjustment*, Basingstoke: Palgrave Macmillan, (2002):201–35.

Goldberg, P. K. and G. Maggi, "Protection for Sale: an Empirical Investigation," *American Economic Review* 89 (1999):1135–55.

Golden M., M. Wallerstein, and P. Lange, "Union Centralization Among Advanced Industrial Societies," National Science Foundation (1998).

Gottschalk, P. and T. M. Smeeding, "Cross-national Comparisons of Earnings and Income Inequality," *Journal of Economic Literature* 35 (1997):633–87.

Grossman, G. M. and E. Helpman, "Protection for Sale," *American Economic Review* 84 (1994):833–50.

Hall, H. K. and D. Nelson, "Institutional Structure and the Political Economy of Protection: Administered versus Legislated Protection," *Economics and Politics* 4 (1992):61–77.

STRUCTURAL CHANGE AND THE LABOR-MARKET EFFECTS   789

——, "The Peculiar Political Economy of NAFTA," manuscript, Murphy Institute of Political Economy (2001).

Haskel, J., B. Kersley, and C. Martin, "Labour Market Flexibility and Employment Adjustment: Micro Evidence from UK Establishments," *Oxford Economic Papers* 49 (1997):362–79.

Helpman, E., "A Simple Theory of International Trade with Multinational Corporations," *Journal of Political Economy* 92 (1984):451–71.

Huber, E. and J. Stephens, "Internationalization and the Social Democratic Model," *Comparative Political Studies* 31 (1998):353–97.

Hymer, S., *The International Operations of National Firms: a Study of Direct Foreign Investment*, Cambridge, MA: MIT Press (1960).

Jones, R. and H. Kierzkowski, "A Framework for Fragmentation," in S. Arndt and H. Kierzkowski (eds.), *Fragmentation: New Production Patterns in the World Economy*, New York: Oxford University Press (2001):17–34.

Katzenstein, P., *Small States in World Markets*, Ithaca: Cornell University Press (1985).

Kau, J. B. and P. H. Rubin, "The Impact of Labor Unions on the Passage of Economic Legislation," *Journal of Labor Research* 2 (1981):133–45.

Kohler, W., "A Specific-factors View on Outsourcing," *North American Journal of Economics and Finance* 12 (2001):31–53.

Koskela, E. and R. Schöb, "Alleviating Unemployment: the Case for Green Tax Reforms," *European Economic Review* 43 (1999):1723–46.

Krugman, P., "Domestic Policies in a Global Economy," *Brookings Trade Forum—1999*, Washington, DC: Brookings Institution (1999):73–93.

Leamer, E., "The Heckscher–Ohlin Model in Theory and Practice," *Princeton Studies in International Finance* 77 (1995).

Martin, J., "Measures of Replacement Rates for the Purpose of International Comparisons: a Note," *OECD Economic Studies* 26 (1996):99–115.

Mayer, F., *Interpreting NAFTA: the Science and Art of Political Analysis*, New York: Columbia University Press (1998).

Organisation for Economic Co-operation and Development (OECD), *Employment Outlook*, Paris: OECD (1997).

Pemberton, J., "A 'Managerial' Model of the Trade Union," *Economic Journal* 98 (1988):755–71.

Persson, T., "Do Political Institutions Shape Economic Policy?" *Econometrica* 70 (2002):883–905.

Persson, T. and G. Tabellini, "Is Inequality Harmful for Growth?" *American Economic Review* 84 (1994):600–21.

——, "Political Economics and Public Finance," in A. J. Auerbach and M. Feldstein (eds.), *Handbook of Public Economics*, Vol. 3, Amsterdam: North-Holland (2002).

Rama, M. and G. Tabellini, "Lobbying by Capital and Labor over Trade and Labor Market Policies," *European Economic Review* 42 (1998):1295–316.

Rodrik, D., "Why Do More Open Economies Have Bigger Governments?" *Journal of Political Economy* 106 (1998):997–1032.

Rowthorn, R. E., "Centralisation, Employment and Wage Dispersion," *Economic Journal* 102 (1992):506–23.

Saint-Paul, G., "Exploring the Political Economy of Labour Market Institutions," *Economic Policy* 23 (1996):263–315.

Saint-Paul, G. and T. Verdier, "Inequality, Redistribution and Growth: a Challenge to the Conventional Political Economy Approach," *European Economic Review* 40 (1996):719–28.

Shleifer, A. and R. W. Vishny, "Corruption," *Quarterly Journal of Economics* 108 (1993):599–617.

Slaughter, M., "What Are the Results of Product–Price Studies and What Can We Learn from Their Differences?" in R. Feenstra (ed.), *The Impact of International Trade on Wages*, Chicago: University of Chicago Press/NBER (2000):129–65.

Steinmo, S., "The End of Redistribution? International Pressures and Domestic Tax Policy Choices," *Challenge* 37 (1994):9–18.

790   *Noel Gaston and Douglas Nelson*

Swank, D., *Global Capital, Political Institutions, and Policy Changes in Developed Welfare States*, Cambridge: Cambridge University Press (2002).
Tanzi, V., *Taxation in an Integrating World*, Washington, DC: Brookings Institution (1995).
Vousden, N., *Economics of Trade Protection*, Cambridge: Cambridge University Press (1990).
Woldendorp J., H. Keman, and I. Budge, "Party Government in 20 democracies: an Update (1990–1995)," *European Journal of Political Research* 33(1) (1998):125–64.
Zweimüller, J. and E. Barth, "Bargaining Structure, Wage Determination, and Wage Dispersion in 6 OECD Countries," *Kyklos* 47 (1994):81–93.

Notes

1. Hall and Nelson (2001) develop a simple, preliminary analysis of this sort.
2. As Gaston and Nelson (2002) argue, the one-sector model used by labor economists has the virtue of providing clear guidance for empirical work, but must introduce the effect of standard globalization shocks (trade, immigration, foreign direct investment) in an essentially ad hoc way. That is, they shift either demand or supply, but there is no essential equilibrium relationship between globalization and the labor market.
3. The surveys of this literature are now almost sufficiently numerous to warrant a survey of their own. We make do with a reference to Slaughter's (2000) survey of work explicitly rooted in the Stolper–Samuelson theorem.
4. Consider a two-good model in which one sector decides to outsource. Either the original sector disappears, producing a three-good model (i.e., the original good unchanged good, and the two new sectors created by splitting the old technology) or a four-good model (if some firms continue to produce the final good under a unified technology). In either case, the dimensionality of both the price vector and the technology matrix must change, rendering standard comparative static methods problematic.
5. See Persson (2002) for a recent discussion with application to macroeconomic policy, and Hall and Nelson (1992) give an early institutional comparative static analysis of trade policy.
6. Rama and Tabellini (1998) refer to these as the "formal" and informal" sectors of the economy.
7. Most OECD countries rely on payroll taxes to fully, or to partially, fund their unemployment insurance systems (Ehrenberg, 1994; Koskela and Schöb, 1999).
8. If aggregate imports are negative, then $\tau > 0$ can be interpreted as an export subsidy. Similarly, if $\tau < 0$, then τ can be interpreted as an import subsidy if aggregate imports are positive, or as an export tax if aggregate imports are negative.
9. Strictly speaking, m denotes the fallback utility level of the union leadership should the sector's employees quit union membership. For example, if the union operates in more than one sector of the economy, it represents union membership in those other sectors (see Pemberton, 1988, and discussion below). In the present context, we assume that there are m incumbent workers employed elsewhere in the organization. We follow Pemberton (1988) and Burda (1997) in assuming that $n > m$, so that $(n - m)$ represents the incremental utility gain to the union leadership from the bargaining agreement.
10. Farber (1986, p. 1063) summarizing his own earlier research on the United Mine Workers states that the union "seems to have placed more weight on employment relative to compensation than rent-maximization would imply." On the other hand, Clark and Oswald (1993) show that unions often care more about wages than employment.
11. It is debatable whether firms and unions negotiate *both* wages and employment or just wages alone. Empirical evidence in favor of efficient bargaining is mixed (Farber, 1986, p. 1067). On the other hand, negotiation over work rules may ensure that bargains are efficient. Notwithstanding, in this paper when unions and firms agree to wage–employment combinations on the firm's labor demand curve is given by the special case $\gamma = 0$.
12. Haskel et al. (1997) show that increasing labor market flexibility in the United Kingdom has resulted in labor input being more closely aligned to the business cycle. This implies that

STRUCTURAL CHANGE AND THE LABOR-MARKET EFFECTS   791

wage and employment contracts lie closer to the marginal revenue product or demand-for-labor curve.

13. Given our focus on indirect effects of globalization in the context of a politically active union, some form of lobbying model is clearly the preferred political-economy framework. Grossman and Helpman's (1994) implementation of the menu auction model is particularly attractive because it makes the government an active participant in the political process (unlike previous lobbying models) as well as the organized interests (unlike the political-response-function models). However, we are well aware that both political-response-function models and lobbying models with a passive register government yield essentially the same qualitative results.

14. Goldberg and Maggi (1999) emphasize that the Grossman–Helpman formulation is formally equivalent to choosing the unemployment benefit that maximizes the joint surplus of all the parties involved.

15. Since employment is affected by both taxes and unemployment benefits, there are certain permissible values of both t and b for our problem to be well-defined. To illustrate, suppose that tariff revenues are not used to finance benefits, that we have a constant elasticity of production, and that $l = 1$. We require that $bg_n n_t < 1$, where $g(n) = (1 - n)(nw)^{-1}$, which implies that $t(1 + t)^{-1} < (1 - \alpha)(1 - n)$. The condition for the tax rate also ensures that we are on the Laffer-efficient side of the tax revenue function. This requires that the tax elasticity of employment is not "too" elastic; i.e., $n_t t n^{-1} > -1$ (or that $t(1 + t)^{-1} < (1 - \alpha)$).

16. The risk neutrality allows us to focus on the political contestability of unemployment benefits, rather than on the role of benefits as providing insurance, per se. (See also note 19, below.) We also leave aside the issue of whether unemployment insurance benefits might optimally be provided privately, rather than socially; see Casamatta et al. (2000).

17. From equation (7b), assuming $l = 1$, the slope of the NBC is $-(1 - \alpha)wn^{-1}$; and from equation (8), the slope of the indifference curve evaluated at (w^*, n^*) is $-(1 - \alpha)\delta w[(\gamma + \alpha)n]^{-1}$ (using equations (7b) and (8) to simplify). Comparing the two expressions, the NBC has a relatively steeper slope when $\gamma + \alpha > \delta$. In addition, evaluated at (w^*, n^*), the slope of the union leadership's indifference curve has a steeper slope than the worker's indifference curve as long as $\gamma > \delta$; i.e., when the union leaders are relatively more concerned with employment growth than with higher wages.

18. The maximand is the same regardless of whether τ is an export tax or subsidy or an import tariff or subsidy. See note 14.

19. Acemoglu and Shimer (1999) focus on the effects of unemployment benefits on workers' job search behavior. They show that firms may be willing to invest more in high-risk capital if the costs of searching for high-wage/high-unemployment-risk jobs by risk-averse workers are lowered by positive levels of unemployment insurance. An increase in the value of nonmarket time would have similar effects.

20. Such budgetary considerations may provide a theoretical explanation for Blank and Freeman's (1994) argument that some European countries, in the face of increased international competition, tried to reduce the "generosity" of their social programs.

21. In contrast, when an import subsidy is lowered there is pressure on benefits to be reduced due to higher internal prices, but there is also a relaxation of the government's balanced-budget constraint making the payment of more generous benefits possible. (Likewise, there are offsetting effects for export taxes and subsidies.)

22. It should be clear that asymmetric weighting of groups makes for a more complex relationship.

23. Some authors have interpreted a as measuring a policymaker's incorruptibility or the willingness of a government to adhere to welfare-maximizing policies (Shleifer and Vishny, 1993; Fredriksson and Svensson, 2003). However, in the context of pluralist democracies like those of the OECD, which make up our empirical sample, this is clearly a problematic interpretation of public political effort by organized groups.

24. For example, the globalization of capital markets and the increased mobility of capital, coupled with the fact that lobbying and political contributions are costly, may reduce the attractiveness of lobbying for capital owners (Fredriksson and Gaston, 2000). However, this sort of

792   *Noel Gaston and Douglas Nelson*

argument is usually associated with governments being strongly pro-capital as well—i.e., fear of alienating "the capital market" induces governments to adopt market conforming regulation, low rates of capital taxation, etc.

25. The OECD produces these data for odd-numbered years from 1961 to 1999. Martin (1996) provides a detailed description of this variable. The OECD Directorate for Education, Employment, Labour and Social Affairs, Social Policy Division, was kind enough to provide these data.

26. The lag of the dependent variable is a control for first-order autocorrelation. We are constrained to use a two-year lag because the variable is calculated only biennially.

27. Our sample countries are essentially the high-income OECD countries for which we could get at least 10 years of data: Australia, Austria, Belgium, Canada, Denmark, Finland, France, Germany, Ireland, Italy, Japan, Netherlands, Norway, Sweden, Switzerland, UK, and US. In fact, our preferred specification also excludes Italy as a result of problems with the dependent variable (see the annex to Martin, 1996). We initially suspected that there might be problems with the German data as a result of unification, but exclusion of Germany has no qualitative effect, and only very small quantitative effects, on our results.

28. We considered random-effects specifications of all the reported fixed-effects specifications. In addition to the usual problems with interpreting random effects, in all but one case the Hausman test rejected the random-effects specification in favor of the fixed-effects specification.

29. The reported estimates were produced in PcGive, using the panel data models module (Doornik et al., 2001). We checked the results by estimating the models in TSP and EViews with no significant differences in results. That is, although these packages use somewhat different corrections to the standard errors, the qualitative and quantitative differences in significance were small.

30. See the discussions in Garrett (1998) and Swank (2002).

31. See Friedrich (1982) for an extended discussion of the use of interaction terms and their interpretation.

Journal of
INTERNATIONAL
ECONOMICS

ELSEVIER   Journal of International Economics 71 (2007) 167–186

www.elsevier.com/locate/econbase

Can compensation save free trade? ☆

Carl Davidson [a,b], Steven J. Matusz [a,b,*], Douglas R. Nelson [b,c]

[a] Michigan State University
[b] GEP, University of Nottingham
[c] Tulane University

Received 29 March 2004; received in revised form 8 May 2006; accepted 17 May 2006

Abstract

When the median voter loses from trade reform, liberalization is blocked. Allowing the electorate to vote for compensatory subsidies may reverse this outcome. However, the order of the agenda may matter. The winners who pay the compensation may be sufficiently powerful to block compensation if trade is first liberalized. Seeing the inevitable outcome of sequential votes, the median voter realizes he will not be compensated for his losses and opposes liberalization. In contrast, liberalization can be achieved if compensation is placed first on the agenda. Finally, there is a significant chance that the least efficient compensation scheme will be chosen.
© 2006 Elsevier B.V. All rights reserved.

Keywords: Liberalization; Median Voter; Compensation

JEL classification: F130; D720

1. Introduction

Welfare economics generally, and the welfare economics of international trade in particular, has long understood that there is a close connection between liberalization and the need for compensation. While liberalization generally implies gains, it also implies adjustment, and, loosely speaking, the bigger the gains, the bigger the adjustment. For a country unable to influence its terms of trade, we have a sizable number of results, under quite general conditions,

☆ We thank seminar participants at the University of Nottingham and Syracuse University, two anonymous referees, and a co-editor, for insightful comments on earlier drafts of this paper.
* Corresponding author: Department of Economics; Michigan State University; East Lansing, MI 48824. Tel.: +1 517 353 8719; fax: +1 517 432 1068.
   E-mail address: matusz@msu.edu (S.J. Matusz).

0022-1996/$ - see front matter © 2006 Elsevier B.V. All rights reserved.
doi:10.1016/j.jinteco.2006.05.001

168   *C. Davidson et al. / Journal of International Economics 71 (2007) 167–186*

showing that free trade dominates limited trade and, under more restricted conditions, that existing forms of protection could be liberalized in such a way as to produce an increase in aggregate economic welfare. These results, however, rely on two fundamental abstractions: first, these are long-run/comparative static results that do not consider the short-run costs of adjustment from the distorted to the undistorted equilibrium; and, second, these results implicitly or explicitly assume that compensation is carried out in such a way as to ensure that a potential welfare gain is made actual. While both sorts of questions have produced research seeking to evaluate the robustness of gains from trade results to their concerns, in this paper we are interested in the positive political economy of the second question.[1]

The great majority of research on the positive political economy of domestic trade policy can be seen as an attempt to answer the question: if protection is so bad, why is there so much of it? The key result, presented most clearly in Mayer's (1984) fundamental paper: under the assumptions of the 2-good, 2-factor small HOS model, with heterogeneity in household factor ownership, and determination of equilibrium policy by simple referendum, except in the razor's edge case in which the median household factor ownership happens to be identical to that of the economy as a whole, free trade will not generally be an equilibrium policy.[2] This result, of course, relies on an assumption that the government does not possess a redistributive instrument (or does not choose to use it). Given the goals of that paper, and the plausible empirical claim that governments do not, in fact, seem to do much in the way of trade-contingent redistribution, this was an appropriate strategy.

In this paper, we follow Mayer's lead and adopt a referendum-based approach to the political economy of trade policy in which both protection and redistribution are essential components. Specifically, we construct a simple model in which a continuum of heterogeneous agents is inefficiently distributed between two industries due to protection. We assume that these agents face a choice between liberalization and protection, in which they will also choose whether to redistribute (some of) the gains from trade from (some of) the gainers to (some of) the losers. The particular institution involves three stages of voting: in the first stage, voters decide whether to liberalize trade. If liberalization is chosen, then in the second stage they vote on whether to provide compensation to the dislocated workers. Finally, if compensation is chosen, then in the third stage the workers vote on the method of compensation. We then compare the outcome of this political process with the outcome that would emerge if the only choices were uncompensated free trade or no liberalization. As in Mayer, the continuum assumption and the median voter framework allow us to focus on the fundamental question of policy choice/sustainability without getting bogged down in institutional details that have little claim to descriptive accuracy and even less claim to generating additional insight. That is, we can see the referendum as a reduced form for a more detailed representation of the political process.

In the context of this model, we address two interesting questions. First, would coupling trade liberalization measures with policies aimed at compensating dislocated workers increase the chances that free trade will emerge as the outcome of the political process? Many economists have argued that, in addition to moving trade liberalization in the direction of actual, as opposed to

---

[1] See Davidson and Matusz (2004) for an overview and extension of research on the first question. Fundamental normative research on the second question goes back to debates on the status of potential gain criterion of the Kaldor–Hicks sort, eventually evolving into questions about the feasibility of, and limits to, various compensation schemes. Examples of this latter research include Dixit and Norman (1986), Kemp and Wan (1986), Brecher and Choudhri (1994), Feenstra and Lewis (1994), Hammond and Sempere (1995), Guesnerie (2001), and Spector (2001).

[2] For all of the massive boom in research on the political economy of trade policy, there is surprisingly little substantive content beyond this result.

simply potential, Pareto improvement, compensation makes liberalization politically more sustainable (Lawrence and Litan, 1986). However, most attempts to evaluate this claim proceed under the assumption that the government seeks to maximize national welfare, but is constrained politically in the pursuit of this goal (Feenstra and Bhagwati, 1982; Magee, 2003). Our approach proceeds by considering the simple referendum model in the institution described above.[3] Second, we ask whether or not the optimal compensation policy will be chosen if workers are allowed to vote on the design of that policy. In the context of our model, we consider three policies that have received some attention in the policy debates on compensation: unemployment compensation, wage subsidies, and employment subsidies. We show that in this model the wage subsidy is preferred to the other two policies on efficiency grounds and then ask whether the wage subsidy is preferred in the referendum.[4]

Our results offer much hope for those that favor compensating displaced workers; but, they also raise one small concern. On the positive side, we find that in many instances allowing for compensation increases the likelihood that liberalization will emerge as the equilibrium outcome regardless of the order of the agenda. There does, however, exist a non-trivial portion of the parameter space for which the sequencing of decisions determines the outcome. In this portion of the parameter space, liberalization can be achieved if compensation is agreed upon beforehand, but not if the vote to compensate post dates the vote to liberalize. Finally, the one new concern that we uncover has to do with the choice of the compensation policy. We find that in some instances in which the agents vote in favor of liberalization with compensation, they also select an inefficient compensation policy.

2. The model

2.1. Overview

We assume that labor is the only input, but workers differ by ability (a). We assume that ability is uniformly distributed over the unit interval, implying that (with exceptions spelled out below) the worker for whom $a = 1/2$ is the median voter and is therefore decisive.

Workers can produce one of two goods. We refer to the first good as the "low-skill" good and assume that each worker, regardless of ability, can produce 1 unit of this good. We call the other good the "high-skill" good and assume that a worker with ability a can produce a units of this good. Workers are perfectly mobile across sectors and can immediately find employment in the low-skill sector, but must search for a job in the high-skill sector. We assume that time is continuous and that job offers arrive according to a Poisson process in the high-skill sector, with e representing the rate at which unemployed workers find jobs. Moreover, jobs in the high-skill sector do not last forever, with involuntary separations also following a Poisson process. We use b to denote the rate of job separation.

We assume that all markets are perfectly competitive and choose the high-skill good to serve as numeraire. All employed workers are paid the value of their marginal product.[5]

---

[3] We return to a comparison of our results with those of Feenstra/Bhagwati and Magee in the conclusion.

[4] In a slightly more complex model, Davidson and Matusz (2006) provide a detailed analysis of the relative efficiency of all three instruments.

[5] This assumption is used to ensure that the free trade equilibrium will be efficient. As is well known, search models are generally rife with externalities generated by the search process. We want to make sure that our results are not driven by how different compensation policies affect these search-related externalities.

We assume that the country under study has a comparative advantage in the high-skill good, and that the initial equilibrium (status quo) is distorted by a tariff levied on imports of the low-skill good. Following Mayer (1984), we assume that tariff revenue is neutral in that it is rebated to workers in proportion to their wage income. We describe below how the tariff rate is initially determined.

We only consider a subset of all possible parameterizations of the model. In particular, we are interested in exploring situations in which the median voter is initially employed in the protected low-skill sector and decides to switch sectors and search for a high-skill job in the event of liberalization. That is, we are interested in situations where the group of trade-displaced workers includes the median voter. It will become evident as we present the details of the model that other parameterizations are less interesting. For example, if the median voter is initially employed in the export sector, the status quo will be characterized by free trade (see below), and policies aimed at compensating trade-displaced workers cannot affect the political equilibrium if the median voter is trapped in the import-competing sector subsequent to liberalization.

To determine the status quo, we note that each worker has a most-preferred tariff. There are three groups that we must consider. First, there are those who would choose to work in the import-competing sector under free trade. For these workers, there exists a strictly positive tariff $\tilde{t}$ which leads to their globally optimal outcome. This is due to the fact that a tariff raises the wage of a worker in the import-competing sector and (to a point) increases tariff revenue. Thus, $\tilde{t}$ is higher than the tariff that maximizes tariff revenue. Indeed, the optimal tariff for these workers may be prohibitive, but need not be if tariff revenue constitutes a significant portion of income. Note that $\tilde{t}$ is independent of ability since the import-competing wage does not depend on ability.

The second group consists of the workers that would choose to seek employment in the export sector with $\tilde{t}$ in place. For this group, a zero tariff always leads to their most-preferred outcome.

This leaves us with the third group: those that would seek employment in the export sector under free trade but would work in the import-competing sector when the tariff is set at $\tilde{t}$. For these workers, preferences are not single-peaked and the optimal outcome is found by comparing utility with $\tilde{t}$ in place with utility under free trade.

To summarize to this point, $\tilde{t}$ and 0 are two obvious candidates for the status-quo tariff. Since we are concerned with the problem of liberalization, we assume that the status-quo tariff is $\tilde{t}$. With trade preferences determined by the median voter, this will in fact be the status-quo tariff if the median worker prefers $\tilde{t}$ over free trade. In this case, a simple referendum on liberalization unaccompanied by any compensating policies is doomed to fail.

However, there are parameterizations of the model for which the globally optimal tariff for the median worker is zero. Consequently a referendum on liberalization will succeed even in the absence of compensating policies. In these cases, we can justify our assumption that the status-quo tariff is $\tilde{t}$ in a variety of ways. For example, we could appeal to an un-modeled history where the initial distribution of ability may have been skewed in favor of low-skill workers, where import-competing workers may have had political power disproportionate to their numbers, or where the government may have had some non-economic objective for protecting the low-skill sector. Alternatively, this could be viewed as a short cut to a more complicated problem in which the economy recently experienced a significant improvement in the terms of trade, causing the median worker to switch his preference in favour of uncompensated liberalization. In this latter case, the status-quo tariff would differ slightly from the value of the status-quo tariff modelled in this paper (in that it would depend on the initial terms of trade), but the substance of the analysis would not be affected.

Starting from the status quo, we consider a series of votes. The first vote is on the issue of trade liberalization, consisting of complete removal of the initial tariff. If the majority votes for

C. Davidson et al. / Journal of International Economics 71 (2007) 167–186   171

liberalization, a second vote occurs. The issue addressed by the second referendum is whether displaced workers ought to be compensated for their losses. If the majority votes in favor of compensation, a final vote is held to select the instrument by which compensation is undertaken. As usual, the solution method requires us to start at the end of the process and work backwards. In most cases, the order of the vote is irrelevant. However, we highlight one case where the agenda does indeed matter.

2.2. Status-quo equilibrium

Workers choose between finding a low-paying job with certainty in the low-skill sector or searching for a high-paying job in the high-skill sector. Our assumption that tariff revenue is rebated to workers in proportion to their wage implies that the distribution of tariff revenue does not distort this decision, though the tariff itself clearly does create a distortion.

In order to determine the allocation of workers between sectors, we first begin by formulating the asset–value equations for each group of workers: those employed in a low-skill job (L), those who are unemployed and looking for a high-skill job (U), and those employed in a high-skill job (H). In doing so, we use $w_i(a)$ to denote the ability-specific wage, measured in terms of the numeraire, paid to a sector i worker, where $i=$ L,H, and we simplify the exposition by assuming that all workers have identical, Cobb–Douglas preferences, spending a fraction of their income ($\beta \leq 1$) on the low-skill good and their remaining income on the high-skill good. Defining the discount rate as ρ, the asset–value equations are then written as

$$\rho V_L(a, P_{sq}) = w_L(a)(1+r)P_{sq}^{-\beta} \tag{1.a}$$

$$\rho V_U(a, P_{sq}) = e[V_H - V_U] \tag{2.a}$$

$$\rho V_H(a, P_{sq}) = w_H(a)(1+r)P_{sq}^{-\beta} - b[V_H - V_U] \tag{3.a}$$

where P_{sq} is the status-quo price (i.e., the domestic price inclusive of the tariff $\tilde{t}$), $P_{sq}^{-\beta}$ is the price index, and r is the ratio of tariff revenue to total wages. Each of the above equations is formulated in the standard way, namely the right hand side of each represents the instantaneous real income earned by the worker adjusted for expected capital gains or losses.

The status-quo tariff is implicitly defined by the difference between the status-quo price and the free-trade price (P_{ft}) of the low-skill good. Moreover, given the world price, r is clearly a function of the status-quo price. For example, tariff revenue is zero (and therefore $r=0$) if the status-quo price equals the autarky price (a prohibitive tariff) or the world price (free trade).

Using the assumptions $w_L(a)=P_{sq}$ and $w_H(a)=a$, we can solve Eqs. (1.a), (2.a), and (3.a) to obtain:

$$V_L(a, P_{sq}) = (1+r)\frac{P_{sq}^{1-\beta}}{\rho} \tag{1.b}$$

$$V_U(a, P_{sq}) = (1+r)\frac{e}{\rho+b+e}\frac{aP_{sq}^{-\beta}}{\rho} \tag{2.b}$$

$$V_H(a, P_{sq}) = (1+r)\frac{\rho+e}{\rho+b+e}\frac{aP_{sq}^{-\beta}}{\rho} \tag{3.b}$$

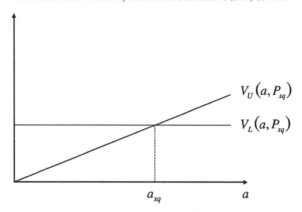

Fig. 1. Determining the status-quo distribution of workers.

Equating Eq. (1.b) with Eq. (2.b), we solve for the ability of the marginal worker who, given the status-quo price, is just indifferent between working in the low-skill sector (earning V_L) or searching for a job in the high-skill sector (earning V_U). Defining this marginal worker's ability as a_{sq}, we have:

$$a_{sq}(P_{sq}) = \frac{\rho + b + e}{e} P_{sq}. \tag{4}$$

Workers with less ability choose to work in the low-skill sector, those with higher ability are either looking for a job in the high-skill sector or are actually employed in that sector. This outcome is illustrated in Fig. 1, where we graph Eqs. (1.b) and (2.b) as functions of worker ability, taking as given the parameters of the model and the status-quo price.

For purposes of numeric analysis, we set the status-quo price equal to the price that would maximize present discounted utility for a low-skill worker. Our choice is based on the assumption that the median worker is employed in the low-skill sector in the status quo. That is, we only look at parameterizations such that $a_{sq} \geq 1/2$. From Eq. (1.b), it is clear that the real wage of a low-skill worker is monotonically increasing in the status-quo price, but tariff revenue first increases and then decreases as the domestic price increases from equality with the world price to the autarky price. The status-quo price therefore lies between the price that maximizes tariff revenue and the autarky price. While there is no closed-form solution for this price, it can be shown that the status-quo price is implicitly a function of P_{ft} and β.[6] We lighten the notation by suppressing this functional dependence.

3. Liberalization and compensation

Suppose that this economy now liberalizes trade, allowing the domestic relative price to fall to the exogenously-given free-trade price. We illustrate in Fig. 2 the resource-allocation and welfare

---

[6] In our numeric analysis, we solve for the *status-quo* price for every parameter pair by first calculating the equilibrium outcome (including tariff revenue) as a function of P_{sq}, P_{ft} and β. We then allocate aggregate tariff revenue (found as the difference between domestic and world prices multiplied by the quantity of imports) to workers in proportion to their wage income. Finally, we search over all P_{sq} to find the value that maximizes the utility of a worker employed in the low-skill sector.

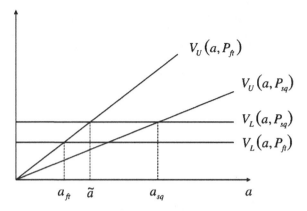

Fig. 2. Effects of liberalization.

effects of uncompensated liberalization. Clearly, low-skill employment now generates lower discounted utility than before since liberalization simultaneously reduces the real wage and removes any tariff revenue that low-skill workers might have been receiving in the status quo. In contrast, high-skill workers benefit from liberalization. This necessarily follows since liberalization benefits the economy as a whole (there are no distortions other than the tariff) and the only other group in the economy is harmed by liberalization.

We use a_{ft} to represent the ability of the marginal worker who is just indifferent between sectors under a regime of free trade. This value is calculated by substituting the free trade price into the right hand side of Eq. (4).

Several different groups of workers can be identified in Fig. 2. All workers with $a > a_{sq}$ unambiguously benefit from liberalization. These workers are originally tied to the high-skill sector (either employed or searching for a job) and remain there after liberalization. We refer to this group of workers as the "incumbents". On the opposite end, all workers with $a < a_{ft}$ are harmed by liberalization. Their real wage decreases and they receive no tariff revenue. Moreover, their ability is too low to make it worthwhile to switch sectors. These workers are trapped in the low-skill sector. We refer to this group as the "stayers". Finally, we refer to those with ability $a \in [a_{ft}, a_{sq}]$ as "trade-displaced" workers, an expression in line with the terminology used by Jacobson et al. (1993), Kletzer (2001) and others who have attempted to measure the financial impact that globalization has had on this group of workers. Among trade-displaced workers, those with $a \in [a_{ft}, \tilde{a}]$ are harmed by liberalization, while the remaining workers in this group benefit. That is, trade-displaced workers with lower ability can soften the blow of liberalization by switching sectors, but they cannot completely eliminate their losses. However higher-ability trade-displaced workers actually benefit. This is entirely consistent with Kletzer's (2001) empirical findings.[7]

Some of the losses suffered by the trade displaced workers are due to the adjustment costs that they must incur to switch occupations. We have chosen to model these adjustment costs in the form of search costs, but, in reality, these workers often face retraining and other costs as well.

---

[7] Kletzer (2001) reports that more than one third of re-employed workers earn the same or higher wages at their new job compared with their pre-displacement job.

174	*C. Davidson et al. / Journal of International Economics 71 (2007) 167–186*

Recent research suggests that these costs may be significant. For example, Jacobson, LaLonde and Sullivan (1993) found that the average dislocated worker suffers a loss in lifetime income of roughly $80,000 (see also Kletzer, 2001). Concerns about the magnitude of these costs have led many in the policy community to call for programs aimed at compensating these workers for their losses.[8] For this reason, in this paper we restrict attention to programs aimed at compensating all trade displaced workers for the losses they incur due to liberalization. That is, we do not consider policies aimed at compensating those that remained trapped in the previously protected sector. However, it should be clear that our analysis can easily be extended to consider the policy implications of compensating those trapped in the low-skill sector.

The primary policy used for compensation in the U.S. is trade adjustment assistance (TAA) which is essentially an extension of unemployment insurance for trade displaced workers. This program has been criticized in the policy community because of its unintended consequences: since unemployment insurance lowers the cost of remaining unemployed, it tends to lengthen jobless spells. Many in the policy community have suggested replacing TAA with a wage subsidy program (often referred to as 'wage insurance'), a program that rewards workers for finding new jobs and encourages them to return to work relatively quickly.[9] Following the success of the "reemployment bonus experiments" sponsored by the federal government during the 1980s, others have argued in favor of employment subsidies (often referred to as 'reemployment bonuses').[10] For example, a reemployment bonus program was included in President Clinton's 1996 Workforce Investment Act and the Bush Administration recently introduced legislation (referred to as the 'Growth and Jobs Plan') that includes provisions for the establishment of "personal reemployment accounts" which would provide cash bonuses for unemployed workers who return to work within 13 weeks of losing their jobs.

The challenge for the government is to craft policies that fully compensate all trade-displaced workers and that can be implemented with minimal information.[11] In this paper we focus attention on the program currently in use (TAA) and the two types of programs that have been suggested: wage subsidies and employment subsidies. Thus, we consider three distinct policies: unemployment compensation (μ), an employment subsidy (η) or a wage subsidy (ω). To the extent that unemployment benefits are based upon a worker's previous wage, they are, in this model, independent of the displaced worker's ability (all displaced workers earn the same wage in the status quo). Similarly, the magnitude of the employment subsidy is independent of ability. In this sense, the two policies are isomorphic. However, at least some workers have incentive to "cheat" with unemployment compensation. For example, unemployment compensation is likely to be higher than the value of the marginal product of labor for the lowest ability workers, suggesting a strong incentive to remain unemployed even when a job offer arrives. We therefore

---

[8] See, for example, Baily et al., 1993; Jacobson et al., 1993; Brander and Spencer, 1994; Brecher and Choudhri, 1994; Feenstra and Lewis, 1994; Burtless et al., 1998; Parsons, 2000; Hufbauer and Goodrich, 2001; Kletzer, 2001; Kletzer and Litan, 2001.

[9] See the papers referenced in the previous footnote.

[10] For more on the reemployment bonus experiments see Woodbury and Spiegelman (1987) or Robins and Spiegelman (2001).

[11] In our simple two-sector model it would be fairly easy for a government to implement a Dixit and Norman (1986) type of scheme whereby consumption taxes are levied so that consumers face pre-liberalization prices while producers face world prices. The resulting budget surplus could then be redistributed among all consumers to generate a Pareto gain. However, the complexity of this sort of scheme increases dramatically as the number of goods expands. By comparison, the complexity of a system of worker subsidies is relatively insensitive to the number of goods. The primary reason for the difference lies in the very demanding informational requirements for the former policy.

argue in the next section that unemployment compensation will never be the outcome of the political equilibrium and confine our analysis to a comparison of wage and employment subsidies.[12]

Policies can either be permanent or temporary. From the point of view of the recipient, all that matters is the expected discounted value of the subsidy, taking any expected termination into account. In the numeric examples constructed for this paper, we model policies as temporary. In particular, we assume that each subsidy (wage or employment) is given only to a displaced worker during his first spell of employment subsequent to liberalization. One can show that expected discounted utility for a displaced worker searching for his first job subsequent to liberalization is then[13]

$$V_{U\eta}(a, P_\text{ft}) = \left[\frac{\rho}{\rho + b}(a + \eta) + \frac{b}{\rho + b}\frac{e}{\rho + e + b}a \right] \left[\frac{e}{\rho + e} \right] \frac{P_\text{ft}^{-\alpha}}{\rho} \tag{5.a}$$

$$V_{U\omega}(a, P_\text{ft}) = \left[\frac{\rho}{\rho + b}(1 + \omega) + \frac{b}{\rho + b}\frac{e}{\rho + e + b} \right] \left[\frac{e}{\rho + e} \right] \frac{aP_\text{ft}^{-\alpha}}{\rho} \tag{5.b}$$

where the subscript signifies either an employment subsidy (η) or wage subsidy (ω).

All trade-displaced workers are unemployed immediately subsequent to liberalization. All compensation packages work by increasing the discounted utility for unemployed workers. The idea is to choose the size of the policy parameter (e.g., the magnitude of η, the employment subsidy) such that the worker with ability a_ft is indifferent between searching for a high-skill job under free trade and being employed in the low-skill sector when that sector is protected by a tariff. The effects of the two compensating policies are illustrated in Fig. 3.

The employment subsidy results in a parallel upward shift of the curve representing the discounted utility earned by an unemployed worker. This follows from the observation noted above that the employment subsidy does not depend upon worker ability. In contrast, the wage subsidy shifts this curve up while simultaneously increasing its slope. In this case, the marginal trade-displaced worker earns a wage of $a_\text{ft}(1 + \omega)$ while the subsidy is in effect. Each displaced worker is subsidized by the same percentage, implying that the actual magnitude of the subsidy increases with ability.

We assume that compensation is calibrated to the marginal trade-displaced worker, but it is given to any worker who switches sectors subsequent to liberalization. This gives rise to a class of policy-displaced workers: that is, workers who would continue to maintain employment in the low-skill sector in the absence of compensation, but who find that searching for a job in the high-skill sector is more attractive if compensation is being offered.[14]

In terms of Fig. 3, all workers with ability $a \in [a_\omega, a_\text{ft}]$ are characterized as policy-displaced if a wage subsidy is used to compensate trade-displaced workers, while an employment subsidy expands this set to include all of those workers with $a \in [a_\eta, a_\omega]$.

---

[12] Unemployment compensation would be isomorphic to a wage subsidy if the marginal product of workers varies with ability in both sectors and if unemployment compensation is related to a worker's wage prior to the spell of unemployment. This case was modeled in Davidson and Matusz (2006). It would still be the case, however, that some recipients of unemployment compensation would find it in their interest to cheat, suggesting that a majority would always prefer a wage subsidy to unemployment compensation in this case.

[13] See Appendix A for details.

[14] Davidson and Matusz (2006) refer to these workers as *temporary movers* because they return to the low-skill sector once their initial spell of high-skill employment terminates.

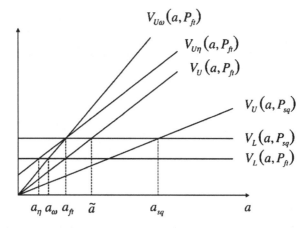

Fig. 3. Liberalization with compensation.

The creation of policy-displaced workers distorts the equilibrium, partially offsetting the gross gain from liberalization. This raises two questions. First, what is the most efficient way to compensate displaced workers? That is, which policy creates the smallest distortion while fully compensating the marginal trade-displaced worker? Second, could the deadweight loss generated by the compensation policy outweigh the gains from free trade? Both of these issues are addressed in Davidson and Matusz (2006). Regarding the second issue, while it is clearly an empirical question as to whether the distortion is larger or smaller than the gross gain from liberalization, Davidson and Matusz (2006) show that it is highly unlikely that the distortion can outweigh the gross gain. In any event, the net gain from liberalization is always positive for all of the parameterizations explored in this paper.

As for the first issue, Davidson and Matusz (2006) show that a wage subsidy program is the most efficient way to compensate trade displaced workers. While it is not quite this simple, the gist of the argument is as follows: since it is the creation of the policy-displaced workers that creates the distortion, then for any given compensation goal, the program that generates the smallest group of policy displaced workers is the most efficient policy. Fig. 3 shows that the wage subsidy is therefore superior to the employment subsidy, since it leads to a smaller set of policy-displaced workers.

Clearly, the compensation that we are analyzing has to be net of any taxes paid in order to effectively increase the discounted utility of trade-displaced workers. It is simplest, therefore, to assume that this group of workers is untaxed. Moreover, it seems unreasonable to tax stayers, who have lower income than trade-displaced workers. Therefore, all taxes used to pay for compensation come from the group of incumbents.[15] In essence, our tax scheme is a stylized progressive income tax where the marginal tax rate is zero for workers with income below some

---

[15] This is an entirely innocuous assumption. We could assume instead, as we did in Davidson and Matusz (2006), that the compensation scheme is financed by taxing all workers at a constant marginal rate without altering our qualitative results.

C. Davidson et al. / Journal of International Economics 71 (2007) 167–186   177

critical wage and $t > 0$ for workers with higher income.[16] The results of our numeric example follow directly as long as the critical wage is below a_{sq}.[17]

4. Preferences over policies

We start by assuming that two votes have been completed, resulting in a majority of voters opting for compensated liberalization. The third vote determines the form of compensation.

We argue that unemployment compensation, which is currently the primary instrument used to compensate trade displaced workers (through TAA), will never be the choice for the majority. Unemployment compensation and the employment subsidy both have the same effect on the utility of a trade-displaced worker; hence trade-displaced workers are indifferent between these two policies.[18] The two policies differ, however, for at least some policy-displaced workers. In instances in which the expected duration of unemployment is short relative to the expected duration of a high-skill job, the magnitude of the unemployment benefit necessary to fully compensate the marginal trade displaced worker is likely higher than the wage that would be earned by a low-ability worker employed in a high-skill job. Indeed, this compensation may even be higher than the low-skill wage. As such, there may be some workers who would continue to collect unemployment benefits for as long as possible; refusing any job offers that might come their way. Unless the unemployment program is perfectly monitored, the ultimate cost of providing fully compensating unemployment benefits will exceed the cost of a fully-compensating employment subsidy. By offering a slightly higher employment subsidy, incumbents can entice trade-displaced workers to vote for an employment subsidy over unemployment compensation. These two groups together constitute more than half of the population. As such, we eliminate unemployment compensation from further consideration, focusing instead on comparing the wage and employment subsidies.

We next observe that workers with $a \in [0, a_\eta]$ have no stake in the outcome of the political process. These workers do not pay taxes nor do they receive compensation. Therefore the voting population consists only of workers with $a \in [a_\eta, 1]$. Trade-displaced workers clearly prefer the wage subsidy, since this generates a larger transfer than the fully-compensating employment subsidy for all but the marginal trade-displaced worker. On the other side, workers with $a \in [a_\eta, a_\mathit{fl}]$ prefer the employment subsidy, since this policy generates for them a larger transfer than the equivalent wage subsidy (see Fig. 3). Incumbents prefer the policy that generates the smallest aggregate subsidy, since this generates the smallest tax burden. While the wage subsidy is more generous to trade-displaced workers, an employment subsidy creates more policy-displaced workers, raising the aggregate cost of the transfer. In the next section (and Appendix A), we show that it is possible to divide the parameter space such that incumbents prefer the wage subsidy for

---

[16] A worker in the high-tech sector who faces the positive marginal tax rate has a net wage of $a(1-t)$. Eqs. (2.b) and (3. b) are then simply modified by multiplying the right hand side of each by $(1-t)$.

[17] Workers with ability between a_fl and a_{sq} are net recipients of transfers, and therefore are unaffected by the tax structure. Those with ability below a_fl care about the tax structure, but the tax structure itself does not change their ranking of policy instruments, nor does it change their preferences regarding the status quo versus liberalization. Liberalization becomes more difficult if the critical value is above a_{sq}, since a smaller share of the population bears the burden of compensation. It is conceivable in this case that the magnitude of the transfer is larger than the gross gain from liberalization that is captured by this group of taxpayers, inducing them to vote against liberalization in instances where they foresee a majority in favor of compensation. We leave analysis of this case for future work.

[18] See Davidson and Matusz (2006) for a more complete discussion of the equivalency of various compensation policies.

one set of parameters, while preferring the employment subsidy for another set of parameters. Our numeric exercise indicates that none of the three groups form a majority on their own, therefore the preferences of incumbents are decisive in this vote.

We now back up to the vote on whether compensation should be offered, assuming that liberalization has been approved. Rational agents look forward to see the form of compensation that would be offered in the event that a majority favors compensation. If the perfect-foresight outcome is an employment subsidy, all workers with $a \in [a_\eta, a_{sq}]$ prefer compensation, while all incumbents oppose it. The remaining workers have no stake in the outcome, since they do not pay taxes nor receive compensation. The outcome is only modestly different if the perfect-foresight outcome is a wage subsidy, in which case all workers with $a \in [a_\omega, a_{sq}]$ prefer compensation, all incumbents continue to oppose it, and the remainder are indifferent.

Finally, consider the vote on whether or not to liberalize. Forward-looking agents anticipate whether or not compensation will be offered. They also anticipate the form that the compensation will take in the event that it is offered. Workers with $a \in [0, a_{ft}]$ lose relative to the status quo even when compensation is offered; therefore these workers always oppose liberalization. Workers with $a \in [a_{ft}, \tilde{a}]$ join in the opposition in the event that compensation is not offered, while all remaining workers support liberalization. All trade-displaced workers with $a \in [a_{ft}, a_{sq}]$ support liberalization with compensation, regardless of the form that the compensation takes. Incumbents join in support for liberalization if the total transfer required under compensation is smaller than the gross gains from liberalization that accrue to them.

5. Constructing the parameter space

The nature of the political equilibrium depends on the parameters of the model. Taking labor market turnover rates and the discount rate as given, a_η, a_ω, a_{ft}, $\tilde{a}$, and a_{sq} can all be written as functions of the free trade price (P_{ft}) and the preference parameter (β).

In order to focus on situations where the group of displaced workers contains $a = 1/2$, we have to limit the range of P_{ft}. If P_{ft} is too high, the worker with $a = 1/2$ would prefer to remain in the low-skill sector after liberalization, and if P_{ft} is too low, that worker would locate in the high-skill sector even under the status quo. Therefore, we assume that $P_{min} \leq P_{ft} \leq P_{max}$. The maximum price is the price at which the worker with $a = 1/2$ is just indifferent between low-skill employment and searching for a high-skill job under free trade, and is found by replacing $a_{sq}(P_{sq})$ in Eq. (4) with $1/2$ and letting $P_{sq} = P_{max}$, so that

$$P_{max} = \frac{1}{2} \frac{e}{\rho + e + b}. \tag{6}$$

The minimum price is the price at which the worker with $a = 1/2$ is just indifferent between low-skill employment and searching for a high-skill job assuming that this worker's most-preferred tariff is levied. To solve for this price, we first observe that if the autarky price (P_a) is too low, even a prohibitive tariff could not dissuade a worker with $a = 1/2$ from seeking employment in the high-skill sector. We show in Appendix A that

$$P_a(\beta) = \sqrt{\frac{e}{\rho + b + e}} \sqrt{\frac{\beta e}{(2 - \beta)(b + e) + \beta \rho}} \tag{7}$$

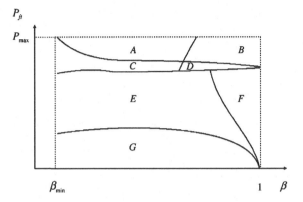

Fig. 4. Division of the parameter space.

so that the autarky price is increasing in the preference parameter. A minimum value of the autarky price therefore translates to a minimum bound on β, which can be found by replacing $a_{sq}(P_{sq})$ in Eq. (4) with 1/2 and letting $P_{sq}=P_a(\beta)$. Doing so and solving for β, we obtain

$$\beta_{min} = \frac{2(b+e)}{3\rho + 5(b+e)}. \tag{8}$$

We can then use Eq. (4) to solve for P_{min} when $\beta > \beta_{min}$. To see this, first recall that P_{sq} depends upon P_{ft} and β. Then P_{min} is a function of β and is implicitly defined as the free trade price that solves Eq. (4) when $a_{sq}=1/2$.

Note that $P_{max}=P_a(\beta_{min})$, from which it follows that $P_{max} \leq P_a(\beta)$ for all $\beta \geq \beta_{min}$ since the autarky price is increasing in β. Therefore, our restrictions guarantee that $P_{ft} \leq P_a(\beta)$ for all $\beta \geq \beta_{min}$ so that the economy has a comparative advantage in the high-skill good.

Finally, for every β there exists a free trade price at which the worker for whom $a=1/2$ is indifferent between the status quo and uncompensated free trade. Let $P_I(\beta)$ represent this price. Then $P_I(\beta)$ is implicitly defined as the solution to $V_U(a,P_{ft})=V_L(a,P_{sq})$ evaluated at $a=1/2$, where we once again recognize that P_{sq} depends upon both P_{ft} and β. The median worker strictly prefers the status quo (uncompensated liberalization) for $P_{ft}>(<)P_I(\beta)$. This follows because the status-quo price is chosen to maximize discounted utility, so a small change in the free trade price has only a second-order effect on discounted utility of a low-skill worker under the status quo, whereas the utility of a high-skill worker is strictly decreasing in P_{ft}.

We illustrate the relevant parameter space in Fig. 4, which we divide into seven regions. This figure was computer generated based on a particular parameterization of the model, however experimentation with a wide range of parameters suggests that the qualitative features of the figure are not sensitive to the choice of parameters.[19]

---

[19] Specifically, we constructed this figure assuming that $\rho=0.05$, $b=0.1$, and $e=4$. The parameter value for b implies that the expected duration of a high-skill job is 10 years, while the parameter for e suggests that the expected duration of a spell of unemployment is 3 months.

Region G in Fig. 4 represents combinations of P_{ft} and β for which the median worker would locate in the high-skill sector under the status quo (and remain there after liberalization). In contrast, in regions A–F the median worker starts out in the low-skill sector and moves to the high-skill sector after liberalization. The border dividing G from E is defined by $P_{\text{min}}(\beta)$. For our purposes, G is uninteresting, since a majority of agents would clearly prefer uncompensated liberalization. We therefore restrict attention to A–F for the remainder of the paper.

In regions C, D, E, and F the median worker would prefer uncompensated liberalization to the status quo; whereas in regions A and B, the median worker would prefer the status quo to uncompensated liberalization.[20] The border separating C and D from A and B (respectively) is defined by $P_{\text{I}}(\beta)$. It follows that a simple referendum on liberalization would result in free trade in C–F and the status quo in A and B. It follows that if the parameters lie in A or B, liberalization can only be obtained as a political outcome if compensation is provided to displaced workers.[21]

Finally, we turn to preferences over compensation policies. As we noted in the previous section, we need to know how the magnitude of the aggregate transfer associated with an employment subsidy compares with that associated with a wage subsidy in order to determine the incumbents' preferences over the compensation programs. In contrast, we know that trade-displaced workers always prefer the wage subsidy, whereas policy-displaced workers always prefer the employment subsidy.

The border separating regions E and F from C and D (respectively) is defined as the set of parameters for which the two policies generate the same discounted value of the transfer.[22] The employment subsidy generates a smaller aggregate transfer for all parameter combinations lying above this border, with the wage subsidy generating the smaller transfer for all combinations lying below this border. Therefore, incumbents prefer the employment subsidy if parameters lie in regions A, B, C, or D, while they prefer the wage subsidy otherwise.

6. The political equilibrium

We now combine information on policy preferences with information summarized in Fig. 4 to solve for the equilibrium outcome. As noted earlier, the solution technique is backwards induction.

Suppose that the majority has already voted in favor of compensated liberalization. All that remains is to determine the form of the compensation program. In describing policy preferences, we argued that all trade-displaced workers (of whom there are $a_{\text{sq}} - a_{\text{ft}}$) prefer the wage subsidy, while all policy-displaced workers (of whom there are $a_{\text{ft}} - a_n$) prefer the employment subsidy. Since those trapped in low-skill jobs are not affected by the form of compensation, they do not vote, implying that the voting population consists of $1 - a_n$ workers. In all of our numeric analysis, neither trade-displaced workers nor policy-displaced workers alone form a majority of this population. The policy that wins the majority is therefore the policy

---

[20] Refer back to our discussion in Section 2.1 where we justify the initial tariff in C, D, E, and F as a legacy from past circumstances.

[21] The existence of regions A and B indicates that, as Mayer (1984) emphasized, free trade may not be the equilibrium outcome when the median voter's preferences determine trade policy. Our approach here is a bit different from Mayer's. In his model, agents have preferences over tariffs and he shows that the equilibrium tariff is the one preferred by the median voter. Since this tariff is zero only if the median voter's factor ownership is identical to that of the economy as a whole, his result is that free trade is not likely to be the outcome when agents vote on the level of protection. In contrast, we are assuming that protection is already in place and ask under what conditions society will choose to liberalize.

[22] In Appendix A we show how to solve for this border.

C. Davidson et al. / Journal of International Economics 71 (2007) 167–186 181

favored by the group of incumbents who align themselves with trade-displaced workers if parameters lie in regions E or F (where the wage subsidy is less costly to finance), or align themselves with policy-displaced workers if parameters fall into regions A, B, C, or D (where the employment subsidy is less costly).[23]

Knowing the outcome of the final stage of voting, we now step back to ask whether a majority would favor compensation in the event of liberalization. There are two cases to consider. Suppose first that parameters lie in A, B, C, or D, so that the final stage of voting results in an employment subsidy. In this case, workers with $a \in [a_\eta, a_{sq}]$ favor compensation, while those with $a > a_{sq}$ are opposed. Workers at the very bottom of the ability distribution have no stake in the outcome, since they would not be affected either way. The border in Fig. 4 that divides regions A and C from regions B and D (respectively) is defined as the set of parameters for which $1 - a_{sq} = a_{sq} - a_\eta$. If the parameters lie in B or D, displaced workers constitute a majority of the voting population and therefore compensation will be approved, whereas compensation will be defeated if the parameters lie in regions A or C.

Similar reasoning separates E from F. The difference here is that the wage subsidy will carry the day in the event that compensation is approved. Under these circumstances, workers with $a < a_\omega$ have no stake in the outcome, so the voting population is smaller. The border between E and F is therefore the set of parameters for which $1 - a_{sq} = a_{sq} - a_\omega$. Displaced workers have a majority if parameters fall in F, whereas the incumbents are in the majority if the parameters fall in E.

To summarize to this point, no compensation will be offered if parameters lie in A, C, or E. If parameters lie in B or D, an employment subsidy will be used to compensate displaced workers, while a wage subsidy will be used to compensate these workers if parameters fall in F.

Turning to the initial vote, it is easy to see now that the status quo wins out if parameters fall in A. In this case, the median worker who opposes uncompensated liberalization recognizes that incumbents are strong enough to block all compensation if trade is liberalized. Therefore the median worker opposes liberalization.

If parameters lay in C or E, the median worker will vote to liberalize. Despite the recognition that there will ultimately be no compensation, the median worker prefers uncompensated liberalization to the status quo.

For parameters in A, C, or E, placing the issue of compensation on the table does not affect the outcome. However, the outcome is affected if parameters lie in B, D, or F. Compensation does buy liberalization in B, where the median worker opposes uncompensated liberalization but realizes that compensation will be forthcoming if trade is liberalized. Regions D and F will also result in liberalization, as they would in the absence of compensation, however the outcome will not be a complete removal of all distortions. In these two cases, compensation will be offered, distorting the equilibrium by creating a class of policy-displaced workers. In all of our numeric analysis, however, the distortion created by offering compensation is smaller than the distortion generated by the status-quo tariff. Hence, the net gain is positive.

We close this section by noting that the order of voting only matters in A. To see this, suppose that the economy first voted on compensation. This would be defeated in C and E, where incumbents hold a majority, but the median worker prefers uncompensated liberalization to the status quo, so liberalization would still occur. In B, D, and F, incumbents are in the minority, so compensation passes and liberalization occurs. Incumbents prefer compensated liberalization to

---

[23] As already noted, region G will be associated with uncompensated liberalization since the median worker is an incumbent. We therefore need not consider choice of instrument in this region.

182   *C. Davidson et al. / Journal of International Economics 71 (2007) 167–186*

the status quo, they would therefore find it in their interest to vote for compensation if parameters lie in A, since this is the only way to assure a favorable vote on liberalization.

7. Discussion

We see this paper as making two contributions. First, we have extended the standard referendum model of political economy of trade policy to incorporate compensation. Second, our specific application considered the issue of whether compensation can "save free trade".

Our first contribution involves the extension of a Mayer-type referendum model to endogenize the compensation, as well as the trade policy, decision.[24] Although there is a sizable literature on the common-sense notion that compensation, in addition to moving a potentially Pareto-improving policy in the direction of an actual Pareto improvement, increases the political sustainability of trade liberalization, there is very little in the way of systematic political economic analysis on this question. Early work by Johnson and McCulloch (1973) argued that a welfare maximizing government that was politically constrained to offer protection might gain relative to a tariff by using the distribution of quota revenues to support lower levels of protection. Feenstra and Bhagwati (1982) apply similar reasoning in a model in which a welfare maximizing government uses tariff revenues to induce lower levels of lobbying on the part of a protection-seeking labor union. While Feenstra and Bhagwati do present an explicit model of political-economic interaction, the assumption of a welfare-maximizing government seems broadly inconsistent with the underlying goals of political economic analysis. More closely related to our work is Magee (2003). As with Feenstra and Bhagwati, in Magee's model the government is an active player, but unlike Feenstra and Bhagwati, instead of seeking purely to maximize welfare the government is of the Grossman and Helpman (1994) sort. Contrary to Feenstra and Bhagwati, Magee finds that, precisely because it lowers the cost of any given level of protection, the presence of compensation permits the government to offer more protection.[25] In particular, at low levels of protection (such as those currently applied in virtually all industrial countries) compensation may hinder further liberalization.[26]

There are two major differences between Magee's analysis and ours. First, where Magee's analysis evaluates the contribution of compensation to liberalization at the margin, our analysis focuses on the contribution of compensation to the overall sustainability of liberalization. That is, our model considers a choice between fixed, finite policy options. Second, and perhaps more importantly, Magee's analysis, like Feenstra and Bhagwati's, is really only indirectly about liberalization. As in Grossman and Helpman, what is really for sale is protection. In our analysis the issue on the agenda is liberalization. We think it is worth noting that trade policy in the post Second World War era has been overwhelmingly about liberalization, and that arguments about compensation have been directly related to this policy and not to protection per se. Furthermore, this commitment to liberalization has been only very indirectly related to the sorts of forces modeled in standard work on political economy (Nelson, 2003). Thus, while the details of inter-sectoral variation in protection may be well-modeled in something like a Grossman–Helpman

---

[24] See Mayer (1984).

[25] This effect is particularly large in Magee's simulations because he takes the result of Goldberg and Maggi (1999) that the government's weight on aggregate social welfare is 50 to 70 times the weight placed on contributions.

[26] This result is contrary to that obtained by Fung and Staiger (1996) who analyze compensation in a model without domestic political competition. Their model treats domestic compensation as part of the *international* political economy of trade policy. In their paper the implicit bribe is not directed to domestic factors of production but to one's negotiating partners in a trade agreement.

framework, we believe that the issue of overall sustainability of a liberalization policy (adopted for some un-modeled reason) is more clearly treated in a framework such as that developed here.

Directly related to the last comment, our second contribution is an evaluation of claims that a well-constructed compensation program can help "save free trade" (Lawrence and Litan, 1986). In the context of our model we find that allowing for the possibility of compensating trade-displaced workers does lead to liberalization in instances where it would have otherwise been blocked, but there are situations where compensation results in a distorted outcome when a Pareto efficient outcome would have been obtained in the absence of compensation.

We close by offering some suggestions for extensions. With respect to the political economy model: first, it would be interesting to consider alternative structures of referendum; second, introducing an active government with alternative objectives would seem to be a useful extension; and third, it would seem important to consider the sustainability of compensation in the context of less robust information than considered here. Finally, with respect to the specific issue of "saving free trade", it would be interesting to bring more concrete structure to the analysis to permit some more specific evaluation of the role of compensation (i.e., What part of the parameter space do we find ourselves in?).

Appendix A

Autarky

Let $\bar{a}$ represent the ability of the worker who is just indifferent between low-skill employment and searching for a job in the high-skill sector when the economy is in autarky. Given that ability is uniformly distributed over the unit interval, the allocation of labor implies that $\bar{a}$ is the fraction of workers employed in the low-skill sector with all remaining workers either employed in the high-skill sector or searching for a job in that sector. Of the $1 - \bar{a}$ workers affiliated with the high-skill sector, steady-state conditions imply that the fraction $\left(\frac{b}{e+b}\right)$ are unemployed, with the remaining $\left(\frac{e}{e+b}\right)$ employed. We can therefore solve for the supplies of the two goods as a function of relative price $(S_i(P), i=H,L)$

$$S_L(P) = \int_{0\bar{a}} \mathrm{d}a = \bar{a} \tag{A.1}$$

$$S_H(P) = \left(\frac{b}{e+b}\right) \int \bar{a}^{1} a \mathrm{d}a = \left(\frac{b}{e+b}\right) \left(\frac{1+\bar{a}}{2}\right)(1-\bar{a}) \tag{A.2}$$

Our assumption that all workers share the same Cobb–Douglas preferences implies that the demands for the two goods are related in the following way:

$$PD_L(P) = \frac{\beta}{1-\beta} D_H(P). \tag{A.3}$$

In the absence of trade, the demand for each good must equal its supply. We then use Eqs. (A.1), (A.2), and (A.3) to obtain Eq. (7) in the text.

Tariff revenue

Let R represent tariff revenue. Then

$$R(P_{sq}) = (P_{sq} - P_{ft})(D_L(P_{sq}) - S_L(P_{sq})). \tag{A.4}$$

The supply of the low-skill good is given in Eq. (A.1). Demand for the low-skill good has to satisfy Eq. (A.3) for $P = P_{sq}$ and the economy-wide budget constraint:

$$P_{ft} D_L(P_{sq}) + D_H(P_{sq}) = P_{ft} S_L(P_{sq}) + S_H(P_{sq}) \tag{A.5}$$

Therefore, demand for the low-skill good is:

$$D_L(P_{sq}) = \frac{\beta(P_{ft} S_L(P_{sq}) + S_H(P_{sq}))}{\beta P_{ft} + (1-\beta)P_{sq}} \tag{A.6}$$

where we again note that P_{sq} is itself a function of P_{ft} and β.

Tariff revenue is distributed to each worker in proportion to the wage earned by the worker:

$$r(P_{sq}) = \frac{R(P_{sq})}{P_{sq} S_L(P_{sq}) + S_H(P_{sq})}. \tag{A.7}$$

Discounted utility with a temporary employment subsidy

We assume that the employment subsidy is given to a displaced worker only during the duration of his first post-liberalization job. The asset value equations are then as follows:

$$\rho V_H = a P_{ft}^{-\alpha} - b[V_H - V_U] \tag{A.8}$$
$$\rho V_U = e[V_H - V_U] \tag{A.9}$$
$$\rho V_{H\eta} = (a + \eta) P_{ft}^{-\alpha} - b[V_{H\eta} - V_U] \tag{A.10}$$
$$\rho V_{U\eta} = e[V_{H\eta} - V_{U\eta}] \tag{A.11}$$

Where $V_{H\eta}$ represents discounted income for a displaced worker employed for the first time in the high-skill sector.

An analogous system can be written for a wage subsidy, replacing $(a+\eta)$ in Eq. (A.10) with $a(1+\omega)$. The two systems can then be solved for Eqs. (5.a) and (5.b) in the text.

Discounted value of the employment subsidy

Everyone with ability $a \in [a_\eta, a_{sq}]$ receives the employment subsidy during the first spell of employment. Let $\Omega_{U\eta}$ represent the present discounted value of the employment subsidy received by a worker searching for his first job and let $\Omega_{H\eta}$ represent the present discounted value of the subsidy received by a worker in his first job. Then:

$$\rho \Omega_{U\eta} = 0 + e[\Omega_{H\eta} - \Omega_{U\eta}] \tag{A.12}$$
$$\rho \Omega_{H\eta} = \eta - b \Omega_{H\eta} \tag{A.13}$$

Solving these two equations:

$$\Omega_{U\eta} = \frac{1}{\rho + b} \frac{e}{\rho + e} \eta \tag{A.14}$$

C. Davidson et al. / Journal of International Economics 71 (2007) 167–186   185

so T_η, the total present discounted value of the transfer at the moment of liberalization is:

$$T_\eta = \left\{ \frac{1}{\rho + b} \frac{e}{\rho + e} \eta \right\} \left\{ a_{sq} - a_\eta \right\}. \tag{A.15}$$

Eqs. (A.16) and (A.17) are the analogues for a wage subsidy:

$$\Omega_{U\omega} = \frac{1}{\rho + b} \frac{e}{\rho + e} (1 + \omega) P_{ft} a \tag{A.16}$$

$$T_\omega = \frac{1}{\rho + b} \frac{e}{\rho + e} \frac{a_\omega^2 + a_{sq}^2}{2} (1 + \omega) P_{ft}. \tag{A.17}$$

Setting $T_\eta = T_\omega$ provides the border dividing C and D from E and F in Fig. 4. We can compare T_η and T_ω with the discounted value of the gains from liberalization that accrue to incumbents:

$$G = \frac{b}{e + b} \int_{a_{sq}}^1 \{V_H(P_{ft}, a) - V_H(P_{sq}, a)\} da + \frac{e}{e + b} \int_{a_{sq}}^1 \{V_U(P_{ft}, a) - V_U(P_{sq}, a)\} da. \tag{A.18}$$

In all of our numeric calculations, the discounted gain to the incumbents was larger in magnitude than the discounted value of either subsidy.

References

Baily, M.N., Burtless, G., Litan, R., 1993. Growth with Equity. Brookings Institution, Washington D.C.

Brander, J., Spencer, B., 1994. Trade adjustment assistance: welfare and incentive effects of payments to displaced workers. Journal of International Economics 36, 239–261.

Brecher, R., Choudhri, E., 1994. Pareto gains from trade, reconsidered: compensating for jobs lost. Journal of International Economics 36, 223–238.

Burtless, G., .Lawrence, R., Litan, R., Shapiro, R., 1998. Globaphobia: Confronting Fears about Open Trade. Brookings Institution, Washington D.C.

Davidson, C., Matusz, S.J., 2004. International Trade and Labor Markets: Theory, Evidence and Policy Implications. W.E. Upjohn Institute, Kalamazoo.

Davidson, C., Matusz, S.J., 2006. Trade liberalization and compensation. International Economic Review 43, 723–747.

Dixit, A., Norman, V., 1986. Gains from trade without lump-sum compensation. Journal of International Economics 21, 111–122.

Feenstra, R., Bhagwati, J., 1982. Tariff seeking and the efficient tariff. In: Bhagwati, J. (Ed.), Import Competition and Response. University of Chicago Press/NBER, Chicago, pp. 245–258.

Feenstra, R., Lewis, T., 1994. Trade adjustment assistance and Pareto gains from trade. Journal of International Economics 36, 201–222.

Fung, K.C., Staiger, R., 1996. Trade liberalization and trade adjustment assistance. In: Canzoneri, M., Ethier, W., Grilli, V. (Eds.), The New Transatlantic Economy. Cambridge University Press/CEPR, Cambridge, pp. 265–286.

Goldberg, P., Maggi, G., 1999. Protection for sale: an empirical investigation. American Economic Review 89, 1135–1155.

Grossman, G., Helpman, E., 1994. Protection for sale. American Economic Review 84, 833–850.

Guesnerie, R., 2001. Second best redistributive policies: the case of international trade. Journal of Public Economic Theory 3, 15–25.

Hammond, P., Sempere, J., 1995. Limits to the potential gains from trade. Economic Journal 105, 1180–1204.

Hufbauer, G., Goodrich, B., 2001. Steel: Big Problems, Better Solutions. Policy Brief. Institute for International Economics, Washington D.C.

Jacobson, L., LaLonde, R., Sullivan, D., 1993. Earnings losses of displaced workers. American Economic Review 83, 685–709.

Johnson, H.G., McCulloch, R., 1973. A note on proportionally distributed quotas. American Economic Review 63, 726–732.

Kemp, M., Wan, H., 1986. Gains from trade with and without compensation". Journal of International Economics 21, 99–110.

Kletzer, L., 2001. Job Loss from Imports: Measuring the Costs. Institute for International Economics, Washington D.C.

Kletzer, L., Litan, R., 2001. A prescription to relieve worker anxiety. Policy Brief, vol. 73. Brookings Institution, Washington D.C.

Lawrence, R., Litan, R., 1986. Saving Free Trade: A Pragmatic Approach. Brookings Institution, Washington D.C.

Mayer, W., 1984. Endogenous tariff formation. American Economic Review 74, 970–985.

Magee, C., 2003. Endogenous tariffs and trade adjustment assistance. Journal of International Economics 60, 203–222.

Nelson, D., 2003. Political economy problems in the analysis of trade policy. Inaugural Lecture, University of Nottingham.

Parsons, D., 2000. Wage insurance: a policy review. Research in Employment Policy 2, 119–140.

Robins, P., Spiegelman, R., 2001. Reemployment Bonuses in the Unemployment Insurance System. W.E. Upjohn Institute for Employment Research, Kalamazoo.

Spector, D., 2001. Is it possible to redistribute the gains from trade using income taxation? Journal of International Economics 55, 441–460.

Woodbury, S., Spiegelman, R., 1987. Bonuses to workers and employers to reduce unemployment: randomized trials in Illinois. American Economic Review 77, 513–530.

4. The politics of (anti-)globalization: what do we learn from simple models?

David Greenaway and Douglas Nelson*

INTRODUCTION

Contrary to some of the more overheated rhetoric on globalization, this process is, in fact, quite reversible. Sometimes lost in the attempts to determine whether current levels of globalization are higher or lower than those in the late 19th century is the fact that globalization came to a screaming halt in the 1930s.[1] Simple technological determinism misses the essential role of politics in supporting, or undermining, globalization.[2] Such determinism also distracts from at least one fundamental difference between the late 19th-century globalization and the late 20th-century version: the former was characterized by far more restricted democratic politics in the core countries than the latter. As we observe an increasingly confident and aggressive anti-globalization movement, proponents of a liberal international order, to say nothing of stable liberal domestic political economies, need to think hard about both the roots of anti-globalism and the nature of its politics. In this chapter we focus on the latter.

Our focus is a preliminary investigation of the link between democratic politics and the stability of globalization in three steps. First, we briefly develop two key distinctions that will provide an analytical framework for our discussion. Specifically, we shall argue that most of the literature on political economy of trade and immigration fails to distinguish between the average level of a policy (say, a tariff) and the variance of that policy (for example, the dispersion of the tariff across sectors), and we shall distinguish between two very broad classes of political economy model (Weberian models and interest-group models). Second, we shall consider how well these models account for policy outcomes, both mean and variance, in trade and immigration policies. We conclude that the pattern of successes and failures is difficult to account for within any of the standard political economy frameworks. This will lead us to the third part of the

69

chapter in which we propose what, for want of a better label, we call the social values extension of both the Weberian and interest-group models.

MODELING THE DOMESTIC POLITICS OF GLOBALIZATION: TRADE AND IMMIGRATION

At least among economists, there are two broad approaches to the systematic explanation of policy – the Weberian model and the interest-group model.[3] In both cases, analysis proceeds by constructing a model of the underlying economy of an essentially neoclassical sort. That is, we assume a given set of households and firms: the former are characterized by preferences over final consumption goods as well as endowments of goods and factors; and the latter by technologies for transforming inputs into outputs. Most research on trade and immigration further simplifies by assuming that households are endowed only with factors of production and firms produce only final consumption goods, technologies are constant returns to scale, markets for all goods and factors exist and are perfectly competitive, and there are no externalities in production or consumption.[4] Finally, it is quite often assumed that all consumers share the same, generally homothetic, preferences.

With a well-specified model of the economy in place, we can complete the political economy model by identifying the politically relevant agent(s), the policy space, and the institutions that constrain policy choice. In both the Weberian and the interest-group models, individual household preferences play a fundamental role. In the former an ideal bureaucrat seeks to choose the policy which is, in some sense, best for society. For the economist, this is an invitation to transform the Samuelsonian social planner of welfare economics into Weber's ideal bureaucrat, thus transforming normative into positive theory. If we are willing to endow the ideal bureaucrat with a utilitarian objective function and assume that preferences are identical and homothetic (thus aggregable), the analysis becomes trivially easy.

The group politics (class of) model is inherently more complex. Where the ideal bureaucrat operates directly on individual welfares and selects an optimal policy based on his or her own objective function, the analysis of group politics proceeds from individual preferences over policy. Each of these must be derived relative to household preferences over final consumption, for each household, and then be mapped somehow into a final policy choice. It is well known, at least since Arrow's (1951) pioneering work, that this final selection will not generally satisfy a small set of normative axioms intended to reflect minimally democratic commitments.

The positive version of Arrow's theorem is that we cannot generally expect to predict an equilibrium policy based on detailed knowledge of preferences in a minimally complex institutional environment (that is, we cannot generally expect a preference-induced equilibrium to exist).[5] As a result, all analyses make very restrictive assumptions on preferences, economic structure, and political institutions. Standard referendum models, such as Mayer's (1984) classic paper, generally assume identical, homothetic preferences with a key, but little noticed, assumption of single-peakedness over the one-dimensional policy space, and policy determination by direct referendum. Similarly, the currently popular model of Grossman and Helpman (1994) rests on an exceptionally restrictive model of preferences (identical quasi-linear), economic structure (perfect competition in all markets, specific factors with a freely traded Ricardian numeraire), and political institution (direct sale of clearly delimited policy to a unitary, rational policy maker with a very simple objective function).[6] While these restrictions render the models highly dubious as frameworks for structural estimation, the clarity they bring makes them extremely useful as loose guides to both research and thinking about the future. It is this latter purpose for which we use them in this chapter.

Specifically, we want to use the Weberian and group politics models to look at the ways that domestic politics respond to changes in international trade and immigration. Because we are particularly interested in the potential for transformation in support for globalization, we argue that it is essential to distinguish between change in the average level of policy and in the dispersion of policy around that average. For example, in the case of international trade policy, considered as level of protection, it is well known that there was a break in the average level of US protection occurring around the time of the Reciprocal Trade Agreements Act of 1934 (RTAA). As Figure 4.1 shows, the US went from being a country characterized by rather highly variable tariffs around a high average, to quite stable low tariffs. While widely commented upon, this systemic transformation has received very little systematic research. At the same time, the variance of the tariff across sectors has continued to be substantial.[7] Similarly, overall levels of immigration have varied over time, while dispersion across sources of immigrants as well as a wide variety of other immigrant characteristics (skill/education, gender, age, family status) is also substantial.

The distinction between mean and variance in the dependent variable has not generally been made in systematic analysis of the political economy of globalization, so the next two sections consider this issue for trade and immigration policy in both the Weberian and the group politics frameworks.

72   *Globalization and economic integration*

Note: The average tariff here is defined as (tariff revenues)/(total value dutiable imports).

Source: *Historical Statistics of the United States: From Colonial Times to 1970*,
Washington, DC: US Bureau of the Census; updated from Census Bureau data.

Figure 4.1   US average tariff

UNDERSTANDING THE POLITICS OF GLOBALIZATION: THE WEBERIAN MODEL

For our purposes, Max Weber's theory of the modern state characterizes the ideal state as autonomous from group pressure, unitary, and legitimate.[8] It is the first attribute that distinguishes the Weberian model from the group politics model. The second attribute, along with the rationality that is so central to all of Weber's analysis, allows us to treat state decision making as if it were done by an individual. We shall return later to legitimacy; at this point we simply assume that the objective function characterizing the policy preferences of the state is widely accepted as legitimate. In fact, we shall assume that the state's objective is to maximize social welfare. That is, we now conceive of the state as an ideal Samuelsonian social planner.

    It is well known that, under quite general conditions, free trade can be shown to dominate protection for a small economy. From a comparative

The politics of (anti-)globalization 73

static perspective, again for a small country, a liberalizing change is welfare improving.[9] There are, of course, a virtually infinite number of exceptions. The theory of economic policy, as applied to international trade policy, deals with the major cases of such exceptions.[10] For a country like the US it might seem that the optimal tariff argument (application of monopoly power in trade) would be relevant, but there is very little evidence that politicians in the US have ever considered this a credible argument for protection. As a practical matter, the optimal tariff structure of the US would be as complex as the economy itself. Thus, at least when thinking about the average tariff, free trade is probably as good a baseline as any for thinking about the optimal policy. The striking thing about US policy (in common with virtually all major trading countries), as illustrated in Figure 4.1, is that current policy is strikingly close to this optimum. With an average tariff of less than 4 percent in all the main trading countries of the industrial world, the Weberian model would seem to do an excellent job of accounting for current trade policy in the average sense.[11] Furthermore, again as illustrated for the US in the figure, the direction of change in the average has been consistently in the direction of the optimum.

When we turn to dispersion of tariff rates, the story would appear to be quite different. While a very small number of countries have a uniform tariff (for example, Chile), not a single major trading nation has adopted such a policy. Not only are statutory tariff rates highly varied, but administered protection mechanisms generate rates that are sizable multiples of bound rates for very specific imports. While any one of these rates might be justified in terms of the theory of economic policy, the structures would appear to be incoherent from an overall perspective. Thus, while the Weberian model seems to provide a coherent account of the average tariff, it appears to fail completely to account for the variance. This, in fact, is the opening wedge for the group politics model of trade policy making that we consider in the next section.

When we turn to immigration policy, the content of the state's objective function is considerably less certain. Immigrants carry many traits that enter only very indirectly in economic welfare, usually proxied by income, but may be highly relevant to social welfare more broadly construed. However, if we apply the same objective function that we used for the case of trade policy, in the context of the same sort of underlying economy, the implication is fairly clear. Even in this case, there are tricky issues about where to count the welfare of the immigrants, but if we use the same utilitarian framework and perfectly competitive baseline, something like free migration would seem to be the central policy prediction of the Weberian model.[12] However, where most of the industrial countries that make up the core of the liberal international economy are committed to something approximating free trade, none of them is committed to anything like free immigration.[13] With considerably less confidence than for the case of trade, we conclude that the Weberian model fails to account for the average immigration policy.

As with trade, we suppose that the "average" immigration flow (for example, the annual total) is fixed, and consider the allocation of that number across categories of potential immigrants. Sticking with national income as shorthand for aggregate welfare, Borjas (1999) argues that policy should seek to admit "high quality" immigrants – that is, immigrants with a high value of marginal product given the existing technology, tastes and endowment in the host country. Borjas further suggests that this can be implemented by focusing on labor market properties (education or other measures of relevant skills) as well as any directly productive capital that might be brought.[14] While most industrial countries are constrained by non-economic objectives, such as family unification, to give some weight to these goals, virtually all countries give some considerable weight to such economic considerations. By comparison with trade policy, and again with less confidence than for the case of trade policy, we conclude that the Weberian model does a better job of accounting for variance in immigration policy.[15]

UNDERSTANDING THE POLITICS OF GLOBALIZATION: THE GROUP POLITICS MODEL[16]

As we noted above, it is the failure of the Weberian model to account for cross-section variance in protection that is the usual opening wedge for the group politics (class of) model. We are using the phrase "group politics model" to refer to all models in which policy is determined fundamentally by more-or-less organized citizen preferences, where those are determined by selfish preferences defined over bundles of final consumption goods. Based on those, it is straightforward to derive preferences over policy. Under the standard assumptions that fundamental preferences are identical across households and factor markets are perfectly competitive so all factors of a given type earn the same rental in equilibrium, preferences over policy are primarily driven by the effect of policy on factor rentals and any government transfers. That is, representing preferences with the indirect utility function

$$\mu_h = v^h(p; \gamma^h); \text{ where } \gamma^h = \sum_{i \in I} r_i z_i^h + T_h, \qquad (4.1)$$

where z_i is factor $i \in I$, r_i is the return to factor i, T_h is the transfer to h, and $h \in H$ refers to a given household. Since the direct effect of increases in

The politics of (anti-)globalization   75

the elements of **p** on $v^h(\cdot)$ is negative for all households, through the effect on cost of consumption, heterogeneity in policy preference comes though endowment and transfer heterogeneity (that is, $\mathbf{z}^h$ and T_h vary among households).

While the literature on the political economy of trade policy does not make the distinction between average and variance of policy, one approach is to think of low-dimensionality models (that is, models with one importable and one exportable good) as being about the average level of policy and high-dimensionality models (many goods, many factors) as being about its variance. For the low-dimensionality case, the comparative static effects of a change in trade policy are clear: the Stolper–Samuelson theorem yields factor-based preferences for the case of two inter-sectorally mobile factors and two goods; while the equivalent result for the case of two goods, two sector-specific factors and one mobile factor yields sector-based preferences. In terms of the equation above, these results tell us about the r_j, not about household income (or welfare). The way the models are usually used is to assume that each household is endowed with some quantity of a single factor, so that household income can be tied to returns to that factor. When we turn to the high-dimensionality case, things get considerably trickier. Only analytically local effects for single-factor households can be determined, and these are unlikely to be very useful in thinking about the sorts of non-marginal changes that characterize the sorts of major change in policy that induce political economy analysis.[17] It is analytically straightforward to derive the effects of a change in the policy vector on household portfolios, but virtually impossible to identify these portfolios in the data.[18] It is probably not surprising that, even in papers that use data with many factors and many goods, the fundamental intuition for interpreting the results runs off low-dimensionality results like Stolper–Samuelson or restrictive economic structures like the specific-factors model.

For the case of the average level of protection, we can draw on the sizable literature on citizen preferences over trade policy based on public opinion surveys. As columns two and three in Table 4.1 (from Mayda and Rodrik, 2005) illustrate, with the exceptions of the Netherlands and Japan, majorities of respondents to questions about support for trade restrictions show majorities in favor.[19] Loosely speaking, in the context of the referendum model, the median voter in nearly all countries supports trade restriction. To the extent that we have historical data on such opinions, it would appear that in most industrial countries, for most historical periods, and for the period of dramatic liberalization beginning some time in the 1930s in particular, the median voter has been a supporter of protection, or at least an opponent of further liberalization.[20] Without reference

76   Globalization and economic integration

Table 4.1   Average opinion on trade and immigration

	Pro-trade	Anti-trade	Pro-immigration
Germany West	0.36	0.39	0.03
Germany East	0.22	0.56	0.02
Great Britain	0.14	0.63	0.04
USA	0.13	0.64	0.08
Austria	0.16	0.70	0.04
Hungary	0.09	0.71	0.01
Italy	0.23	0.60	0.04
Ireland	0.22	0.66	0.20
Netherlands	0.37	0.29	0.05
Norway	0.28	0.38	0.07
Sweden	0.24	0.41	0.07
Czech Republic	0.27	0.52	0.02
Slovenia	0.24	0.51	0.02
Poland	0.14	0.65	0.09
Bulgaria	0.08	0.77	0.06
Russia	0.22	0.60	0.08
New Zealand	0.25	0.52	0.11
Canada	0.28	0.46	0.20
Philippines	0.16	0.66	0.11
Japan	0.34	0.31	0.16
Spain	0.10	0.71	0.08
Latvia	0.13	0.71	0.00
Slovak Republic	0.25	0.55	0.03
Mean	0.22	0.54	0.07
Standard deviation	0.41	0.50	0.26

Sources: For trade question: Mayda and Rodrik (2005); for immigration question: Mayda (2006).

to the roots of preference, we can already see that the group politics model has trouble accounting for average policy. This is what we have elsewhere called "the mystery of missing protection" (Nelson, 2003; Greenaway and Nelson, 2005).[21]

Attempts to account for cross-sectional variation in protection (or liberalization) constitutes the core of empirical research on the political economy of trade. This large body of research ranges from essentially ad hoc search for correlates of sectoral protection, through work that is loosely motivated by one or another model of group pressure, to putative structural estimates that take a given model very seriously indeed. The results of this large literature, which examines tariff and non-tariff barriers,

The politics of (anti-)globalization   77

voting on trade policy by legislators, and implementation of the administered protection mechanism, are consistent with both informed knowledge
about the actual politics involved in the making and enforcement of trade
policy and loosely consistent with standard group pressure models.[22] In
particular, variables intended to capture the return to political activity, the
ability to organize, access (for example, representation in key committees,
chairmanship of key committees, and so on), and resources invested (for
example, Political Action Committee (PAC) contributions and testimony
in hearings on trade legislation) consistently and significantly appear
with the signs predicted by the theory. Overall, our judgment is that these
models do a rather good job of accounting for cross-sectional variance in
levels of protection.

The inference in group pressure models of immigration is the same as
that for trade: we identify the predicted effect of immigration flows on
citizen-agents and then identify an equilibrium policy (or comparative
static change in policy) based on the distribution of those preferences
(or change in the distribution of those preferences). As with trade, for
a first cut at explaining the average level of policy, we can examine the
distribution of preferences over immigration policy without reference
to the underlying determinants of preferences. Like trade (in fact, even
more strongly so) the median voter would seem to reject liberalization of
the immigration regime. Column four of Table 4.1, drawn from Mayda
(2006), shows that in no country is there more than a small proportion of
the population willing to support liberalization of a national immigration
regime.[23] That is, in all countries polled, the median voter would seem to
support a regime no less restrictive than the existing regime. Unlike trade,
most of the governments involved have adopted restrictive regimes and, at
least in recent years, have tightened up those regimes. Thus, at least with
respect to average policy, the group pressure model performs reasonably
well.

The situation is different when we turn to cross-section variance in
policy. We have already noted that there are a number of possible ways
in which immigrants could be differentiated, but we shall focus on the
one most commonly considered in the political economy literature: labor
market characteristics and, specifically, skill. Most political economy
research that focuses on direct labor market effects as the basis of policy
preferences follows the literature in labor economics in assuming a single
final output (GDP) produced by a variety of inputs, with a particular focus
on various types of labor. This framework naturally drives all adjustment
through the wage and makes the attachment of standard trade-theoretic
political economy models particularly easy.[24] That is, for the small open
economy (that is, a country for which the **p** vector is fixed) an increase

in the endowment of a factor (say, unskilled labor) reduces the return to that factor and raises the return to all others, while raising aggregate income. In the context of a lobbying model, all citizen-agents should resist immigration by factors that compete with their factor and support immigration by others.[25] The problem with this research is that, while there is a certain prima facie plausibility to this prediction, the existence of generally restrictive immigration regimes, and occasional outbreaks of aggressive anti-immigrant politics, seems far out of scale relative to estimated labor market effects of immigration.[26] Furthermore, public opinion data suggest that it is precisely those groups for whom there are statistically significant wage effects that are less opposed to immigration. Thus, where average trade policy is characterized by a "mystery of missing protection", variance of immigration policy is characterized by a "mystery of too much protection".

An alternative channel via which immigration might produce a political response based on material interest recognizes the presence of a redistributive state as an essential part of the political economy of immigration. In terms of equation (4.1), we need to focus on the T_h terms. In addition to a number of insightful, if informal, analyses of the effect of immigration on the welfare state (for example, Freeman, 1986) a sizable literature has developed seeking to model interactions between immigration and various aspects of the welfare state.[27] While this work helps organize thinking about the topic, the results tend to be very model specific and cover a very wide range, with the varying results depending on which redistributive programs are considered (pensions, unemployment, and so on) and what is assumed about the properties of the immigrants and the size and timing of shocks. It is not surprising that there is very little in the way of systematic empirical research based on this theory, and that what there is must be seen as very preliminary. There is a body of empirical research based only loosely on this sort of theory, but seeking to link institutional detail to underlying economics.[28] Most of this work is by political scientists and tends to assume the existence of the sorts of labor market effects that we have already seen are hard to establish. Thus, it is hard to see this work as representing a successful account of existing patterns of policy across categories of immigrant.

In the context of the federal political system in the US, there are two components of the redistributive system: a federal welfare state and a state welfare state. Simplifying, considerably, the former deals with pensions while the latter deals with health and education. Immigrants tend to be relatively expensive in the state welfare because they tend to: have more school-age children; be poorer and thus receive more state-funded aid; and have lower incomes and, thus, pay less in property and other state taxes.

The politics of (anti-)globalization   79

The National Academy of Sciences study of immigration in the US estimated that, as a result of state welfare expenditures, immigrants in major immigrant gateways resulted in net negative effects, while the effects in the rest of the country were net positive – with an aggregate effect near zero (the members of the commission that produced the report differed on the aggregate effect). In only one gateway was this effect large: in California the central estimate was that the average Californian household paid an additional $1,178 (for the 1994/95 tax year) in taxes as a result of immigration (Smith and Edmonston, 1997, Chapter 6).[29] This makes it relatively easy to understand the highly politicized nature of immigration politics in California, but it is not very useful in understanding the overwhelming rejection of a liberal immigration regime in parts of the US that seem to gain via the welfare state channel. On the other hand, if the Borjas/national labor market model is correct, it is hard to understand why the aggressive public politics of unskilled immigration are so locally focused in California. Overall, and again in contrast to trade policy, it is hard to see that either the direct labor effect models or the indirect redistributive state models provide much explanatory power of variance across categories of immigrant.

The central mystery this chapter sets out to identify is illustrated in Table 4.2. It is not clear at all why, for either the Weberian or the group politics model: the politics of average and variance should differ within either policy domain; or why the pattern of success and failure in accounting for these should differ across policy domains. The core of both the standard Weberian and group pressure models are that citizen preferences, derivable from observable, self-regarding, material conditions, fundamentally determine policies. While we can construct a consistent account for each separate case, looking at the average and variance of policy, for two fundamental components of globalization leads us to the puzzle identified in Table 4.2. In the next section we offer the beginnings of an approach to this puzzle.

Table 4.2   Summary of argument

		Policy domain is:	
		Trade	**Immigration**
Dependent variable is	**Average**	Fails	Works (?)
	Dispersion	Works	Fails

UNDERSTANDING THE POLITICS OF GLOBALIZATION: PUBLIC POLITICS AND SOCIAL VALUES

In this section, we argue that the difference between the politics of international trade and immigration is not due to any underlying material difference between the issues, but rather to the fact that one, international trade, is treated as a technical issue, while the other, immigration, is treated, when it is treated at all, as a public political issue. We shall argue that the more private the issue, the more it can approach the pure group-theoretic ideal modeled in the endogenous policy framework, while the more public the issue, the more it becomes attached to broad considerations of social values and the less predictable its outcomes.

The first step in developing this argument is to provide greater clarity by developing a distinction due to Schattschneider (1960) between "group politics" and "democratic politics". For Schattschneider, and as we have used the expression above, group politics is about the pursuit of relatively narrowly defined private interests. In US parlance, group politics is "inside the Beltway" politics – the politics of lobbying. Because group politics are solidly rooted in relatively stable interests, they are predictable and change in predictable ways in response to the, generally marginal, changes in the environment embedding these interests. Not surprisingly, group politics is the focus of virtually all endogenous policy analysis. Early research in the group-theoretic tradition (often called "pluralist theory" by political scientists) saw group politics as a natural mechanism for aggregating preferences.[30] Where voting could not convey much information about intensity of preference and, except in the relatively rare case of single-issue referenda, could not convey much specific information about policy, lobbying does both.[31]

While accepting the positive analysis of group politics, critical pluralists rejected group politics as a normative basis for democratic theory. Much research by critical pluralists involved detailed case studies of particular policy areas which demonstrated the presence of severe asymmetries in representation, resulting in biased outcomes.[32] One of the earliest, and most influential, of these critical pluralist analyses was Schattschneider's (1935) classic study of the making of the Hawley–Smoot tariff. Because of the link between group politics and democracy, many saw critical pluralists as making the argument that democracy was a sham.[33] It was in this context that Schattschneider produced his "realist's view of democracy in America" as a response to this line of argument. Specifically, he argued that while democracies, in common with every other form of political organization known to man, were characterized by a group politics system

The politics of (anti-)globalization   81

possessing all of the biases identified by the critical pluralists, what distinguished democracies from other systems was the presence of a democratic political system that acted as a check on the group politics system.

For Schattschneider, democratic politics revolves around the public attempt to identify collectively satisfactory policies. That is, democratic politics is seen as the public politics through which a democratic civil society constitutes itself and through which it is linked to the policy-making apparatus. It is about the legitimation of policies and the governments that formulate them. While elections are the final defense of democratic politics, as well as the key stimulus to the public discourse, as stressed by theorists of deliberative democracy, the core of democratic politics is the public discourse itself. For our purposes, one of the essential attributes of this discourse is that its terms emphasize public interests/values and downplay private/individual interests. Note that the claim is not that private interests are unimportant in defining one's interpretation of the public interest, or one's position in the public discourse, but only that widely held notions of the public interest (as well as attendant notions like "fairness") constrain that discourse.

One of the main sources for the constraining power of these widely held notions is that they affect the willingness of unengaged citizens to take sides in the public discourse. This is one of the keys to the link between democratic and group politics. Stable group politics depends on the participants being generally satisfied with the outcomes. This does not mean that there are not winners and losers, but that both prefer the outcomes under the group politics regime to their expected outcome from public politics. When this condition fails, the loser(s) in the interaction may seek to change the structure by turning to public politics. Similarly, the emergence of new groups may produce a dynamic in which those groups seek to use democratic politics as a resource in their bid to enter the group politics system, or even to overturn the existing group politics in the interest of more radical goals. In either case, success in such strategies involves recruiting citizens who have not taken strong positions, and that involves explicit attempts to link the issue to broadly held normative commitments. Given the relatively unstable nature of such commitment, these strategies tend to be risky.[34]

At the founding of the Republic, trade was sufficiently central to the definition of the state to be written into the Constitution as a defined responsibility of Congress. In the first century of its existence the tariff was primarily about revenue, however with the end of Reconstruction (1877) both parties cast about for an issue to replace the "Bloody Shirt" and settled on "The Tariff".[35] The capitalization is appropriate here since the issue was not any specific tariff, but the system of high tariffs, often referred to in the period as "the American system". With the emergence of the tariff as a, if not the, major basis of continuing electoral contestation between Republicans and Democrats, both parties sought to attach a tariff to a wide range of national goals. Broadly speaking, to the Republicans "The Tariff" was a symbol of national strength, independence, and a strong central government; to the Democrats it was "the mother of trusts", a symbol of the corruption of national government. However, as a number of ethno-cultural studies of 19th-century voting suggest, the meaning of "The Tariff" varied greatly across elections and regions.[36] This is the characteristic of democratic politics in which we are particularly interested.

For reasons that are still far from clear, "The Tariff" disappears as a public issue sometime between the writing of the Hawley–Smoot tariff (when classic tariff politics were very much on display) and the Trade Expansion Act of 1962 (when the structure of new trade politics was firmly established).[37] Given the suspicion with which the general public treats trade liberalization (as reflected in the poll data) it seems clear that this transition was more-or-less independent of public preference and fundamental to the long period of general trade liberalization. However, while the democratic politics of "The Tariff" disappear, individual tariffs continued to be determined by group politics.[38] Even while the Executive branch negotiated steady reductions in the average level of protection, the lobbying system surrounding both the legislation setting the rules under which protection is given (administered protection) and the quasi-judicial process actually granting that protection has become even better established. Part of the reason why standard political economy models do such a good job of accounting for cross-sector dispersion of protection is the isolation of the group politics of trade from democratic politics. On the other hand, the failure of such models to account for the average is a result of the decoupling of the setting of the average from democratic politics.[39]

Unlike trade policy, the early Republic of the US was essentially unconcerned with immigration. The basic immigration law of the US simply asserted that free, white males were free to enter and become citizens. This remained the basic law until the late 19th century when immigration of Chinese and then Japanese became a major public issue in California – resulting in the first major change in the immigration law (the Chinese Exclusion Act of 1882). Even before this, however, nativism (that is, anti-immigrant political activity) had occasionally been a feature of public politics. Like the public politics of trade, and like contemporary anti-globalization politics, there appears to have been a strong link between poor macroeconomic conditions and the attractiveness of restrictive

The politics of (anti-)globalization   83

policies. Also like the public politics of trade, the presence of direct economic foundations (that is, factor-market foundations) of anti-immigrant politics is hard to identify.[40] As with contemporary anti-immigrant politics, these public politics tended to be local, episodic, and intense. That is, unlike the politics of trade, immigration tended not to be a continuing issue of national political competition. Rather, anti-immigrant politics tended to emerge in what are now called "gateway" communities, and to emerge primarily in times of economic and/or political stress. Because there was an obvious target, these moments of anti-immigrant politics were often characterized by violence.

Perhaps most strikingly, to the extent that group politics grew up around the immigration issue, it did not bear nearly the strong relationship to underlying material interests that characterize the group politics of trade. One of the most telling facts is that there is no equivalent, long-lived, group-based politics surrounding immigration. Following the establishment of the national origin quotas in the Johnson–Reed Act (1924), immigration more or less disappears as a political issue (democratic or group) for forty years – not because it is taken off the table, as with trade, but because the public seem to have no particular interest in the issue. Interestingly, the Immigration and Nationality Act of 1965, which ended the quota system, reflected neither the emergence of new public pressure nor the operation of group politics, but rather derived from its attachment to civil rights issues and, to some extent, to a liberal framing of US international obligations (Gimpel and Edwards, 1999). By the time of the landmark Immigration Reform and Control Act of 1986, while there was a more established set of groups in play: these groups do not have the long history that groups on trade do (that is, most of the established groups go back no further than the politics surrounding the 1965 Act); and, more importantly, there is not the same straightforward material foundation, or broad base, in immigration-related groups.[41] It is interesting that, although there is interest-based organization on the immigration issue, this organization does not cover the wide range of economic interests that organization on trade does, and, as we have just noted, much of it focuses on issues that are essentially orthogonal to economic issues in general, and distributive issues in particular. Comparing the lack of both broad interest-based organization and sustained interest-based politics on immigration, to the presence of both on trade would seem to provide strong evidence in favor of our central claim.[42] Thus, to the extent that standard political economy models account well for average immigration policy it is because these politics are public politics; while their failure to account for dispersion reflects the lack of a clear material basis for those politics.

CONCLUSIONS

Overall, then, the peculiar pattern of success and failure of the group-theoretic model across dependent variables (average and variance) and issue domains (trade and immigration) does not seem to rely on any obvious material basis. Thus, it seems unlikely that it will be compellingly accounted for by reference to standard political economy models. So, what do we learn from simple political economy models about the coming politics of globalization? It seems likely that, to the extent that globalization becomes a public issue, group-theoretic models (especially those with a strong analytical link to lobbying) will be of very limited use. Globalization politics seem much more likely to be like the politics of immigration than the politics of trade. General public attitudes will play an important role in setting the terms of the democratic politics of globalization, but those terms will be highly contestable. The terms of the public discourse will not be set by economists, and will not likely be identifiable in any simple way from economic self-interest of identifiable groups. At least as important will be how globalization is related to widely, but loosely, held notions like "fairness". Some steps in the direction of a more systematic understanding of such notions have been taken by scholars working in behavioral economics, but we need much more systematic research on how these work in aggregate in the political economy.[43] This is an area where new work on public opinion would be useful – but the emphasis needs to be less on the material foundations of policy attitudes (since these seem weakly held in any event), and more on how citizens see globalization attaching to broader social values.

As we noted above, there have been a number of studies of the ways in which the public discourse of democratic politics works, but similar studies on the evolution of trade policy would be very useful. Specifically, the transition in the political economy of trade that we mentioned above is an ideal laboratory for understanding the interaction among insiders, outsiders, institutions, and policy equilibrium. We know too little about how elite attitudes on trade changed so dramatically at a time when citizen attitudes appear not to have changed to the same degree. We still know too little about which institutional changes were essential to the transition, and which less so. And we know too little about how immigration remained a public issue, when trade did not. There is clearly a major agenda for research on the domestic political foundations of a Liberal international political economy, but we shall make little headway if we continue to focus exclusively on the political economy of protection.

The politics of (anti-)globalization 85

NOTES

* This chapter was presented at the 2005 CESifo workshop on Global Economic Negotiations, held in Venice on 20–21 July 2005. The authors are grateful to the conference participants for very useful discussions. Financial support from the Leverhulme Trust under Programme Grant F114/BF is gratefully acknowledged.

1. James (2001) is an excellent treatment of the reversal of globalization during the Great Depression. Bordo et al. (1999) present a useful overview of the data on globalization in the late-19th and late-20th centuries. On these latter issues, also see the papers collected in Bordo et al. (2003).

2. While much political economy research on globalization focuses on the ways in which globalization constrains democratic politics, in this chapter we emphasize the ways in which democratic politics constrains globalization.

3. We abstract from the "stuff happens" approach, according to which all policy acts are specific and require specific explanation involving shifting mixes of ignorance and chance along with the sort of systematic effects on which the Weberian and interest-group models focus.

4. There are, of course, a number of more technical assumptions that yield sufficient structure to carry out standard comparative static analysis. Virtually any trade theory text develops these assumptions and the fundamental results derivable from such models. Particularly useful texts are: Dixit and Norman (1980); Woodland (1982); and Wong (1995).

5. The logic of this result has been developed in most detail for the case of majority rule in the context of more than one issue, but the point is quite general (as Arrow's theorem suggests). Among the many excellent presentations of this literature, see Riker (1982) for a sophisticated development of the relationship between results of this sort and the theory of democracy. For an admirably clear development of the formal theory, see Austen-Smith and Banks (1999).

6. This should not be taken as a criticism of the theory. Both the Mayer and the Grossman–Helpman models are paragons of political economy theory. Rather, we simply note that the attempt to capture the structure and dynamics of political economy for complex policy areas, like globalization, require radical simplification to get any results at all.

7. As a result of formula cuts in the GATT/WTO, the absolute dispersion has almost certainly fallen. However, I know of no research suggesting whether this dispersion has fallen relative to the average (that is, change in the variance). Furthermore, the domestic factors affecting the dispersion have certainly changed far less than whatever are the factors that determine the average.

8. See Weber (1978) for the classic treatment and Weber (1921) for a short, but admirably clear, development of key aspects of this theory. Recall that this is an *ideal* type. Actually existing states will possess these properties only to a greater or lesser extent. This is directly parallel to the treatment of individuals in standard microeconomic theory.

9. For the analysis of policy change, one of the essential assumptions, especially from a positive perspective, is the existence of an ideal redistributive mechanism (lump-sum transfers). While such a mechanism does not exist, the presence of a sizable welfare state surely goes a long way toward moving a potential welfare improvement in the direction of an actual welfare improvement. Bordo et al. (1999), among others, argue that the existence of a welfare state has played a role in supporting trade liberalization for precisely this reason.

10. See Bhagwati et al. (1998) for an admirably clear presentation of all the issues in this paragraph, and the theory of economic policy in particular.

11. The Weberian model does not, at least without some additional work, provide an account for why the tariff was so high prior to the change that occurred in the 1930s. It is in some sense correct, but trivial, to say that the content of the state's objective

86   *Globalization and economic integration*

function changed. What is clearly needed is a more general account of the content of state preferences and sources of change in those preferences. We return to this question following our discussion of group politics.

12. One of the earliest treatments of this issue is by Henry Sidgwick (1891). Sidgwick concludes that free immigration is the implication of a thoroughgoing utilitarian position, but ultimately rejects that position on practical political grounds. Borjas (1999) simply asserts that maximizing national income is the obvious objective function for immigration policy. In fact, one is far less able to predict a scholar or an activist's position on immigration based on knowledge of the usual predictors (political commitments: left versus right; normative position: (utilitarian versus Rawlsian versus libertarian versus communitarian; and so on) than it is to predict their position on trade policy. Most economists are perfectly willing to contemplate a smoothly operating redistributive system when advocating free trade, but see only barriers to such redistribution when considering immigration.

13. Contemporary levels of immigration are quite high – approaching the extraordinary levels of the 19th century. These levels, however, only very imperfectly reflect policy. In fact, all countries maintain highly restrictive immigration regimes that tend to be overwhelmed by large illegal flows as well as refugee flows that are only very tangentially related to policies of the sort considered by models of immigration policy. On the evolution of immigration policy, which includes some comparison with trade policy, see the important work reported in Williamson (2004), Hatton (2005), and Hatton and Williamson (2006).

14. Borjas (1999) also suggests that, as a result of the close correlation between country of origin and labor market properties, country of origin could be used as a proxy for policy orientation.

15. From a comparative perspective, countries vary considerably in the degree to which such economic objectives figure in the construction of immigration policy. For example, Australia and Canada have explicit point systems with sizable weight assigned to economic factors, while the US system of preferences assigns much higher weight to non-economic factors. As with trade, explaining a shift in preferences, such as that implied by the US Immigration Reform and Control Act of 1986, requires an explicit account of the preference shift from a Weberian perspective.

16. This section provides only representative references. For a more detailed survey of the relevant research, see Greenaway and Nelson (2005).

17. See Jones and Scheinkman's (1977) analysis of friends and enemies for the classic presentation. Ethier (1984) is the industry standard presentation of the results in the high-dimensionality case.

18. See Cassing (1981) for the first paper that showed how using such portfolios allows identification of determinate household income effects, and thus preferences over policy, in the high-dimensional case. For useful generalizations, see Lloyd and Schweinberger (1997) and Lloyd (2000).

19. Based on ISSP question: "(Respondent's country) should limit the import of foreign products in order to protect the national economy". The pro- and anti- categories come from aggregating the "agree" and "strongly agree", and "disagree" and "strongly disagree" responses.

20. Scheve and Slaughter (2001a) provides some of the historical data for the US.

21. This is revealed most clearly in papers of the Goldberg and Maggi (1999) sort, in which a state "preference" parameter accounts for the overwhelming majority of (lack of) protection in cross-section. Given that this parameter has no analytical foundation, these results are essentially the same as saying that the average level of protection is unaccounted for by the model.

22. For surveys with good coverage of the empirical literature, see: Baldwin (1984); Anderson and Baldwin (1987); Rodrik (1995); Magee (1997); and Gawande and Krishna (2003). On administered protection, see Blonigen and Prusa (2003) and Nelson (2006).

The politics of (anti-)globalization 87

23. The question Mayda (2006) focuses on asks: "Do you think the number of immigrants to the country should be a) reduced a lot; b) reduced a little; c) remain the same as it is; d) increased a little; or e) increased a lot". The number reported in the table is the share of the population expressing a "pro-immigration" attitude – that is, a response of (d) or (e).

24. See Bilal et al. (2003) for a derivation of policy preferences over immigration policy, and for examples of papers that derive equilibrium immigration policy in such an environment, see Grether et al. (2001) who use a median voter framework or Facchini and Willmann (2005) who use a menu auction framework.

25. The theoretical extension to domestic and immigrant households endowed with multiple factors is as straightforward as its empirical implementation is difficult.

26. With the exception of recent work by George Borjas (for example, 2003), the overwhelming majority of research on labor market effects agrees that these are small and concentrated on very narrowly defined groups made up primarily of earlier cohorts of immigrants with essentially identical labor market traits. For a recent evaluation of this literature, see Card (2004). Borjas's work proceeds from a fundamental critique of earlier work based on comparison of local labor markets. The key claim is that the US labor market is essentially national, since highly mobile workers will adjust their internal migration decisions to avoid labor markets faced with large immigration shocks. There are two problems with this analysis: first, Card (2001) finds little evidence of such effects on the pattern of migration by native workers; and, more importantly, from a political economy perspective, it is precisely the highly localized nature of public response to immigration that is most striking.

Gaston and Nelson (2000, 2002) argue that the standard trade-theoretic model is identical to the standard labor theoretic model in all details but dimensionality. If there are at least as many productive sectors as inter-sectorally mobile factors of production, then Leamer's (1995) factor-price insensitivity result holds. Intuitively, and without taking factor-price insensitivity as a perfect description of reality, the trade-theoretic model emphasizes adjustment on the output margin as an alternative to adjustment on the wage margin. Given that most estimates of wage adjustment are small, the prima facie plausibility of the trade model as a basic framework for intuition in this case seems established. As a matter of fact, technological change seems to have played a major role in this case. But that just pushes the analysis back to the issue of how to conceive of technological change. If such change were a random phenomenon, unrelated to the immigration shock, then we might still retain the labor model as our intuition driver. That is, citizen-agents unable to count on an appropriate technological shock, should still be expected to resist immigration based on an expectation of negative wage effects. However, if the technological change were a rational response to the immigration shock, then from the perspective of political economy modeling, that is essentially the same as adjustment on the output margin. That is, rational agents should expect adjustments in input mix that will tend to protect the existing wage structure. Recent work by Ethan Lewis (2004a, b, 2005; Card and Lewis, 2005) presents strong evidence that the technological response is endogenous in this latter sense.

27. For representative work of this sort, see Razin and Sadka (2001, 2005), Razin et al. (2002), and Facchini et al. (2005).

28. For representative work of this sort, see: Gimpel and Edwards (1999) on the US; Lahav (2004) on Europe; and Money (1999) for a very interesting comparative study.

29. The next largest negative impact was in New Jersey, where the estimated effect was $232.

30. Greenstone (1975) is still an excellent overview of the classic work in the group-theoretic tradition, with particular reference to the link between group theory and democratic theory more broadly, both the early work that emphasized the democratic virtues of lobbying and the later critical pluralism emphasizing asymmetries and democratic problems.

31. We are referring here to actual lobbying on an issue. The data most commonly used to

88   *Globalization and economic integration*

represent this variable in empirical studies, total lobbying expenditure (on any issue) by organization, are really little more informative than voting data. Note that exactly the same data are used in congressional voting studies on every other issue, so interpretation is bedeviled by exactly the same problem as giving meaning to a vote in a multiple issue referendum or election.

32. Critical pluralism was given the beginnings of a solid theoretical foundation by Mancur Olson's (1965) *The Logic of Collective Action*, which provided a systematic account of asymmetric organization among groups seeking private outcomes from government.

33. Many Marxists at the time made this claim quite explicitly. More generally, this research was seen as related to results from the early voting studies suggesting that large numbers of citizens had very little detailed knowledge of the candidates or issues on which they were casting votes. Together with the detailed case studies of critical pluralists, this led to something of a crisis in normative democratic theory.

34. Schattschneider (1960) likens this to the process by which a fight is transformed into a brawl as participants in the fight seek allies from the crowd. Riker (1986) develops a more formal analysis of such strategies, which he calls "heresthetic". For case studies, see Baumgartner and Jones (1993, 2002) and Rochefort and Cobb (1994).

35. "The Bloody Shirt" refers to the wounds suffered by the Union soldiers in the Civil War. The transition to the use of trade as the most important ongoing issue between Republicans and Democrats is well described in Reitano (1994).

36. McCormick (1974) is an excellent overview of this research.

37. The literature on the transformation of US trade politics in this period is large and has produced no compelling account of the transformation. Among such accounts are those stressing: elite learning; domestic institutional change (specifically adoption of an income tax and the Reciprocal Trade Agreements Act of 1934); international institutional change (mainly the General Agreement on Tariffs and Trade); female franchise; and change in the mobility of factors of production. Reviews of these accounts can be found in Hiscox (1999) and Nelson (2003).

38. In addition to Schattschneider's (1935) classic, which we have already mentioned, the importance of group politics to the determination of early tariff politics is made clear in Taussig (1931).

39. This is also why poll data on general public preferences over trade data are of very little use in understanding the politics of trade policy: they have essentially nothing to do with the average level of protection because of this decoupling; and they tell us very little about the politics of dispersion because dispersion is set by lobbying, not by public politics. That is, the great majority of citizens, whose preferences may be well measured by the polls, are simply unrepresented in the politics of trade.

40. The literature on public opinion on immigration is large and suggests strongly that broad social values have a major impact on preferences for immigration policy. A number of recent studies have identified a significant element of material interest (Scheve and Slaughter, 2001b; O'Rourke and Sinnott, 2002; Mayda, 2004; Hatton, 2005). However, recent work by Hainmueller and Hiscox (2004) successfully shows that these results, which use education to identify labor market position, are more likely to be identifying general values.

41. The best treatment of the politics of this period is Schuck (1992). A couple of exceptions require careful consideration. On the one hand, there are a small number of groups with clear material interests that have been involved in immigration politics on more or less the same terms as trade-related groups. Southwestern farmers, orchard owners, and ranchers have been actively involved in immigration politics. More recently are employers in the computer industry that have aggressively sought liberalization of entry for skilled labor. However, the narrowness of these interests relative to the wide base of economic interests makes the immigration groups exceptions that prove the rule. On the other hand, immigration lawyers have played an important role in the politics of immigration policy. In understanding their role, however, it is useful to compare the immigration bar with the trade bar. Both have an obvious interest in the details of the

The politics of (anti-)globalization 89

law regulating their areas of practice, but these two groups of lawyers do very different things: the trade bar is essentially in the lobbying business, they represent broad parts of American industry and labor; the immigration bar represents a much less obviously material interest and what they do seems different. In addition, a range of humanitarian, religious, and other groups play large roles that they do not play in the trade context.

42. It may be that part of the reason why the group politics of immigration appear so different from those of trade is that the opportunities to engage in group-based politics are so few. In addition to fairly regular legislation on trade issues, there are anti-dumping, countervailing duty, escape clause, unfair trade practices (301: that is, Section 301 of the 1974 (US) Trade Act), (a few) national security cases, and so on. In all of these the plaintiff is an industry. This is also, indirectly, true in the Court of International Trade cases. And we should not forget that there is virtually always Geneva-based action of one kind or another. All of these induce broad sector-based, and, since unions are actively involved, factor-based organization on the issue. There do not appear to be nearly the range of opportunities for group-based politics on immigration.

43. For a very preliminary effort in this direction, with some related references, see Davidson et al. (2005).

REFERENCES

Anderson, K. and R. Baldwin (1987), "The political market for protection in industrial countries", in A.M. El-Agraa (ed.), *Protection, Cooperation, Integration and Development*, New York: Macmillan.

Arrow, K. (1951 [1968]), *Social Choice and Individual Values*, New Haven, CT: Yale.

Austen-Smith, D. and J.S. Banks (1999), *Positive Political Theory, I: Collective Preference*, Ann Arbor, MI: University of Michigan Press.

Baldwin, R. (1984), "Trade policies in developed countries", in R. Jones and P. Kenen (eds), *Handbook of International Economics*, vol. 1, Amsterdam: North-Holland.

Baumgartner, F. and B. Jones (eds) (1993), *Agendas and Instability in American Politics*, Chicago, IL: University of Chicago Press.

Baumgartner, F. and B. Jones (eds) (2002), *Policy Dynamics*, Chicago, IL: University of Chicago Press.

Bhagwati, J., A. Panagariya and T.N. Srinivasan (1998), *Lectures in International Trade*, 2nd edn, Cambridge, MA: MIT Press.

Bilal, S., J.-M. Grether and J. de Melo (2003), "Attitudes towards immigration: a trade-theoretic approach", *Review of International Economics*, **11** (2), 253–67.

Blonigen, B. and T. Prusa (2003), "Antidumping", in E.K. Choi and J. Harrigan (eds), *Handbook of International Trade*, Oxford: Blackwell, pp. 251–84.

Bordo, M., B. Eichengreen and D. Irwin (1999), "Is globalization today really different from globalization a hundred years ago?", in S. Collins and R. Lawrence (eds), *Brookings Trade Forum, 1999*, Washington, DC: Brookings Institution, pp. 1–72.

Bordo, M., A. Taylor and J. Williamson (2003), *Globalization in Historical Perspective*, Chicago, IL: University of Chicago Press/NBER.

Borjas, G. (1999), *Heaven's Door: Immigration Policy and the American Economy*, Princeton, NJ: Princeton University Press.

Borjas, G. (2003), "The labor demand curve *is* downward sloping: reexamining the impact of immigration on the labor market", *Quarterly Journal of Economics*, 118 (4), 1335–74.

Card, D. (2001), "Immigrant inflows, native outflows, and the local labor market impacts of higher immigration", *Journal of Labor Economics*, 19 (1), 22–64.

Card, D. (2004), "Is the new immigration really so bad?", IZA Discussion Paper 1119, Institute for the Study of Labor, Bonn.

Card, D. and E. Lewis (2005), "The diffusion of Mexican immigrants during the 1990s: explanations and impacts", NBER Working Paper 11552, National Bureau of Economic Research, Cambridge, MA.

Cassing, J. (1981), "On the relationship between commodity price changes and factor-owners real positions", *Journal of Political Economy*, 89 (3), 593–5.

Davidson, C., S. Matusz and D. Nelson (2005), "Fairness and adjustment to trade in a simple political economy model", Manuscript, Michigan State University.

Dixit, A. and V. Norman (1980), *Theory of International Trade*, Cambridge: Cambridge University Press.

Ethier, W. (1984), "Higher dimensional issues in trade theory", in R. Jones and P. Kenen (eds), *Handbook of International Economics*, vol. 1, Amsterdam: North-Holland, pp. 131–84.

Facchini, G., A. Razin and G. Willmann (2005), "Welfare leakage and immigration policy", *CESifo Economic Studies*, 50 (4), 627–45.

Facchini, G. and G. Willmann (2005), "The political economy of international factor mobility", *Journal of International Economics*, 67 (1), 201–19.

Freeman, G. (1986), "Migration and the political economy of the welfare state", *Annals of the American Academy of Political and Social Science*, no. 485, 51–63.

Gaston, N. and D. Nelson (2000), "Immigration and labour-market outcomes in the United States: a political-economy puzzle", *Oxford Review of Economic Policy*, 16 (3), 104–14.

Gaston, N. and D. Nelson (2002), "The wage and employment effects of immigration: trade and labour economics perspectives", in D. Greenaway, R. Upward and K. Wakelin (eds), *Trade, Investment, Migration and Labour Market Adjustment*, Basingstoke: Palgrave-Macmillan, pp. 201–35.

Gawande, K. and P. Krishna (2003), "The political economy of trade policy: empirical approaches", in E. K. Choi and J. Harrigan (eds), *Handbook of International Trade*, Oxford: Blackwell, pp. 213–50.

Gimpel, J. and J. Edwards (1999), *The Congressional Politics of Immigration Reform*, Boston, MA: Allyn & Bacon.

Goldberg, P. and G. Maggi (1999), "Protection for sale: an empirical investigation", *American Economic Review*, 89 (5), 1135–55.

Greenaway, D. and D. Nelson (2005), "The distinct political economies of trade and immigration policies", in F. Foders and R.J. Langhammer (eds), *Labor Mobility and the World Economy*, New York: Springer-Verlag, pp. 295–327.

Greenstone, J.D. (1975), "Group theories", in F. Greenstein and N. Polsby (eds), *Micropolitical Theory*, Reading, MA: Addison-Wesley, pp. 243–318.

Grether, J.-M., J. de Melo and T. Muller (2001), "The political economy of migration in a Ricardo–Viner model", in S. Djajic (ed.), *International Migration: Trends, Policy, Impact*, London: Routledge, pp. 42–68.

Grossman, G. and E. Helpman (1994), "Protection for Sale", *American Economic Review*, 84 (4), 833–50.

Hainmueller, J. and M. Hiscox (2004), "Educated preferences: explaining attitudes

The politics of (anti-)globalization   91

toward immigration in Europe", Manuscript, Harvard University, Cambridge, MA.

Hatton, T. (2005), "Trade policy and migration policy: why the difference?", Manuscript, Australian National University, Canberra.

Hatton, T. and J. Williamson (2006), *Global Migration in the World Economy: Two Centuries of Policy and Performance*, Cambridge, MA: MIT Press.

Hiscox, M. (1999), "The magic bullet? The RTAA, institutional reform and trade liberalization", *International Organization*, **53** (4), 669–98.

James, H. (2001), *The End of Globalization: Lessons from the Great Depression*, Cambridge, MA: Harvard University Press.

Jones, R. and J. Scheinkman (1977), "The relevance of the two-sector production model in trade theory", *Journal of Political Economy*, **85** (5), 909–35.

Lahav, G. (2004), *Immigration and Politics in the New Europe: Reinventing Borders*, Cambridge: Cambridge University Press.

Leamer, E. (1995), "The Heckscher–Ohlin model in theory and practice", *Princeton Studies in International Finance*, no. 77.

Lewis, E. (2004a), "Local open economies within the US: how do industries respond to immigration?", Federal Reserve Bank of Philadelphia Working Paper 04-1.

Lewis, E. (2004b), "How did the Miami labor market absorb the Mariel Immigrants?", Federal Reserve Bank of Philadelphia Working Paper 04-3.

Lewis, E. (2005), "Immigration, skill mix, and the choice of technique", Federal Reserve Bank of Philadelphia Working Paper 05-8.

Lloyd, P. (2000), "Generalizing the Stolper–Samuelson theorem: a tale of two matrices", *Review of International Economics*, **8** (4), 597–613.

Lloyd, P. and A. Schweinberger (1997), "Conflict generating product price changes: the imputed output approach", *European Economic Review*, **41** (8), 1569–87.

Magee, S. (1997), "Endogenous protection: the empirical evidence", in D.C. Mueller (ed.), *Perspectives On Public Choice: A Handbook*, New York: Cambridge University Press, pp. 526–61.

Mayda, A.M. (2004), "Who is against immigration? A cross-country investigation of individual attitudes towards migrants", IZA Discussion Paper 1115, Institute for the Study of Labor (IZA), Bonn.

Mayda, A.M. (2006), "Who is against immigration? A cross country investigation of individual attitudes toward immigrants", *Review of Economics and Statistics*, **88** (3), 510–30.

Mayda, A.M. and D. Rodrik (2005), "Why are some people (and countries) more protectionist than others?", *European Economic Review*, **49** (6), 1393–430.

Mayer, W. (1984), "Endogenous tariff formation", *American Economic Review*, **74** (5), 970–85.

McCormick, R. (1974), "Ethno-cultural interpretations of nineteenth century voting behavior", *Political Science Quarterly*, **89** (2), 351–77.

Money, J. (1999), *Fences and Neighbors: The Political Geography of Immigration Control*, Ithaca, NY: Cornell University Press.

Nelson, D. (2003), "Political economy problems in the analysis of trade policy", Inaugural Lecture, University of Nottingham.

Nelson, D. (2006), "The political economy of antidumping: a survey", *European Journal of Political Economy*, **22** (3), 554–90.

O'Rourke, K. and R. Sinnott (2002), "The determinants of individual trade policy

92 *Globalization and economic integration*

preferences: international survey evidence", *Brookings Trade Policy Forum 2001*, pp. 157–96.

Olson, M. (1965), *The Logic of Collective Action*, Boston, MA: Harvard University Press.

Razin, A. and E. Sadka (2001), "Interactions between international migration and the welfare state", in S. Djajic (ed.), *International Migration: Trends, Policy, Impact*, London: Routledge, pp. 69–88.

Razin, A. and E. Sadka (2005), *The Decline of the Welfare State: Demography and Globalization*, Cambridge, MA: MIT Press/CESifo.

Razin, A., E. Sadka and P. Swagel (2002), "Tax burden and migration: a political-economy theory and evidence", *Journal of Public Economics*, **85** (2), 167–90.

Reitano, J. (1994), *The Tariff Question in the Gilded Age*, University Park, PA: Pennsylvania State University Press.

Riker, W. (1982), *Liberalism against Populism: A Confrontation between the Theory of Democracy and the Theory of Social Choice*, San Francisco, CA: W.H. Freeman.

Riker, W. (1986), *The Art of Political Manipulation*, New Haven, CT: Yale University Press.

Rochefort, D. and R. Cobb (eds) (1994), *The Politics of Problem Definition: Shaping the Policy Agenda*, Lawrence, KS: University Press of Kansas.

Rodrik, D. (1995), "Political economy of trade policy", in G. Grossman and K. Rogoff (eds), *Handbook of International Economics*, vol. 3, Amsterdam: North-Holland, pp. 1457–94.

Schattschneider, E.E. (1935), *Politics, Pressure, and the Tariff*, Englewood Cliffs, NJ: Prentice-Hall.

Schattschneider, E.E. (1960), *The Semi-Sovereign People: A Realist's View of Democracy in America*, New York: Holt, Rinehart.

Scheve, K. and M. Slaughter (2001a), *Globalization and the Perceptions of American Workers*, Washington, DC: Institute for International Economics.

Scheve, K. and M. Slaughter (2001b), "Labor market competition and individual preferences over immigration policy", *Review of Economics and Statistics*, **83** (1), 133–45.

Schuck, P. (1992), "The politics of rapid legal change: immigration policy in the 1980s", *Studies in American Political Development*, **6**, 37–92.

Sidgwick, H. (1891), "Principles of external policy", Chapter XVIII of *The Elements of Politics*, London: Macmillan, pp. 285–315.

Smith, J. and B. Edmonston (eds) (1997), *The New Americans: Economic, Demographic, and Fiscal Effects of Immigration*, Washington, DC: National Academies Press.

Taussig, F. (1931), *The Tariff History of the US*, New York: G.P. Putnam's Sons.

Weber, M. (1921), "Politics as vocation", Translation in H.H. Gerth and C. Wright Mills (eds) (1946), *From Max Weber: Essays in Sociology*, New York: Oxford University Press, pp. 77–128.

Weber, M. (1978), *Economy and Society*, Berkeley, CA: University of California Press.

Williamson, J. (2004), *The Political Economy of World Mass Migration*, Washington, DC: AEI Press.

Woodland, A. (1982), *International Trade and Resource Allocation*, Amsterdam: North-Holland.

Wong, K. (1995), *International Trade in Goods and Factor Mobility*, Cambridge, MA: MIT Press.

Learning from Behavioral Economics: Fairness in Trade and Trade Policy

Journal of
INTERNATIONAL
ECONOMICS

ELSEVIER   Journal of International Economics 70 (2006) 451–469

www.elsevier.com/locate/econbase

Fair wages, unemployment and technological change in a global economy

Udo Kreickemeier [a],*, Douglas Nelson [a,b]

[a] *GEP, University of Nottingham, School of Economics, University Park, Nottingham NG7 2RD, United Kingdom*
[b] *Murphy Institute of Political Economy, 108 Tilton Hall, Tulane University, New Orleans, Louisiana 70118-5698 USA*

Received 1 March 2005; received in revised form 5 October 2005; accepted 17 November 2005

Abstract

This paper analyzes the effects of global and national technological change on employment and relative wages in an integrated two-country world ("Europe" and "America"), where both countries are characterized by equilibrium unemployment due to fair wage constraints. The asymmetry between the countries arises from country-specific preferences towards wage inequality, with Europe's preferences being more egalitarian. Furthermore, we look at integration between this two-country world and a third country ("low-wage south"). We derive an analytical tool, the Virtual Integrated Equilibrium, that allows us to adapt Dixit and Norman's Integrated Equilibrium approach to a situation where both countries have endogenous unemployment levels.
© 2006 Elsevier B.V. All rights reserved.

Keywords: Fair wages; Unemployment; Virtual integrated equilibrium; Factor price equalization

JEL classification: F11; F16

1. Introduction

As with many issues, there would appear to be a sizable gap between the way economists view the effects of real globalization (i.e. trade, direct investment, immigration) and the way citizens in general view these phenomena. At least as revealed by current research, economists seem to believe that globalization is no big deal, at least as far as labor market effects are concerned, while citizens appear to be quite concerned about the effects of globalization. Among the many possible

* Corresponding author. Tel.: +44 115 951 4289; fax: +44 115 951 4159.
E-mail addresses: udo.kreickemeier@nottingham.ac.uk (U. Kreickemeier), dnelson@tulane.edu (D. Nelson).

0022-1996/$ - see front matter © 2006 Elsevier B.V. All rights reserved.
doi:10.1016/j.jinteco.2005.11.003

452   U. Kreickemeier, D. Nelson / Journal of International Economics 70 (2006) 451–469

reasons for this gap is that economists and citizens are looking at different things. Specifically, we economists have invested most of our effort in analyzing the effect of trade (and other forms of globalization) on wages. Public opinion data suggest that most citizens are far more concerned with levels of employment, and unemployment, than wages.[1] One specific claim that has received some attention is that the differing labor market institutions in the US and Europe have resulted in systematically different outcomes as a result of globalization (Davis, 1998a; Krugman, 1995). In this paper, we extend a simple, but plausible, model of equilibrium unemployment to a model of trade between large economies. Ours is not the first paper to examine this question so, prior to presenting our analytical framework and results, we begin by briefly situating our work relative to the related research.

Broadly speaking, we need a framework with: equilibrium economy-wide unemployment; sufficient sectoral structure to permit international trade; and, because we are interested in the effect of international asymmetries in labor market institutions on the effects of globalization, we will need to introduce these asymmetries. Much of the literature on unemployment works with a one-sector model. As a result, any institutional structure that supports wages above the market clearing level will produce equilibrium unemployment. Among the variety of models producing equilibrium unemployment are: minimum wages; insider–outsider/union models; implicit contracts; search; and effciency wages.[2] As Solow (1980) points out, all of these might play a role in any given firm or sector and contribute to the existence of equilibrium unemployment at the macroeconomic level.

In this paper we choose to focus on a source of unemployment for which there is considerable microeconomic evidence across virtually all sectors as well as experimental evidence: the fair wage model. Recent reviews of the evidence can be found in Howitt (2002) and Bewley (2005). Both stress the wide extent and strength of evidence supporting the fair wage model from a range of sources including: surveys of managers and workers; firmlevel studies of pay and termination patterns; experiments; and common sense/personnel management textbooks.

Beginning with now classic papers by Solow (1979), Akerlof (1982), and Akerlof and Yellen (1988, 1990) a sizable literature has developed deriving efficiency wages from a fairness constraint. The basic idea is that worker effort is a function of the perceived fairness of the wage: $\varepsilon_k = f(w_k/w_k^*)$, where ε_k is effort, w_k is the wage of worker type k and the star denotes the wage perceived as fair by workers of type k. Like in all efficiency wage models, firms are induced to pay wages above the market clearing wage, resulting in equilibrium unemployment. From both a theoretical and empirical point of view, the difficult thing is identifying a plausible and observable basis for the evaluation by workers of the fairness of a wage offer. In this paper we will follow Akerlof and Yellen (1990) in supposing that there are two types of labor (skilled and unskilled) and

---

[1] Slaughter (2000) provides an overview of research on the link between changes in commodity prices and changes in the skill premium. Chapter 2 of Scheve and Slaughter (2001) does a nice job of reviewing the results of current poll data on questions related to globalization. We are not arguing that research of the sort reviewed in Slaughter (2000) is misguided. What provoked this research was the striking rise in the skill premium in the 1980s, a period characterized by an increase in the supply of skill. What the research reviewed in Slaughter shows is that, at least in the context of the competitive general equilibrium model, changes in the relative prices of traded goods cannot account for more than a small share of the change in the skill premium. The analysis in this paper is provoked by an interest in the link between globalization and unemployment, a link that obviously cannot be understood in a model which posits full employment as an equilibrium condition. It should be noted, however, that if unemployment is generated by downward inflexibility of wages, which varies across types of labor and industries, inference based on mandated wage regressions may be problematic.

[2] Davidson (1990) and Layard et al. (1991) provide clear discussions of these alternatives.

U. Kreickemeier, D. Nelson / Journal of International Economics 70 (2006) 451–469 453

that the fair wage has two determinants: the market wage of the other group, and their own expected wage if they become separated from their current job (taking into account the possibility that they might be unemployed).

Where most theoretical work on unemployment proceeds under the assumption of a single productive sector, our interest in international trade requires that we develop a model with at least two sectors. Furthermore, since we are interested in equilibrium unemployment, we will need the fairness constraint to be binding in both sectors. In previous work, Agell and Lundborg (1995) have provided a two-sector general equilibrium model of a trading fair wage economy that is loosely related to the Akerlof/Yellen model.[3] In contrast, the framework we use is a direct extension of the Akerlof/Yellen model to two sectors. The closer resemblance to the Akerlof/ Yellen setup makes our paper different from Agell and Lundborg (1995) in two important ways: First, the fair wage mechanism in the present paper operates for both types of workers, and the outcome with full employment of skilled workers and unemployment for unskilled workers arises endogenously. In contrast, Agell and Lundborg *assume* that the fair wage mechanism operates only for one of the factors. While this may be appropriate in their setup with the two factors labor and capital, it would be hard to justify in a model with two types of labor. Second, in our model, as in Akerlof and Yellen (1990), both types of workers provide a well-defined level of full effort in equilibrium. Due to a different specification of the effort function, there is no full effort in Agell and Lundborg (1995), and equilibrium effort is variable. It is the simplification of a constant equilibrium effort which will allow us to represent our model in a simple graphical framework.[4]

Finally, in contrast to Agell and Lundborg who analyze a small–open economy, we are interested in the interaction between two large economies and the impact of asymmetries between labor market institutions in the two economies. In this, our analysis is motivated by the important work of Krugman (1995), Davis (1998a,b), and Xu (2001). In his analysis of the effect on OECD countries of manufactured exports from low-wage developing countries, Krugman develops two models of the OECD — a flexible wage "American" model and a "European" model with fixed wages in which adjustment occurs on the employment margin. Davis (1998a) extends Krugman's analysis by considering the impact of economic linkage between the American and European economies on their respective adjustments to the opening of trade with a low-wage South. In that paper, the American economy is a standard Heckscher–Ohlin economy with flexible wages in both sectors, while the European economy is characterized by an economy-wide minimum wage of the sort analyzed by Brecher (1974). Davis shows that the asymmetry between economies produces spillovers in the form of higher unemployment in Europe and higher wages in the US as a result of liberalized trade with developing country exporters of manufactures. In the words of Davis' title, European unemployment props up American wages. Davis gets very strong results from a model of very stark differences between the European and American economies. This was useful in a first presentation, but it is important to audit results of this sort by considering less stark assumptions.[5]

In this paper both the American and European economies are characterized by fair wage constraints. The asymmetry between the two countries remains, however, because the European

---

[3] Agell and Lundborg (1992) examine the introduction of a fair wage constraint in a Harberger model. Rapanos (1996) extends Agell and Lundborg's (1995) model to an examination of technical change.

[4] The Akerlof/Yellen specification of the effort function with a well-defined level of full effort is furthermore compatible with the empirical observation that workers' effort falls when they are underpaid but does not increase when they are overpaid.

[5] Another example of such auditing is Oslington (2002), which retains Davis' labor market assumptions but looks at the case where Europe becomes completely specialized in production of the skill intensive good, and hence factor prices are not equalized. Under this assumption, Oslington shows that some of Davis' results do not hold.

454   *U. Kreickemeier, D. Nelson / Journal of International Economics 70 (2006) 451–469*

fair wage constraint is, in a sense specified below, tighter than that in the American economy. As a result, while both countries will have equilibrium unemployment, the levels of unemployment will differ between the two in empirically plausible ways.[6] This framework produces results that differ in interesting ways from those in the minimum wage model without losing the fundamental linkage between economies emphasized by Davis.

One of the premier issues in evaluating empirical results on the relationship between international trade and the skill premium is the relationship between various forms of technical change, trade, and wages.[7] Leamer (1998) and Krugman (2000) engage with one another on the issue of the relative importance of the factor-bias versus sector-bias of technological change for the skill premium in the context of a small–open economy. Xu (2001) presents a sophisticated and comprehensive analysis of this question in the context of a two-country world in which both countries are large and characterized by perfect competition in factor and commodity markets. Davis (1998b) addresses the effects of technical change in his model of a flexible wage America and a Europe with a binding minimum wage. In this paper, we extend the analyses of Xu and Davis by considering the effect of technical change in our two-country world with fair wages and equilibrium unemployment. As with the case of falling prices for the unskilled good, we derive distinctive results for this case as well.

Our analysis proceeds by developing our notation in the standard competitive 2-good × 2-factor case (Section 2.1), introducing the fair-wage constraint (Section 2.2), and then developing the 2-country world economy (Section 2.3). In this last section we introduce the virtual integrated equilibrium (VIE), a key concept for the rest of our analysis. In Section 3 we develop our main results on reactions to trade shocks (Section 3.1) and technology shocks (Section 3.2). Section 4 concludes.

2. The model

The model is set up in three steps. First, the well-known two-sector full employment model of a closed economy is introduced. This mainly serves to introduce the notation. Second, we introduce the fair wage mechanism and show that it generates involuntary unemployment in equilibrium. Third, we show how the equilibrium in the closed fair wage economy can be related to the equilibrium in an asymmetric two-country trading world consisting of America and Europe. The asymmetry is generated by the assumption that workers' attitudes towards wage inequality are different across countries. This third step builds on Dixit and Norman's (1980) well-known integrated equilibrium (IE) approach.

2.1. The closed economy with full employment

The closed flexible-wage economy is assumed to produce the two goods X and Y using the factors unskilled labor L and skilled labor H. Good Y serves as the numéraire and is assumed to be unskilled labor intensive relative to X at all common factor price ratios. Product markets are

---

[6] See Nickell (1997) for an argument, and supporting data, to the effect that US and European labor markets are not nearly as distinctive as common beliefs suggest. In particular, unemployment rates between the US and Continental European countries are not dramatically different.

[7] The classic treatments of these relationships for the two-sector competitive model are Findlay and Grubert (1959) and Jones (1965). More recent work in the small economy context includes: Jones (1997, 2000); Leamer (1998); Krugman (2000); and Neary (2002).

U. Kreickemeier, D. Nelson / Journal of International Economics 70 (2006) 451–469 455

perfectly competitive, and production functions in both sectors exhibit constant returns to scale. Both factors of production are supplied inelastically in the quantities L^W and H^W, respectively. Finally, preferences are assumed to be homothetic with both goods being essential in consumption. With w_L as the return to labor, w_H as the return to skill, and P as the relative price of X, the zero profit conditions for the two sectors are given by the equality of goods prices to unit costs, i.e.

$$c_X(w_L, w_H) = P \qquad c_Y(w_L, w_H) = 1. \tag{1}$$

It is assumed at this stage that flexible factor prices clear the markets for both skill and labor. Hence, the employment ratio of skill relative to labor, denoted by h, equals their endowment ratio $h^W \equiv H^W / L^W$. Furthermore, ω is defined as the ratio of w_L and w_H. Equilibrium in the closed economy is then given by the following two relations:

$$P = \lambda(h) \quad \text{with} \quad \lambda'(h) < 0 \tag{2}$$

$$\omega \equiv \frac{w_L}{w_H} = \psi(P) \quad \text{with} \quad \psi'(P) < 0 \tag{3}$$

For a given $h = h^W$, Eq. (2) gives the equilibrium relative goods price and Eq. (3) gives the equilibrium relative factor price. The sign of λ' follows from the assumptions of good X being skill intensive and consumers having homothetic preferences. Under these assumptions, the Heckscher–Ohlin theorem ensures that the higher the skill-to-labor endowment of a country, the lower is its autarky price of the skill intensive good. The sign of ψ' is implied by the factor intensity assumption alone. Under this assumption, it follows from the Stolper–Samuelson theorem that an increase in the price of X decreases the relative price of unskilled labor.

2.2. Fair wages in the closed economy

In the next step, the fair wage mechanism is introduced into the closed economy. Involuntary unemployment is generated by a variant of the Akerlof and Yellen (1990) model. The adaptations made serve the sole purpose of making their one-sector model work in a two-sector general equilibrium framework. The two factors L and H are supplied inelastically, and both types of workers are able to choose their effort at work. In doing so, workers take into account the effort norm ε^n, and they maximize their utility by providing effort ε equal to ε^n. This is formalized by defining the utility function for a worker of group k as

$$v = \upsilon(X, Y) + \Delta \varepsilon_k \tag{4}$$

where $\Delta \varepsilon_k \equiv -|\varepsilon_k - \varepsilon_k^n|$ is the degree of norm violation, and $\upsilon(\cdot)$ is assumed to be homothetic. Workers' effort norms are determined by

$$\varepsilon_k^n = \min\left(\frac{w_k}{w_k^*}, 1\right) \quad k = L, \ H \tag{5}$$

where w_k^* denotes the fair wage for workers of group k. From Eq. (4), utility maximizing workers of group k will always choose $\varepsilon_k = \varepsilon_k^n$. Hence it follows from Eq. (5) that workers provide the normal level of effort, which is normalized to one, if they are paid at least their fair wage.

Firms are wage setters but they are assumed to treat the fair wage, which is determined in general equilibrium, parametrically. Under this assumption, profit maximization can be thought of as a two-

456   *U. Kreickemeier, D. Nelson / Journal of International Economics 70 (2006) 451–469*

stage process, just as in the standard efficiency wage model of Solow (1979). In step one, firms set the wage rate for each type of labor k to minimize the wage paid for an effciency unit, which is w_k/ε_k. In step two, they hire workers up to the point where the value marginal product of labor is equal to the wage set in step one. It can be seen from Eq. (4) together with $\varepsilon_k = \varepsilon_k^n$ that the wage rate for an effciency unit of labor (skilled or unskilled) stays constant (at w_H^* and w_L^*, respectively) if a firm pays a wage below the fair wage. We can therefore safely assume, following Akerlof and Yellen (1990), that firms choose to pay wages at least as high as the fair wage for the respective factor.

For each of the two groups, the fair wage has two determinants: first the market wage of the respective other group, and second the remuneration they could expect outside their own job, taking into account that they might be unemployed with a probability that is equal to the factor-specific rate of unemployment.[8] Hence, we have

$$w_L^* = \theta w_H + (1-\theta)(1-U_L)w_L \tag{6}$$

$$w_H^* = \theta w_L + (1-\theta)(1-U_H)w_H \tag{7}$$

where U_L and U_H are the factor-specific rates of unemployment, and θ is the weight attached to the respective other factors remuneration in one factor's determination of its fair wage.

We assume that in a perfectly competitive labor market the wage for skilled workers would be higher than the wage for unskilled workers. Under this condition it is straightforward to see that the following must be true in equilibrium:

$$U_L > U_H = 0 \tag{8}$$

$$w_H > w_H^* > w_L = w_L^* \tag{9}$$

$$\varepsilon_L = \varepsilon_H = 1 \tag{10}$$

i.e., there is a strictly positive rate of unemployment $U = U_L$ for unskilled workers but full employment for skilled workers, the fair wage is binding only for unskilled workers, and both types of workers provide the normal effort.[9]

Using Eqs. (6), (8), (9) and (10), one can derive an equilibrium relationship between the wage differential and the rate of unemployment. Using $\omega \equiv w_L/w_H$, we get

$$\omega = \alpha(U, \theta) = \frac{\theta}{\theta + (1-\theta)U}. \tag{11}$$

Following Akerlof and Yellen (1990), Eq. (11) is called the *fair wage constraint*. For a given value of θ, the fair wage constraint describes equilibrium combinations between the rate of

---

[8] Instead of the expected wage rate, Akerlof and Yellen (1990) use the (hypothetical) market clearing wage rate of the respective group as the second determinant of the fair wage. The two approaches yield similar results as in the presence of involuntary unemployment for the respective factor both its expected wage and its market clearing wage lie below the actual wage. The approach used here is more straightforward to apply in a multi-sector model.

[9] These results are the same as in the model of Akerlof and Yellen (1990). A strictly positive unemployment rate U_L ensures that the fair wage of unskilled workers – which is also their market wage – is below the market wage of skilled workers in equilibrium. For skilled workers, the fair wage can never be binding because it is a weighted average of two variables that would both be smaller than the fair wage itself were this wage paid in equilibrium. With w_H^* non-binding, w_H does not affect skilled workers' effort, and it adjusts to ensure market clearing.

U. Kreickemeier, D. Nelson / Journal of International Economics 70 (2006) 451–469 457

unemployment of unskilled workers and the relative gross wages of skilled and unskilled workers.[10] Partial differentiation gives

$$\frac{\partial \alpha}{\partial U} = \frac{-\theta(1-\theta)}{(\theta + (1-\theta)U)^2} < 0 \quad \text{and} \quad \frac{\partial^2 \alpha}{\partial U^2} = \frac{2\theta(1-\theta)^2}{(\theta + (1-\theta)U)^3} > 0,$$

and hence the fair wage constraint is negatively sloped and convex in $\omega - U$-space, i.e. higher rates of unemployment (for unskilled workers) lead firms to paying them relatively lower wages. This is because with higher rates of unemployment, the fair wage needed to elicit normal effort from unskilled workers is lower. Considering the extreme cases $U=0$ and $U=1$, we have $\alpha(0, \theta)=1$ and $\alpha(1, \theta)=\theta$. Hence, relative wages can vary over the range $[\theta, 1]$, and the model gives us an intermediate case between full wage flexibility and a fixed wage differential.[11]

Furthermore, given that skill is fully employed, there is by definition a relationship between the rate of unemployment U, the endowment ratio h^W and the employment ratio h:

$$U = 1 - \frac{h^W}{h} \equiv \beta(h, h^w) \quad \text{with} \quad \frac{\partial \beta}{\partial h} > 0. \tag{12}$$

This relation is identical to the "Brecher relation" stated in Davis (1998a) but for the fact that we have divided both sides by L^W.[12] Taken together, Eqs. (2), (3), (11) and (12) determine the endogenous variables P, ω, U and h in the closed fair wage economy. Note that contrary to the full employment model, the goods market equilibrium condition (2) now describes possible combinations between two endogenous variables.

It is convenient to illustrate the determination of equilibrium in Fig. 1, which is similar to Fig. 1 of Davis (1998a). The graphical representations of Eqs. (2), (3), and (12) in quadrants I, II and IV are straightforward and do not need further elaboration. The fair wage constraint, Eq. (11) is depicted in quadrant III. The upward sloping curve in quadrant I, labelled $\mu(h)$, is implied by Eqs. (3), (11) and (12): For a given zero profit relation (3), it gives combinations of h and P which are compatible with workers supplying the profit maximizing level of effort along the fair wage constraint.[13] It can be easily verified that there is a unique equilibrium for the closed economy, with the equilibrium values of the respective variables being denoted by a "$-$".

The welfare properties of the closed economy equilibrium can now be derived. Given the utility function (4), we can draw standard indifference curves in goods space to measure social welfare. As goods prices determine factor prices in our model and relative factor prices determine the level of unemployment, there is a production possibility frontier (along which employment of

---

[10] In deriving Eq. (11) unemployment benefits have been set to zero. If we were to assume instead that unskilled workers are entitled to unemployment benefits of γw_L, $\gamma < 1$, which are financed lump-sum, the fair wage constraint becomes $\omega = \alpha(U, \theta, \gamma) = \theta/[\theta + (1-\theta)(1-\gamma)U]$, and an increase in γ pivots the fair wage constraint outwards, i.e. for a given level of unemployment the fair wage increases.

[11] With perfectly competitive markets for both types of labor, ω can vary between 0 and 1, assuming – as we did – that under perfect competition skilled workers are paid the higher wage.

[12] Note that the form of Eq. (12) does not depend on the particular mechanism generating unemployment. Observing this, we will not use the term "Brecher relation" in the following because it appears to suggest a connection to the minimum wage model originally due to Brecher (1974).

[13] Formally, we have $\mu(h, h^W, \theta) \equiv \psi^{-1}\{\alpha[\beta(h, h^W), \theta]\}$, where $\psi^{-1}\{\omega\}$ is the inverse of $\psi(P)$. Partial differentiation gives $\frac{\partial \mu}{\partial h} \equiv (\psi^{-1})' \frac{\partial \alpha}{\partial U} \frac{\partial \beta}{\partial h} > 0$.

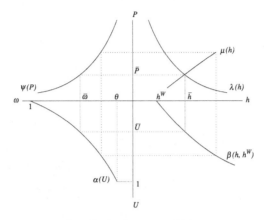

Fig. 1. The closed economy equilibrium.

both factors is constant) for each relative goods price. The tangency points of all price-contingent production possibility frontiers with the respective price lines give the locus along which production in the fair wage economy takes place. Following the terminology used by Brecher (1974), we label this locus the *transformation curve* of our model.[14]

The welfare properties of the closed economy equilibrium are illustrated by means of Fig. 2. $R(\tilde{P})$ and $R(\bar{P})$ denote production possibility curves for two arbitrarily picked relative prices $\tilde{P}$ and $\bar{P}$, and the transformation curve is given by TT. The unique equilibrium is at point A, where the social indifference curve II is tangent to the price line with slope $-\tilde{P}$ and to the production possibility frontier $R(\tilde{P})$. As in the familiar minimum wage model of Brecher (1974), there is a non-tangency between TT and II, and welfare in the closed economy can be increased by paying a subsidy on either the consumption or the production of unskilled labor intensive good Y. The second-best subsidy $\tau* > 0$ (measured in per cent of the producer price) brings about tangency between a social indifference curve and TT. With $P*$ as the relative producer price, we have $MRS = P*/(1-\tau*) = MRT$, and $P*$ equal to the slope of $R(P*)$. It is easily verified that $P*/(1-\tau*) > \tilde{P} > P*$.[15]

2.3. Conditions for factor price equalization

In this section, the equilibrium for the closed fair wage economy just derived is reinterpreted as describing the situation of a world economy in which both goods and factors are freely mobile. Then Samuelson's angel (Samuelson, 1949), descends from the theorist's heaven and allocates the factors among two countries (Europe and the US). Following Dixit and Norman (1980), we then

---

[14] An analogous locus appears in Agell and Lundborg (1995) under the name "fairness constrained production possibilities frontier". Along this locus, both physical labor input and effort are variable, in contrast to the present model where effort is constant along the transformation curve.

[15] Unemployment benefits, modeled as set out in fn. 10, are a shift variable of the transformation curve. It is easily checked that lowering unemployment benefits shifts the transformation curve outwards and increases welfare in the closed economy.

U. Kreickemeier, D. Nelson / Journal of International Economics 70 (2006) 451–469 459

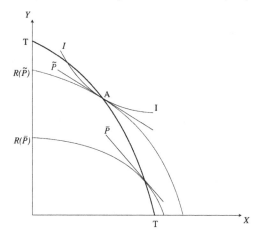

Fig. 2. Welfare in the closed economy.

examine the conditions under which free trade in goods, but not in factors, can replicate the integrated equilibrium.

It is shown in the following that a modified IE approach can be used to derive conditions for factor price equalization in an asymmetric trading world consisting of Europe and America. We assume that the two countries differ in their attitudes towards wage inequality, with European workers disliking high skill premiums to a larger extent. Formally, this is captured here by the assumption $0 < \theta^A < \theta^E < 1$, where A and E are country superscripts applying to America and Europe, respectively. From Eq. (11) we have that $\partial \alpha / \partial \theta > 0$ for $U > 0$, and hence the European fair wage constraint lies above the American fair wage constraint for all strictly positive values of U. Linking the two-country case to the integrated equilibrium, we assume that Europe inherits all properties – and in particular the value for θ – of the closed economy in the previous section. It is clear from Eq. (11) that in the absence of technological differences and with diversified production in both countries as well as free goods trade, factor prices will be equalized internationally. This implies, as can be seen in Fig. 3 for the equilibrium relative wage $\bar{\omega}$, that the rate of unemployment is higher in Europe than in America in any diversified equilibrium with free trade and identical technologies.

As a preliminary step, we show that the standard version of the IE approach cannot be applied to our case of differing values for θ, i.e. different attitudes towards wage inequality, between countries. Let $H^W = H^A + H^E$ and $L^W = L^A + L^E$ describe the distribution of endowments across countries, with W being the superscript for the integrated world. We then have the following result.

Lemma 1. *It is impossible to find a division of labor between the two countries that leads to both countries having the same factor prices as the integrated world.*

The proof is by contradiction. Assume that the endowment split leaves world factor prices unaltered. An unaltered wage rate elicits the profit maximizing effort from the European workers – and hence is chosen by European firms – if and only if after the endowment split Europe has the same rate of unemployment as the integrated world had before. But a constant rate of unemployment

460   *U. Kreickemeier, D. Nelson / Journal of International Economics 70 (2006) 451–469*

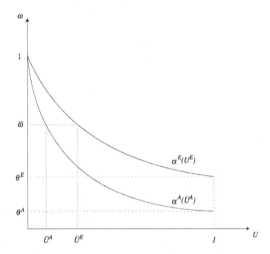

Fig. 3. European and American fair wage constraints.

in Europe implies a decreasing average rate of unemployment in the world compared to the integrated equilibrium. This means a lower *average* skill intensity of production and hence a higher relative price of the skill intensive good. Any change in relative goods prices however is incompatible with both countries having the same factor prices as in the integrated equilibrium.

It is now checked whether there are allocations of factors to the two countries that lead to free trade equilibria in which factor prices, although different from the integrated equilibrium, are the same in both countries. To this end, we construct a hypothetical one-country world with fair wages which has

(i) the same skill endowment as the two-country world,
(ii) the same average skill intensity of production as the two-country world, and
(iii) the same rate of unemployment as Europe.

In analogy to the Dixit–Norman terminology, this hypothetical one-country world is called the *virtual integrated equilibrium* (VIE). Let s^L be the European share of the unskilled labor force. With different rates of unemployment across countries, the average unemployment rate in the world is $U^E s^L + U^A (1 - s^L)$. Let $a \equiv U^A / U^E$ denote the ratio between the American and European unemployment rate and $d \equiv \omega^E / \omega^A$ the ratio between European and American relative wages. From Eq. (11), it follows that

$$a = \frac{d - \omega^E}{1 - \omega^E} \frac{\theta^A (1 - \theta^E)}{\theta^E (1 - \theta^A)}. \tag{13}$$

With equal technologies between countries and diversified production it follows that $d = 1$ and $a < 1$. Furthermore, one can see from Eq. (13) that under FPE a is constant as it only depends on the preference parameters θ^E and θ^A. Using this, as well as the condition $U = U^E$, the average rate

U. Kreickemeier, D. Nelson / Journal of International Economics 70 (2006) 451–469 461

of unemployment for the two-country world becomes $U(s^L+(1-s^L)a)$. Hence, the equivalent to Eq. (12) in the asymmetric two-country world becomes

$$U = \frac{1}{s^L + (1-s^L)a}\left(1 - \frac{h^W}{h}\right) \equiv \beta(h, h^W, s^L, a), \tag{14}$$

where

$$h \equiv \frac{H^W}{L^W[1-U(s^L + (1-s^L)a)]}$$

in this new context is reinterpreted as the average skill intensity of world production. Denote the variables pertaining to this VIE by a "˜". In order to satisfy conditions (i) (ii) and (iii), the virtual endowment ratio $\tilde{h}^W \equiv H^W / \tilde{L}^W$ has to solve the equation $\beta(h, \tilde{h}^W) = \beta(h, h^W, s^L, a)$, holding h constant at the level of the two-country world. Substituting from Eqs. (12) and (14) yields

$$\tilde{h}^W = h + \frac{h^W - h}{s^L + (1-s^L)a}, \tag{15}$$

and solving for $\tilde{L}^W$ this becomes

$$\tilde{L}^W = L^W \frac{1-U(s^L + (1-s^L)a)}{1-U} \tag{16}$$

It is clear from Eq. (16) that $\tilde{L}^W > L^W$ because $a < 1$. Crucially, Eq. (16) shows that $\tilde{L}^W$ does not depend on the allocation of the world skill endowment between the two countries.

The concept of VIE can now be illustrated in Fig. 4. European and American factor endowments are measured from origins O^E and O^A, respectively. The width of the *solid* box gives the world labor endowment, its height the world skill endowment. The European labor endowment $L^E = s^L L^W$ is given by $\overline{O^E B}$, the European unemployment rate U by $\overline{O^E A}/\overline{O^E B}$. Analogously, the American labor endowment is equal to $\overline{GO^A}$, and the American rate of unemployment aU is given

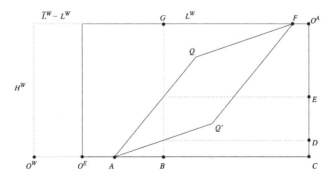

Fig. 4. The virtual integrated equilibrium.

by $\overline{FO^A}/\overline{GO^A}$. Then the virtual labor endowment $\tilde{L}^W$, and hence O^W, is determined by the the condition that $(\overline{O^WA} + \overline{FO^A})/\overline{O^WC}$, the rate of unemployment in the VIE, be equal to $\overline{O^EA}/\overline{O^EB}$. Vectors $\overline{AQ}$ and $\overline{AQ'}$ are the factor inputs into X and Y production, respectively, in the VIE. Let s^H be the European share of the world skill endowment. It is now immediate that the two-country world replicates the VIE if and only if $\overline{CD}/\overline{CO^A} \le s^H \le \overline{CE}/\overline{CO^A}$. Note that Fig. 4 shows only the "snapshot" for a given value of s^L. Changing the allocation of unskilled labor between countries leads to a different VIE.

More generally, it follows from Eq. (16) that there is a unique and finite $\tilde{L} > L$ for every admissible combination of L^W, s^L, U, and a. And one can easily verify by inspecting Fig. 4 that for *every* value of s^L point B lies strictly to the right of point A (as the European unemployment rate is strictly smaller than one). Finally, given the assumption that X production is more skill intensive than Y production at all common factor price ratios, point E lies strictly above point D. This proves that there is a non-degenerate FPE set in the following sense:

Proposition 1. *Let s^L and s^H be the fractions of the world labor and skill endowments, respectively, which are allocated to Europe. Then, for every s^L with $0 < s^L < 1$ there exists a range of skill allocations $[s^H_1, s^H_2]$ with $0 < s^H_1 < s^H_2 < 1$ which leads to factor price equalization.*

Now, the FPE set can be described formally in a manner very similar to the standard model. Let goods be indexed by i, countries by j. Then, the divisions of world factor endowments that replicate the VIE can be described as

$$
\text{FPE} = \left\{ \begin{array}{c} [(H^A, L^A), (H^E, L^E)] \exists \lambda_{ij} \ge 0 \\ \text{such that } \sum_j \lambda_{ij} = 1 \\ (H^A, L^A) = \sum_i \lambda_{iA}\left(\tilde{H}(i), \tilde{L}(i)\right) + (0, L^A \cdot aU) \\ (H^E, L^E) = \sum_i \lambda_{iE}\left(\tilde{H}(i), \tilde{L}(i)\right) + (0, L^E \cdot U) \\ i = X, Y \; j = A, E \end{array} \right\}
\tag{17}
$$

Here, $\tilde{H}(i)$ and $\tilde{L}(i)$ denote the amounts of skill and labor, respectively, employed in sector i in the VIE with factor endowments $(H^W, \tilde{L}^W)$, where $\tilde{L}^W$ is given by Eq. (16). These conditions state that in order to replicate the VIE it must be possible for the two-country world to use the skill intensities of the VIE and thereby achieve full employment for skilled labor in both countries as well as unemployment rates of U and aU for unskilled labor in Europe and America, respectively, where U is the unemployment rate of the VIE and $a = [\theta^A(1 - \theta^E)]/[\theta^E(1 - \theta^A)]$ (from Eq. (13)).

It has been stressed that every redistribution of labor between Europe and America, implying a change in s^L, leads to a change in the corresponding VIE. Clearly, this involves a change in skill intensities. Therefore, in contrast to both the full employment model and the minimum wage model considered by Davis (1998a), the FPE region of the present model is characterized by non-constant goods and factor prices.[16] The effects can be verified by means of Fig. 5. It follows from Eq. (14)

---

[16] On a general level, this result is due to the assumed asymmetry between the two countries. An analogous result can be produced in a full employment model if it were assumed that consumers in the two countries have different preferences over goods. In this case, redistributing consumers between countries would influence prices. See Uzawa (1959) and Albert (1994). In Davis (1998a), prices are constant within the FPE region despite the asymmetry between the countries because of the exogenously fixed wage.

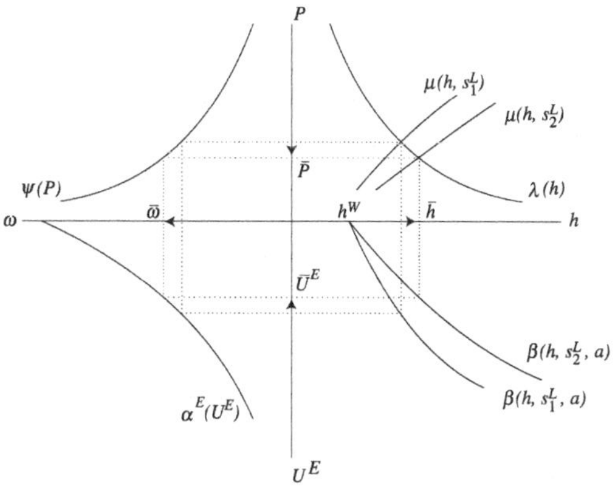

Fig. 5. Varying the relative size of Europe's labor force.

that $\partial\beta/\partial s^L < 0$, which implies that increasing the relative size of the European labor force within the FPE region from s_1^L to s_2^L rotates $\beta(\cdot)$ inwards. If FPE holds throughout, changes in equilibrium values of the variables of interest are indicated by arrows.[17] This gives the following result:

Proposition 2. *Increasing the relative size of the European labor force leads to a higher average skill intensity of world production, a lower relative price of the skill intensive good, a higher relative (and absolute) wage of unskilled workers and to a lower rate of unemployment in both countries.*

It is now straightforward to show that, as in Davis (1998a), there is a sense in which labor market characteristics in one country spill over into labor market outcomes in the other. Plugging Eq. (13) into Eq. (14) and differentiating gives $\partial\beta/\partial\theta^A < 0$. Hence, changes in America's fairness preference have effects on the European labor market that are analogous to those of changes in s^L. In Fig. 5, an increase in θ^A rotates $\beta(\cdot)$ inwards. We therefore have:

Proposition 3. *With more egalitarian preferences of American workers, the unemployment rate of European unskilled workers as well as the skill premium in Europe fall.*

Hence European unskilled workers are negatively affected by the less egalitarian preferences of American workers. It is straightforward to see (by re-labeling countries in Fig. 5) that the reverse is true as well: American unskilled workers are positively affected in terms of relative wages and employment levels by the more egalitarian preferences of European workers.

3. Comparative statics

We now conduct two comparative static exercises which appear to have particular interest from a policy point of view. First, we look at the entry of newly industrializing countries into the trading

[17] In Fig. 5, $\tilde{h}^W$ for each of the two equilibria can be found by drawing a β-curve with $s^L = 1$ through the respective equilibrium point $(\bar{U}, \bar{h})$. The resulting (endogenous) intersection points with the h-axis give the values for $\tilde{h}^W$. One can easily verify that increasing s^L leads to an increase in $\tilde{h}^W$.

464   *U. Kreickemeier, D. Nelson / Journal of International Economics 70 (2006) 451–469*

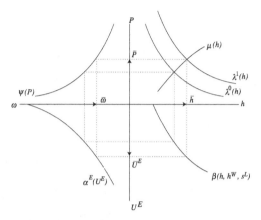

Fig. 6. The entry of NICs into world trade.

world. Second, we look at global and national technical progress. For both cases, the minimum wage model used by Davis (1998a,b) generates strong results. Part of the aim of this section is to examine the extent to which the special nature of the labor market distortion assumed by Davis is responsible for these results. An obvious second benchmark case would be given by the full employment model. However, we will consider instead the more general benchmark of a constant rate of unemployment which is not necessarily zero. With respect to the comparative static effects, it is immaterial whether the rate of unemployment is constant at some positive level or zero. And using a positive rate of unemployment as a starting point allows us to sensibly compare comparative static effects of our model, which is characterized by unemployment in the initial equilibrium, to this benchmark.

3.1. Entry of NICs into world trade

Consider the entry of newly industrializing countries (NICs) into the trading world, i.e. the virtual integrated equilibrium comprising America and Europe. It is assumed that at the relative world market price of the VIE, the NICs as a group are net exporters of the labor intensive good.[18] Again, the comparative static effects can be shown by a variant of the familiar four-quadrant diagram, assuming that factor price equalization between America and Europe continues to hold.

In Fig. 6, the entry of NICs into world trade shifts the goods–market–equilibrium relation outwards, i.e. from position λ^0 to position λ^1. The vertical distance between the two curves measures the amount by which this change would make P, the relative world market price of the skill intensive good, go up for a given average skill intensity of production in the VIE countries. This would be the price change occurring in a model with a constant rate of unemployment. The horizontal distance between the two curves measures the amount by which the average skill

---

[18] This assumption is quite general in the sense that restrictions for the trade between NICs and the VIE countries are not ruled out. Similarly, technology differences between both groups of countries are allowed for. Clearly, if trade was restricted or technologies between the two groups of countries were different, factor prices between NICs and the VIE countries would not be equalized.

U. Kreickemeier, D. Nelson / Journal of International Economics 70 (2006) 451–469 465

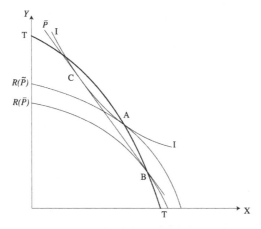

Fig. 7. Globalization shock.

intensity of production in the VIE countries would have to increase in order to accommodate the entry of the NICs into world trade at constant relative goods prices. This is the case described by Davis (1998a). The equilibrium changes in P, ω, U^E and h are indicated in Fig. 6 by arrows.[19] The β-function does not move because from Eq. (13) the ratio of unemployment rates between the two countries is constant as long as factor prices are equalized between them. Hence, we have

Proposition 4. *The entry of NICs into the world trading system decreases relative wages of the unskilled in Europe and America, and it proportionally increases the unemployment rates in both countries.*

Unskilled workers in both countries who remain employed experience a loss in real wages through a standard Stolper–Samuelson effect induced by the decrease in the relative price of the labor intensive good. In addition, some of them become unemployed, and hence their wage income falls to zero. The results of the present model are in marked contrast to the minimum wage model where American workers are not affected at all by the entry of NICs into world trade. This strong implication of the Davis (1998a) model no longer holds in a world with endogenously determined prices.

The welfare effects of the globalization shock just described on both countries can be analyzed using Fig. 7, which is analogous to Fig. 2. Here, TT is the aggregate transformation curve of the integrated two-country world. The autarky equilibrium is at A, with relative price $\tilde{P}$ (the price line has been omitted in order to avoid clutter). As shown above, the globalization shock leads to an increase in P and a decrease in employment. In Fig. 7, the new price is $\bar{P}$, production occurs at B, and consumption at C. As drawn, the globalization shock leaves aggregate welfare for the two-country world, measured by the indifference curve II, unchanged. This is a borderline case, where

---

[19] It is possible for h and P to rise at the same time because the VIE countries as a group are now exporting the skill intensive product.

the positive consumption and production effects from opening up to trade, which are well-known from the standard model, are exactly offset by the negative employment effect. Clearly this is only by construction, and there is no presumption as to which effect might dominate. This result is in marked contrast to the minimum wage model where, as shown by Brecher (1974), aggregate welfare falls if the economy moves from autarky to becoming an exporter of the capital (or skill) intensive good, while still producing both goods.[20]

In the borderline case shown in Fig. 7, welfare in both countries can be seen to move in opposite directions. There is nothing country specific in the employment effect, as shown above. However, in the pre-globalization equilibrium one of the two countries has to be the exporter of labor intensive good *Y*, while the other country imports it. For the old exporter (importer) of *Y*, opening up to trade with the NICs means a negative (positive) terms of trade shock. Together, this implies that national welfare for the old *Y*-exporter falls as a consequence of the globalization shock, while national welfare increases for the old importer of *Y*. It is now straightforward to see that with aggregate globalization gains for the two-country world, the old importer of *Y* gains while the effect for the old exporter is ambiguous. On the other hand, with aggregate losses for the two-country world, the old exporter of *Y* loses while the effect for the old importer of *Y* is ambiguous. In Davis (1998a), aggregate welfare in minimum-wage Europe falls along with the level of employment, while welfare in America is unchanged. The pre-globalization trade pattern plays no role here.

3.2. Technological change

In a recent paper, Xu (2001) derives the effects of sector-specific technological change on relative factor prices in a full employment model. His analysis of different cases is exhaustive in considering different elasticities of substitution in demand as well as different types of technological progress (TP). Davis (1998b) looks at the effects of sector-specific TP on relative wages and unemployment in the asymmetric two-country world where "Europe" has a binding minimum wage that is fixed in terms of the numéraire good, and "America" has fully flexible wages. In the context of our model with positive but different unemployment rates in both countries, the additional question arises as to whether TP can explain divergent unemployment paths in the two countries.

Equipped with the results derived in the previous section, it is immediately clear that a global technology shock that leaves both countries diversified in production will leave *relative* unemployment rates between them constant: Factor prices continue to be equalized internationally in this case, which from Eq. (13) gives the stated result. Furthermore, from Eq. (11), unemployment rates in both countries increase (decrease) whenever the skill premium increases (decreases). The effect of sector-specific TP on the skill premium in turn is determined by exactly the same variables as in the well-known full employment case: At constant goods prices, TP in the skill intensive (labor intensive) sector increases (decreases) the skill premium, while the induced relative goods price effect works in the opposite direction. Ceteris paribus, a higher elasticity of substitution in demand makes it more likely that the impact effect (i.e. the effect at constant goods prices) dominates, because the higher the elasticity of substitution the lower the relative price effect that is needed to absorb the excess

---

[20] This is because due to the absence of relative price effects in the minimum wage model consumption and production effects are zero, leaving only the negative employment effect.

U. Kreickemeier, D. Nelson / Journal of International Economics 70 (2006) 451–469   467

supply of the sector experiencing the TP. Induced employment effects in our model dampen the relative wage effects but never reverse them.[21,22]

In the case of national – rather than global – technological change, we focus on the case where technologies are identical ex ante, and both countries are diversified before and after TP in one of the countries occurs. Clearly, factor prices are no longer equalized between countries after the technology shock. For concreteness, assume TP in the skill intensive sector of one of the countries. By standard Heckscher–Ohlin reasoning, the country experiencing this TP will then have a higher skill premium than the other country because the relative demand for skilled workers increases. The reverse is true with TP in the labor intensive sector. The result on relative unemployment rates between Europe and America can now be inferred from Eq. (13):

Proposition 5. *National technical progress in the skill intensive (labor intensive) sector increases (lowers) the unemployment rate of the country experiencing it relative to the unemployment rate of the other country.*

Hence, TP in America's labor intensive sector and Europe's skill intensive sector widen the international unemployment differential, while TP in America's skill intensive sector and Europe's labor intensive sector narrow it. In principle, the latter type of shocks could even reverse the ranking of unemployment rates between countries, as can be seen from Eq. (13). In particular we need $d > \omega^E + (1 - \omega^E)[\theta^E(1 - \theta^A)]/[\theta^A(1 - \theta^E)]$ for this outcome, where the term on the right hand side of the inequality is strictly larger than one.

4. Conclusion

Unemployment is clearly an important part of the policy environment within which trade policy is evaluated. Furthermore, at least since the important work of Davis (1998a) it has been clear that trade between economies with heterogeneous labor markets may produce very different outcomes for the economies. Where Davis made his analysis in the context of very stark institutional assumptions to throw his central point into high relief, we have sought to develop a complementary analysis in terms of a model with a macroeconomically plausible empirical referent (the fair wage model) and a relatively simple form of international heterogeneity (relative strength of preference for fairness).

In this context, we have considered both increased trade with a low-wage south and technological change. While the central point of Davis' analysis (interdependent adjustment to shocks) comes through strongly, some of his results turn out to be specific to his modeling framework. In the fair wage context considered here, neither a global technology shock nor increased trade with

---

[21] For a more detailed discussion of the relative wage and unemployment effects described in this section, see our working paper, Kreickemeier and Nelson (2005).

[22] These results are in marked contrast to those in Davis (1998b). In his minimum wage framework, TP in the non-numéraire sector leaves relative wages unchanged, while TP in the numéraire sector leads to an increase in the skill premium. Neither the skill intensity of the sector in which TP occurs nor the elasticity of substitution in consumption plays a role for this result. The intuition is straightforward. With TP in the non-numéraire sector, the zero profit condition in the numéraire sector is unchanged. As w_L is fixed in terms of the numéraire, w_H remains constant as well. The relative goods price adjusts in order to make these wages compatible with zero profits in the non-numéraire sector. In contrast, TP in the numéraire sector changes this sector's zero profit condition, giving room for factor price increases. As w_L is fixed, w_H increases and hence so does the skill premium. Again, the relative goods price adjusts in order to restore zero profits in the non-numéraire sector.

the low-wage south – but only technology shocks with a country-specific component – can explain divergent unemployment paths between countries. Internally to the development of trade theory, we have also seen how the powerful integrated equilibrium approach can be adapted to this class of model.

We have argued that the fair wage model constitutes an empirically plausible and theoretically useful framework for analyzing equilibrium unemployment in trade models. In future work this framework can be extended in a number of directions. A number of standard trade theoretic questions still remain to be studied systematically — e.g. issues of policy competition, dynamics, outsourcing, etc. In addition, as suggested by Solow's remark that the sources of equilibrium unemployment are likely to be many, it also seems useful to consider the interaction of these sources. For example, following recent work in labor economics, the interaction between fair wage constraints and union bargaining seems a particularly fruitful avenue for future research.

Acknowledgements

We thank two referees and the editor for helpful comments. Financial support from The Leverhulme Trust under programme grant F114/BF is gratefully acknowledged. The usual disclaimer applies.

References

Agell, J., Lundborg, P., 1992. Fair wages, involuntary unemployment and tax policies in the simple general equilibrium model. Journal of Public Economics 47, 299–320.

Agell, J., Lundborg, P., 1995. Fair wages in the open economy. Economica 62, 335–351.

Akerlof, G., 1982. Labor contracts as partial gift exchange. Quarterly Journal of Economics 97, 543–569.

Akerlof, G., Yellen, J., 1988. Fairness and unemployment. American Economic Review 78, 44–49.

Akerlof, G., Yellen, J., 1990. The fairwage-effort hypothesis and unemployment. Quarterly Journal of Economics 105, 255–283.

Albert, M., 1994. Das Faktorpreisausgleichstheorem. J.C.B. Mohr, Tübingen.

Bewley, T., 2005. Fairness, reciprocity, and wage rigidity. In: Gintis, H., Bowles, S., Boyd, R., Fehr, E. (Eds.), Moral Sentiments and Material Interests: The Foundations of Cooperation in Economic Life. MIT Press, Cambridge, pp. 303–338.

Brecher, R., 1974. Minimum wage rates and the pure theory of international trade. Quarterly Journal of Economics 88, 98–116.

Davidson, C., 1990. Recent Developments in the Theory of Involuntary Unemployment. W.E. Upjohn Institute for Employment Research, Kalamazoo.

Davis, D.R., 1998a. Does European unemployment prop up American wages? National labor markets and global trade. American Economic Review 88, 478–494.

Davis, D.R., 1998b. Technology, unemployment, and relative wages in a global economy. European Economic Review 42, 1613–1633.

Dixit, A., Norman, V., 1980. Theory of International Trade. Cambridge University Press, Cambridge.

Findlay, R., Grubert, H., 1959. Factor intensities, technological progress and the terms of trade. Oxford Economic Papers 11, 111–121.

Howitt, P., 2002. Looking inside the labor market: a review article. Journal of Economic Literature 40, 125–138.

Jones, R., 1965. The structure of simple general equilibrium models. Journal of Political Economy 73, 557–572.

Jones, R., 1997. Trade, technology, and income distribution. Indian Economic Review 32, 129–140.

Jones, R., 2000. Technical progress, price adjustments and wages. Review of International Economics 8, 497–503.

Kreickemeier, U., Nelson, D., 2005. Fair Wages, Unemployment and Technological Change in a Global Economy, GEP Research Paper 2005/05. University of Nottingham.

Krugman, P., 1995. Growing world trade: causes and consequences. Brookings Papers on Economic Activity 327–362.

Krugman, P., 2000. Technology, trade and factor prices. Journal of International Economics 50, 51–71.

U. Kreickemeier, D. Nelson / Journal of International Economics 70 (2006) 451–469   469

Layard, R., Nickell, S., Jackman, R., 1991. Unemployment: Macroeconomic Performance and the Labor Market. Oxford University Press, Oxford.

Leamer, E., 1998. In search of Stolper–Samuelson effects on US wages. In: Collins, S. (Ed.), Imports, Exports and the American Worker. Brookings Institution, Washington, DC, pp. 141–214.

Neary, J.P., 2002. Competition, trade and wages. In: Greenaway, D., Upward, R., Wakelin, K. (Eds.), Trade, Investment, Migration and Labour Market Adjustment. Palgrave–Macmillan, Houndmills, pp. 28–46.

Nickell, S., 1997. Unemployment and labor market rigidities: Europe versus the United States. Journal of Economic Perspectives 11, 55–74.

Oslington, P., 2002. Factor market linkages in a global economy. Economics Letters 76, 85–93.

Rapanos, V., 1996. Technical change in a model with fair wages and unemployment. International Economic Journal 10, 99–121.

Samuelson, P., 1949. International factor price equalisation once again. Economic Journal 59, 181–197.

Scheve, K., Slaughter, M., 2001. Globalization and the Perceptions of American Workers. Institute for International Economics, Washington, DC.

Slaughter, M., 2000. What are the results of product–price studies and what can we learn from their differences? In: Feenstra, R. (Ed.), The Impact of International Trade on Wages. University of Chicago Press/NBER, Chicago, pp. 129–165.

Solow, R., 1979. Another possible source of wage stickiness. Journal of Macroeconomics 1, 79–82.

Solow, R., 1980. Theories of unemployment. American Economic Review 70, 1–11.

Uzawa, H., 1959. Prices of the factors of production in international trade. Econometrica 27, 448–468.

Xu, B., 2001. Factor bias, sector bias, and the effects of technical progress on relative factor prices. Journal of International Economics 54, 5–25.

The World Economy (2006)
doi: 10.1111/j.1467-9701.2006.00832.x

Fairness and the Political Economy of Trade

Carl Davidson[1], Steve Matusz[1] and Doug Nelson[2]

[1]*Michigan State University and GEP, University of Nottingham, and* [2]*Tulane University and GEP, University of Nottingham*

1. INTRODUCTION[1]

THE language of fairness is extensively deployed in the politics of international trade virtually everywhere in the world. The legal structures providing protection through administered mechanisms are generally referred to as 'fair trade laws', the formula 'free and fair' is widely used in the public politics of international trade, by both supporters and opponents of trade liberalisation, as characterising the ideal state of international commercial relations. As economists, we are justifiably sceptical of the rhetoric of fairness when applied to arguments for protection. On the one hand, again as economists, we collectively tend to be strong supporters of liberalisation and opponents of protection, so we find ourselves opposed to positions that appear to have their strongest support in fairness-based arguments. On the other hand, our most characteristic normative methods – based in straightforward individualistic utilitarian consequentialism – dismisses notions of rights, justice and fairness as, at best muddled, and more likely welfare worsening (Kaplow and Shavell, 2002). Unlike the archetypal two-handed economist, at least in this area, both of our hands are pushing in the same direction: rejection of fairness-based arguments for trade policy.

The authors are grateful to the participants of the 'Fairness and the Political Economy of Globalization' conference. They are also especially grateful for conversations with Simon Gächter on the model. Doug Nelson gratefully acknowledges financial support from the Leverhulme Trust under Programme Grant F114/BF.

[1] This paper was presented at a conference on 'Fairness and the Political Economy of Globalization', funded by the Murphy Institute (Tulane University) and the Leverhulme Centre for Research on Globalisation and Economic Policy (University of Nottingham), held in New Orleans on 1 and 2 April, 2005. The organisers of the conference (Udo Kreickemeier and Doug Nelson) are grateful to both organisations for their generous support. In addition, the organisers are grateful to all conference participants.

990   C. DAVIDSON, S. MATUSZ AND D. NELSON

In this paper, and without prejudice to either of the pre-dispositions of most economists identified in the previous paragraph, we want to argue that, as a matter of positive political economy, fairness plays a non-trivial role in the politics of trade policy. In the next section, we argue that, as a matter of fact, widely held notions of fairness, that are identifiable at the micro level, have macro effects not only in the social and political systems, but even in the economy. Furthermore, as we argue in Section 3, these notions systematically constrain public officials in the construction and pursuit of trade policy. In the final section we provide concluding comments.

2. FAIRNESS IN THE ECONOMY AND SOCIETY

Stigler (1981, p. 176), in his 1980 Tanner Lecture, asserted that:

> in situations where self interest and ethical values with wide verbal allegiance are in con-
> flict . . . most of the time the self-interest-theory will win.

As a methodological assertion this has much to offer, as its overwhelming, and generally highly valuable, application throughout economics suggests. However, as an ontological statement, it is almost surely wrong.[2] It seems (at least to us) obvious, that relatively widely held notions of fairness have potentially powerful effects on political outcomes in general, and the outcomes of trade politics in particular. More specifically, such notions increase the influence of people seeking to achieve 'fair' outcomes and lower the influence of people seeking to achieve 'unfair' outcomes. The result is that there is a genuine stake in attaching a policy goal to such widely held notions of fairness as well as to affecting those notions (usually by appeal to even more primitive notions of fairness). This obvious claim is affected not at all by the equally obvious fact that the people most aggressively asserting fairness claims expect to benefit from general acceptance of those claims.[3] In this section we discuss the evidence that fairness considerations play a significant role in economics and politics generally, and then argue that these considerations merit more serious analysis in the specific case of trade policy.

Before considering more systematic evidence, it is worth noting that introspection should provide a first level of evidence. All of us have been children and

---

[2] It should be noted that many economists, who apply standard methods in much of their research, have long recognised the importance of extending that framework to include fairness considerations. Useful surveys can be found in Moulin (2003) and Zajac (1996). More generally, fairness considerations are obviously one of the types of 'non-welfaristic' information that scholars such as Sen (e.g. 1979) have long argued are necessary to a welfare economics sufficiently rich to be useful in many applied situations.

[3] This last fact does certainly mean that we cannot accept such claims at face value. It is, however, effective testimony to the potential importance of fairness claims to the final outcome of political conflict. Were this not the case, such language would long since have passed out of political use.

FAIRNESS AND THE POLITICAL ECONOMY OF TRADE   991

many of us have been parents. A considerable part of the socialisation process revolves precisely around the attempt to instil in children a sense of what the community considers fair behaviour and fair outcomes. These lessons virtually never leave us. We respond strongly to perceived unfairness – not only against ourselves, but to others. Even Economics Departments consider fairness in the allocation of both unpleasant tasks and rewards. Fairness considerations are often not dispositive, but they constitute constraints that need to be taken into account. These considerations recognise an irreducibly social element even in the context of what is essentially a market relationship. Some of the most compelling evidence offered by Akerlof (1982) and Akerlof and Yellen (1990) in support of the fair wage variant of efficiency wage theory involves a survey of personnel texts. Those texts reflect an explicit understanding of fairness considerations in wage-setting. In recent years a sizeable body of research has developed providing more systematic evidence that fairness considerations play a major role in the determination of even economic behaviour.

The evidence of fairness constraints in markets that is most closely linked to the evidence of introspection is given by surveys.[4] Important work has been done with respect to both markets for final goods and labour markets (e.g. Bewley, 1999). In the former it has been argued that, in cases where firms are concerned with repeat business, firms adopt pricing strategies that reflect a concern with widely held notions of fairness among consumers (Okun, 1981). This can result in both excess demand when upward price adjustment is constrained by fairness considerations as well as excess supply when consumers are punishing firms. Kahneman et al. (1986b) carried out household surveys seeking to identify these widely held norms. Based on the results of those surveys, the authors proposed a number of implications for Okun-type 'customer markets':

Proposition 1: When excess demand in a customer market is unaccompanied by increases in suppliers' costs, the market will fail to clear in the short run.

Proposition 2: When a single supplier provides a family of goods for which there is differential demand without corresponding variation of input costs, shortages of the most valued items will occur.

Proposition 3: Price changes will be more responsive to variations of costs than to variations of demand, and more responsive to cost increases than to cost decreases.

Proposition 4: Price decreases will often take the form of discounts rather than reductions in the list or posted price.

---

[4] For more detailed overviews of the empirical research on fairness constraints in markets, see Kahneman et al. (1986a) and Bewley (1999 and 2005).

992   C. DAVIDSON, S. MATUSZ AND D. NELSON

The authors find evidence supporting all of these propositions. Similar results are found in the much more extensive literature on fairness in the labour market context. Bewley (1999) reports extensive surveys of managers (246) and labour leaders (19) in the US in the early 1990s, when the US was in a recession. The core question was why wages were not cut during a recession. The answer had two parts, both interesting: first, the main source of resistance to wage cutting was management, not labour; and, more importantly, the main reason given by management for avoiding wage cutting was concern with morale. Furthermore, fairness considerations appear to play a major role in explaining the effect on morale. As Bewley's (2005) survey of this literature suggests, the great majority of work by economists is consistent with these conclusions.

An alternative source of evidence on the operation of fairness constraints comes from experimental economics.[5] From the earliest work on ultimatum games (Guth et al., 1982), experimental game theory has generated a steady flow of results that strongly suggest the operation of fairness constraints in economic environments. The ultimatum game involves a *proposer* making a take-it-or-leave-it offer of a division of some amount of money and a *responder* accepting or rejecting the offer. If the offer is accepted, the division is made; if the offer is rejected, neither player receives a positive payoff. The obvious Nash equilibrium in this game is for the proposer to offer the smallest positive payoff possible and for the responder to accept. As reported in Camerer (2003), in a wide range of treatments, proposers offer much larger shares (around 40 per cent of the total) and responders tend to reject offers below a threshold well above the minimum (around 20 per cent, with considerable variance). These experiments show that there are widely held and commonly understood notions of fairness that affect behaviour both because they are internalised (altruism) and enforced (punishment).[6]

One particularly important set of experiments from the perspective of this paper are those that relate to labour markets. An important research programme, developed by Ernst Fehr, with a large number of co-workers has developed experimental labour markets with the express purpose of evaluating (among other things) the role of fairness considerations in wage-setting (Fehr and Gächter, 2000). These experiments construct a horserace between a standard moral hazard model in which expectation of minimum effort induces firms to pay a minimum wage and the Solow-Akerlof-Yellen efficiency wage model (Solow,

---

[5] Excellent overviews of the experimental literature and its implications for economics and game theory can be found in: Camerer (2003, Ch. 2), Camerer and Thaler (1995), Fehr and Gächter (1998 and 2000), Fehr and Schmidt (2003) and Rabin (1993 and 2002).

[6] As Camerer notes, the power of internalised norms (altruism) without punishment is rather weak, though certainly not zero. This evidence comes from dictator games – i.e. games in which only the responder cannot reject offers. Closely related to the ultimatum games are both prisoners' dilemma and public good games, in which levels of cooperation are generally much higher than predicted by theory (Ledyard, 1995).

FAIRNESS AND THE POLITICAL ECONOMY OF TRADE   993

1979; Akerlof, 1982; and Akerlof and Yellen, 1990) in which firms pay a premium and are rewarded by high effort. The results are strongly consistent with the Solow-Akerlof-Yellen model and, importantly, with the survey evidence reported by Bewley and others.

Overall then: in the surveys, people assert that they would take actions based on considerations of fairness that would have macroeconomic consequences; and in the experiments people appear to take economically costly actions based on fairness considerations of precisely this type. When considered along with the evidence of introspection, one needs to be very narrow-minded indeed not to recognise the operation of fairness constraints even in the economy. It is important to note that this research does *not* suggest that fairness considerations are an alternative to self-interested behaviour, but that they complement it. In many cases little is lost by abstracting from fairness considerations. However, the presence of these effects, even where tightly constrained by competitive considerations, can have macroeconomic effects. When we turn to the political domain, where fairness considerations are less tightly constrained, we should not be surprised to find both stronger evidence of their presence, nor should we expect their macro-political consequences to be smaller.[7]

In the specific case of preferences over policy it does seem that fairness considerations play an important role independent of (i.e. not reducible to) considerations of pure self-interest. Some considerable effort has been expended by political scientists in the attempt to identify the politically relevant components of fairness. With respect to economic (as opposed to racial or gender) issues, most of this research has focused on issues of equality, redistribution and support for the welfare state. While most of this research is based on public opinion surveys, it is interesting to note that there is also a body of experimental research on these issues which is both broadly consistent with the survey research noted here and the experimental research on markets noted above (Frolich and Oppenheimer, 1993).

Political science research on the economic foundations of political evaluation has struggled to disentangle two sorts of effects: retrospective versus prospective

---

[7] The notion that the economy and civil society are characterised by fundamentally different normative structures under capitalism is widely shared by political economists of virtually all sorts. The notion that these two normative systems are in fundamental conflict in the context of genuinely democratic politics (i.e. politics that enfranchise the relatively risk averse and relatively poor) has been argued by analysts as different in their political commitments as Joseph Schumpeter (1942) and Karl Polanyi (1944). For Schumpeter and Polanyi this conflict was seen to be fatal to capitalism, but for later scholars the success of capitalism in the wake of the Depression and the Second World War – both at avoiding further depression and securing widespread legitimacy in the context of democratic politics – became the core research question for macro political economy. This research has identified a central role for the state in mediating this relationship and, more recently, has focused particularly on the redistributive (i.e. 'welfare') state. Most recently, this research has sought to identify the ways in which welfare states have supported increased globalisation. From the perspective of this paper, we are interested in the ways that claims about fairness emerge from civil society to underwrite claims for intervention in the economy.

994   C. DAVIDSON, S. MATUSZ AND D. NELSON

evaluation; and personal versus sociotropic evaluation. In all cases these refer to
characterisations of the ways that rational individuals evaluate the performance
of incumbent or potential governments.[8] It is the issue of personal versus
sociotropic voting that interests us here. Starting with important research by
Kinder and Kiewiet (1979 and 1981) a body of research developed which chal-
lenged the consensus on economic voting, the same consensus that currently
exists in research on the political economy of trade policy, that policies/candi-
dates were evaluated based on their (expected or retrospective) impact on individual well-being. Kinder and Kiewiet present micro-level survey research showing
that there was very little correlation between perceptions of individual well-being
and voting behaviour, developed the concept of *sociotropic voting*:

> In reaching political preferences, the prototypic sociotropic voter is influenced most of all by the
> *nation's* economic condition. Purely sociotropic citizens vote according to the country's pocket-
> book, not their own. Citizens moved by sociotropic information support candidates that appear
> to have furthered the nation's economic well-being and oppose candidates and parties that seem
> to threaten it. Thus the party in power suffers at the polls during hard times because voters act
> on their negative assessments of national economic conditions – quite apart from the trials and
> tribulations of their own economic lives. (Kinder and Kiewiet, 1981, p. 132)

Kinder and Kiewiet presented preliminary survey research supporting this hypothesis, and while successive research has fairly consistently found evidence of
personal voting, the current consensus would seem to support a strong role for
sociotropic evaluation as well (Mutz and Mondak, 1997; Funk and Garcia-Monet,
1997; and Gomez and Wilson, 2001).[9]

As a bridge to our discussion of fairness in the context of trade policy, it is
worth noting that while there is little systematic work seeking to identify the micro-
foundations of sociotropic evaluation, there is some reason to believe that unemployment plays a particularly central role. A provocative paper by Conover et al.
(1986), in addition to finding evidence consistent with both personal and sociotropic
evaluation, found that the public responded more quickly to information about
unemployment than to information about inflation. Specifically, the people in
their sample (a panel survey from 1981–1983) generally had a more accurate
perception of the state of unemployment than of inflation. Furthermore, even
people without accurate knowledge of the unemployment rate were generally
knowledgeable about its trend. By contrast, only those who had accurate knowledge of the inflation rate were also knowledgeable about the trend (although
there was evidence of learning over time). The authors suggest that, at least in the
early 1980s, the public appeared to be more responsive to unemployment than to

---

[8] While we are interested in the second of these pairs, it is interesting to note that in research on the
political economy of trade policy, theoretical analysis tends to assume prospective evaluation while
empirical research (usually implicitly) assumes retrospective evaluation.
[9] Some recent research has found quite strong evidence of other-regarding preferences in experimental settings in which agents vote on redistribution: Tyran and Sausgruber (forthcoming) and
Bolton and Ockenfels (2002).

FAIRNESS AND THE POLITICAL ECONOMY OF TRADE   995

inflation. This result finds more general support in the macroeconomic research on the relative effects of unemployment and inflation on reported happiness in the US and Europe (di Tella et al., 2001 and 2003).

These results are consistent with recent work, also based on opinion surveys, on the foundations of 'happiness'. There exists a substantial and growing empirical literature indicating that job loss generates a loss of utility or sense of well-being that goes beyond the loss attributed to the concurrent loss of income. The non-pecuniary value of employment appears to be quite large. Using panel survey data of German males aged 20–64, Winkelmann and Winkelmann (1998) find that the 'non-pecuniary costs of unemployment by far exceed the pecuniary costs associated with loss of income while unemployed'. As the authors suggest, 'employment is not only a source of income but also a provider of social relationships, identity in society and individual self-esteem'. In a separate study using data from three waves of the World Values Survey covering more than 30 countries, Helliwell (2003) compares the effect of job loss on individual well-being with a variety of other life events. For example, respondents were asked to evaluate their health on a scale of 1 to 5, with 1 representing very good health, and 5 representing very poor health. When including the health variable and employment status in the same regression (along with other control variables, including measures of income), Helliwell finds that unemployment reduces self-reported satisfaction by the same magnitude as a one-point reduction in self-reported health. Other research has found that satisfaction levels are related to the overall level of unemployment.[10]

Our reading of the literatures sketched in this section suggests that the public politics of economic issues are likely to be strongly conditioned by broad fairness considerations that are closely linked to concerns about unemployment. We now focus on the political economy of trade policy. Although there is quite compelling evidence that unemployment affects preferences over trade policy, there has been very little work to date seeking to make this link. At the same time, while the public rhetoric of trade policy often makes reference to fairness, there is literally no systematic research on the way fairness considerations affect the political economy of trade.

3. FAIRNESS IN THE DOMESTIC POLITICAL ECONOMY OF TRADE POLICY

We noted in the introduction that the language of fairness is extensively used in the public politics of international trade policy. In this section we do three

---

[10] A convenient, non-technical overview of this research can be found in Oswald (2003). Broad overviews of research on 'happiness' with some discussion of unemployment can be found in Darity and Goldsmith (1996), Frey and Stutzer (2001) and Layard (2005).

996   C. DAVIDSON, S. MATUSZ AND D. NELSON

things: first, we briefly discuss the apparent foundations of fairness-related concerns with trade policy; second, we illustrate the way that individual-level fairness concerns result in aggregate-level policy outcomes; and third, raise some broader issues in the positive analysis of fairness as applied to trade policy.

Among the many things that surely are relatively widely held components of a public notion of fairness, we focus on three here: exogeneity, unemployment and inequality.[11] Unlike outcomes that are the result of poor, or even unfortunate, choices by individuals, trade shocks appear to be essentially exogenous to those choices. Like epidemics, earthquakes and hurricanes, a trade shock has widespread effects that produce a sympathetic response from unaffected citizens. In all of these cases, claims in fairness to a positive response meet with considerable support from such citizens. This is precisely the basis of arguments for trade adjustment assistance (Lawrence and Litan, 1986).[12] Also like epidemics, earthquakes and hurricanes, the exogeneity of trade shocks also carries a strong implication of unpredictability. There is a sizeable literature that seeks to account for trade policy activism in terms of insurance motives and, while the insurance motive can be rooted in purely self-oriented preferences, general support for social insurance surely contains an element of concern for fairness as well.[13]

The role of unemployment in public evaluations of trade policy is well-documented. A standard finding in the public opinion literature on trade policy is that questions linking trade to unemployment systematically induce stronger support for protection than questions which make no such link (Scheve and Slaughter, 2001; Mayda and Rodrik, 2005; and Hiscox, 2004). This link is sufficiently strong that Hiscox (2004) characterises questions which make the link as an 'anti-trade' framing. Our discussion of unemployment in the previous

---

[11] Suranovic (2000) presents a catalogue of arguments that might be used to justify various trade policy positions as fair or unfair; and Risse (2005) provides an analysis of fairness claims in protection policy. Neither of these is a positive analysis in the sense suggested here – i.e. an attempt to understand the implications of widely held notions of fairness for equilibrium trade policy.

[12] The 'foreignness' of the shock is also clearly relevant. The current consensus among economists (if not among the public at large) is that technological change is at least as significant as trade/globalisation in producing income redistribution and insecurity, but, except for hardcore Luddites, there is very little resistance to technological change. We do not mean to suggest that there is no resistance to technological change. We can see a sort of diffuse Luddism in response to new retail technologies. In the middle of the twentieth century this showed up in attempts to regulate the activities of chain stores (e.g. resale price maintenance) and currently we see this in resistance to Wal-Mart. Nonetheless, these concerns seem considerably less potent than anti-globalisation concerns.

[13] The classic paper on insurance motives in trade is Newberry and Stiglitz (1984). Eaton and Grossman (1985), Cassing et al. (1986) and Dixit (1987 and 1989), among others, extend that analysis. In addition, there is an interesting body of work that seeks to understand the link between support for openness and the presence of a redistributive state in terms of insurance motives (e.g. Cameron, 1978; and Rodrik, 1998).

FAIRNESS AND THE POLITICAL ECONOMY OF TRADE 997

section suggests why this effect is so strong: we all understand that (involuntary) unemployment has large pecuniary and psychic effects. When linked to the claim that trade-related unemployment is unfair due to the generally unfair nature of trade shocks, it is clear why even people with little risk of unemployment still respond strongly to a framing in terms of unemployment. Hiscox's presentation of his results in terms of framing suggests that people have no fixed preference over trade policy, but rather can be manipulated due to framing effects. An alternative interpretation is that, if the politics of trade policy come to be seen as about unemployment, the general support for trade intervention will be high.[14]

Finally, one of the most fundamental foundations for public claims about fairness in Liberal society is (in)equality.[15] Conditional on a wide variety of contextual information, there is considerable evidence that people possess some preference for equality.[16] With specific reference to trade policy, Baldwin (1985) and Anderson and Baldwin (1987), among others, have noted that trade policy seems to protect relatively unskilled workers.[17] Since this result continues to hold even when the analysis controls for factors that might make such workers politically effective (e.g. unionisation), this seems strongly consistent with the operation of some kind of equality norm and this is precisely the interpretation given by Baldwin.

We now turn to a simple illustration of the impact of such preferences on equilibrium trade policy. Specifically, we will abstract from exogeneity and unemployment to illustrate this effect in the simplest environment – one in which the only issue is the presence or absence of a preference for equality. To do this we draw on recent research suggesting that a simple form of preference for fairness as equality rationalises many of the experimental results on this topic. Specifically, we will introduce Fehr/Schmidt preferences (Fehr and Schmidt, 1999, hereafter F/S) into Mayer's model of endogenous tariff formation (Mayer, 1984). We then discuss some extensions and implications.

---

[14] It is hard not to see some of the hysteria among trade economists on trade and wages, and trade and unemployment, as being driven by precisely this concern.

[15] The literature here is vast. An excellent discussion of many relevant issues is Nagel (1991) and Clayton and Williamson (2002) who collect a number of fundamental contributions that provide an excellent overview of the main positions. Miller (1992) provides an interesting overview that seeks to relate the empirical research on the actual beliefs of people about distributive justice to the philosophical literature. Philosophers often abstract from empirically relevant, but philosophically tangential issues and focus directly on equality, while empirical political scientists find the costs of such simplification too high, and thus focus on equity.

[16] Scholars like Hochschild (1981), Fong (2002) and Corneo and Grüner (2002) have pursued the positive analysis of public values of distributive equity and their implications for political behaviour.

[17] Standard surveys of the empirical political economy of trade by Baldwin (1984) and Rodrik (1995) both document the fact that, controlling for a variety of other factors, sectors which are characterised by low skill-intensity/low wages/labour intensity are relatively highly protected.

998   C. DAVIDSON, S. MATUSZ AND D. NELSON

Mayer (1984) considers a small open economy which produces two goods, from two factors, under standard Heckscher-Ohlin-Samuelson conditions. That is, production functions in each sector are characterised by constant returns to scale, with both factors essential in the production of both goods.[18] If we take the two factors of production to be skilled and unskilled labour, the standard no factor-intensity reversal assumption means that we can refer to one of the goods as the skill-intensive good and one as the (basic) labour-intensive good. These assumptions (along with differentiability and strict concavity of the production functions) ensure that there is a one-to-one relationship between relative commodity prices and relative factor prices and, more importantly, that the Stolper-Samuelson theorem holds:

Stolper-Samuelson theorem: Under the assumptions of the Heckscher-Ohlin-Samuelson model, a fall in the price of one of the goods lowers the return to the factor used intensively in the production of that good, relative to all other prices, and raises the return to the other factor, relative to all other prices.

To generate heterogeneity among agents, although all agents share identical, homothetic preferences, Mayer assumes that every agent is endowed with one unit of unskilled labour and some non-negative endowment of skilled labour.

The key to Mayer's analysis is that, under the assumptions of the model, every agent has an optimal self-interested tariff dependent only on her endowment. Under the assumptions that tariff revenues are redistributed according to and in proportion to the agent's income as a share of national income and that utility functions are strictly concave in the tariff, Mayer shows (p. 974) that: (1) any agent whose endowment is identical to that of the economy as a whole prefers the economy's optimal tariff (zero for the small economy case assumed here and in Mayer); (2) that the agent's optimal tariff is positive (negative) for agents well-endowed with the scarce (abundant) factor relative to the economy's endowment; and (3) this preference is increasing in the distance between the agent's endowment and the economy's endowment. Black's (1948) theorem is then used to identify the equilibrium tariff:

Black's theorem: In a majority rule contest in which preferences are single-peaked over a one-dimensional issue, the most preferred policy of the median voter cannot be defeated.[19]

---

[18] A bit more technically, in addition to linear homogeneity, we take both production functions to be twice differentiable and strictly concave.
[19] In political economy applications the usual mechanism is given by two-party competition over the issue space, and Hotelling's (1929) result that the Nash equilibrium of that game is for both parties to offer the most preferred point of the median voter. The classic development of spatial political competition is Downs (1957), and an admirably clear pedagogical treatment can be found in Enelow and Hinich (1984).

FAIRNESS AND THE POLITICAL ECONOMY OF TRADE   999

Once the median voter has been identified, we know from Mayer's result and Black's theorem that the optimal tariff of the median voter will be the equilibrium tariff for the economy. For our purposes, Mayer's essential result is that, as long as the median voter's proportional endowment of skilled to unskilled labour differs from that of the economy as a whole, the equilibrium policy will not be free trade.[20] Furthermore, to the extent that ownership of skill is skewed toward the right, the equilibrium will involve a positive tariff.

Now we suppose that, instead of strictly selfish preferences, all agents possess a preference for a fair distribution of income. Following Fehr and Schmidt (F/S, 1999) we assume that all agents have preferences of the following form:[21]

$$U^k(\mathbf{x}_k; \mathbf{x}_{-k}) = u^k(\mathbf{x}_k) - \alpha_k \int_{e_k}^{1} [u^h(\mathbf{x}_h) - u^k(\mathbf{x}_k)] f(k(e)) de$$

$$- \beta_k \int_{0}^{e_k} [u^k(\mathbf{x}_k) - u^h(\mathbf{x}_h)] f(k(e)) de, \qquad (1)$$

where $k, h \in H$ denote agents, $\mathbf{x}_k$ is the consumption vector of agent k, $\mathbf{x}_{-k}$ is a matrix of consumption bundles of all other agents, e_k is the endowment index for agents with a given endowment, and $f(k(e_k))$ is the proportion of agents with that endowment. Thus, in addition to the standard utility function, defined over own consumption, F/S preferences reflect a general distaste for inequality composed of both a dislike for others being better off than oneself (the term preceded by α_k) and for oneself being better off than others (the term preceded by β_k).[22] That is, for a given level of own utility from consumption, total individual utility is maximised if income could be redistributed such that everyone has the same

---

[20] It is one of the striking facts of this analysis, in this general case, the optimal choice of a social choice function (majority rule) which is Arrovian differs from the optimal choice of a Kaldor-Hicks social welfare function (i.e. free trade).

[21] We are grateful to Simon Gächter for suggesting that we consider these preferences. F/S are concerned with accounting for experimental results in which some good is simply divided, so their utility function is defined over a scalar quantity allocated to the individual, say x_k and its allocation to others x_h. Because we assume identical preferences, agents are assumed able to make the relevant comparisons in utilities. In addition, we have taken advantage of the natural ordering of incomes, and utilities, induced by our assumptions on agent endowments and identical preferences. That is, since all agents have the same preferences, the self-regarding utilities $u^k(\mathbf{x}_k)$ differ only as a function of incomes and incomes rise with the size of the skill endowment. Under free trade and no redistributive policy, an agent's position in the income distribution and the utility distribution is given by her endowment ratio. Given this, we can associate every agent with their endowment ratio and, following Mayer, associate this ratio with an index, e, such that $k(e) = k(0) = 0$, $k(e) = k(1) = k^{max}$, and $\partial k / \partial e > 0$.

[22] While it is not essential for our purposes, F/S assume that $\beta_k \leq \alpha_k$ and $0 \leq \beta_k < 1$. That is: agents dislike being worse off than others more than they dislike being better off than others; and that no agents like to be better off than others. The first of these seems sensible given the general concern with fairness; the latter is surely counter-factual, but is a useful simplification in an attempt to evaluate the impact of preferences for fairness at the aggregate level.

1000   C. DAVIDSON, S. MATUSZ AND D. NELSON

utility from consumption (i.e. the second and third r.h.s. terms in (1) are zero) without reducing the economy's total income.

We have already noted that, in the Mayer (strictly self-regarding preferences) model, free trade will only obtain for a small economy if the median voter happens to have the same endowment ratio as the economy. Under the assumption that the median voter is unskilled relative to the aggregate endowment (i.e. the skill endowment is skewed to the right) in a skill-abundant economy, this implies that the equilibrium tariff will be positive. We now argue that an economy with F/S preferences will have a higher endogenous tariff than the Mayer economy. Note that the identity of the median voter will not change – this is determined by the natural ordering of agent endowments. Since all agents possess one unit of unskilled labour and some non-negative endowment of skilled labour, all agents to the left of the median voter are poorer than the median voter and all agents to the right are richer. Furthermore, since, via the Stolper-Samuelson theorem, an increase in the tariff transfers income from skilled to unskilled labour, the welfare of the median voter is raised both because the income of all agents to her right are reduced and because the income of all agents to her left are raised. Thus a small increase in the tariff from the self-regarding optimum will reduce aggregate inequality and raise the welfare of the median voter, so the equilibrium tariff must be higher under F/S preferences than under self-regarding preferences. There is also, of course, an aggregate efficiency cost that will work against increasing the tariff; however, it is notable that experimental work by Bolton and Ockenfels (2002) suggests that agents may generally have a rather strong preference for equity relative to efficiency.[23]

A similar argument applies to the case of a trade shock. That is, suppose that our initial state is an equilibrium with a tariff and F/S preferences. For some reason, say China liberalises its trade regime and the world price of the unskilled good falls. Now the Stolper-Samuelson effects redistribute income generally from unskilled labour to skilled labour and specifically from agents to the left of the median voter ('poor' agents) to agents to the right of the median voter ('rich' agents). By the same argument as in the previous paragraph, a small increase in the tariff will undo some of the negative distributional effect. This is just a specific version of what Corden (1974 and 1986) called the conservative social welfare function argument for protection.[24]

---

[23] This is also the opening wedge of the argument for the superiority of using an alternative instrument to secure the welfare optimum – i.e. some combination of free trade and a less distorting means of transferring income. As a practical matter, it is probably the case that stably low tariffs in the post-Second World War era are associated with the presence of a redistributive welfare state for more-or-less this reason. See, among others, for an argument of this sort, in addition to the work cited in footnote 13, Bordo et al. (1999).

[24] Also see Deardorff (1993) for a development of the logic of a conservative social welfare function.

FAIRNESS AND THE POLITICAL ECONOMY OF TRADE   1001

4. CONCLUDING COMMENTS

It is particularly easy to illustrate the effect of a preference for a fair income distribution, or a fairness-based insurance motive as with the above version of the conservative social welfare function, but it should be clear that a similar sort of analysis could be generated for a social concern with unemployment in a model with equilibrium unemployment. However, this approach simply illustrates an effect in a simple, reduced-form model of a political economy. The great virtue of the referendum model is its simplicity, but if we are trying to understand the role of fairness it has the fundamental weakness of portraying the politics as essentially public. However, one of the most distinctive attributes of the politics of trade policy in the GATT/WTO era is precisely that those politics are not public. Unlike the politics of the tariff during the era of classic tariff politics (essentially from the end of Reconstruction until the Reciprocal Trade Agreements Act of 1934), trade policy is an 'inside the beltway' issue. This provides much less opportunity for trade politics to be *about* fairness. Inside the beltway, the politics of trade is about balancing interests with very little rhetoric about fairness. In a sense, public deployment of the language of fairness in this context (e.g. fair trade laws, rhetoric of 'level playing fields' and trade adjustment assistance) is more about keeping the public out of the politics of trade than delivering anything that is identifiably about fairness.[25]

If, and as, the politics of trade policy become public politics, the role of fairness language will become much more important. In the context of essentially technical politics like those related to trade policy, public fairness claims constitute a first step in the process of making those politics more public, more democratic and less predictable. The purpose of a fairness claim in the public political discourse is to increase the political weight of agents who are, in some sense, losing the political struggle (either as direct participants or as a result of being marginalised).[26] In an era of striking Liberality and relatively rapid globalisation, it is not surprising that it is opponents of globalisation who seek to use the language of fairness to increase their influence. We are only at the very beginning of a systematic understanding of the public politics of trade policy, but it seems likely that an understanding of the politics of fairness will be central to any advance in this area.

---

[25] It is interesting, and essential, to note that the reason for keeping the public out is to support a more Liberal trade policy than could be sustained under public determination of trade policy. Thus, as Pastor (1981) and Destler (2005), among others, have argued, when the politics of protection threaten to become public, political elites can point to these institutional commitments to fairness, thus deflecting that pressure. This particular subtlety is usually lost on us as economists. We tend to see fairness language as empowering protection seekers even inside the beltway.

[26] This is a specific instance of Schattschneider's (1960) classic account of the unpredictability of democratic political struggle – as opposed to the much greater predictability of what he called 'group politics'.

1002   C. DAVIDSON, S. MATUSZ AND D. NELSON

REFERENCES

Akerlof, G. (1982), 'Labor Contracts as Partial Gift Exchange', *Quarterly Journal of Economics*, **97**, 4, 543–69.

Akerlof, G. and J. Yellen (1990), 'The Fair Wage-effort Hypothesis and Unemployment', *Quarterly Journal of Economics*, **105**, 2, 255–84.

Anderson, K. and R. Baldwin (1987), 'The Political Market for Protection in Industrial Countries', in A. El-Agraa (ed.), *Protection, Cooperation, Integration and Development: Essays in Honor of Professor Hiroshi Kitamura* (London: Macmillan), 20–36.

Baldwin, R. (1984), 'Trade Policies in Developed Countries', in R. Jones and P. Kenen (eds.), *Handbook of International Economics, Vol. 1* (Amsterdam: Elsevier), 571–619.

Baldwin, R. (1985), *The Political Economy of U.S. Import Policy* (Cambridge, MA: MIT Press).

Bewley, T. (1999), *Why Wages Don't Fall During a Recession* (Cambridge, MA: Harvard University Press).

Bewley, T. (2005), 'Fairness, Reciprocity and Wage Rigidity', in H. Gintis, S. Bowles, R. Boyd and E. Fehr (eds.), *The Moral Sentiments: Origins, Evidence and Policy* (Cambridge, MA: MIT Press).

Black, D. (1948), 'On the Rationale of Group Decision-making', *Journal of Political Economy*, **56**, 1, 23–34.

Bolton, G. and A. Ockenfels (2002), 'The Behavioral Tradeoff between Efficiency and Equity when a Majority Rules', Working Paper (Max Planck Institute for Research into Economic Systems).

Bordo, M., B. Eichengreen and D. A. Irwin (1999), 'Is Globalization Today Really Different than Globalization a Hundred Years Ago?', *Brookings Trade Forum – 1999* (Washington, DC: Brookings Institution Press), 1–72.

Camerer, C. (2003), *Behavioral Game Theory: Experiments in Strategic Interaction* (Princeton, NJ: Princeton University Press).

Camerer, C. and R. Thaler (1995), 'Ultimatums, Dictators, and Manners', *Journal of Economic Perspectives*, **9**, 2, 209–19.

Cameron, D. (1978), 'The Expansion of the Public Economy: A Comparative Analysis', *American Political Science Review*, **72**, 4, 1243–61.

Cassing, J., A. Hillman and N. van Long (1986), 'Risk Aversion, Terms of Trade Uncertainty and Social Consensus Trade Policy', *Oxford Economic Papers*, **38**, 2, 234–42.

Clayton, M. and A. Williamson (eds.) (2002), *The Ideal of Equality* (Basingstoke: Palgrave Macmillan).

Conover, P., S. Feldman and K. Knight (1986), 'Judging Inflation and Unemployment: The Origins of Retrospective Evaluations', *Journal of Politics*, **48**, 3, 565–88.

Corden, W. M. (1974), *Trade Policy and Economic Welfare* (Oxford: Oxford University Press).

Corden, W. M. (1986), 'Policies Towards Market Disturbance', in R. Snape (ed.), *Issues in World Trade Policy* (London: Macmillan).

Corneo, G. and H. P. Grüner (2002), 'Individual Preferences for Political Redistribution', *Journal of Public Economics*, **83**, 1, 83–107.

Darity, W. and A. Goldsmith (1996), 'Social Psychology, Unemployment and Macroeconomics', *Journal of Economic Perspectives*, **10**, 1, 121–46.

Deardorff, A. (1993), 'Safeguards and the Conservative Social Welfare Function', in H. Kierzkowski (ed.), *Protection and Competition in International Trade* (Oxford: Blackwell), 22–40.

Destler, I. M. (2005), *American Trade Politics* (4th edn., Washington, DC: Institute for International Economics).

Downs, A. (1957), *An Economic Theory of Democracy* (New York: Harper).

Di Tella, R., R. J. MacCulloch and A. J. Oswald (2001), 'Preferences Over Inflation and Unemployment: Evidence from Surveys of Happiness', *American Economic Review*, **91**, 1, 335–41.

Di Tella, R., R. J. MacCulloch and A. J. Oswald (2003), 'The Macroeconomics of Happiness', *Review of Economics and Statistics*, **85**, 4, 809–27.

FAIRNESS AND THE POLITICAL ECONOMY OF TRADE 1003

Dixit, A. (1987), 'Trade and Insurance with Moral Hazard', *Journal of International Economics*, **23**, 3/4, 201–20.

Dixit, A. (1989), 'Trade and Insurance with Adverse Selection', *Review of Economic Studies*, **56**, 2, 235–48.

Eaton, J. and G. Grossman (1985), 'Tariffs as Insurance: Optimal Commercial Policy when Domestic Markets are Incomplete', *Canadian Journal of Economics*, **18**, 2, 258–72.

Enelow, J. and M. Hinich (1984), *The Spatial Theory of Voting: An Introduction* (Cambridge: Cambridge University Press).

Fehr, E. and S. Gächter (1998), 'Reciprocity and Economics: The Economic Implications of *Homo Reciprocans*', *European Economic Review*, **42**, 3/4/5, 845–59.

Fehr, E. and S. Gächter (2000), 'Fairness and Retaliation: The Economics of Reciprocity', *Journal of Economic Perspectives*, **14**, 3, 159–81.

Fehr, E. and K. Schmidt (1999), 'A Theory of Fairness, Competition, and Cooperation', *Quarterly Journal of Economics*, **114**, 3, 817–68.

Fehr, E. and K. Schmidt (2003), 'Theories of Fairness and Reciprocity: Evidence and Economic Applications', in M. Dewatripont, L. Hansen and S. Turnovsky (eds.), *Advances in Economics and Econometrics – 8th World Congress* (Cambridge: Cambridge University Press), 208–57.

Fong, C. (2002), 'Social Preferences, Self-interest and the Demand for Redistribution', *Journal of Public Economics*, **82**, 2, 225–46.

Frey, B. and A. Stutzer (2001), *Happiness and Economics: How the Economy and Institutions Affect Human Well-being* (Princeton, NJ: Princeton University Press).

Frolich, N. and J. Oppenheimer (1993), *Choosing Justice: An Experimental Approach to Ethical Theory* (Berkeley, CA: University of California Press).

Funk, C. and P. Garcia-Monet (1997), 'The Relationship between Personal and National Concerns in Public Perceptions about the Economy', *Political Research Quarterly*, **50**, 2, 317–42.

Gomez, B. and J. M. Wilson (2001), 'Political Sophistication and Economic Voting in the American Electorate: A Theory of Heterogeneous Attribution', *American Journal of Political Science*, **45**, 4, 899–914.

Güth, W., R. Schmittberger and B. Schwarze (1982), 'An Experimental Analysis of Ultimatum Bargaining', *Journal of Economic Behavior and Organization*, **3**, 4, 367–88.

Helliwell, J. F. (2003), 'How's Life? Combining Individual and National Variables to Explain Subjective Well-being', *Economic Modelling*, **20**, 2, 331–60.

Hiscox, M. (2004), 'Through a Glass and Darkly: Framing Effects and Individuals' Attitudes Towards International Trade' (Manuscript, Harvard University).

Hochschild, J. (1981), *What's Fair: American Beliefs about Distributive Justice* (Cambridge, MA: Harvard University Press).

Hotelling, H. (1929), 'Stability in Competition', *Economic Journal*, **39**, 41–57.

Kahneman, D., J. Knetsch and R. Thaler (1986a), 'Fairness and the Assumptions of Economics', *Journal of Business*, **59**, 4, Pt. 2, s285–s300.

Kahneman, D., J. Knetsch and R. Thaler (1986b), 'Fairness as a Constraint on Profit Seeking: Entitlements in the Market', *American Economic Review*, **76**, 4, 728–41.

Kaplow, L. and S. Shavell (2002), *Fairness versus Welfare* (Cambridge, MA: Harvard University Press).

Kinder, D. and D. R. Kiewiet (1979), 'Economic Discontent and Political Behavior: The Role of Personal Grievances and Collective Economic Judgements in Congressional Voting', *American Journal of Political Science*, **23**, 3, 495–527.

Kinder, D. and D. R. Kiewiet (1981), 'Sociotropic Politics: The American Case', *British Journal of Politics*, **11**, 2, 129–61.

Lawrence, R. and R. Litan (1986), *Saving Free Trade: A Pragmatic Approach* (Washington, DC: Brookings Institution Press).

Layard, R. (2005), *Happiness: Lessons from a New Science* (London: Penguin).

Ledyard, J. (1995), 'Public Goods: A Survey of Experimental Research', in J. Kagel and A. Roth (eds.), *The Handbook of Experimental Economics* (Princeton, NJ: Princeton University Press), 111–94.

1004   C. DAVIDSON, S. MATUSZ AND D. NELSON

Mayda, A. M. and D. Rodrik (2005), 'Why Are Some People (and Countries) More Protectionist than Others?', *European Economic Review*, 49, 6, 1393–430.

Mayer, W. (1984), 'Endogenous Tariff Formation', *American Economic Review*, 74, 5, 970–85.

Miller, D. (1992), 'Distributive Justice: What People Think', *Ethics*, 102, 3, 555–93.

Moulin, H. (2003), *Fair Division and Collective Welfare* (Cambridge, MA: MIT Press).

Mutz, D. and J. Mondak (1997), 'Dimensions of Sociotropic Behavior: Group-based Judgements of Fairness and Well-being', *American Journal of Political Science*, 41, 1, 284–308.

Nagel, T. (1991), *Equality and Partiality* (New York: Oxford University Press).

Newberry, D. and J. Stiglitz (1984), 'Pareto Inferior Trade', *Review of Economic Studies*, 51, 1, 1–12.

Okun, A. (1981), *Prices and Quantities: A Macroeconomic Analysis* (Washington, DC: Brookings Institution Press).

Oswald, A. (2003), 'How Much do External Factors Affect Well-being?', *The Psychologist*, 16, 3, 140–41.

Pastor, R. (1981), *Congress and the Politics of U.S. Foreign Economic Policy* (Berkeley, CA: University of California Press).

Polanyi, K. (1944), *The Great Transformation* (New York: Rinehart).

Rabin, M. (1993), 'Incorporating Fairness in Game Theory and Economics', *American Economic Review*, 83, 5, 1281–302.

Rabin, M. (2002), 'A Perspective on Psychology and Economics', *European Economic Review*, 46, 4/5, 657–85.

Risse, M. (2005), 'Fairness in Trade' (Manuscript, Kennedy School of Government).

Rodrik, D. (1995), 'Political Economy of Trade Policy', in G. Grossman and K. Rogoff (eds.), *Handbook of International Economics, Vol. 3* (Amsterdam: Elsevier), 1457–94.

Rodrik, D. (1998), 'Why Do More Open Economies Have Bigger Governments?', *Journal of Political Economy*, 106, 5, 997–1032.

Scheve, K. and M. Slaughter (2001), *Globalization and the Perceptions of American Workers* (Washington, DC: Institute for International Economics).

Schumpeter, J. (1942), *Capitalism, Socialism and Democracy* (New York: Harper & Brothers).

Sen, A. (1979), 'Personal Utilities and Public Judgements: or What's Wrong with Welfare Economics?', *Economic Journal*, 89, 355, 537–58.

Solow, R. (1979), 'Another Possible Source of Wage Stickiness', *Journal of Macroeconomics*, 1, 1, 79–82.

Stigler, G. (1981), 'Economics or Ethics?', in S. McMurrin (ed.), *Tanner Lectures in Human Value, Vol. 2* (Cambridge: Cambridge University Press), 145–91. [Also Chapters 1–3 in *The Economist As Preacher, and Other Essays*, Chicago: University of Chicago Press.]

Suranovic, S. (2000), 'A Positive Analysis of Fairness with Applications to International Trade', *The World Economy*, 23, 3, 283–307.

Tyran, J.-R. and R. Sausgruber (forthcoming), 'A Little Fairness May Induce a Lot of Redistribution in Democracy', *European Economic Review*.

Winkelmann, L. and R. Winkelmann (1998), 'Why are the Unemployed So Unhappy? Evidence from Panel Data', *Economica*, 65, 257, 1–15.

Zajac, E. (1996), *The Political Economy of Fairness* (Cambridge, MA: MIT Press).

ECONOMICS & POLITICS   DOI: 10.1111/j.1468-0343.2011.00393.x
Volume 24   March 2012   No. 1

A BEHAVIORAL MODEL OF UNEMPLOYMENT, SOCIOTROPIC CONCERNS, AND THE POLITICAL ECONOMY OF TRADE POLICY

CARL DAVIDSON*, STEVEN J. MATUSZ AND DOUGLAS NELSON

We present a behavioral model in which agents are concerned about the scarring effects from unemployment for themselves and others and explore the manner in which unemployment matters for trade policy. We derive three policy implications: the government has an incentive to increase employment in sectors characterized by "good jobs," where the good job/bad job characterization depends on an industry's job creation and destruction rates; the government has an incentive to pursue this policy in a gradual fashion by channeling new and unemployed workers into the appropriate sector; and opposition to trade liberalization can be reduced by welfare state policies.

Customs tariffs which implied profits for capitalist and wages for workers meant, ultimately, security against unemployment, stabilization of regional conditions, assurance against liquidation of industries and, perhaps most of all, the avoidance of that painful loss of status which inevitably accompanies transference to a job at which a man is less skilled and experienced than at his own. (Polanyi, 1944)

When economists think about the labor market effects of trade, we think about wages; when everyone else thinks about the labor market effects of trade, they think about jobs. Thinking in terms of wages, especially as represented by generalizations of the Stolper–Samuelson theorem as embodied in the mandated wage regression approach, we have pretty much convinced ourselves that trade is essentially irrelevant to labor markets (Slaughter, 2000). Unfortunately, this framework has nothing to say about jobs.[1] This is particularly problematic when it comes to the positive analysis of trade policy, where there is little direct evidence that relative wage effects matter at all and considerable evidence that unemployment matters a great deal.[2] Thus, in this article, we build on earlier work that analyzes the link between trade and unemployment to provide a new analysis of trade policy and unemployment.

Our main goal is to draw on recent work in behavioral economics in order to examine the implications of unemployment for the design of trade policies. Specifically, we argue that, in addition to affecting individual wellbeing, unemployment plays a central role in citizen evaluation of government performance. The economic and psychological foundations for this centrality are obvious from introspection and increasingly supported by empirical research. Most obviously, it should be clear that unemployment

---

*Corresponding author: Carl Davidson, Department of Economics, 110 Marshall-Adams Hall, Michigan State University, East Lansing, MI 48824, USA. E-mail: davidso4@msu.edu

[1]Not only is it the case that full employment is an equilibrium condition, but in the even case (i.e., the number of factors is equal to the number of goods) that is generally deployed, the zero profit conditions, from which the Stolper–Samuelson theorem is derived, are separable from the full employment conditions.
[2]We discuss the evidence supporting this below, but the basic fact is that unemployment variables are always significant in macro tariff regressions. In addition, the public opinion data, which are often taken as providing evidence supporting a significant role for relative price effects (e.g., Slaughter, 2000), are ambiguous in this regard, while it is widely agreed that framing questions in terms of unemployment has the effect of increasing protectionist sentiment significantly (Hiscox, 2006; Scheve and Slaughter, 2001a, 2001b).

can be psychologically, as well as economically, traumatic. Current research suggests that the economic consequences of job loss are nontrivial.[3] Perhaps more importantly, this is consistent with considerable evidence in the growing literature on the economics of happiness which suggests that job loss is considered one of life's most traumatic events (e.g., Winkelmann and Winkelmann, 1998; Helliwell, 2003; Oswald, 2003; and/ or Layard, 2005). Some of this evidence is quite startling. For example, Helliwell (2003) reports that in surveys in which subjects were asked to rank the impact of certain life events on their wellbeing, unemployment ranked as more traumatic than separation or divorce from a spouse! There is also evidence that unemployment brings with it significant health risks – layoffs more than double the risk of heart attack and stroke for older workers and workers losing their jobs face an 83% greater chance of developing stress related health problems.[4] Furthermore, evidence indicates that even short jobless spells have longer-term scarring effects on workers.[5] Additional support for our claim that individuals, in particular in their role as voters, show more concern for unemployment than for price (and wage) effects comes from surveys of attitudes toward (and knowledge of) the macroeconomic environment suggesting that voters are more concerned about (and aware of) unemployment than inflation (Conover et al., 1986; Di Tella et al., 2001, 2003).

Our interpretation of the evidence is that in addition to the consequential reduction in income, unemployment generates two sources of welfare losses for individuals. First, there is a scarring effect from losing one's job that lowers utility even if reemployment is found relatively quickly. Second, individuals are concerned about the employment risk faced by others – through some combination of empathy rooted in introspection on the economic and psychic costs of unemployment, and social attachment to a community – and thus, suffer a loss in welfare when others are unemployed. We refer to the latter as a "sociotropic" or "fairness" concern and argue that this is the effect that most individuals are primarily concerned about when they refer to "fair trade."[6] We note here that calls for "fair trade" are common in the public political discourse about trade policy, and there is considerable evidence that fairness considerations have played a significant role in shaping trade policy for generations (e.g., Stiglitz and Charlton, 2005). For example, legal structures that provide protection through administered mechanisms are commonly referred to as "fair trade laws." In addition, fairness is often cited as a primary justification for policies aimed at aiding workers displaced by changes in trade patterns. Examples of this would include trade

---

[3]See Jacobson et al. (1993); or, with reference to job losses associated with international trade, see Kletzer (2001). In addition, in a recent paper Krishna and Senses (2009) find that trade has a significant effect on lifetime income risk. While their focus is on income, the fact that this risk derives largely from switching industries suggests that employment risk plays a part as in the work of Kletzer.

[4]See "At Plant Closing, Ordeal Included Heart Attacks" in the *New York Times*, Feb. 24, 2010.

[5]The scarring effects relate to both future labor market performance (Arulampalam, 2001; Gregg, 2001; Gregg and Tominey, 2005; Gregory and Jukes, 2001) and to future "happiness" (Clark et al., 2001; Lucas et al., 2004).

[6]The term "sociotropic" comes from political science and refers to other-regarding preferences, usually in the context of voting. Specifically, that voters are concerned with *national* wellbeing when casting their votes. The term was used in this context originally by Kinder and Kiewiet (1979, 1981) and studied extensively (e.g., Cowden and Hartley, 1992; Funk and Garcia-Monet, 1997; Hibbs, 1993; Kiewiet, 1983; Kinder et al., 1989; Lanoue, 1994; Lewis-Beck, 1988; MacKuen et al., 1992; Markus, 1988, 1992; Romero and Stambough, 1996). Two important papers for us are Mutz and Mondak (1997), who provide a strong link between sociotropic evaluation and fairness, and Mansfield and Mutz (2009), who focus directly on attitudes toward international trade. The results overwhelmingly show that both self-regarding and national-level sociotropic evaluation are central to individual political decision-making.

74   DAVIDSON ET AL.

adjustment assistance (e.g., Lawrence and Litan, 1986) and calls for wage insurance (e.g., Kletzer and Litan, 2001). Survey research also indicates that the public is unlikely to support liberalization if there is a perception that some workers will be unfairly harmed by such a policy (Hiscox, 2006; Mayda and Rodrik, 2005; Scheve and Slaughter, 2001a, 2001b).[7] It is our contention that such concerns are rooted in a view that job losses tied to changes in trade patterns are somehow "unfair" and that society has an obligation to reduce the hardship associated with such life-changing events.

We therefore present a behavioral model in which agents are concerned about the scarring effects from unemployment both for themselves and for others. We then explore the manner in which unemployment matters for trade policy. We show that this framework provides a natural representation of the widely held notion that long-lasting jobs are "good jobs," with the characterization of a job as "good" or "bad" tied to an industry's job creation and job destruction rates. The model yields three policy implications: the government has an incentive to increase employment in sectors characterized by "good jobs"; the government has an incentive to pursue this policy in a gradual fashion by channeling new and unemployed workers into the good job sector; and opposition to trade liberalization can be reduced by welfare state policies. We argue that there is at least indirect evidence consistent with each of these propositions.

In the next section, we introduce our behavioral model and explore its implications for trade policy in the presence of scarring effects and sociotropic concerns tied to employment risk. In Section 3, we examine the link between openness and the generosity of the welfare state.

This article is not the first to deal with international trade and unemployment. Nearly 40 years ago, Brecher (1974) used a minimum wage to introduce unemployment into a standard trade model and Davidson and Matusz, along with their coauthors, have developed trade models with search generated unemployment since the mid-1980s.[8] In this vein, there are three papers that offer results on unemployment and trade policy. Davidson et al. (1999) embed search frictions into an HOS model and examine the link between trade and factor returns. They show that the return to employed factors is a convex combination of Stolper–Samuelson and Ricardo–Viner forces with the weights tied to the sectoral turnover rates. The Ricardo–Viner forces are generated by the search costs that must be incurred to find employment. Since these costs are relatively low in high turnover industries, factor returns are mainly driven by Stolper–Samuelson forces in such industries. In contrast, when turnover rates are relatively low, employed factors have strong ties to their industries and the Ricardo–Viner forces dominate. The link between preferences over trade policies and unemployment then follows directly from the fact that the sectoral unemployment rates are determined by the turnover rates.

---

[7]The Hiscox study is particularly relevant for our purposes since it shows that protectionist arguments couched in terms of job destruction significantly increase opposition to trade liberalization *and* that such arguments clearly trump pro-trade arguments couched in terms of job creation and lower prices. While Hiscox focuses on framing as the key issue, we believe that there are additional substantive issues tied to attitudes toward unemployment and trade policy that are revealed by this study. We provide a more detailed analysis of this issue in Section 2 of our working paper precursor to this article, Davidson et al. (2010).

[8]In addition to Davidson et al. (1987, 1988), work on trade and unemployment includes, but is not limited to, Copeland (1989), Brecher (1992), Matusz (1994, 1996), and Davis and Harrigan (2011) who model unemployment using efficiency wages; Kreickemeier and Nelson (2006) and Egger and Kreickemeier (2008, 2009) who use models with fair wages constraints; Davis (1998) who assumes minimum wages; and Helpman and Itskhoki (2010) and Felbermayr et al. (2011) who use search models.

UNEMPLOYMENT AND TRADE POLICY   75

Costinot (2009) uses a model with search frictions and specific human capital to examine the relationship between trade policy and unemployment. In his model, the government uses trade policy to reallocate workers and he shows that any parameter that is positively (negatively) related to unemployment is also positively (negatively) related to trade taxes. Costinot's results are driven by the nature of the externalities generated by search activity; an issue that is present in our analysis as well. Finally, Davidson et al. (1994) develop an overlapping-generations model with search and show that changes in employment transfer income across generations and produce a social surplus. The size of the surplus varies across sectors, with job creation and job destruction rates playing key roles, therefore having implications for trade policy. It is worth noting that the results of Costinot (2009) and Davidson et al. (1994) identify optimal policy as a response to a distortion in traditional welfare-theoretic terms, while the current paper emphasizes political economic (i.e., noneconomic) considerations.[9]

In addition to work on the link between trade policy and unemployment, there is a small body of work on the link between unemployment and the politics of trade.[10] To start with, macro tariff regressions consistently find a positive link between the unemployment rate and protection (e.g., Hall et al., 1998; Magee and Young, 1987; Takacs, 1981).[11] A recent paper by Magee et al. (2005) tests the predictions of Davidson et al. (1999) on the link between sectoral unemployment, preferences over trade policy and lobbying behavior. The empirical work reported in that paper is supportive of a link between sectoral turnover rates and political activity that plays a central role in the theory developed in this article. An important early paper by Wallerstein (1987) developed an analysis of the link between unemployment and demand for protection based on a model with unions that are active in bargaining on the wage and in the politics of protection. The union wage is above market clearing and, thus, creates sectoral unemployment that generates a demand for protection. Where Wallerstein, like Magee, Davidson and Matusz, is primarily concerned with the demand side of the market for protection, recent work by Bradford (2006) embeds a bargaining model in a model of labor market search like that of Davidson and Matusz, and political lobbying derived from that of Grossman and Helpman (1994).[12] Bradford's model

---

[9]It is worth noting that in Bradford (2006) the government uses trade policy to buy the votes of the unemployed. Thus, Bradford's explanation is also political.

[10]The Grossman–Helpman (1994) "Protection for Sale (PFS)" model, which has become the workhorse of current theoretical and empirical research on the political economy of trade, is characterized not only by full employment, but a fixed wage for all labor in the economy. Thus, contrary to the empirical and policy literatures, labor issues cannot play a role in the determination of trade policy.

[11]The purpose of macro tariff regressions is generally not to examine the effect of unemployment, in fact unemployment is usually one of several variables intended to capture business cycle effects. All of these variables are quite closely correlated. In addition to econometric studies, a wide range of policy comments draw a connection between cyclical downturn and protection, and these comments virtually always stress that the variable of most political significance is unemployment. This link will figure prominently in our analysis of the link between unemployment and public support for protection.

[12]An earlier paper by Bradford (2003) focused on the link between *employment* and protection, in an economy characterized by sectoral minimum wages and unemployment. He finds that protection is increasing in sectoral employment, but not output (as predicted by the Grossman-Helpman model). A recent paper by Matschke and Sherlund (2006) focuses on unionization and labor mobility, but is not directly concerned with unemployment. Interestingly, unions and specific capital are allowed to lobby independently or together. The empirical results are strongly supportive of their model relative to the basic Grossman–Helpman model with passive labor.

76   DAVIDSON ET AL.

predicts that protection should be decreasing in sectoral turnover and increasing in unionization, both of which are supported in his empirical work.[13]

Interestingly, the majority of this research treats the essential link between unemployment and trade policy as being mediated by lobbying (primarily following Grossman and Helpman). In this article, we argue that this focus may be misguided. Greenaway and Nelson (2010) develop a distinction, due originally to Schattschneider (1960), between group and democratic politics. The basic idea is that the group politics (lobbying) of trade policy have primarily to do with distributive politics (and thus very little to do with unemployment). By contrast, democratic politics are public politics and when trade policy becomes the focus of democratic politics, it is likely that activists on the issue will seek to link trade to unemployment. As a result, in an effort to keep trade policy from becoming a focus of public politics, and in addition to the general attempt to keep unemployment low, politicians will attempt to be seen as responding to trade-linked unemployment with trade-linked policies. This suggests that a preliminary approach to modeling the connection between unemployment and trade policy can fruitfully focus on the link between unemployment and aggregate social welfare.

2. SCARRING, SOCIOTROPIC CONCERNS, AND TRADE POLICY

In this section we introduce a simple model with search generated unemployment that takes into account both the scarring effects of unemployment and sociotropic concerns about employment risk faced by others. After the model has been developed, we explore the implications of our behavioral assumptions for trade policy.

The novelty of our approach is the manner in which we treat preferences. To model the scarring effect of unemployment, we assume that each agent suffers a disutility of s while unemployed. Moreover, agents care about the welfare of others, resulting in an additional welfare loss which is increasing in the unemployment rate (μ) that captures agents' sociotropic concerns. However, the level of hardship associated with unemployment depends on the generosity of the welfare state. This generosity is measured by the level of support provided to unemployed workers by the government (unemployment compensation), which we denote by b. The total loss in utility for each agent due to their sociotropic concerns (i.e., the employment risk face by others) is therefore measured by $\varphi(\mu; b)$ with $\varphi_\mu > 0 > \varphi_b$. Finally, since a more generous welfare state may reduce the scarring from unemployment, we assume that s is also a decreasing function of b.[14,15] Formally, for an agent earning an income of ω and facing a consumer price index of p, we assume that indirect utility is given by $v(p)\omega - s(b)I - \varphi(\mu; b)$ where I is an indicator function which equals 1 while the agent is unemployed and 0 otherwise. Note that this form of the indirect utility function implies risk neutrality.

---

[13]Also related to our work is the sizable literature on the link between globalization and welfare states. For example, Gaston and Nelson (2004a) develop a model of the political economy of unemployment benefit in an open, unionized economy. Their model of the political process is also derived from Grossman and Helpman.

[14]This assumption plays no major role in our analysis. In fact, it only affects our results on openness and the welfare state, where we find an ambiguous relationship. As we explain in footnote 29 below, this ambiguity would be moderated somewhat if we were to assume that s was independent of b (or even increasing in b).

[15]Empirical support for our assumptions about the impact of the welfare state on the utility losses from unemployment can be found in Di Tella et al. (2003), Gangl (2004), and Pacek and Radcliff (2008).

We consider a continuous time small open economy with a fixed number (L) of ex ante identical infinitely lived risk neutral workers who each inelastically supply a unit of labor at each point in time. There are two goods and each good is produced in a different sector using labor as the only input. For simplicity, we assume that the production of two units of good i requires two agents working as a team (for $i = 1, 2$). Thus, agents seeking a sector i job must find a partner in order to produce. We introduce unemployment by assuming that there are labor market frictions so that it takes time and effort for agents seeking partners to find each other. This means that some agents seeking a partner will be unsuccessful and will be "unemployed." Those agents that find partners and produce are "employed." Unemployed workers choose a sector in which to search based on the expected lifetime utility that each sector offers.

Once a match is formed, the workers produce output, sell it on the world market and split the proceeds evenly until the match is destroyed. Sector-i matches are destroyed involuntarily by an idiosyncratic shock according to a Poisson process. The rate at which shocks occur is defined as $\delta_i \in (0, \infty)$. A match may also break up voluntarily if the partners expect to earn more by searching for a new match in another sector rather than continuing to produce in their current sector. Thus, a change in the terms of trade (or trade policy) can cause the agents to reassess their options and voluntarily break up an already-formed productive partnership, though all break ups are involuntary in a steady-state. Regardless of the reason for the breakup, whenever a match dissolves both agents must re-enter the search process.

The number of new matches created in a sector is a function of the number of agents searching in that sector. Thus, if we let U_i denote the number of unemployed agents in sector-i, then the number of new matches created in that sector is given by $M_i(U_i)$.[16] We assume that $M_i(U_i)$ is increasing and strictly concave with $M_i(0) = 0$. The assumption of concavity, implying congestion externalities in the search process, is required to generate an equilibrium with diversified production. Since all agents are identical, we assume that each unemployed worker in a given sector is equally likely to find a match. This implies that the sector-i job acquisition rate is given by

$$\pi_i(U_i) = \frac{2M_i(U_i)}{U_i}. \tag{1}$$

Note that the numerator of π_i gives the number of new jobs created while the denominator reflects the number of agents competing for those jobs.

Since search decisions are driven by the desire to maximize expected lifetime utility, we now turn to the value equations which describe expected utility in different labor market states. To make our point, it is sufficient to focus on steady-states. If we use V_i^E to denote the expected lifetime utility for an employed sector i worker and V_i^U to denote the expected lifetime utility for an unemployed worker in sector i then we have

$$rV_i^E = v(p)[p_i - \tau(b)] - \varphi(\mu; b) - \delta_i(V_i^E - V_i^U) \tag{2}$$

$$rV_i^U = v(p)[b - \tau(b)] - s(b) - \varphi(\mu; b) + \pi_i(U_i)(V_i^E - V_i^U), \tag{3}$$

---

[16]Allowing agents to influence the probability of finding a partner by altering search effort would not change our results. See Davidson et al. (1994) for details.

where p_i denotes the world price of good i; r denotes the interest rate; and $\tau(b)$ is the *lump-sum* tax paid by all agents to fund the welfare state. Since each match produces two units of output, a sector-i employed worker earns p_i from the sale of output and pays $\tau(b)$ in taxes. This worker loses his/her job at rate δ_i, in which case there is a capital loss of $V_i^E - V_i^U$. Unemployed workers receive a transfer payment of b from the government but must also pay taxes of $\tau(b)$. These workers find jobs at rate π_i, in which case there is a capital gain of $V_i^E - V_i^U$. In addition, unemployed workers suffer a loss in utility of $s(b)$ due to the scarring effects from unemployment while all agents lose utility of $\varphi(\mu; b)$ due to concerns about the employment risk faced by others.

We can solve (2) and (3) to obtain:

$$V_i^E - V_i^U = \frac{v(p)(p_i - b) + s(b)}{r + \delta_i + \pi_i(U_i)} \tag{4}$$

$$V_i^U = \frac{v(p)\pi_i(U_i)p_i + (r + \delta_i)[v(p)b - s(b)]}{r[r + \delta_i + \pi_i(U_i)]} - \frac{v(p)\tau(b) + \varphi(\mu; b)}{r}. \tag{5}$$

Unemployed workers select a sector to search in based on the relative values of V_1^U and V_2^U; whereas a worker employed in sector i will sever his/her partnership if a shock to the economy causes V_i^E to fall below V_j^U.

The number of new jobs created in any given sector must equal the number destroyed in any steady state. If we use X_i to denote sector-i output (and hence employment) we have the following steady-state condition:

$$\pi_i(U_i)U_i = \delta_i X_i. \tag{6}$$

In (6), the left-hand side gives the number of unemployed workers finding jobs in sector i while the right-hand side measures the number of employed workers who lose their jobs.

Next, let L_i denote the number of workers attached to sector i at any point in time. Then, we must have the following two accounting identities

$$L_i = X_i + U_i \tag{7}$$

$$\bar{L} = L_1 + L_2. \tag{8}$$

And, for a balanced budget we need

$$\tau(b) = \frac{b(U_1 + U_2)}{\bar{L}}. \tag{9}$$

Finally, in any diversified equilibrium, unemployed workers must sort themselves so that they expect to earn the same lifetime utility in both sectors. Thus,

$$V_1^U = V_2^U. \tag{10}$$

This completes the description of the model. The novelty of our approach is in the agents' attitudes toward unemployment as captured by the personal scarring effect of unemployment, $s(b)$, and our fairness measure, $\varphi(\mu; b)$.

To examine the model in greater detail, we begin by focusing on the case in which $b = \tau(b) = 0$. Our goal is to show that the steady-state equilibrium is unique.

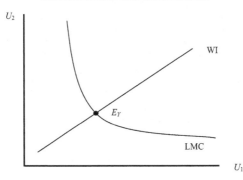

Figure 1.   Equilibrium is unique.

Straightforward substitution into (8) and (10) allows us to reduce the model to two equations in two unknowns, U_1 and U_2. Using good 2 as the numeraire and defining $p = p_1$ we obtain

$$\frac{\pi_1(U_1)v(p)p - s(b)(r + \delta_1)}{r + \delta_1 + \pi_1(U_1)} = \frac{\pi_2(U_2)v(p) - s(b)(r + \delta_2)}{r + \delta_2 + \pi_2(U_2)} \tag{11}$$

$$U_1 + \frac{2M_1(U_1)}{\delta_1} + U_2 + \frac{2M_2(U_2)}{\delta_2} = \bar{L}. \tag{12}$$

Equation (11), which comes from (10), is the Worker Indifference (WI) condition. Since $\pi_i'(U_i) < 0$, this condition is clearly upward sloping. Intuitively, an increase in U_1 reduces the returns to search in sector 1 (due to the congestion externalities) and makes that sector less attractive. To restore equality, sector 2 must become less attractive, requiring an increase in U_2.

Equation (12) is the Labor Market Clearing (LMC) condition. It is downward sloping and strictly convex (see Figure 1). The convexity comes directly from the concavity of the matching technologies. To see this, note that the absolute value of the slope of the LMC curve is $\frac{\delta_1 + 2M_1'(U_1)}{\delta_2 + 2M_2'(U_2)} \frac{\delta_2}{\delta_1}$. As we move up and to the left on the LMC curve, U_1 falls and U_2 rises. By concavity, $M_1'(U_1)$ must rise while $M_2'(U_2)$ falls so that the slope rises.

The steady-state equilibrium is given by the intersection of the LMC and WI curves. We now have our first result, which follows directly from Figure 1.

Proposition 1. There is a unique steady-state equilibrium.

For later use, we note that changes in trade policy or unemployment compensation shift the WI curve up or down. In particular, protecting sector 1 shifts the WI curve down (since $\pi_i'(U_i) < 0$) causing sector 1 to expand and sector 2 to contract. We examine the impact of changes in unemployment compensation below.

2.1 Social Welfare in the Free Trade Equilibrium

To begin our discussion of trade policy, we start by calculating welfare (continuing to focus on the case in which $b = \tau(b) = 0$). We assume that Social Welfare is the sum of the individual agents' welfare. Thus, in any steady state we have

$$W = \text{Welfare} \equiv \sum_i \left\{ X_i V_i^E + U_i V_i^U \right\} = \sum_l \left\{ L_i V_i^U + X_i (V_i^E - V_i^U) \right\}. \tag{13}$$

Substituting from (4) to (7) we obtain

$$W = \frac{1}{r} \left\{ \sum_i \left\{ v(p) p_i X_i - s(0) U_i \right\} - \bar{L} \varphi(\mu; 0) \right\}. \tag{14}$$

Equation (14) illustrates how concerns about the scarring effects of unemployment and sociotropic concerns enter into social preferences. In particular, (14) indicates that in our behavioral model welfare consists of three components: the value of output, the personal costs from unemployment, and the utility loss due to sociotropic concerns.

It is clear from (11) that workers internalize the scarring effect of unemployment when selecting a sector. Even so, congestion externalities in the search process suggest that the free trade equilibrium would not maximize the value of output net of the scarring costs of unemployment, $Y = \sum_i \left\{ v(p) p_i X_i - s U_i \right\}$. Moreover, sociotropic concerns play no role in allocating resources. This is evident from the observation that the worker indifference condition (11) is independent of $\varphi(\mu; b)$.[17] The presence of congestion externalities combined with the absence of fairness considerations in the worker decision-making process strongly suggests that the free trade equilibrium will not maximize welfare as defined in (14).

In the Appendix of our working paper (Davidson et al., 2010), we show that the allocation of resources that maximizes Y satisfies

$$\frac{2M_1'(U_1) v(p) p - s(0)(r + \delta_1)}{r + \delta_1 + 2M_1'(U_1)} = \frac{2M_2'(U_2) v(p) - s(0)(r + \delta_2)}{r + \delta_2 + 2M_2'(U_2)}. \tag{15}$$

Yet, in the free trade equilibrium unemployed workers sort themselves across sectors so that (11) holds (with $b = 0$). A quick comparison of (11) and (15) confirms that since $2M_i'(U_i) \neq \pi_i(U_i)$, the two allocations are different. The reason for this outcome is clear. Individual choices are driven by the *average* job acquisition rates [i.e., the $\pi_i(U_i)$ terms in equation 11]; whereas (15) tells us that labor should be allocated based on the *marginal* job acquisition rates (in sector i this would be $2M_i'(U_i)$) in order to maximize the value of output net of scarring effect (Y). With congestion externalities present, the marginal and average rates are not equal.[18] Thus, even if we ignore sociotropic considerations, the free trade equilibrium is distorted. Even for a small country, a trade tax or subsidy can be welfare enhancing by tilting incentives to induce a worker allocation consistent with (15).

As noted in the introduction, the implications of search generated externalities for trade policy have been explored at length elsewhere (e.g., Costinot, 2009; Davidson

---

[17]This follows from the two facts – (a) sociotropic concerns enter into V_1^U and V_2^U in the same manner and cancel out and (b) workers treat total unemployment as fixed, since they are small relative to the market.

[18]Without congestion externalities the equilibrium would be efficient but the model would have Ricardian properties in that countries would specialize in production unless world prices equaled autarkic prices.

UNEMPLOYMENT AND TRADE POLICY   81

et al., 1987, 1988) and are well understood. And, since these externalities are not the focus of this article, we will not explore how they distort the allocation of resources. Thus, in order to highlight the manner in which sociotropic concerns affect trade policy (which is the primary focus of this article), we side-step this issue by assuming that in the initial free trade equilibrium the government corrects for search generated externalities by implementing the appropriate production subsidy. This production subsidy equates the marginal and average job acquisition rates in each sector. With this assumption in place, we are now in a position to derive our main results.

2.2 Sociotropic Concerns and Trade Policy

We now turn to the question of how sociotropic concerns about the employment risk faced by others alter trade policy. With the optimal production subsidy in place the free trade allocation of labor maximizes Y. By the Envelope Theorem, small changes in the allocation of labor away from this point create only second order losses. From (14), it follows that the government has an incentive to marginally reduce total unemployment: doing so will have no impact on the first two terms in (14) but will increase welfare by reducing the sociotropic measure $\varphi(\mu; b)$.

Proposition 2. When free trade cum production subsidy maximizes the value of output net of the scarring costs from unemployment, the government can raise welfare by instituting policies that marginally reduce total unemployment.

In the Appendix to our working paper (Davidson et al., 2010), we show that the allocation of labor that minimizes total unemployment [therefore minimizing $\varphi(\mu; b)$] satisfies

$$\frac{2M_1'(U_1)}{r + \delta_1} = \frac{2M_2'(U_2)}{r + \delta_2}. \tag{16}$$

For low discount rates, (16) indicates that sociotropic concerns about unemployment are minimized when the ratio of the marginal job creation rate to the job destruction rate is equalized across sectors. Given the convexity of the LMC curve, there is a unique point on that curve where (16) is satisfied. This point is labeled E_μ in Figures 2 and 3.

While Proposition 2 indicates that the government should marginally reduce unemployment to increase welfare, it does not tell us how to do so. In order to answer that question, we need to compare E_μ to the initial equilibrium. There are two cases to consider, illustrated in Figures 2 and 3. In each figure, the initial equilibrium is represented by E_Y, where the subscript is a reminder that we are starting from an equilibrium that would emerge if the production subsidy that maximizes Y were levied. The sectoral allocation of searchers satisfies both the Worker Indifference condition and the LMC condition at this point.

In Figure 2, E_μ lies to the southeast of E_Y. Unemployment is monotonically decreasing as we move along LMC from E_Y toward E_μ. Since the government's goal is to marginally reduce unemployment, the optimal policy when sociotropic concerns matter must shift WI down toward E_μ, which expands sector 1. However, protecting sector 1 introduces production and consumption distortions, with the optimal policy balancing the reduction in unemployment with the increased magnitude of the

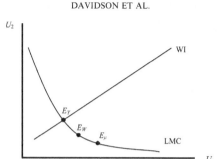

Figure 2. Protecting sector 1 will increase welfare.

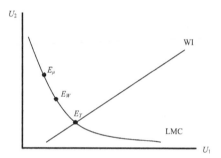

Figure 3. Protecting sector 2 will increase welfare.

production and consumption distortions.[19] In other words, the policy-induced allocation of resources that maximizes welfare will not minimize unemployment, but rather
must lie between E_μ and E_Y. We label this point E_W.
The conditions under which it is optimal to expand sector 1 can be found by comparing marginal job creation and job destruction rates at E_μ and E_Y. Given the relative positions of E_μ and E_Y and the concavity of the matching functions, it follows
that $2M_1'(U_1^Y) > 2M_1'(U_1^\mu)$ and $2M_2'(U_2^Y) < 2M_2'(U_2^\mu)$, where U_i^Y represents the number
of unemployed workers in sector i corresponding to the allocation at Y, with the
remaining variables defined analogously. Combining these inequalities with (16) we
now know that at E_Y we have

---

[19]Since protection introduces a consumption distortion, it is not the first-best policy – a production subsidy would be superior. The optimal production subsidy balances the loss in welfare from reducing the value
of output with the gain in welfare that comes about as sociotropic concerns are reduced (and, with this subsidy in place, free trade would be optimal). Since this policy does not distort consumption, it entails *more*
labor market reallocation than the optimal trade policy. However, a common public view is that production
subsidies simply trade one set of domestic jobs for another, while protection saves domestic jobs from foreign competition and thus, protection may be an easier way to reallocate resources politically (especially
since a production subsidy must also be financed). Since our focus is on how concerns about unemployment
alter trade policy, we assume that the first-best domestic policy alternative is politically infeasible.

$$\frac{2M_1'(U_1^Y)}{r+\delta_1} > \frac{2M_2'(U_2^Y)}{r+\delta_2}. \tag{17}$$

Thus, sociotropic concerns lead us to protect sector 1 when (17) holds in the initial equilibrium.

The second case, depicted in Figure 3, is analogous. Now E_μ lies to the northwest of E_Y. As above, the policy when sociotropic concerns matter must shift the WI curve toward E_μ, meaning that we must now expand sector 2. Formally, we have $2M_1'(U_1^Y) < 2M_1'(U_1^\mu)$ and $2M_2'(U_2^Y) > 2M_2'(U_2^\mu)$; and, using the definition of E_μ we find that at the initial steady-state

$$\frac{2M_1'(U_1^Y)}{r+\delta_1} < \frac{2M_2'(U_2^Y)}{r+\delta_2}. \tag{18}$$

Thus, sociotropic concerns lead the government to institute policies designed to expand sector 2 whenever (18) holds. Both cases are summarized in Proposition 3.

Proposition 3. Suppose that the current allocation of labor maximizes the value of output net of the personal costs of unemployment. Then if sociotropic concerns about total unemployment are present, the government can reduce unemployment and therefore increase welfare by shifting resources to the sector in which $\frac{2M_i'(U_i)}{r+\delta_i}$ is highest.

Proposition 3 tells us that when agents are concerned about the fairness of trade policy, governments will have an incentive to protect sectors that offer durable jobs (those for which δ_i is low) and sectors in which it is relatively easy to create new jobs (where the marginal job creation rate, $M_i'(U_i)$, is high). It is in this sense that some jobs are better than others in our framework. The "good jobs" offer a high level of job security and can be found in sectors with high marginal job creation rates. These jobs are better than others to the extent that they are associated with smaller social losses from the sociotropic component of welfare. We note that Bradford (2006) provides some empirical support for Proposition 3 in that he finds that protection is lower in industries with high job destruction rates.

We are not the first to offer a rationale for a good jobs/bad jobs distinction. Many were offered back in the 1980s in response to the debate over industrial policy aimed at expanding sectors with "good jobs." During this debate, Bulow and Summers (1986) correctly pointed out that industrial policy makes little or no sense in a competitive economy: "Competition equalizes the marginal productivities of all equivalent workers. There is no such thing as a good or bad industry." One of the main points of the Bulow/Summers paper is to show that when labor markets are distorted such a distinction makes sense. In their model, the economy is distorted by the inability of firms to observe worker effort. As a result, firms need to motivate employees to work hard and efficiency wages and unemployment provide the necessary motivation. The labor market distortions sever the link between wages and productivity making it possible to increase welfare by expanding some sectors at the expense of others. Similar rationales for the good job/bad job distinction can be found in Acemoglu (2001) and Costinot (2009) where the distortions are generated by labor market frictions or Davis and Harrigan (2011) where efficiency wage considerations are present.[20] It is important to emphasize we are offering an explanation that is fundamentally different from this previous work (where the good jobs/bad jobs distinction is mainly about high paying jobs vs. low paying jobs). In our setting, the government has already internalized the congestion externalities by instituting a production subsidy – as a result, the initial steady-state equilibrium maximizes the value of output net of the scarring costs of unemployment. The good jobs/bad jobs distinction follows instead from the behavioral aspects of our model – some jobs are better than others because their durability lowers the loss in welfare that is inherently tied to employment risk. Thus, our framework suggests that rather than characterizing jobs as "good" or "bad" it might be more appropriate to label jobs as "more secure" and "less secure."

2.3 Gradualism

Our next result is related to how the new policies alter the steady-state. In this environment, the government has an incentive to gradually phase in all new policies. There are two reasons for this: the presence of congestion externalities in the search process and the existence of scarring effects and sociotropic concerns tied to unemployment. The result that congestion externalities in the labor market can lead to gradualism is not new. This result can be found in Cassing and Ochs (1978) and in Davidson and Matusz (2004).[21] The argument is straightforward. Suppose that the government decides to implement a tariff to increase welfare by expanding sector 1. There are both costs and benefits from phasing in the higher tariff gradually. The cost is that it takes longer to reach the new equilibrium in which welfare is permanently higher. The benefit is that by phasing in the new tariff the government can reduce the congestion externalities generated as sector 1 expands. Davidson and Matusz (2004) show that as long as congestion externalities are present, the benefits may outweigh the costs and gradualism may be optimal. It follows that if the government wants to alter the composition of employment it should gradually phase in policies that provide incentives for unemployed workers to seek new matches in the targeted industries. In other words, it is better to have labor market reallocation take place slowly with only the unemployed changing their career paths.

In Cassing and Ochs (1978) and Davidson and Matusz (2004), the appropriate measure of welfare is the value of output. In our behavioral model, we have two additional terms in our welfare function that are tied to scarring effects and fairness concerns, both of which depend solely on unemployment. The presence of these new terms makes the case for gradualism stronger by adding benefits without adding new costs. If we assume that the optimal policy is large enough to cause employed workers to quit their jobs and switch sectors if implemented fully and immediately, then unemployment would be lower all along the transition path if the policy would be phased in instead. Phasing in the policy would allow adjustment to take place through the reallocation of *unemployed* workers with all existing employment relationships kept intact. This implies that the total scarring effects from unemployment and the welfare losses associated with sociotropic concerns would be lower with gradualism. Therefore, societies with stronger sociotropic concerns should be more likely to gradually phase in new policies.

We see this issue of good jobs/bad jobs and gradualism as being related to active labor market policies (ALMP). The primary goal of an ALMP is to promote labor

---

[20]A somewhat different rationale can be found in the overlapping generation model of Davidson et al. (1994) where "good jobs" transfer more resources across generations than "bad jobs."

[21]See also the related work of Karp and Paul (1994, 1998, 2005) and Gaisford and Leger (2000).

market adjustment through a variety of policies, generally including: job training; search assistance; and employment subsidies. An essential element of ALMP is the attempt to move people to "better" jobs, where this is generally seen as higher paying and/or more stable jobs.[22] From the early 1950s, with the inauguration of the Rehn–Meidner plan in Sweden, until today, ALMPs have figured prominently in Northern European countries. ALMPs have been promoted as part of the OECD's jobs program (OECD, 1990, 1991, 1994, 2006) and the EU's European Employment Strategy (European Commission, 2002, 2004).[23] A major textbook treatment of unemployment even recommends ALMP as an appropriate policy for dealing with labor market adjustment (Layard et al., 1991). In particular, we see the gradualism result as being directly related to the strategy of ALMP. That is, ALMP does not conceive of moving currently employed people from "bad" to "good" jobs, as a simple comparative static result (or some form of *dirigiste* picking of winners) might suggest, but rather seeks to move people as they become unemployed.

3. OPENNESS AND THE WELFARE STATE

There is a widely held belief, among scholars and policy-makers, that openness to trade is supported by welfare state effort. This relationship was identified by Cameron (1978) and discussed at length in a pair of books by Katzenstein (1984, 1985). Since then, this hypothesis has been extensively studied by economists, political scientists and sociologists. The main justifications for this relationship are broadly plausible: a political economic story in which the welfare state buys support of organized labor that would otherwise oppose greater openness; and an insurance story in which greater openness increases income risk and citizens are more willing to support openness if that risk is insured. Given the plausibility of these stories, and the early empirical support, it is somewhat surprising that more recent research has not consistently found support for this hypothesis.[24] Most of this literature emphasizes econometric work relative to the above, essentially ad hoc, hypotheses.[25]

---

[22]Not only is our approach consistent with the emphasis on improving matching efficiency as an essential part of the strategy of moving people from bad jobs to good jobs, but Estevao's (2007) suggestion that one of the gains from ALMP is that "active policies may lower the disutility of being unemployed, because they provide an occupation to otherwise unemployed workers, some income, and a hope of keeping their labor skills" seems closely related to our scarring effects. Gangl (2006) presents more systematic empirical support for this claim.

[23]ALMPs have been evaluated at length. An early and influential example is Calmfors (1994), while Heckman et al. (1999) took 233 pages of the *Handbook of Labor Economics* for a survey. Research on the effects of ALMP continue up to the present (e.g., Estevao, 2007). The results in this literature are mixed, to say the least, but for our purposes the essential point is that governments and international agencies continue to see ALMP as a potentially important component of labor market policy.

[24]For example, Rodrik's (1998) paper finds support, with particular reference to the insurance story; Alesina and Glaeser (2004) provides evidence to the contrary. Hicks (1999) and Swank (2002) find evidence supporting the redistributive story, while Garrett (1998) and Pontusson (2005) find a negative relationship. Iversen and Cusack (2000) argue that there is no relationship, that technological change is the central driving force in accounting for change in levels of welfare state provision. A particularly interesting result is that there is a strong positive relationship between globalization and welfare state expansion during what people studying welfare states often call the golden age (i.e., the post-War period up to the early 1970s); but that this relationship disappears following in the current period (Eichengreen, 2006; Huber and Stephens, 2001).

[25]There are, of course, exceptions. Adsera and Boix (2002) offer a game theoretic analysis; Davidson et al. (2007) offer a simple general equilibrium analysis under a referendum; Rama and Tabellini (1998) consider a unionized economy with full employment and a PFS political economy; and Gaston and Nelson (2004b) examine a unionized economy with unemployment and a PFS political economy.

86   DAVIDSON ET AL.

Many studies emphasize that the origins and continued support for welfare states are related to notions of fairness, especially with respect to concerns about lack of work, via notions of citizenship rights. The model we have developed in this article contains all of these elements. Thus, in this section, we examine the relationship between welfare state provision and trade policy implied by our theoretical framework. In particular, we ask if countries with more generous welfare programs might have less protection. In our framework, the answer is not clear cut. We first provide an intuitive explanation of the conflicting forces that are present. We then illustrate our results by focusing on a simple example. Our approach in this subsection is consistent with our approach above. We assume that the initial steady-state equilibrium is given by E_Y and that the government then institutes a welfare program by offering unemployment insurance to all workers.[26] We then want to investigate whether countries with larger welfare states (higher b) will tend to be more open to trade. This approach allows us to take into account the distortions created by the welfare state and analyze their implications for trade policy.

Increasing b has two effects. First, increasing b reduces lifetime income loss, the psychic scarring effect, and the sociotropic effect of unemployment. This seems intuitive: for any level of unemployment, transfers to the unemployed will raise their welfare; and the same introspection that reduces the welfare of the currently employed in the face of unemployment will lead to increased welfare as the welfare of the unemployed rises. One of the main reasons that we are concerned about the unfairness of unemployment is that unemployment implies hardship. With a more generous welfare state, this hardship is diminished, implying that we should be less concerned about the scarring effects from unemployment and the costs imposed on others (this is the rationale for our assumptions that s and our fairness measure φ are both decreasing in b). Thus, as b increases, the welfare-maximizing policy places relatively more weight on output and less on minimizing unemployment. This will result in a less interventionist trade policy. We refer to this as the *direct effect* of b, and this is the effect that underlies most assertions to the effect that larger welfare states are associated with greater openness.[27]

However, there is a second effect that is not generally considered in the literature on welfare states and openness: by reducing the personal cost of unemployment, an increase in b should make the high-unemployment sector relatively more attractive; and this should lead to an inefficient expansion of that sector. As resources are reallocated toward the high unemployment sector, we would expect total unemployment to rise and when we take sociotropic concerns into account we will now tend to need a larger trade intervention to lower total unemployment.[28] Since this reallocation of resources is an unintended outcome triggered by an expansion of the welfare state, we refer to this as the *indirect effect* of an increase in unemployment compensation.[29] It

[26]That is, we assume that the government has already instituted policies aimed at correcting for the congestion externalities before the unemployment insurance program is implemented.

[27]Some of the arguments are complicated versions of the above analysis. Rodrik's (1998) analysis, for example, emphasizes the insurance role of the welfare state in the context of an expectation that trade makes incomes in the traded sector riskier. In our model, agents are risk neutral and so it cannot reflect this consideration, but it should be clear that the logic is in the same class as what we have called the "direct effect."

[28]Although one must be careful here – as the sector sizes change, the job acquisition rates change and this alters the sectoral unemployment rates. This is one of the reasons that this analysis is not quite clear cut. We return to this issue below.

[29]Note that magnitude of the indirect effect would be smaller if s were independent b (or increasing in b) since this would moderate the reallocation of labor toward the high-unemployment sector when the welfare state expands. Thus, as we noted in footnote 14, this would reduce the ambiguity of our results by making it more likely that the direct effect would dominate.

follows that where the direct effect reduces the importance of unemployment in the social welfare function, the indirect effect of an increase in b is to increase unemployment, so the overall implication for the link between the generosity of the welfare state and overall protection should be ambiguous.

To formally illustrate these arguments, first note that the LMC curve is independent of b and remember that the economy's initial steady-state is at E_Y. Now, when unemployment insurance is first introduced, the WI curve shifts. To see how, first note that with $b > 0$, the worker indifference condition (11) becomes

$$\frac{\pi_1(U_1)v(p)p + (r + \delta_1)[v(p)b - s(b)]}{r + \delta_1 + \pi_1(U_1)} = \frac{\pi_2(U_2)v(p)p + (r + \delta_2)[v(p)b - s(b)]}{r + \delta_2 + \pi_2(U_2)}.$$

(11b)

Next, note that both the left-hand side (V_1^U) and right-hand side (V_2^U) of (11b) increase as b increases, but the left-hand side increases by a larger magnitude if

$$\frac{\pi_2(U_2)}{r + \delta_2} > \frac{\pi_1(U_1)}{r + \delta_1}.$$

(19)

With $V_1^U > V_2^U$, unemployed workers start to flow out of sector 2 and into sector 1. As sector 1 expands, congestion causes U_1 to increase, while the flow of unemployed workers out of sector 2 causes U_2 to fall. This reallocation continues until the equality in (11b) is restored. Geometrically, the changes in unemployment are represented by a rightward and downward shift of the WI curve in Figures 1–3. Clearly, WI shifts in the opposite direction if the inequality in (19) is reversed.

The inequality in (19) compares the increase in expected lifetime utilities due to the increase in b across sectors. The sector that experiences the bigger increase expands. Inequality (19) tells us that a low average job acquisition rate (which contributes to high unemployment in a sector) and/or a high job destruction rate (which also contributes to high unemployment in a sector) make it more likely that the sector will expand when b rises. So, our general result is that an increase in the generosity of the welfare state will increase the size of the sector in which $\frac{\pi_i(U_i)}{r + \delta_i}$ is the lowest.

To proceed further, we turn to a specific example in which the matching technologies in the two sectors are identical and given by $M_i(U_i) = \left(\frac{U_i}{2}\right)^\lambda$ with $\lambda < 1$. Under this assumption, the only difference between sectors is the job destruction rates. This simplifies matters because with this matching technology $2M'_i(U_i) = \lambda\pi_i(U_i)$, which implies that $\frac{2M'_1(U_1)}{2M'_2(U_2)} = \frac{\pi_1(U_1)}{\pi_2(U_2)}$. To see why this matters, note that Figure 2 is relevant if (17) holds; and, if (17) holds we have

$$\frac{\pi_1(U_1)}{\pi_2(U_2)} = \frac{2M'_1(U_1)}{2M'_2(U_2)} > \frac{r + \delta_1}{r + \delta_2},$$

(20)

so that, by (19) an increase in b causes the WI curve to shift up and to the left and away from E_μ. Since this shift moves the economy away from E_μ, unemployment is increasing and since it also moves the economy away from E_Y and E_W this expansion of unemployment is inefficient. Further increases in the size of the welfare state push the WI curve further up to the left, causing additional increases unemployment and additional distortions. This requires greater government intervention to undo the damage and lower unemployment. This is the indirect effect described above. The direct effect follows from the fact that the increase in b lowers our sociotropic measure φ,

88   DAVIDSON ET AL.

causing E_W to move away from E_μ toward E_Y – that is, the welfare-maximizing point moves closer to the steady-state equilibrium. As a result, a *smaller* government program will be needed to maximize welfare. Thus, as our intuition suggested, the direct and indirect effects have opposing implications for the level of government intervention. Note that the same conclusions apply to Figure 3 since the inequality in (20) is then reversed, implying that an expansion of the welfare state causes the WI curve to move down to the right and away from E_μ.

In summary, in this case, when the generosity of the welfare state increases, we expect the high unemployment sector to expand and concerns about scarring and fairness to be reduced. The first effect leads to more protection aimed at reducing unemployment but the second effect leads to less protection because concerns about the hardship associated with unemployment have been reduced. The net effect for protection is ambiguous.

It is worth noting that if we compare (19) with (16), the condition that defines E_μ, it is clear that things will not always work out exactly as our intuition or this example suggests. A complication arises because, from (19), it is the *average* job creation rate that dictates whether the WI curve will shift up or down while, as (16) indicates, it is the *marginal* job creation rates that determine where total unemployment is minimized. This makes it difficult to tell how total unemployment will change when the welfare state expands – that is, it is not clear whether an increase in b causes the steady-state equilibrium to move toward E_μ or away from it. Our specific example allows us to avoid this issue, because the ratio of marginal job creation rates equals the ratio of average job creation rates – but this will not always be the case.

However, for more general matching functions, the additional case that arises actually leads to cleaner results. This case arises when an increase in b causes the WI curve to shift toward E_μ, thereby lowering unemployment. This could happen, for example, if the low-unemployment sector is relatively large. In that case, an increase in b would reallocate resources toward the high-unemployment sector and the subsequent reduction in congestion in the low-unemployment sector would lower that sector's unemployment rate. Since the economy-wide unemployment rate is a convex combination of the sectoral rates and since the low-unemployment sector is relatively large, this could lead to a reduction in the economy-wide rate of unemployment. In such a case, the direct and indirect effects work in the same direction – they both imply that economies with a larger welfare state should be more open.

We have seen that, in the general equilibrium model developed in this article, even with explicit inclusion of sociotropic concerns, the link between welfare state provision and trade openness is ambiguous due to the simultaneous occurrence of the direct and indirect effects. This is weakly consistent with the ambiguous results in the empirical literature on this relationship. At a minimum, this sort of general equilibrium relationship, which seems quite appropriate given the broadly macroeconomic impact of both openness and welfare state provision, suggests greater care in econometric modeling of this relationship. Stronger evidence of the causal forces we identify might exploit the break in the relationship identified by Huber and Stephens (2001) and Eichengreen (2006) as occurring some time after the post-War "golden age" of welfare state capitalism. That is, our framework suggests that one might look for factors that either weaken the direct effect or strengthen the indirect effect over the post-War period.

In closing this subsection, is worth noting that the ambiguity of our results highlights the need for a more careful examination of optimal social insurance programs in open economies. The welfare state in our model simply provides unemployment insurance. Perhaps a program that combines wage or training subsidies with an unemployment insurance program might be superior and might have different implications for the indirect effect. Although we are always quick to point out that those harmed by trade can be compensated without exhausting the gains from trade, surprisingly little work has focused on how this might be accomplished with politically feasible labor market programs. And, while there has been significant work in macroeconomics on optimal social insurance programs, the same cannot be said for the field of international economics. The insights derived in the macro literature, which are based on closed economy models, may not generalize to open economy setting in which labor market policies, labor market structure and the pattern of trade are likely to be linked. We would argue that it is now time for trade economists to start to think seriously about how to design programs aimed at compensating trade displaced workers in a manner that makes increased openness easier to attain.

4. CONCLUSIONS AND DIRECTIONS FOR FUTURE RESEARCH

In this article, we have focused on how the scarring effects from unemployment and sociotropic concerns about the employment risk faced by others are likely to shape trade policy. Of course, these concerns also have implications for industrial policy, an issue that we have not addressed here. The main reason for this is that in many countries (including the United States) it is common for politicians to call for trade policy to combat pockets of high unemployment. Sometimes the calls are for freer trade, aimed at expanding exports markets and creating new domestic jobs; while at other times the calls are for barriers to trade aimed at protecting domestic jobs in a particular sector. It far more rare for politicians to push for domestic policies with similar objectives, perhaps because such policies are viewed as "zero-sum" with new domestic jobs in one sector coming at the expense of domestic jobs in another sector; whereas trade policy is viewed as producing or protecting domestic jobs at the expense of foreigners. This is, of course, very much at odds with the way trade economists view the world but it is consistent with other views that seem to be held by the public. As Paul Krugman and others have pointed out, the public seems to think that trade is all about exports, since they generate jobs, while imports are considered a necessary evil. Given that the public and our political leaders hold such views, it seems reasonable to ask how concerns about unemployment are likely to affect trade policy.

Finally, we close by pointing out that the analysis presented here suggests a new way of interpreting the relationship between two bodies of research on the political economy of international trade policy that seem to coexist somewhat awkwardly at present: empirical research based on public opinion data (e.g., Mayda and Rodrik, 2005; O'Rourke and Sinnott, 2002; Scheve and Slaughter, 2001a, 2001b); and theoretical and empirical work based on the Grossman and Helpman's (1994) "PFS" model. The former are often presented as providing information with respect to individual preferences on trade policy that are presumed, somehow, to be translated into policy – either via the lobbying channel or via the political decision-maker's concern with aggregate welfare. However, as we argue above, there are serious problems with this interpretation. From the point of view of aggregation, it is not clear how we are supposed to get from this information to trade policy: on the one hand, there have virtually never been referenda on trade, and only very rarely have there been elections in recent times that turned on trade; while, on the other, citizens rarely participate in

90   DAVIDSON ET AL.

lobbying. Perhaps more importantly, there is, in fact, little evidence that citizens understand trade in the way that our models presume they do (Guisinger, 2009; Hainmueller and Hiscox, 2006; Hiscox, 2006; Mansfield and Mutz, 2009). This latter fact does not render citizen opinion unimportant, but it does mean that we need to theorize the relationship with some care. We have argued that citizen preferences, such as they are, act as a constraint on governmental policy choice very much in the way that the aggregate welfare constraint is modeled by Grossman and Helpman. However, we have also argued that there is considerable evidence that, when citizens think about trade policy, unemployment plays a major role in their calculation and that this calculation contains a major sociotropic element. The political decision-maker must obviously take these elements into account. Our analysis draws these elements together. The next step in the program begun in this and our previous paper (Davidson et al., 2006) is to analyze the full political economic equilibrium with lobbying.

CARL DAVIDSON   DOUGLAS NELSON
Michigan State University and GEP,   *Tulane University and GEP,*
University of Nottingham   *University of Nottingham*

STEVEN J. MATUSZ
Michigan State University and GEP,
University of Nottingham

REFERENCES

Acemoglu, D., 2001, Good jobs versus bad jobs. *Journal of Labor Economics* 19, 1–21.
Adsera, A. and C. Boix, 2002, Trade, democracy, and the size of the public sector: the political underpinnings of openness. *International Organization* 56, 229–262.
Alesina, A. and E. L. Glaeser, 2004, *Fighting Poverty in the US and Europe: A World of Difference* (Oxford University Press, Oxford).
Arulampalam, W., 2001, Is unemployment really scarring? Effects of unemployment experiences on wages. *Economic Journal* 111, F585–F606.
Bradford, S., 2003, Protection and jobs: explaining the structure of trade barriers across industries. *Journal of International Economics* 61, 19–39.
———, 2006, Protection and unemployment. *Journal of International Economics* 69, 257–271.
Brecher, R., 1974, Minimum wage rates and the pure theory of international trade. *Quarterly Journal of Economics* 88, 98–116.
———, 1992, An efficiency-wage model with explicit monitoring: unemployment and welfare in an open economy. *Journal of International Economics* 32, 179–191.
Bulow, J. I. and L. H. Summers, 1986, A theory of dual labor-markets with application to industrial-policy, discrimination, and Keynesian unemployment. *Journal of Labor Economics* 4, 376–414.
Calmfors, L., 1994, Active labor market policy and unemployment – a framework for the analysis of crucial design features. *OECD Economic Studies* 22, 7–47.
Cameron, D. R., 1978, Expansion of the public economy – comparative analysis. *American Political Science Review* 72, 1243–1261.
Cassing, J. and J. Ochs, 1978, International trade, factor market distortions, and the optimal dynamic subsidy: comment. *American Economic Review* 68, 950–955.
Clark, A. E., Y. Georgellis, and P. Sanfey, 2001, Scarring: the psychological impact of past unemployment. *Economica* 68, 221–241.
Conover, P. J., S. Feldman, and K. Knight, 1986, Judging inflation and unemployment – the origins of retrospective evaluations. *Journal of Politics* 48, 565–588.

Copeland, B., 1989, Efficiency wages in a Ricardian model of international trade. *Journal of International Economics* 27, 221–244.

Costinot, A., 2009, Jobs, jobs, jobs: a "new" perspective on protectionism. *Journal of the European Economic Association* 7, 1011–1041.

Cowden, J. A. and T. Hartley, 1992, Complex measures and sociotropic voting. *Political Analysis* 4, 75–95.

Davidson, C. and S. Matusz, 2004, An overlapping-generations model of escape clause protection. *Review of International Economics* 12, 749–768.

——, L. Martin, and S. Matusz, 1987, Search, unemployment, and the production of jobs. *Economic Journal* 97, 857–876.

——, ——, and ——, 1988, The structure of simple general equilibrium-models with frictional unemployment. *Journal of Political Economy* 96, 1267–1293.

——, ——, and ——, 1994, Jobs and chocolate – Samuelsonian surpluses in dynamic-models of unemployment. *Review of Economic Studies* 61, 173–192.

——, ——, and ——, 1999, Trade and search generated unemployment. *Journal of International Economics* 48, 271–299.

——, S. Matusz, and D. Nelson, 2006, Fairness and the political economy of trade. *World Economy* 29, 989–1004.

——, ——, and ——, 2007, Can compensation save free trade? *Journal of International Economics* 71, 167–186.

——, ——, and ——, 2010, A behavioral model of unemployment, sociotropic concerns and the political economy of trade policy. Michigan State University Working Paper. Available at http://www.msu.edu/~davidso4/currentnew.html (accessed December 22, 2011).

Davis, D., 1998, Does European unemployment prop up American wages? National labor markets and global free trade. *American Economic Review* 88, 478–494.

—— and J. Harrigan, 2011, Good jobs, bad jobs, and trade liberalization. *Journal of International Economics.* 84, 26–36.

Di Tella, R., R. J. MacCulloch, and A. J. Oswald, 2001, Preferences over inflation and unemployment: evidence from surveys of happiness. *American Economic Review* 91, 335–341.

——, ——, and ——, 2003, The macroeconomics of happiness. *Review of Economics and Statistics* 85, 809–827.

Egger, H. and U. Kreickemeier, 2008, International fragmentation: boon or bane for domestic employment? *European Economic Review* 52, 116–132.

—— and ——, 2009, Firm heterogeneity and the labor market effects of trade liberalization. *International Economic Review* 50, 187–216.

Eichengreen, B., 2006, *The European Economy since 1945: Coordinated Capitalism and Beyond* (Princeton University Press, Princeton, NJ).

Estevao, M., 2007, Labor policies to raise employment. *IMF Staff Papers* 54, 113–138.

European Commission, 2002, *Taking Stock of Five Years of the European Employment Strategy* (European Commission, Brussels).

European Commission, 2004, *Growth, Competitiveness, Employment (White Paper)* (European Commission, Brussels).

Felbermayr, G., J. Prat, and H.-J. Schmerer, 2011, Globalization and labor market outcomes: wage bargaining, search frictions and firm heterogeneity. *Journal of Economic Theory* 146(1), 39–73.

Funk, C. L. and P. Garcia-Monet, 1997, The relationship between personal and natonal concerns in public perceptions about the economy. *Political Research Quarterly* 50, 317–342.

Gaisford, J. and L. Leger, 2000, Terms-of-trade shocks, labor-market adjustment, and safeguard measures. *Review of International Economics* 8, 100–112.

Gangl, M., 2004, Welfare states and the scar effects of unemployment: a comparative analysis of the United States and West Germany. *American Journal of Sociology* 109, 1319–1364.

——, 2006, Scar effects of unemployment: an assessment of institutional complementarities. *American Sociological Review* 71, 986–1013.

Garrett, G., 1998, *Partisan Politics in the Global Economy* (Cambridge University Press, Cambridge, UK/New York).

Gaston, N. and D. Nelson, 2004a, Structural change and the labor-market effects of globalization. *Review of International Economics* 12-#5, 769–792.

92   DAVIDSON ET AL.

—— and ——, 2004b, Structural change and the labor market effects of globalization. *Review of International Economics* 12, 769–792.

Greenaway, D. and D. Nelson, 2010, The politics of (anti-) globalization: what do we learn from simple models? in: N. Gaston and A. Khalid, eds., *Globalization and Economic Integration: Winners and Losers in the Asia-Pacific* (Edward Elgar, Cheltenham, UK) pp. 69–94.

Gregg, P., 2001, The impact of youth unemployment on adult unemployment in the NCDS. *Economic Journal* 111, F626–F653.

—— and E. Tominey, 2005, The wage scar from male youth unemployment. *Labour Economics* 12, 487–509.

Gregory, M. and R. Jukes, 2001, Unemployment and subsequent earnings: estimating scarring among British Men 1984–94. *Economic Journal* 111, F607–F625.

Grossman, G. and E. Helpman, 1994, Protection for sale. *American Economic Review* 84, 833–850.

Guisinger, A., 2009, Determining trade policy: do voters hold politicians accountable? *International Organization* 63, 533–557.

Hainmueller, J. and M. Hiscox, 2006, Learning to love globalization: education and individual attitudes toward international trade. *International Organization* 60, 469–498.

Hall, H. K., C. Kao, and D. Nelson, 1998, Women and tariffs: testing the gender gap hypothesis in a Downs-Mayer political-economy model. *Economic Inquiry* 36, 320–332.

Heckman, J. J., R. J. Lalonde, and J. A. Smith, 1999, The economics and econometrics of active labor market programs, in: O. Ashenfelter and D. Card, eds., *Handbook of Labor Economics* (North-Holland, Amsterdam) pp. 1865–2097.

Helliwell, J. F., 2003, How's life? Combining individual and national variables to explain subjective well-being. *Economic Modelling* 20, 331–360.

Helpman, E. and O. Itskhoki, 2010, Labor market rigidities, trade and unemployment. *Review of Economic Studies* 77(3), 1100–1137.

Hibbs, D. A., 1993, *Solidarity or Egoism? The Economics of Sociotropic and Egocentric Influences on Political Behavior: Denmark in International and Theoretica Perspective* (Aarhus University Press, Aarhus).

Hicks, A. M., 1999, *Social Democracy and Welfare Capitalism: A Century of Income Security Politics* (Cornell University Press, Ithaca, NY).

Hiscox, M., 2006, Through a glass darkly: framing effects and individuals' attitudes toward trade. *International Organization* 60, 755–780.

Huber, E. and J. D. Stephens, 2001, *Development and Crisis of the Welfare State: Parties and Policies in Global Markets* (University of Chicago Press, Chicago, IL).

Iversen, T. and T. R. Cusack, 2000, The causes of welfare state expansion – deindustrialization or globalization? *World Politics* 52, 313–349.

Jacobson, L. S., R. J. Lalonde, and D. G. Sullivan, 1993, Earnings losses of displaced workers. *American Economic Review* 83, 685–709.

Karp, L. and T. Paul, 1994, Phasing in and phasing out protectionism with costly adjustment of labor. *Economic Journal* 104, 1379–1392.

—— and ——, 1998, Labor adjustment and gradual reform: when is commitment important? *Journal of International Economics* 46, 333–362.

—— and ——, 2005, Intersectoral adjustment and policy intervention: the importance of general equilibrium effects. *Review of International Economics* 13, 330–355.

Katzenstein, P. J., 1984, *Corporatism and Change: Austria, Switzerland, and the Politics of Industry* (Cornell University Press, Ithaca, NY).

——, 1985, *Small States in World Markets: Industrial Policy in Europe* (Cornell University Press, Ithaca, NY).

Kiewiet, D. R., 1983, *Macroeconomics and Micropolitics: The Electoral Effects of Economic Issues* (University of Chicago Press, Chicago, IL).

Kinder, D. R., G. S. Adams, and P. W. Gronke, 1989, Economics and politics in the 1984 American presidential election. *American Journal of Political Science* 33, 491–515.

—— and D. R. Kiewiet, 1979, Economic discontent and political behavior: the role of personal grievances and collective economic judgements in congressional voting. *American Journal of Political Science* 23, 495–527.

—— and ——, 1981, Sociotropic politics – the American case. *British Journal of Political Science* 11, 129–161.

Kletzer, L., 2001, *Job Loss from Imports: Measuring the Costs* (Institute for International Economics, Washington, DC).

——— and R. Litan, 2001, *A Prescription to Relieve Worker Anxiety* (Institute for International Economics, Washington, DC).

Kreickemeier, U. and D. Nelson, 2006, Fair wages, unemployment and technological change in a global economy. *Journal of International Economics* 70, 451–469.

Krishna, P. and M. Z. Senses, 2009, International trade and labor income risk in the United States. NBER Working Paper No. 14992.

Lanoue, D. J., 1994, Retrospective and prospective voting in presidential year elections. *Political Research Quarterly* 47, 193–205.

Lawrence, R. and R. Litan, 1986, *Saving Free Trade: A Pragmatic Approach* (Brookings, Washington, DC).

Layard, R., 2005, *Happiness: Lessons from a New Science* (Penguin, New York).

———, S. J. Nickell, and R. Jackman, 1991, *Unemployment: Macroeconomic Performance and the Labour Market* (Oxford University Press, Oxford, England/New York).

Lewis-Beck, M. S., 1988, *Economics and Elections: The Major Western Democracies* (University of Michigan Press, Ann Arbor, MI).

Lucas, R. E., A. E. Clark, Y. Georgellis, and E. Diener, 2004, Unemployment alters the set point for life satisfaction. *Psychological Science* 15, 8–13.

MacKuen, M., R. Erikson, and J. A. Stimson, 1992, Peasants or bankers? The American electorate and the U.S. economy. *American Political Science Review* 86, 597–611.

Magee, C., C. Davidson, and S. Matusz, 2005, Trade, turnover, and tithing. *Journal of International Economics* 66, 157–176.

Magee, S. P. and L. Young, 1987, Endogenous protection in the United States, 1900-1984, in: R. Stern, ed., *U.S. Trade Policies in a Changing World Economy* (MIT Press, Cambridge) pp. 145–195.

Mansfield, E. D. and D. C. Mutz, 2009, Support for free trade: self-interest, sociotropic politics, and out-group anxiety. *International Organization* 63, 425–457.

Markus, G. B., 1988, The impact of personal and national economic conditions on the presidential vote: a pooled cross-sectional analysis. *American Journal of Political Science* 32, 137–154.

———, 1992, The impact of personal and national economic conditions on presidential voting: 1956–1988. *American Journal of Political Science* 36, 829–834.

Matschke, X. and S. Sherlund, 2006, Do labor issues matter in the determination of U.S. trade policy? An empirical reevaluation. *American Economic Review* 96, 405–421.

Matusz, S. J., 1994, International trade policy in a model of unemployment and wage differentials. *Canadian Journal of Economics* 27, 939–949.

———, 1996, International trade, the division of labor, and unemployment. *International Economic Review* 37, 71–84.

Mayda, A. M. and D. Rodrik, 2005, Why are some people (and countries) more protectionist than others? *European Economic Review* 49, 1393–1430.

Mutz, D. C. and J. J. Mondak, 1997, Dimensions of sociotropic behavior: group-based judgments of fairness and well-being. *American Journal of Political Science* 41, 284–308.

O'Rourke, K. and R. Sinnott, 2002, The determinants of individual trade policy preference: international survey evidence, in: S. Collins and D. Rodrik, eds., *Brookings Trade Forum* (Brookings, Washington, DC) pp. 157–206.

OECD, 1990, *Labour Market Policies for the 1990s* (Organization for Economic Cooperation and Development, Paris).

OECD, 1991, *Evaluating Labour Market and Social Programmes* (Organizaton for Economic Cooperation and Development, Paris).

OECD, 1994, *The OECD Jobs Study: Facts, Analysis, Strategies* (Organization for Economic Cooperation and Development, Paris).

OECD, 2006, *OECD Employment Outlook–2006* (Organization for Economic Cooperation and Development, Paris).

Oswald, A. J., 2003, How much do external factors affect well-being? *Psychologist* 16, 140–141.

Pacek, A. and B. Radcliff, 2008, Assessing the welfare state: the politics of happiness. *Perspectives on Politics* 6, 267–277.

94 DAVIDSON ET AL.

Polanyi, K., 1944, *The Great Transformation: The Political and Economic Origins of Our Time* (Farrar & Rinehart, New York/Toronto).

Pontusson, J., 2005, *Inequality and Prosperity: Social Europe Vs. Liberal America* (Cornell University Press, Ithaca, NY).

Rama, M. and G. Tabellini, 1998, Lobbying by capital and labor over trade and labor market policies. *European Economic Review* 42, 1295–1316.

Rodrik, D., 1998, Why do more open economies have bigger governments? *Journal of Political Economy* 106, 997–1032.

Romero, D. W. and S. J. Stambough, 1996, Personal economic well-being and the individual vote for congress: a pooled analysis, 1980–1990. *Political Research Quarterly* 49, 607–616.

Schattschneider, E. E., 1960, *The Semisovereign People: A Realist's View of Democracy in America* (Holt, New York).

Scheve, K. and M. Slaughter, 2001a, *Globalization and the Perceptions of American Workers* (Institute for International Economics, Washington, DC).

——— and ———, 2001b, What determines individual trade-policy preferences? *Journal of International Economics* 54, 267–292.

Slaughter, M., 2000, What are the results of product-price studies and what can we learn from their differences? in: R. Feenstra, ed., *The Impact of International Trade on Wages* (University of Chicago Press, Chicago, IL) pp. 129–165.

Stiglitz, J. E. and A. Charlton, 2005, *Fair Trade for All: How Trade Can Promote Development* (Oxford University Press, Oxford).

Swank, D., 2002, *Global Capital, Political Institutions, and Policy Change in Developed Welfare States* (Cambridge University Press, Cambridge).

Takacs, W. E., 1981, Pressures for protectionism – an empirical-analysis. *Economic Inquiry* 19, 687–693.

Wallerstein, M., 1987, Unemployment, collective-bargaining, and the demand for protection. *American Journal of Political Science* 31, 729–752.

Winkelmann, L. and R. Winkelmann, 1998, Why are the unemployed so unhappy? Evidence from panel data. *Economica* 65, 1–15.

Trade Theory

Journal of International Economics 36 (1994) 309–331. North-Holland

Incentive compatible regulation of a foreign-owned subsidiary

Thomas A. Gresik

Department of Economics, The Pennsylvania State University, University Park, PA 16802, USA

Douglas R. Nelson*

Murphy Institute of Political Economy, Tulane University, New Orleans, LA 70118, USA

Received June 1991, revised version received June 1993

Transfer prices are administered charges for intra-firm transfers of factors of production. For a multinational firm, transfer prices for international transfers provide the means to redistribute costs and increase global profits given variations in national tax and profit repatriation policies. Local regulation of a subsidiary may thus be necessary to limit the welfare costs of strategic transfer pricing. Prusa (*Journal of International Economics*, 1990, 28, 155–172) characterizes the welfare-maximizing regulations for a monopoly subsidiary that induce the firm to report transfer prices truthfully. We show, however, that it can be more efficient to implement regulations that encourage the firm to misrepresent its true transfer costs.

Key words: Transfer prices; Multinational regulation; Incentive compatibility
JEL classification: F13; F23; D82 C72

1. Introduction

Transfer prices are administered charges for intra-firm transfers of goods and factors of production. By misrepresenting the cost of a transfer, a firm can shift the apparent location of profits across national boundaries. For multinational enterprises (MNEs), transfer prices represent one of the more effective tools for dealing with disparate national tax and repatriation policies.[1] The fact that MNEs can circumvent national tax and regulatory policies through the strategic use of transfer prices may explain, in part, why

Correspondence to: Professor Thomas Gresik, Department of Economics, The Pennsylvania State University, University Park, PA 16802, USA.
*We thank Rick Bond, Keith Crocker, Nancy Lutz, Roger Myerson and several referees from this journal whose comments have significantly improved the presentation of our results. As always, we alone are responsible for any errors.

[1]See Lall (1973) for an extensive discussion of the incentives to engage in strategic transfer pricing. Benvignati (1985) presents a useful empirical study of the transfer-pricing behavior of U.S. firms.

MNEs tend to be larger and more profitable than the average firm in the relevant industry.[2] This same fact also provides an explanation for the interest on the part of national governments, especially those with protectionist interests, to regulate the transfer pricing of MNEs whose local subsidiaries represent foreign direct investment. One might therefore assume that national welfare is best served by implementing regulations that induce MNEs to report transfer prices truthfully. We will show that national welfare may in fact be best served by regulations that allow the firm to earn positive or negative transfer price profits.

Given the prominence of foreign direct investment and the significance of transfer pricing, it is not surprising that there is a substantial and sophisticated literature studying the phenomenon.[3] Starting with the foundational papers by Copithorne (1971) and Horst (1971), a number of scholars have studied the effect of various tax/tariff regimes on the pricing and production decisions of MNEs and, conversely, the optimal regimes for regulating the profit-maximizing MNE.[4] Until recently, however, the literature on the regulation of MNEs assumed that the national tax/regulatory authority possessed the information necessary to implement its optimal tax policy [Horst (1977, 1980), Diewert (1985), Hartman (1985)]. Thus, Prusa's (1990) recent extension of Baron and Myerson's (1982) model of optimal regulation of a domestic monopolist under incomplete cost information to the case of a multinational monopolist constitutes a considerable advance on the previous literature.[5]

Because national regulations can create incentives to strategically misrepresent the cost of intra-firm transfers, a sophisticated government should adopt regulatory objectives that are incentive compatible with respect to the MNE's transfer pricing behavior. Following the literature on regulating a domestic monopolist, Prusa focuses attention on direct two-part regulatory schemes – that is, schemes in which the regulator sets a price and a lump-sum subsidy given the MNE's report of its marginal cost (in this case,

---

[2]See Caves (1982) for a review of research on MNEs. See Graham and Krugman (1990) and Julius (1990) for recent presentations of aggregate data on foreign direct investment. Recent research by Benvignati (1987) is particularly relevant to the profitability of MNEs.

[3]In general, direct investment is distinguished from portfolio investment in terms of managerial control. Portfolio investment is undertaken as a function of the risk–return properties of a given investment, while a direct investment is undertaken to acquire managerial control over the production, pricing, and other activities of a firm located in a different national market. This economic distinction should not be confused with the balance-of-payments distinction which turns on the degree of ownership (i.e. more than 10 percent constitutes direct investment, less than 10 percent constitutes portfolio investment).

[4]See the useful survey paper by Eden (1985) for an introduction to this literature. The other papers collected in Rugman and Eden (1985) provide theoretical extensions and empirical observations on the phenomenon of transfer pricing and its regulation.

[5]In addition to the paper by Baron and Myerson (1982), see the excellent surveys by Besanko and Sappington (1986) and Baron (1989) for more recent developments on regulation under uncertainty.

marginal cost is determined by the cost of a transferred intermediate good from one division of the MNE to a subsidiary operating in another country). The MNE's report is also assumed to be the transfer price charged to the division receiving the transfer. Regulating the subsidiary then is treated as a principal–agent problem in which the national regulatory/tax authority is the principal and the MNE is the agent possessing private information about the cost of production. As is usual in the literature that has grown out of Baron and Myerson's work, the national authority uses a subsidy to induce compliance with a second-best pricing/output scheme, where the second-best nature of the solution flows from the fact that the MNE must receive private information rents.

Prusa's analysis of the transfer price regulation problem is incomplete, however, because he restricts attention to regulatory schemes that induce the MNE to truthfully report the cost of its intermediate good. In many models, such a restriction involves no loss of generality because of the Revelation Principle.[6] In the model Prusa analyzes, this is not necessarily true. A problem arises because the MNE's transfer price in Prusa's model serves two purposes. It redistributes the MNE's costs between its subsidiary and the parent firm and it communicates cost information to national authorities. If an MNE's transfer prices only played an informational role, inducing truthful cost reporting would not by itself create an additional welfare cost. But because transfer prices allow an MNE to increase its global post-tax profits via cost redistribution, they also have the potential to limit the national authority's ability to adequately control the MNE's global profits. Any attempt to induce truthful transfer prices may generate additional welfare costs by restricting how the national authority allows the MNE to earn its information rents. Therefore any analysis of optimal regulations must either disentangle the two tasks currently served by transfer prices or it must provide a proper accounting of the welfare costs associated with limiting transfer price distortions.

Disentangling the two roles played by transfer prices represents an application of Myerson's (1982) 'generalized Revelation Principle'. Although Myerson was concerned with moral hazard issues, of which none exists in this paper, his basic idea of expanding the set of available regulatory instruments still applies. In our paper, this involves the MNE reporting its transfer cost to the government. The government then uses the report to set the level of regulation and the MNE's transfer price. By setting the transfer price, the national authority gains control of both relevant dimensions of the MNE's profit: monopoly distortion and cost distribution. We refer to this option as direct transfer price regulation. Added flexibility in analyzing

---

[6] For the foundational work on the Revelation Principle, see Dasgupta et al. (1979), Myerson (1979), Rosenthal (1979), and Harris and Townsend (1981).

optimal regulations occurs because the transfer price need not equal the MNE's reported costs. In fact, the two will generally not be equal under the optimal regulations.

If explicitly setting the MNE's transfer price is not feasible for institutional or political reasons, then we are back to Prusa's model. To properly account for a transfer price's effect on national welfare, we use a technique first developed by Mirrlees (1971) by which identifying optimal regulations involves defining a set of performance targets – desirable price, repatriation, and subsidy levels – and then constructing a set of regulations that implement the performance targets. We refer to this option as indirect transfer price regulation because the government indirectly sets the MNE's transfer price via the incentives created by its choice of regulations. If the optimal direct regulations include a strictly monotonic transfer-price rule, the optimal indirect regulations are payoff equivalent with the optimal direct regulations. If the optimal direct transfer-price rule is not strictly monotonic, the government strictly prefers direct regulation to indirect regulation.

The optimal regulations include features common in the regulation literature such as marginal cost plus pricing that reflects the second-best nature of the regulations and the fact that the MNE collects information rents. Features specific to the multinational case depend on the relative weights given consumer and producer surplus by the national regulator. When the value placed on producer surplus relative to consumer surplus is small (in a sense to be made precise below), the optimal regulations generally require zero operating profits for the local subsidiary and positive transfer-price profits. This case also supports a continuum of 'knife-edge' regulations that are optimal, including Prusa's regulations that require truthful cost reporting.[7] On the other hand, when the relative value of producer surplus is high, the optimal regulations require positive operating profits. Transfer-price profits can be either positive or negative and honest transfer pricing is never optimal.

The economic intuition for these results is straightforward. Although the government's price regulation determines the level of information rents an MNE can earn, the MNE can collect these rents either as transfer-price profits or as operating profits from its subsidiary. This means that the government's problem is to decide how best to distribute the MNE's rents between these two sources. If the government restricts attention to regulations that induce truthful transfer prices, all of the MNE's rents must take the form of operating profits. As we have suggested above, national welfare

---

[7]It is important to note that by invoking the Revelation Principle, the optimality of any resultant solutions can only be asserted and not proven unless the antecedents of the Revelation Principle are satisfied. In Prusa's model they are not. Moreover, we will show that Prusa's solution is optimal under certain economic conditions only if several modifications to his model are adopted.

can be enhanced by allowing the MNE to earn non-zero transfer-price profits.[8]

Finally, we show that if the government requires the MNE's transfer price to fall within a prespecified interval, then with a minor modification of our model, there exist economic conditions under which the limit transfer pricing policies found in Copithorne (1971) and Horst (1971) are optimal direct regulations. It is not known whether limit transfer pricing is supported by optimal indirect regulations.

We begin our analysis in section 2 where we present Prusa's model of an MNE, describe the set of incentive compatible regulations that he claims maximize expected welfare for the country playing host to the subsidiary, and point out where his analysis is incomplete. In section 3 we characterize optimal direct regulations and in section 4 we characterize optimal indirect regulations. We conclude our discussion with some remarks in section 5.

2. A simple model of an MNE

We begin by presenting Prusa's model of an MNE which has its origin in the papers of Copithorne (1971) and Horst (1971).[9] This model will provide a reference point for our arguments.

Consider the case of a parent company located in its Home country that owns and operates a subsidiary in a Host country. The parent company produces an intermediate product at Home and ships it to the subsidiary at a total constant marginal cost, θ. The subsidiary then transforms the imported intermediate good under fixed costs, k.[10] While the subsidiary's fixed cost is known to the Host government and the MNE or firm, only the MNE knows its marginal cost. The Host government believes that the firm's marginal cost is distributed according to $G(\theta)$ with continuous positive density $g(\theta)$ on the interval $[\theta_0, \theta_1]$. Finally, there is assumed to be some sort

[8]Two related studies of transfer pricing by an MNE are Raff (1991) and Stoughton and Talmor (1991). Raff derives the optimal transfer-price regulations when the MNE is involved in exporting intermediate goods to the parent firm. The focus on export transfer prices instead of import transfer prices allows him to avoid the complications associated with the Revelation Principle that we encounter. Stoughton and Talmor focus on the internal transfer-price policies of an MNE when the subsidiary has better information about its operations than does the parent. Their study then differs from ours in that our focus is on the problems of regulating an MNE when the informational asymmetry is between the MNE and the foreign government.
[9]While the Horst and Copithorne models are formally equivalent, Horst analyzes transfer pricing in a horizontally integrated firm while Copithorne analyzes transfer pricing in a vertically integrated firm. Thus, our study more closely parallels that of Copithorne's. For numerous other examples in which the Horst and Copithorne models have been used, see Eden (1985).
[10]This assumption, that the marginal cost of production in the affiliate is entirely due to the cost of the imported intermediate good, is fairly standard.

of exogenously determined interest differential between the two countries, $i \geqq 0$, so that the parent company weakly prefers to repatriate the subsidiary's profits.[11]

The subsidiary is a monopolist in the Host country facing a strictly decreasing inverse demand curve, $P(\cdot)$. Moreover, we assume that market demand is large enough so that an unregulated subsidiary could earn positive economic profits regardless of its true costs. The Host government wishes to regulate the subsidiary's operations through control of the market price, p, a profit repatriation limit, β, and a production subsidy, S. Actually, we assume the regulator sets a market price indirectly by setting an output level, q. Clearly, $p = P(q)$. In addition, the subsidiary faces a corporate profit tax, $\gamma \in [0,1]$, and an ad valorem tariff, t, on the imported intermediate product that are outside the control of the regulator.[12]

Generally speaking the regulatory scheme the Host government uses will present the parent company with an incentive to distort the price it charges its subsidiary for the intermediate product. In so doing it can repatriate foreign earned profits in a manner not subject to the Host country's regulations. The subsidiary earns operating profits of

$$\pi(\theta_h) = P(q(\theta_h))q(\theta_h) - (1+t)\theta_h q(\theta_h) - k + S(\theta_h) \tag{1}$$

and pays Host taxes equal to $\gamma\pi(\theta_h)$ when it reports a marginal cost of θ_h to the Host government and faces the regulatory scheme, $(q(\theta_h), \beta(\theta_h), S(\theta_h))$. Thus, given the interest differential, the MNE's global post-tax profit from its foreign operations (measured in the Host country's currency) is

$$\tau(\theta_h, \theta) = (1+i)(\theta_h - \theta)q(\theta_h) + (1-\gamma)(1+\beta(\theta_h)i)\pi(\theta_h). \tag{2}$$

We assume that knowing θ and faced with the regulations $Q = (q, \beta, S; t, \gamma)$ abroad, the firm chooses θ_h to maximize (2). Let $\theta_h^*(\theta)$ denote the firm's optimal transfer-price strategy. In general it will be easier to define a regulatory scheme as a quantity schedule, a repatriation rate, and an

[11]Prusa argues that the interest differential can be given a broad interpretation, incorporating such factors as exchange risk and political risk. While Prusa's assumption that $i > 0$ is perfectly reasonable, it may also be the case that $i = 0$ for a broad range of cases. For example, the European Community under a unified currency/financial regime would, presumably, fall into this case. Thus, our analysis covers both cases. The case for which $i < 0$ represents the situation where the Host government places restrictive limits on foreign direct investment. Faced with such limits a firm can use its transfer prices to indirect increase its investment in the Host market. Since studying this case requires explicit modelling of the investment opportunities in the Host market, it is beyond the scope of this paper.

[12]The exogenous specification of the profit tax and the tariff simplify our analysis and involve no loss of generality. In a model in which the profit tax and the tariff are also set by the regulator, it is easy to demonstrate that the tariff and the subsidy are perfect substitutes for achieving any incentive feasible level of welfare and the profit tax and the subsidy are close (but imperfect) substitutes. Thus, our admittedly ad hoc focus on the role of production subsidies as a regulatory tool will not affect the general implications of our analysis.

operating profit schedule, that is as $Q = (q, \beta, \pi; t, \gamma)$. Without loss of generality we will use (1) and adopt this second definition.[13]

The Host government wishes to choose a regulatory scheme that maximizes a weighted sum of expected consumer surplus, producer surplus, and tax revenues. The weights on consumer surplus and tax revenues are equal and normalized to 1 while the weight on producer surplus equals α, where $0 \leqq \alpha < 1$. If we denote gross consumer benefit by $V(q) = \int_0^q P(t)\,dt$, then the Host regulator's social welfare function equals

$$\int_{\theta=\theta_0}^{\theta_1} \{V(q(\theta_h^*(\theta))) - P(q(\theta_h^*(\theta)))q(\theta_h^*(\theta)) - S(\theta_h^*(\theta)) + t\theta_h^*(\theta)q(\theta_h^*(\theta))$$

$$+ [\gamma + \alpha(1-\gamma)(1 - \beta(\theta_h^*(\theta)))]\pi(\theta_h^*(\theta))\}g(\theta)\,d\theta. \tag{3}$$

Using (1) to eliminate S and (2) to eliminate $\theta_h^*(\theta)q(\theta_h^*(\theta))$ allows us to write the Host regulator's problem as

$$\max \int_{\theta=\theta_0}^{\theta_1} \left\{ V(q(\theta_h^*(\theta))) - \theta q(\theta_h^*(\theta)) + (1-\gamma)\left(\alpha - \frac{i}{1+i}\right) \right.$$

$$\left. (1 - \beta(\theta_h^*(\theta)))\pi(\theta_h^*(\theta)) - \frac{\tau(\theta_h^*(\theta), \theta)}{1+i} \right\} g(\theta)\,d\theta - k \tag{4}$$

s.t. (a) $\tau(\theta_h^*(\theta), \theta) \geqq 0$,

    (b) $0 \leqq \beta(\theta_h^*(\theta)) \leqq 1$,

    (c) $\theta_h^*(\theta) \in \underset{\tilde{\theta}}{\operatorname{argmax}}\ \tau(\tilde{\theta}, \theta)$.

The rationale behind constraint (a) is that the firm can always guarantee itself zero global post-tax profits by shutting down. Thus, any feasible set of regulations must provide an adequate incentive for the firm to operate the subsidiary. Constraint (b) simply reflects the fact that the repatriation rate is a fraction between 0 and 1. Constraint (c) is the incentive compatibility constraint.

A useful benchmark is the welfare-maximizing regulatory scheme when the Host government has complete cost information. The complete information problem is defined by dropping the integral in the maximand of (4) and incentive constraint (c). We will show that honest transfer pricing is not welfare maximizing. When $\theta_h^*(\theta)$ is assumed to equal θ, the complete

---

[13]To minimize on notation the reference to t and γ will generally be omitted.

information solution is $P(q(\theta)) = \theta$, $\beta(\theta) = 0$, and $\pi(\theta) = 0$. The Host country, however, can generate greater welfare by regulating the MNE's transfer price so that it can differ from θ.[14] Let $\rho(\theta_h)$ denote the regulated transfer price. Because the Host country and the MNE view operating profits and transfer-price profits as perfect substitutes (α and i are constant), the complete information problem is unbounded. When $\alpha < i/(1 + i)$, the optimal regulations set $\pi = -\infty$ which must be offset by $\rho = +\infty$ so that $\tau = 0$. When $\alpha > i/(1 + i)$, $\pi = +\infty$ and $\rho = -\infty$. This discussion is summarized in Lemma 1.

Lemma 1.   With complete cost information, the welfare-maximizing regulations involve marginal cost pricing, zero repatriation, and zero global profits. Moreover, if the transfer must equal actual cost, the subsidiary's operating profit equals zero while if the transfer price can differ from actual cost, either operating profit equals $+\infty$ and the transfer price equals $-\infty$ or vice versa.

Another benchmark is Prusa's solution. It is described in Lemma 2. He obtains his solution by adding to (4) the constraint, $\theta_h^*(\theta) = \theta$. This constraint is analogous to the restriction in the complete information problem that transfer price equal actual cost. Call the optimization problem formed by adding this additional constraint to (4), (4'). The reasoning behind this assumption will be discussed shortly. The reader is referred to Prusa (1990) for the proof of Lemma 2.

Lemma 2.   Assume that $\theta + G(\theta)/g(\theta)$ is increasing.[15] Then the solution to (4') satisfies: (i) $P(q(\theta)) = \theta + (1 + i)\mu(\theta)/g(\theta)$, where $\mu(\theta) = G(\theta)/(1 + i)$ if $\alpha < i/(1 + i)$ and $\mu(\theta) = (1 - \alpha)G(\theta)$ if $\alpha \geq i/(1 + i)$; (ii) $\beta(\theta) = 1$ if $\alpha < i/(1 + i)$ while $\beta(\theta) = 0$ if $\alpha \geq i/(1 + i)$; and

(iii) $\tau(\theta) = \pi(\theta) = (1 + i) \int\limits_{w = \theta}^{\theta_1} q(w)\,dw.$[16]

Three features of Lemma 2 are important to note. First, marginal-cost pricing occurs only when the firm's marginal cost equals θ_0. Second, the subsidiary's global post-tax profit equals the information rents paid to the firm by the regulator. It is strictly positive except when the firm's marginal cost equals θ_1. In light of Lemma 1, the regulatory scheme described in Lemma 2 is clearly not first-best. Third, the justification for the additional constraint in (4') is the Revelation Principle which asserts that, for many

---

[14]Prusa's model does not formally provide the Host country with this option.
[15]This condition is satisfied by a large class of distributions including those most often used in applications.
[16]Remember that the regulations can be functions of only the firm's report, θ_h. However, given the additional truth-telling constraint, we know that $\theta_h = \theta$.

economic problems, there is no loss of generality in restricting attention to regulations requiring a cost report, such as (q, β, π), that induce the firm to honestly report its private cost information. What this means is if the Revelation Principle can be applied to (4), (4) and (4') will be payoff equivalent. Unfortunately, this is not true.

A quick way to verify that (4) and (4') are not equivalent is to note that like its complete information counterpart in which the transfer price need not equal actual cost, (4) is unbounded. (4') is not. The unboundedness arises because none of the constraints in (4) places any bounds on the term in the maximand, $(1-\gamma)\{\alpha-[i/(1+i)]\}(1-\beta)\pi$, and the remaining terms in the maximand are functions of only q. So if $\alpha-i/(1+i)>0$, the optimal operating subsidy equals $+\infty$ and the optimal transfer price equals $-\infty$. Global post-tax profits are positive and finite. If $\alpha-i/(1+i)<0$, the optimal subsidy equals $-\infty$ while the optimal transfer price equals $+\infty$. Global post-tax profits are the same as before. Expected welfare in either case is infinite.

The economic reason (4) is unbounded is related to the fact that a dollar of producer surplus left in the Host country is worth only $1/(1+i)$ dollars to the MNE. This means the MNE should be willing to pay up to $i/(1+i)$ dollars to repatriate this profit. Thus, $i/(1+i)$ equals the Host government's opportunity cost of keeping a dollar of operating profit in the country. Whether the Host government wants to allow or enjoin repatriation depends upon whether the value it places on a dollar of producer surplus (α) is greater or less than the opportunity cost of retaining operating profits in the Host country. In other words, $\alpha-i/(1+i)$ is the Host country's marginal rate of substitution between operating profits and transfer-price profits. Since it is a constant in Prusa's model, these two types of profit are perfect substitutes. Setting $\rho=\theta$ prohibits the regulator from substituting between transfer-price profits and operating profits and prevents unbounded solutions. Once ρ and θ can differ, assuming that the Host country treats both types of profits as perfect substitutes becomes questionable on economic grounds and suggests the need for more natural economic assumptions. We will offer a set of such assumptions in the next section.

This initial analysis of both complete and incomplete information versions of Prusa's model identifies the assumption that the transfer price equal actual cost as the source of the lack of generality in Prusa's analysis. The complete information analysis shows that the restriction is costly and the incomplete information analysis shows that the incentive constraints need not eliminate this cost. As a result, a certain degree of strategic transfer pricing may be welfare enhancing.

There is a second way to understand how, by solving (4') instead of (4), one overlooks some important economic costs. In order to maximize expected welfare, the Host country must be able to control two aspects of the MNE's activities: the size of its monopoly distortion and its cost distribution.

The latter must be controlled because the MNE's report provides it with a direct benefit from cost redistribution which in turn can lead to a reduction in welfare.[17]

That is, the MNE's information rent is correlated with its output distortion (the closer the subsidiary's output to the unregulated monopoly level, the lower the MNE's information rent). To balance the welfare gains from reducing the MNE's output distortion with the attendant information costs, the Host country needs both quantity regulation and a lump-sum subsidy to achieve a second-best level of welfare. But the Host government also needs to control the MNE's cost distribution in order to present the firm with reporting incentives consistent with its welfare objectives. Problem (4') does not necessarily capture the relevant incentive costs due to the two functions the MNE's cost report plays. A simple example confirms this fact.

Suppose $\gamma = 1$. (Remember that γ is an exogenous parameter.)[18] In this case, direct revelation requires that $q(\theta_h) \equiv 0$. Consequently, the firm's global post-tax profit equals zero as does the Host country's welfare. Such a scheme cannot be optimal since the Host country can always decide not to regulate the firm in which case the firm earns monopoly profits and generates positive welfare levels (consumer surplus) for the Host country. Clearly, no regulation Pareto dominates any direct revelation regulation when $\gamma = 1$.

Since (4') does not account for possible 'limited-control' welfare costs, we will, in the next two sections, characterize the expected welfare-maximizing regulations and identify conditions under which the regulations (q, β, π) give the Host country sufficient control over the MNE's global profits to generate second-best welfare levels. When these conditions fail to hold, the Host country can benefit from also regulating the MNE's transfer price.

3. Direct transfer price regulation

Because the Revelation Principle cannot be applied to the model in section

---

[17]We are grateful to a referee for pointing out that direct payoff relevance of the MNE's report is not sufficient to conclude that the Revelation Principle does not hold. For example, when $\gamma = i = 0$, our model reduces down to Baron and Myerson's (1982) model, a model for which the Revelation Principle holds. (That is, the transfer-pricing problem is fundamentally a consequence of tax and capital interest differentials.) However, instead of asking the firm to report its cost, the government could indirectly solicit cost information by asking the firm to set output and then offer a subsidy schedule defined in terms of the firm's output choice. In this case, the firm's choice is clearly payoff relevant. In our model, direct payoff relevance becomes a factor because we are considering regulations that solicit cost information directly and because Host country welfare is affected by changes in the value of the source of this direct payoff relevance – cost redistribution.

[18]The choice of $\gamma = 1$ may appear pathological. In the next section we will show that this is not the case by solving (4) for any value of γ (and α, i, and t). The sole purpose of setting $\gamma = 1$ at this point in the paper is to provide a very simple example to help convince the reader that something is amiss with the application of the Revelation Principle in Prusa's paper.

2, another method is needed for working with the complex association between a government's choice of regulations, the MNE's cost report, and the consequent effect on the country's welfare. In this section we augment the set of instruments available to the Host government by assuming it sets ρ, the MNE's transfer price, as well as (q, β, π). Giving the Host government control over the firm's transfer price breaks the link between the MNE's cost report and cost distribution and gives the Host government full control of the MNE's global profits. Alternatively, we could assume that the government offers the MNE a fully repatriatable subsidy, ρq, and a partially repatriatable subsidy, S.[19]

Allowing ρ to differ from θ gives the Host regulator greater flexibility in deciding how the MNE will earn its information rents. Before, the information rents took the form of greater operating profits. Now, the MNE can collect information rents either as operating profits or as transfer-price profits. Moreover, since negative operating profits or negative transfer-price profits (but not both) are now possible, we must take account of certain economic costs that are inconsequential in a model that proscribes non-zero transfer-price profits.[20] The modifications to Prusa's model which we use to account for these costs are described below.

First, we consider changes related to the possibility that $\pi < 0$. Given (q, β, π, ρ), the subsidiary's operating profit equals

$$\pi(\theta_h) = P(q(\theta_h))q(\theta_h) - (1+t)\rho(\theta_h)q(\theta_h) - k + S(\theta_h). \tag{5}$$

If $\pi > 0$, the MNE's global post-tax profit equals

$$\tau(\theta_h, \theta) = (1+i)(\rho(\theta_h) - \theta)q(\theta_h) + (1-\gamma)(1+\beta(\theta_h)i)\pi(\theta_h). \tag{6}$$

On the other hand, if $\pi \leq 0$, the profit tax and repatriation rate are no longer relevant (effectively, $\gamma = 0$ and $\beta = 1$) and

$$\tau(\theta_h, \theta) = (1+i)[(\rho(\theta_h) - \theta)q(\theta_h) + \pi(\theta_h)]. \tag{7}$$

Eq. (7) implies that the MNE must repatriate its subsidiary's losses. Without this assumption, the subsidiary would have to find alternative financial resources when $\pi < 0$ or close down. In reality, then, our assumption is that the MNE is the subsidiary's only external source of funds. As long as $\tau > 0$

---

[19]We thank one of the referees for this interpretation.

[20]Negative transfer-price profits provide an alternative channel for increased foreign direct investment, something an MNE would be willing to consider if its subsidiary's operations were suitably rewarded. At the same time an MNE would be willing to accept regulations that imply negative *economic* operating profits for its subsidiary if the transfer-price regulations provided adequate transfer-price profits. Empirical evidence for both types of trade-offs can be found in Alworth (1988), Rugman and Eden (1985), and Razin and Slemrod (1990).

for almost all θ, the MNE will want to repatriate subsidiary losses to maintain an ongoing concern and the opportunity cost of each dollar of such support is $1+i$.

There is also the issue of how negative producer surplus enters the Host country's welfare function. We prefer to think of α as the opportunity cost of producer surplus when $\pi < 0$. For our model there is no loss of generality in assuming that α is a constant for all $\pi \leq 0$.

Second, we consider changes related to the possibility of negative transfer-price profits that arise when $\rho < \theta$. Here we dispense with the assumption that consumer and producer surplus are perfect substitutes as implied by the constant weight put on producer surplus in the Host country's welfare function. The reason for assuming a decreasing marginal rate of substitution between consumer and producer surplus is that larger transfer-price losses must necessarily be coupled with larger operating profits in order to cover the MNE's information rents. Larger operating profits at some point can only be achieved via larger operating subsidies and large subsidies carry with them non-trivial economic costs. These include opportunity costs that reflect general equilibrium distortions when the Host government raises the subsidy with taxes and a capital market distortion when it raises the subsidy by borrowing. In addition one can also expect that the marginal benefit of producer surplus is decreasing and that the marginal cost of producer surplus due to increased political instability is increasing. Individually or together these reasons imply that consumer and producer surplus are not perfect substitutes. Alternatively one could point out that negative transfer-price profits imply increased capital investment in the subsidiary and that this additional capital will eventually generate increasing opportunity costs for the MNE because of capital market imperfections. That is, if the capital investment in the subsidiary is large enough, the MNE will need to borrow funds. Imperfect capital markets imply an increasing marginal cost of these funds. All three of these costs, increasing marginal opportunity costs of capital for the MNE, increasing marginal costs of subsidy dollars for the Host government, and a decreasing marginal rate of substitution between consumer and producer surplus, affect the relative returns to various levels of regulation in similar ways. In order to limit the complexity of the model, we will only model the last of these three costs by assuming that for $\pi > 0$, the weight on producer surplus is a function of the subsidiary's operating profits.

Assumption 1. (i) $0 \leq \alpha(0) \leq 1$, (ii) $\alpha(\infty) = 0$, and (iii) $\alpha'(\pi) < 0$ *for* $\pi \geq 0$.

Assumption 2. (i) α *is continuously differentiable and* (ii) $\pi(\theta) = \hat{\pi}$ *uniquely maximizes* $\{\alpha(\pi(\theta)) - [i/(1+i)]\}\pi(\theta)$ *when* $\alpha(0) > i/(1+i)$.

Assumption 1 requires that the net marginal benefit of producer surplus is initially positive, that it is generally less than the marginal benefit of consumer surplus, that it is strictly decreasing, and that it converges to 0. Assumption 2 is included to simplify the technical exposition.

These assumptions naturally bound the Host country's problem. Recognizing the different tax and repatriation treatments of negative operating profits bounds the problem from below while allowing for a variable weight on producer surplus bounds the problem from above.

Finally we modify Prusa's model by assuming that $\beta = 0$. If β was chosen endogenously, its optimal value would either be 0 or its value would be irrelevant (with one exception that we will mention below). Thus we exogenously set β to 0 to economize on notation.

Together these changes alter the Host country's social welfare function. Let $W(q(\theta_h), \pi(\theta_h), \rho(\theta_h, \theta)$ denote this welfare function for a reported cost of θ_h and a true cost of θ. Combining these changes with (5), (6), and (7) implies that if $\pi(\theta_h) > 0$,

$$W = V(q(\theta_h)) - \theta q(\theta_h) + (1 - \gamma)\left(\alpha(\pi(\theta_h)) - \frac{i}{1+i}\right)\pi(\theta_h) - \frac{\tau(\theta_h, \theta)}{1+i} - k, \quad (8)$$

and if $\pi(\theta_h) \leqq 0$,

$$W = V(q(\theta_h)) - \theta q(\theta_h) + \alpha(\pi(\theta_h))\pi(\theta_h) - \frac{\tau(\theta_h, \theta)}{1+i} - k. \quad (9)$$

Of course, the most important change in this section is letting the Host government set the MNE's transfer price. Since the MNE's cost report is no longer directly payoff relevant we can, without loss of generality, invoke the Revelation Principle and restrict attention to direct revelation regulations. Lemma 3 characterizes these regulations.[21]

Lemma 3. The regulations (q, β, π, ρ) are direct revelation regulations if, and only if,

$$\tau'(\theta) \equiv \frac{d\tau(\theta, \theta)}{d\theta} = -(1+i)q(\theta) \quad (10)$$

and

$$q'(\theta) \leqq 0. \quad (11)$$

Intuitively, (10) tells us that to support honest reporting, the firm's global post-tax profits must be negatively correlated with its cost report and (11)

---

[21]Prusa's (1990) proof of his Proposition 2 is analogous to the proof of Lemma 3.

tells us that higher cost reports must result in lower output levels. In light of Lemma 3, let $\tau(\theta) \equiv \tau(\theta, \theta)$.

We can now write down the Host country's optimization problem as

$$\max \int_{\theta = \theta_0}^{\theta_1} W(q(\theta), \pi(\theta), \tau(\theta), \theta) g(\theta) \, d\theta \qquad (12)$$

s.t. (a) $\tau(\theta, \theta) \geq 0$,
   (b) $\tau'(\theta) = -(1 + i)q(\theta)$,
   (c) $q'(\theta) \leq 0$.

The easiest way to solve (12) is to drop constraint (c) and then verify that it is satisfied by the solution. Theorem 1 describes the regulations that solve (12). The proof is in Appendix A.

Theorem 1.   Assume that $\theta + G(\theta)/g(\theta)$ is increasing.[22] Let (q^*, ρ^*, π^*) denote the solution to (12) and let τ^* denote the MNE's global post-tax profit given (q^*, ρ^*, π^*). Then

$$P(q^*(\theta)) = \theta + G(\theta)/g(\theta),$$

$$\tau^*(\theta) = (1 + i) \int_{w = \theta}^{\theta_1} q^*(w) \, dw,$$

and

$$\rho^*(\theta) = \theta + \frac{\tau^*(\theta)}{(1 + i)q^*(\theta)} - \frac{1 - \gamma}{1 + i} \frac{\pi^*(\theta)}{q^*(\theta)}.$$

For $\alpha(0) \leq i/(1 + i)$, $\pi^*(\theta) = 0$. For $\alpha(0) > i/(1 + i)$, $\pi^*(\theta) = \hat{\pi}$ and $\alpha(\hat{\pi}) + \alpha'(\hat{\pi})\hat{\pi} = i/(1 + i)$.

The economic reason that two cases arise was discussed earlier in reference to the unboundedness problem. Regardless of which case we wish to discuss, Lemma 3 makes it quite clear that the MNE must earn cost-information rents and hence non-negative global post-tax profits. As a result the Host government must address two questions: How large should the MNE's information rents be? What is the optimal distribution of these rents between transfer-price profits and operating profits? For the first question the problem is that in welfare terms the Host country would like to increase market output up to the first-best level of Lemma 1. However, as the Host government increases output beyond the unconstrained monopoly level, the

---

[22]This condition, which is satisfied by many common densities, ensures that the solution satisfies constraint (12c). See Baron and Myerson (1984) or Prusa (1990) for details.

T.A. Gresik and D.R. Nelson, Incentive compatible regulation of a foreign-owned subsidiary 323

information rents due the firm also increase. Thus, the output schedule should only be increased out to the point where the marginal gain in surplus equals the Host country's marginal cost of the MNE's information rents. That is what the pricing rules accomplish.

Up to this point there are only minor differences between Prusa's solution in Lemma 2 and the solution above in Theorem 1. Where the two solutions differ, however, is in the way the Host government allows or encourages the MNE to collect its information rents. By assuming that $\rho(\theta) = \theta$, Prusa was effectively requiring the Host government to pay the MNE all of its rents via a production subsidy. The following corollary identifies the expected welfare costs of this assumption. Its proof is in Appendix A.

Corollary 1.   *Let* $\theta + G(\theta)/g(\theta)$ *be increasing. If* $\alpha(0) < i/(1 + i)$, *then for all* $\theta \in [\theta_0, \theta_1)$, $\rho^*(\theta) > \theta$ *and* $(\rho^*)'(\theta) > 0$. *For* $\alpha(0) > i/(1 + i)$, *let* $\hat{\theta} = \min \{\theta \mid \tau^*(\theta) \leq (1 - \gamma)\hat{\pi}\}$. *Then for all* $\theta < \hat{\theta}$, $\rho^*(\theta) > \theta$ *and* $(\rho^*)'(\theta) > 0$, *and for all* $\theta > \hat{\theta}$, $\rho^*(\theta) < \theta$ *and* $(\rho^*)'(\theta) < 0$.

Corollary 1 makes it clear that a policy that induces honest transfer pricing for any level of true costs θ is never welfare maximizing. In addition, if the marginal value of producer surplus starts out greater than $i/(1 + i)$ and decreases fast enough, then the optimal regulations may include both positive transfer-price profits and positive operating profits. If the rate of decrease is slower, then the Host country will elect to use operating profits exclusively to pay the MNE its information rents.

It is important to note that if the repatriation rate, β, is set endogenously, then when $\alpha(0) \leq i/(1 + i)$, another set of solutions emerges. In this case, $\beta = 1$ and any value of $\pi(\theta)$ is optimal. The implication of this result is that $\rho(\theta) < \theta$, $\rho(\theta) = \theta$, $\rho(\theta) > \theta$, or any combination of these possibilities can be consistent with expected welfare maximization. In particular, the component of Prusa's solution when $\alpha < i/(1 + i)$ is optimal. These alternative solutions would disappear if the profit tax is levied on positive accounting profits instead of just positive economic profits (or at least to some arbitrarily small fraction of economic profits less accounting profits). It would also be true in this case that the optimal regulations would result in zero accounting profits for the subsidiary. In this way these alternative solutions can be viewed as knife-edge solutions.

The optimal transfer-price behavior also does not correspond to the limit transfer-pricing strategies found in the complete-information models of Copithorne (1971) and Diewert (1985). With limit transfer pricing the MNE's transfer price equals either θ_0 or θ_1. Limit transfer pricing is also found in Prusa's Proposition 1, but then only as the MNE's response to fixed, ad hoc repatriation and subsidy levels. Given the model used in this section, limit transfer pricing cannot be optimal because it is impossible for $\rho^*(\theta) \geq \theta_1$ for all θ when $\alpha(0) \leqq i/(1+i)$. However, if the profit tax is levied on positive accounting profits rather than positive economic profits and if $\rho \in [\theta_0, \theta_1]$, conditions exist under which limit transfer-pricing behavior is welfare maximizing. This change requires that we assume $k = k^a + k^o$, where k^a equals the accounting cost of the MNE's fixed investment and k^o equals the opportunity cost of the MNE's fixed investment. If $|\alpha'(\cdot)|$ is sufficiently small and k^o is sufficiently large, then the optimal transfer price equals either θ_0 or θ_1. When $\alpha(0) > i/(1+i)$, the slower the rate at which the marginal benefit of producer surplus decreases as the level of produce surplus increases, the higher is the optimal level of operating profit for the subsidiary. If this operating profit level is sufficiently large, the optimal regulations will imply $\rho(\theta) \leqq \theta_0$. But since we now require $\rho \geqq \theta_0$, ρ will equal θ_0. When $\alpha(0) \leqq i/(1+i)$, negative economic operating profits implies positive transfer-price profits. Since the optimal regulations do not cover k^o with operating profits they must be covered with transfer-price profits. Thus, ρ will be larger the larger k^o. But $\rho \leqq \theta_1$. So if k^o is large enough, $\rho(\theta) = \theta_1$. Consequently, conditions exist under which limit transfer pricing can be seen as an optimal policy given a profit tax on accounting profit and an exogenous requirement that the MNE's transfer price agree with the support of the Host country's beliefs.

4. Indirect transfer price regulation

Instead of adopting direct transfer price regulations, governments often use regulations that allow the MNE to set its transfer price but provide incentives that 'guide' the MNE's choice. Such indirect regulations, however, reintroduce the Revelation Principle problems identified in section 2. In this section we characterize optimal indirect transfer-price regulations and compare their welfare properties with the optimal direct regulations of section 3. The approach we use is due to Mirrlees (1971). It involves first writing (4), with the assumptions from section 3 used to bound the problem, in terms of what we will call performance targets. This new problem differs from (12) in that it does not restrict attention to regulations that induce truth-telling. We then solve for the optimal performance targets and derive the regulations $Q = (q, \pi)$ that implement these targets.[23]

We need to define two targets, one for each regulatory instrument. Denote these targets by $\delta = (\delta_q, \delta_\pi)$ where

$$\delta_q(\theta) = q(\theta_h^*(\theta)) \quad \text{and} \quad \delta_\pi(\theta) = \pi(\theta_h^*(\theta)). \tag{13}$$

These performances targets specify the output and operating profit levels the Host government would like to realize for each value of θ given the MNE's

[23]We will continue to assume that $\beta = 0$.

optimal transfer-price strategy $\theta_h^*(\theta)$.[24] Certainly, if we start with a set of regulations, it is possible to derive the corresponding performance targets. However, we need to work in the opposite direction. That is, given some performance targets we need to associate them with regulations that satisfy (13). We will call the targets δ *incentive compatible* if, and only if, there exist regulations Q such that (13) holds. If such a set of regulations exists, we will say that Q *implements* δ. If $Q = \delta$, then Q is a set of direct revelation regulations.

If we ignore the implementation issue for a moment, it turns out that the optimal targets, $\delta^* = (\delta_q^*, \delta_\pi^*)$, coincide with the optimal regulations of Theorem 1. That is, $\delta_q^*(\theta) = q^*(\theta)$ and $\delta_\pi^*(\theta) = \pi^*(\theta)$. If δ^* is incentive compatible, then it must also be true that $\theta_h^*(\theta) = \rho^*(\theta)$. Since $q^*(\theta)$ is strictly decreasing, a necessary and sufficient condition for implementation is that ρ^* be invertible. According to Corollary 1, this is true only when $\alpha(0) \leq i/(1+i)$ or when $\alpha(0) > i/(1+i)$ and $(1-\gamma)\hat{\pi} \geq \tau^*(\theta_0)$ because these conditions are necessary and sufficient for ρ^* to be strictly monotonic. In both cases, the optimal direct and indirect regulations are welfare equivalent, i.e. they generate the same market price, the same operating and transfer-price profits, and the same transfer prices. Still δ^* only defines target quantity and operating profit levels. The actual regulations that implement these targets, call them q^{*i} and π^{*i}, are those that satisfy (13) and for which

$$\frac{\partial \tau^*(\theta_h^*(\theta), \theta)}{\partial \theta_h} = 0, \tag{14}$$

where

$$\tau(\theta_h, \theta) = (1+i)(\theta_h - \theta)q(\theta_h) + (1-\gamma)\pi(\theta_h) \tag{15}$$

when $\pi(\theta_h) > 0$ and

$$\tau(\theta_h, \theta) = (1+i)[(\theta_h - \theta)q(\theta_h) + \pi(\theta_h)] \tag{16}$$

when $\pi(\theta_h) \leq 0$. Eq. (14) is the first-order condition for $\theta_h^*(\theta)$ to be a profit-maximizing reporting strategy. Because $\pi^*(\theta)$ is a constant in both cases, (13) can only be satisfied if $\pi^{*i}(\theta_h) = 0$ when $\alpha(0) \leq i/(1+i)$ and if $\pi^{*i}(\theta_h) = \hat{\pi}$ when $\alpha(0) > i/(1+i)$. Moreover, $\pi^*(\theta)$ constant implies that (14) is equivalent to

$$q(\theta_h^*(\theta)) + (\theta_h^*(\theta) - \theta)q'(\theta_h^*(\theta)) = 0. \tag{17}$$

---

[24]Because $P(\cdot)$ is common knowledge and strictly decreasing, one can alternatively think of indirect transfer pricing as price regulation in the final good market.

326   T.A. Gresik and D.R. Nelson, Incentive compatible regulation of a foreign-owned subsidiary

The solution to the differential equation in (17) defines $q^{*i}(\theta_h)$. The details are provided in the Appendix B.

In the remaining case, ρ^* does not fully separate or distinguish among different cost levels, θ, even though q^* requires full separation.[25] Although describing the optimal indirect regulations for this third case must be left for future research, it is possible to conclude from the above discussion that in this case the optimal direct regulations generate strictly greater expected welfare than the optimal indirect regulations.[26] Theorem 2 summarizes this discussion.

Theorem 2. If $\alpha(0) \leq i/(1+i)$ or $\alpha(0) > i/(1+i)$ and $(1-\gamma)\hat{\pi} \geq \tau^*(\theta_0)$, then the expected welfare-maximizing direct regulations and the expected welfare-maximizing indirect regulations are welfare and profit equivalent. If $\alpha(0) > i/(1+i)$ and $(1-\gamma)\hat{\pi} < \tau^*(\theta_0)$, then the Host country strictly prefers the expected welfare-maximizing direct regulations over the expected welfare-maximizing indirect regulations.

5. Conclusion

When we talk about international transfer pricing, the most common example associates the United States with the Home country and some developing country with the Host. However, recent events like 'Europe 1992' and the establishment of productive capacity by Japanese firms in the United States will quickly, if they have not already, upset these stereotypes. Recent congressional concern over the transfer-price practices of the Japanese suggests that confronting these issues from the perspective of the Host government is already a very real issue in U.S. trade policy. While our analysis of the problem is far from complete, we believe our work makes several important points.

First, the fact that the MNE's transfer has both direct and indirect payoff relevance can invalidate studies arising from a standard application of the Revelation Principle. To address this fundamental problem in the study of strategic trade issues the transfer price must either be placed under the direct control of the Host government or the optimal regulations that allow the MNE to control its transfer price must be defined using techniques common to the optimal taxation literature.

---

[25]We thank one of the referees for pointing out a problem related to this fact in an earlier draft.

[26]The same problem arises in the model variant in which limit transfer pricing emerges as an optimal direct policy. Since $(\rho^*)'(\theta) = 0$, the MNE's cost report under indirect regulation is uninformative. As a result, all indirect regulations generate fewer welfare gains than the best direct regulation.

Second, although international transfer pricing necessarily creates opportunities to skirt local tax policies and other financial regulations it also creates an opportunity for a Host government to induce compliance with its regulations in a way that reduces the welfare costs of the information rents the MNE will inevitably collect. As long as the Host government places sufficient value on producer surplus, any attempt to eliminate the incentives that encourage a firm to distort its transfer prices and that also fail to eliminate the underlying incomplete information problems will result in lower welfare for the Host country.

Third, given that tariffs on imported intermediate goods often have distortionary effects from a general equilibrium perspective, they should be eliminated since in both cases they serve only to increase the subsidy the government must pay the firm. Moreover, for each dollar collected via a tariff, the subsidy must be increased by a dollar.

Fourth, the direction in which the firm strategically manipulates its price is directly related to the Host country's attitudes towards producer surplus. With a sufficiently strong value placed on producer surplus, the Host country benefits from regulations that increase the level of foreign direct investment it receives.

Fifth, while there can exist an equivalence between the optimal direct and indirect regulations, one need not exist in general.

A number of areas of future research are also suggested by our results. Among them we mention two that we will pursue in future papers. First, in this paper we studied optimal regulation of a foreign-owned subsidiary that operates as a monopolist. If instead the subsidiary faces local competition, the set of regulatory instruments available to the Host government may change and competition may diminish the value of the MNE's private information. These changes may then alter the structure of optimal transfer-pricing regulation. Second, the regulation of a MNE by a Host country may create incentives for the Home country to offer the parent company countervailing incentives. Thus, the regulation of an MNE might best be viewed as a problem of common agency since both countries can influence the firm's behavior through the choice of local regulations. Given this potential interaction among competing regulations it may be important to delineate when it is appropriate to analyze a firm's transfer-price activities as a pair of disjoint principal–agent problems and when it is necessary to adopt an integrated common agency approach. For examples of this type of problem see Baron (1985), Gal-Or (1991), van Egteren (1991) and Stole (1992).

Appendix A: Proofs

Proof of Theorem 1. The Hamiltonian associated with (12) is

328	T.A. Gresik and D.R. Nelson, Incentive compatible regulation of a foreign-owned subsidiary

$$\mathcal{H} = W(q, \pi, \tau, \theta)g(\theta) - \mu(\theta)(1 + i)q(\theta),$$

where τ is the state variable, μ is the co-state variable, q and π are the controls, and

$W(q, \pi, \tau, \theta) =$

$$\begin{cases} V(q(\theta)) - \theta q(\theta) - \dfrac{\tau}{1+i} + (1-\gamma)\left(\alpha(\pi(\theta)) - \dfrac{i}{1+i}\right)\pi(\theta) - k, & \text{if } \pi(\theta) > 0, \\[3mm] V(q(\theta)) - \theta q(\theta) - \dfrac{\tau}{1+i} + \alpha(0)\pi(\theta) - k, & \text{if } \pi(\theta) \leq 0. \end{cases}$$

The Euler conditions with respect to q and τ are

$$(P(q(\theta)) - \theta)g(\theta) - \mu(\theta)(1 + i) = 0 \tag{A.1}$$

and

$$\mu'(\theta) = \frac{g(\theta)}{1+i}. \tag{A.2}$$

Eq. (A.2) implies that $\mu(\theta) = G(\theta)/(1 + i)$. Thus, (A.1) implies that

$$P(q^*(\theta)) = \theta + \frac{G(\theta)}{g(\theta)}.$$

When $\alpha(0) < i/(1 + i)$, $W_\pi < 0$ for $\pi > 0$ and $W_\pi > 0$ for $\pi \leq 0$. Thus, $\pi^*(\theta) = 0$. When $\alpha(0) > i/(1 + i)$, $W_\pi > 0$ for $\pi = 0^+$. Hence, $\pi^*(\theta) > 0$ and satisfies

$$\alpha'(\pi(\theta))\pi(\theta) + \alpha(\pi(\theta)) = i/(1 + i). \tag{A.3}$$

For this latter case, let $\Gamma(\pi) = (\alpha(\pi) - i/(1 + i))\pi$. Because $\Gamma(0) = 0$, because there exists a $\bar{\pi}$ such that for all $\pi > \bar{\pi}$, $\Gamma(\pi) \leq 0$, and because $\Gamma'(0) > 0$, a local maximum of Γ (and hence $\mathcal{H}$) exists. Therefore a global maximum also exists and must satisfy (A.3). Finally, $P' < 0$ guarantees that the second-order conditions for a maximization are also satisfied.

$\tau^*(\theta, \theta)$ can be derived from (10) and by noting that the implicit transversality condition requires that $\tau^*(\theta_1, \theta_1) = 0$. (6) and (7) can then be used to derive $\rho^*(\theta)$.

Finally, if $\theta + G(\theta)/g(\theta)$ is non-decreasing, then $q'(\theta) \leq 0$. Given Lemma 3, (q^*, π^*, ρ^*) must be direct revelation regulations.	Q.E.D.

Proof of Corollary 1.	Given Theorem 1, (6), and (7),

$$\rho^*(\theta) = \theta + \frac{\tau^*(\theta)}{(1+i)q^*(\theta)} \tag{A.4}$$

and

$$(\rho^*)'(\theta) = \frac{-\tau^*(\theta)(q^*)'(\theta)}{(1+i)q^*(\theta)^2} \tag{A.5}$$

if $\alpha(0) \leq i/(1+i)$; while

$$\rho^*(\theta) = \theta + \frac{\tau^*(\theta) - (1-\gamma)\hat{\pi}}{(1+i)q^*(\theta)} \tag{A.6}$$

and

$$(\rho^*)'(\theta) = \frac{(q^*)'(\theta)}{(1+i)q^*(\theta)^2} [(1-\gamma)\hat{\pi} - \tau^*(\theta)]. \tag{A.7}$$

if $\alpha(0) > i/(1+i)$. Thus, $\rho^*(\theta) > \theta$ in (A.4) and as $(q^*)'(\theta) < 0$, $(\rho^*)'(\theta) > 0$ in (A.5). The signs of both $\rho^*(\theta) - \theta$ from (A.6) and $(\rho^*)'(\theta)$ from (A.7) equal the sign of $\tau^*(\theta) - (1-\gamma)\hat{\pi}$.   Q.E.D.

Appendix B: The solution to differential equation (17) – The optimal indirect quantity schedule

Because $\delta_q'(\theta) < 0$ and because there are no exogenous bounds on the MNE's reported transfer price, (17) is both necessary and sufficient for implementation. Part of the difficulty in solving (17) is the fact that $\theta_h^*(\theta)$ depends on q.

To solve (17) multiply both sides by $(\theta_h^*)'(\theta)$, which equals $(\rho^*)'(\theta)$, and thus is non-zero by Corollary 1. Then substitute (13) into (17) noting that $\theta_h^*(\theta) = q^{-1}(\delta_q(\theta))$ and $(\theta_h^*)'(\theta) = (q^{-1})'(\delta_q(\theta))\delta_q'(\theta)$, where $\delta_q(\theta) = q^*(\theta)$. This yields

$$\frac{\mathrm{d}}{\mathrm{d}\theta} [\delta_q(\theta)q^{-1}(\delta_q(\theta))] = \theta\delta_q'(\theta). \tag{B.1}$$

(B.1) is an ordinary differential equation in $q^{-1}(\cdot)$ the solution of which is

$$wq^{-1}(w) = \delta_q(\theta_1)q^{-1}(\delta_q(\theta_1)) - \int_{x = \delta_q^{-1}(w)}^{\theta_1} x\delta_q'(x)\,\mathrm{d}x.$$

The initial condition

330 T.A. Gresik and D.R. Nelson, Incentive compatible regulation of a foreign-owned subsidiary

$$
\delta_q(\theta_1)q^{-1}(\delta_q(\theta_1)) = \theta_h^*(\theta_1)q(\theta_h^*(\theta_1)) =
\begin{cases}
\theta_1\delta_q(\theta_1), & \text{if } \alpha(0) \leq \dfrac{i}{1+i}, \\[4mm]
\theta_1\delta_q(\theta_1) - \dfrac{(1-\gamma)\hat{\pi}}{1+i}, & \text{if } \alpha(0) > \dfrac{i}{1+i},
\end{cases}
$$

ensures that $\tau(\theta_h^*(\theta_1), \theta_1) = 0$.

References

Alworth, J., 1988, The finance, investment, and taxation decisions of multinationals (Blackwell, Oxford).

Baron, D., 1985, Noncooperative regulation of a nonlocalized externality, Rand Journal of Economics 16, 553–568.

Baron, D., 1989, Design of regulatory mechanisms and institutions, in: R. Schmalensee and R. Willig, eds., Handbook of industrial organization, Vol. 2 (North-Holland, Amsterdam) 1347–1447.

Baron, D. and R. Myerson, 1982, Regulating a monopolist with unknown costs, Econometrica 50, 911–930.

Benvignati, A., 1985, An empirical investigation of transfer pricing by US manufacturing firms, in: A. Rugman and L. Eden, eds., Multinationals and transfer pricing (St. Martins, New York) 193–211.

Benvignati, A., 1987, Domestic profit advantages of multinational firms, Journal of Business 60, 449–461.

Besanko, D. and D. Sappington, 1986, Designing regulatory policy with limited information, in: M. Crew, ed., Fundamentals of pure and applied economics, Vol. 20 (Harwood Press, New York).

Caves, R., 1982, Multinational enterprise and economic analysis (Cambridge University Press, Cambridge).

Copithorne, L., 1971, International corporate transfer prices and government policy, Canadian Journal of Economics 4, 324–341.

Dasgupta, P., P. Hammond and E. Maskin, 1979, The implementation of social choice rules: Some general results on incentive compatibility, Review of Economic Studies 46, 185–216.

Diewert, E., 1985, Transfer pricing and economic efficiency, in: A. Rugman and L. Eden, eds., Multinationals and transfer pricing (St. Martins, New York) 47–81.

Eden, L., 1985, The microeconomics of transfer pricing, in: A. Rugman and L. Eden, eds., Multinationals and transfer pricing (St. Martins, New York) 13–46.

Gal-Or, E., 1991, A common agency with incomplete information, Rand Journal of Economics 22, 274–286.

Graham, E. and P. Krugman, 1990, Foreign direct investment in the United States (Institute for International Economics, Washington, DC).

Harris, M. and R. Townsend, 1981, Resource allocation under asymmetric information, Econometrica 49, 33–64.

Hartman, D., 1985, Tax policy and foreign direct investment, Journal of Public Economics 26, 107–121.

Horst, T., 1971, Theory of the multinational firm: Optimal behavior under differing tariff and tax rates, Journal of Political Economy 79, 1059–1072.

Horst, T., 1977, American taxation of multinational firms, American Economic Review 67, 376–389.

Horst, T., 1980, A note on the optimal taxation of international income, Quarterly Journal of Economics 44, 793–798.

Julius, D., 1990, Global companies and public policy (Royal Institute for International Affairs, London).

T.A. Gresik and D.R. Nelson, *Incentive compatible regulation of a foreign-owned subsidiary* 331

Lall, S., 1973, Transfer pricing by multinational manufacturing firms, Oxford Bulletin of Economics and Statistics 35, 173–195.
Mirrlees, J., 1971, An exploration in the theory of optimum income taxation, Review of Economic Studies 28, 175–208.
Myerson, R., 1979, Incentive compatibility and the bargaining problem, Econometrica 47, 61–73.
Myerson, R., 1982, Optimal coordination mechanisms in generalized principal–agent problems, Journal of Mathematical Economics 10, 67–81.
Prusa, T., 1990, An incentive compatible approach to the transfer pricing problem, Journal of International Economics 28, 155–172.
Raff, H., 1991, Intra-firm exports and optimal host country commercial policy under asymmetric information, Mimeo. (Université Laval).
Razin, A. and J. Slemrod, eds., 1990, Taxation in the global economy (NBER, Chicago, IL).
Rosenthal, R., 1979, Arbitration of two-party disputes under uncertainty, Review of Economic Studies 45, 595–604.
Rugman, A. and L. Eden, eds., 1985, Multinationals and transfer pricing (St. Martins, New York).
Stole, L., 1992, Mechanism design under common agency, Mimeo. (University of Chicago, Chicago, IL).
Stoughton, N. and E. Taylor, 1991, A mechanism design approach to transfer pricing by the multinational firm, Mimeo. (University of California, Irvine, CA).
van Egteren, H., 1991, State versus federal environmental regulation in a non-cooperative monopoly screening model, Mimeo. (University of Illinois, Urbana, IL).

Intra-Industry Trade as an Indicator of Labor Market Adjustment

By

Mary E. Lovely and Douglas R. Nelson

Contents: I. Introduction. – II. Adjustment Costs under Inter-Industry Versus Intra-Industry Trade. – III. A Specific-Factors Model with IIT. – IV. Effects of Liberalization. – V. Measures of MIIT and Labor Adjustment. – VI. Conclusions. – Appendix.

I. Introduction

T he relationship between international trade and labor markets has been a central concern of pamphleteers, politicians, and academics for virtually as long as "international trade" has been a coherent concept.[1] While much of the current concern is motivated by the apparent deterioration in the returns to unskilled labor (both absolutely and relative to skilled labor), issues of adjustment cost have figured prominently in both theoretical and empirical research for some time. In the 1990s, a sizable body of work developed attempting to use intra-industry trade (IIT) as an indicator of "non-disruptive trade growth" (Dixon and Menon 1997: 234). This work extends from Balassa's (1966) observation that adjustment to IIT might involve lower costs than adjustment to inter-industry trade.

Balassa's observation explains the powerful attraction of the IIT approach: it promises to isolate the role of trade changes on labor reallocations. Many factors influence labor markets, and, as the "trade and wages debate" shows, parceling responsibility for labor market outcomes to trade, technological change, labor supply shifts, etc., is fraught with difficulty. The IIT approach offers a way around these difficulties in that it promises readily available information about trade's ability to generate disruptive structural change. Its importance to trade policy-making is obvious; predictions about the structure of trade changes flow-

Remark: We thank Wilfred Ethier and Ted To for helpful comments. All remaining errors are our own.

[1] Viner (1937: 52–57) discusses the mercantilist's "stress on employment" and Irwin (1996) illustrates the continuing importance of labor-related issues in the evaluation of international trade from Graeco-Roman times down to our own.

ing from any particular agreement can be viewed as predictions about the political costs of the agreement.

Measurement issues are at the heart of the recent literature on IIT and adjustment. Hamilton and Kniest (1991) argue that using the change in the Grubel–Lloyd index of IIT to identify low-adjustment-cost trade can lead to potentially serious measurement error. In response, a growing body of papers examines the algebraic properties of various measures of *marginal intra-industry trade* (MIIT), seeking to determine their relative suitability as measures of the low-adjustment-cost component of increased trade (Azhar et al. 1998). These measures, which disaggregate the change in total trade in various ways, are claimed to be superior to simply measuring the change in the Grubel–Lloyd index, based on arguments that a particular calculation better represents the structure of the *change* in trade flows and, thus, better represents the effects of innovations in trade on labor allocation. Table 1 summarizes the recent literature and indicates the data used to calculate the authors' preferred IIT and/or MIIT measures (see pp. 189–191).

Despite the obvious importance of this empirical work for general assessment of the desirability of trade agreements, the theoretical foundations for MIIT measures have been examined in only a rudimentary way.[2] The purpose of this paper is to extend the theoretical analysis of MIIT, and in particular to embed it in an explicitly general-equilibrium environment. Working within a general-equilibrium context is essential because these measures are used to gauge an essentially general-equilibrium phenomenon: how labor is reallocated in response to broad trade agreements. We posit a model that reflects the literature's concern with short-run labor adjustment, and we use it to derive analytical expressions for MIIT and labor reallocation. We then compare these expressions to identify the conditions under which popular measures of (marginal) intra-industry trade are informative with respect to intra- versus inter-industry labor adjustment. Our results indicate the need to control for trade-induced changes in domestic demands, a fea-

---

[2] Much of this work focuses on measures of IIT for a given sector, without incorporating adjustments of the overall equilibrium, making algebraic analysis of these measures equivalent to a partial-equilibrium analysis. Brülhart's (1999) approach is ostensibly general-equilibrium, but he makes extreme assumptions that render the treatment of questionable value. One such assumption is that the structure of demand remains unaltered by changes in trade and domestic production. As we shall argue, MIIT measures fail to measure labor adjustment pressures, even under the best of production circumstances, precisely because of concomitant demand changes.

ture that is absent from the existing literature. Controlling for such changes offer a way to improve the current MIIT program, and the lack of such controls may explain the inability of researchers to find a systematic relationship between MIIT and direct measures of labor adjustment.

We begin by tracing the development of IIT as a measure of low-adjustment-cost trade and by describing the measures commonly used in the literature. In Section II we present our analytical framework, while Section III provides a comparative static analysis of liberalization in that framework. In Section IV we use this analysis to assess MIIT measures as indicators of labor reallocation. We conclude in Section V by placing our formal analysis in the context of the ongoing research program.

II. Adjustment Costs under Inter-Industry versus Intra-Industry Trade

Analysis of IIT has developed in close relationship with both the analysis of trade liberalization and the analysis of adjustment to international trade. In their now classic analyses of the trade effects of early European efforts at economic integration, Verdoorn (1960), Drèze (1960, 1961), and Balassa (1966), all emphasized the empirical importance of IIT. Balassa's work, in particular, laid the foundation for what has become an enormous empirical literature on the measurement of IIT.[3] It was also Balassa (1966) who suggested that adjustment to IIT might be expected to involve lower costs than inter-industry trade:

> It would appear that the difficulties of adjustment to freer trade have been generally overestimated. It is apparent that the increased exchange of consumer goods is compatible with unchanged production in every country while changes in product composition can be accomplished relatively easily in the case of machine building, precision instruments and various intermediate products. These considerations may explain why the fears expressed in various member countries about the demise of particular industries have not been realized. (1966: 472)

This theme, which has figured prominently in the literature on IIT, is also central to this paper. Thus, we first review the literature on IIT and industrial adjustment, which proceeds under the assumption that intra-industry adjustment is less costly than inter-industry adjustment, and

---

[3] Grubel and Lloyd (1975) is an essential landmark. See Greenaway and Milner (1986) for an extremely useful survey of the state of the art on all aspects of research on IIT. Greenaway and Torstensson (1997) provides an update.

182 Weltwirtschaftliches Archiv 2002, Vol. 138 (2)

then we review some recent research in labor economics that provides evidence of this assumption.

We need to consider three key causal connections: the link between liberalization and IIT; the link between IIT and inter- *versus* intra- industry labor mobility; and the relative cost of intra- *versus* inter-industry labor movement.[4] The last two make up what is sometimes called the "smooth adjustment hypothesis." That is, the claim that IIT generates smaller inter-industry factor movement than inter-industry (or "net") trade, and that inter-industry mobility is higher cost than intra-industry mobility.

Following early studies that appeared to show that intra-EEC IIT grew rapidly relative to total intra-EEC trade and relative to IIT growth outside the EEC, the question of whether there was an association between liberalization, and especially preferential liberalization, and growth in IIT was addressed in a large proportion of the research on IIT.[5] There seems to be fairly widespread acceptance of the existence of such an empirical relationship, even though empirical research has provided only mixed support.[6] The difficulty with this result is that there is no particular reason for there to be such a relationship based on economic fundamentals. Even in a world characterized by IIT, there is no particular reason for general liberalization, whether preferential or

---

[4] Our review of this early literature will be brief. For more detail with a particular focus on the adjustment implications of IIT in the EC context, see: White (1984), Greenaway and Milner (1986: ch. 11), Greenaway and Tharakan (1986), Greenaway (1987), and Greenaway and Hine (1991).

[5] In addition to the papers by Verdoorn, Drèze, and Balassa that we have already mentioned, important early papers by Kojima (1964) and Grubel (1967) also showed an apparently strong connection between liberalization and IIT. Similar results are recorded by Menon (1994) for the case of the Australia-New Zealand Closer Economic Relations Pact (CER).

[6] Key papers supporting the presence of a link between IIT and preferential liberalization are: Loertscher and Wolter (1980), Havrylyshyn and Civan (1983), Balassa and Bauwens (1987), and Globerman and Dean (1990). Pagoulatos and Sorenson (1975) and Caves (1981) consider measures of tariff level and tariff similarity between countries to test the hypothesis that multilateral liberalization induces IIT – i.e. tariff levels should be negatively associated and tariff similarity positively associated with IIT. Pagoulatos and Sorenson interpret their findings as supportive of this relationship. Caves, for whom levels had the wrong sign, found the relationship unconvincing on a priori grounds and took his results as insufficiently strong to change his priors. More recent research on protection levels or openness measures continues to generate mixed results, with Balassa and Bauwens (1987, 1988), Lee (1989), Clark (1993), and Stone and Lee (1995) providing support for some relationship, but Toh (1982) agreeing with Caves, and Torstensson (1996) arguing that protection variables are not robust in sensitivity analyses.

multilateral, to generate more IIT than would be present in the general evolution of trading patterns.[7] The peculiarity of the apparent connection between liberalization and IIT has led a number of investigators to conjecture that the causation actually runs from IIT (or, rather, potential for IIT) to liberalization. The argument proceeds from the claim, already present in the quotation above from Balassa (1966), that adjustment to IIT is less costly than adjustment to inter-industry trade, to the claim that countries negotiating liberalization will be predisposed to agree to liberalize sectors characterized by significant IIT, via a straightforward political economy argument. This suggestion was first studied in detail by Hufbauer and Chilas (1974), in the context of an analysis of trade among industrial countries, arguing:[8]

> "GATT negotiations very much favor intra-industry over inter-industry specialization. ... It is easier to secure one industry's consent for lower trade barriers if that *same* industry stands to gain from reciprocal concessions. ... Thus, GATT concessions typically foster intra-industry specialization." (1974: 6)

The authors then compare inter-industry specialization within the European Community to that between states in the United States, finding substantially higher inter-industry specialization within the United States. That is, in an environment where local (i.e., national in the EC context) governments are able to resist market reallocation, we observe the same pattern of IIT-dominated trade that we observe under GATT liberalization.

---

[7] This is particularly true given that the relationship between liberalization and IIT seems to be present in both south-south (Balassa 1979; Havrylyshyn and Civan 1983, 1985) and north-south (Tharakan 1984, 1986) trade. As Havrylyshyn and Civan (1983) make clear, while the trade of LDCs contains significant IIT, it is important to note that the volume of intra-industry trade declines as GNP per capita declines for any country, and also declines with the difference in GNP per capita between trading partners. The existence of substantial north-south IIT has led to a sizable literature on vertical IIT (see Hine et al. 1999). An essential point is that vertical IIT may be endowment-based and generate adjustment pressure more like that of inter-industry trade than intra-industry trade.

[8] One might note that this is also the basis of the common claim that free trade areas/customs unions are easier to create among countries between which IIT might be expected to be intense – i.e. relatively developed countries with similar factor endowments. Thus, whether preferential or multilateral, the liberalization process is expected to be most successful when it begins with partners and goods that are expected to involve relatively low adjustment costs and builds on that base. This would seem to be the model of the EU, NAFTA (which began not just with the United States and Canada, but with autos), and the GATT/WTO. Difficulties developed in all three cases in extending the logic of liberalization to both new products and new members. Thus, it is probably not surprising that such expansions have led to a boom in research on adjustment.

184   Weltwirtschaftliches Archiv 2002, Vol. 138 (2)

The suggestion that political economy forces help account for the prominence of IIT is widely cited and has received additional systematic study in the United States case by Finger and DeRosa (1979), Marvel and Ray (1987), and Ray (1991). Finger and DeRosa estimate a cross-industry regression of nominal or effective (post-Kennedy round) tariff rates on capital, labor, and human capital inputs as well as measures of intra-industry trade, finding a highly significant positive effect of labor use, and highly significant negative effects of human capital use and IIT for the case of nominal tariffs. That is, independently of the commonly noted tendency of industrial countries to protect labor, and controlling for factors generating export success, Finger and DeRosa find evidence of an independent effect of IIT on protection. Marvel and Ray (1987) regress measures of nominal or effective tariffs on instruments for import share, export share, and an interaction of the two, finding support for the claim that "as imports rise, additional exports limit significantly the protectionist impulse that the imports engender" (1987: 1288).[9] Lundberg and Hansson (1986) examine the relationship between protection and IIT for the case of Sweden finding only a weak and insignificant correlation (1959) or a positive and significant correlation (1972). However, when Lundberg and Hansson consider changes, they find a strong positive correlation between the initial level of IIT in 1959 and the reduction in tariffs from 1959 to 1972.[10] They take this as evidence in favor of the claim that adjustment costs are lower for IIT than inter-industry adjustment.

If we accept that IIT really is intra-*industry* (i.e., not the result of problems with categorical aggregation), we can take advantage of substantial direct evidence from research by labor economists on the question of the relative costs of inter- versus intra-industry adjustment. Specifically, a substantial body of research uniformly finds that the cost of being unemployed in terms of lower wages is higher under inter-industry adjustment (Neal 1995; Kletzer 1996; Kim 1998; Haynes et al. 2002). The modal explanation is quite clear: workers accu-

---

[9] Nelson (1990) and Ray (1991) provide discussions of the implications of this intersectoral pattern of protection on the prospects for LDC exports.

[10] This can be compared with Finger and DeRosa who find no cross-sectional relationship between their factor-input and IIT measures and changes. In the Finger–DeRosa case, because they were looking at effects generated by the Kennedy Round, which, as Jan Tumlir points out in a comment on the paper, was the first round to use a linear cut, this was to be expected. Similarly, since Lundberg and Hansson examine only correlation and not a regression, their cross-section results on levels of protection are not strictly comparable with those of Finger and DeRosa.

mulate human capital which is portable between firms in the same sector, but is not portable between sectors; when a sector contracts (as the importable sector does under liberalization in the HOS model), labor is forced to move to the expanding exportable-producing sector. The IIT case is thought to be different: firms may go out of business, but liberalization does not generate (high cost) inter-industry adjustment.

An interesting body of recent research, however, has questioned whether evidence of increases in IIT, as measured in conventional ways, provides a sufficient basis for accurate inferences about adjustment. This research accepts, as do we, the causal connection, based on findings by labor economists that intra-industry adjustment is associated with lower adjustment cost than inter-industry adjustment, but suggests alternative measures of the trade forces inducing the adjustment. Before turning to a consideration of this literature, we note that our fundamental focus, in this and the companion paper (Lovely and Nelson 2000), is the second causal link – from IIT to intra-industry adjustment. We now turn to a discussion of the appropriate measure of IIT for the study of factor-market adjustment, which will provide a fundamental input to our modelling in the next section.

Virtually all of the work we have considered to this point measures IIT by the Grubel–Lloyd index, or one of its variants.[11] If we let X_j and M_j denote exports and imports of commodity j, the Grubel–Lloyd index of IIT in sector j is given by:[12]

$$G_j := \frac{IIT_j}{TT_j} = \frac{X_j + M_j - |X_j - M_j|}{X_j + M_j} \equiv 1 - \frac{|X_j - M_j|}{X_j + M_j}. \tag{1}$$

G_j gives IIT as a share of total trade in commodity j, TT_j, and, thus, takes values between 0 (no IIT) and 1 (all trade is IIT). These indices can be studied directly or aggregated to study broad sectoral or economy-wide trends in IIT. To do the latter, it is common to use an average of the form:

---

[11] The variants attempt to correct for problems related to categorical aggregation or unbalanced trade, neither of which will concern us in our theoretical development, so we will focus on the Grubel–Lloyd index. For details on other measures, see chapter 5 of Greenaway and Milner (1986).

[12] The Grubel–Lloyd index follows straightforwardly from the fact that $IIT_j := 2 \min[X_j, M_j] = X_j + M_j - |X_j - M_j|$, and normalization by TT. One interprets G_j by noting that since net trade, $NT_j := |X_j - M_j|$, we can use the identity $TT \equiv IIT + NT$ and divide by TT to get an index that takes values in [0,1].

$$G_J := \sum_{j \in J} w_j G_j,$$

where J is a subset of industries (often manufacturing), at some level of aggregation (commonly 3-digit SITC), and where the w_j are aggregation weights such that $\sum_{j \in J} w_j = 1$. The research we reviewed above, implicitly or explicitly, takes change in the (sectoral or aggregate) Grubel–Lloyd index to indicate the magnitude of that part of new trade that does not generate high adjustment cost. That is, for the case of IIT in sector j, this research considers:

$$\Delta G_j := G_{j,t+1} - G_{j,t}. \tag{2}$$

Starting with a paper by Hamilton and Kniest (1991), however, it has been argued that (2) cannot provide accurate information on adjustment pressure.[13] Hamilton and Kniest emphasize, following Caves (1981: 213), that what is relevant is not whether the share of IIT has increased, but whether the share of IIT in *new* trade has increased. That is, if one is interested in the effect of changed trading conditions on adjustment, it is necessary to identify the contributions of change in IIT and change in net trade (NT) to change in total trade. Thus, they propose a measure of *marginal* IIT (MIIT). Following a critical evaluation by Greenaway et al. (1994), which identified some serious shortcomings in Hamilton and Kniest's indices, the bulk of empirical research on IIT and adjustment has focused on two, closely related, sets of measures of MIIT – one set due to Jayant Menon and Peter Dixon, the other due to Marius Brülhart.[14] Because Menon and Dixon are fundamentally concerned with measurement of MIIT and its contribution to change in total trade, whereas Brülhart is ultimately interested in issues of adjustment, we will start with Menon and Dixon's analysis and then take up Brülhart's.

In a useful series of papers, Menon and Dixon develop the theory of MIIT measurement in considerable detail.[15] Menon and Dixon's ba-

---

[13] See Azhar et al. (1998) for a very useful geometric comparison of the empirical properties of the various marginal IIT indices, and Brülhart (1999) for a detailed review of measures and empirical results, with particular reference to adjustment issues.

[14] We follow the literature in this attribution, but it should be noted that Shelburne (1993) first presented what is essentially Brülhart's *A* index, while Greenaway et al. (1994) give the first use of what we will call Menon and Dixon's first index (*MD*1).

[15] Dixon and Menon (1997) lays out the basic theory, Menon and Dixon (1996a) develops the application to regional trade arrangements, and Menon and Dixon (1996b) develops a framework within which the contributions of exports and imports of a commodity are separately considered.

sic measure of the contribution of the change in IIT to the percent change in total trade is:

$$MD1_j := \frac{\Delta IIT_j}{TT_j} = \hat{IIT}_j \, G_j,$$ (3)

where the "^" denotes a proportional change and G_j is the Grubel–Lloyd index for commodity j. Menon and Dixon prefer $MD1_j$ to ΔG_j because the latter can lead to quite misleading inferences about the significance of MIIT in changing trade. Specifically, an increase in G_j is generally taken to imply an increase in the significance of IIT relative to NT. However, as Menon and Dixon (1996a: 7–8) show analytically, it is possible for $\Delta G_j > 0$ to be associated with a smaller marginal increase in intra-industry trade than in net trade. Perhaps more importantly, they develop extensive empirical evidence of precisely such an implication. Dixon and Menon (1997) use Australian data at the 3-digit SITC level to illustrate the empirical significance of the measure one chooses to use in analyzing the effect of IIT in changing aggregate trade. Specifically, they find that, of the 133 manufacturing industries that make up their data set, about 14 percent in 1981–1986, and 31 percent in 1986–1991, were characterized by increases in G_j but larger contributions of marginal net trade than marginal IIT.

Dixon and Menon (1997) point out that $MD1_j$ may itself lead to faulty inference if the goal of the analysis is to identify that share of trade growth characterized by low adjustment costs. As an alternative, they propose:

$$MD2_j := \frac{2\min[\Delta X_j, \Delta M_j]}{TT}.$$ (4)

Since $2\min[\Delta X_j, \Delta M_j] \neq \Delta IIT$, it is clear that the indices in (3) and (4) are distinct.[16] $MD2_j$ is a measure of the part of trade change accounted for by matched changes in imports and exports, which is a measure of the share of trade change that creates low adjustment costs. Specifically, Dixon and Menon (1997, at equations 17–20) show that $MD1_j$ will overestimate the "non-disruptive" part of change in trade (i.e. $MD1_j \geq MD2_j$).[17] As they argue, since $MD2_j$ is a direct measure of matched changes in imports and exports, relative to total trade, it is precisely a

---

[16] It is straightforward to show that $\Delta IIT = \Delta X_j + \Delta M_j + |X_j - M_j| - |X_j + \Delta X_j - M_j - \Delta M_j|$ and that $2\min[\Delta X_j, \Delta M_j] = \Delta X_j + \Delta M_j - |\Delta X_j - \Delta M_j|$.

[17] Specifically, $MD1_j > MD2_j$ if $\text{sgn}[X_j - M_j] \neq \text{sgn}[\Delta X_j - \Delta M_j]$.

188   Weltwirtschaftliches Archiv 2002, Vol. 138 (2)

measure of that part of the change in trade which has been widely seen as non-disruptive. With reference to the same Australian data used to evaluate the inferential implications of ΔG_j relative to $MD1_j$, Dixon and Menon find that the strict inequality applies in 21 percent and 34 percent of the 133 industries. Perhaps more damaging from this perspective, in many of the cases, the signs are even different, with $MD2_j$ taking negative signs.

Brülhart is particularly interested in generating a measure with properties like those of the Grubel–Lloyd index. Specifically, Brülhart proposes an index of MIIT:

$$A_j := 1 - \frac{|\Delta X_j - \Delta M_j|}{|\Delta X_j| + |\Delta M_j|} \tag{5}$$

Like G_j, A_j takes values in [0,1], with a 0 indicating that the entire change in trade is inter-industry and a 1 indicating that the entire change is intra-industry. Also, like G_j, A_j can be aggregated to give a measure of broad sectoral or economy-wide MIIT.[18] On the other hand, A_j seems to lack a clear derivation of the sort Dixon and Menon give for $MD1$ and $MD2_j$.[19]

In addition to considerable discussion of the algebraic properties of these indices, recent years have seen a considerable amount of application to data as well, as summarized in Table 1. There are two distinct types of research using MIIT measures. The first is primarily interested in pointing out that ΔG is a poor measure of "non-disruptive trade growth." While the research is always motivated by an interest in adjustment issues, the empirical work in these papers is generally undertaken to illustrate that ΔG and the author's preferred measure are not empirically related to one another. This permits a conclusion to the effect that ΔG is a poor measure of "non-disruptive trade growth." These papers can be identified by the "N. A." ("Not Applicable") in the column listing measures of structural adjustment and method.

The second group of papers, also summarized in Table 1, are considerably more ambitious. These papers seek to evaluate the claim that

---

[18] We note, however, that Oliveras and Terra (1997) show that Brülhart's A index does not fully share the aggregation properties of G_j. They argue that where G_j can be consistently aggregated across time, and has systematic (and thus known) aggregation bias across sectors, A_j does not have these properties. Rather, A_j is sensitive to both the temporal and sectoral levels of aggregation, but not in generally predictable directions.
[19] The problem is that, since $|\Delta X_j| + |\Delta M_j| \geq \Delta X_j + \Delta M_j$, with strict inequality if ΔX_j or ΔM_j or both are negative, the A_j index does not follow from an obvious operation on the identity $\Delta TT_j = \Delta IIT + \Delta NT$ or $\Delta TT = 2 \min[\Delta X_j, \Delta M_j] + |\Delta X_j - \Delta M_j|$.

Table 1: *Summary of Empirical Studies of MIIT*[20]

Author(s)	Sample year	Sample country	MIIT measure	Struct. adj. measure	Method	Result
Hamilton/ Kniest (1991)	1981/82, 1986/87	ANZCERTA	ΔGL, HK	Nhat, Lhat, Yhat, (Y/N)hat	Comp. Avgs. by Lo and Hi IIT	Weak supporting evidence of a relationship between MIIT and adjustment
Shelburne (1993)	1980– 1987	NAFTA	ΔGL, A	N. A.	N. A.	Trade pattern conclusions differ depending on measure of MIIT
Greenaway, Hine, Milner, and Elliott (1994)	1979– 1985	UK (Chemicals)	ΔGL, HK, GHME, MD1	N. A.	N. A.	Trade pattern conclusions differ depending on measure of MIIT
Brülhart (1994)	1985– 1990	Ireland (Chemicals)	ΔGL, HK, GHME, MD1, A, B, C	N. A.	N. A.	Trade pattern conclusions differ depending on measure of MIIT
Brülhart/ McAleese (1995)	1985– 1990	Ireland	ΔGL, A, B	Lhat, Yhat	Comp. avgs. by MIIT category, and correlation	ΔGL misleading, MIIT correlated with measures of industrial performance
Menon/ Dixon (1996a)	1981/86, 1986/91	ANZCERTA	ΔGL, MD1, MD1iu, MD1eu	N. A.	N. A.	ΔGL misleading, useful to consider independent contributions of inter-union and extra-union MIIT
Menon/ Dixon (1996b)	1981/86, 1986/91	Australia	ΔGL, MD1, MD1x, MD1m	N. A.	N. A.	ΔGL misleading, useful to consider independent contributions of exports and imports to MIIT
Menon (1996)	1981/86, 1986/91	ASEAN	ΔGL, MD1	N. A.	N. A.	ΔGL misleading

[20] MIIT measures are as defined in the text, except that *MD1iu* and *MD1eu* refer to individual indexes for intra-union trade and extra-union trade, and *MD1x* and *MD1m* refer to individual indexes calculated on exports and imports. The structural adjustment measures are changes in: number of establishments in the sector (*N* hat), sectoral employment (*L* hat), sectoral output (*Y* hat); and output per establishment ([*Y/N*] hat).

Table 1: *Continued*

Author(s)	Sample year	Sample country	MIIT measure	Struct. adj. measure	Method	Result
Menon (1997)	1981/86, 1986/91	Japan-US	ΔGL, MD1, MD1x, MD1m	N. A.	N. A.	ΔGL misleading, useful to consider independent contributions of exports and imports to MIIT
Dixon/ Menon (1997)	1981/86, 1986/91	Australia	ΔGL, MD1, MD2	N. A.	N. A.	Trade pattern conclusions differ depending on measure of MIIT
Menon/ Dixon (1997)	1985– 1990	Ireland (Chemicals)	UMCIT	N. A.	N. A.	Trade pattern conclusions differ depending on measure of MIIT
Oliveras/ Terra (1997)	1988/92, 1992/94	Uruguay	A	N. A.	N. A.	A index sensitive to temporal and sectoral aggregation
Brülhart/ Elliott (1998)	1980– 1990	Ireland	A A	ΔL	OLS	Weak supporting evidence of a relationship between MIIT and adjustment
Brülhart (1998)	1961– 1990	EU	ΔGL	Locational concentration	Correlation	No evidence of a relationship between IIT and specialization
Thom/ McDowell (1999)	1989– 1995	EU-CSFR	A	N. A.	N. A.	A index works badly with vertical IIT
Tharakan/ Calfat (1999)	1980– 1990	Belgium	GHME, A, B	ΔL	OLS	No evidence of a relationship between MIIT and sectoral change, or of EU-generated inter-sectoral adjustment
Harfi/Montet (1999)	1979– 1990	France	ΔGL, A	ΔL	Correlation	Modest relationship between MIIT and sectoral adjustment
Smeets (1999)	1980– 1987	Germany	ΔGL, A, B, GHME	ΔN, ΔL, ΔY, ΔVA	Correlation	No evidence of a relationship between MIIT and sectoral change, or of EU-generated inter-sectoral adjustment

Lovely/Nelson: Intra-Industry Trade 191

Table 1: *Continued*

Author(s)	Sample year	Sample country	MIIT measure	Struct. adj. measure	Method	Result
Sarris, Papadimitriu, and Mavrogiannis (1999)	1978– 1978/7	Greece	ΔGL, A, B, GHME	ΔL	OLS	Evidence of a significant relationship between MIIT and sectoral employment change
Brülhart, McAleese, and O'Donnell (1999)	1961/67, 1978/87	Ireland	ΔGL, A, B, GHME, C	ΔL, ΔY, specialization	Comp. avgs. by MIIT category, and correlation	Evidence of a significant relationship between MIIT and sectoral employment/output change
Rossini/ Burrattoni (1999)	1978– 1987	Italy	ΔGL, A, B	ΔL, ΔY	Correlation	No evidence of a relationship between MIIT and sectoral change, or of EU-generated inter-sectoral adjustment
Kol/Kuijpers (1999)	1972– 1990	Netherlands	ΔGL, A, B	ΔL, specialization	Comp. avgs. by MIIT category, and correlation	Evidence of a significant relationship between MIIT and sectoral employment
Porto/Costa (1999)	1986– 1989	Portugal	ΔGL, A, B	ΔL, ΔY, specialization	Comp. avgs. by MIIT category, and correlation	Evidence of a significant relationship between MIIT and sectoral employment and output change
Brülhart/ Murphy/ Strobl (1998)	1980– 1990	Ireland	ΔGL, A, C	Intra-sectoral L reallocation	Panel	Weak supporting evidence of a relationship between MIIT and adjustment

IIT is "non-disruptive." Most of these papers seek simple correlations between some measure of MIIT (usually ΔGL and either the A index or MD1) and some measure of adjustment. A few attempt to control for a small set of other factors in an OLS framework. The most sophisticated of these studies creates parallel measures of labor adjustment from firm level data in a panel method (Brülhart, Murphy and Strobl 1998). Regardless of the measures or the method, the usual result is that there

192   Weltwirtschaftliches Archiv 2002, Vol. 138 (2)

is little evidence of a systematic relationship between MIIT and adjustment.

We argue here, and in Lovely and Nelson (2000), that there is a fundamental problem in the economics underlying the asserted link between the measures of MIIT in use and any plausible measure of labor adjustment. The problem stems from the fact that changes in labor allocation reflect changes in production structure while changes in trade patterns reflect changes in production *and* demand. Brülhart, Murphy and Strobl (1998) note that, while the Grubel–Lloyd index has been systematically incorporated in theoretical frameworks that generate IIT, there has been no similar development with respect to MIIT.[21] Given the importance of MIIT measures for inference on the link between trade and adjustment, Brülhart et al. argue that this is a serious shortcoming in the theoretical literature. We agree and now turn to a first attempt to fill this gap.

III. A Specific-Factors Model with IIT

As noted above, we use a general-equilibrium model to explore analytically the relationship between measures of MIIT and measures of labor adjustment. An implicit assumption of the MIIT literature is that labor reallocation is positively correlated with production changes – expanding industries employ more labor, contracting industries employ less.[22] To assess MIIT as a metric for labor adjustment, we choose to use a model that has this characteristic – a model with sector-specific capital.[23] The resulting measures of labor reallocation may be viewed, in this context, as measures of short-run pressure for labor adjustment.

---

[21] For derivation of the Grubel–Lloyd index in well-specified general-equilibrium models, see Helpman (1981, at eqs. 42 and 43) and Helpman and Krugman (1985: Ch. 8) for the case of trade in differentiated final goods, or Ethier (1982, at eq. 24) for the case of trade in differentiated intermediate goods. Lovely and Nelson (2000) develop various MIIT measures in the context of Ethier's division-of-labor model.

[22] This relationship is made explicit in Brülhart's (1999) theoretical treatment, where he "formalizes the intuition behind the proposed measures of MIIT". Our goal here is to stay as close to the spirit of this intuition as possible, while emphasizing the relationships imposed by general-equilibrium conditions.

[23] This model treats intra-industry trade in the simplest way possible, by positing distinct intermediates that form an "industry." Models that introduce intra-industry trade through increasing returns and imperfect competition offer a more satisfying basis for such trade, but are unlikely to add additional clarity to our understanding of how MIIT measures and labor adjustment are related. For the present purposes, we chose not to introduce the additional complexity associated with these models. For an exploration of the link between MIIT and labor adjustment in a model of international increasing returns, see Lovely and Nelson (2000).

Labor is treated as a mobile factor, moving freely between subsectors of the economy. Like the rest of the literature, we do not explicitly model adjustment costs, relying instead on the assertion that movement across industries is more "costly" to labor than movement between subsectors. We associate movements of labor between subsectors of a given industry with intra- industry, and thus low-cost, labor adjustment.

Part of the intuition underlying MIIT analysis is that expanding subsectors may absorb some of the labor freed from contracting subsectors in the same industry. To permit such adjustment patterns, we posit a production structure in which distinct groups of intermediate inputs are used in production of each of two final goods. We capture the possibility for substitution among inputs by positing a pair of intermediates in each industry. To close the model, we assume that the economy is small, taking trading prices as given. This simple structure allows us to highlight the neglected role of demand in discussions of the theoretical foundation for MIIT measures while maintaining the literature's focus on short-run labor adjustment.

Final goods are costlessly assembled from intermediate inputs. Denoting final goods output as Y_1 and Y_2, the production functions for final goods are:

$$Y_j = F^j(A_{1j}, A_{2j}), \quad j = \{1, 2\}, \tag{6}$$

where F^j is assumed to be a linearly homogeneous and twice-differentiable function, and A_{ij} is domestic absorption of intermediate ij. Final goods producers take input and output prices as given, so equilibrium requires zero profits in final goods assembly.

The economy trades intermediate inputs and places an ad valorem tax on imports of intermediates in each industry. We assume that the inputs labeled 21 and 22 are imported while the inputs labeled 11 and 12 are exported. Thus, within each industry there is an import-competing subsector as well as an exporting subsector. Because the economy is small, a change in home tariffs results in a proportional change in the price of imported intermediates. To avoid tariff jumping through final goods trade, we assume a tariff is levied on final goods imports at the same rate as is levied on imported inputs. This tariff implies that there is no trade in final goods. Consequently, the economy produces all the final goods it consumes through assembly from domestically produced and imported intermediates.

Production of intermediate inputs requires labor and subsector-specific capital. Production functions for the four intermediate inputs are:

$$X_{ij} = f^{ij}(L_{ij}, \bar{K}_{ij}), \tag{7}$$

where $i = \{1, 2\}$ denotes the input type and $j = \{1, 2\}$ denotes the output sector. Total labor supply is fixed, fully mobile, and fully employed among the four subsectors of the economy:

$$\bar{L} = L_{11} + L_{12} + L_{21} + L_{22}. \tag{8}$$

Demand for final goods is assumed to be a function of the domestic relative price, p where $p = P_2/P_1$, and domestic aggregate income, inclusive of tariff revenue, Γ. That is, domestic demand functions are:

$$Z_j = D^j(p, \Gamma). \tag{9}$$

Because no final goods are traded, equilibrium requires domestic final goods markets to clear:

$$Y_j = Z_j, \quad j = \{1, 2\}. \tag{10}$$

In contrast with final goods, intermediate goods are traded. Net exports of intermediate good ij are $N_{ij} = X_{ij} - A_{ij}$. Balanced trade requires the value of net exports to sum to zero:

$$\sum_i \sum_j q_{ij}^* N_{ij} = 0, \tag{11}$$

where q_{ij}^* is the world price of intermediate ij. The domestic price of exported intermediates is the same as the world price, i.e. $q_{1j} = q_{1j}^*$ (for $j = 1, 2$). Imported intermediates may be taxed, so $q_{2j} = q_{2j}(1 + \tau_{2j})$.

IV. Effects of Liberalization

The liberalization we consider is an equiproportionate reduction in all tariffs on imported intermediates (thus, we can drop subscripts on the τ_{2j}). In this section we derive the effects of this tariff change on labor allocation and on net exports. In the next section, we use these results to form MIIT and labor adjustment measures.

Liberalization implies reductions in the price of the imported intermediates:

$$\hat{q}_{21} = \hat{q}_{22} = \hat{\tau} < 0. \tag{12}$$

Because the economy is small, q_{11} and q_{12} remain unchanged. Domestic final goods prices change to reflect the reduction in input costs. Using zero-profit conditions in final goods assembly, we have:

$$\hat{P}_1 = \theta_{11}\hat{q}_{11} + \theta_{12}\hat{q}_{21},$$
$$\hat{P}_2 = \theta_{12}\hat{q}_{12} + \theta_{22}\hat{q}_{22}. \tag{13}$$

Here the θ_{ij} are distributive shares (i.e. $\theta_{ij} = [a_{ij} q_{ij}]/p_j$). Given the intermediate input price changes,

$$\hat{p} = \hat{P}_2 - \hat{P}_1 = (\theta_{22} - \theta_{21})\hat{\tau}. \tag{14}$$

Whether the relative price of good 2 rises or falls depends on the value shares of imported intermediates in production. Only if imported intermediates account for the same share of value in each assembly process does the relative final goods price remain unchanged.

Domestic demand may respond to this change in relative prices as well as to the income change caused by liberalization:

$$\hat{Z}_j = \varepsilon_{jp}\,\hat{p} + \varepsilon_{j\Gamma}\,\hat{\Gamma}, \quad j = \{1, 2\}, \tag{15}$$

where ε_{jp} is the price elasticity of demand for final good j and $\varepsilon_{j\Gamma}$ is the income elasticity of demand for final good j. The income change $\hat{\Gamma}$ is itself a function of the tariff change, but for our purposes it is sufficient to note that such an income effect occurs and that it may influence domestic demand.

To derive measures of MIIT, we need to understand how liberalization affects net exports. Defining the value of net exports, V_{ij}, as net exports valued at domestic prices, total differentiation yields:

$$\hat{V}_{ij} = \delta_{ij}^x\,\hat{X}_{ij} - \delta_{ij}^A\,\hat{A}_{ij} + \hat{q}_{ij}, \tag{16}$$

where $\delta_{ij}^x = [q_{ij} X_{ij}]/V_{ij}$ and $\delta_{ij}^A = [q_{ij} A_{ij}]/V_{ij}$. That is, the change in V_{ij} depends on the change in domestic production, X_{ij}, the change in domestic absorption, A_{ij}, and the change in domestic prices, q_{ij}. The price changes are given in (12). Changes in domestic production depend entirely on labor reallocation caused by price decreases for import-competing intermediates.[24] With subsector-specific capital, this reallocation accords with partial-equilibrium reasoning; the quantity of labor used in both exporting subsectors rises, while labor used in the import-competing sectors is reduced. Consequently, production changes are:

$$\hat{X}_{11} = \varphi_{11}\,\hat{L}_{11} > 0$$
$$\hat{X}_{21} = \varphi_{21}\,\hat{L}_{21} > 0$$
$$\hat{X}_{12} = \varphi_{12}\,\hat{L}_{12} > 0$$
$$\hat{X}_{22} = \varphi_{22}\,\hat{L}_{22} > 0, \tag{17}$$

---

[24] The Appendix provides the fully differentiated system of equations describing labor allocation.

where φ_{ij} is the elasticity of output in intermediate sector ij with respect to labor input.[25]

Changes in domestic absorption are a bit more complicated as they involve both final demand response and changes in intermediate input usage by final goods assemblers. Note that $A_{ij} = a_{ij}Y_j$, where a_{ij} is the quantity of input ij used to produce one unit of final good j. Totally differentiating gives

$$\hat{A}_{ij} = \hat{a}_{ij} + \hat{Y}_j, \quad i = \{1, 2\}, \quad j = \{1, 2\}. \tag{18}$$

Changes in input coefficients depend on input price changes and the elasticity of substitution. As in the Heckscher–Ohlin–Samuelson model (Jones 1965: 560):

$$\hat{a}_{1j} = -\sigma_j \theta_{2j} (\hat{q}_{1j} - \hat{q}_{2j}), \quad j = \{1, 2\}$$
$$\hat{a}_{2j} = \sigma_j \theta_{1j} (\hat{q}_{1j} - \hat{q}_{2j}), \quad j = \{1, 2\}, \tag{19}$$

where σ_j is the (positive) elasticity of substitution in final good j assembly. Final goods markets must clear, so $\hat{Y}_i = \hat{Z}_j$. Using (15) and (19) in (18), and recalling that $\hat{q}_{1j} = 0$ and $\hat{q}_{2j} = \hat{\tau}$, we have:

$$\hat{A}_{1j} = [\sigma_j \theta_{2j} + \varepsilon_{jp} (\theta_{22} - \theta_{21})] \hat{\tau} + \varepsilon_{i\Gamma} \hat{\Gamma}$$
$$\hat{A}_{2j} = [-\sigma_j \theta_{1j} + \varepsilon_{jp} (\theta_{22} - \theta_{21})] \hat{\tau} + \varepsilon_{i\Gamma} \hat{\Gamma}. \tag{20}$$

These expressions show how changes in domestic absorption depend on production and demand elasticities, as well as on the pattern of tariff changes.

V. Measures of MIIT and Labor Adjustment

To illustrate the relationship between MIIT measures and labor adjustment, we use the measure referred to above as $MD1$, defined by (3). The heart of this measure, a disaggregation of the change in total trade into changes in IIT and NT, is the basis for several other measures. Therefore, the issues we identify as problematic for $MD1$ apply as well to other measures based on total trade disaggregation, regardless of how they are scaled.

---

[25] Solutions for the $\hat{L}_{ij}$ are given in the Appendix.

When we consider changes in total trade, we must account for changes in quantity and price.[26] If we let $\hat{N}_{ij} = \hat{V}_{ij} - \hat{q}_{ij}$, then we can use (16) to get the change in real net exports:

$$\hat{N}_{ij} = \delta_{ij}^X \hat{X}_{ij} - \delta_{ij}^A \hat{A}_{ij}. \tag{21}$$

Noting that, by assumption, the $N_{1j} > 0$ and the $N_{2j} < 0$, the real value of total trade may be measured as

$$TT = \sum_i \sum_j |N_{ij}|. \tag{22}$$

In this context, $MD1$ may be expressed as

$$MD1 = \sum_i \sum_j |\psi_{ij} \hat{N}_{ij}| - \sum_j |\psi_{1j} \hat{N}_{1j} + \psi_{2j} \hat{N}_{2j}|, \tag{23}$$

where $\psi_{ij} = N_{ij}/\left(\sum_i \sum_j |N_{ij}| \right)$, i.e. the share of total trade accounted for by net exports in subsector ij. We note that the $\psi_{1j} > 0$ and the $\psi_{2j} < 0$.

To illustrate the relationship of this measure to labor reallocation, we now assume that liberalization causes all trade volumes to expand, in a manner consistent with trade balance – every $\hat{N}_{ij} > 0$. We also assume that net exports in industry 1 fall (imports rise more than exports), while net exports in industry 2 rise.[27] These assumptions permit us to know the sign of each term in (23) and allow us to express our MIIT measure as:

$$MD1 = 2(\psi_{11} \hat{N}_{11} - \psi_{22} \hat{N}_{22}). \tag{24}$$

Using the expressions in (21) for $\hat{N}_{ij}$, and the first and fourth expressions for output change in (17), we get

$$MD1 = 2\left[\psi_{11}(\delta_{11}^X \varphi_{11} \hat{L}_{11} - \delta_{11}^A \hat{A}_{11}) \right.$$
$$\left. - \psi_{11}(\delta_{22}^X \varphi_{22} \hat{L}_{22} - \delta_{22}^A \hat{A}_{22}) \right]. \tag{25}$$

---

[26] As with most trade theory, all of our magnitudes are taken to be real. Following comments in Greenaway et al. (1994) empirical applications on MIIT deflate the trade data so that the results are informative with respect to real changes.

[27] These assumptions allow us to illustrate the relationship between MIIT and a measure of labor reallocation for a particular pattern of trade changes. The lessons we draw from this case do not depend on the patterns used to illustrate them.

198   Weltwirtschaftliches Archiv 2002, Vol. 138 (2)

Note that $\psi_{11}\delta_{11}^X = q_{11}X_{11}/TT$ and $\psi_{11}\delta_{11}^A = q_{11}A_{11}/TT$, and similarly for subsector 22. Using these expressions, we get

$$MD1 = \frac{2}{TT}\left[(q_{11}X_{11}\varphi_{11}\hat{L}_{11} - q_{22}X_{22}\varphi_{22}\hat{L}_{22}) \right.$$

$$\left. - (q_{11}A_{11}\hat{A}_{11} - q_{22}A_{22}\hat{A}_{22})\right]. \qquad (26)$$

The first term of expression (26) reflects changes in domestic production, while the second term reflects changes in domestic absorption of intermediates.

We begin our examination of (26) by considering only the first term of $MD1$. We show that this term represents labor reallocation, perhaps explaining why MIIT is such a tempting measure of adjustment. Let us define a measure of labor reallocation that is analogous to $MD1$ in that it disaggregates total labor reallocation into within and between industry shifts and scales these shares by total labor.[28] Letting $\lambda_{ij} = L_{ij}/\bar{L}$ the share of total labor in sector ij, this measure of intra-industry labor shifts is:

$$\hat{L}^{II} = \sum_i \sum_j |\lambda_{ij}\hat{L}_{ij}| - \sum_j |\lambda_{1j}\hat{L}_{1j} + \lambda_{2j}\hat{L}_{2j}|, \qquad (27)$$

which is the weighted sum of all proportionate labor movements less inter-industry movements. In the context of our model, movement between subsectors of the same final goods industry is intra-industry labor reallocation.

To illustrate, we assume that there is net reallocation of labor from final sector 1 to final sector 2. Using this assumption,

$$\hat{L}^{II} = 2(\lambda_{11}\hat{L}_{11} - \lambda_{22}\hat{L}_{22}). \qquad (28)$$

We may now compare $\hat{L}^{II}$ with the first term in our expression for $MD1$ in (26). The weights on labor movements in (26) are $q_{11}X_{11}\varphi_{11}$ and $q_{22}X_{22}\varphi_{22}$. The elasticity φ_{ij} is the ratio of labor's marginal product to its average product in subsector ij. Marginal product in each sector equals the real wage in that sector. Based on these relations, we have:

$$\varphi_{ij} = \frac{wL_{ij}}{q_{ij}X_{ij}}, \qquad (29)$$

---

[28] Brülhart (1999) explicitly proposes a measure of intra-industry labor movement (IILM) that is analogous to his A index. In our illustrative case, this measure is the same disaggregation we use here, except that Brülhart scales by total labor movement rather than by total labor.

the output elasticity equals labor's share of total product. The first term of $MD1$ can now be expressed as:

$$\frac{2}{TT}(q_{11}\,X_{11}\,\varphi_{11}\,\hat{L}_{11} - q_{22}\,X_{22}\,\varphi_{22}\,\hat{L}_{22})$$
$$= \frac{2w}{TT}(L_{11}\,\hat{L}_{11} - L_{22}\,\hat{L}_{22}). \tag{30}$$

In contrast, the intra-industry labor reallocation measure is:

$$\hat{L}^{II} = \frac{2}{L}(L_{11}\,\hat{L}_{11} - L_{22}\,\hat{L}_{22}). \tag{31}$$

Comparing (30) and (31) it can easily be seen that, if absorption changes are absent:

$$\frac{MD1}{\hat{L}^{II}} = \frac{w\,\bar{L}}{TT}, \tag{32}$$

so these measures differ by a scaling factor.

While this type of analysis exemplifies the intuition underlying the use of MIIT as a metric for labor reallocation (see Brülhart 1999 for a formal statement of precisely this logic), the unfortunate fact remains that trade changes involve more than production patterns. The second term of (26), reflecting changes in domestic absorption, simply cannot be ignored. Because trade changes result from the endogenous response of production *and* domestic demand, it makes no sense to identify trade changes with production changes while, in *ceteris paribus* fashion, assuming demand is unaltered. The same liberalization that prompts labor reallocation induces changes in input usage and consumption. They are part and parcel of the same system.

Moreover, changes in domestic absorption do not depend directly on how labor shifts within the production sector and, thus, make $MD1$ and similar measures unreliable guides to economy-wide labor reallocation. As shown in equations (20), absorption changes depend on the elasticity of substitution in production as well as on price and income elasticities of domestic demand. These absorption terms "disappear" only under very extreme assumptions. The assumptions are:

(1) the elasticity of substitution in production is zero;
(2) there is no change in final goods relative prices (which in the present model requires that $\theta_{22} = \theta_{21}$); and
(3) demands are quasi-linear or income effects of the liberalization are compensated.

200   Weltwirtschaftliches Archiv 2002, Vol. 138 (2)

In general, we would not expect these assumptions to hold. Consequently, the share of new trade that is new intra-industry trade generally will not indicate the share of labor reallocation that is intra-industry, even when the production sector works in a manner consistent with partial-equilibrium reasoning.

The observation that demand changes make MIIT an unreliable measure of labor reallocation may explain why attempts to find correlations between MIIT measures and indicators of production or labor adjustment have been largely unsuccessful. A priori, we would not expect any particular relationship to exist. For example, even if most of labor reallocation is intra-industry, most of the change in trade could be accounted for by change in net trade.[29] Such a situation could occur if final goods demand shifts were large.

Given the attraction of using trade data to gauge the effect of trade alone on labor markets, it may be possible to adjust trade-based measures to better reflect production shifts by themselves. Inspection of (26) suggests that such an empirical strategy requires information on changes in domestic final goods demand and changes in input usage. Because MIIT analysis it typically performed at the 3-digit level of aggregation, it may be possible to find suitable elasticity estimates created for other purposes, such as applied general-equilibrium analysis. Such a procedure also would require the analyst to specify the price changes induced by the liberalization under study. Because agreements like the EU, ANZCERTA, and NAFTA are such complex undertakings, such specification is difficult. The need to avoid an exact characterization of liberalization is, after all, one of the attraction of using MIIT measures alone. Amending MIIT measures to reflect absorption is admittedly burdensome, both in the data required and in the leaps of faith needed to represent demand changes. It is difficult, however, to see how such a burden is less troubling than assuming that trade liberalization has no effect on domestic absorption.

VI. Conclusions

Paul Samuelson famously argued that one of the important roles of theory is to serve an auditing function with respect to empirical intuition. One of the most prominent applications of this insight has been the role of general-equilibrium theory in auditing essentially partial-equilibrium intuition. The idea that intra-industry trade induces relatively lower adjustment

---

[29] Lovely and Nelson (2000) presents a model in which precisely the opposite occurs as a result of liberalization – the change in total trade is all intra-industry while labor reallocation is all inter-industry.

costs than inter-industry trade is prima facie extremely plausible. Furthermore, for the case of relatively small changes in a single sector, the analysis strikes us as unexceptionable as a rule of thumb. However, as the literature surveyed in Section I indicates, this is not the purpose for which these measures are intended, nor for which they have been used. Rather, they have been applied to cases of large-scale, multi-sector liberalizations like the EU, ANZCERTA, and NAFTA; and their purpose is to provide guidance with respect to the likely adjustment consequences of future liberalizations. It has been the essential claim of this paper, and of the companion paper (Lovely and Nelson 2000), that a careful examination of the theoretical foundation for this work leads to doubt about the usefulness of MIIT as an indicator of labor market adjustment. Where the earlier paper used a division of labor model of the Ethier (1982) type to show that pure intra-industry trade generates inter-industry effects essentially via the resource constraint, in this paper we use a simpler structure in which inter- and intra-sector movement are transparent to illustrate problems that emerge via demand- as well as supply-side adjustments.

Because there are few general propositions of general-equilibrium theory, it is often the case that assertions of the form, "such-and-such claim cannot be sustained in general equilibrium," are nihilistic with respect to attempts to quantify seemingly plausible economic relationships. We hope it is clear that this is not the purpose of this paper. We have shown that current measures lack solid economic foundations, and suspect that this may help explain the generally weak results in empirical work on the link between IIT and adjustment. We emphasize the essential difference between trade structure and production structure and we offer expression (26) as the basis for amendment of existing measures. However, it should be noted that the informational burden in estimating (26) is not much different than that required to directly study the effects of trade on adjustment.

Appendix

This appendix provides solutions for the production changes induced by import liberalization. Equations (12) and profit maximization imply that:

$$\hat{w} = \eta_{11} \hat{L}_{11} + \hat{q}_{11} \tag{A1}$$

$$\eta_{11} \hat{L}_{11} + q_{11} = \eta_{21} \hat{L}_{21} + q_{21} \tag{A2}$$

$$\eta_{21} \hat{L}_{21} + \hat{q}_{21} = \eta_{12} \hat{L}_{12} + \hat{q}_{12} \tag{A3}$$

$$\eta_{12} \hat{L}_{12} + \hat{q}_{12} = \eta_{22} \hat{L}_{22} + \hat{q}_{22} \tag{A4}$$

202   Weltwirtschaftliches Archiv 2002, Vol. 138 (2)

where η_{ij} is the elasticity of the marginal product of labor with respect to labor input in the subsector ij ($\eta_{ij} < 0$). The labor constraint (13) can be totally differentiated to give:

$$\lambda_{11}\,\hat{L}_{11} + \lambda_{12}\,\hat{L}_{12} + \lambda_{21}\,\hat{L}_{21} + \lambda_{22}\,\hat{L}_{22} = 0. \tag{A5}$$

where the factor-shares are $\lambda_{ij} = L_{ij}/\bar{L}$.

As discussed in the text, we assume that liberalization takes the form of an equiproportionate reduction in the tariffs on intermediate imports. Because the economy is assumed to be small and open, liberalization leads to the intermediate price changes given by (12).

Using these exogenous price changes and equations (A1)–(A5), it is straightforward to derive the following solutions for proportionate changes in labor allocations and the wage:

$$\hat{L}_{11} = \frac{1}{\Lambda}\left\{\eta_{12}\,\eta_{22}\,\lambda_{12} + \eta_{21}\,\eta_{12}\,\lambda_{22}\right\}\hat{\tau}$$

$$\hat{L}_{21} = -\frac{1}{\Lambda}\left\{\eta_{11}\,\eta_{22}\,\lambda_{12} + \eta_{12}\,\eta_{22}\,\lambda_{11}\right\}\hat{\tau}$$

$$\hat{L}_{12} = \frac{1}{\Lambda}\left\{\eta_{11}\,\eta_{22}\,\lambda_{21} + \eta_{11}\,\eta_{11}\,\lambda_{22}\right\}\hat{\tau}$$

$$\hat{L}_{22} = -\frac{1}{\Lambda}\left\{\eta_{12}\,\eta_{21}\,\lambda_{12} + \eta_{21}\,\eta_{12}\,\lambda_{11}\right\}\hat{\tau}$$

$$w = \frac{1}{\Lambda}\left\{\eta_{11}\,\eta_{12}\,\lambda_{21} + \eta_{11}\,\eta_{21}\,\eta_{12}\,\lambda_{22}\right\}\hat{\tau},$$

where $\Lambda := \eta_{11}\,\eta_{21}(\eta_{12}\lambda_{22} + \eta_{22}\lambda_{12}) + \eta_{12}\,\eta_{22}(\eta_{21}\lambda_{11} + \eta_{11}\lambda_{21}) < 0$. Because $\eta_{ij} < 0$ and $\hat{\tau} < 0$, L_{11} and L_{12} both increase as a result of liberalization, while L_{21} and L_{22} both decrease. In accordance with partial-equilibrium intuition, liberalization reduces production in the import-competing sectors, while raising output in the exporting sectors. We note also that the liberalization reduces the nominal wage.

References

Azhar, A., R. Elliott, and C. Milner (1998). Static and Dynamic Measurement of Intra-Industry Trade and Adjustment: A Geometric Reappraisal. *Weltwirtschaftliches Archiv* 134 (3): 404–422.

Balassa, B. (1966). Tariff Reductions and Trade in Manufactures Among the Industrial Countries. *American Economic Review* 56 (3): 466–473.

Balassa, B. (1979). Intra-Industry Trade and the Integration of Developing Countries in the World Economy. In H. Giersch (ed.), *On the Economics of Intra-Industry Trade*. Tübingen: J. C. B. Mohr.

Balassa, B., and L. Bauwens (1987). Intra-Industry Specialization in a Multi-Country and Multi-Industry Framework. *Economic Journal* 97 (December): 923–239.

Balassa, B., and L. Bauwens (1988). The Determinants of Intra-European Trade in Manufactured Goods. *European Economic Review* 32 (6): 1421–1437.

Brülhart, M. (1994). Marginal Intra-Industry Trade: Measurement and Relevance for the Pattern of Industrial Adjustment. *Weltwirtschaftliches Archiv* 130 (3): 600–613.

Brülhart, M. (1998). Trading Places: Industrial Specialization in the European Union. *Journal of Common Market Studies* 36 (3): 319–346.

Brülhart, M. (1999). Marginal Intra-Industry Trade and Trade-Induced Adjustment. In M. Brülhart and R. Hine (eds.), *Intra-Industry Trade and Adjustment: The European Experience*. London: Macmillan.

Brülhart, M., and R. Elliott (1998). Adjustment to the European Single Market: Inferences from Intra-industry Trade Patterns. *Journal of Economic Studies* 25 (3): 225–247.

Brülhart, M., and R. Hine (eds.) (1999). *Intra-Industry Trade and Adjustment: The European Experience*. London: Macmillan.

Brülhart, M., and D. McAleese (1995). Intra-industry Trade and Industrial Adjustment: The Irish Experience. *Economic and Social Review* 26 (2): 107–129.

Brülhart, M., D. McAleese, and M. O'Donnell (1999). Ireland. In M. Brülhart and R. Hine (eds.), *Intra-Industry Trade and Adjustment: The European Experience*. London: Macmillan.

Brülhart, M., A. Murphy, and E. Strobl (1998). Intra-Industry Trade and Job Turnover. University of Manchester, manuscript.

Caves, R. (1981). Intra-Industry Trade and Market Structure in the Industrialised Countries. *Oxford Economic Papers* 33 (2): 203–223.

Clark, D. P. (1993). Recent Evidence on Determinants of Intra-Industry Trade. *Weltwirtschaftliches Archiv* 129 (2): 332–344.

Dixon, P., and J. Menon (1997). Measures of Intra-industry Trade as Indicators of Factor Market Disruption. *Economic Record* 73 (September): 233–237.

Drèze, J. (1960). Quelques Réflexions Sereines sur l'Adaptation de l'Industrie Belge au Marché Commun. *Comptes-rendus des Travaux de la Société d'Economie Politique de Belgique* 275: 3–37.

Drèze, J. (1961). Les Exportations Intra-CEE en 1958 et la Position Belge. *Recherches Economiques de Louvain* 27 (8): 717–738.

Ethier, W. (1982). National and International Returns to Scale in the Modern Theory of International Trade. *American Economic Review* 72 (3): 388–405.

Finger, J. M., and D. DeRosa (1979). Trade Overlap, Comparative Advantage and Protection. In H. Giersch (ed.), *On the Economics of Intra-Industry Trade*. Tübingen: J. C. B. Mohr.

Globerman, S., and J. Dean (1990). Recent Trends in Intra-Industry Trade and Their Implications for Future Trade Liberalization. *Weltwirtschaftliches Archiv* 126 (1): 25–48.

Greenaway, D. (1987). Intra-Industry Specialization, Intra-Firm Trade and European Integration. *Journal of Common Market Studies* 26 (2): 153–172.

204   Weltwirtschaftliches Archiv 2002, Vol. 138 (2)

Greenaway, D., and R. Hine (1991). Intra-Industry Specialization, Trade Expansion, and Adjustment in the European Economic Space. *Journal of Common Market Studies* 29 (6): 603–621.

Greenaway, D., and C. Milner (1986). *The Economics of Intra-Industry Trade*. Oxford: Basil Blackwell.

Greenaway, D., and P. K. M. Tharakan (1986). Imperfect Competition, Adjustment Policy, and Commercial Policy. In D. Greenaway and P. K. M. Tharakan (eds.), *Imperfect Competition and International Trade: The Policy Aspects of Intra-Industry Trade*. Brighton: Wheatsheaf.

Greenaway, D., and J. Torstensson (1997). Back to the Future: Taking Stock on Intra-Industry Trade. *Weltwirtschaftliches Archiv* 133 (2): 249–269.

Greenaway, D., R. Hine, C. Milner, and R. Elliott (1994). Adjustment and the Measurement of Marginal Intra-Industry Trade. *Weltwirtschaftliches Archiv* 130 (2): 418– 427.

Grubel, H. (1967). Intra-Industry Specialization and the Pattern of Trade. *Canadian Journal of Economics and Political Science* 33 (3): 374–388.

Grubel, H., and P. J. Lloyd (1975). *Intra Industry Trade: The Theory and Measurement of International Trade with Differentiated Products*. London: Macmillan.

Hamilton, C., and P. Kniest (1991). Trade Liberalisation, Structural Adjustment and Intra-Industry Trade. *Weltwirtschaftliches Archiv* 127 (2): 356–367.

Harfi, M., and C. Montet (1999). France. In M. Brülhart and R. Hine (eds.), *Intra-Industry Trade and Adjustment*. London: Macmillan.

Havrylyshyn, O., and E. Civan (1983). Intra-Industry Trade and the Stage of Development: A Regression Analysis of Industrial and Developing Countries. In P. K. M. Tharakan (ed.), *Intra- Industry Trade: Empirical and Methodological Aspects*. Amsterdam: North-Holland.

Havrylyshyn, O., and E. Civan (1985). Intra-industry Trade among Developing Countries. *Journal of Development Economics* 18 (2/3): 253–271.

Haynes, M., R. Upward, and P. Wright (2002). Estimating the Wage Costs of Inter- and Intra-Sectoral Adjustment. *Weltwirtschaftliches Archiv*, this volume.

Helpman, E. (1981). International Trade in the Presence of Product Differentiation, Economies of Scale and Monopolistic Competition: A Chamberlin-Heckscher-Ohlin Approach. *Journal of International Economics* 11 (3): 305–340.

Helpman, E., and P. Krugman (1985). *Market Structure and Foreign Trade: Increasing Returns, Imperfect Competition, and the International Economy*. Cambridge: MIT Press.

Hine, R., D. Greenaway, and C. Milner (1999). Vertical and Horizontal Intra-Industry Trade: An Analysis of Country-Specific and Industry-Specific Determinants. In M. Brülhart and R. Hine, (eds.), *Intra-Industry Trade and Adjustment: The European Experience*. London: Macmillan.

Hufbauer, G. C., and J. Chilas (1974). Specialization by Industrial Countries: Extent and Consequences. In H. Giersch (ed.), *The International Division of Labor: Problems and Perspectives*. Tübingen: J. C. B. Mohr.

Irwin, D. A. (1996). *Against the Tide: An Intellectual History of Free Trade*. Princeton: Princeton University Press.

Jones, R. (1965). The Structure of Simple General Equilibrium Models. *Journal of Political Economy* 73 (6): 557–572.

Kim, D. I. (1998). Reinterpreting Industry Premiums: Match-Specific Productivity. *Journal of Labor Economics* 16 (3): 479–504.

Kletzer, L. (1996). The Role of Sector-Specific Skills in Post-Displacement Earnings. *Industrial Relations* 35 (4): 473–490.

Kojima, K. (1964). The Pattern of International Trade among Advanced Countries. *Hitotsubashi Journal of Economics* 5 (1): 17–36.

Kol, J., and B. Kuijpers (1999). The Netherlands. In M. Brülhart and R. Hine (eds.), *Intra-Industry Trade and Adjustment: The European Experience.* London: Macmillan.

Lee, Y. S. (1989). A Study of the Determinants of Intra-Industry Trade among the Pacific Basin Countries. *Weltwirtschaftliches Archiv* 125 (2): 346–358.

Loertscher, R., and F. Wolter (1980). Determinants of Intra-Industry Trade: Among Countries and Across Industries. *Weltwirtschaftliches Archiv* 116 (2): 281–293.

Lovely, M. E., and D. R. Nelson (2000). Marginal Intra-Industry Trade and Labor Market Adjustment. *Review of International Economics* 8 (3): 436–447.

Lundberg, L., and P. Hansson (1986). Intra-Industry Trade and Its Consequences for Adjustment. In D. Greenaway and P. K. M. Tharakan (eds.), *Imperfect Competition and International Trade: The Policy Aspects of Intra-Industry Trade.* Brighton: Wheatsheaf.

Marvel, H. P., and E. J. Ray (1987). Intra-Industry Trade: Sources and Effects of Protection. *Journal of Political Economy* 95 (6): 1278–1291.

Menon, J. (1994). Trade Liberalisation, Closer Economic Relations, and Intra-Industry Specialization. *Australian Economic Review* (2): 31–42.

Menon, J. (1996). The Dynamics of Intra-Industry Trade in ASEAN. *Asian Economic Journal* 10 (1): 105–115.

Menon, J. (1997). Japan's Intraindustry Trade Dynamics. *Journal of the Japanese and International Economies* 11 (2): 123–142.

Menon, J., and P. Dixon (1996a). Regional Trading Agreements and Intra-Industry Trade. *Journal of Economic Integration* 11 (1): 1–20.

Menon, J., and P. Dixon (1996b). How Important Is Intra-Industry Trade in Trade Growth? *Open Economies Review* 7 (2): 161–175.

Menon, J., and P. Dixon (1997). Intra-Industry versus Inter-Industry Trade: Relevance for Adjustment Costs. *Weltwirtschaftliches Archiv* 133 (1): 164–169.

Neal, D. (1995). Industry-Specific Human Capital: Evidence from Displaced Workers. *Journal of Labor Economics* 13 (4): 653–677.

Nelson, D. (1990). The Welfare State and Export Optimism. In D. Pirages and C. Sylvester (eds.), *The Transformations in the Global Political Economy.* London: St. Martins Press.

Oliveras, J., and I. Terra (1997). Marginal Intra-Industry Trade Index: The Period and Aggregation Choice. *Weltwirtschaftliches Archiv* 133 (1): 170–178.

Pagoulatos, E., and R. Sorensen (1975). Two-Way International Trade: An Econometric Analysis. *Weltwirtschaftliches Archiv* 111 (3): 454–465.

Porto, M., and F. Costa (1999). Portugal. In M. Brülhart and R. Hine (eds.), *Intra-Industry Trade and Adjustment: The European Experience.* London: Macmillan.

Ray, E. J. (1991). U. S. Protection and Intra-Industry Trade: The Message to Developing Countries. *Economic Development and Cultural Change* 40 (1): 169–187.

206   Weltwirtschaftliches Archiv 2002, Vol. 138 (2)

Rossini, G., and M. Burattoni (1999). Italy. In M. Brülhart and R. Hine (eds.), *Intra-Industry Trade and Adjustment: The European Experience*. London: Macmillan.

Sarris, A. H., P. Papadimitriou, and A. Mavrogiannis (1999). Greece. In M. Brülhart and R. Hine (eds.), *Intra-Industry Trade and Adjustment: The European Experience*. London: Macmillan.

Shelburne, R. C. (1993). Changing Trade Patterns and the IIT Index: A Note. *Weltwirtschaftliches Archiv* 129 (4): 829–833.

Smeets, H.-D. (1999). Germany. In M. Brülhart and R. Hine (eds.), *Intra-Industry Trade and Adjustment: The European Experience*. London: Macmillan.

Stone, J., and H.-H. Lee (1995). Determinants of Intra-Industry Trade: A Longitudinal, Cross-Country Analysis. *Weltwirtschaftliches Archiv* 131 (1): 67–85.

Tharakan, P. K. M. (1984). Intra-Industry Trade Between the Industrial Countries and the Developing World. *European Economic Review* 26 (1/2): 213–227.

Tharakan, P. K. M. (1986). The Intra-Industry Trade of Benelux with the Developing World. *Weltwirtschaftliches Archiv* 122 (1): 131–148.

Tharakan, P. K. M., and G. Calfat (1999). Belgium. In M. Brülhart and R. Hine (eds.), *Intra-Industry Trade and Adjustment: The European Experience*. London: Macmillan.

Thom, R., and M. McDowell (1999). Measuring Marginal Intra-Industry Trade. *Weltwirtschaftliches Archiv* 135 (1): 48–61.

Toh, K. (1982). A Cross-Section Analysis of Intra-Industry Trade in US Manufacturing Industries. *Weltwirtschaftliches Archiv* 118 (2): 281–300.

Torstensson, J. (1996). Determinants of Intra-Industry Trade: A Sensitivity Analysis. *Oxford Bulletin of Economics and Statistics* 58 (3): 507–524.

Verdoorn, P. J. (1960). The Intra-Bloc Trade of BENELUX". In E. A. G. Robinson (ed.), *Economic Consequences of the Size of Nations*. London: Macmillan.

Viner, J. (1937). *Studies in the Theory of International Trade*. New York: Harper and Brothers.

White, G. (1984). Intra-Industry Trade Adjustment and European Industrial Policies. In A. Jacquemin (ed.), *European Industry: Public Policy and Corporate Strategy*. Oxford: Oxford University Press, Clarendon Press.

* * *

Abstract: Intra-Industry Trade as an Indicator of Labor Market Adjustment. – A growing body of recent empirical research uses measures of change in intra-industry trade as indicators of labor market adjustment. In this paper, we argue that the theoretical foundations for this work are problematic. To make this argument we develop a simple model with both inter- and intra-industry trade and adjustment. We find that changes in domestic absorption, which influence trade flows but which are distinct from production changes, make changes in IIT an unreliable guide to labor market pressure. JEL no. F10, F14.

The Economic Journal, **112** (*July*), 649–678. © Royal Economic Society 2002. Published by Blackwell Publishers, 108 Cowley Road, Oxford OX4 1JF, UK and 350 Main Street, Malden, MA 02148, USA.

A GEOMETRY OF SPECIALISATION*

Joseph F. Francois and Douglas Nelson

Division of labour models have become a standard analytical tool, along with competitive general equilibrium models (Ricardian, HOS, Ricardo–Viner), in public finance, trade, growth, development and macroeconomics. Yet unlike the earlier models, these models lack a canonical graphical representation. This is because they are both new and complex, characterised by multiple equilibria, instability and emergent structural properties under parameter transformation. We develop a general framework for such models, illustrating results from current research on specialisation models, and explaining why one sub-class of these models is particularly difficult to illustrate.

One of the great traditions in the analysis of international trade is the use of canonical models: Ricardian, Ricardo–Viner, and Heckscher–Ohlin–Samuelson. Furthermore, each of these models has a simple graphical representation, useful for both intuition generation and for pedagogical purposes. Over the last fifteen years, two additional classes of model have joined the big three: strategic trade models and division of labour models.[1] The strategic trade models entered the literature with simple graphical representations developed in the industrial organisation literature, while the division of labour models have proven to be considerably more resistant to simple representation.

Recent applications work with specific functional forms, and often involve numeric simulation, obscuring for some the general properties of these models. Even so, a set of general results (low-level equilibrium traps, catastrophic adjustment, agglomeration effects) do stand out from this somewhat diverse collection of special models. Because our starting point in this paper involves examination of this class of models in the context of relatively general functional forms and technologies (linear homothetic, concave, etc.), we are able to offer a generalised treatment that links this pattern of results to the general properties of models with increasing returns due to specialisation. In the process, we demonstrate that important results in the recent literature depend critically on the stability and transformation properties that characterise the general framework highlighted here. These properties are closely related to those explored in the context of scale economy models by an earlier generation of trade and development economists.

* Thanks are due to Kym Anderson, Richard Baldwin, Jan Haaland, Mary Lovely, Anthony Venables and the participants at the CEPR sponsored European Research Workshop in International Trade (ERWIT), held in Helsinki. Special thanks are due to the reviewer and editor of this JOURNAL for a very careful reading of the paper and the provision of several useful suggestions. While working on this paper, the authors benefited from support provided by the Tinbergen Institute (Nelson) and the Center for International and Economic Studies at the University of Adelaide (Francois) while visiting those institutions. All remaining errors are due to confusion on the part of the authors.
[1] Strategic trade models refer to essentially partial equilibrium models of strategic competition rooted in modern industrial organisation theory (Brander, 1995). Division of labour models refer to a wide class of models attempting to formally characterise and analyse the Adam Smith–Allyn Young notion of division of labour. See Buchanan and Yoon (1994) for a useful selection of papers in this literature. We focus on one member of this class of models.

The central role of division of labour models in modern economic analysis is undeniable. They are prominent in international trade theory, public economics, regional/urban economics and macroeconomics (both growth theory and business cycle theory). Following Ethier's (1979, 1982*a*) original presentation of the model as a framework for studying the interaction between national and international returns to scale, the framework diffused rapidly throughout economic analysis. The reasons why a division of labour is 'limited by the extent of the market' that were loosely discussed by Smith and examined more deeply in Young's (1928) classic analysis are here provided a simple and tractable formal structure. In international trade theory, the model has been used to study trade patterns (Ethier, 1979, 1982*a*; Markusen, 1988, 1989; van Marrewikj *et al.*, 1997), trade policy (Markusen, 1990*a*; Francois, 1992, 1994; Lovely, 1997) and factor-market adjustment to trade (Burda and Dluhosch, 1999; Francois and Nelson, 2000; Lovely and Nelson, 2000). One of the most interesting recent applications uses the multiple equilibrium property of these models to derive north–south trade structures endogenously (Markusen, 1991; Krugman and Venables, 1995; Krugman, 1995; Venables, 1996*a*; Puga and Venables, 1996; Matsuyama, 1996). Following the important work of Romer (1987, 1990), the Ethier model has also become a standard framework in endogenous growth theory (Barro and Sala-I-Martin, 1995, ch. 6) and has been used extensively in development theory (Rodriguez-Clare, 1996; Rodrik, 1996) and regional economics (Holtz-Eakin and Lovely, 1996*a,b*; Fujita *et al.*, 1999).

In this paper, we proceed as follows. To provide some structure to the exercise, we have divided the general family of specialisation models into four types, as specified in Table 1. We begin with two versions of national production externality (NPE) models. In the first, a closed-economy version of the model (unimaginatively called model Type I in Table 1), we develop our basic geometric framework in the simplest environment. Even in this simple context, we are able to illustrate basic mechanisms that have been highlighted in the literature on endogenous growth and development. From there, we develop a NPE model of trade in final goods only (called model Type II), and demonstrate that this model is operationally identical to standard models of trade with national external economies of scale. The greatest conceptual and analytical difficulties emerge with international production externalities (IPE), which surface once trade in intermediate goods is permitted (model Types III and IV). The graphical analysis makes the locus of this difficulty clear. The general treatment of IPE models is followed by an examination of trading costs (an important issue in the recent literature) in Ricardian and Heckscher–Ohlin versions of the IPE model.

1. National Production Externalities (NPEs) in Autarky: Model I

1.1. *The Basic Model*

Although there are a wide range of variants, for pedagogical purposes we start with the NPE formulation closest to the Heckscher–Ohlin–Samuelson (HOS) model beloved of trade economists. That is, we will assume that there are two factors of production, labour (*L*) and capital (*K*); and two final consumption goods, wheat (*W*) and manufactures (*M*). Wheat is taken to be produced from *K* and *L* under a

Table 1

A Classification of Specialisation Models

		Trade structure	Description
NPE Models	I	Closed economy	The properties of this type of model are those of an external scale economy model (Markusen, 1990*a*).
	II	Open economy (trade in final goods only)	*Markusen Model:* Final goods production in each region will exhibit increasing returns due to specialisation (Markusen, 1989). However, without direct trade in intermediates, trade has no effect on the production structure of the economy. Model behaves like standard model of trade under external economies of scale.
IPE Models	III	Trade in intermediates only (or intermediates and the standard good)	*Ethier model:* International economies of scale. Trade affects production conditions, so transformation functions are no longer technological facts (Ethier, 1982*a*).
	IV	Trade in intermediates and final goods	Without trading costs, this is identical to type III, and this is where the scale of one regional sector will directly effect the efficiency of other sectors. Types III and IV diverge in interpretation with trading costs.

standard neoclassical technology represented by a production function $f(K_w, L_w)$ which is twice differentiable, linear homogeneous and strictly concave. Both factors are costlessly mobile between sectors and the markets for K, L, W and M are perfectly competitive. Where demand is needed, it will be taken to be generated by a representative agent whose preferences can be represented by a twice differentiable, strictly quasi-concave, homothetic utility function defined over consumption of W and M. Division of labour models diverge from standard trade models in the technology of M production. M is produced by costless assembly of components (x). Components are produced from 'bundles' of K and L – denoted m. The market for components is monopolistically competitive and bundles production is perfectly competitive.

Ethier's key insight was that the Spence (1976)–Dixit and Stiglitz (1977) model of preference for variety, applied to international trade by Krugman (1979, 1980), when applied to production constitutes the basis of a model of division of labour. The model contains two main elements:

(1) a technology reflecting increasing returns to 'division of labour'; and
(2) something limiting the division of labour (ie 'the extent of the market').[2]

The first element is given by a CES function that costlessly aggregates components (x_i) into finished manufactures:

$$M = \left(\sum_{i \in n} x_i^{\phi} \right)^{1/\phi}. \tag{1}$$

Here, n types of components are costlessly assembled into final manufactures and ϕ is an indicator of the degree of substitutability between varieties of inputs (x_i).[3]

---

[2] The appendix contains a full development of the Ethier model.
[3] Note the harmless abuse of good mathematical notation: n being used as both the label of an index set and the number of elements in that set.

In particular, note that if $x_i = x \; \forall I \in n$, (1) reduces to $M = n^{1/\phi}x$. Then, for n constant, output of manufactures is linearly related to output of components and if $0 < \phi < 1$ (as we assume it to be) there are increasing returns to the variety of inputs, i.e.

$$\frac{\partial M}{\partial n} = \frac{1}{\phi} n^{\frac{1-\phi}{\phi}} x > 1.^4$$

The smaller is ϕ, the stronger are the returns to the division of labour. As in the SDS formulation, fixed costs in the production of intermediates and finite resources limits the number of types of components produced and thus, since aggregate output of M is increasing in varieties of component types, economies of scale are limited by the extent of the market.

The transformation of the SDS model of preferences into a model of the division of labour, along with the trick of using 'bundles' of inputs in the production of intermediates, not only makes the model exceptionally tractable from an analytical point of view, but also lends itself to straightforward graphical representation. The first element of this representation is the *bundles transformation function*: $w = B(m)$. In each industry, 'bundles' of capital and labour are produced according to standard neoclassical production functions of K and L: $m = g(K_m, L_m)$ and $w = f(K_w, L_w)$. Since capital and labour exist in finite quantities, $\{\bar{K}, \bar{L}\}$, and if we assume, say, manufacturing is K-intensive relative to wheat at all relative factor prices, the bundles transformation function will have the usual concave shape. This is plotted in Fig. 1 in the SW quadrant. The NW and SE quadrants contain functions mapping bundles into final good outputs: $W = \psi(w)$ and $M = \theta(m)$. In the HOS case, $\psi(\cdot)$ is just a 45° line.[5]

The real core of the graphical analysis is the $\theta(\cdot)$ function. In mapping bundles into final manufactures, this function embodies the market structure assumptions in both production of intermediates (internal increasing returns due to fixed cost and monopolistic competition) and final assembly (external increasing returns due to division of labour). Following the development in the Appendix, we are able to show that

$$M = \theta(m) = Am^{\frac{1}{\phi}} \tag{2}$$

where A is a constant and, as shown in (1), ϕ is an indicator of the degree of substitutability between varieties of inputs. It will be useful in the later analysis to have expressions for the first and second derivatives of θ:

$$\theta'(m) = \frac{1}{\phi} Am^{\frac{1}{\phi} - 1} > 0$$

$$\theta''(m) = \frac{\frac{1}{\phi} - 1}{\phi} Am^{\frac{1}{\phi} - 2} > 0 \tag{3}$$

Following Mayer's (1972, Fig. 1) analysis of production and trade under increasing returns to scale, we can use the information contained in the bundles transformation function and the two mapping relations to derive the transformation relation between final manufactures and wheat, $W = T(M)$, presented in

---

[4] Since, as we show in the Appendix, x is constant in equilibrium, it is easy to see that the production of M is homogeneous of degree $1/\phi > 1$.

[5] That is, the 'bundles', w, used in wheat production are just the inputs from standard analysis.

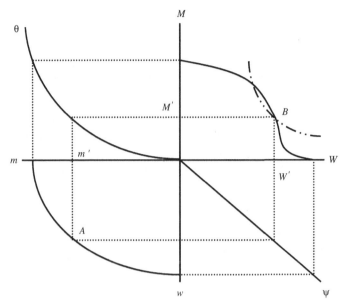

Fig. 1.

the NE quadrant in Fig. 1. That is, every point on the bundles transformation curve, $B(\cdot)$, is mapped to a point on the final goods transformation curve, $T(\cdot)$.

Herberg and Kemp (1968) and Mayer (1972) have intensively studied precisely the system we have just described for the case of variable returns to scale in both sectors (in our notation, θ and ψ are both permitted to be nonlinear). From Mayer (1972, p. 103), we have expressions for $T'(\cdot)$ and $T''(\cdot)$ in terms of θ, ψ, and $B(m)$. Note that, in these expressions, we are working with the inverses of B and T. That is, $\beta = B^{-1}$ and $\tau = T^{-1}$.[6]

$$\tau' = \frac{\mathrm{d}M}{\mathrm{d}W} = \left(\frac{\theta'}{\psi'}\right)\beta'$$

and

$$\tau'' = \frac{\mathrm{d}^2 M}{\mathrm{d}W^2} = \frac{\theta'}{(w')^2}\left[\left(\frac{\theta''}{\theta'}\right)(\beta')^2 - \left(\frac{\psi''}{\psi'}\right)\beta' + \beta''\right]. \tag{4}$$

In the baseline case of HOS structure for bundles production, $\psi' = 1$ and $\psi'' = 0$, so the expressions in (4) are considerably simplified to

$$\tau' = \frac{\mathrm{d}M}{\mathrm{d}W} = \theta'\beta'$$

---

[6] Since $B(m)$ is the standard HOS production frontier, we know that it possesses a unique inverse. We adopt this both for expositional convenience and because, as graphically portrayed, the slope in W–M space is naturally seen as $\mathrm{d}M/\mathrm{d}W$.

and

$$\tau'' = \frac{d^2 M}{dW^2} = \theta' \left[\left(\frac{\theta''}{\theta'} \right) (\beta')^2 + \beta'' \right]. \tag{5}$$

The expressions for τ' show the interaction between $B(\cdot)$, θ, and ψ that are illustrated at any point on $T(\cdot)$ frontier in the right panel of Fig. 1. As with Herberg, Kemp and Mayer, we are particularly interested in $T''(\cdot)$ if we want to know about the curvature of $T(\cdot)$.

We can show that if $\theta''/\theta' \to \infty$ as $m \to 0$, then the transformation function must be convex in the neighbourhood of zero manufacturing output.[7] Given the derived expressions in (3), it is easy to see that

$$\frac{\theta''}{\theta'} = \frac{\frac{1}{\phi} - 1}{m} > 0 \tag{6}$$

which (since $0 < \phi < 1$) clearly approaches ∞ as m approaches zero. This equation is just a measure of local curvature (like the Arrow–Pratt measure of absolute risk aversion). Thus, because the function taking m into M is extremely (ie almost infinitely) tightly curved in the neighbourhood of zero manufacturing output, the transformation function is pulled in toward the origin. As the β'' term in the expression for τ'' suggests, the concavity of $B(m)$ works against the convexity of θ and can produce a concave portion of $T(M)$ in the neighbourhood of zero W output. In particular, it is easy to see that (6) and β' both become smaller as the output of M increases, implying that the first term in the square brackets in (5) becomes smaller. Unfortunately, while the first term should decline monotonically, unless we are willing to make some strong assumptions about the magnitude of T'', we are unable to say anything *definite* about curvature away from the neighbourhood of zero M output. This is an important point. The frontier may, in general, be characterised by multiple convexities and alternative stable and unstable regions. (Stability is discussed below.) With specific functional forms and parameter values, the approach in the literature has basically been to make implicit assumptions about where these regions occur.

1.2. Ricardian Variations

Given the structure that we have developed to this point, it is easy to illustrate two standard variants of the basic model: the Ricardian and Ricardo–Viner technologies for bundle production. In the Ricardian case (Chipman, 1970; Ethier, 1982*b*; Gomory, 1994), labour is the only productive factor, as a result the resource constraint takes the simple form of a straight line with a slope of negative unity in the SW quadrant. (Fig. 2*a*). Wheat is produced with a constant returns to scale production function, components are produced with a fixed and variable component (now paid entirely in labour) and manufactures are produced from components according to (1). We now have that the 'bundles' transformation

---

[7] This is a result of Mayer's (1972, pp. 106–9) which refines a result originally presented in Herberg and Kemp (1968).

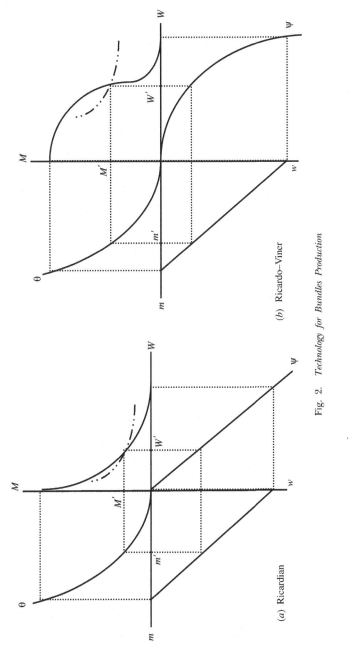

(a) Ricardian

(b) Ricardo–Viner

Fig. 2. *Technology for Bundles Production*

function (ie the labour constraint) is characterised by $B' = -1$ and $B'' = 0$. Since ψ is still a linear map with a slope of 1, we derive $T' = -\theta'$ and $T'' = \theta''$. That is, the shape of the transformation function between finished manufactures and wheat is defined entirely by θ, and T is concave throughout its length. The explanation of this is quite clear in Fig. 2a since the θ function is the only source of curvature, while both B and ψ have unit slopes.

The Ricardo–Viner structure (Fig. 2b) has been extensively used in an important series of papers by Markusen (1988, 1989, 1990a,b, 1991). Consider the simplest version of this model: wheat is produced with mobile labour and specific capital; components are produced with labour only (again there is a fixed and a variable part needed in production of components); and manufactures are produced by costless assembly of components. As with the Ricardian model, the resource constraint for the Ricardo–Viner model is given by the labour constraint, which will again be a straight line with a slope of negative one. The θ function, determined by monopolistic competition among component producers and the CES aggregator, has the same qualitative properties and graphical appearance as in the HOS and Ricardian cases. Unlike the two previous cases, however, the ψ function is no longer linear but, reflecting the presence of the specific capital, shows diminishing returns to mobile labour (ie $\psi' > 0$ and $\psi'' < 0$). As a result, we cannot use the expressions for τ' and τ'' in (5) but must use those in (4). On the other hand, the Ricardian resource constraint still permits us to take $B' = B'' = -1$ and $B' = \beta'' = 0$, so we can write

$$\tau' = \frac{dM}{dW} = -\left(\frac{\theta'}{\psi'}\right)$$

and

$$\tau'' = \frac{d^2M}{dW^2} = \frac{\theta'}{(\psi')^2}\left[\left(\frac{\theta''}{\theta'}\right) + \left(\frac{\psi''}{\psi'}\right)\right]. \tag{7}$$

As with the HOS case, in the Ricardo–Viner case the term in square brackets contains a strictly positive term and a strictly negative term. The first term in the square brackets, still given by (6), goes to positive infinity in the neighbourhood of zero output of final manufactures. The second (negative) term is strictly finite at that point, so T will be convex at that point. We also know that the first term will decline smoothly as output of finished manufactures increases. Unfortunately, other than sign, we have very little information about the properties of the negative term, so we cannot be certain about the *structure of T* away from the neighbourhood of zero manufacturing output.[8] This is an important source of multiple equilibria in the literature.

---

[8] Following Markusen (1989), we can obtain some additional leverage by considering specific functional forms. For example, in the Cobb–Douglas case, we have $\psi''/\psi' = (\alpha - 1)/L_w < 0$. This expression goes to negative infinity as output of wheat goes to zero. Mayer (1972), again expositing a result due to Herberg and Kemp (1968), shows that, in this case, T must be strictly concave in the relevant neighbourhood. Since both ψ''/ψ' and θ''/θ' decline smoothly with increases in L applied to W and M respectively, we can say, for this case, that T will have a single inflection (at the unique point where $-\psi''/\psi' = \theta''/\theta'$). For additional discussion of the curvature of $T(\cdot)$ in the Ricardo–Viner case, see Markusen and Melvin (1984), Herberg and Kemp (1991) and Wong (1996).

1.3. The Closed Economy Equilibrium and Nontangencies

We turn next to the equilibrium structure of the closed economy. This involves consumption along the MW frontier in Fig. 1. While under S-D-S type monopolistic competition, the closed economy produces the optimal number of varieties for a given allocation of resources to m production, average cost pricing and returns to specialisation mean that, even so, the relative size of the manufacturing sector will be sub-optimal.[9] As a result of average cost pricing, while autarky consumption will be at some point like B in Fig. 1, domestic prices will not be tangent to the $T(\cdot)$ frontier at this point (Markusen, 1990a,b). This leaves scope for policy interventions that target expansion of the manufacturing sector.

With the addition of Cobb–Douglas preferences, it can be shown that the production side of the economy exhibits the standard features of more classical models. In particular, the combination of Cobb–Douglas preferences (with fixed expenditure shares) and homotheticity of wheat and bundles production yields a subsystem of equations that is purely Heckscher–Ohlin. As a result, as shown in Ethier (1982a,b), the standard Rybczynski and Stolper–Samuelson results hold (in terms of wheat and bundles). However, the welfare calculus is complicated by aggregate scale effects in the transformation of bundles in final manufactures – which is what matters for welfare.

1.4. Economic Growth

In addition to the implications of returns to specialisation for the shape of the static production frontier $T(\cdot)$, such returns also carry important dynamic implications. The critical difference is captured in the θ function, which is strictly linear in the neoclassical model. With capital accumulation in the classical model, there will be an expansion of the production possibility frontier (the $T(\cdot)$ frontier), with a bias toward the capital intensive sector. With labour in fixed supply (and assuming a standard final demand system), the new equilibrium return to capital will fall. Identically, the incremental gain from an additional unit of capital will also decline. Because of these declining returns, the classical model will exhibit the dynamic property, under classical savings or Ramsey specifications, of a fixed long-run capital–labour ratio and zero growth. This process can be fundamentally altered, however, by the simple addition of returns to specialisation. Because the θ function is no longer linear, the decline in the return to capital is moderated by returns to specialisation (Grossman and Helpman, 1991, ch. 4). If returns to specialisation are sufficiently large that they effectively bound the return to capital from below, the model will produce sustained economic growth. This depends on the relative curvature of the θ function. Even if the model exhibits local long-run Solow properties (with a unique steady-state level of capital and income in the long-run), the curvature of the θ function still implies a longer period of transitional growth, and a magnification

---

[9] See Bhagwati et al. (1998) for a concise discussion of the optimal variety issue.

effect related to efficiency shocks (as may follow from policy intervention). In conjunction with average cost pricing, the externalities related to resource accumulation mean that the laissez faire equilibrium in the model exhibits not only a sub-optimal static allocation of resource, but also a sub-optimal dynamic one.

The curvature of the θ function also carries dynamic implications for the effects of learning by doing. For example, we can represent the accumulation of production knowledge in the manufacturing sector by temporal shifts in the $B(\cdot)$ frontier – simply reinterpret K as knowledge capital. Even in the neoclassical model, this may lead to sustained economic growth. This depends, critically, on whether there are diminishing returns to knowledge accumulation. Externalities following from knowledge accumulation – variations on $A(K)$-type growth – can lead to sustained growth. Specialisation economies can deliver the required externalities. It is the curvature of the θ function that proves critical to determining whether specialisation economies are sufficient to generate sustained economic growth, or whether, instead, they simply provide a magnification of static effects (and boost the Solow residual in the process).

2. NPE with Trade: with Trade: Model II

We turn next to the open economy version of the NPE model. If we are willing to permit trade in final goods only (ie in W and M, but neither in components nor in factors), $B(\cdot)$, $\theta(m)$, and $\psi(w)$ continue to be technological properties of a country's economy. (By a 'technological property', we refer to properties of an economy that are not changed by opening international trade.) Since factors are taken to be immobile (except when factor mobility is the subject of analysis), it should be clear that trade will not have any effect on the bundles transformation function. Similarly, $\psi(w)$ is defined purely in terms of a national technology. Finally, examination of (1) reveals that, as long as only nationally produced intermediates are available to producers of final manufactures, $\theta(m)$ is also determined solely in terms of national magnitudes. Thus, Figs 1–2 continue to characterise production conditions whether or not there is trade in final goods only. This is exceptionally convenient because it permits us to appropriate the substantial body of work on international trade under increasing returns to scale virtually unchanged (Helpman, 1984).

The Type II model is an extreme version of a model with local agglomeration effects. We say extreme because there are no moderating effects related to cross-border spillover of production externalities. Because the reduced form structure of the model is identical to the older external scale economy literature, we are free to stand on the shoulders of this literature when drawing policy implications about trade policy and the location of industry. One important feature of the Type II model is that, Dr Pangloss to the contrary notwithstanding, there will generally be multiple, Pareto-rankable equilibria. For small countries, in particular, there is the strong likelihood that they will specialise in wheat production and may suffer a welfare loss relative to autarky. This fact underlies the modern versions of Frank Graham's argument for protection (Panagariya, 1981; Ethier, 1982*b*).[10] Many of the insights of the recent literature on forward linkages, development and specialisation (Rodrik, 1996; Rodriguez-Clare, 1996; Rivera-Batiz and Rivera-Batiz, 1991; Venables, 1996*b*) follow directly from this property of local agglomeration models. Basically, because specialised primary/wheat production involves a stable equilibrium, and because more developed economies, by definition, have cost advantages related to larger and more specialised upstream industries, there is a tendency for underdeveloped countries to stay that way.

3. International Production Externalities (IPEs): Models III and IV

3.1. *Introducing IPE in the Basic Model*

While, as we have seen, Ethier's model of the division of labour has provided extremely useful microfoundations for the analysis of strictly national returns to scale, in its maiden application, it was actually used to examine internationally increasing returns to scale. The notion that access to international markets permits beneficial specialisation has been an essential element of trade theoretic analysis at least since Adam Smith and David Ricardo. What is new in Ethier's formulation is the formalisation of a direct link between international trade and the technology of production: access to a wider variety of component inputs permits an increased division of labour in the production of manufactures. As we shall see, however, it is precisely the link between trade and technology that makes the analysis difficult to visualise in simple graphical form: production conditions (especially as represented by the transformation function between final goods) are no longer a 'technological fact', determined only by nationally fixed production functions and endowments, but will now be dependent on the international equilibrium.[11]

We now assume that all R countries share identical tastes, technologies for producing factor bundles ($w = f(K_w, L_w)$ and $m = g(K_m, L_m)$), technologies for producing components from factor bundles and the technology for transforming w into wheat (ie $\psi(w)$). In all countries, all markets are taken to be perfectly competitive, except the market for components which is monopolistically

---

[10] Where Panagariya and Ethier adopt a Ricardian model, Markusen and Melvin (1984, proposition 1) and Ide and Takayama (1993, proposition 4) present an equivalent result for the HOS case. In deriving these results, fundamental use is made of the stability properties of these models under a Marshallian adjustment process in the final goods sector. The only peculiarity, for stability analysis, of our models relative to the standard external economy models, is the monopolistic competition in the intermediate sector. However, Chao and Takayama (1990) have shown that, as long as production functions are homothetic, monopolistic competition of this sort is stable under the obvious firm entry process. Since homothetic production functions characterise all of our models in this paper, for models I/II, we can fully appropriate the stability results developed by Eaton and Panagariya (1979) and Ethier (1982*b*) for the Ricardian case, Panagariya (1986) for the Ricardo–Viner case and Ide and Takayama (1991, 1993) for the HOS case.

[11] A variation of the basic model type developed here incorporates value-added at the final assembly stage of intermediates into final goods. This leads to explicit interaction between division of labour effects and intermediate linkages. See, for example, Brown's (1994) discussion in the context of large applied general equilibrium models, and Puga and Venables' (1998) similar application in the context of smaller numerical models.

competitive. A given country, $j \in R$, assembles components into final manufactures according to the aggregator function

$$M^j = \left[\sum_{r \in R} \sum_{i \in n_r} \left(x_i^r \right)^\phi \right]^{\frac{1}{\phi}} \tag{8}$$

Roman subscripts and superscripts are country identifiers, Greek superscripts are numbers (ie powers). In the two-country case, the Home country will have no superscript and foreign magnitudes will be starred, ie, when $n = 2$, $n = \{ , *\}$. With traded intermediate goods, it will no longer be the case that, at the level of a given national economy, the amount produced by a given component producer (which we now denote by y_r) will be equal to the amount of that component consumed in the country (x_r). In fact, since some strictly positive share of every component producing firm's output is exported, $x_r < y_r$. As a result, we can no longer simply substitute the expression for y – (A5) in Appendix 1 – into (8) unless we are working with global output. We can, however, exploit the fact that, under the assumption of a constant elasticity of substitution among varieties of components and zero transportation costs, if price per unit of every component is the same, every final manufacturing firm will purchase the same quantity of the intermediate from every intermediate producer in the world. Thus, we can set $x_i^r = x^r \forall i$ and r.[12] As a result, since $\sum_{i \in n_r} \left(x_i^r \right)^\phi = n_r x_r^\phi$, and letting $n^G = \sum_{r \in R} n^r$, we can write (8) as

$$M^j = \left[\sum_{r \in R} n^r (x^r)^\phi \right]^{\frac{1}{\phi}} = \left(n^G \right)^{\frac{1}{\phi}} x. \tag{9}$$

Furthermore, since all component producers produce the same quantity, given by (A5), and all manufacturing firms consume the same quantities of each component, it will be the case that $x^j = \delta_j y_r$. Since country j consumes δ_j of every variety, it is implicitly consuming δ_j of the total allocation of factors to bundle production, and denoting implicit consumption of bundles in country j by m^j, we have

$$\delta^j = \frac{m^j}{m^G}. \tag{10}$$

What we are really interested in is an expression for $\theta(m)$ incorporating the possibility of imported intermediate components. The aggregator in (9) is essentially the same as that in (1), so for national component producers the underlying competitive conditions are essentially unchanged from those underlying the analysis presented above. Thus, we can now write[13] $M^j = \theta(m^j, \mathbf{m}^{-j})$:

$$M^j = \theta^j \left(m^j, \mathbf{m}^{-j} \right) = A \left(\sum_{r \in R} m_r \right)^{\frac{1}{\phi} - 1} m^j \tag{11}$$

where θ is now functions of the *global* level of component production.

---

[12] That is, every final assembly firm will buy the same quantity of every type of component and, since M production is produced by competitive firms under identical technologies, we can treat the economy's output as being produced by a single firm with that technology.

[13] Appendix 2 presents the analytics underlying this claim.

Before considering the two-country case (as an approach to the R country case), we briefly note the analytical simplification purchased by assuming that the country in question is either the only economically large country or is economically small. In the first case, the analysis is identical to that in the closed economy case (the Type I model). In the small country case, ROW (or large country) production completely determines the magnitude of the term in parentheses on the right-hand side making $M^j = A^+ m_j$ (where A^+ is a constant that includes everything but m_j). This is, of course, a linear function, so the small country behaves like a small country under constant returns to scale.

3.2. Allocation Curves and Policy Ranking

Now suppose that there are two countries (Home and Foreign), both large. Ethier's allocation curves, graphed below the SW quadrant in Fig. 3, are used to identify the equilibrium quantities m and m^*.[14] At this equilibrium, m and m^* are determined and so θ is a linear function.[15] That is, θ is a linear function (shown in the NW quadrant of Fig. 3). The allocation curve diagram picks out the equilibrium point on the bundles transformation function (point A in the figure) which, via ψ and the linear θ, is mapped to equilibrium outputs of final goods (point B). If point A is an interior point on $B(\cdot)$, competitive conditions and technology ensure that the slope of the tangent at that point gives the equilibrium price (in units of wheat) per unit of m (which we denote p). If there is trade in intermediate goods only (ie all trade is intra-industry trade), consumption occurs at point B as well: $m_P{}^j = m_C{}^j$.

The same logic will also work for the case of trade in components and wheat (the Type III model), with local assembly of components into final manufactures for local consumption (the case considered in Ethier). However, if intermediate goods can be exchanged for wheat (as well as other intermediate goods), it will no longer be generally true that $m_P{}^j = m_C{}^j$. We have already seen how to find the production point on the bundles frontier (A) and the implicit final goods production point (B). The equilibrium at the intersection of the allocation curves reflects an equilibrium price of manufactures (P, taking wheat as the numeraire). As a result of zero-profits, full-employment of the factor-endowment and balanced trade, we know that consumption will occur on the national income line through point B (with a slope of $-P$). As illustrated at point C in Fig. 3, this will be a tangency between an indifference curve and the national income line. Using the equilibrium (linear) θ and ψ again, this time from point C, we can find the pair of factor bundles ($m_C{}^j$, $w_C{}^j$) needed to produce the consumption bundle of final goods. We know that the national income line tangent to the bundles frontier (at A) reflects the same national income as that given by the line through B, with an adjustment

---

[14] Recall that the allocation curves give, for either country, the (m, m^*) combinations that are consistent with domestic equilibrium for that country – i.e. where the domestic supply price is equal to the world demand price. The intersection of these curves identifies an (m, m^*) combination consistent with simultaneous equilibrium in both national markets and, thus, the world market.

[15] In terms of equation (B1) in Appendix 2, the equilibrium value of $k = \bar{k}$. From this we have $\theta = \bar{k}m$, a linear function in m.

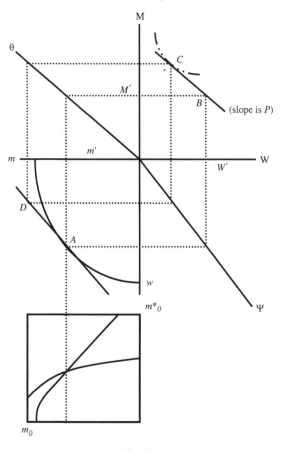

Fig. 3.

for scale.[16] Thus, D will lie on the national income line through A, the slope of which is $-p$ (i.e. the price per unit m). This is a full characterisation of equilibrium in the Ethier model with trade in intermediate goods and wheat (model III).

It is essential to note that we have not yet drawn a production set in the northeast quadrant. This is because of the fundamental difference between models I/II and models III/IV highlighted by the general equilibrium nature of θ in the latter case. Since θ is not a technological fact, we cannot draw a purely technological production frontier. There are only equilibrium points. In fact, at the equilibrium defined by the allocation curve intersection, we have taken the equilibrium θ as linear to draw Fig. 3. As a result, there cannot be offer curves or excess supply curves

---

[16] That is, we must make adjustment for the fact that $kP = p$.

of the usual sort. This, of course, is why Ethier developed the allocation curve technique.

As an aid to visualising the role of economic policy, we now construct an *experiment dependent set of production and consumption schedules*.[17] Recall that $B(\cdot)$ is a technological fact (it depends only on a fixed technology and a fixed factor endowment). Appropriate economic policy can pick out any point on the $B(\cdot)$ frontier. Consider, for example, a subsidy for home intermediate manufactures production. Such a subsidy will have a direct effect related to home output, and a second effect that captures the interaction between home production and rest of world production in the manufacturing sector. The net effect, involving changes in m and m^*, reflects the shifts in the home and foreign allocation curves that will be realised in the fifth quadrant in Fig. 3, see Ethier (1979) on this point. From (11), these, in turn, imply a shift in the efficiency of the economy in transforming m into M. As discussed more formally in the Appendix, every level of home m output is associated with a new policy dependent equilibrium characterised by a new production point in final goods space, a new relative price for manufactured goods P, and a new consumption point related back to implicit trade in bundles.

Moving to our graphic apparatus, we define Θ as the locus of all equilibrium points on the linear θ functions in mM space. This embodies the interaction between changes in the subsidy and changes in $(m + m^*)$. The Θ function can now be used to trace out the experiment dependent production frontier $T(\cdot)$ in Fig. 4, which we will refer to as the realised product transformation (RPT) frontier, defined in terms of final consumption goods.[18] This is effectively the production side of the economy. The next step involves finding the locus of all points identified by consumption of final goods at the experiment equilibria along the RPT. This follows from the imposition of final preferences and an income identity for consumption. If we impose identical homothetic preferences, we can then map the consumption locus as follows. First, along the RPT curve in Fig. 4, we have a price P associated with each point on the surface. One such price line is P_0 – associated with production point e_0. At the same time, from our imposition of homothetic preferences, this price P_0 also has associated with it an income expansion path E_0. The intersection of the price line, projected from the production point e_0, and the income expansion path E_0 projected from the origin gives us the associated consumption point C_0. We can map such consumption points for each production point on the RPT curve, yielding the consumption locus FN.

We can actually go a step further, and discuss welfare rankings along the policy-dependant consumption locus in Fig. 4. This is also discussed formally in Appendix C. The bottom line is that we are able to represent welfare ranking through shifts along social indifference curves in Fig. 4. Hence, in Fig. 4, social welfare U_1 is greater than U_0.

---

[17] Appendix C contains the algebra underlying the analysis of this section.
[18] In this section, we are speaking in terms of trade in intermediates (an Ethier model). Identically, the same discussion can be viewed in terms of specialised consumer goods, with M denoting the subutility index for differentiated consumer manufactures.

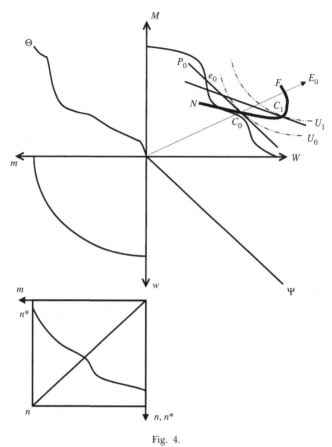

Fig. 4.

3.3. Production and Stability

Because the Θ function reflects a general equilibrium relationship rather than a technological fact, the same is true of the $T(\cdot)$ frontier – it is also an experiment-dependent artifact. The stability properties are also more elusive. We can demonstrate that internal equilibria sufficiently close to the vertical axis will be Marshallian stable, and that internal equilibria sufficiently close to the horizontal axis will be Marshallian unstable. The region in the middle, however is a theoretical free zone, with multiple stable and unstable equilibria allowed by the rules.[19]

[19] As Ethier (1979) makes clear, if we assume Mill–Graham preferences, there cannot be multiple equilibria. However, with more general demands, multiple equilibria emerge as a general property once again. Ethier (1979) also presents the stability analysis for this case.

Their existence will depend on the relative curvature of home and foreign $B(\cdot)$ frontiers and the relative importance of returns to specialisation.

Recall that we have drawn an experiment-dependent $T(\cdot)$ frontier in Fig. 4, where we add additional information about the home and foreign industries for equilibria along the RPT. In drawing the figure, we have forced the economy to move along its $B(\cdot)$ frontier, while allowing the rest of the global economy to adjust and clear all markets. Each point on the $T(\cdot)$ frontier, therefore, represents an equilibrium level of production (though a tax-cum-subsidy scheme may be required to sustain the equilibrium.) We have also represented, in the box at the lower left, the relative size of home and foreign industry, as indexed by the number of intermediate firms. Because we are mapping the implications of movements along the $B(\cdot)$ frontier, the number of home firms will be a linear function of m. (Recall the properties of the model, where m expansion involves entry of identical firms.) We cannot make such a statement about foreign firms, since their entry and exit (or identically the size of the m^* sector) is driven by the nature of the general equilibrium system, which will include the relative and absolute curvatures of the home and foreign bundles frontiers, the relative importance of specialisation economies, and the underlying preference structure. When we have a foreign region made up of many countries, the nonlinearity of n^* will be even more evident. It is, in fact, the nonlinearity of the mapping of n to n^* (or identically from m to m^*) that leads directly to the varied curvature of the $\Theta(m)$ function. This is immediately evident from inspection of (19).[20]

4. The IPE Model and Trading Costs

4.1. *The Ricardian IPE Model and Trading Costs*

An important application of Type IV models involves the implications of trading costs (Venables, 1996*a,b*; Krugman and Venables, 1995; Venables and Krugman, 1996; Fujita *et al.*, 1999). Trading costs are used, alternatively, to represent actual trading costs (transport, paperwork etc.) and government imposed costs, like tariffs and non-tariff barriers.

What do trading costs look like in the generic system? For expositional purposes, we start with a simple Ricardian model with identical home and foreign technologies, as illustrated in Fig. 5*a*. The autarky transformation frontier $T(\cdot)$ is represented in the upper right quadrant by the curve *142*. Consider next the integrated

---

[20] It is useful to note that, for the example developed in Fig. 4, we have shown an economy gaining from squeezing its own manufacturing sector out. From the box in the lower left, we see that this is accompanied by some relocation of industry (indexed by n and n^*) from home to foreign. Along with this, there is an increase in the price of M, implying that home had some natural comparative advantage in m. As drawn, this price increase is sufficient to generate terms of trade gains. The point highlighted by the diagram is as follows: the fact that a country can relocate industry to within its own borders, including the capture of associated agglomeration benefits, is insufficient to justify such a move on welfare grounds. In actuality, if the country is a net exporter of manufactured goods, terms of trade effects may justify intervention that squeezes the manufacturing sector out. In other words, in general equilibrium, the benefits of agglomeration effects must be weighed against potential terms-of-trade effects. Net exporters of manufactured goods are likely to gain from forcing prices up instead of down. Net importers of manufactures are more likely to benefit from a forced increase in global supply (with consequent agglomeration effects). See Francois (1994).

equilibrium (Dixit and Norman, 1980). The equilibrium level of M production is represented by the horizontal dashed line. With trade, the $T(\cdot)$ frontier (now represented by 1432) will be linear up to the point where the home level of M exactly matches the M that we would observe in the integrated equilibrium.[21] In this range, there is a one-for-one displacement of home and foreign firms, with the allocation of firms between countries being indeterminate. This linear relationship between n and n^* is represented in the box in the lower left corner. The linear region of the $T(\cdot)$ frontier also corresponds to a linear section of the $\Theta(m)$ function.[22] Beyond point 4, the home $T(\cdot)$ frontier will correspond to the autarky frontier (and the trade-based Θ function will rejoin the autarky one). It is also beyond this point that the home industry completely displaces the foreign industry. Interestingly, if production in the convex region of the home $T(\cdot)$ frontier improves home welfare, it will also improve foreign welfare. This is because of the basic non-tangency condition first discussed in Section 2, which will also characterise the integrated equilibrium. In the absence of terms-of-trade effects (which we have sterilised with our assumption of identical Ricardian countries), the world is actually better off if a single country (or set of countries) can capture the complete industry and then introduce a nationally optimal subsidy strategy. In this case, the nationally optimal subsidy will correspond to the globally optimal value.[23]

Next, consider the effect of transport costs as represented in Fig. 5b. We will have an inward shift of the $T(\cdot)$ frontier in regions where both countries produce m.[24] Whether or not either country specialises will depend on relative trading costs for intermediate and final goods. If the foreign country does specialise in W production at some point on the $T(\cdot)$ frontier, then, beyond that point, the frontier will again correspond to the autarky frontier. We will also have a shift in the n to n^* mapping, as represented in the lower left box. The complete specialisation point on the n^* curve will correspond to the point on the $T(\cdot)$ frontier where it rejoins the autarky frontier. There will also be an associated inward shift in the Θ function (see the upper left

---

[21] In terms of the analytics in Appendix B, the expression for k' in the region of an internal equilibrium, with identical Ricardian technologies, collapses to zero for the Type III/IV model.

[22] The linear section of Θ is determined where k remains constant as long as we are reproducing the integrated equilibrium.

[23] For groups of countries, the nationally optimal subsidy will be proportional to their share of the global industry, *if* we sterilise terms of trade effects (Francois, 1992).

[24] While beyond the scope of this paper, an alternative way to represent the model graphically in product space is with variety-scaled output. In particular, if we represent the introduction of trading costs as a break in the symmetry of weights on the regional CES aggregation functions, then we can represent the effects of regional variety changes in the productivity of m when used in production through a scaling term based on the size of local industry. Viewed this way, the production side of the economy, in terms of variety-scaled intermediates (Francois and Roland-Holst, 1997) and W, collapses to the Type II class of models. We then have Armington demand for intermediates indexed over regions (which reflects differential CES weights in different regions). These are produced regionally under increasing returns. The full effect of variety can again be represented by the Θ function, where this now transforms m into variety-scaled intermediates. Increases in foreign variety boost productivity of domestic varieties through marginal product increases in the CES aggregation function. The only non-concave feature of the model, represented this way, follows from the technological Θ relationship. For the Ricardian example developed here, the frontier for variety-scaled output (call it Z) and W will be convex over its entire length. The basic non-tangency result will still obtain along this frontier. Local agglomeration effects will be reflected in the CES weights, which will be higher for local goods. Hence, specialisation economies (and related convexities) will carry downstream to local M production.

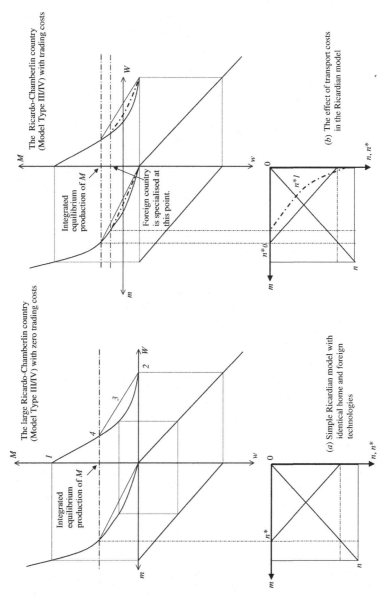

Fig. 5. *Ricardian Models with IEPS*

quadrant), with the Θ mapping also rejoining the autarky mapping at the point where the foreign country specialises.

The appearance of the $T(\cdot)$ frontier, with trading costs, closely resembles the frontier for the Type II class of models. In particular, in the present example of the Ricardian model, we have the type of frontier examined by Kemp (1964) and Kemp and Negishi (1970).[25] The critical difference is that, while Kemp was able to take world prices as fixed, we are unable to do so. From the point of view of the home country, border prices will shift as we move along the $T(\cdot)$ frontier, with the expectation that prices will be flatter as we move closer to the horizontal axis. The similarity to Kemp-type external scale economies leads us directly to a generalisation, in our generic framework, of a basic result of the location literature. In trade equilibria, there are again good and bad equilibria, and there may be instances of catastrophic collapse due to instability of internal equilibria along regions of the $T(\cdot)$ frontier. The possibility of foreign collapse also means that the $T(\cdot)$ frontier mapping from the horizontal axis to the point of foreign specialisation will not necessarily be continuous (hence also for the Θ mapping).

4.2. The Heckscher-Ohlin IPE Model and Trading Costs

We turn next to the characterisation of the $T(\cdot)$ frontier for the Type IV version of the economy developed in section 2. Recall that the economy is characterised by a Heckscher–Ohlin structure underlying the $B(\cdot)$ frontier. In autarky, the structure of the economy can be represented as in Fig. 6a. The Bundles frontier $B(\cdot)$ is strictly concave to the origin, while the existence of specialisation economies, imply increasing returns in production of M, and hence we have a realised product transformation frontier $T(\cdot)$ in the upper right quadrant that is characterised by concave and convex regions. We have represented the number of intermediate firms n (which is a strictly linear function of m) in the box at the lower left.

In developing the RPT frontier for the Type IV version of the Heckscher–Ohlin model, Fig. 6 proves to be an important reference case. Another useful reference case is the integrated equilibrium (Dixit and Norman, 1980). Recall from Helpman and Krugman (1985, ch. 7) that, for a global set of factor endowments F within the factor price equalisation set (which is bounded by the relative factor intensities for m and w in the integrated equilibrium), a trading economy will replicate the integrated equilibrium.[26] Hence, within F, we know that the production of m and w will be that necessary to allow reproduction of the integrated equilibrium level of output. This defines one equilibrium point on

---

[25] The effective collapse of Type III/IV models to a complex version of the Type II class of models in the presence of trading costs is not limited to the Ricardian case, but will instead hold as long as bundle cost functions are homothetic. The proof, however, is beyond the scope of this paper. See the discussion in note 24.

[26] If we introduce additional sectors, the pattern of production and trade becomes indeterminate within F. This implies flat regions on the RPT hypersurface, where production patterns are indeterminate nationally but the global level of production of $(m + m^*)$ will be fixed at the integrated equilibrium value.

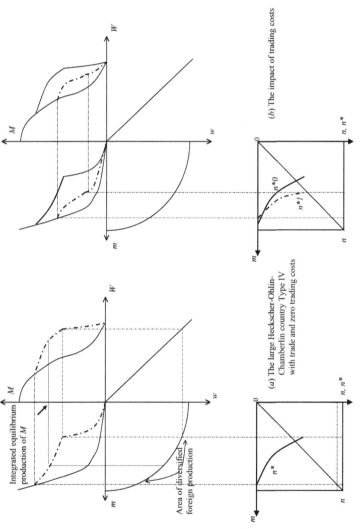

(b) The impact of trading costs

(a) The large Heckscher-Ohlin-
Chamberlin country Type IV
with trade and zero trading costs

Fig. 6. Type IV Heckscher–Ohlin–Chamberlin Country

the $B(\cdot)$ frontier, and also on the RPT curve, as represented in Fig. 6a. When we move left from this point on the $B(\cdot)$ frontier, we will induce exit of foreign firms (though the total $n+n^*$ will be increasing). Movements left/right in the region of the integrated equilibrium will map the RPT curve in the region of the integrated equilibrium level of production on the $T(\cdot)$ frontier, through Θ. If the home country is sufficiently large, sufficient movement along the $B(\cdot)$ frontier will induce specialisation of the foreign country, either in m^* or in W^*. In the case of full foreign specialisation in W, the properties of the Θ function are determined strictly by home production of m, so that the relevant Θ function collapses to the corresponding region of the Type I θ function. As a consequence, the RPT curve rejoins the autarky RPT curve past the point of foreign specialisation in W. In terms of the mapping of n to n^* in the box at lower left, this is also the point where n^* reaches zero. Alternatively, at the point of foreign specialisation in m^*, the contribution of m^* to the Θ function becomes linear, and we are in a situation of strictly national returns to scale (where such returns are greater than in the autarky case). This is represented in the lower left quadrant of the figure, defining the regions of the $B(\cdot)$ frontier where we will observe diversified foreign production.

Consider next the implications of trading costs for intermediate manufactures. Formally, we can represent this by a shift in relative weights in the CES aggregator function for the national producers of M. Graphically, this means that Θ will be strictly lower (unless the foreign region is specialised in W) than without trading costs, and hence that Θ in Fig. 6b will shift in. Again, for points beyond where the foreign region specialises in W, the RPT will correspond to the autarky $T(\cdot)$ frontier. For those regions where the RPT remains above the autarky $T(\cdot)$ frontier, we have the general result that with increasing trading costs, the RPT curve will converge on the autarky $T(\cdot)$ frontier.

It should be evident by now that an important implication of trading costs is that the RPT curve is endogenous with respect to trading costs, including tariffs. Hence, a country can affect the efficiency of its national economy through commercial policy. In general, trade protection targeting trade in manufactures will reduce the efficient set for the economy, because of its impact on international agglomeration effects. This may be welfare improving if the country benefits from the consequent increase in manufactures prices (though it does not come close to being a first-best option for industrial policy, which would involve production subsidies and taxes). Transport costs will also have an important effect on the RPT curve, with declining transport costs boosting the national frontier.

The graphical analysis of tariff policy and transport costs in Fig. 6b, when compared to a classic Heckscher–Ohlin setting, or even to the setting of the Type II Heckscher–Ohlin model, is complicated by the endogeneity of the $T(\cdot)$ frontier. It is also complicated by the endogeneity of price along the frontier. Depending on where we locate along the old and new RPT frontiers, we may also observe catastrophic agglomeration (or collapse) of the foreign region (such that n^* reaches zero or its upper bound in the lower box), meaning that net m exporters may become net importers or vice versa.

5. Summary

Division of labour models have become a standard analytical tool, along with competitive general equilibrium models (like the Ricardian, Heckscher–Ohlin–Samuelson, and Ricardo–Viner models), in public finance, trade, growth, development and macroeconomics. Yet unlike these earlier general equilibrium models, specialisation models so far lack a canonical representation. This is because they are both new, and also highly complex. Typically, they are characterised by multiple equilibria, instability and emergent structural properties under parameter transformation.

Given the prominence of specialisation models in modern economics, the value of a generic representation seems considerable. In this paper, we have developed such a framework. In the process, we demonstrate that important results in the recent literature depend critically on the stability and transformation properties that characterise the generic model. We have also highlighted why one sub-class of these models is particularly difficult to illustrate easily.

Tinbergen Institute and CEPR
Tulane University and Leverhulme Centre for Research on Globalisation and Economic Policy

Date of receipt of first submission: April 2000
Date of receipt of final typescript: August 2001

Appendix A: Structure of Ethier's division of Labour Model

Recall from the text that the first element of the model is given by a CES function that costlessly aggregates components (x_i) into finished manufactures:[27]

$$M = \left(\sum_{i \in n} x_i^\phi \right)^{1/\phi} \tag{A1}$$

Here n types of components are costlessly assembled into final manufactures and ϕ is an indicator of the degree of substitutability between varieties of inputs (x_i).[28] In particular, note that if $x_i = x \; \forall I \in n$, (A1) reduces to $M = n^{1/\phi} x$. Then, for n constant,

---

[27] Ethier's original formulation is actually slightly different:

$$M = n^\alpha \left(\sum_{i \in n} \frac{x_i^\phi}{n} \right)^{1/\phi} \tag{A1a}$$

Note that, in both formulations, the elasticity of substitution between varieties is given by $1/(1 - \phi)$ – ie the higher is ϕ, the more easily can the x_i be substituted for one another in production. In (A1a) there are effects operating both through market power (reflected in imperfect substitution among components – $0 < \phi < 1$) and returns to variety $(\alpha > 1)$. It should be clear, though that the formulations in (A1) and (A1a) are identical if $x_i = x \; \forall I \in n$ and $\alpha = 1/\phi$. Since the distinct effects of market power and returns to variety are not essential to our analysis, we will use the simpler form in (A1), where returns to division of labour emerge directly from the imperfect substitutability between varieties of inputs. For an analysis of policy that exploits the distinct effects in (A1a) see Holtz-Eakin and Lovely (1996a,b).

[28] Note the harmless abuse of good mathematical notation: n is being used as both the label of an index set and the number of elements in that set.

output of manufactures is linearly related to output of components and if $0 < \phi < 1$ (as we assume it to be) there are increasing returns to the variety of inputs, i.e.[29]

$$\frac{\partial M}{\partial n} = \frac{1}{\phi} n^{\frac{1-\phi}{\phi}} x > 1$$

The smaller is ϕ, the stronger are the returns to the division of labour.

Component production is the final essential element of the standard division of labour model – and the locus of the actual division of labour. Where production of final manufactures is characterised by external economies of scale, components are produced under internal decreasing costs. Specifically, we assume (again following Ethier) that production of x_i units of components requires the purchase of *bundles* of capital and labour (denoted m) according to the relation

$$m_i = ax_i + b \tag{A2}$$

Note that both the fixed (b) and marginal (a) costs are paid in bundles and are constant across firms in the component producing sector. If we let $m = \sum m_i$, and $x_i = x_i \, \forall i \in n$, then $m = n(ax + b)$. As a result of decreasing costs, no two firms will produce the same type of component. Fig A1 shows the overall production relations in manufacturing and wheat.

The supply side of the model is closed by the resource constraint. With a fixed endowment of factors of production $\{\bar{K}, \bar{L}\}$ this is summarised by the transformation function between bundles of factors used in the production of components and wheat. For this purpose, we assume that bundles used in the production of components are produced according to a standard neoclassical production function, $m = g(K_m, L_m)$, which is linear homogeneous, twice differentiable, and strictly concave. Along with the equivalent assumptions on the production of wheat, and no factor-intensity reversal, we know that the function $W = B(m)$ is the strictly concave transformation function of the HOS model. In particular, we know that $B'(m) < 0$ and $B''(m) \le 0$. Since wheat just is bundles of K and L, one might also think of the transformation process as involving bundles used in components and bundles used in wheat, where the former are transformed linearly into wheat. Where it is not confusing, we adopt the purely rhetorical simplification of referring to as 'wheat' both wheat and bundles of K and L used in producing wheat. Where necessary, we will denote bundles of K and L in wheat production as $w = f(K_w, L_w)$ and relate bundles to wheat via $W = \psi(w)$, where

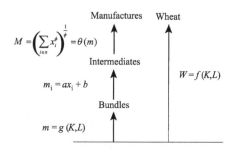

Fig. A1. *Schematic Representation of Production Structure*

[29] Since, as we shall see, x is constant in equilibrium, it is easy to see that the production of M is homogeneous of degree $1/\phi > 1$.

ψ is a linear relationship, ie $\psi(w) = a_{wW}\,w$. We will usually take the technical coefficient a_{wW} to be unity. The exception will be in the Ricardo–Viner case, where $\psi(w)$ is a nonlinear function.

Furthermore, given perfect competition in wheat and bundles (ie in m), and taking wheat as the numeraire, the relative cost of factor bundles for component production is

$$P_m = -B'(m). \tag{A3}$$

Now we want to link bundles to final production of manufactures: $M = \theta(m)$.[30] θ will serve as a basis for our graphical analysis, so we will need to pursue its properties, which will depend on both technology and the monopolistic competition among component producers, in some detail. Since component producers purchase bundles under competitive conditions, total cost for a representative component producing firm is $-B'(m)(ax_j + b)$ and total revenue is just $p_j x_j$, so the condition that marginal revenue equals marginal cost can be rearranged to obtain an expression for p_j:

$$p_j = -B'(m)\frac{a}{\phi} \tag{A4}$$

In deriving (A4), we substitute

$$\frac{\mathrm{d}x_j}{\mathrm{d}p_j} = \frac{1}{(1-\phi)}\frac{x_j}{p_j}$$

which can be derived from the demand curve for component j (Ethier, 1982, eq. (4)). The profit of each component producing firm is $\pi_j = p_j x_j + B'(m)(ax_j + b)$ which will be driven to zero by free entry and exit (abstracting from integer problems). Thus, setting $\pi_j = 0$ and substituting for p_j from (A4) gives

$$x_j = \frac{b\phi}{a(1-\phi)}. \tag{A5}$$

Since this is made up entirely of parameters that are constant across component producing firms, (A5) underwrites our treatment of x as identical across firms. Thus, from the fact that $m = n(ax + b)$, we can solve for the number of firms as a function of aggregate output of bundles:

$$n = \frac{(1-\phi)}{b}m. \tag{A6}$$

Note the implication that m and n are linearly related. Ethier works with a function $k(m)$, given by $M = km$. We can use (A5) and (A6), along with the fact that $M = n^{1/\phi}x$, to obtain an expression for $k = M/m$:[31]

$$k = \left\{ \left[\frac{(1-\phi)}{b}\right]^{\frac{1}{\phi}-1}\frac{\phi}{a} \right\} m^{\frac{1}{\phi}-1}. \tag{A7}$$

Furthermore, since the expression in parentheses is made entirely of parameters, we can write this as $k = Am^{\frac{1}{\phi}-1}$. Since $0 < \phi < 1$, k is clearly an increasing function of m, ie $k' > 0$, and since $k'' > 0$, θ is a strictly convex function, reflecting strictly increasing

---

[30] This type of analysis begins with Herberg and Kemp (1968), where the equivalent function is denoted h^{-1}. Mayer (1972), whose graphical analysis we build on, also refers to this function as θ. In both of these papers, the θ function is derived from a multiplicative relationship involving a scale multiplier and a kernel constant returns production function: $M = \gamma(M)g(K_m, L_m)$. Ethier (1982) works with a slightly different formulation which, as we shall see, yields an even simpler form for the θ function. See Helpman (1984) for a clear review of models with variable returns to scale.

[31] This expression is equation (8) in Ethier (1982). Note that while $k(m)$ is explicitly a function of bundles in Ethier, the equality to M/m makes it clear that it serves the same purpose as $\gamma(M)$ in the Herberg–Kemp/Mayer analysis.

returns in the production of M. From this, it is easy to define the function $\theta(m)$ that maps bundles into final outputs as

$$M = \theta(m) := km = \left(Am^{\frac{1}{\phi}-1}\right)m = Am^{\frac{1}{\phi}} \tag{A8}$$

which is (2) in the text.

Summarising the resource constraint and the bundles part of the model by the bundles transformation function, we can derive the transformation function between W and M via a pair of mapping relations from bundles to outputs. This system is

$$w = B(m)$$
$$W = \psi(w) \tag{A9}$$
$$M = \theta(M) := Am^{\frac{1}{\phi}}.$$

Given the production structure assumed above, and summarised in (10), the supply side of the model has a simple graphical representation (Mayer, 1972, Fig. 1). We plot the bundles transformation curve with the usual smoothly concave curvature. The SE quadrant contains the ψ function, a ray from the origin with a slope of 1. The NW quadrant contains the strictly convex θ function. This information can be used to plot the transformation function between W and M ($W = T(M)$): every point on $B(\cdot)$ is mapped to a point on $T(\cdot)$ by ψ and θ.

Appendix B

As we note in the text, the aggregator in (9) is essentially the same as that in (1), so, for national component producers, the equilibrium marginal conditions are still given by (A4), the volume of output of each component producing firm is still a constant determined by parameters as in (A5), and the number of component producers (and, thus, varieties of components) in country r (n_r) is still a linear function of the volume of bundle production (A6). Since all producers of final manufactures have access to all varieties, we can denote the global number of varieties by

$$n^G = \frac{1-\phi}{b}\left(\sum_{r\in R} m_r\right).$$

Using these facts, we can derive an expression for k^j in exactly the same way as we derived (A7):

$$k^j = \left[\left(\frac{1-\phi}{b}\right)^{\frac{1}{\phi}-1}\frac{\phi}{a}\right]\left(m^G\right)^{\frac{1}{\phi}-1}$$
$$= A\left(m^G\right)^{\frac{1}{\phi}-1}. \tag{A10}$$

Note that this, in fact, is precisely the same expression that we derived in (A7). Thus, we can still write $M^j = \theta(m^{\ j}, \mathbf{m}^{-j}) = km^j$:

$$M^j = \theta^j\left(m^j, \mathbf{m}^{-j}\right) := km^j = A\left(\sum_{r\in R} m_r\right)^{\frac{1}{\phi}-1} m^j \tag{A11}$$

where k and θ are now functions of the *global* level of component production, which is (11) in the text. It is also useful to note that, since k is the same for all countries in equilibrium, we can rewrite (10) as

$$\delta^j = \frac{m^j}{m^G} = \frac{km^j}{km^G} = \frac{M^j}{M^G}. \tag{10'}$$

Appendix C: Policy Ranking and the *FN* Schedule

In this section, we provide a more formal treatment of the ranking of economic policy, as discussed in section 3.2. Consider, for example, a subsidy for home intermediate manufactures production. From (11), we then have

$$M = km = \Theta(m)$$
$$k = A(m + m^*)^{\frac{1}{\phi}-1}.$$
(A12)

With the introduction of (or change in) a production subsidy, the change in k will be

$$\frac{\mathrm{d}k}{\mathrm{d}s} = \left(\frac{1}{\phi} - 1\right)(m + m^*)^{\frac{1}{\phi}-2}\left[\frac{\partial m}{\partial s} + \left(\frac{\partial m^*}{\partial m}\right)\left(\frac{\partial m}{\partial s}\right)\right]$$
$$= \left[\frac{1 - \phi}{\phi k(m + m^*)}\right]\left[1 + \left(\frac{\partial m^*}{\partial m}\right)\right]\left(\frac{\partial m}{\partial s}\right).$$
(A13)

In (A13), the first term in square brackets captures the direct effect of subsidies on home output given ROW output, while the second captures the interaction between home production and ROW production in the manufacturing sector.

We move from this functional relationship to our graphic apparatus as follows. We have effectively defined Θ in (A12) as the locus of all equilibrium points on the linear q functions in mM space. The Θ function can now be used to trace out the experiment dependent production frontier $T(.)$ in Fig. 4. From there, the next step involves finding the locus of all points identified by consumption of final goods at the experiment equilibrium along the RPT. This follows from the imposition of final preferences and an income identity for consumption. Formally, we first impose identical homothetic preferences, such that we can specify a social welfare function of the form

$$U^i = \Pi^i f(P)$$
$$\Pi^i = M^i P + W^i$$
(A14)

where Π denotes national income measured in units of wheat, and the term P is the price of final manufactures. With identical homothetic preferences, we can specify demand as

$$P = \eta\left(\frac{W^h + W^{\mathrm{row}}}{M^h + M^{\mathrm{row}}}\right)$$
(A15)

where $\eta > 0$. In addition, relative world supply of M and W can be specified in reduced form as

$$\left(\frac{W^h + W^{\mathrm{row}}}{M^h + M^{\mathrm{row}}}\right) = \varsigma(P, s) \qquad \varsigma_1 = \partial\varsigma/\partial P < 0, \varsigma_2 = \partial\varsigma/\partial s < 0.$$
(A16)

Taken together, (A15) and (A16) imply a mapping from the subsidy rate s to the price level P. In particular, we will have

$$P = \eta\varsigma(P, s) \Rightarrow \frac{\mathrm{d}P}{\mathrm{d}s} = \frac{\eta\varsigma_2}{(1 - \eta\varsigma_1)}.$$
(A17)

Consider next the welfare rankings of policy – in this case a subsidy. Given (A14)–(A17), we can show that the welfare effect of shifting our subsidy – and hence moving consumption along *FN* – will be

$$\frac{\mathrm{d}U^h}{\mathrm{d}s} = f(P)[(A + BD) + CD]$$
(A18)

where

$$A = \left(\frac{\partial M^h}{\partial s}\right)P + \left(\frac{\partial W}{\partial s}\right)$$

$$B = \left(\frac{\partial M^h}{\partial P}\right)P + \left(\frac{\partial W}{\partial P}\right)$$

$$C = M + \left(\frac{\Pi}{f(P)}\right)\left(\frac{\partial f}{\partial P}\right)$$

$$D = [\eta \varsigma_2 / (1 - \eta \varsigma_1)].$$

(See the precise derivation of this expression in Francois (1992).) In (A18), the term D is identical to the derivative found in (A17), and represents the general equilibrium shift in P as we induce movements along the bundles frontier through a subsidy. The first term in square brackets $(A+BD)$ is zero at the level that maximises national income in terms of the numeraire good W. The second term then measure the interaction of shifts in world prices with welfare as consumption moves along the FN frontier.

References

Barro, R. and Sala-I-Martin, X. (1995). *Economic Growth.* New York: McGraw Hill.
Bhagwati, J., Panagariya, A. and Srinivasan, T. N. (1998). *Lectures in International Trade.* Cambridge MA: MIT Press.
Brander, J. (1995). 'Strategic trade policy', in (G. Grossman and K. Rogoff, eds.), *Handbook of International Economics,* Vol. III. Amsterdam: Elsevier, pp. 1395–455.
Brown, D. (1994). 'Properties of applied general equilibrium trade models with monopolistic competition and foreign direct investment', in (J. Francois and C. Shiells, eds.), *Modeling Trade Policy: Applied General Equilibrium Assessments of North American Free Trade,* Cambridge: Cambridge University Press, pp. 124–50.
Buchanan, J. and Yoon, Y. eds (1994). *The Return to Increasing Returns.* Ann Arbor: University of Michigan Press.
Burda, M. and Dluhosch, B. (1999). 'Globalization and European labour markets', in (H. Siebert, ed.), *Globalization and Labour,* Tübingen: Mohr Siebeck, pp. 181–207.
Chao, C. C. and Takayama, A. (1990). 'Monopolistic competition, non-homotheticity, and the stability of the Chamberlinian tangency solution', *International Economic Review,* vol. 31, pp. 73–86.
Chipman, J. (1970). 'External economies of Acale and competitive equilibrium', *Quarterly Journal of Economics,* vol. 84, pp. 347–85.
Dixit, A. and Norman, V. (1980). *Theory of International Trade.* Cambridge: Cambridge University Press.
Dixit, A. and Stiglitz, J. (1977). 'Monopolistic competition and optimum product diversity', *American Economic Review,* vol. 67, pp. 297–308.
Eaton, J. and Panagariya, A. (1979). 'Gains from trade under variable returns to scale, commodity taxation, tariffs and factor market distortions', *Journal of International Economics,* vol. 9, pp. 481–501.
Ethier, W. (1979). 'Internationally decreasing costs and world trade', *Journal of International Economics,* vol. 9, pp. 1–24.
Ethier, W. (1982a). 'National and international returns to scale in the modern theory of international trade', *American Economic Review,* vol. 72, pp. 388–405.
Ethier, W. (1982b). 'Decreasing costs in international trade and Frank Graham's argument for protection', *Econometrica,* vol. 50, pp. 1243–68.
Francois, J. (1992). 'Optimal commercial policy with international returns to scale', *Canadian Journal of Economics,* vol. 25, pp. 184–95.
Francois, J. (1994). 'Global production and trade: factor migration and commercial policy with international scale economies', *International Economic Review,* vol. 35, pp. 565–81.
Francois, J. and Nelson, D. (2000). 'Victims of progress: globalization, specialization, and wages for unskilled labour', CEPR discussion paper 2527.
Francois, J. and Roland-Holst, D.W. (1997), 'Scale economies and imperfect competition', in (J. F. Francois and K. A. Reinert, eds.), *Applied Methods for Trade Policy Analysis: A Handbook,* Cambridge: Cambridge University Press, pp. 331–63.

2002]   A GEOMETRY OF SPECIALISATION   677

Fujita, M., Krugman, P. and Venables, A. (1999). *The Spatial Economy: Cities, Regions, and International Trade.* Cambridge: MIT Press.
Gomory, R. (1994). 'A Ricardo model with economies of scale', *Journal of Economic Theory*, vol. 62, pp. 394–419.
Grossman, G. and Helpman, E. (1991). *Innovation and Growth in the Global Economy.* Cambridge, MA: MIT Press.
Helpman, E. (1984). 'Increasing returns, imperfect markets and trade theory', in (R. Jones and P. Kenen, eds.), *Handbook of International Economics*, vol. 1, Amsterdam: North-Holland, pp. 325–65.
Helpman, E. and Krugman, P. (1985). *Market Structure and Foreign Trade.* Cambridge, MA: MIT Press.
Herberg, H. and Kemp, M. (1968). 'Some implications of variable returns to scale', *Canadian Journal of Economics*, vol. 2, pp. 403–15.
Herberg, H. and Kemp, M. (1991). 'Some implications of variable returns to scale: the case of industry specific factors', *Canadian Journal of Economics*, vol. 24, pp. 703–4.
Holtz-Eakin, D. and Lovely, M. (1996a). 'Scale economies, returns to variety, and the productivity of public infrastructure', *Regional Science and Urban Economics*, vol. 26, pp. 105–23.
Holtz-Eakin, D. and Lovely, M. (1996b). 'Technological linkages, market structure, and production policies', *Journal of Public Economics*, vol. 61, pp. 73–86.
Ide, T. and Takayama, A. (1991). 'Variable returns to scale, paradoxes and global correspondences in the theory of international trade', in (A. Takayama, M. Ohyama, and H. Ohta, eds.), *Trade, Policy, and International Adjustments*, San Diego: Academic Press, pp. 108–54.
Ide, T. and Takayama, A. (1993). 'Variable returns to scale, comparative statics paradoxes, and the theory of comparative advantage', in (H. Herberg and N. V. Long, eds.), *Trade, Welfare and Economic Policies*, Ann Arbor: University of Michigan Press.
Jones, R. (1968). 'Variable returns to scale in general equilibrium theory', *International Economic Review*, vol. 9, pp. 261–72.
Kemp, M. C. (1964). *The Pure Theory of International Trade.* Englewood Cliffs, NJ: Prentice-Hall.
Kemp, M. C. and Negishi, T. (1970). 'Variable returns to scale, commodity taxes, factor market distortions and their implications for trade gains', *Swedish Journal of Economics*, vol. 72, pp. 1–11.
Krugman, P. (1979). 'Increasing returns, monopolistic competition, and international trade', *Journal of International Economics*, vol. 9, pp. 469–79.
Krugman, P. (1980). 'Scale economies, product differentiation, and the pattern of trade', *American Economic Review*, vol. 70, pp. 950–9.
Krugman, P. (1995). 'Complexity and emergent structure in the international economy', in (J. Levinsohn, A. Deardorff, and R. Stern, eds.), *New Directions in Trade Theory*,' Ann Arbor: University of Michigan Press, pp. 23–46.
Krugman, P. and Venables, A. (1995). 'Globalization and the inequality of nations', *Quarterly Journal of Economics*, vol. 110, pp. 857–80.
Lovely, M. (1997). 'Playing by the new subsidy rules: capital subsidies as substitutes for sectoral subsidies', *Journal of International Economics*, vol. 43, pp. 463–82.
Lovely, M. and Nelson, D. (2000). 'Marginal intraindustry trade and labour adjustment', *Review of International Economics*, vol. 8, pp. 436–47.
Markusen, J. (1988). 'Production, trade, and migration with differentiated, skilled workers', *Canadian Journal of Economics*, vol. 21, pp. 492–506.
Markusen, J. (1989). 'Trade in producer services and in other specialized inputs', *American Economic Review*, vol. 79, pp. 85–95.
Markusen, J. (1990a). 'Micro-foundations of external economies', *Canadian Journal of Economics*, vol. 23, pp. 495–508.
Markusen, J. (1990b). 'Derationalizing tariffs with specialized intermediate inputs and differentiated final goods', *Journal of International Economics*, vol. 28, pp. 375–83.
Markusen, J. (1991). 'First mover advantages, blockaded entry, and the economics of uneven development', in (E. Helpman and A. Razin, eds.), *International Trade and Trade Policy*, Cambridge MA: MIT Press, pp. 245–69.
Markusen, J. and Melvin, J. (1984). 'The gains from trade theorem with increasing returns to scale', in (H. Kierzkowski ed.), *Monopolistic Competition and International Trade*, New York: Oxford University Press, pp. 10–33.
Matsuyama, K. (1996). 'Why are there rich and poor countries? Symmetry-breaking in the world economy', *Journal of the Japanese and International Economies*, vol. 10, pp. 419–39.
Mayer, W. (1972). 'Homothetic production functions and the shape of the production possibility locus', *Journal of Economic Theory*, Vol. 8, pp. 101–10.
Panagariya, A. (1980). 'Variable returns to scale in general equilibrium once again', *Journal of International Economics*, vol. 10, pp. 221–30.

Panagariya, A. (1981). 'Variable returns to scale in production and patterns of specialization', *American Economic Review*, vol. 71, pp. 221–30.

Panagariya, A. (1986). 'Increasing returns, dynamic stability, and international trade', *Journal of International Economics*, vol. 20, pp. 43–63.

Puga, D. and Venables, A. (1996). 'The spread of industry: spatial agglomeration in economic development', *Journal of the Japanese and International Economies*, vol. 10, pp. 440–64.

Puga, D. and Venables, A. (1998). 'Trading arrangements and industrial development', *World Bank Economic Review*, vol. 12, pp. 221–49.

Rivera-Batiz, F. and L. (1991). 'The effects of direct foreign investment in the presence of increasing returns due to specialization', *Journal of Development Economics*, vol. 34, pp. 287–307.

Rodríguez-Clare, A. (1996). 'The division of labour and economic development', *Journal of Development Economics*, vol. 49, pp. 3–32.

Rodrik, D. (1996). 'Coordination failures and government policy: a model with applications to East Asia and Eastern Europe', *Journal of International Economics*, vol. 40, pp. 1–22.

Romer, P. (1987). 'Growth based on increasing returns due to specialization', *American Economic Review*, vol. 77, pp. 56–62.

Romer, P. (1990). 'Endogenous technical change', *Journal of Political Economy*, vol. 98, pp. s71–102.

Spence, A. M. (1976). 'Product selection, fixed cost and monopolistic competition', *Review of Economic Studies*, vol. 43, pp. 217–35.

van Marrewikj, C., Stibora, J., de Vaal, A. and Viaene, J. M. (1997). 'Producer services, comparative advantage, and international trade patterns', *Journal of International Economics*, vol. 42, pp. 195–220.

Venables, A. (1995). 'Economic integration and the location of firms', *American Economic Review*, vol. 85, pp. 296–300.

Venables, A. (1996*a*). 'Trade policy, cumulative causation, and industrial development', *Journal of Development Economics*, vol. 49, pp. 179–97.

Venables, A. (1996*b*). 'Equilibrium location of vertically linked industries', *International Economic Review*, vol. 37, pp. 341–58.

Venables, A. and Krugman, P. (1996). 'Integration, specialization, and adjustment', *European Economic Review*, vol. 40, pp. 959–67.

Wong, K. Y. (1996). 'A comment on "Some implications of variable returns to scale: The case of industry-specific factors"', *Canadian Journal of Economics*, vol. 29, pp. 240–4.

Young, A. (1928). 'Increasing returns and economic progress', ECONOMIC JOURNAL; vol. 38, pp. 527–40.

Credits

Chapter 1

Reprinted with permission from the American Economic Association:
Finger, J. Michael, H. Keith Hall and Douglas R. Nelson. 1982. "The Political Economy of Administered Protection." *American Economic Review*, 72(3), 452–466.

Chapter 2

Reprinted with permission from John Wiley and Sons:
Hall, H. Keith and Douglas R. Nelson. 1992. "Institutional Structure in the Political Economy of Protection: Legislated v. Administered Protection." *Economics and Politics*, 4(1), 61–77.
Permission conveyed through Copyright Clearance Center, Inc.

Chapter 3

Reprinted with permission from MIT Press:
Egger, Peter and Douglas R. Nelson. 2011. "How Bad is Antidumping? Evidence from Panel Data." *Review of Economics and Statistics*, 93(4), 1374–1390.

Chapter 4

Reprinted with permission from Cambridge University Press:
Nelson, Douglas R. 1989. "Domestic Political Preconditions of US Trade Policy: Liberal Structure and Protectionist Dynamics." *Journal of Public Policy*, 9(1), 83–108.
Permission conveyed through Copyright Clearance Center, Inc.

Chapter 5

Reprinted with permission from Taylor & Francis (http://www. tandfonline.com), on behalf of The Instituto Affari Internazionali:
Hall, H. Keith and Douglas R. Nelson. 1989. "Institutional Structure and Time Horizon in a Simple Model of the Political Economy: The Lowi Effect." *The International Spectator*, 24(3/4), 153–173.
Permission conveyed through Copyright Clearance Center, Inc.

Chapter 6

Reprinted with permission from John Wiley and Sons:
Hall, H. Keith, Chihwa Kao and Douglas R. Nelson. 1998. "Women and Tariffs: Testing the Gender Gap Hypothesis in a Downs-Mayer Political-Economy Model." *Economic Inquiry*, 36(2), 320–332.
Permission conveyed through Copyright Clearance Center, Inc.

Chapter 7

Reprinted with permission from Emerald Group Publishing:
Hall, H. Keith and Douglas R. Nelson. 2004. "The Peculiar Political Economy of NAFTA: Complexity, Uncertainty and Footloose Policy Preferences," in A. Panagariya and D. Mitra (eds), *The Political Economy of Trade, Aid and Foreign Investment Policies*. Amsterdam: Elsevier, pp. 91–109.

Chapter 8

Reprinted with permission from John Wiley and Sons:
Gaston, Noel and Douglas R. Nelson. 2004. "Structural Change and the Labor-market Effects of Globalization." *Review of International Economics*, 12(5), 769–792.
Permission conveyed through Copyright Clearance Center, Inc.

Chapter 9

Reprinted with permission from Elsevier:
Davidson, Carl, Steven J. Matusz and Douglas R. Nelson. 2007. "Can Compensation Save Free Trade?" *Journal of International Economics*, 71(1), 167–186.
Permission conveyed through Copyright Clearance Center, Inc.

Chapter 10

Reprinted with permission from Edward Elgar Publishing Ltd:
Greenaway, David and Douglas R. Nelson. 2010. "The Politics of (Anti-) Globalization: What Do We Learn from Simple Models?," in N. Gaston and A. Khalid (eds), *Globalization and Economic Integration: Winners and Losers in the Asia-Pacific*. Cheltenham: Elgar, pp. 69–92.

Chapter 11

Reprinted with permission from Elsevier:
Kreickemeier, Udo and Douglas R. Nelson. 2006. "Fair Wages, Unemployment and Technological Change in a Global Economy." *Journal of International Economics*, 70(2), 451–469.
Permission conveyed through Copyright Clearance Center, Inc.

Chapter 12

Reprinted with permission from John Wiley and Sons:
Davidson, Carl, Steven J. Matusz and Douglas R. Nelson. 2006. "Fairness and the Political Economy of Trade." *World Economy*, 29(8), 989–1004.
Permission conveyed through Copyright Clearance Center, Inc.

Chapter 13

Reprinted with permission from John Wiley and Sons:
Davidson, Carl, Steven J. Matusz and Douglas R. Nelson. 2012. "A Behavioral Model of Unemployment, Sociotropic Concerns, and the Political Economy of Trade Policy." *Economics and Politics*, 24(1), 72–94.
Permission conveyed through Copyright Clearance Center, Inc.

Chapter 14

Reprinted with permission from Elsevier:
Gresik, Thomas A. and Douglas R. Nelson. 1994. "Incentive Compatible Regulation of a Foreign-owned Subsidiary." *Journal of International Economics*, 36(3–4), 309–331.
Permission conveyed through Copyright Clearance Center, Inc.

Chapter 15

Reprinted with permission from Institut für Weltwirtschaft:
Lovely, Mary E. and Douglas R. Nelson. 2002. "Intra-Industry Trade as an Indicator of Labor Market Adjustment." *Weltwirtschaftliches Archiv-Review of World Economics*, 138(2), 179–206.

Chapter 16

Reprinted with permission from John Wiley and Sons:
Francois, Joseph F. and Douglas R. Nelson. 2002. "A Geometry of Specialisation." *Economic Journal*, 112(481), 649–678.
Permission conveyed through Copyright Clearance Center, Inc.

Printed in the United States
By Bookmasters